ON THE SIDE OF
THE ANGELS

ON THE SIDE OF
THE ANGELS

An Appreciation of Parties and Partisanship

———◆———

Nancy L. Rosenblum

PRINCETON UNIVERSITY PRESS • PRINCETON AND OXFORD

Copyright © 2008 by Princeton University Press
Published by Princeton University Press, 41 William Street, Princeton,
New Jersey 08540

In the United Kingdom: Princeton University Press,
6 Oxford Street, Woodstock, Oxfordshire OX20 1TW

All Rights Reserved

Library of Congress Cataloging-in-Publication Data
Rosenblum, Nancy L., 1947–
On the side of the angels : an appreciation of parties and partisanship /
Nancy L. Rosenblum
p.   cm.
Includes bibliographical references and index.
ISBN 978-0-691-13534-2 (hardcover : alk. paper)   1. Political parties
2. Political science   3. Political parties—United States.   I. Title.
JF2051.R7576   2008
324.2—dc22   2008002317

British Library Cataloging-in-Publication Data is available

This book has been composed in Minion, University Light, and Futura Light

Printed on acid-free paper. ∞

press.princeton.edu

Printed in the United States of America

1 3 5 7 9 10 8 6 4 2

To Oliver and Leonardo, on the side of the angels

CONTENTS

—⟫◦⟪—

ACKNOWLEDGMENTS

My thanks go to colleagues and students who heard, read, and responded to lectures that previewed the material in this book. I am indebted to colleagues at Stanford University, where I delivered the Wesson Lectures in 2006 at the kind invitation of Deborah Rhode; at Yale Law School where, at the invitation of Dean Harold Koe, I delivered the Storrs Lectures in 2006; at the Olin Lectures at the University of Chicago in 2005; and at the Gilbane Lectures at Brown University the same year. I am also grateful to students and faculty at the Priestley Lectures at University College, University of Toronto in 2002.

Several colleagues read and commented on parts of the manuscript: Dennis P. Thompson, William Galston, and Alan Wolfe. Richard Pildes and Kathleen Sullivan, readers for Princeton University Press, suggested ideas and changes of emphasis that improved the manuscript immeasureably.

Joseph Kochanek, Eric Lomazoff, and Bettina Scholz, graduate students in the Department of Government at Harvard, assisted in research over the course of several summers. Their imagination brought material to my attention and their careful documentation saved me from many errors.

An early version of chapter 8 appeared as "Liberalism and Illiberalism: 'Extremism' and Anti-Extremism in American Party Politics," *Journal of Contemporary Legal Issues* 12, no. 2 (2002): 843–85. Chapter 9, "Militant Democracy," appeared in an earlier version in "Banning Parties: Religious and Ethnic Parties in Multicultural

Democracies," *Law and Ethics of Human Rights* 1 (2007): 18–75. "Political Parties as Membership Groups," my first foray into the subject, appeared in *Columbia Law Review* 100, no. 3 (April, 2000): 813–44.

The poem by Alan Dugan, "Portrait of a Local Politician," from *Poems Seven: New and Complete Poetry*, copyright © 2001 by Alan Dugan, is reprinted with the permission of Seven Stories Press, www.sevenstories.com.

The attention I pay here to political science owes to the stimulation of my colleagues in the Department of Government at Harvard, whose fascination with parties and elections inspired me to look beyond political theory; it has been an education.

ON THE SIDE OF
THE ANGELS

INTRODUCTION

An Appreciation of Parties and Partisanship

Antipartyism and its partner in negativity, antipartisanship, have a distinguished, even brilliant pedigree. *On the Side of the Angels* is my assessment of antipartyism, designed to map the field, to facilitate comparison among enduring aversions to political parties, to see whether contemporary antiparty thinkers echo orthodox arguments or are creative in their loathing. The materials I draw on to represent antipartyism are scholarly and literary, with added dollops of political commentary. From the furious railings of what I call the "glorious traditions of antipartyism" before democracy to the "post-party depression" that stretches to the present and shows few signs of lifting, antipartyism is one subject where the usual chasm between philosophy and common understanding is shrunk, closed really. I expect that my readers share the aversions I record, are frustrated with parties in practice, are quick to express antipathy, or are confirmed in their indifference. It is likely that any acceptance of parties is pragmatic, unexuberant, unphilosophical, grudging. I expect readers to be skeptical of a sympathetic theory of parties.

Yet that is my challenge: to rehabilitate parties and partisanship in readers' minds. From the long history of antipartyism, I retrieve rare moments of appreciation. I also propose my own. Parties are truly "the orphans of political philosophy,"[1] and I show why democratic theorists should adopt them and take them in. Rehabilitation of parties in practice is another matter, deserving of whatever scrap of utopianism is in us.

Disregard: The Bad Attitude of Contemporary Political Theory

Parties and partisanship are indisputably orphans of political philosophy. The list of advocates of parties and partisanship in contemporary political theory is spare. The classic work on the concept of representation, for example, pays them scant attention.[2] When they address the subject at all, political theorists reproduce the antiparty temper that dominates the history of political thought. In democratic theory today, parties either are the object of reflexive antipathy or suffer utter disregard.

It is hardly surprising that *philosophers* derogate partisanship. Whether their aspirational perspective is subversive Socratic questioning or Humean impartiality, a transcendent "view from nowhere" or stringent "public reason," it is the antithesis of a partisan perspective. That is expected. More remarkable is that contemporary democratic theorists who describe their work as "nonideal theory" have little to say. Democratic theorists refer to parties rarely or accusingly in passing. The problem is not that democratic theorists are inattentive to institutions generally. On the contrary, their interests extend to just about every institution for participation, representation, decision making, and political education *except* parties. Here is a brief rundown of the true objects of political theorists' affections: advocacy groups (self-styled public interest groups chief among them) and social movements; direct democratic institutions such as referenda, and experiments such as "citizen juries" and "deliberative polls." Theorists of multiculturalism and the "politics of difference" value self-organized identity groups and arrangements for guaranteed representation.[3] Democratic theorists of almost every stripe look to the associations of civil society to cultivate civic virtue and political engagement, and affirm that hope for democracy rests on "exploring the unrealized possibilities in ... institutions such as schools, workplaces, churches and synagogues, trade unions and social movements."[4] The exclusion of parties from exhaustive catalogues of the associations of civil society is particularly curious, given the foundational concern with mediating institutions that bridge society and government. Finally, for stern proponents of deliberative democracy for whom overcoming disagreement is a regulative ideal, partisanship is anathema. Even those who do not aim at consensus would assign disciplined deliberation a place of its own, removed from conventional political arenas, elections, and parties, such as specially created "mini-publics" with participants chosen to represent "lay citizens and nonpartisans."[5] It would be too harsh to cast these dominant strains of democratic theory as antipolitical, but contemporary theorists write—sometimes expressly—as if democracy could and should do without parties and partisanship.

If parties are the orphans of political philosophy, they are the darlings of political science. They are built into the standard definition of democratic government as "one chosen periodically by means of popular elections in which two or more parties compete for the votes of all adults."[6] The touchstone of governments that call themselves democratic is frequent and fair elections, made meaningful by party competition.[7] Political science puts parties at the core of its signature preoccupation with voting and elections. Democracy is "unthinkable save in terms of parties,"[8] and "democratic deficit" typically cites their absence.

The disjuncture between political science and political theory is striking. Political theorists have abandoned the field, and the study of parties and partisanship is carried on in political science terms (or in terms set by constitutional and election law). I have gone on a scouting expedition into the territory of political science, off the usual paths of political theory. My discussion of contemporary antipartyism moves back and forth between political science and political theory, imagining a conversation, and using resources from both to assess the achievement parties represent and the moral distinctiveness of partisanship.

The Sounds of Silence

The plain disproportion between a record of relentless, ferocious opposition to parties and moral disdain for partisans, on the one hand, and reticence bordering on silence when it comes to defending parties, on the other, brings to mind classical writings on democracy. With the partial exception of Aristotle's *Politics*, the great Greek texts reveal their authors' hostility to democracy.[9] They broadcast its failings. Philosophic arguments undermined democratic premises; Socrates' subversion of popular opinion is the most powerful instance. Why was there no corresponding philosophical defense of democracy?[10] One thought is that Athenian democracy in the fourth and fifth centuries was so deeply entrenched as popular ideology and practice that it stimulated no theoretical justification. No wonder "it was much easier for John Adams to find a thousand quotations and historical examples from the ancients in support of mixed government than for any Anti-federalist to find even one endorsing simple democracy."[11]

Something similar may hold for political parties, at least after the consolidation of electoral democracy when parties competing in regular elections became a familiar feature of the political landscape. Today, parties are acknowledged as "convenient vehicles for conducting" elections,[12] mechanisms for "reducing the transaction costs" of democracy.[13] Further justification seems superfluous. The energy of thought is committed instead to identifying the pathologies of "the system" and devising correctives.

We might assume that partisanship itself is a defense of parties. Not so: when partisans had to justify organizing, they typically argued for the necessity of combining in their own particular case, not for the respectability of parties per se. ("When bad men conspire, the good must associate."[14]) Whether partisans adopt the standard historical defense that theirs is "a party to end parties" or simply affirm that theirs is on the side of the angels, they give little thought to the value of parties in general or to partisanship as a political identity.

Established party systems have not stopped antiparty political theorists from aspiring to democracy without parties and proposing designs to contain or circumvent or eliminate them. But entrenched parties *do* appear to inhibit theorists from challenging utopias in which all citizens are Independents, and from acknowledging the

4

value of parties and partisanship. I take Bernard Crick's warning to heart; "boredom with established truths is the great enemy of free men."[15]

Speculating about silence is hazardous, of course. I will simply note that the absence of appreciation is not the result of disillusion. There was no initial enthusiasm for parties' promise followed by inevitable dashing of hopes. Disgust with parties as "unscrupulous power groups" and moral disdain for partisans as "little more than a Conspiracy of Self-Seekers"[16] dominate the history of political thought, and contemporary thinkers have not dissented from that view. Canonical political theory from antiquity is studded with precursors and echoes of the philosopher Hume, who famously wrote: "As much as legislators and founders of states ought to be honored and respected among men, as much ought the founders of sects and factions to be detested and hated."[17] And Jefferson, co-founder of the first popular political party, nonetheless contended, "If I could not go to heaven but with a party, I would not go there at all."[18] There are few corresponding champions of political parties. Parties' positive contributions to regulating political conflict, governing, exciting political participation, and deliberating go mostly unacknowledged. Parties do have one classic defender, Edmund Burke, of whom William Goldsmith wrote in 1774, "Here lies our good Edmund. Who, born for the universe, narrowed his mind. And to party gave up what was meant for mankind."[19]

Political theory harbored no great political expectations parties could disappoint, then. Burke's positive definition—"a body of men united, for promoting by their joint endeavors the national interest, upon some particular principle in which they are all agreed"[20]—was rejected by dour detractors from the start. One writer juxtaposed a definition of party as a group held together by the "cohesive power of public plunder."[21] In any case, the charge that parties and partisans have not lived up to Burke's principled concern for the national interest is only one thread of antipartyism, hardly the sole cause of universal antipathy. Simply, no aspiration for what parties could be or might do, and no account of the virtues of partisanship existed, or was sufficiently believed, to give rise to disillusion. Parties' failings were reported, and the reports mounted once parties took shape as permanent institutions for organizing elections and governing. But antipathy is not disappointment. As for partisans, they have always been mistrusted as blind loyalists or hacks, manipulated or bought. "Sounds of silence" refers to appreciation, not aversion.

Excoriation of politicians as power-hungry and treacherous, deformed by hypocrisy, tainted by personal and institutional corruption is as old as ruling and being ruled. It preceded party politics and will doubtless carry on after. I will show that distinctive moral and political pathologies are said to taint partisanship and parties: the very existence of parties signals a falling off from wholeness or original unity, for one, and the fatal divisiveness of party strife for another. If nothing else, parties make vivid the politics—the ceaseless strategies, collective efforts to exercise power and to deny its exercise to others, the arrant partiality of legislating and governing (and shaping public opinion). And there is the sheer indignity of partisanship.

One explanation for the loud and nearly ubiquitous sounds of antipartyism is that antipartyism is everywhere because parties are everywhere. In the words of one scholar, "parties are potential in every regime where they are not actual; and where they are actual, there are also potential parties lurking beneath every opinion taken for granted by the actual parties."[22] And why are parties everywhere? One answer is, because politics is partisan. In saying politics is partisan, I am saying the obvious: politics is about disagreement that brings conflict. Politics exists only when the fact of pluralism is accepted and there is latitude for open agitation of groups with rival interests and opinions.[23] In this respect, parties might be expected everywhere that they are not brutally repressed. The problem with this logic is that both historically and today, parties are *not* everywhere. They are not the only way to organize political conflict, and are seldom the favored way. Of course politics is partisan, but parties are not the only carriers of partisanship. (Partisans of a cause form caucuses, alliances, associations, and movements, to say nothing of subversive groups bent on revolutions, coups, and civil wars.) If political parties were inevitable, irrepressible, and ubiquitous, they would not be achievements.

Appreciation

Between carping and disapproval of parties and partisanship, on the one hand, and taking their uses for granted or utter disregard, on the other, we lose sight of the achievement of parties and partisanship. We miss the historical innovation of regular party rivalry, and the conceptual breakthroughs required to imagine and accept the political work parties do. Above all, we miss the creativity of party politics and the moral distinctiveness of partisanship. Parties create, not just reflect, political interests and opinions. They formulate "issues" and give them political relevance. Party antagonism "stages the battle"; parties create a system of conflict and draw the lines of division.[24] Moving back and forth between metaphors of natural and artistic creation, Maurice Duverger tried to capture this shaping power: parties crystallize, coagulate, synthesize, smooth down, and mold. Creativity in politics is almost always identified with founding moments, constitutional design, transformative social movements, or revolution, not with "normal politics." Modern party politics is the ordinary, not (ordinarily) extraordinary locus of political creativity.

Partisanship warrants appreciation, too. We do not need to admit the virtues of partisanship or admire partisans even an iota to see that representative democracy benefits from them. Ardent partisans may not be deliberative personally and individually, but at the level of the polity partisanship fuels collective discussion of men and measures; partisans are the agents of "trial by discussion."[25] Important as that is, I think partisanship deserves recognition on its own terms. I advocate for the moral distinctiveness of partisanship and propose reasons to elevate partisanship over its nemesis, the much vaunted pose of "Independence." Partisanship is the only political identity that does not see pluralism and political conflict as a bow to necessity, a pragmatic recognition of the inevitability of disagreement. It demands severe self-discipline to acknowledge that my party's status is just one part in a permanently pluralist politics, and hence the provisional nature of being the governing party and the charade of pretending to represent the whole. Partisanship, I argue, is *the* political identity of representative democracy. It may seem like an

7

unsettling reversal of the common-sense view that partisans supports parties to argue, as I do, that one value of political parties is to serve as "carriers" of partisanship. Political theorists today do not connect the practice of democratic citizenship with partisanship, or the virtues of citizenship with the qualities of partisanship. I intend to repair this lapse.

Partisanship is separable from parties, and in the sense of advocacy for an interest or cause is always with us. Partiality and disagreement are universal and irrepressible too, as are political groups organized in opposition to one another. But once again political parties in representative democracy are not, and neither is partisanship tied to parties, "party ID." I will show why we should recognize them as achievements.[26]

I argue that on their own terms democratic theorists' inattention or antipathy to parties is indefensible—or demands a defense that is not offered. We should charge parties with carrying some of the heavy moral water of democracy, including for example deliberation, which has become the academic touchstone for democratic legitimacy; indeed, for some theorists deliberation defines representative democracy. Parties do a lot of this work already, even if that is no partisan's noble intention. And no other institution, actual or imagined, is positioned to do more. Although I respond directly to antipartyism in political theory, I do not mean to say that philosophical standards such as deliberation are the only standards that apply to parties, or that every failing of party politics can be repaired by making partisans more deliberative. Still less that every deviation from deliberation (or any other regulative ideal) is damning. Rescuing politics from the unreasonable is unreasonable. I have kept this caution in mind: "no recipe can be given for founding an enduring political party . . . that will contain the exact dosages required for satisfying every human sentiment," for there will always be a fusion of lofty sentiments and low passions, of precious metal and base metal—"otherwise the alloy will not stand the wear and tear."[27] Valuing parties entails accepting this alloy. In this spirit, Duverger introduced his "general theory of parties" by advising that the subject is one where "high feeling and special pleading are the rule."[28] High feeling and special pleading are perfectly appropriate for partisans, certain they are on the side of the angels. High feeling and special pleading on behalf of parties in general are defensible, too. There is no way to rally the ideas and energy needed to make a crack in the great wall of antipartyism without sentiments as strong as arguments. That is the temper appreciation demands.

A dispassionate, outside views of parties was seldom attempted, at least not until political science made parties and elections its signature subject. Only a few philosophers have assumed a detached perspective. Hume examined parties from the standpoint of the impartial observer, and Mill envisioned parties engaged in "a serious conflict of opposing reasons,"[29] each party "deriving its utility from the deficiencies of the other,"[30] providing a dynamic of mutual correction, even progress. Neither philosophical standpoint offers a satisfactory view of parties, I argue, and neither pose is appropriate for partisans. Nonetheless, these philosophical moments of appreciation are significant, and I mention them here at the outset as indicative of the stern rejection of high feeling and special pleading by those few theorists who entertain the subject. Contemporary political philosophers may concede that "the clash of political beliefs, and of the interests and attitudes that are likely to influence them, are ... a normal condition of human life," but they still rue that "much political debate betrays the marks of warfare ... rallying the troops and intimidating the other side."[31] Nothing could arouse revulsion more dependably than Teddy Roosevelt's urging that fearless criticism and high principles are not enough, that thoughtful men should not be too delicate for party politics and must "show them that one is able to give and to receive heavy punishment without flinching."[32] Contemporary philosophers are averse to "high feeling and special pleading" by partisans or on their behalf.

Readers may judge that I go too far in the direction of appreciation, or that I apologize for parties without sufficient attention to their content, or that I am inadequately appalled by partisans' characteristic intemperateness, or "extremism," or, equally likely, their blind loyalty or passive acquiescence to "leading strings." So I have made it my aim, along with assessing antipartyism and retrieving grounds for appreciating parties, to suggest elements of an ethic of partisanship. My goal is to chip away at the moral high ground claimed by partisans' adversaries, Independents, and to provide partisanship with at least an iota of dignity.

In 1880 Henry Adams, the historian and heir of two presidents, published a novel, *Democracy*.[33] Adams's heroine is a New York socialite, Madeline Lightfoot Lee. Mrs. Lee suffers from ennui. She has lost interest in salons, in philanthropy, in business. "She had resorted to desperate measures," Adams writes: "she had read philosophy in the original German, and the more she read, the more she was disheartened that so much culture should lead to nothing—nothing." Desperate, Mrs. Lee transplants herself in Washington, where enthralled by "the clash of interests" of forty million people, she is revived. The human interest of politics attracted her: the personalities and ambition, the indignities and betrayals, the occasional heroic successes of poet Alan Dugan's "winner," whom people bet on and bet against. Party politics is a dramatic agonistic contest, and not surprisingly a favorite subject for literature (and American musical theater[34]). Every writer on democratic politics, no matter how severely analytic or social scientific, was once gripped by "the great game of politics,"[35] the high stakes waged by those who believe they are on the side of the angels. I will try not to lose sight of the game entirely.

Plan of the Book

Readers who want to go directly to my appreciation of parties and partisanship can make their way to chapter 3, "Moments of Appreciation," chapter 7, "The Moral Distinctiveness of 'Party ID,'" and chapter 8, "Centrism and Extremism and an Ethic of Partisanship." These set out my account of the achievement parties represent and their worth as a subject for political theory. Be advised, however, that the surrounding chapters on historical and contemporary antipartyism provide more than context and setup for this work of reclamation. They hold independent interest, bringing to light antipartyism as a significant, understudied element of the history of political thought. These chapters also reveal the striking lapse in contemporary democratic theory, where parties are the objects of antipathy or studied neglect. As this plan of the book explains, my challenge is to create a typology that makes the ceaseless story of antipartyism manageable and to assess in some detail attempts to circumscribe, circumvent, or eliminate parties and to transform errant partisans into judicious Independents.

My objective in part 1 is to introduce two of the high points on my map of the terrain of antipartyism. The two "glorious traditions of antipartysim" that are the subjects of chapters 1 and 2 derive from the etymology and literal meaning of the term "party." Parties are parts. And in Latin *partire* means to divide. The two traditions can be thought of in terms of abhorrence of parties as "unwholesome parts" and abhorrence of parties as literally "divisive." From the standpoint of what I call "holism," all social and political groups threaten the unity and integrity of political order. Because parties have partiality and opposition *as their aim*, they stand out among parts as the most morally, politically, and aesthetically unabidable. The second high point on the antiparty terrain accepts social and political parts and partiality but sees parties as fatally divisive. These two antiparty traditions held sway from antiquity, losing their dominance only in the late nineteenth century. This discussion is historical but it will be apparent that my inquiry is from the standpoint of the present. I invite readers to consider how much contemporary antipartyism rests on either the latent appeal of holism or antipathy to the divisiveness that is the necessary work of political parties.

Apart from its intrinsic importance and centrality to the story of antipartyism, holism is not safely in the past. Partisans of holism exploit electoral politics in order to erase pluralism and impose an ideal, undivided order. A party to end parties is the pose of utopian and revolutionary parties—Puritan Levelers, Jacobins, Communists; it is the pose of parties of virtue, of national unity, of ethnic purity. I look at several living variations of holism: parties of virtue, "one-partyism" (why one party instead of no party?[36]), and majoritarianism when it assumes the form I call "shadow holism." Resistance to parties and partisanship in the holist tradition rests on ideas that are widely rejected today as antipluralist and antidemocratic. Rejection is not total, however. When parties claim the moral ascendancy that

11

comes from earning the approval of "the great body of the people," represent the minority as a sinister interest opposed to the people, and invoke a majority (a moral majority, a silent majority) as if it were the whole, we recognize the semblance of holism.

Holists cast parties as *parts against* rather than *parts of* the whole. In contrast, the second "glorious tradition" of antipartyism accepts pluralism but does not follow the logic of pluralism to parties. The objection to parties here is not to their partiality per se but to the fact that they are dangerously divisive, and there are myriad historical expressions of the view that parties are wantonly selfish and sinister factions, engines of destructive partiality. In chapter 2 I try to make this array of charges manageable by identifying several major themes: the Roman archetype, "the irrepressible hydra," and the classification of parties as a way of taming by categorization. The distinguishing mark of this glorious tradition of antipartyism is that parts and partiality are acceptable, but parties are not. They impede balance or harmony among recognized social parts. The mixed constitution is the most important and enduring example of the recognition and representation of pluralism without parties. After its decline, thinkers struggled to conceive how to organize government and manage political pluralism without parties. I illustrate the persistence of this tradition of antipartyism in American and European thought with the Federalists and Antifederalists, Sieyes's theory of political representation, and Hegel's corporatism.

Reconciliation to parties is possible from the standpoint of the second antiparty tradition because parties are less symptoms of deeper intolerable division than drivers of arrant divisiveness, disrupters of political equilibrium. They can conceivably be tempered and put to use. It is in response to the second glorious tradition of antipartyism that we get grudging acceptance of the divisions parties create and the trouble partisanship causes.

The episodic defense of parties of constitutional necessity is a halfway house between absolute condemnation and sympathy. In addition to acceptance of the exceptional party of necessity, there are three genuine "moments of appreciation," my subject in chapter 3. One moment sees parties as a form of regulated rivalry and acknowledges managed conflict as an achievement: "The Parties who are Out, are always a Curb, and a Bridle to those which are In, and the Parties which are In, are always a Terror and a Stirrer up to Vigilance in those which are Out."[37] A second appreciates parties as a way of organizing government and recruiting governors. These moments of appreciation owe to experience and are grasped by partisans themselves. A third is philosophical, the view from outside, remote from the ordinary self-understanding of partisans. This moment of appreciation casts parties as complementary, bearers of partial truths, agents of progress. In eclipse, I bring these moments of appreciation out of the shadows to serve as guides to the achievement of parties. They are the work of Burke, Hegel, Hume, and Mill.

These moments of appreciation were articulated before the rise of electoral parties, and remind us that orthodox standards of representativeness or responsiveness or accountability are not the only ones. Regulated rivalry, governing, and fruitful conflict have independent merit. They are touchstones for rehabilitating parties, and they provide groundwork for the ethics of partisanship I propose in part 3. These initial points on the terrain of antipartyism and moments of appreciation are sharply defined and surprisingly fixed. I illustrate them by drawing from the canon of European and American political thought and show that often contemporary opponents of parties and partisanship stand on well-worn spots of ground. Holism and fatal divisiveness are not the only sites of antipartyism, however. The landscape of antipartyism is also marked by high points shaped by later experience with broad electorates and institutionalized parties, what I call "post-party depression."

Beginning in the nineteenth century, extended suffrage, regular elections, and legalized party systems gave rise to a fresh set of attacks and prescriptions I gather under the rubric "progressive antipartyism" in chapter 4. Parties are reviled as corrupt and corrupting ("There can be no question that a great many men do deteriorate very much morally when they go to Albany"[38]). Parties' "open, conscious appeal to the body of the citizens"[39] is not salutary. Parties pander to voters or special interests; their business is "trafficking in policies."[40] As for partisans, they are seen as blind loyalists or craven "hacks" or, only slightly better, as rational calculators out for spoils. Partisans' undisputed moral superiors are "Independents," and a recurrent progressive fantasy is a party of Independents. Progressive hope for reform is not easily sustained, though. "The fundamental trouble," Teddy Roosevelt offered in uniquely vivid fashion, "was that the country was sick and tired of reform." "The average man was tired of decency in politics," and "the dog returned to its vomit."[41] Antipartyism raises the troubling question: if parties are central to elections and elections integral to democracy, "Is Democracy a failure?"[42]

The array of complaints that comprise "progressive antipartyism" dominate political theory today. Although historical Progressivism is a parochial American pose, a latitudinarian view of progressive aversions resonates widely. So do the anxieties and correctives I discuss in chapters 5 and 6. The same holds for the normative arguments I make in Part III in defense of parties and partisanship. My materials in these chapters are predominantly American. This is not a project in comparative politics, clearly. But neither do the arguments apply exclusively to the United States. Some antipathies and correctives speak mainly to two-party systems, but for the most part they are familiar throughout democracies and democratic theory today.

Post-party depression is a tenacious political mood, and progressive antipartyism articulates its discontents. Virtually every element of contemporary antipartyism and every scheme for correcting the system by eliminating, circumventing, or containing parties echoes progressive antipartyism. In chapter 5, I show the persistence of progressive antipartyism in charges leveled at parties entrenched in what is aptly called "the system." In these accounts of party convergence, collusion, and cartel, parties fall short of the basic achievement of regulated rivalry. And insofar as parties are competitive, they are not responsive to "the common, recognizable interests of ordinary people, and nothing more."[43] The confounding ambiguity dividing critics is whether parties should be seen as agents of corporate predators, captured by "special interests," or as principals advancing their own special interests, extortionists involved in their own "elaborate influence-peddling scheme."[44] Is the "invisible government" behind the "ostensible government" actually run by parties, or by forces that work through them? I call this the "anxiety of influence" and trace the flip back and forth about the direction in which "undue influence" flows. I illustrate the phases of the anxiety of influence by looking at justifications for campaign finance reform.

Progressive antipartyism gives rise to a persistent set of schemes for "correcting the system," my subject in chapter 6. Like progressive aversions, these corrections remain the principal touchstones of antipartyism today. Two correctives stand out, sturdy features of American political life, which is my focus, and evident in other democracies as well. One is voluntarism, first put into self-conscious use as an antiparty alternative during the Progressive era. Nothing is more familiar than confidence in people's ability to organize associations in the public interest in opposition to special interests. "The group principle" and "good" civil society are democratic expectancies. They promise resources and motivation for civic engagement, potential counterweights to sinister interests, and, collectively, a democratic alternative to "the system" of parties and partisanship. The sometimes fanciful reflections of civil society theorists do not pose a grave challenge to parties and partisanship, on my view, but the actual explosion of groups—advocacy groups, interest groups, self-styled public interest groups—does. These groups embody an unreconstructed pluralism that inhibits the work of parties, and reflect a plurality of political identities in competition with and often in opposition to partisanship.

A second corrective to the party system concedes the centrality of voting and elections but sees parties as corrosive of democratic participation. These reforms are designed to address a new charge: that both for strategic reasons and as the unintended consequence of their failings, parties depress participation, demobilize citizens, "turn voters off." The interventions theorists propose would revive and refashion electoral participation, making it deliberative and nonpartisan. We recognize contemporary political theorists of civil society and deliberative democracy as heirs of early progressives in disposition and political imagination, in their implacable antipartyism, and in their visions of reform.

Unquestionably, the high point of antipartyism today is aversion to partisanship specifically. Part 3 is my appreciation of parties and

15

partisanship, and I begin by answering the charges laid on partisanship. At moments of party polarization such as the one in which I write, the barb "partisan" comes out of improbable mouths, a virtual reflex. It is no virtue to cultivate the disposition that your party is "on the side of the angels." We recognize "partisan" as invective. Even if parties have their uses, it seems, partisanship is abhorrent. While partisans battle one another, all claiming to be on the side of the angels, critics demonize them all and see Independents as virtuously above the fray. Antipartisanship is rooted in a view of partisans as degraded citizens, political dependents. Whatever the source of dependency—clientelism, capture, sheer gullibility, or abandonment of personal judgment—the partisan exhibits not an iota of political self-reliance. "Independence" is a superior status, morally and politically. It is more than simple nonpartisanship; independence is a distinct political identity. The luster of independence, its positive valence, can be explained. It borrows from a broader civic ideal of independence with deep roots in American political ideology, replanted in the soil of electoral politics. An ideology of independence may be distinctively American, but turning away from partisanship and favoring independence is a widespread phenomenon. The luster of independence can be dulled, as I attempt to do, by demonstrating its "weightlessness." In chapter 7, I take sides—not between opposing partisans but between partisanship and independence. I make a case for the moral distinctiveness of "party ID," and sketch an ethic of partisanship for private citizens.

An ethic of partisanship for party officials, activists, and partisan representatives is my subject in chapter 8, "Centrism and Extremism." "Extremist" is not a neutral term of political geography. It is leveled by partisans against the opposition and by political pundits selecting the strongest possible negative label. "Extremist" is a radical intensification of "partisan" as a term of attack, the ultimate political opprobrium. "Centrism" is not neutral, either; it is meant to offer political reassurance. The title of this chapter poses a puzzle: the disjuncture between regular accusations of extremism in day-to-day politics, on the one hand, and what is often described as the characteristic centrism of major American parties, on the other. Political science's "spatial model" and "median voter" go only partway toward explaining incessant appeals to the terms "centrist" and "extremist." Also at work, I argue, are normative ideas about democracy, and in this respect the subject is not uniquely American. Extremism is something more than a reference to ideological positioning, an electoral strategy, or a term of political abuse. "Extremist" is convenient shorthand for three ways in which parties and partisans are unfaithful to democratic expectations and violate elements of an ethic of partisanship. "Extremist" signals abdication of responsibility for educating and mobilizing voters; it signals unresponsiveness to the comprehensive range of problems major parties are uniquely able to identify and address; and it signals the adoption of intransigence as a public value at the expense of getting the public business done.

Throughout *On the Side of the Angels* I defend parties and partisanship. Not all parties are defensible, of course. Not all parties are lawful, or should be. "Militant democracy" is the name for self-defense against parties that would exploit regulated rivalry in order to undo it. It is democracy's response to parties that do not accept that they are parts. The grounds for banning parties confirm, in the negative, the value of parties and virtues of partisanship. In chapter 9, I look at justifications for banning political parties, drawing on materials from a wide range of democracies. Violence, incitement to hate, existential challenges to political identity, and outside interference and control are the principal reasons for criminalizing parties. This list of reasons alerts us that in recent decades thinking about the bounds of permissible party organization has shifted away from the original terms of democratic self-defense that defined "militant democracy." The orthodox justification for banning parties with overtly antidemocratic political ideologies such as fascism or communism cannot be neatly applied to parties that incite hatred against an ethnic or regional group, to religious parties that oppose some aspect of secular government, to parties with separatist programs, or to parties that pose existential challenges to national identity.[45]

This final chapter points up the parameters of my study. The appreciation of parties and partisanship I set out has meaning in the context of freedom of political association and competitive elections, where pluralism expressed in the form of the regulated rivalry of political parties is accepted. *On the Side of the Angels* is not an account of politics per se, and my appreciation does not apply, or not without serious accommodation, where pluralism is effectively thwarted.

Antipartyism: Coherence via Aversion

"Antipartyism" suggests that its object, "party," is an identifiable kind of political group. What is a political party? Jefferson encouraged the thought that political parties are universal: "Men have differed in opinion, and been divided into parties by these opinions, from the first origin of societies, and in all governments where they have been permitted freely to think and to speak, the terms whig and tory belong to natural as well as to civil history."[46] The claim that parties have persisted through all of history, much less the specific opposition between Whigs and Tories, is hyperbole, of course. I do not take up Jefferson's claim, nor do I trace the institutional history of parties, their changing types. That is the work of historians who struggle to define "party" in specific periods and political contexts. Interpretive debates about Roman factions have occupied scholars since the 1930s, to take one example. Did the Romans have stable political associations that could be called parties? If using modern ideological and electoral parties as a standard is inapt, what are the criteria for designating a political group a faction or party? Or, to take another example, which criteria determine the point at which political groupings in post-revolutionary America became political parties proper? Did the "fledgling parties" of the 1790s "define issues, shape public awareness, wage election campaigns, and organize government on a continental scale" and "successfully create a workable machinery to manage national politics"? Does it matter that creators themselves called the machinery "a party"?[47] The confident assertion that "parties are a phenomenon of the last 150 years, and as such are creatures of modernity"[48] begs the question.

Analytically, too, "party" is incoherent. If we recall the definition proposed by their chief defender, Burke, a party is "a body of men united, for promoting by their joint endeavors the national interest, upon some particular principle in which they are all agreed."[49] This is no definition, but a target of interpretation and quarrel. Not all parties are parties of principle; the emphasis should be on *particular*, not principle. Not all partisans share politically relevant preferences, even. Unsympathetic definitions substitute the pursuit of private interests for the national interest. Madison famously defined faction as a number of citizens united and actuated by some common impulse of passion or of interest adverse to the rights of other citizens, or to the permanent and aggregate interest of the community.

Cognizant of the vicissitudes of the history of parties and the variety of contexts in which they operate, and eschewing the normative quagmire, political scientists instead propose typologies and developmental steps. A fair culling of the literature suggests three main moves. First came parties as associations or caucuses of officeholders within legislative assemblies. Parties in government preceded the party in the electorate and the organization connecting officials to the world outside government. Mass electoral parties came later, products of extended suffrage, which incorporated large numbers of people into the political process. (Duverger subdivided mass parties further on the basis of origin—"internal parties" created by officials within government and "external parties" mobilized outside and often against the dominant forces in representative institutions— Socialist or Christian Democratic parties, for example.) Finally, on the view that at least some contemporary parties constitute a third type, political scientists struggle to characterize it. A modicum of consensus casts these parties as service organizations to candidates in a system described as "audience democracy," with "catch-all" parties geared to immediate electoral success and marked by the dominance of candidate-centered choice over platforms and programs.[50] The extreme of this type has been called the "instant party," which exploits communication technology and marketing strategy to appeal directly to voters; the exemplar is Silvio Berlusconi's Forza Italia born from the ambition and financial capital of one man.[51] A much discussed question in political science is whether the typology and evolutionary story of parties based on West European and American experience applies to newer European democracies, post-communist states, and others transitioning to representative democracy. Do they follow a similar trajectory and arrive at similar party forms, or diverge from them?[52]

Historical and social science studies of party go some way toward satisfying the great scholar of parties who complained about the confusion that results "from the tendency of lazy people to imagine that all things known by the same name must be the same."[53] It is wrong to assume that "a party is a party whether found in the United States in 1800 or in 1940." But too much delicacy and thick description can thwart understanding, too. I am encouraged to assert something general for the purposes of my work, even if it is something less than a full account of the defining characteristics of parties.

Parties are associations organized for political conflict; they are one form political conflict takes. That is a start, but this most basic element—political groups in opposition to one another, organized to exercise power—fails to distinguish parties from cabals, say, or revolutionary groups or what Mosca called "the struggles between gangs and gangsters."[54] When Madison said that parties arise in every *political* society, his point was telling. Parties do not arise in every society but only in political society where there is government with political offices to be occupied. "Parties live in a house of power," Weber wrote.[55] The aim of party conflict is to hold office and participate in government, not just a general "bid for power."[56] This distinguishes parties from revolutionary attempts to overturn rather than occupy office, from secret political clubs and societies tarred with the brush of sedition, from enterprising interest groups and pressure groups that seek political influence but not office,[57] from "movements" engaged in what Hofstadter usefully called "a nonresponsible critique of government," meaning they are not organized to govern.[58]

In short, a party is a group organized to contest for public office; it is avowed in its partisanship and operates not conspiratorially but in public view; it is not an ad hoc coalition or arrangement for vote trading and compromise on a specific issue, but an institution formed for ongoing political activity; and it can claim a substantial number of followers, in current terms, a partisan "base." Today, of course, the definition of party includes an additional element: parties contest for electors' votes. Hence Sartori's definition, which we now recognize as time-bound and truncated: "any political group identified by an official label that presents at elections, and is capable of placing through elections . . . candidates for public office."[59] There is one more notable piece. After saying that parties are "office-seeking," Weber goes on: their action is oriented toward the acquisition of social power . . . *no matter what its content may be.*"[60] A main theme of my project is just this: creating the content, drawing the lines of division, is the achievement of parties and partisans.

I suspend any further hunt for conceptual coherence, for what I think is a good reason. Before the emergence of modern governing and electoral parties, "party" was principally an aversive label. To put simply what I hope to demonstrate in detail, "party" was an accusatory term. Not all partial, political groups aspiring to govern were considered parties, and political pluralism was defended without extending acceptance to parties. Parties were often contrasted, in accusatory mode, with benign social divisions and political groups, organized classes or interests. Staple accusations against a noxious political group earn it the dishonorable label "party." These aversions have endured over time, and I take the latitude of referring to them as traditions of antipartyism. It is less party that gives *On the Side of the Angels* coherence than antipartyism. And it is antipartyism that paradoxically provides the terms for moments of appreciation and the elements of an ethic of partisanship. I begin, then, with "glorious traditions of antipartyism."

PART I

Glorious Traditions of Antipartyism and
Moments of Appreciation

CHAPTER 1

———⟫•◇•⟪———

Glorious Traditions of Antipartyism: Holism

While the character, organization, and purpose of parties vary over history and in local political context, the negative content of the label "party"—the reference to despised groups—is surprisingly steady. The coherence of my subject is supplied not by any expectation that "party" is a distinct and well-defined concept or singular institution, then, but by identifiable streams of antipartyism. It is less the object of loathing that provides unity to my discussion than the reasons why "party" and its counterparts, faction and sect, have been accusatory terms. "Party" may not have coherence, but aversions do.

In this chapter and the next I map the terrain of antipartyism up to the time when parties became accepted first as governing and then as electoral parties in a regular party system. The terrain of historical antipartyism has two high points, two "glorious traditions." The first sees parties as unwholesome parts. From the standpoint of what I call "holism," all social and political groups threaten the unity and integrity of political order. Because parties have partiality and opposition *as their aim*, they stand out among parts as the most esthetically, morally, politically unabidable. The second high point on the antiparty terrain accepts social and political parts and partiality but sees parties as dangerously divisive. It is one thing to accept divisions and to institutionalize pluralism in a system of political representation. It is another thing to organize political conflict within or among acceptable parts by means of the accusatory "party." For parties turn accepted social and political divisions into warring factions. Or they create novel divisions for the sole purpose of contesting for power. In this second glorious tradition, recognition and acceptance of pluralism and partiality is compatible with antipathy toward parties. Division and divisiveness are distinct dangers, then, each with its antiparty tradition. These themes persist in politics today.

Because the holist tradition rejects pluralism, it is a more profound challenge than the tradition that accepts pluralism but rejects parties as fatally divisive. "Moments of appreciation" of parties emerge when experience and reflection suggest that parties are not necessarily destructive and can have their uses. Holism in contrast is hostile to every political manifestation of pluralism and division; parties are particularly virulent, but they are not holism's only target. For philosophical holists, parties are a second-order concern. Holism deserves attention even though it is not the most prevalent form of antipartyism today, and not only because holist antipartyism is the position of philosophers. Beyond that, the spirit of antipathy toward pluralism, the longing for unity, is always with us. It remains a source of antipartyism today. It is an element of aversion to parties and partisanship even among democratic thinkers. Holism deserves attention, too, because avowed partisans of holism exploit party politics in order to erase pluralism and impose an ideal undivided order. This form of antipartyism is not purely philosophical and is not safely in the past then. After examining the basic contours of holism, I explore three contemporary incarnations.

Unwholesome Parts

This antiparty tradition, which I call the holistic account, attacks parties as parts. It insists that political society should be a unity and that divisions are morally unwholesome and politically fatal. The formulations are familiar: an organic body politic, an indivisible nation or people, unitary royal or popular sovereignty, a general will that cannot err, one determinable common good. The basis of holism may be metaphysical (divine creation or an orderly cosmos), ideological (classlessness), or prudential (the severe requirements of civil peace).

Holism can be hierarchical or communitarian and egalitarian. Often it has a pronounced esthetic dimension, which pictures divisions as hideous imperfections. (The monstrous image of a body politic with two heads captures this horror.[1]) Marks of this form of antipartyism are the supreme value placed on integrity, and the identification of division with alienation—a falling off from original unity.

From a holist perspective, every partial group and association draws off loyalty and attachment and fosters particular interests and opinions. Every division signals disunity. Even relatively stable social groupings and entrenched, aptly named social "orders," such as estates of the realm, undermine unity. No form of pluralism is benign. That is why "harmony" and "balance" are poor formulations for this anti-party tradition. "Balance" in particular is accepting of parts and counterparts. If division is thinkable—like the mythic division of labor in Plato's *Republic*—the parts must be cast as natural, unalterable elements of an indivisible city or soul. This was precisely Aristotle's criticism of holism and the impetus to his account of the polis as a compound and of the mixed polity as the best possible regime. For holists, however, parts, especially if they are awarded political recognition, are disfiguring and signal disunity. Singleness is the watchword. Antipartyism is simply the most ferocious expression of holism's global antipathy to pluralism, the most ferocious because partiality in the form of political parties is the final failure. Parties are seen as parts *against*, not parts *of*, a whole.

Holism is antipolitical, and holist utopias make this vivid. In every perfectionist community, the absence of political institutions is the ideal. Where there is true unity, no coercion or constraint is necessary. Political authority, even the most rational or democratic, is evidence of conflict. Thus philosophical creators of utopia prescribe anarchy or technical superintendence, the wisdom of sages or Fourier's high priestesses guaranteeing every member of the phalanx his or her personal, gratifying "sexual minimum." Politics means absence of order, not a way to create or maintain order. In saying "holism is antipolitical" I am also making a theoretical point about politics. Politics is motivated by pluralism, by divisions that become the basis for conflict over holding political office and exercising political power.

For holist thinkers, no division, hence no politics, and certainly no party, is tolerable. It makes little difference whether the basis of divisions that give rise to partiality and political conflict is material goods, or honor, or opinion—including opinion about the common good, or sheer ambition and love of intrigue. Any political authority, especially any mixed constitution or system of political representation, concedes the plurality of parts; politics is fit only for circumstances of pluralism and conflict, which holism cannot abide.[2]

Two holist assumptions dictate aversion to politics and therefore to parties: first, that there is an identifiable common good or good of the whole and, second, that no political recognition and arrangement of parts, no dynamic of cooperation, and certainly no dialectic of conflict can illuminate the common good and move from fragmentation to unity. To drive this point home, holists typically insist that ordinary political actors will always fail to understand the common good and prevent alienation. Instead, this is the business of the creative founder, the iconic legislator—Moses, the disinterested expert, the philosopher, the unchallenged sovereign. In Rousseau's terms, unity is the work of a semi-divine intelligence molding a generation of children:

> Individuals must be obliged to subordinate their will to their reason; the public must be taught to recognize what it desires. Such public enlightenment would produce a union of understanding and will in the social body. . . . Hence the necessity of a lawgiver.[3]

Holism is antipolitical. It may also be classically utopian in the sense of picturing an ideal order that is less prescriptive than cautionary: meant not as an aspiration for revolutionary transformation but rather as a demonstration in thought of how far we always are from the community we can imagine. The heart of utopian holism is an image of perfection, and the point is plain: what is perfect cannot be improved. There is no reason or room for politics in utopia. Perfect, whole, it is immune to change. In classical utopias the best order is one that is "always and ever the same."

Mortality, not ordinary instability or injustice, haunts holism, and thoughts about eternal life can be found in classical utopias ancient and modern, in Christian idylls of life before the fall or the Puritan "Eternal City" on earth, and in modern political thought. Mortality is a theme running through the great texts *Leviathan* and *The Social Contract*. Mortals and governments die, Hobbes wrote, but the artificial man can have an artificial eternity of life: "For by the nature of their Institution, they are designed to live, as long as Man-kind, or as the Lawes of Nature, or as Justice it selfe, which gives them life."[4] Rousseau's lawgiver has "a task which is beyond human powers and a non-existent authority for its execution" because the body politic begins to die the day it is born.[5] Neither author was historically hopeful. Both speculated that perpetuation if not immortality was closely tied to an undivided whole. The contrast with pluralist theories of every kind is striking. Where there is pluralism, change is expected. Political institutions are human achievements that, like constitutions themselves (and despite their name) are complex, changeable, and good for the living or perhaps for posterity but not for eternity.[6]

Metaphysical versions of holism and classical utopias with their extraordinary legislators cast all parts as unwholesome. Sweeping in their condemnation of pluralism, many philosophers of holism have little to say about parties specifically. They are beneath contempt or notice. For my purposes, this tradition of antipartyism is best exemplified by the secular, skeptical, defensive holism of Hobbes and Rousseau. Hobbes describes Leviathan as an artificial man in which the sovereign is the artificial soul, giving life and motion to the whole body.[7] Rousseau's ideal was a public person formed by the union of all other persons, an artificial and collective body acquiring "its unity, its common ego, its life and its will."[8] Discriminating in their assessment of the dangerousness and dysfunction of partial groups and associations, Hobbes and Rousseau singled out parties as the most threatening. Parties are particularly anathema because division is their origin and aim. Preventatives aim at suppressing parties and partisanship above all.

"Worms in the Bowels"

The great question for Hobbes was how to unite, not just combine individuals, who are willful and self-protective and fall naturally into a war of all against all, to form Leviathan. Only the absolutely central role of conflict in Hobbes explains the ferocious temper of his anti-partyism, and the nature of his solution. To Judge what is necessary for security is natural to individuals born to preserve themselves and their own advantage; so is association with others in self-defense. The private judgment of individuals and groups, and conflicts of judgment, first over the imperatives of survival and then extending to every imaginable aspect of social life, cannot be extirpated and cannot be dependably suppressed. Hobbes's grim, exhaustive account of the sources of division says it all. Disagreements arise in connection with riches, reputation, and every other thing that is valued and that, along with fearful anticipation of insecurity, produces "a perpetual and restless desire of power after power." Diseases of the commonwealth proceed from the poison of seditious doctrine, chief among them "that every private man is Judge of Good and Evil actions."[9] Hobbes's principal concern was opinion as the basis for factions that organize and express disagreement. Opinion is the source of political divisions, and organized opinion *about* political order is fatal to it. *Leviathan* is a picture of an ongoing state of emergency; there is no room for politics, no safe partisanship.

Private judgment could not be suppressed but it could be renounced, and the wills of individuals could be aligned. Hobbes's effort was to show that each subject could take a unified sovereign's will as his or her own.[10] Men may reduce all their wills to one will, by appointing one man "to bear their person." This is more than consent, Hobbes writes; it is a real unity of them all. A multitude of men are made one person by being represented by one person; unity cannot otherwise be understood in multitude.[11] The unified sovereign's judgment of right and wrong, good and evil, lawful and unlawful, constitutes the civil law and the public conscience. The implications were radical. Plainly, so-called mixed constitution is not government at all on this view, but fragmentation of the commonwealth into factions. Hobbes attributed the civil war to widespread belief in mixed monarchy—the division of governmental powers among king, lords, and commons. Similarly, voting as a mechanism to decide between parties and policies is simply the replication of the conflict that was supposed to end with exit from the state of nature. Hobbes's description of voting literally echoes the language he uses to describe the state of nature, where equality causes and perpetuates conflict: "the Votes are not so unequall, but that the conquered have hopes by accession of some few of their own opinion at another sitting to make the stronger Party."[12] Hobbes's is a theory of sovereign absolutism in the service of a stable whole. He laid out in detail a system of public education through the discipline of language, law, and religion to reinforce this ongoing, act of renunciation of division and appreciation of unity.

Hobbes also offers concrete counsel to the sovereign for warding off division. His recommendations are simple: criminalize or if necessary license and regulate groups. He provides an elaborate discussion of "systems," by which he meant numbers of men joined in one interest or business: systems "regular" and "irregular," lawful and unlawful. His catalogue includes public bodies (licensed corporations for trade, for example), armed leagues of subjects, associations based on the popularity of ambitious men. The variety of what Hobbes tellingly called "bodies politiques subordinate and subject to a sovereign power" is virtually unlimited, and groups formed for every imaginable business and to advance every imaginable opinion are latently if not actively political. They are all divisions, bound to make political claims and demand political recognition, if not a share of political authority. (Hobbes's fearful conviction is echoed today to opposite purpose in the hopeful claim of democratic pluralists and theorists of civil society that "any association, however innocent it might seem, is potentially a center of resistance."[13]) General "concourse" is lawful, Hobbes concedes, but as in everything else associations are assessed for their public utility and the sovereign's judgment of benign versus seditious is final. "All uniting of strength by private men for evil intent, unjust; if for intent unknown, dangerous to the public and unjustly concealed." Cabals in assemblies are always unlawful. So are factions disputing church government. Worst of all are parties organized around contesting opinions about public policy or who should exercise authority. Holism is undone when a "body politique of subjects" is free to "divide the dominion, contrary to peace and defense." Leviathan is a prescription for preventatives and purging. Hobbes's revulsion was patent; unwholesome is the right word. He called corporations "worms in the bowels of the commonwealth," which it is the sovereign's duty to expel.[14]

"The General Will"

Hobbes's canonical counterpart in this tradition of holist antiparty-ism is Rousseau. Rousseau's antagonism to *Leviathan* is a set-piece in the history of modern political thought, but on this matter the philosophers are of one mind. True, in place of Hobbes's account of conflict springing from judgments about personal security and opinions about good and evil, Rousseau put a sophisticated social psychology of the invention of needs and dynamic of dependence. Also, Rousseau imbibed as Hobbes did not the *Republic*'s notion that in the best social order all the members *feel* their connection to the whole and to the common good. An immediate sense of identification and unity, an absence of personal experience of tension between obligation and inclination, marks a well-ordered republic. Finally, then, Rousseau's single will was republican, not absolutist. That said, like Hobbes, Rousseau gave central place to will and willfulness and agreed that there can be just one authoritative view on every matter concerning the common good. And both conceived of a radically transformative politics. Like Hobbes's sovereign, Rousseau's general will must be created, and to persist the general will requires severe preventative institutions, stern pedagogies, and elaborate rituals that repress and redirect temptations to pluralism and partiality.[15] The aim is not a neutral judge, an impartial Lockean umpire to resolve disagreements, but real unity. Pluralism is anathema.

The general will was everything to Rousseau.[16] The general will is inalienable and indivisible, and *The Social Contract* is one long investigation of how to prevent division and alienation. Because private life is a distraction from public life, there should be no civil society or a radically enfeebled one. Because every private will inclines by its nature to partiality, every private association or "sectional society" is formed at the expense of the whole. Citizens' "relations among themselves should be as limited, and relations with the entire body as extensive, as possible." The point of perfection is reached "if each citizen can do nothing whatever except through cooperation with [all] others." Rousseau's judgment is famous: "When particular interests begin to make themselves felt and sectional societies begin to exert an influence ... the common interest becomes corrupted" and "the meanest interest impudently flaunts the sacred name of the public good."[17]

Motivated by radical holism, Rousseau, like Hobbes, rejected political theories of mixed government, which I argue is one mark of the distinction between the two glorious traditions of antipartyism. Like Hobbes, Rousseau in *The Social Contract* opposed any political recognition of parts.[18] For Rousseau, government conceived in terms of checks and balances makes of the sovereign "a fantastic creature, composed of bits and pieces." His characterization of mixed government, that mainstay of ancient and modern constitutionalism, is withering:

> It is said that Japanese mountebanks can cut up a child under the eyes of the spectators, throw the different parts into the air, and then make the child come down, alive and all of a piece. This is more or less the trick that our political theorists perform—after dismembering the social body with a sleight of hand worthy of the fairground, they put the pieces together again any how.[19]

Rousseau extends this stricture to political representation, at least when it comes to legislating. The moment a people adopts representatives to make laws, it is no longer a people, he insists.[20] "The people as a whole makes rules for the people as a whole." "Sovereignty cannot be represented for the same reason it cannot be alienated." We, the communal we, obey ourselves.[21]

In *The Social Contract*, everything is geared to seeing that the people's will is expressed without resort to partial associations, above all to parties. Deliberation, discussion, persuasion about public matters are invitations to parties; they assume partial and interested perspectives, even if these are perspectives on the common good. Rousseau uses "deliberation" to signal something dramatically different from the guiding idea of contemporary deliberative democracy.[22] Today, deliberation is a collective process of shaping informed opinions in assemblies or in other public fora. Rousseau does not imagine that a citizen's understanding or disposition to will the general will needs public consideration of alternatives and reasoned arguments for and against. Each sole citizen possesses the "criteria for evaluation."[23] The general will exists, and simply needs to be affirmed and expressed. The best hope for people wishing the public good and affirming it is for each to decide on the acceptability of a proposal alone. The surest corruption and seduction is initiating proposals and debating them in an assembly, much less in partial associations; that is a recipe for the representation of interests and for parties. This explains Rousseau's stern requirement that ratification of laws must be in person, with no abstention. It explains his requirement that citizens vote without communicating with one another, deliberating only with oneself.[24] It explains, too, why the division of the public into majority and minority is a sign that considerations other than the common good are the basis for decision. Any outcome short of unanimity (and even unanimity when consensus does not correspond to the general will) is an expression of partiality.[25]Anything less than assent by all is abhorrent. Unanimity is not just an ideal but the premise of Rousseau's republicanism. The holist spirit of Rousseau's republic of virtue is pervasive; a falling off is a profound, moral disappointment: "Not all the realism in the world can make it easier to forgive the world the inability to accommodate . . . [these] principles."[26]

In holist accounts, organized classes, social group, and voluntary associations threaten unity. Parts just are partial. They are actual or latent political parties. We see that antipartyism is a second-order thesis of holism. Parties are most despised because their raison d'être is partiality and conflict. They organize around conflicting opinions about authority and the exercise of power. They seek to impose partial interests, or their own particular opinion of the public interest. Where political order is a single, coherent whole, parties do not arise. If they do, unity and effective government require their extirpation or suppression or renunciation. Love of party is inseparable from subdivision by cabal, from "cantonizing" the state. Small wonder that holists see parties as the work of vicious intent and partisans as public enemies.

Partisans of Holism

In chapter 2, I turn to the dominant historical tradition of antipartyism, which accepts pluralism and the political representation of parts without conceding anything to parties. This second tradition of antipartyism is wonderfully various, and I will lay out as much as possible of its rich detail. First, however, I want to reflect that while holist antipathy often owes to the timeless distance between philosophy and political practice, it is not the exclusive preserve of philosophers and designers of utopia. Holist antipartyism is a real political force. Modern holists want to repress or extirpate pluralism, above all its expression in political parties. Moreover, contemporary holists must reckon with the claims of democracy and with parties as a defining element of representative democracy. The object of aversion is not just social and political division in general, then, but governing and electoral parties specifically. Partisans of holism confront both the political pluralism that is the universal circumstance of parties and the actuality of parties. Their party is a means to erase or repress the rest.

So, I must qualify the conclusion of the last section. Holists see parties as the work of vicious intent and partisans as public enemies, with one exception. They offer dispensation to a party aimed at arresting alienation and restoring wholeness. Partisans of holism claim that only one party represents the nation or people and is the vanguard of unity. Communists and fascists, partisans of holism emerging from post-colonialism and crises of national integration, and theocratic parties fit this mold.[27] Parties of virtue, of national unity, of ethnic purity, of revolutionary transformation are holists. A party to end parties is the pose of utopian, revolutionary, and "movement" parties—Puritan Levelers, Jacobins, communists—shared by conservative, organicist advocates of holism. "The builders of utopias . . . had no place for anything so cluttered, so persistently unresolved, as party competition, for it seemed to be the enemy of all who wished to be permanently, universally, and gloriously right."[28] Hegemony is not enough; any manifestation of political pluralism is repulsive.[29] For partisans of holism: "In the cracked mirror of parties the country no longer recognizes its image."[30]

To be clear: historically, it was common for partisans to deny that they comprise a party, as I show in some detail in the next chapter. Disavowal of partisanship was the rule before governing and electoral parties became accepted institutions and the legitimacy of a party system was established. The self-designation "a party to end all parties" was standard political fare. In a well-studied example, Lord Bolingbroke's party was supposed to be the last party; its aim was to eliminate the conditions that gave an excuse for party.[31] Other instances come readily to mind. At their inception, American Federalists and Republicans each declared themselves defender of the Constitution. Each saw the opposition as intractably subversive, treasonously allied with foreign powers. Each anticipated uniting all parties for the general welfare—an end of parties.[32] Similarly, the French revolutionaries agreed only in their opposition to parties. Danton's assertion can stand in for Condorcet's view on one side and Robespierre's on the other: "If we were to exasperate each other we would end up with forming parties, whereas we only need one, that of reason."[33]

The claim to be a party to end all parties was common enough, then. Before a regular party system was well conceived or even tentatively experienced, denial of partiality was a regular feature of political organization. As Madison cautioned, there is every incentive for factions to claim to represent the nation, the people, or the public good. But this standard repudiation of partisanship was not rooted in a holist political philosophy or "derive[d] from a thoroughly metaphysical compulsion."[34] Holist parties that arise after the introduction of modern party systems indicate clearly the difference between what had been the normal historical disavowal of partiality, on the one hand, and genuine holist ambition, on the other. Holist parties are distinguished by their radical aim: to overturn the present political order, triumph over enemies, put an end to every political manifestation of faction, indeed to every eruption of pluralism and social division, to achieve complete and final, not contingent, success. Holists maintain a vision of unity as the overarching ideal and their practical political goal. They take on the party form to take parties out. Ordinary partisans in democratic states do not intend to eliminate all challengers. They accept party opposition as regular and legitimate. When we hear a party claim to represent the people today, we ordinarily understand it as hypocrisy or rhetorical flourish. True, partisans do often see themselves as carriers of an account of justice for all. And as I discuss shortly, majoritarianism can take the form of "shadow holism." That said, partisans today accept their status as parts in a system of regulated rivalry. When they do not, when a party of virtue seeks to erase political pluralism, democracies may be justified in banning them, and I return to justifications for "militant democracy's" self-defense against partisans of holism in chapter 9.

I want to take a brief look at three living variations of holism: the party of virtue, "one-partyism," and majoritarianism when it assumes a form I call "shadow holism." Each is a step or more removed from the philosophical holism I set out above; they can be described as holism with weak foundations or none at all. Each is a step away from utopianism, too. Each living version of holism makes its appearance in a context where political pluralism is recognized, and each assumes the form of the enemy, that is, refers to itself as a party. Together, the party of virtue, one-partyism, and majoritarianism as "shadow holism" indicate the range and persistence of holist impulses. I am not attempting an exhaustive account of partisans of holism or proposing a taxonomy here, but rather illustrating the turns holist antipartyism can take, some of them dreadfully familiar. My intention in what follows is to take this glorious tradition of antipartyism out of the study and into the lit arena of politics.

Parties of Virtue

For holists, party organization is an opportunistic route to power; election results are described as revolutionary; and once in office, rival parties are outlawed. The goal is not just political victory but eliminating rivals by devouring, crushing, or criminalizing opposition parties or by breaking up old combinations and absorbing them as clients, becoming the *pater* of the whole, resonant of Caesarism.[35] (We can understand why German thinkers in the 1930s, motivated by the desire to understand the domination of a leader of a party identified with the whole state, produced studies of Roman parties and the rise of Caesar.[36])

An early and exemplary holist party is the Jacobins. Starting out as a parliamentary party, one among others, the Jacobins assumed the mantle of "*the* revolutionary party." In *On Revolution*, Hannah Arendt describes Robespierre and St. Just battling against spontaneously organized communal groups—the districts of Paris, the council system, popular societies—as well as against competing parties. These entities stood for pluralism and the notion of divided power. They all had to be emasculated. Multipartyism rests on recognition that the opposition is a legitimate institution and "is possible only under the assumption that the nation is not *une et indivisible*."[37] The party of virtue was the party with transformative ambitions for a general will and centralized power. "Robespierre's rule of terror was indeed nothing else but the attempt to organize the whole French people into a single gigantic party machinery through which the Jacobin club would spread a net of party cells all over France."[38]

Whatever its philosophy of unity—and not all holists could be described as partisans of virtue—the goal of engaging in party conflict is to put an end to politics. For Marx, "winning the battle of democracy" was one possible avenue to dictatorship of the proletariat. Only vulgar Marxists, devoid of Marx's own sense of political contingency and opportunism and convinced of "iron necessity," think it "peculiar to organize a political party for the achievement of a coming eclipse of the sun."[39] Everywhere party systems existed, communists were divided about whether electoral activity would undercut their self-proclaimed role as the leading edge of a world revolutionary movement, and whether to disavow the overthrow of government by force.[40] Depending on circumstances, some were prepared to exploit the electoral process as a transitional moment. Given this purpose, the holist party often has distinguishing features. The Communist Party USA stated plainly that it did not seek its strength in numbers but in "selected, dedicated, indoctrinated, and rigidly disciplined members."[41] ("Every revolution is a Puritan revolution."[42]) Holist parties are marked by organizational singularities: secrecy, front organizations, conspiratorial activity, central control.[43] Their organization and practice are antithetical to normal party politics with its invitation to mass membership and party leadership responsive to supporters. Communists faced the charge that the CP was only "pretending to be but another political party."[44]

Rule by a communist party is democracy in its original meaning: in classical political thought democracy is partial, class rule. But for partisans of holism, democracy was intended to culminate in the transcendence of class and party, freeing and realizing humanity. In what C. B. MacPherson apologetically called "the real world of democracy," the general will can express itself only through a single party, a monopolistic and monolithic force standing for the whole classless society.[45] Pluralism and competitive parties are justifiably suspended in the name of a democracy that only the party, with its superior consciousness, can create. Understanding one's own time correctly, that is, why this is the final struggle and the resolution of all contradictions, justifies one-party rule. The logic behind the formation of a holist party is not perverse if the leading role of the party is provisional, a phase of social evolution, and if—after all enemies are vanquished and pluralism smoothed away—the party would cease to be one. For the party, "the need for action itself was transitory, and they had no doubt that after the victory of the revolution further action would simply prove unnecessary or subversive," that politics would disappear, that the substance of politics would become administration.[46] Partisans of holism have "a privileged relation with history."[47] "After the nation . . . had stepped into the shoes of the absolute prince, it became, in the course of the twentieth century, the turn of the party to step into the shoes of the nation."[48]

The German National Socialists are the modern touchstone of holism in Western Europe.[49] Arendt's famous thesis has it that unlike ordinary parties, totalitarian parties were not held together by identifiable economic, social, or political interests. They were massive organizations of the indifferent, comprising people who never join parties and hardly ever go to the polls, now recruited and "mobilized" in opposition to pluralism. "Society" with its divisions, was a disintegrated, disintegrative morass; "the class-ridden and party-ridden nation-state" was loathsome.[50] Repudiation of regular parties and political organization

> transformed the slumbering majorities behind all parties into one great unorganized, structureless mass of furious individuals who had nothing in common except their vague apprehension that the hopes of party members were doomed, that, consequently, the most respected and articulate and representative members of the community were fools and that all the powers that be were not so much evil as that they were stupid and fraudulent.[51]

We do not have to accept Arendt's thesis that atomism and absence of social ties are the condition for totalitarian mobilization. Recent historical accounts propose a different set of conditions that allowed these parties to come to power.[52] But historians concur in the broad conclusion. Party fragmentation and abdication of responsibility for forming coalitions and governing, the absence of legislative majorities, the "outsider" antiparty stance of the president and rule by decree all contributed, and Holist parties rushed to fill the political vacuum.[53] The holist party to end parties placed itself outside and against the party system. It rested on a "new terrifying negative solidarity" in what has been described as a passionate struggle against democracy and parliamentarism; a view of parties as moral aberration.[54] The holist party exploited deep antipathy toward political pluralism. It claimed completeness and infallibility. Its aspirations were inclusive: control of the church, regular state bureaucracy, military, business elites, labor unions, media. It eliminated "islands of separateness."[55] The party "invade[s] the private and social domains of family life, education, cultural and economic concerns." The aim was to penetrate the interior lives and wills of subjects: a "*Weltanschauung* by which they would take possession of man as a whole."[56] As the head of the Nazi Labor Office put it, "in the Nazi state the only private individual was someone asleep."[57] Control of government was neither the end nor the principle means, then. The party aimed at precedence over government.

Unifying, purging, repairing divisions, or casting groups out as aliens and enemies were the great holist aims that motivated and justified antiparty partisans. We know from experience that sham avowals of support for democracy are compatible with disgust at parties, with political division as abomination, with revulsion at arrant pluralism. Indeed, the background circumstance of holist parties is widespread aversion to the perceived impotence, the "chatter and intrigue," of divisions represented in parliamentary democracy, the "cancers" and "disorders" of parties. "In so many places the cry has gone up that *the* party or *the* leader is defending the people against *the* politicians."[58] So that "even the simple step of becoming a party could seem a betrayal to some purists . . . a descent into the soiled arena of bourgeois parliamentarism."[59] The promise to unite the people, to dissolve other parties, gives the "prepotent and monolithic" claims of holist parties their appeal.[60]

Carl Schmitt studied Caesarism and looked to the "uninhibited voluntarism" of the Bolsheviks and to the Fascist March on Rome.[61] The party had no need to be tested in elections. "The concurrence of the masses is necessary, but not their participation,"[62] meaning the popular will can be expressed through "acclamation" better than through "the statistical apparatus" that makes democracy "a registration system for secret ballots." "The will of the people is always identical with the will of the people, whether a decision comes from the yes or no of millions of voting papers, or from a single individual who has the will of the people even without a ballot, or from the people acclaiming in some way."[63] The phrase "direct mobilization" is revealing. There is the tenor of ecstasy, a palpable wave of unity. It overrides politics understood as representation and negotiation of particulars. There is only consolidation of national homogeneity in the plebiscitarian executive by spontaneous acclamation en masse.

The experience of holist parties—disciplined organizations, vehicles for spectacularly vicious claims to unity, organizational bases for totalitarianism, carriers of the logic of acting in lieu of the popular will until it is properly educated and unified—produced an apprehensiveness about parties difficult to overcome. It remains a source of antipartyism in parts of Europe today.[64] It spawned the theory of "militant democracy," justifying exceptions to freedom for political association and criminalization of certain parties. Observers grimly acknowledge that democracy "not merely stabilizes free regimes, it makes stronger unfree regimes, and it has made possible totalitarianism."[65] We recognize this wary response as political prudence and that "militant democracy" is not antiparty. The prescription is not to eliminate political pluralism but to ensure competitive parties with connections to the associational life of civil society. That is the bulwark against holist antipartyism, against believers able "to think with complacency that everybody not of the Christian faith will be damned."[66]

There are other histories of holist parties in Western Europe, among them the aspirations of confessional parties beginning in the nineteenth century and persisting until after World War II. These parties eventually relaxed their antipluralist, antipolitical ambitions, and the reasons and processes by which some religious parties were integrated into the political systems they loathed and had intended to subvert have been well studied.[67] I mention them because some religious and ethnic parties today have the appearance of holism and raise many of the same fears. Do Islamist parties exploit electoral systems—relatively established systems, as in Turkey, or nascent ones—in order to supplant pluralist politics with the rule of the party of virtue? ("Is democracy a means or an end? . . . We say that democracy is a means, not an end."[68]) Is accepting one's status as just one part strategic—to avoid criminalization and survive as a haven for zealots and a focal point of militancy? (Is the partisan "a theocrat in a necktie"?[69]) Or does party organization and electoral activity signal acceptance of pluralism, accommodation to constitutional constraints and counterbalances, including multiple parties?

Holist parties that exploit electoral competition with the intention of eliminating parties as unwholesome expressions of pluralism are one modern incarnation of this tradition of antipartyism. Their party is a party to put an end to the whole rotten business.

One-Partyism

Another living version of holism is "one-partyism." Here, too, unity and singleness are watchwords. These partisans of holism share the tradition's aversion to division; they abhor pluralism and see competitive parties as its most repulsive expression. Only where European holists emerged from existing party systems and aimed at dismantling them, partisans of a single party typically emerge from colonialism or traditional societies where there are few modern political institutions and no established party system. Also in contrast, these holist partisans are committed to the permanence of their single party. One-partyism is not a transitional moment but a permanent cure for the pathologies of pluralism. Their party without counterparts is not supposed to be transcended "after the revolution."[70] Partisans of holism normalize their single party. They establish a "one-party system."

The glorious tradition of holist antipartyism began as the preserve of philosophers and designers of utopia. But philosophical underwriting of holism is rare in the case of one-partyism; so is a theological foundation or ideology of the sort we find articulated by parties of virtue. From the standpoint of philosophical holism we could say that one-partyism exploits holism, just as from the standpoint of pluralism it exploits the name "party." What one-partyism shares with this tradition of antipartyism is antipolitics. In this respect the fundamental complementarity between one-partyism and holism is plain: the aim is to erase pluralism, above all partisan political pluralism. Parties in opposition represent politics. ("The real worry is not that Ghana is not a democracy, which it plainly is not, but that with the intolerance of the government to opposition even as criticism, it may not even be political."[71]) One-partyism aims at political "prohibition, privation, privatization."[72] Its goal is "to monopolize public discourse absolutely, *to kill politics*, to eliminate politics as a means of defending oneself or expressing oneself."[73] Leaders justify one-partyism and the absence of competitive elections in holist terms.

Justifications for one-partyism take the form of standard holist aversions to pluralism, then. Only one nationalist party can take on external threats and challenge the imperial power. Only one party can counter internal threats to the nation. Tribal, racial, and religious divisions ensure that multiple parties would threaten national unity. Partisans of holism confront head on party competition as a defining characteristic of democracy. When Nasser organized the Egyptian National Union in the 1950s, he denounced multiparty systems as an instrument of reactionary landlords and capitalists; parties were responsible for the dissension and chaos of Egyptian national politics.[74] A Syrian Ba'thist party member explained that the party's raison d'être is "to protect the Arab nation from factionalism, backwardness, and corruption."[75] As in every variation of holism, multiple parties are parts *against*, not parts *of* a whole.

> The apologists for the one-party state are not unlikely to play both sides of the street; that is, to assert that the single party can appropriately exist without violating democratic precepts because it is essentially a continuation of the national unity won in the anti-colonial struggle, and at the same time, perhaps less overtly, to plead the necessity of having a single party if the break-up of the society is to be prevented.[76]

Referring to post-independence expectations for Nigerian unity, one leader asked, "Having just come inside from the rain, why should they be expected to return outside"?[77]

But why a *party*? Why not a dynasty or authoritarian military dictatorship, bureaucratic control or personal rule? Why one party instead of no parties?[78] Is the title "party" nominal, a borrowed authority? Do these partisans suffer "a bad conscience"?[79]

To be clear, holist one-partyism should not be confused with a hegemonic party.[80] Hegemonic parties acknowledge pluralism and oppositional parties, even though only one party has the electoral strength and capacity to govern. Alternation in office is practically impossible; still, formal competition and the existence of multiple parties is the rule. A dominant party may even behave competitively in the absence of viable opposition. In contrast, the holist party rejects opposition as an intolerable manifestation of pluralism. One-partyism is something other than dominance, simply.

Again, why a party? To say that the label "party" lends democratic legitimacy to what is basically personal or autocratic rule begs the question.[81] Political science is challenged to understand one-partyism.[82] Case studies associate it with political modernization, where the goal is "the ability of the government to make its writ run throughout the entire territory."[83] Fertile soil for the emergence of a single party is nation building following independence from colonial rule; so is the transition from traditional social systems to unified states.[84] (Contrary to the suggestion implicit in the phrase "transitional regime," "transition" does not presume a path to pluralism and party competition.[85]) Samuel Huntington provided the foundation of the answer to "why (one) party?" in his classic study of political order in changing societies. It is captured by his provocative claim that "Marx was a political primitive. Where Marx imagined social class was the key to revolution, Lenin saw it was the political party." Lenin "substituted a consciously created, structured, and organized political institution for an amorphous social class."[86] The party is a distinctive, autonomous *political* organization. Contra Marx, it can be independent of social forces and can manipulate them. The party is the instrument for centralizing and expanding power. "The triumph of revolution is the triumph of party government"[87] pertains, revolution or not, when the goal is filling the vacuum of authority.

In a modernizing, nationalizing context, party organization moves from mobilization to institutionalizing roots in the population to governing. The party is the vehicle for enlisting large numbers of people in overturning colonialism, conceiving a nation, eclipsing the political importance of traditional social divisions. The party brings people previously excluded from the nation into the community in whose name it governs.[88] The party's orientation is to the whole. It articulates new, public interests. It welds national identity. In the strongest terms, the party creates the nation. In this limited respect the holist party, which is antiparty, points ahead to moments of appreciation of parties. That is, it reminds us that the significance of party is not exhausted by electoral activity, representativeness, or accountability. It is a vivid, if grimly exaggerated reminder of parties' capacity to create and organize, rather than just to mirror interests, and to shape society. That party is not unique to democracies reminds us too of their centrality to governing.

Political scientists argue that under conditions of political modernization, monolithic one-party systems tend to be more stable than pluralist systems.[89] They point in this connection to the incentives for forming a party and the organizational mechanisms for party building and control that partisans of holism share with party builders generally. The single party produces members.[90] It recruits leaders.[91] It builds field organizations and regional and local networks. The party provides patronage in the form of jobs, and party connections provide avenues for advancement in every sphere, particularly where the bulk of resources is publicly controlled. One-partyism is underwritten by the fact that

> The requirement that incumbents accept the principle of turnover in office is the most difficult to institutionalize, particularly in poor nations with state-dominated economies, where yielding office means not only that incumbent leaders must give up their source of status, power, and income but also that a large coterie of their followers (sometimes millions of people) must yield preferments.[92]

The single party is *the* organizational form for partisans of holism where a goal is popular support. Modern party organization is always about the exhibition of support, ordinarily through competitive elections. As one-partyism shows, performance of partisanship takes other forms, including the "acclamation" of choreographed elections or plebiscites. Of course, "support" implies that the grant is conditional, and there is no actual chastening of one-party authority, only public affirmation through the party's condoned channels, compliance in the presence of varying kinds and degrees of repression. Creating a general opinion in favor of holism, persuading a majority—much less all the people—is not a necessity, but exhibitions of support, rituals of unity, are. "Lack of inner conviction is acceptable as long as every single party member and official is prepared to demonstrate publicly his/her commitment to party and President."[93] So apathy, cynicism, and depoliticization are compatible with one-partyism. One-partyism is "a notoriously useful instrument for the limitation of conflict and depression of political participation."[94] One-partyism requires the "contingent consent" of particular elites, but popular support requires precisely what the holist party does not allow—conflict and revocability.

"No government or authority can govern and survive unless it is based on consent—be it only the consent of the praetorian guard or the officer corps," wrote the brilliant, indefatigable pluralist Bernard Crick.[95] He went on:

> There are good grounds for thinking that politics is often a more effective way of ensuring survival than the absolute rule of Leviathan. Whether Leviathan is a monarch, a dictator, a party, or a "nation in arms," he is apt to be a pretty clumsy fellow who has few reliable ways of knowing what is really going on (representative electoral institutions, for instance, seem a fairly good way by which a government can find out what people will do and what they will stand for).[96]

"How does one find out what people think except by giving them real choices to discuss and real freedom to criticize and choose their government?" Crick asks. This suggests one more answer to the question, why one party? One-partyism is the holist attempt at two-way communication without political pluralism.[97] The party spreads the message of unity. It exercises "authoritative communication."[98] As important, the party is a source of information about the population. "The main purpose . . . is to establish perfect communication channels between the base and the leadership . . . and vice versa on an everyday basis. In this way we can keep track of the party activities and learn about the demands of the masses."[99]

A monolithic party can endure, but partisans of holism cannot maintain it on their own fantastic terms. The promise of wholeness, even if it functions provisionally and is widely believed, is cracked. Even without manifest external opposition, the party faces internal divisions.[100] It must exclude, repress, or absorb recalcitrant political aspirations. "In practice . . . the solidarity of the ranks of the national leaders is gravely impaired . . . by the substantial number of distinguished figures or potential contributors to national well-being who are held in preventive detention, otherwise jailed, or have vanished into exile."[101] It is not simply that political pluralism is ineradicable. Rather, despite its antipolitical claims, the name "party" is a give-away: one-partyism is partisan. It holds interest here as a vehicle for partisans of holism. It is a reminder that holist assaults on pluralism and parties are not the exclusive prerogative of philosophers or safely in the past.

Majoritarianism as "Shadow Holism"

Contemporary holist antipartyism often represents itself as democratic, but the examples I have offered suggest that partisans of holism deviate wildly and deliberately from recognizably democratic dispositions and aims. This is not to say that democracy without parties is inconceivable, only that it is not rooted in holism. Antipartyism has a firm foothold in prescriptions for direct democracy and for representation without partisan elections, for example, and these are my subject in part 2. Is there a living example of a genuinely democratic holism? There is something very close. I give the name "shadow holism" to invocations of a majority—actual or imagined—as if it were the whole people.

What is majoritarianism? In formal terms it is a decision rule. Wherever people in groups must move from disagreement to action, majority rule is a common device for getting to a decision.[102] It is not an exclusively political institution, either, though I am unaware of literature that answers the question whether the origin of majority decision is politics and other settings are derivative, or vice versa. Philosophical anthropology suggests a political origin. Familiar accounts characterize majority decision as logical and necessary once political society has developed past the authority of fathers, and past the stage in which the "beginners of commonwealths" consent to the government of one fit and trusted man.[103] Locke presents the introduction of majoritarianism in these terms:

> And thus every man, by consenting with others to make one body politic under one government, puts himself under an obligation to every one of the society to submit to the determination of the majority and to be concluded by it; or else this original compact . . . would signify nothing, and be no compact . . . Such a constitution as this would make the mighty leviathan of a shorter duration than the feeblest creatures, and not let it outlast the day it was born.[104]

Two latent considerations coexist here. On one view, majoritarianism is a necessary and justifiable substitute for unanimity, which is the ideal. On another view, difference is welcome, disagreement permanent, and majoritarianism is a "convenient convention" for accommodating it.[105] Locke represents the second, but not all assessments of this convention are as sanguine as his. In contrast to Locke's logic of consent, Benjamin Constant bluntly characterized it as sheer force of numbers:

> The prerogative of the majority is that of the strongest. It is unjust. It would be still more unjust, however, if the will of the weakest were to prevail. If society has to make a decision, the strongest or the weakest, the most or the least numerous, [the strongest] must triumph. If the right of the majority, that is, the strongest, were not recognized, the right of the minority would be. This is to say that injustice would weigh down on a greater number of people.[106]

For Constant, majoritarianism is the lesser evil. His formulation indicates plainly why political theorists often see majoritarianism as compelling in only the literal sense. Thus: a "purely statistical determination of whether there are more members in favor of a bill than against it" suggests that "bills do not reason themselves into legal authority; they are thrust into authority with nothing more credible than numbers on their side." Majoritarianism contributes to "the indignity of legislation."[107]

From this standpoint, determination by sheer numbers must be cabined. Liberals and democrats of many stripes insist, as Constant did, on setting bounds to the kinds of decisions that fall within the majority's competence and on preventing entrenchment, protecting future majorities against present ones. Among the securities: ensuring rights through constitutional constraints and judicial review and designing institutions such as the separation of powers, in which, short of a working majority in all branches, no party has plenary authority even between elections. (And not even then if institutional rules give minorities a role in agenda setting, calls for information and investigation, and so on.) We expect a certain disposition of constraint on the part of majorities, too. Normally, a majority does not claim that the right to constitute government goes so far as to assume all power without regard for the minority; the minority's assent if not consent is required.[108] Majoritarianism is not absolutist.[109] Nevertheless, majoritarianism as a decision rule entails decision. Pluralism and disagreement must be provisionally set aside. "On this point, Hobbes's argument has lost none of its force."[110]

It would seem from what I have said so far that characterizing majoritarianism as "shadow holism" is wrong-headed. After all, majoritarianism expressly acknowledges division and political conflict. If disagreements were resolved according to a norm of consultation and consensus, or a decision rule requiring unanimity, majoritarianism would have no warrant. Majoritarianism is quite unlike that bewildering doctrine, "the sovereignty of the people," with its implied indivisibility. So in speaking of majoritarianism as "shadow holism," I am obviously suggesting that the majority is identified with something more than superior numbers.

One aspect of majoritarianism as "shadow holism" is so familiar it is liable to go unnoticed. Majoritarianism entails bowing to the decision of the half plus one *as if* it were the decision of the whole. It compounds the winner's victory; in the context of a partisan contest, the majority gets the whole prize. Again, unmitigated majoritarianism is seldom defended philosophically and seldom let loose in practice: it is typically constrained by substantive limitations on the matter and scope of majority decisions, by institutional checks, by the internal rules of specific bodies. In matters subject to majority rule, however, the majority gives direction to the whole. And the minority agrees to accept it, albeit provisionally and generally for a specified period, as if it were the decision of the whole. A sentimental note is sometimes struck: for example, the typical "honeymoon" period of a new American president, entitled to "the good wishes of the whole community."[111] The appeal to marriage, a presumably sacred union, is apt. For the priority value here is political cohesion, effective unity. This was perfectly clear to thinkers opposed to majoritarianism. Calhoun's polemics against majority despotism are a denial of the "as if" of the whole. Slavery in the American territories was a defining challenge to national unity, and Calhoun's nullification thesis would replace "numerical majority" with a "concurrent majority" that would give a veto to "each interest or portion of the community."[112] He recognized and sought to disentangle the presumptive connection between majoritarianism and unity.

Here we see the shadow of holism: majoritarianism rests on the assumption that the cohesion of the whole has priority over the minority's claims. The minority accepts its loss. It does not secede or revolt, go underground or lead an armed resistance, disappear or go into eclipse. At the same time, the concept of majority assumes the right of existence of a minority. Although majority decision making is compelling, for every majority there is a minority. Majoritarianism is not Sieyes's "transfiguration of majority will into unanimous will as a practical necessity."[113] For it acknowledges the remains of disagreement. Commitment to the whole, taking the majority as if it were the whole, is perfectly compatible with recognizing that the majority is a part and its status as stand-in is provisional.

This deceptively mundane face of "shadow holism" takes the majority decision as if it were the decision of the whole. What is the basis for this "as if" if not a prudent retreat in the face of greater numbers? ("Voting constitutes 'flexing muscles': a reading of chances in the eventual war."[114]) The insight here is that a system and set of procedures that could be said to be called into being out of necessity, as Locke claimed, "convert that necessity into a positive moral opportunity"[115]—that is, the opportunity for sustained political unity, at best extending to the felt experience of unity. "The majority principle operates as psychologically binding in a democracy because the dissenting minority considers itself as belonging to the same community as the majority.... Should such a bond of unity ... not exist ... then the majority principle would no longer function as a method of unifying in cooperation the wills of the citizens, but would become a mere condition of the fact of rulership."[116] Theorists have characterized the moral aspects of this opportunity variously. Locke's explanation, again, takes majoritarianism to be a logical tendency of a proposition about consent rather than force.[117] In the terms of contemporary democratic theory, majoritarianism is more often cast as recognition and respect for the political equality of citizens; it takes differences of interest and opinion seriously and weighs them equally,[118] so that "if I chance to be in the minority, I cannot morally claim to prefer my own judgment to that of my equals."[119] (By the same token, equal weighing dignifies the minority: it takes opposition into consideration and "institutionalizes the admission that there were also reasons not to desire the solution finally adopted."[120]) An earlier generation of political theorists de-emphasized equality and demonstration of respect; they appealed instead to freedom: the majority principle represents "the relatively closest approach to the idea of freedom." Equality is a precondition for majoritarianism, on this view, but if it bears the whole weight of the majority principle, the result is "purely mechanical," again, "the roughly formalized expression of the experience that the many are stronger than the few." Instead, the real significance of majoritarianism is that as many as possible should be free; "as few people as possible should find their wills in opposition to the general will of the social order."[121] The sturdy "as if" of majoritarianism also owes to the habit of majority rule reinforced daily in nonpolitical arenas. The shadow of holism is plain in the defensible "as if," which treats the majority decision, provisionally and for a determined period, as the decision for the whole. This is only a shadow of holism because majority and minority are conceived as *parts of*, not *parts against*, this whole.

I have not finished with "shadow holism." In some circumstances it has an even stronger resonance of unity and integrity and approaches a real manifestation of holist antipartyism. Majoritarianism is the primary reality of electoral politics in the United States, and in American political thought nothing is more striking than "the centrality of majorities and minorities as basic units of political life around which so much reflection turns."[122] The notion of majority rule was an indispensable feature of early American ideology. To grasp this as "shadow holism" it helps to look at the majority's counterpart, the minority, and at hostility toward the politically empowered minorities of the day. The minority that seized the attention of the Founders was not in the first instance a weak group requiring protection but the successful, ambitious, and above all politically influential few. The fear was not only that the minority opposes its sinister interest to the public interest but that its doctrines subvert the people's own understanding of its interests. "Majority" evoked both democratic pride and uneasiness that social and economic inequalities would undermine the people's ability to decide how they wanted to be governed.[123]

Majority as the moral equivalent of the people and minority as a separate sinister interest and a subversive antipopular force was standard fare. Even Madison, the famous pluralist, could be Manichean. Republicans cherish the people and are offended at every measure that "does not appeal to the understanding and to the general interest of the community," he wrote. Antirepublicans are "more partial to the opulent than to the other classes of society, and having debauched themselves into a persuasion that mankind are incapable of governing themselves, it follows with them . . . that government can be carried on only by the pageantry of rank, the influence of money and emoluments, and the terror of military force." The mass of people in every part of the union and every occupation "must at bottom be with them [republicans], both in interest and sentiment." Madison goes on to draw the conclusion we would expect from a semblance of holism: republicans' "superiority of numbers is so great, their sentiments are so decided and the practice of making a common cause . . . is so well understood" that this party would "ultimately establish its ascendance," which he equates with the ascendance of "the great body of the people."[124] This is unsurprising during the early years of the republic, certainly. It is an echo of the commitment that had enabled revolution: "Without passionate devotion to the cause, they would never have had the audacity to speak in the name of 'We the People' at Philadelphia."[125]

One more step completes this sketch of majoritarianism as "shadow holism." What makes majoritarianism so crucial in American political thought is that "the people" was not a corporate body or class; there were no English commoners or Roman plebs. The minority was not a fixed, designated corporate group, either (though conspiracies to revive ranks and orders were a recurrent fear). Without a designable majority, it was impossible to assign genuine political meaning to "aristocrats," or "monocrats," or "the money power," or elites exercising "undue influence." They had to be set off and apart from the people, made visible and concrete. We see why American political thought is preoccupied almost obsessively with the status of the majority. The majority stood for "the great body of the people" and was an oppositional idea. Minorities were not just outvoted but identified in the process. The status majoritarianism conferred was "the democracy."

Tocqueville saw perfectly clearly that majoritarianism signified more than a procedural requirement for political victory. "The parties have a great interest in determining the election in their favor, not so much to make their doctrines triumph with the aid of the president-elect as to show by his election that those doctrines have acquired a majority," he wrote.[126] The constant burden of challengers is to struggle against the opposition's status as the majority party—a struggle required by more than just the rule-bound necessity of winning the requisite number of votes in order to attain political office. The object, again, is "to show by his election that those doctrines have acquired a majority." It is the moral ascendancy that comes from earning the approval of "the great body of the people" for their doctrines. In short, the urgency of not only winning but winning by a majority and, what is more, claiming to be the majority party is a matter of having both the authority to govern and to represent the whole. Tocqueville could not have been clearer about the stakes. Parties contest for majorities wherever they can, he observed; "When they lack it among those who have voted, they place it among those who have abstained from voting, and when it still happens to escape them there, they find it among those who did not have the right to vote."[127] Tocqueville anticipated partisan invocations of silent and moral majorities, and he saw why these phantom majorities are so important. If many citizens do not vote at all and electoral majorities are not majorities of the eligible citizenry (or claimed as silent elements of the majority), the status of a majority is purely technical. The moral force of majoritarianism is its resonance with "the great body of the people."

In the next chapter I show that early American thinkers were vehemently antiparty, and in chapter 3 I turn to the notion of a party of "constitutional necessity" as the entering wedge of parties.[128] The point for now is the prevailing thought that there existed a body called "the democracy" that must be organized in its own defense: "'The democracy' ... was the great mass of Americans devoted to the constitutional principle of majority rule."[129] Party came into the picture as the institutional device by which "the democracy" might exercise its authority in practice. Martin Van Buren's Democratic Party claimed to be the heir of Jefferson's republicans, to embody the majority. "To Van Buren, Jackson had been the tribune of the democracy, protecting the people against the factions. But tribunes were temporary; the Democratic party must be as permanent as the Constitution."[130] Large-scale organization would create a party that embodied undivided democracy.[131] The idea was to replace law making by a deliberative Congress of superior types—influential gentlemen of reputation and independent judgment refining and enlarging the public view—with a party bearing the popular will: a republican (not partisan) institution to interpret the constitutional principle of popular sovereignty, a majority party. The party's platform and substantive goals, its "normal politics," were less important than its commitment to majority rule: the claim to represent the "suprapartisan sovereignty of the democracy contemplated in the Constitution."[132] Even after nominating meetings began to adopt party labels, they continued to "insist on their status as primary assemblages of the people ... claiming that their nominations bound all supporters of the democratic Constitution ... the only possible incarnations of popular sovereignty because they were based on no principle but majority rule."[133] The division of democracy into parties was anathema, but a party organization for governance by "the democracy" was imperative. This is "shadow holism."

"Shadow holism" helps to explain why the ambition of partisans is not victory simply. Winning is often by plurality, after all. Strategic approaches to parties and elections are standard practice, of course; I argue in Part II that this contributes to antiparty sentiment, and I argue in Part III that it violates the ethic of partisanship. Here, suffice to say that the ambition is to be a majority party and thus to have a morally compelling claim to speak for the great body of the people. Granted, in what is patently overreaching, bare electoral winners frequently claim a "mandate." The plebiscitarian president is particularly prone to hyperbole of this kind.[134] Nonetheless, at certain moments majoritarianism as "shadow holism" has plausibility. We recognize the presence of majoritarianism as "shadow holism" when the minority comprises a separate interest opposed to "the democracy," and I return to this in chapter 4. We recognize it too when mandates have a certain radical character.[135] That is, when a party is uniquely creative, identifies a significant, simple, and usually single issue, casts it in terms of urgent "reform" of some antidemocratic minority turpitude, and brings this deep line of division over national direction home to people.[136] It is not surprising that Bruce Ackerman capitalizes the "People" in his account of these electoral transformations in *We the People.*

Democratic theorist George Kateb has drawn attention to the imagination it takes to comprehend elected authority. Double-vision is at work. With one eye we glimpse the unity created by taking the majority "as if" it were the whole. We recognize that some minorities, identified definitively through elections, are opposed to democracy, to the great body of the people. We see the semblance of holism. With the other eye we see that majorities are partisan parts and divisions are not lost sight of; then, the electoral system "supplies a vivid, public, and continuous imparting of the moral lesson that the only tolerable authority is a deliberately chastened authority."[137]

The Disappearing Shadow

True to its name, "shadow holism" is always on the verge of disappearing from view. Rightly so. Political pluralism is richer than the episodic division between "the democracy" and a sinister elite. Early on in the history of theorizing about representative democracy, Benjamin Constant cautioned that the majority is often represented as a "real person whose existence is protracted and which always comprises the same part." In fact, Constant went on, it happens all the time that a section of the population that was in the majority yesterday forms today's minority. "Everyone in turn finds himself in the minority. . . . To grant the majority unlimited power is to offer to the people en masse the slaughter of the people piecemeal."[138] The mystique of the majority as a stand-in for the whole or as the moral equivalent of the whole cannot be maintained for long in the course of actual political contests. In pluralist politics, divisions are changeable, attenuated, amenable to political delineation. That is the famous insight of the other, pluralist Madison.

So a chastening knowledge of pluralism is always there, on the periphery of our vision if not in full view. A particular majority is temporary, vulnerable to the next shaping event, the next campaign. Parties conjuring shifting majorities are the routine players playing routine parts in the pluralist politics of representative democracy. We know "shadow holism" has faded when the majority party is seen as a temporary political alliance. Or when majorities are produced automatically, as they often are in two-party systems: "the voters have no other place to go."[139] There is an iota of regret for the disappearance of the shadow—the eclipse of "the democracy" with its substantive common good and sense of wholeness, but also welcome for the sober return to numbers and a decision rule, bare and without holist resonance, to pluralism and regulated rivalry.

One disappearance of the shadow of holism is indisputably lamentable, however, and troubling because it amounts to an invitation to the real thing: to a party of virtue or one-partyism. Any semblance of holism is erased by awareness of the dormant population, eligible to participate in politics, but inactive. "The indifferent and inarticulate sections of the people," whose silent approbation or acquiescence or apathy is almost always taken for granted, are not part of it. When "what the [then] sixty million quarrel about evidently does not excite the forty million," majoritarianism loses its force as a semblance of "the democracy." When passive citizens are figured in, and the active majority is literally a minority, people, including the inactive, may be persuaded that political majorities are spurious and do not correspond to the realities of the country. Not only can they make no believable claim to stand for the whole; they are in fact a meaningless minority. Massive nonvoting, compounded in the United States by chronic antipartyism, can produce "a nonpolitical antimajoritarian democracy."[140] This political cynicism strikes at majoritarianism and beyond, at the whole democratic apparatus of parties and partisanship, a condition that makes the promise of real holism dangerously tempting.

Democratic majoritarianism is conceivable without parties, as we know from plebiscites, referenda, and "independent" or nonpartisan candidates for election. But we can see why its internal logic pushes in the direction of parties and partisanship. There is no natural party of the people. No majority exists spontaneously, ready to be contested for. It is identified in the course of drawing lines of division. That is what political activity generally and party activity specifically is about. Where majorities and minorities are "the basic units of political life," parties attempt to create a majority, and in doing so they identify a minority. "Irresistible developments lead . . . to the organization of the people into political parties."[141] Political scientists propose that majorities are formed by bringing diverse groups together into a governing majority.[142] As important as practical coalition building is, more important is the fact that parties create majorities by inventing lines of division.[143] Parties fashion as well as mobilize majorities, and I attach this as a friendly amendment to E. E. Schattschneider's claim:

> Parties are the special form of political organization adapted to the mobilization of majorities. . . . If democracy means anything at all it means that the majority has the right to organize for the purpose of taking over the government. Party government is strong because it has behind it the great moral authority of the majority and the force of strong traditional belief in majority rule.[144]

As I have described it, majoritarianism as "shadow holism" takes two forms. It is "the great body of the nation," the unity and integrity of the people, "the democracy." And it is the "as if" of governing. Both are giant steps away from genuine holism, clearly. Majoritarianism has no metaphysical roots. It is not utopian. It does not abhor parts in principle. It does not conceive of an organic body politic, an indivisible nation or people, a general will that cannot err. For their part, genuine holists have no more appetite for and give no more weight to majority/minority than to any other division. Partisans of holism—leaders of parties of virtue, erectors of one-partyism do not recognize the principle of majority rule. They are undeterred by being in the minority. The terms have no meaning for holists. Their claim to act in the name of the whole, as the vanguard of the people or nation or virtue or faith, has no necessary basis in actual support, much less respect for the electoral rules that condition majoritarianism. Moreover, the majority is explicitly and by definition only a part, although it acts and decides for the whole. Holist antipartyism is the tradition that sees all parts as potential parties, that is, once again, as parts *against*, rather than parts *of*, the whole. This brings me to the second glorious tradition of antipartyism, which accepts political pluralism and partiality but not parties. Not division but dividiveness is anathema, and parties instigate and exacerbate conflict.

CHAPTER 2

———>•◇•<———

Glorious Traditions of Antipartyism: Fatal Divisiveness

In this chapter I continue mapping the terrain of antipartyism up to the time when parties became governing and then electoral parties in a regular party system. The first glorious tradition of antipartyism despises parties as parts. The second tradition does not adhere to an ideal of a coherent and indivisible political whole. Instead, it recognizes social and political parts as legitimate, and incorporates them into the frame of government. In this second tradition, and in contrast to holism, not all parts are parties. The objection to parties—what earns a group the accusatory label—is not that they are partial but that parties impede balance or harmony among recognized social parts. Parties are dangerously divisive. Partisanship in the general sense of advocacy on behalf of groups and causes is natural and acceptable, but parties as instruments for practicing partisanship are not. Divisions and divisiveness are distinct dangers, then, each with its antiparty tradition. Recognition and acceptance of parts is compatible with antipathy toward parties in this second glorious tradition, and I point to the mixed constitution as a principal way in which social divisions were recognized and brought into government. A well-ordered constitution has parts without parties.

A terse summary of this type of antipartyism is this: permanent social divisions may be inevitable, even natural, but parties exploit them. Not all parts are despised, and the charge of fatal divisiveness identifies parties as those groups that exploit divisions or, what may be worse, invent and organize new divisions. They are wantonly selfish and sinister factions, engines of destructive partiality. Political thinkers from every period repeat that parties are "associated with painfully deep and unbridgeable differences in national politics, with religious bigotry and clerical animus, with treason and the threat of foreign invasion, with instability and dangers to liberty."[1] The language is telling: fury, madness, fatal divisions. Nothing makes this point more forcefully than the analogy often drawn in modern political thought between party and religious schism—"What the term 'schism' connoted in religious affairs, 'faction' covered in politics"[2]—with its implication of angry severance among those who had shared a faith. What could be more fearful than scheming clergy, religious incendiaries, and violent civil (and foreign) war among religiously inspired partisans who see themselves literally on the side of the angels? This is the nub of the tradition of antipartyism that opposes parties as divisive: parties fracture, agitate, and produce disorder. Divisiveness and instability alone, leaving aside substantive objections to the goals of particular parties or the presumed corruption of judgment and morals that accompanies partisanship, explain why they are intolerable. Parties are groups that sometimes invent and always agitate divisions; partisans are agitators. In Hume's words: "Factions subvert government, render laws impotent, and beget the fiercest animosities . . . and what should render the founders of parties more odious is the difficulty of extirpating these weeds when once they have taken root in any state."[3]

Until party government and electoral systems based on organized parties were regularized and accepted, this view of parties as dangerously divisive dominated the political and philosophical literature and was an indelible feature of political experience. Parties were considered aberrations, or better, because they were nearly ubiquitous, aberrant. Put simply, parties were "forbidden by traditional morality and political wisdom."[4] Because the view of parties as fatally divisive is rhetorically familiar from canonical writings in ancient and modern political thought, it is tempting to pass over it quickly. But there are good reasons to identify the main themes of this type of antipartyism.

For one thing, even brief immersion in the mood of "fatal divisiveness" reminds us of the enduring force of this antiparty tradition. It is a spur to reflect on "divisiveness" as an element in antipathy to parties and partisanship today, and on the parameters of acceptable division. For another, the record of opposition to parties as divisive reveals a generally neglected but critical, defining characteristic of parties that is a guiding thread of my project: parties do not just reflect but also create lines of division. Writers in this antiparty tradition were keenly aware of the willful creation of divisions by partisans, and appalled by the way parties bring them to political life. This capacity can be recast positively and valued, and I turn at the end of this chapter to the way partisans, in Tocqueville's words, "introduce a new power into the political world." My main business here, however, is to explore this tradition of antipartyism.

Like holism, the tradition of antipartyism that sees parties as fatally divisive does not offer a coherent conceptual distinction between partial groups and associations and parties. "Party" is an accusatory label, applied in context. But for holists, parties were second-order concerns—pluralism of any sort was abhorrent. Social and political pluralism are accepted in this second antiparty tradition, and applying the accusatory label "party" is a first-order concern. At the same time, the identifying marks of "party" as instigator of divisiveness are not easily generalized. The contours of this diffuse tradition of antipartyism are not easily traced. I provide what I think is a good handle by focusing on four characteristic themes: the invocation of archetypical examples of fatal party strife, the irrepressibility of parties, the classification of parties with an implicit hierarchy of dangerous divisiveness, and the move from antipartyism to even more virulent antipartisanship. With the main themes of "fatal divisiveness" in hand, I go on to illustrate the ways in which political pluralism was accommodated even as parties were not: first in the enduring ideal of the mixed constitution, and later in three key accounts of pluralism and partiality without parties.

The Roman Archetype

For antiparty writers beginning in the early modern period, the touch-stone case of fatal divisiveness comes from cautionary histories of the Roman republic. Post-mortems, "great necrological argumentations"[5] about the decline of Rome, converge on "civil discords and hateful conspiracies" fueled by the consuming desire to hold office.[6] The political system itself was rarely inculpated, largely because both Roman historians and later scholars viewed the republic as the positive essence of Rome. It was better to attribute calamity to the rancorous, rival-rous ruling class and to adopt Livy's moralistic terms.[7] The canonical view, and a staple of antipartyism, is that "the fierce strife of nobles for political advancement" marked two centuries of Rome's history and that Rome lost its freedom through increasingly violent party conflict when it extended to generals and the armies loyal to them.[8]

The difficulty of settling on an analytic definition of party emerges here. Neither ancient writers nor modern historians agreed on how to characterize political divisions in the republic. Interpretive debates about Roman factions have long occupied historians.[9] Were there coherent associations that could be called parties? The question as posed used modern ideological electoral parties as a standard, which is plainly inapt.[10] Roman political divisions were social and personal, based on clientele relations, and later in the republic on shifting alliances and enmities among leading families. Politics was dominated by "cliques." Were these alliances coherent or stable enough to be called parties or factions at all in light of evidence that Roman "friends," as political allies were sometimes called, did not necessarily have the same enemies and common enmities did not cement friendship? Cicero reflected repeatedly on whether the *fides* on which friendship was based included mutual assistance and political services, and whether friendship rooted in mutual respect could survive divergent political interests and principles.[11] Certainly, *amicitia* entailed political relationships: "A man expected from his friends not only support at the polls but aid in the perils of public life, the unending prosecutions brought from political motives by his personal enemies, his *inimici*, his rivals in the contest for office and for the manifold rewards of public life. . . . Cicero, in writing to Crassus to clinch their reconciliation, urged Crassus to consider his letter a treaty."[12] Still, political advantage was not the foundation of friendship, and friendship did not amount to partisanship. The main thing to emerge from this historical analysis is the accusatory force of designating a group a party, and the connection ceaselessly made between parties and civil war.[13]

Antiparty thinkers invoking the Romans commonly point to a division within the Roman senatorial ranks between those who championed the authority of the senate and those who championed the rights of the people. "All those who convulsed the state alleged the public good under fair names," Sallust observed, "some that they were defending the rights of the People, others that the authority of the Senate should predominate. In fact each was striving for his own power."[14] These groupings were described as *pars* or *partes* or *factio*, and were grimly associated by both ancient and modern writers with civil war and decline. The Roman designations are telling. Allies called themselves "good men," *optimates*, who rested their claim to power on moral worth. They called their opponents *populares*, or demagogues. In response, their enemies called them a *factio*.[15] Hence Sallust's observation: "haec inter bonos amicitia, inter malos factio est."[16] One classicist's conclusion serves as summary: "The Republic was destroyed not by an external enemy, not by some abstract and inexorable process of economic or historical development, but by the ruinous lust for power and position of that very class which had traditionally identified itself most closely with the *respublica*—the *nobiles*."[17]

Comparison between the divisive parties of Rome and contemporary groups organized for political conflict was common fare in early modern political thought. It gave way only with tentative experience and tentative notice (not yet establishment or justification) of regulated party rivalry and party government. Machiavelli's is the classic appeal to Rome as the archetype. He used the Roman republic as a caution to free Italian city states, though as I will indicate, his discussion is nuanced.[18] In his *Florentine Histories*, Machiavelli's vocabulary was condemnatory: "discordia (civile), divisione, odio, inimicizie, disunione, disordine, disparere, parti, sette."[19] "In Rome, as everybody knows . . . the discord between the nobles and the plebs emerged, and this division continued until the ruin of the republic."[20] Machiavelli's application to Florence was not one to one. Unlike republics undone by parties of nobles and plebs, in Machiavelli's city things were more complex:

> First the nobles were divided among themselves, then there was a division between the nobles and the popolo, and finally between the popolo and the plebs, and it often happened that one of these parties, having gained the upper hand, split in two. From these divisions there came as many deaths, as many exiles, as many destructions of families, as ever arose in any city whose history is known to us.[21]

Still, the standard accusation holds: Florence's citizens "never organized for the general good but always with the view of benefiting their own party, which instead of establishing order in the city only tended to increase disorders," and Machiavelli pointed approvingly to Roman Consuls who restored peace between patricians and plebeians by killing the chiefs of the opposing factions.[22]

To complicate matters, Machiavelli conceded the uses of faction. "Tumult" could be beneficial. The Romans were able to set the parties against one another for a long time before a series of changes, including economic interests and the determination not to take a part in government but to rule exclusively, resulted in violence and ultimate ruin. Similarly, the division of the barons of Rome into the two factions Orsini and Colonna kept the pope weak; the temporal force of the papacy increased only when Alexander VI eliminated the barons with the help of a French invasion.[23] "True it is that some divisions injure republics, while others are beneficial to them. When accompanied by factions and parties they are injurious; but when maintained without them they contribute to their prosperity."[24]

Machiavelli stands out among writers for whom Rome is the archetype of "fatal divisiveness" for the careful attention he paid to institutions that mitigated the bad effects of parties. He reflected on the possibility that parties could function "to dissipate the frustrations which might otherwise erupt against a well-disposed government."[25]

He decided that they did not vent agitation safely, however, and contrasted parties with the regular and beneficial institution of public accusation brought by any private citizen against officials and ambitious men. Popular accusation and punishment were formalized precisely for the purpose of preventing the organization of parties, on his account. Without these regular procedures, with recourse only to private "calumny" and unsubstantiated charges, Machiavelli argued, private retaliation and factional violence were the rule. Accusation was a substitute for arrant factionalism. Parties arise from "bad orders, because inside that wall there is no order able, without extraordinary modes, to vent the malignant humors that arise in men—for which one fully provides by ordering accusation there before many judges." Machiavelli spelled this out, pointing to the accusation of Coriolanus: "consider how much ill would have resulted to the Roman republic if he had been killed in a tumult; for from that arises offense by private individuals against private individuals, which offense generates fear; fear seeks for defense; for defense they procure partisans; from partisans arise the parties in cities; from parties their ruin."[26] Better known are Machiavelli's other proposals for checks on divisiveness: an external enemy and expansion. "Inward pressure from tumults will lead it to seek outlets for its *animus dominandi*, and will therefore lead it to expand. At that point, its encounter with the outside world will require its constituent parts to rearrange their priorities, set their differences aside, and focus on what unites them."[27]

What is Machiavelli's verdict on parties? He casts doubt on the strategy proposed by later thinkers of playing factions against one another. He anticipated only to reject British and French notions that a masterful prince can maintain a balance of power and can govern parties rather than govern by them.[28] Machiavelli was uncharacteristically plain: there is "nothing to be gained by attempting to control cities by means of keeping alive factions."[29] His work can be mined as a source for "fatal divisiveness," then, and he mined Roman history to drive this point home. I want to enter two caveats to this conclusion, however.

As we see, Machiavelli often associated factions with armed cadres, followers of generals or private armies raised by the wealthy—*partizans,* not ordinary civilian partisans. That is, he opposed private political organization in the form of armed factions. Even proponents of parties draw the line at armed groups. If fear of armed conflict is antipartyism, the category is hopelessly broad. Civil war may be a latent possibility wherever there are parties, and Roman history is the model cautionary tale because the civil wars that ensued were fought by party leaders at the heads of armies.[30] But from the standpoint of this tradition of antipartyism, the business of parties is anathema and fatally divisive even if it stops short of insurrection or civil war. One final point mitigates a portrait of Machiavelli as antiparty. He was, after all, author of the view of two distinct and "indelible temperaments" imperfectly embodied in the nobles and the people.[31] These dispositions could be put to political use, checked and handled to serve the common good, or not. The discord of these groups is distinct from the "lobby-like groups" of particular, interested partisans.[32] The former are the life, the latter the death of republics. Looked at closely, Machiavelli's thoughts on parties elude summary. For all that, his work was an important source of the first theme in the antiparty tradition that distinguishes division from divisiveness, parts from parties: Rome as the cautionary archetype.

The Roman path from party enmity to civil war and despotism was a constant, and I conclude with this passage from Washington's farewell address:

> The Alternate domination of one faction over another, sharpened by the spirit of revenge natural to party dissension, which in different ages and countries has perpetuated the most horrid enormities, is itself a frightful despotism. The disorders and miseries gradually incline the minds of men to seek security and repose in the absolute power of an individual; and sooner or later the chief of some prevailing faction . . . turns this despotism to the purpose of his own elevation, on the ruins of public liberty.[33]

The Irrepressible Hydra

Besides Rome as the touchstone of fatal divisiveness, nothing preoccupied writers in this tradition more than parties' irrepressibility.

Philosophers who looked for a preventative for parties were like those in search of a grand elixir or perpetual motion, engaged in impracticable theory, Hume scoffed.[34] He did not think the hydra could be effectively decapitated, and offered a host of examples of the fact that "the spirit of faction is so strong that it is difficult for [even] a social and sanguine temper to guard against."[35] The admitted ubiquity of parties was reason to explore causes and correctives. The catalogue of causes is immense. Aristotle lists seven motives for the instigation of factional strife by rival leaders: profit, dignity, cruelty, fear, excessive power, contemptuous attitudes, and disproportionate aggrandizement, to which he adds lobbying and that umbrella category, "intrigue."[36] "In every political society, parties are unavoidable," Madison wrote in his 1792 essay on the subject, and among the sources of faction he listed opinions concerning religion and government, both speculative and practical; attachment to different leaders in ambitious contention for power; and every manner of interest in property: "there will be rich and poor, creditors and debtors, a landed interest, a monied interest, a mercantile interest, a manufacturing interest." In addition to these "natural distinctions," artificial ones will be founded, on "accidental differences in political, religious or other opinions, or on attachment to the persons of leading individuals. However erroneous or ridiculous these grounds of dissention and faction may appear to the enlightened Statesman, or the benevolent philosopher, the bulk of mankind ... will continue to view them in a different light."[37] Hume made a similar point about the myriad causes of party: "Men have such a propensity to divide into personal factions that the smallest appearance of real difference will produce them"; indeed, "nothing is more usual than to see parties, which have begun upon a real difference, continue after the difference is lost."[38] Madison repeated this tune: "frivolous and fanciful distinctions" suffice to kindle "unfriendly passions" and violent conflicts. We can almost see him throwing up his hands: "A difference of interests, real or supposed, is the most natural and fruitful source of them."[39] There were so many origins that parties seemed to have no origin.[40]

Some thoughtful writers proposed that parties were irrepressible because they were natural. In one sanguine formulation, they reflect "the associating Genius of Man." "Nothing is so delightful as to incorporate," Lord Shaftesbury observed. Distinctions of many kinds are invented, religious societies formed, orders are erected, their interests espoused with "utmost zeal and passion":

> Founders and Patrons of this sort are never wanting. Wonders are perform'd in this wrong social Spirit, by those Members of separate Societies. . . . the very Spirit of Faction, for the greatest part, seems to be no other than the Abuse of Irregularity of that social Love, and common Affection, which is natural to Mankind. For the Opposite of Sociableness is Selfishness."[41]

That is, parties are expressions of sociability, of the sympathetic disposition to form associations. At the same time, the label party or faction is accusatory; it designates a peculiarly nonbenign form of association, a perversion of natural affection.

For Madison, too, "in all civilized societies, distinctions are various and unavoidable."[42] But the benign logic of pluralism does not extend to parties, and he goes a step beyond itemizing causes to explain the dynamic of party formation. We see him thinking this through. As long as reason is fallible and men have liberty to exercise it, different opinions will form. The connection between reason and self-love adds passion to opinion. Add to this the unequal capacity to acquire property, different kinds of property, and the effects of property on sentiments and views, and there "ensues a division of the society into different interests and parties." Notice that up to this point divisions are only latent factions. A property interest or a religious sect is not per se a party. In Madison's terms, they are not yet organized to employ government at the expense of the rights of other citizens or the permanent interests of the nation. The decisive moment for Madison occurs when omnipresent divisions of passion and interest are brought to political life and put into action. That is, when political agents "divided mankind into parties, inflamed them with mutual animosity, and rendered them much more disposed to vex and oppress each other than to cooperate for the common good."[43] Then the state is "violently heated and distracted by the rage of party."[44] Once again, not parts but parties are political anathema.

A proper understanding of the dynamic of party formation may inhibit at least "artificial parties" and "unnecessary opportunities" for "designing men" to foment them.[45] Something *could* be done to eliminate the causes of certain factions, Madison argued. He looked specifically at withholding unnecessary opportunities for parties to form by moderating inequality and reducing extreme wealth.[46]

Madison's debt to Hume on the subject of parties is a staple of intellectual history.[47] He followed Hume in modeling faction on religious sects but rejected Hume's thought that a church Establishment could calm the quarrels of clergy,[48] placing his confidence instead in a plurality of religious sects militating against national establishment and oppression. Madison shared Hume's other characteristic insights, beginning with the understanding that parties are a consequence of, not a security for liberty. Parties arise more easily and propagate themselves faster in free governments, and both authors conceded that suppression would be intolerable and in any case impossible. Attention should focus on schemes to check their *effects*. Above all, Madison took his signature idea for a cure for the "mischief of faction" from Hume's "The Idea of a Perfect Commonwealth."

Hume had suggested that in a large government "the parts are so distant and remote, that it is very difficult, either by intrigue, prejudice, or passion, to hurry them into any measures against the public interest."[49] Madison adapted this insight. He also credited Montesquieu's discussion of federated republics.[50] He brought them together in the proposition that "factious combinations [were] less to be dreaded" in large states and confederated republics. They were irrepressible, but, that said, "The degree of security . . . will depend on the number of interests and sects; and this may be presumed to depend on the extent of the country and the number of people comprehended under the same government."[51] Jefferson admitted one piece of this logic when he wrote that the "extent" of the nation had saved it: "While some parts were laboring under the paroxysm of delusion, others retained their senses and time was thus given to the affected parts to recover their health."[52]

Hume and Montesquieu provided Madison with conceptual tools, which he employed with an eye to the unique danger of a majority faction, something absent from earlier thinking and made concrete by the American electoral framework. Size and constitutional design would help to prevent the existence of a single interest or passion in a majority at the same time. By their plurality and location, groups would hinder a temporary majority, if formed, from acting in concert to carry out their secret wishes and schemes of oppression.[53] The business of political science was to design a preventative to the formation of a permanent majority faction, that is, a majority organized around a single interest or opinion.[54] Madison inaugurated a new political imperative: "The regulation of these various and interfering interests forms the principal task of modern Legislation."[55] Large electoral districts and election's "aristocratic effect" were added insurance that at least some governors were looking out for the "permanent aggregate interests of the community."

Not all Madison scholars are thoroughly admiring of the confidence he put in the jockeying of pluralist groups; the scheme was deliberately tilted against "the grand, dramatic, character-ennobling but society-wrecking opinions about justice and virtue."[56] In fact, Madison himself was not immune to this, nor to the importance of majoritarianism. As I showed in chapter 1 and will reflect on again, he represented his Republican Party as the majority party, as "the democracy," opposed to the sinister antirepublican minority. The point for now is Madison's warning that destructively divisive parties are irrepressible and that the hydra heads must be tamed.

Classifying Parties: Taming by Category

Close behind the touchstone of Rome as the cautionary tale of divisive parties and behind preoccupation with the irrepressibility of parties is a penchant for classification. Antiparty thinkers speak of "party" in accusatory mode, as fatally divisive, but they are also prone to create a hierarchy of dangerous types. Classification could indicate degrees of despicableness. Hume accepted politics, that is, the contest of opinions about the public interest, about the right to power, about the right to property. But partisans pursue these aims without check, spurring one another on. In his words, they are passionate, zealots, extremists, exaggerators of merit and demerit, aggravators without steadiness who speak only in terms of accusation and panegyric, begetters of "extraordinary ferment" and "violent animosities." Partisans suffer "madness of heart."[57]

Some worse than others. Personal factions—the perennial tie between personality and partisan followers—were more common in antiquity, Hume observed, and he pointed in standard fashion to the Romans and to Guelf and Ghibbelline. He contrasted "personal" factions with "real" factions based on some difference of interest or sentiment, principle or affection. Real factions included attachment to a particular dynastic succession; Hume had the Jacobites in mind. Parties of principle, "especially abstract principle," like the parties associated with different understandings of a mixed constitution, were distinctively modern. They were not as destructive as religious parties: "in modern times, parties of religion are more furious and enraged than the most cruel factions that ever arose from interest and ambition."[58] Parties of interest, by which he specifically meant the calculated political interest in places and emoluments, were "the most reasonable and excusable." Hume judged that contemporary court and country parties combined interest and principle (leaders were interested in political places, followers principled).

Tocqueville's classification of great and small parties has had a longer life and holds greater interest for me. He began by distinguishing parties great and small from the "distinct nations" of severely divided societies; parties proper arise "when citizens differ among themselves on points that interest all parts of the country equally." Great parties divide over constitutional change or over even more profound changes in the social state. They are attached to principles rather than consequences, to generalities rather than particular cases, to ideas rather than men. They convulse society. Between "centuries of disorders and miseries one encounters others when societies rest and when the human race seems to catch its breath." That is the moment for small parties. Small parties are "generally without political faith." They are rooted in material interests, not principles. Tocqueville's correspondent, Beaumont, challenged this classification. "Vous n'appelez donc grands parties que ceux qui reposent sur une théorie politique, et vous refusez ce nom à ceux qui on pour base d'immenses intérêst. C'est arbitraire" (You only call those parties great that are based on a political theory, and you refuse this label to those based on great interests. That is arbitrary), and Beaumont pointed to bitter partisan divisions over free trade.[59]

Tocqueville's classification is clearly evaluative; he disdains small parties: "their character is stamped with a selfishness that shows openly in each of their acts. . . . Their language is violent but their course is timid and uncertain. The means that they employ are miserable, as is the very goal they propose for themselves." There are only small parties in America now, he insisted; the country swarms with them. "To a stranger, almost all the domestic quarrels of Americans at first appear incomprehensible or puerile, and one does not know if one ought to take pity on a people that is seriously occupied with miseries like these or envy it the good fortune of being able to be occupied with them." Tocqueville could not bring himself to appreciate "the human race catching its breath" or to find relief in the convulsions of great parties giving way to the agitations of small ones.[60] He responded emphatically to a correspondent who professed indifference toward the machinations of small parties: "You speak to me of what you call your political atheism and ask if I share it," Tocqueville wrote. Emphatically not: "It is not a healthy or virile calm" but "a sort of apoplectic torpor." To turn away from small parties in disgust rather than to point out their miserableness is unacceptable, he continued: "I struggle with all my power against this bastard wisdom, this fatal indifference which in our times is sapping the energy of so many beautiful souls." He had in mind not just America but also France, where the political withdrawal of the legitimists and other principled partisans left in play only the selfishly ambitious.[61]

These classifications—personal and real factions, great and small parties, parties of principle and interest—had their uses. They offered criteria for cataloguing and ranking pathologies and for pointing out occasional, exceptional cases where groups designated parties are not wholly destructive and partisans not thoroughly reprehensible. The types were often elevated into universals and used to attribute patterns to partisan division over time. Of course, great and small, principle and interest, were further classified by substantive aims. The general contours were seen as permanent: a class of men who "cling with fondness to whatever is ancient" and "another class of men, sanguine in hope, bold in speculation, always pressing forward,"[62] or the familiar party of order/party of progress. Recall Jefferson's words quoted at the start of this chapter: "Men have differed in opinion, and been divided into parties by these opinions, from the first origin of societies and in all governments where they have been permitted freely to think and to speak, the terms whig and tory belong to natural as well as to civil history."[63] The substantive division that eclipsed all others and yielded a dominating hierarchy of dangerousness turned on the disposition to protect or oppose the people. John Adams, for example: "The same parties which now agitate the United States have existed through all time. Whether the power of the people or that of the ruler should prevail were questions which kept . . . Greece and Rome in eternal convulsions."[64] Tocqueville described America divided between two opinions "as old as the world and found under different forms and with various names in all free societies. One party wanted to restrict popular power and the other to extend it indefinitely. . . . They touched immaterial interests of the first order, such as love of equality and of independence." These are the "secret instincts" that govern factions in America and that have divided men since there have been free societies; "aristocratic or democratic passions are readily found at the foundation of all parties. . . . They form as it were the sensitive spot and the soul of them."[65]

Madison had argued in *The Federalist Papers* that the sources of faction were as innumerable as interests and opinions, particularly economic ones. In later essays pluralism was eclipsed by this single overriding partisan division "natural to most political societies." What has been called the "Manichean political belief" that the division between parties reflects those who favor and those who would oppress the people dominated American thought.[66] We see it in Madison's 1792 essay "A Candid State of Parties." One partisan division "is likely to be of some duration,"[67] he advised: a republican party, "hating hereditary power and . . . . naturally offended at every public measure that does not appeal to the understanding and to the general interest of the community," drawing strength from the consciousness "that the mass of the people in every part of the Union, in every State, and of every occupation must at bottom be with them, both in interest and sentiment." It stands opposed to an antirepublican party—"more partial to the opulent than to the other classes of society," drawing strength from "men of influence, particularly of moneyed, which is the most active and insinuating influence." He applied this classification, as the essay title tells, to present experience: the Republican Party's "superiority of numbers is so great, their sentiments are so decided and the practice of making a common cause . . . is so well understood" that it would "ultimately establish its ascendance," which he equates with the ascendance of "the great body of the people."[68] Recall from "shadow holism" that this meant more than the approval of a numerical majority; a republican majority is the moral equivalent of "the democracy" and speaks for the people. (The opposition saw the divide differently, of course. On their view, there can be but two parties in the country: the friends of order and its foes.[69])

Notice the dualism, the paired antagonism, long before a two-party system became a virtual tenet of American civic religion. These paired universals appear outside the American context. They are important because they suggest a recurrent partisan dynamic. Theorists in this antiparty tradition used these categories to simplify present crises and to provide a way to frame history as warring alternations between archetypical combatants or as a drama of elusive equilibrium. We see that with a conceptual half-turn parties could be represented as complementary, as antagonistic but equally foundational—party of order/party of progress—philosophically defensible parts of a whole. Parties could be cast—just as the parts of a mixed constitution were cast—as antagonistic parts but at the same time as necessary, even beneficial elements of a reasonable political order. Their dynamic could be viewed as more than simply, devastatingly divisive. A balance of opposition parties, indeed a dynamic even more productive than equilibrium, one of mutual correction or progress, is conceivable. This looks ahead to the philosophical moment of appreciation of parties, to which I turn in the next chapter.

A Turn of the Screw: Antipartisanship

The final theme in this tradition of antipartyism, and a key to grasping party as an accusatory term, is revulsion at partisanship.[70] The two are separable, as we see from contemporary political thought where parties may be grudgingly accepted for instrumental reasons but partisans, both political officials and party-identified voters, are judged inferior to superior "Independents." Historically, too, one theme of this antiparty tradition that defines parties as fatally divisive, and one characteristic that earns a group the accusatory label "party," is the noxious character of partisans. This antiparty tradition is often sternly moralistic. So much so that careful attention to party origins and classification may give way to raw loathing of parties as vehicles for ambitious men in pursuit of office. "The greatest factional split is perhaps that between virtue and depravity," Aristotle wrote, eclipsing his exhaustive catalogue of the sources of division.[71]

Parties are the result of vice and selfishness, the work of incorrigible agitators. In this antiparty tradition defined by fear of fatal divisiveness, the point is less bad faith on the part of particular partisans than nefarious motivation on the part of all partisans. Partisanship is also associated with specific practices (spoils, under-the-table dealing). Motivation is the heart of the matter, though. Fractious men, ambitious personalities excited by "cabal and intrigue," lovers of strategy form parties. Party is the name for a political association aimed at "catching prizes" or "private revenge," personal ambition or venality. Factions are "unscrupulous power groups" bent on spoils.[72] (Bolingbroke defined factions as parties aimed at nothing but spoils.[73]) The only motive for partisanship as despised as power and spoils is status: politics as "a way of rising in the world."[74] With the emergence of electoral parties the charges were also leveled at partisan supporters: parties of voters formed "for what amounts to collective bargaining to extract the maximum payoff from an election."[75] Parties are seen as willfully manufactured vehicles of arrant ambition. Partisans will find any excuse for contesting for office.

Thus, Machiavelli pointed out that a chief source of faction was rich private men, preoccupied with reputation and pursuit of power, who use their wealth for patronage—creating dependents who become partisan followers. Among the methods: "conferring benefits upon individuals, defending them against the magistrates, supporting them with money, and raising them to undeserved honors; or with public games and entertainments gaining the affection of the populace."[76] Machiavelli's point is clear: feuds among powerful political types do not injure a republic unless they take the form of factions, that is, party leaders who create partisans to support them. Recall that Madison made a similar point. As long as men have liberty to exercise their reason, different opinions will form; self-love adds passion to opinion; and inequality of property is added to the stew, and there "ensues a division of the society into different interests and parties."[77] But the critical moment occurs when these divisions are brought to political life: when political men "divided mankind into parties, inflamed them with mutual animosity, and rendered them much more disposed to vex and oppress each other than to cooperate for the common good."[78] "Designing men, by the use of artificial or nominal distinctions do oppose and balance against each other those who never differed as to the end to be pursued, and may no longer differ as to the means of attaining it," Madison wrote. Even after Republicans had gradually adopted Federalist party policies, Federalists were anathema: "Their object is power," Madison wrote, "they are ready to go to every length for which they can train their followers."[79] The obvious corollary is partisan disregard for the public business. "It turneth all Thought into talking instead of doing. Men get a habit of being unuseful to the Publick by turning in a Circle of Wrangling and Railing, which they cannot get out of."[80] George Washington warned of "the baneful effects of the spirit of party," which "distract the public councils and enfeeble the public administration" by their "ill-founded jealousies and false alarms."[81] "In plain English, when it appears that any Set of Men, of whatever denomination, have bellow'd for their Country, only to find a Market for themselves, it must be allow'd the Plague of Faction is visibly among them."[82]

Adam Ferguson was a rare, quasi-defender of partisanship, with all its taints. Ambition and "desires of preferment and profit" are excitements to enter public affairs; the emulation and jealousy "with which parties mutually oppose and restrain one another" draws men in. Partisanship takes a sort of fortitude. Men first enter public life even to have the opportunity to provide public services, to seek valuable ends and exhibit disinterested love of the public. "The suppression . . . of ambition, of party-animosity, and of public envy, is probably, in every such case, not a reformation but a symptom of weakness and a prelude to more sordid pursuits and ruinous amusements."[83] Ferguson's sober judgment that corruption is a substitute for worse private vices, and the price for occasional honor, was not taken up.

One more element of this tradition's antipartisanship is immediately recognizable today. Followers suffer the disease of "party madness"; they credulously "gave up their reason and consciences to party managers."[84] As Halifax put it, "Party is little less than an Inquisition, where Men are under such a Discipline in carrying on the common Cause, as leaves no Liberty of the Private Opinion."[85] To the long-standing accusation that partisans are acrimonious, intemperate, artful, and selfish is the added charge that the machinations of party put "shackles" on the mind. "Party has a more powerful tendency than perhaps any other circumstance in human affairs to render the mind quiescent and stationery. Instead of making each man an individual . . . .it resolves all understandings into one common mass."[86] It took the establishment of electoral parties for this line of argument to achieve full force: partisanship entails the loss of independence. Partisans are blind, errant. My defense of partisanship over independence is the subject of chapter 7.

In this context it is worth remarking on the history of elections, in which elections were consistent with antipartyism and more specifically with antipartisanship. Election of representatives to the English parliament proceeded without choice, much less choice organized by parties. As Mark Kishlansky describes election of representatives in seventeenth-century England, the representation of counties and boroughs by seats in parliament took the literal form of election rather than competitive selection. A single candidate was designated by patrons and acclaimed by popular assent. Instead of voting, there was "voice"; instead of running for office, the dignitary "stood for" office. Election was a confirmation, not conferring, of honor. The ritual of affirmation "knit the local society together" and "recreated their collective identity." Competition for seats by rival candidates and the necessity for a poll was a mark of failure signaling that the natural, harmonious process of patronage and social distinction had broken down. Competition for office was indistinguishable from social conflict. It meant "cost, trouble, fear of riot, challenge to magisterial authority," rooted in "bitter local or personal feuds that rent the fabric of the community," in religious controversy, or in factional infighting intensified and rigidified if rivalry was organized along party lines that cast candidates and electors as partisans. Confirming the self-serving element in contested elections, competition finally emerged among the gentry for ideological reasons combined with contests for social distinction, for patronage, and for influence at court.[87]

In the United States too those who praised representative government and election for its "aristocratic effect" despised parties, for good reason. Gordon Wood has described the early American version of election based on clusters of personal and family influence, social position and manners, patrimonialism and patronage. Wherever ruling colonial families were entrenched, as in Virginia and New Hampshire, contested elections and factionalism were minimal.[88] Edmund Morgan's colorful account looks at representation of geographically defined communities in Maryland and England "stretching the fiction of one man standing for another or for several others to the point where he stood for a whole local community, even for those within the community who had not specifically authorized him."[89] In the colonies the electorate might extend to the majority of free adult males—without changing the type elected (never the "yeoman's own") or the deferential nature of the event. As Wood explains, the expansion of popular participation and contested elections "originated not because the mass of people pressed upward from below with new demands but because competing gentry, for their own parochial and tactical purposes, courted the people and bid for their support by invoking popular whig rhetoric."[90] This confirms the standard picture of self-serving partisanship. The introduction of contests for office presented a challenge not just to aristocracy but to "natural aristocracy," and the door was opened for professional politicians, regular electioneering, and nineteenth-century electoral parties and partisanship, which in turn excited new, virulent forms of antipartyism.

Antipartisanship is a distinct theme in this tradition of antipartyism, then. Parties were represented, indeed, identified as associations of partisans based on nothing but (merely!) political ambition and benefit seeking. Hume remarked on the often trivial sources of faction, the foolish animosity, the persistence of partisanship after the real differences on which it was based have disappeared. Antipathy focuses on ambitious men who create and exploit divisions. Lord Salisbury's scorn was pointed: "parties are formed more with reference to controversies that are gone by than to the controversies which these parties have actually to decide."[91] That parties are based on petty and frivolous divisions, on apparent rather than real differences, did not inhibit antipartyism obsessed with divisiveness. It was another layer of reasons for carping that partisans are vitriolic, create conflict where conflict would not otherwise exist, and obstruct government. Parties can be so "small" as to be hard to distinguish from one another; still, they are despised as divisive. This antiparty focus on partisans without purpose except ambition reverberates today. Contemporary critics characterize the major American parties as indistinct, and party competition as insubstantial. Or they see distinctions as frivolous: "In our day . . . one gets the impression that it is the parties imposing cleavages on society, cleavages that observers deplore as 'artificial.'"[92]

Antipartisanship of the sort sketched here and continuing nonstop in the context of modern democratic parties provokes us to consider whether an ethics of partisanship is conceivable. And both concerns of this antiparty tradition—that parties enflame deep divisions and that parties create trivial ones—provoke us to consider the parameters of a normative justification of parties. How small can they be? How great or extreme? How polarized before the warning of "fatal division" is realized? These are my subjects in part 3.

For now, observe that the two charges—personal ambition and artificial differences among parties—are separable. Partisans can be ambitious, unscrupulous lovers of intrigue and at the same time form great parties, parties of principle. Still, there is something to be gained by examining the twin charge—unprincipled partisans based on frivolous distinctions—as a pair. It suggests that parties do not necessarily reflect deep, pre-existing cleavages or distinct social groups and that party builders may invent differences and conjure up partisans. The creative element of parties is foreshadowed, albeit aversively, in this antiparty tradition, which sees partisanship and parties as dangerously divisive even when the divisions are patently invented.

I have canvassed the four main themes of the antiparty tradition that casts parties as fatally divisive: the Roman archetype, the irrepressibility of parties, the uses of classification, and the separate aversion to partisanship. Recall that in this antiparty tradition, in contrast to the holist tradition, social groups and parts are acceptable. They are not only inevitable, they may be natural and beneficial. But parties are never politically benign—that is what earns a group the accusatory label. Party is the negative, evaluative name for partial groups that are not acceptable, that destructively exacerbate divisions or invent divisions that were not there before, creating unnecessary and dangerous schisms. I want to consider next perhaps the best and most enduring illustration of the appreciation of parts combined with abhorrence of parties: the mixed constitution.

Mixed Constitutions: Representing Parts without Parties

In political theory and institutional design the mixed regime is *the* formulation of the political representation of parts without parties. It is a long-standing form for accommodating recognized social divisions within the frame of government. We have only to think of Aristotle's polity, which combines a role for the people or poor (democracy) with wealth (oligarchy). Aristotle used "polity" or "constitution" as both the generic name for all governments and for this type.[93] Or, we think of Polybius' Rome. Among modern thinkers the model was England's three estates—crown, Lords, and Commons—identified in Polybian fashion with monarchy, aristocracy, and democracy.

There is no better introduction to this theme than Aristotle's quarrel with the *Republic*. Plato portrayed factions in the city and soul as internal enemies. They are meddling, interfering, and rebellious, and in classic holist terms, their existence is always a sign of injustice. Justice, as Socrates said to Thrasymachus, produces unanimity and friendship.[94] Aristotle's objection was that Plato had imposed on politics a unity appropriate to an individual or family—where all the parts of the body feel pleasure and pain together, and where "mine" and "not mine" are unknown. He opened the *Politics* by challenging the premise that "the greatest possible unity of the whole polis is the supreme good." Aristotle explained: "A household is something which attains a greater degree of self-sufficiency than an individual; and a city, in turn, is something which attains self-sufficiency to a greater degree than a household. But it becomes fully a city, only when the association which forms it is large enough to be self-sufficing. On the assumption, therefore, that the higher degree of self-sufficiency is the more desirable thing, the lesser degree of unity is more desirable than the greater."[95] The polis is a compound whole composed of differentiated parts.

Aristotle knew that Socrates was responding to the sophist charge that political life is riven by faction and that political rule is class oppression; the ideal city of the *Republic* was a cure for fractiousness. The ancient typology of regimes—monarchical, aristocratic, democratic—reflected the insight that rule, opinions about the distribution of offices, honors, property, and other goods, and opinions about the common good are all partial and that every regime is partisan.[96] But Aristotle judged the *Republic* the wrong remedy. It is not that he disagreed with unity rightly understood as an ideal.[97] Simply, he took into account all the cities he knew and concluded that the distribution of virtue required for unity was inconceivable. Distinct social orders and deep differences of interest and opinion are permanent, according to Aristotle, and, more important, defensible. The differences can be acknowledged and brought into government. His view, which would become orthodoxy, was that the public good is a judicious arrangement of heterogeneous parts and differing premises about justice. Its institutional expression is the mixed regime. The best polity is not a unity, but it is not divisively partisan, either. The accusatory import of "party" is implicit in Aristotle's characterization of tyranny as the opposite of a mixed regime—not only because the tyrant rejects the constraints and terms of office, but also because the tyrant came to power as the leader of a party stirring resentment and threatening violence.

From the standpoint of mixed constitutionalism, pluralism is an admitted fact of social life, divisions are recognized as legitimate and are politically represented, but nothing is conceded to political parties. The aim is to identify structural elements and to mix or balance them, whether by artful design as in Sparta or in a manner driven by critical struggles over the distribution of property and office, as in Polybius' Rome. In this antiparty tradition, to repeat, parts and parties, divisions and divisiveness, are distinct. Parties are parts that do not respect their limits, or noxious contentious factions within these great, acceptable parts. We see that mixed government is closely tied to antipartyism. I am not making the strong claim that mixed regimes were designed to combat divisive partyism or that antipartyism is an explicit justification of constitutional pluralism. But parts and parties are not the same in the political theory of mixed regimes, and the emergence of parties is both cause and proof of imbalance and disharmony among the parts.

Parties are agents of imbalance or disharmony. They are disconcerting. Why are social classes, in particular their organization for participation in government, not considered to be parties? They *are* parties, on this aversive view, when they disrupt or do not settle for the mix. Even if parties represent the great social divisions recognized and incorporated into government, they are abhorrent for the propensity to enflame conflict and to try to dominate and rule in their own interests, and, as Aristotle warned, the winning side "exacts as the prize of victory a greater share in the constitution."[98] As a plain structural matter, the mixed constitution contains latent factions.

Perhaps no political entity has assumed as many institutional forms as the mixed constitution.[99] The assignment of social parts to institutions was varied, as were prescriptions for guarding against their devolution into parties. What could inhibit groups from bringing their divisive ambitions and discontents into government with the result that shared power dissolves into party strife? Aristotle, the master collector and classifier, enumerated the varying rules for combination.[100] He recommended against assigning different political bodies to represent different social groups; instead, all citizens should participate as individuals in a single assembly, with procedures designed to produce a balanced outcome.[101] "The more perfect the admixture of the political elements, the more lasting will be the constitution," he advised. The ideal polity should look as if it contained both democracy and oligarchy, and as if it contained neither.[102] Aristotle's mixed polity emphasized fusion, not balance; a confrontation of constitutional elements amounts to civil conflict.[103] By contrast, Polybius gave weight to the evolution of mixed regimes out of conflict and to the obstructive effect of each element's power, that is, to checking functions. In the Roman republic legislation was shared between (or moved back and forth between) the senate and the people.[104] Machiavelli lauded Rome for reserving institutions exclusively for the plebeians and elected by them. The Tribunate had specific powers (to veto and to accuse and punish) that protected the people from domination by the nobles and wealthier citizens and kept them vigilant. Montesquieu, reflecting on England, would entrust legislative power to the nobles and representatives of the people in separate assemblies with separate deliberations.[105] "Political liberty," he wrote, "is found only in moderate governments. . . . So that one cannot abuse power, power must check power by the arrangement of things."[106]

Merging, on the one hand, and balance, on the other, are alternative arrangements for mixing parts. Among balancers, proponents differed on whether equilibrium rested on equality of power among groups or on a preponderance of one element to serve as fulcrum. The choice of balancer varied, too. Plutarch pointed to the senate; Montesquieu to the nobility—the intermediate institution that stems the 'boundless sea' of royal power which threatens to inundate the people.[107] The logic of the English system was elusive, and British constitutional history is marked by shifting conceptions of mix; as one historian put it, understanding was "inhibited by familiarity" with constitutions and parties in the ancient world.[108] Was England a mixed regime with the king one of three estates alongside the two houses of parliament (sometimes described as the true republican view)?[109] Or was England a legal monarchy with an independent king balanced by other elements?[110] Or did government comprise interdependent parts that required adjustment? In the eighteenth century when the controversy over royal "influence" reached its height, the constitution and its presumed balance was said to be embodied in the interaction of king, lords, and commons *in* Parliament—the ministry, the peers' retainers, independent members chosen without or in opposition to "influence."[111]

The distinction between parts and parties emerges more sharply if we consider not only formal arrangements but also the rationales for this pluralist, openly antiholist prescription for political order. The reasoning on behalf of parts and against parties turns on representation as a requirement for successful governing. One rationale is a functional division of labor based on experience and skill, knowledge and judgment. Mixed government is not a matter of "privilege unredeemed by function."[112] On the contrary, it takes advantage of the merits and contributions of different classes and their differential aptitude for deliberative, judicial, and magisterial roles. Aristotle's case for combining democracy and aristocracy as the elements of the best regime rested in part on this argument. "The wisdom of the multitude" argues for democracy when it comes to evaluating policy and judging individual cases. Individual citizens have fragments of virtue and prudence; combined, this exceeds the excellence of any one individual. "When they all meet together, the people display a good enough gift of perception, and combined with the better class they are of service to the city."[113] Aristotle's polity has been described as a "weakly democratic political 'alloy' (mass participation in deliberation and judgment, tempered by elite monopoly of offices)."[114] The important point here is the invitation to specific social groups to play defined roles. The dynamic of mix was not balance but "fit." It could be upset if material changes caused partisan agitation to alter the terms of participation. It could be upset if factions arise within groups.[115] From this standpoint, mixed regimes were not hospitable to political representation in general. The objective was not to consult every constituency or part but to combine specific elements necessary for governing well.

The most common proposition in favor of a mixed regime, however, was not function but stability. Stability is possible if groups or classes consent to political arrangements, and reliable consent demands more than regard for each class's partial interest. As Aristotle pointed out, attentiveness to the happiness of all the parts is possible in every simple, good regime in which officials are not using office for private gain and governors have good relations with both citizens and the unenfranchised. The distinctive case for a mixed constitution is that consent is more durable if classes have a share in power. It is a prudential argument. "A city with a body of disenfranchised citizens who are numerous and poor must necessarily be a city which is full of enemies,"[116] Aristotle advised. Cicero argued in *The Republic* that a mixed and evenly balanced combination of the three good, simple forms of government offers equality ("which is a thing free men can hardly do without for any considerable length of time") and protection against revolution.[117] Montesquieu put this vividly in his consideration of the Romans:

> What is called unity in a political body, is a very equivocal thing. When it is genuine it is a harmony which makes all the parts, however opposed they may seem to us, act together for the general good of society. . . . There can be unity in a state in which one can see only discord, and yet it is a real concord that brings happiness. . . . [In immoderate states] there is real conflict and an apparent quiet, not of united citizens, but of dead bodies buried next to each other.[118]

One final point about antipartyism emerges in this connection. Whether grounded in the differential contributions of social orders to public life or in assent, the mixed constitution carries with it the implication of parts acting together for a general good. A monopoly of power by one part leads to unjust rule in the self-interest of the group rather than the common interest. The mixed constitution is more than representation for the purpose of conciliation, achieved by giving groups a share of power proportionate to their importance. Mechanical balance per se is not an adequate guarantee of security; stability also requires cooperation, an arrangement of parts that work in concert. Despite the fact that the framework for discussing mixed constitutions was often balance, the two are not the same.[119] The idea of a balance of power assumes antagonistic interests. It does not require that the parts constitute fixed social orders. It does not anticipate cooperation. The mixed constitution in contrast does incorporate permanent, designated groups or social orders, not shifting interest groups, and aims at cooperation. It requires the parts of the community to work together. Montesquieu observed that as the three powers "are constrained to move, by the necessary motion of things they will be forced to move in concert."[120] What was needed was not just checking and balancing, with its implication of restraint and possibility of deadlock, but coordination for energetic government. (Recall that in early modern and modern thought, the mixed constitution, modeled on Rome and eventually attributed in all its glory—"exquisitely composed," "equally tempered"—to England, was associated with expansion and empire. Mixed regimes, Machiavelli noted, have the greatest ability to acquire glory and greatness.[121]) The accusatory, again, is clear: parties press partial aims as forcefully as they can; they do not accept balance, much less facilitate concert.

The chief challenge to the mixed constitution in modern political thought came from continental advocates of monarchical absolutism. For them, the parts brought into a mixed regime just *are* disruptive factions. They can only fragment and limit power, when what is needed is a strong state. Sovereignty is "the absolute and perpetual power of a commonwealth," Bodin argued; it is indivisible. The coexistence of contradictory types "can incite great troubles in commonwealths and have extraordinary consequences." Moreover, in the face of the nearly overwhelming authority of ancient authors, Bodin insisted that the very category of mixed constitution is a mistake. "There is not now, and never was, a state compounded of aristocracy and democracy, much less of the three forms of state," and Bodin set out to refute "their own reasonings and examples." The universally cited instances of mixed government—Sparta, Rome, and Venice—could not withstand scrutiny. As for France, there is "not a shadow of democratic power in the assembly of the Three Estates as it exists in this kingdom."[122]

The republican challenge to mixed constitutions was less sharp and less potent than monarchical absolutism for the simple reason that it was not considered viable in large states. Besides, the republican exemplars were typically judged to be mixed regimes themselves. Venice, "the most serene republic," was a mixed constitution, idealized precisely for its specific securities against the conditions that give rise to parties, like secret voting and strict laws against electioneering or canvassing for votes.[123] Except for the Commonwealth of 1649 outlawing kingship, English republicans conceded the advantages of mixed constitutions. "If the Commons are sovereign," wrote one thinker of the Rump Parliament, "who will be tribunes of the people to check them?"[124] The conflict between king and commons was framed in terms of mix. In fact, the first influential statement came from Charles I himself in his "Answer to the Nineteen Propositions" addressed to the Long Parliament. (As one historian noted: "The Answer was obviously incompatible with the theory of Divine Right of Kings with which Charles I is commonly associated; but circumstances alter cases, even with sovereigns."[125]) The notion of a mix prevailed during the Civil War and after: law making belonged to king, lords, and commons and concessions by any element would upset the balance of estates. The development of constitutional mix in England has been described as "the republicanization of monarchy": "so confused and blended did monarchy and republicanism become in the 18th century that people, especially in the English-speaking world, had trouble precisely defining them."[126] Montesquieu would solemnize this point with the observation that most modern governments were mixtures of both monarchy and republic to one degree or another.[127] The mixed government idea was sturdy. The dominant English version persisted from 1640 for two centuries. Again, neither mix nor its absolutist and republican challengers made any concession to political parties; partisans were those who urged excess or encroachment.

Mixed constitutions and their theories are dizzyingly variable, but no history has more vicissitudes and circuitous rationales than the way the understanding and practice of mixed constitutions were confounded by, adapted to, and superceded by the constitutional separation of powers. Separation of powers did not connote a mix of classes or other social elements; rather, the "powers" were understood as abstract functions of government that could be assigned to different departments, and in turn to different persons, without any agreed-on expectation that they should represent fixed social parts.[128] The difference between a bicameral system with an executive and a society of orders was not well understood,[129] however, and moves from mixed regimes to separation of powers were made with difficulty. The shift repays attention here. For one thing, it underscores my argument that mixed constitutions were closely tied to antipartyism. For another, it points up the longevity of political theories that accept parts and their political place in government but abhor parties. As the idea of the mixed constitution gave way, and as the social and political divisions that laid claim to representation became more fluid, care was taken to ensure that no entrée existed for parties.

I illustrate the persistence of this tradition of antipartyism with three cases from the post-history of mixed regimes: American pluralism, French simplicity, and corporatism. These flesh out the argument that recognition and acceptance of social divisions is compatible with antipathy toward parties as fatally divisive.

After the Mixed Constitution: American Pluralism and Antipartyism

Interpretations of eighteenth-century American constitutional thought are singularly, almost obsessively focused on the influence of accounts of mixed government modeled on the Roman republic. What stands out, one historian grandly claimed, is "the classicists' rout of the anticlassicists who appealed to enlightenment from God rather than the ancients."[130] In this spirit, historians focus on whether American thinkers got their resources directly from the classics, indirectly via Montesquieu (who wrote, "One can never leave the Romans"[131]), or refracted through seventeenth- and eighteenth-century Whigs?[132] This interpretive perspective has problems, though. For one thing, it is susceptible to overlooking the disunity of "the ancients" on this question.[133] It also overstates the significance for American constitutionalism of the literary history of mixed regimes and underestimates the influence of experience, vaunted "common sense," and the powerful attachment to Paine's maxim "the earth belongs to the living"—with its overt confidence in change as improvement. "Is it not the glory of the people of America that they have not suffered a blind veneration for antiquity?" asks one *Federalist Paper*. Another reads, "Quitting the dim light of historical research," Americans "accomplished a revolution which has no parallel in the annals of human society. They reared the fabrics of governments which have no model on the face of the globe."[134] Madison did not mince words: ancient republics were disasters to be avoided: "little, jealous, clashing, tumultuous commonwealths, the wretched nurseries of unceasing discord and the miserable objects of universal pity and contempt."[135] Even the classicist Jefferson conceded: "History informs us of what bad government is."[136]

The pronounced novelty of American political thought begins of course with the observation that "there was nothing to mix in America."[137] The people were neither Roman plebs nor English commoners. There was little mention of a monarch.[138] Aristocracy in America was "shallow and stunted" in comparison to England. John Adams's grafting of mixed government onto the separation of powers is a good example of the contortions this effort required. The two legislative chambers would respectively represent the two great social classes, the influential few and the common people. ("You are apprehensive of monarchy," Adams wrote to Jefferson, "I, of aristocracy," and argued that by confining "aristocrats" to an upper house, they would remain under public scrutiny.) Adams also proposed an executive for life or, if necessary, a hereditary president, who would serve as balancer.

The key move away from the mixed constitution turned on aristocracy. As my earlier discussion of majoritarianism suggested, there was no great social or legal divide between the wealthy and notable and the rest of the people—certainly none that was usable for institutional design. "Monocrats" and "aristocrats" referred to political dispositions; there was no royal line or noble class. In the American context, "aristocracy" referred to a diffuse and open elite—to anyone with the resources to "create obligations and dependencies that could be turned into political authority,"[139] and to any asset that could produce followers. As John Adams put it in a formulation that embraced

90

wealth, title, and reputation, an aristocrat is "every man who can command or influence two votes; one beside his own."[140] Even so, an aristocratic class understood in these diffuse terms was not inconceivable; it was a constant fear. For Antifederalists, the proposed central government, particularly the Senate, which was remote from the people, was aristocratic for that reason alone. Unaccountable national officials would be able to accumulate property and other bounties of power, and the separation of powers would devolve into a genuine oligarchy of wealth or even a self-assigned titled aristocracy. The national government apparatus with its checks and balances was too distant (Jefferson referred to it as "the foreign branch" of the republic) and too complex. Antifederalists argued that only simple lines of authority and a sharp discrimination of functions would be discernible by the people, enable democratic accountability, and prevent the creation of entrenched classes and creation of an actual aristocracy.[141] For Federalists (and this was no comforting response) the Senate was a small chosen body, a suprapartisan elite of reputation and character, intended to purify opinions and guard against "the confusion of the multitude."[142] In Hannah Arendt's sympathetic judgment, the Senate was the chamber of opinion in which individuals could "exert their reason coolly and freely. The Senate was the medium through which public views must pass."[143] It was meant to triumph over faction-ridden misgovernment of democracy.[144]

Opposition to aristocracy in America was not opposition to a concrete, identifiable legal and social class, then, or to a historically long-standing, native elite. "Aristocracy" had no stable referent. It expressed the perfectly reasonable unease endemic to a representative democracy whose boasted political equality could be undone by social inequality and by partisan associations promoting these interests. That is one reason why majorities and minorities became the basic units of political life.

One great object was to combat the evil of parties formed around specific inequalities—artificial distinctions like titles of nobility or entrenched inequalities of property linked to primogeniture. We have seen Madison's view of the best protection against party: "by withholding unnecessary opportunities from a few, to increase the inequality of property, by an immoderate, and especially an unmerited accumulation of riches." He prescribed laws "which, without violating the rights of property, reduce extreme wealth towards a state of mediocrity, and raise extreme indigence towards a state of comfort."[145] Madison's famous formula for plural factions checking one another and for an intricate government structure designed to make parties ineffective comes into play when this preventative fails. If a strong majority (or minority) party did form, it must be frustrated. It should never be allowed to control government.[146] When Madison wrote, ambiguously, that the regulation of interests "involves the spirit of party and faction in the necessary operations of government," he did not mean that parties should organize government. He meant that well-designed institutions would help to render parties incapable of forming permanent majorities.[147] Parties would, in the words of a modern commentator, "lose and exhaust themselves in futile attempts to fight their way through the labyrinthine framework of government much as an attacking army is expected to spend itself against the defensive works of a fortress"; they "strangle themselves in the machinery of government."[148] (Madison did not anticipate the opposite problem—the difficulty of forming any majority capable of effectively governing in the absence of party organization and partisanship.)

What explains the rise of the first national party system in the First Congress following ratification, given vociferous antipartyism on all sides?[149] The explanation with the most purchase is that the policies pursued by Hamilton were seen by all as a continuation of the founding debates about the Constitution. His policies were viewed by the opposition as opening the way to domination by an aristocratic party, a "junto of unprincipled men" furthering their own interests and hostile to the people. Indeed, majority voting rules in Congress enabled Hamilton's supporters to pass measures they could not have passed under the Articles. As Treasury Secretary, then, Hamilton had begun to forge connections among members of Congress. Madison and Jefferson did the same. Both sides reached out to state and local political leaders for support in their self-described role as "watchdogs." The next step was building an electoral following in the states, for the only recourse for opponents was to muster a majority through elections. Parties, including the first move beyond partisan divisions in the government to organizing electoral bases outside, were justified because partisan organization was necessary until the great question of republicanism was finally settled.

The charges "monocrat" and "Jacobin" show this plainly. Jefferson and Madison formed the Republican Party to resolve the great issue of principle: the popular character of the regime. "Party competition was not among democrats but between democrats and aristocrats."[150] In this cause, and in this crisis, partisan activity was warranted. This new political institution, the first party to turn tentatively to elections and to develop a public political identity, was invented by men who held, sincerely and consistently, to antipartyism.[151] Constitutional politics became party politics—conflict over the meaning of popular sovereignty. In defense of popular majoritarianism, the conflict had to take a party form. (A parallel explanation for parties focuses on defense of the principle of federalism. Legal historians point out that the protector of the contentious state/national balance was not initially thought to be the Court exercising judicial review but popular political action organized and channeled early on by parties. Only parties could span state and national government, creating a flexible federalism instead of the feared confrontation between states and national government.[152])

The mixed constitution gave way to the institutional separation of powers stripped of its resonance of monarchic and aristocratic elements. Yet the notion of recognized, politically represented classes was not entirely moribund and could be revived. Decades before the Civil War, the perception grew in many quarters that a privileged social order had upset the constitutional balance. The national government had been captured by southern oligarchy. The "slave oligarchy" comprised a "lordly Caste," which now for the first time openly proclaimed slavery "the black marble keystone of our National Arch . . . the corner-stone of our Republican edifice." This oligarchy did not respect "time honored" arrangements worked out in the Constitution and the Missouri Compromise. Its members usurped a disproportionate number of high national offices, including the Supreme

Court, an imbalance demonstrated by the Kansas-Nebraska Act and the *Dred Scott* decision. Notably, the Republican Party employed the language of balance but did not promise any longer to act as part of a fragile equilibrium. The mixed constitution was gone. Republicans promised to prostrate the un-American oligarchy.[153]

I have surveyed American moves from mixed constitution to separation of powers with one object in mind: to point out that these changes did not provide an entrée to parties. Pluralism devoid of connection to set social and legal orders, loosed from the classic schematic of people/ aristocracy, made mixed government obsolete. But the eclipse of great social parts built into the structure of government did not signal hospitability to either political groups organized to contest for office or to the party organization of government. Party remained an accusatory label applied to political associations judged needlessly, selfishly, and dangerously divisive. Again, disagreements about the Constitution led to the formation of Federalist and Republican parties—often described as the precursors of modern electoral parties. But as I have shown, they represented themselves as honorable responses to necessity and as temporary; "each hoped instead to eliminate party conflict by persuading and absorbing the more acceptable and 'innocent' members of the other; each side hoped to attach the stigma of foreign allegiance and disloyalty to the intractable leaders of the other, and to put them out of business as a party." "We are attempting by this Constitution," Hamilton said to the New York ratifying convention, "to abolish factions and unite all parties for the general welfare."[154]

After the Mixed Constitution: Sieyes and Simplicity

Like the era of constitutional founding in America, the French Revolution was the occasion for both constitutional creation and renewed antipartyism. In neither did rejection of mixed government and appreciation of a more open political pluralism afford an entrée to parties. Arguably the continent's most important theorist of representative democracy (Condorcet could lay claim to the title as well), Sieyes advocated representation without parts.[155] He also insisted with force on representation without parties. In this he was at one with Condorcet, who wrote that "one of the primary needs of the French republic is to have none."[156]

Sieyes stands out for rejecting not only corporate social orders and mixed government but also separation of powers. He favored a single national assembly. Liberty would be secured by simple government.[157] This meant, of course, the elimination of corporate privileges and representation of estates.[158] The aristocracy was not the only privileged order, but it was certainly the worst, on his view. Sieyes called the nobility the Algerians of France—foreigners with no more claim to representation than the Council of Venice. When in an effort to have their own chamber the French nobility appealed to the British Constitution as a model, Sieyes called the House of Lords "a monument to Gothic superstition."[159] He opposed recalling the French Estates-General and urged a single National Assembly. The National Assembly was emphatically not a House of Commons, then. In a pamphlet said to have "scripted" the events of 1789, Sieyes argued that the Third Estate is "all." He continued to use the phrase even as he rejected the implication that the people were partial, one part among others. The Third Estate alone represented the nation and should refuse to constitute itself as a separate order.[160] Sieyes conceded, but only as a first step toward simplicity, that representation of the third estate in the National Assembly should be doubled, voting should be by head not order, and the Third Estate should demonstrate its pre-eminence by "summoning" the other orders.

> If therefore in France we want to assemble the three orders as one, it will be essential for the noble and the priest to have no other interest than the common interest, and for them to have no other rights by law than those of the simple citizen. Unless this is done you may well be able to bring together the three orders under the same denomination, but they will always form three heterogeneous substances impossible to amalgamate. I cannot be accused of wishing to uphold the distinction between orders . . . . I know only one misfortune which is worse and that is to blend the three orders nominally while leaving them really separate through the maintenance of privileges. This would be to consecrate for ever their triumph over the nation.[161]

Once mixed government was eliminated, Sieyes's title question—"What is the third estate?"—was not easily answered. It is one thing to say that all public officials are representatives of the people because all powers emanate from the people.[162] Or to pronounce: "The nation is prior to all, it is the source of everything. Its will is always legal; it is the law itself."[163] It is another thing, however, to say who the people actually are, how their interests are determined and represented in political institutions, how a national will is created or ascertained.

The question was posed particularly sharply because Sieyes rejected direct democracy. For the Jacobins, the people would make decisions directly (or the vanguard would, acting in their name). Robespierre's was the revolutionary party that represented "the great popular Society of the whole French People."[164] Bur for Sieyes, direct, unmediated rule was always the rule of the few over the many in practice, and he called it false democracy: "The second rate Rousseauists of the revolution repeated Rousseau's fatal mistake."[165] Robespierre brought nothing but the resurgence of a privileged caste, just another absolutism. Benjamin Constant considered Sieyes one of the great political theorists of the age, and like Sieyes he had no urge to summon everyone to politics: "The partisans of ancient liberty [i.e., the Jacobins] grew furious when they saw that the moderns didn't want to be free according to their method."[166] Instead, Sieyes offered a rare, powerful brief for representative democracy: the people delegate powers to the Assembly, and elected representatives are the final decision makers, the constituted authorities. Jefferson's insistence on a public space in which the people would engage in the activities of "expressing, discussing and deciding" was alien, disagreeable to Sieyes.[167] The nation could act only through its assembly. He brooked no check on it. He opposed a royal veto, which he called a "letter-de-cachet directed against the national will."[168] He would not support a channel for the people to appeal beyond representatives to the king, either. "Power belongs only to the whole. As soon as one party appeals against a decision the whole no longer exists. . . . [T]here would be no constitution in a country as soon as the slightest trouble arose between its parts, unless the nation existed independently of all rule and of all constitutional form."[169] Popular sovereignty did not reside in constituencies that chose representatives, in the unorganized people at large, or in convention, but in the assembly. The general will is generated exclusively in the National Assembly.

Sieyes had a strange, stern view of representation, which may be why he avoided using the term "representative democracy": representativeness was not a concern.[170] Neither the assembly as a whole nor its members singly were the agents of any other body or group. The National Assembly was not a federation of small democracies, as instructions from territorially based constituencies imply. Each member represents the nation: "it is not by scrutinizing particular cahiers, if such exist, that he will discover the will of his electors. It is not a question here of conducting a democratic poll, but of proposing, listening, concerting, modifying his opinion, in a word of forming in common a common will."[171] The community confers on its deputies "power of attorney, so that they can meet, deliberate, reconcile their differences, and will in common; thus, instead of simple carriers of votes, it has genuine representatives."[172] The only reason to have political subdivisions at all was to facilitate elections and administration, and Sieyes designed France's uniform system of departments in hopes of *overcoming* existing provincial particularism with its old esprit de corps—ecclesiastical, military, administrative, and judicial. Departments were intended to be a counterforce to the administrative claims of municipality over the nation, *une nation*. In this spirit, Sieyes proposed, contra Paine, a monarch or some strange facsimile of his own invention purely as a symbol of national unity.[173] Sieyes's opposition to a mixed constitution and to politically privileged social orders, his insistence on a single National Assembly, gives a central place to representation, albeit of a strangely severe sort.

We see the consistency and force of Sieyes's theory of representation without parts and parties by taking another look at his answer to the question, who or what did representatives of the Third Estate represent? The nation comprised those who performed all the public functions and private work of a rational society. It was all those who did productive work: "the 40,000 parishes covering the whole territory . . . all the contributors to the public establishment."[174] Sieyes characterized representation as the political counterpart of the vital economic division of labor in commercial society: politically active representatives who pursued the business of government, and citizens who were inactive and inexpressive except for selecting representatives. In fact, Sieyes applied the analogy in reverse: "the division of labor, of professions, etc. is simply the representative system establishing itself spontaneously; it goes hand in hand with the progress of the society it animates. . . . I would even say that representation is confounded with the very essence of social life."[175] The division of labor in politics as in society signified productivity. The analogy had its limits, for the social division of labor, which has often served as a basis for partisan organization (labor parties, plainly) was not supposed to be reflected in representation. There was no mirroring, or politics of presence for Sieyes. Again, representativeness was not a consideration; it only raised the specter of partiality and parties.

Sieyes did not anticipate unanimity in the National Assembly, but neither did he imagine politically organized groups and interests there. He was unwilling to concede any basis for internal divisions, for parties and partisanship. There were only common interests. Sieyes could not have been clearer: with parties, the assembly would be a hive of factions, a fragmented nation. It was not just the experience of aroused and militant parties, fratricidal battles that dictated Sieyes's repulsion. Quite simply, he could see no good from them at all. Divisive parties fatally inhibit the emergence of a national will. Alliances of citizens in the National Assembly "lead to conspiracy and collusion; through it anti-social schemes are plotted; through it the most formidable enemies of the People mobilise themselves. History teems with examples of such misfortunes."[176]

After the Mixed Constitution? Corporate Representation

In the antiparty tradition I have been chronicling, divisions are distinguishable from divisiveness, which is viewed as the entire, reprehensible business of parties. In mixed constitutions, recognition and representation of parts is compatible with antipathy toward parties; the political task was to arrange parts in a way that did not give rise to parties and partisanship. The mixed constitution was overcome with difficulty; and when it was rejected and politics opened to a plurality of social elements, care was taken that this was not an invitation to party organization. Early American political thought illustrates the way mixed constitutions "gave way with difficulty," and Sieyes illustrates a frontal assault aimed at erasing mixed government with one swipe. Hegel's reflections on representation are a good illustration of a third course, in which mixed government comprising social elements was not supplanted but reconceived. Hegel's corporatism rounds out my discussion of the threads that make up the tradition of antipartyism that admits political parts but despises parties.

Hegel had nothing but loathing for the German Assembly of Estates, in which the representation of various sections was a mess of historical privileges. "German constitutional law," he wrote, "is not a science derived from principles but a register of the most varied constitutional rights acquired in the manner of private rights."[177] There was no state, only an assemblage of what were essentially property rights in representation "which the parts have wrested from the whole." Hegel described it as "an anarchy made into a constitution" and spoke of German "obstinate adherence to particularism to the point of madness."[178]

On the other hand, Hegel was contemptuous of rationalist French constitutional design. Sieyes was his favorite target among "the political theories ... partly propounded by would-be philosophers and teachers of the rights of man and partly realized in tremendous political experiments."[179] For similar reasons he targeted the English Reform Bill, which gave central place to "atomistic" political equality, mimicking "French abstractions of mere numbers and quanta of property." This misbegotten notion of political representation was not only theoretically wrong but practically self-defeating. Estates mediated between government and people; they *create* public opinion and within associations people learn how to recognize the true character of their interests. Moreover, voting detached from social anchors breeds political apathy. Hegel was prescient; "the exercise of a wholly occasional calling, like that of being a voter, easily ceases to be of interest ... and in any case depends on an accidental attitude and a momentary preference."[180] Hegel anticipated every contemporary explanation for popular political disengagement, including the insignificance of casting a single vote.[181] He denied that this was representation: "All modern states subsist by representation, and its degeneration alone, i.e. the loss of its true essence, has destroyed France's constitution."[182]

The "true essence" in modern states is representation by estates, which "prevent[s] individuals from having the appearance of a mass, or an aggregate and so from acquiring an unorganized opinion and volition."[183] But historical estates and fixed social orders were no longer the relevant parts, and Hegel admitted a more fluid pluralism:

> The circles of association in civil society are already communities. To picture these communities as once more breaking up into a mere conglomeration of individuals as soon as they enter the field of politics . . . is eo ipso to hold civil and political life apart from one another and as it were to hang the latter in the air, because its basis could then only be the abstract individuality of caprice and opinion."[184]

In *The Philosophy of Right*, he proposed a reformed and modernized account of representation based on the elements of civil society.[185] Certain interests are integral to the modern state, and the importance of these sections justifies representation; they should be "actually present" there. As I show in the next chapter, Hegel was preoccupied with the capacity of representatives to govern, and his rationale for corporate representation was emphatically not a balance of parts; the implication that the elements confronted one another as hostile powers was an entirely false view of the state.[186] Hegel posed the proper understanding of the representation of parts this way: the issue is not *the right* of enfranchisement and therefore of who were to be the constituents, but *the result*, the creation of a legislative assembly. Hegel's appreciation for mixed government reconstituted and properly understood is inescapable: "the development of the state to constitutional monarchy is the achievement of the modern world."[187] (Hegel's philosophic account of the relation of these parts in accord with the state as "the actuality of the ethical Idea"[188] is outside my purview.)

Hegel was the most conceptually adventurous and historically sensitive theorist to recast mixed government. But many other less perceptive and articulate variations of the idea of mix have endured in theory and practice. For example, well into the nineteenth century, Walter Bagehot insisted on a mixed government interpretation of the British Constitution, arguing specifically for an undiluted house of peers (he opposed life peerages, which he called an attempt to "vaccinate" Lords with genius):

> I am exceedingly afraid of the ignorant multitude of the new constituencies. I wish to have as great and as compact a power as possible to resist it. But a dissension between the Lords and the Commons divides that resisting power; as I have explained, the House of Commons still mainly represents the plutocracy, the Lords represent the aristocracy. The main interest of both these classes is now identical, which is to prevent or to mitigate the rule of uneducated members.[189]

Of greater interest is the recurrent appearance of variations of corporate representation in democratic theory, where the representation of pre-existing social parts is set in opposition to divisive parties and arrant partisanship. Here is a short list, certainly not exhaustive, suggesting the scope and persistence of corporate alternatives to parties.

John Calhoun's notion of a "concurrent majority" is one example, assuming as it does stable class and regional interests, like the slaveholding South, and requiring their consent to policy. The "concurrent majority" was conceived as a way to achieve political harmony, an antidote to dread numerical majoritarianism and unscrupulous partisans.[190]

British Idealist philosophers, in their resistance to Leviathan, reincarnated the political pluralism of mixed government, substituting representation by function (producers, workers, industries) for social orders. Corporate representation, G.D.H. Cole wrote, is a corrective to the prevailing perversion of representation, that is, the tendency to "clannishness" among members of Parliament, of which "the party system is an awful, but illuminating example."[191]

"Neo-corporatism" is alive in contemporary constitutional and political theory in the form of proposals for legislation by class or sectoral interests, who cooperate with one another and public authorities to develop and implement policies.[192] Explicitly conceived as a rival to parties for bridging social groups and government is "consociationalism." Compromises among elites circumventing parties and their constituents, coalitions among major blocs of interests, "pacts" among key actors guaranteeing not to harm one another's vital interests all tamp down fractiousness and circumvent the open politics, the divisiveness and disarray of parties.[193]

Political representation of formally recognized social and political divisions is also echoed today in certain accounts of federalism. It is there in schemes for guaranteed representation of racial, ethnic, and religious groups in divided societies, and in stable democracies too. The European Union has been rightly described as a mixed polity whose constitution combines the "powers of society"—in this case national governments, supranational institutions—and "the peoples of the States brought together in Community" represented in the Common Assembly and the European Parliament. (In the EU scheme, as in all mixed regimes, discussion focuses on the trade-offs of balance and capacity for action.[194]) Add to this list the resuscitated ideal of "associational democracy." Also proposals by democratic theorists to recreate institutions like those found in classical mixed government, which discriminate between the wealthy and the rest, or the people and specific elites, giving each separate representation.[195] All of these ideas are in the tradition of political pluralism that admits parts but not parties. I take a closer look at contemporary antipartyism and political theorists' ceaseless efforts to conceive of representative democracy without parties in Part II.

Arrant Divisiveness Reconsidered

I want to return in conclusion to one theme from this antiparty tradition, and use it to begin to cast parties and partisans in a fresh light. The antiparty tradition obsessed with fatal divisiveness sees parties as carriers of deep cleavages, permanently hostile forces. Parties reflect and exacerbate divisions. The aim is to contain divisions through proper mix and balance and to extirpate parties that exploit partiality and upset order. One theme of the tradition that sees parties as fatally divisive is the "turn of the screw" that reorients aversion from parties to partisans. It is bad enough that parties deepen and enflame real social divisions, upset mix and balance. With the emphasis on partisan ambition, parties appear dangerously divisive even if they do not reflect recognized social parts or deep divisions of interest or opinion. Partisans can wreak their havoc even if what defines parties is trivial or ephemeral. Recall: "the smallest appearance of real difference will produce them,"[196] and "a difference of interests, real or supposed, is the most natural and fruitful source of them."[197] By stepping back a bit from this hostile characterization of partisan divisions as "frivolous and fanciful,"[198] we can glimpse what I argue is a defining characteristic of parties, and part of their value. Partisans combine to win office in order to exercise political power, of course. In doing so, they identify and organize politically relevant differences. The creative role of parties is foreshadowed, aversively, in this antiparty tradition.

One point to draw from this antiparty tradition is that parties create differences for the purposes of justifying and effectively pursuing power. In that sense, partisan lines of division are political, relatively autonomous. Social divisions do not automatically give rise to parties, and parties are not necessarily epiphenomena, unwelcome agents of social divisions already recognized and represented. Parties do not necessarily reflect prior, publicly recognized divisions at all. That is implied, in standard accusatory tone, by the phrase "real or supposed." Parties *are* opportunistic responses to political possibilities. Partisans pursue power and use office to govern, and parties are agenda-setting institutions. They present themselves as agents of desirable arrangements and policies different from the status quo (or rallying to preserve it from challenge) and distinct from those advocated by opposition parties.

I do not want to exaggerate this point. In many contexts, modern governing and electoral parties represent social groups with sharply defined interests and views—socialist parties or confessional parties, for example (even so, there was no automatic translation from Catholic Church to Christian Democratic Party). Nor do I want to concede that lines of division created by parties are "supposed" rather than real. Simply, this antiparty tradition recognizes that partisans

103

create politically relevant divisions. That is what makes them doubly anathema to both holists and antiparty thinkers who see them as fatally divisive.

Madison took the lesser evil view of the matter, hoping that party contests "will be either so slight or so transient" as not to threaten profound and permanent divisions.[199] Tocqueville saw something more. He took what had stood as decisive proof of the arrant divisiveness of parties and subtly altered the tenor of discussion. Partisans begin with a private interest or opinion about the public interest, compose lines of division, discover a principle to justify this partiality, and "introduce[e] a new power into the political world":

> Ambition must succeed in creating parties, for it is difficult to overthrow the one who holds power for the sole reason that someone wants to take his place. All the skill of politicians therefore consists in composing parties; a politician in the United States at first seeks to discern his interest and to see what the analogous interests are that could be grouped around his; afterwards, he busies himself with discovering whether there might not by chance exist in the world a doctrine or principle that could suitably be placed at the head of the new association to give it the right to introduce itself and circulate freely. . . . This done, they introduce the new power into the political world.[200]

Tocqueville presented this as a willful, skillful achievement.[201] To compete for office, ambitious men are forced to form coalitions and articulate aims as systems of ideas in competition. That gives them "the right to circulate freely." He was alert to the series of creative moves that make partisanship a political achievement, "introducing a new power into the political world."

This is consistent with a common political science account of parties that is generally (but erroneously) construed as dispiriting and diminishing rather than appreciative:

> The major political party is a creature of the politicians, the ambitious office seeker and officeholder. They have created and maintained, used or abused, reformed or ignored the political party when doing so has furthered their goals and ambitions. . . . These politicians do not have

partisan goals per se. Rather, they have more fundamental goals, and the party is only the instrument for achieving them.[202]

The rapid formation of the Republican Party in the years before the American Civil War illustrates this point. It owed in part to the fact that political men of antiparty sentiment had no vehicle for political organization and in part to experienced public men whose careers could not be advanced through the dissolving Whig Party. The Republican Party offered a "welcome field for their talents and leadership."[203]

Both in pursuit of power and in governing, partisans create lines of division. I want to refine this claim a bit.[204] Parties arise in opposition to one another and present themselves as distinct in politically relevant, even gripping ways. These differences, bases of partiality, are rarely fanciful, but neither are they always already previously recognized cleavages that parties exploit. The creation of party identity elevates a line of division into general political awareness. The dramatic rise of the American Republican Party from its formation in the 1850s to its election of Lincoln in 1860 illustrates this point too. The party did not invent the slavery issue dividing the nation. But Republicans did recast the issue in sectional terms—making it the basis for a sharp North/South divide, and identifying their party with the North. They became the party opposed to the expansion of slavery, and pointed to events that could be interpreted as a conspiracy of southern oligarchs to expand slavery against northern opposition. They successfully labeled the opposition Democratic Party the lackey of the oligarchic South.

Neither social divisions nor popular grievances, no matter how intense, dictate the existence of parties based on these divisions and grievances. In contemporary terms, "issues," "problems," "reforms"—the stuff of party identity—do not arise spontaneously, fully articulated, and electoral victories are not self-interpreting. "Some one has to politicize events, to define their political relevance in terms of a choice between or among parties."[205] The creation and successive political achievements of the Republican Party, which included holding together internal factions from the Emancipation Proclamation through the passage of the Civil War Amendments to the Constitution, epitomize the potential to invent and reinvent the terms of difference.

This idea that parties create lines of division is one important, defining characteristic to emerge from the antiparty tradition that focuses on fatal divisiveness. This antiparty tradition endures because its premise is correct. Parties have to be divisive; they are by definition. "Parties are trouble, or they make trouble; and if not, they are inexcusable."[206] Parties identify lines of division; they have to persuade that these divisions and the conflicts they generate are important, that the stakes in generating an "issue" are real, not supposed. "In politics the most catastrophic force in the world is the power of irrelevance."[207]

From the two glorious antiparty traditions I have presented, we can glean another defining characteristic of parties. Whether they are despised as unwholesome parts or as fatally divisive, critics point out that parties arise in multiples, not singly, in aggressive opposition or reaction to one another. They are by definition rival political associations. Their identity consists in finding an issue, position, principle, or constituency not just distinct from but in opposition to others. Parties are doubly partial, for they represent a particular part and they favor it. Recall that for holists, parties are the worst form of division in what should be indivisible because their business is political conflict. As for partisanship, it is willful identification with the part and advocacy on behalf of that part.

This brings home the fundamental difference between the two glorious traditions of antipartyism I have explored in these opening chapters. For holists, the demand for unity is categorical. No concession to parties and no possibility for reconciliation is conceivable. Holistic antipartyism finds all parts abominable, and parties are just a symptom of abhorrent divisions. By their avowed partiality (a particular interest, opinion, principle, or ambition), a partiality confirmed by the existence of rival parties, parties and partisans resist combination into a unified whole. Again, holists cast parties as *parts against*, rather than *parts of*, the whole. In contrast, the second antiparty tradition accepts pluralism but does not follow the logic of pluralism to parties. Nonetheless, reconciliation to parties is possible from this standpoint. For parties are less symptoms of deeper intolerable division than causes and drivers of arrant divisiveness, disrupters of political equilibrium. They can conceivably be tempered and put to use. Indeed, this reconciliation is potentially robust if parties are seen as mutually complementary and if their dynamic of contest and opposition is seen as potentially fruitful for defending or advancing political understanding or for moderation in government. It is in response to this tradition of antipartyism that we get grudging acceptance of the divisions parties create and the trouble partisanship causes, tenuous moments of appreciation.

These glorious traditions of antipartyism have been tempered but have not disappeared. Antipartyism is rife today, though antipartyism focused on parties as parts and parties as divisive has been supplemented by varieties of antipartyism shaped by the experience of mass electorates and institutionalized party systems. I discuss these additional highpoints in my map of antipartyism in Part II, "Post-Party Depression." In Part III, I answer antipartyism and propose my defense of parties and partisanship, an ethic of partisanship, and an account of the bounds of justifiable parties. Before turning to this facet of my project, I want to cull from the two glorious traditions of antipartyism several tentative moments of appreciation. I have tried to anticipate the points at which the view of parties as unwholesome parts and the view of parties as divisive allow for occasional, contingent, grudging acceptance. Again, "party" was historically an accusatory term, and the history of parties is the history of animadversion. Even today the salutary purposes of parties and partisanship have not gained a foothold in political theory. But there have been rare "moments of appreciation." The existence of parties is greeted with a modicum of acceptance and the beginnings of normative justification. These early thoughts on the achievement of parties are my next subject.

CHAPTER 3

———⟫◆⟪———

Moments of Appreciation

The antiparty tradition that views parties as divisive endures because it is correct. Parties have to be divisive; they are by definition. Parties are doubly partial: they represent a particular part of the political community and they favor that part, even if partiality takes the form of a judgment about the common good. A reluctant acceptance of the divisions that parties create and the trouble that partisanship causes appears in initial, tenuous moments of appreciation. So I want to flag points in the glorious traditions of antipartyism where thinkers paused in their castigation.

True, there is not an iota of appreciation in holist antipartyism. Partisans of holism are purely opportunistic. Party may be an avenue to power, but the aim is to eliminate all opposition and reclaim perfect wholeness. From a holist standpoint, there is no justification for social and political parts, least of all for permanent parties. No reconciliation is possible. In contrast, there *is* room in the antiparty tradition of "divisive" parties for moments of appreciation. We saw Machiavelli's consideration that Roman parties served on occasion "to dissipate the frustrations which might otherwise erupt against a well-disposed government."[1] The moments of appreciation that interest me here arise, as Machiavelli's did, from reflection on particular cases. The still unenthusiastic temper of appreciation is captured by statements of this sort: "Parties in the State, are just of the like nature with Heresies in the Church; sometimes they make it better and sometimes they make it worse."[2] The moments of appreciation I discuss here are tentative and sometimes grudging. With one exception, they do not rise to a systematic defense of parties. But by the eighteenth century a number of thinkers acknowledged that parties were more than occasional political alliances, dangerous instruments, temporary and contingent. They recognized that parties were emerging as regular institutions and that party dynamics were not always aberrant. The mark of this move beyond "a party to end parties" is recognition of their ongoing usefulness, when they are useful. On occasion, too, these thinkers allowed that partisans are not necessarily bent on agitation or subversion and might rise above the moral and political dregs.

This is something. Very few political thinkers have found the messy, ongoing politics of parties or the ceaseless strategies of partisans appealing. Parties make the politics, the sheer partiality, of governing and legislating (and, later, shaping public opinion) explicit. They make differences of interest and value, clashing ambitions, and collective efforts to exercise power and to deny its exercise to others vivid. Antipartyism—whether opposed to parties as parts or to parties as divisive—endures because so many are appalled by what often seems to be the palpable unreason and errant selfishness of party strife, and the latent violence of faction. Each of the moments of appreciation I discuss here finds some good reason for party antagonism. The philosophical moment of appreciation is particularly ambitious, and gives party conflict if not a kind of glow, at least a passable appeal.

My object, then, is to identify the traces of positive in the long history of antipartyism before they were settled theoretical insights, and to underscore their significance. Sartori commented that "great achievements are accomplished in the mental fog of practical experience."[3] Parties were formed and partisans began to manage, not just enflame political conflict without a clear understanding of the process or structure of contestation. As one historian explains, "First, parties had to be created, and then at last they would begin to find theoretical acceptance."[4] A recent account of American parties as the solution to politicians' collective action problems draws the same conclusion: in late eighteenth-century America "none of the principals either foresaw the invention of parties or had any master partisan design in mind." "Politicians confront such circumstances not as theoretical insights, but as practical, substantive problems affecting their ability to achieve goals."[5] That innovations are made untheoretically is no reason to say that the "genius" of practices is what cannot be captured theoretically. It is simply to say that "illegitimacy precedes legitimacy" and that demands for political principles mostly follow rather than precede institutional developments. Justifications come in the train of the creation of political institutions and ways of exercising power. Arendt made the point memorably: "What saves the affairs of mortal men from their inherent futility is nothing but this incessant talk about them, which in its turn remains futile unless certain concepts, certain guideposts for future remembrance, and even for sheer reference, arise out of it."[6]

My purpose here is to retrieve early "moments of appreciation" of parties, to rescue them from futility. They have been partially eclipsed, and I want to bring them out of the shadows to serve as guides to the achievement parties represent. The challenge is to organize traces of positive in the long history of antipartyism so that they have coherence and so that their contemporary significance is plainly in view.

One moment of appreciation sees parties as a form of regulated rivalry and acknowledges managed conflict as an achievement. A second recognizes parties as a way of organizing government. These two were the result of experience and were grasped by partisans themselves. A third moment of appreciation is philosophical. It is the view from outside, not the self-understanding of partisans. It casts parties as carriers of complementary values and party conflict as a constructive dynamic of mutual correction, even progress.

Before turning to these, however, I want to pause at a halfway house between utter condemnation and considered appreciation. In the antiparty tradition that admits social divisions and their political representation but abhors parties, there is room for the possibility that on occasion a particular party might be necessary.

Parties of Constitutional Necessity:
Hume's Insight and Aversion

The argument for necessity focused on securing or restoring constitutional order. It allowed that on occasion a particular party, such as the revolutionary Whigs, could have its moment. The phrase "party of principle" typically denoted constitutional conflict. The English Revolution is one example and is the basis for addressing the question, When is a party of necessity necessary? The political philosopher rightly associated with a defense of parties of constitutional necessity is Hume.[7]

The English Constitution was a mixed one, and wherever social orders are represented in government, one will try to increase its authority at the expense of the others, Hume observed. "The just balance between the republican and monarchical parts of our constitution is really, in itself, so extremely delicate and uncertain, that, when joined to men's passions and prejudices, it is impossible but different opinions must arise concerning it, even among persons of the best understanding."[8] Parties are likely to arise in all regimes, but parties of principle are intrinsic to mixed constitutions: "for we must still have an opposition, open or disguised." During the reigns leading up to the English revolution, conflict over constitutional matters was unceasing, and Hume explored the contours of the disagreement that defined the parties. The royal prerogative, if backed by sufficient resources, would try to breach constitutional limits. Charles employed all the oppressive prerogatives of the crown: forced loans, benevolences, taxes without consent of parliament, arbitrary imprisonments, the billeting of soldiers, martial law. The parliamentary power, too, would be abused; "under colour of advice, they may give disguised orders; and in complaining of grievances, they may draw to themselves every power of government." "From the shock of these opposite pretensions, together with religious controversy, arose all the factions, convulsions, and disorders, which attended that period."[9]

The exceptional case in Hume's account, the reason for admitting parties of constitutional necessity, is the Glorious Revolution. Hume dismissed as devious fiction the Whig claim that they were battling to restore the ancient constitution, but he accepted the overall Whig assessment: "This is constitutional necessity: It is confirmed by the whole ANALOGY of the government and constitution. A free monarchy in which every individual is a slave, is a glaring contradiction." The crown's actions "roused the independent genius of the commons." Subversion of the laws and of religion menaced even the Tories and high clergy, and Hume commended that party's perspicuity too: "their present apprehensions had prevailed over their political tenets." In his account, each party avoided the extreme to which it was peculiarly susceptible—republicanism and unchecked monarchy. Whigs held back from the idea that the crown was forfeited and refrained from expressing a censure of old Tory principles and too open a preference for their own. For their part, Tories held back from insisting on passive obedience. The invitation to William to take the throne was possible because of partisans' mutual moderation in what Hume called "a coalition of parties." He applauded the settlement managed by the parties as a new epoch. "We, in this island, have ever since enjoyed if not the best system of government, at least the most entire system of liberty that was ever known amongst mankind."[10]

Hume appears to have sympathy for the way the parties deferred to each other to achieve the settlement. But almost immediately he tempered his approval and leveled this stern judgment: "both parties, while they warped their principles from regard to their antagonists, and from prudential considerations, lost the praise of consistence and uniformity." Should not this step back from "consistence and uniformity" merit approval from this philosopher of moderation? After all, William's election was effected without violence. And as Hume said of the earlier Petition of Right, "impartial reasoners will confess, that the subject is not, on both sides, without its difficulties."[11] Yet his appreciation flagged. He castigates the parties even at their moment of success: "Never surely was national debate more important, or managed by more able speakers; yet is one surprised to find the topics, insisted on by both sides, so frivolous; more resembling the verbal disputes of the schools than the solid reasoning of statesmen and legislators."[12] And "no sooner was danger past than party prejudices resumed, in some degree, their former authority." "Both parties, be-sides the present dispute, had many latent claims, which, on a favour-able occasion, they produced against their adversaries."[13] From his vantage point in the eighteenth century, Hume charged that Whig and Tory "have continued ever since to confound and distract our government."[14] Moderation is not to be expected of them.[15] At any moment "the controversy may appear so momentous [to partisans] as to justify even an opposition by arms."[16] Having made the case for parties of constitutional necessity, Hume refused to extend it. He did not allow that party moderation is dependable and parties useful outside this exceptional, fortunate instance.

Hume acknowledged at least the possibility of moderate party competition and compromise, then. His term for it was party "coali-tion." He even conceded something in the abstract to the view that governments too steady and uniform "abate the active powers of men; depress courage, invention, and genius; and produce a lethargy in the people."[17] In reaction against Bolingbroke, Hume characterized the attempt to persuade us that we are all of one party composed of common principles, that Whig and Tory are meaningless, is itself an artifice of party. When he wrote that "faction is at an end and Party Distinctions abolished," he meant that hardened divisions throughout the nation were dissolving and that a politics of interest and influence was ascendant.[18] But even if parties were not imminent threats to the dissolution of government, Hume was not prepared to declare party rivalry reliably constrained. Parties were simply not benign. He cau-tioned that uncompromising disputes about succession in particular could still be revived. The parties remain, potentially, "such as enter-tain opposite views with regard to the essentials of government, the succession of the crown, or the more considerable privileges belong-ing to the several members of the constitution." These have justified opposition by arms, and could again. He wrote to Montesquieu that the preference for complex over simple forms of government is too simple if it overlooks that they are liable to be deranged by "le con-traste et l'opposition des parties."[19]

Even without the threat of disorder, Hume reacted against par-ties. One specific complaint is that "the representations of faction" have "extremely clouded and obscured" the events of the revolution. "This event, which in some particulars, has been advantageous to the state, has proved destructive to the truth of history, and has established many gross falsehoods, which it is unaccountable how any civilized nation could have embraced with regard to its domestic occurrences."[20] Partisanship corrupts history, in short. Hume castigated Whig compositions as the means by which "the prevailing faction has celebrated only the partisans of the former . . . at the expense of their antagonists, who maintained those maxims, that are essential to its very existence."[21] Whigs promulgated calumnies that "served to infatuate as well as corrupt the people"; the party proceeded by means of "delusions," the epitome being the "imposture of the popish plot." Hume was evenhandedly allergic. The other faction, too, he noted, "found it necessary to employ like artifices."[22] "Despicable" was his constant refrain.

Hume's aversion to Whig accounts of the revolutionary settlement stemmed in part from his avowed outsider's objection to partisan history and its deformation of political judgment. It also stemmed from his reflection that attempts to ground party rhetoric and positions on the authority of history are dangerously disconnected from present political realities. ("It is ridiculous to hear the commons, while they are assuming by usurpation the whole government, talk of reviving the ancient constitution."[23]) Above all, partisan history misrepresented the real reason why the revolution settlement worked and why constitutional limits were sustained. As Hume saw it, the power of the House of Commons was "so great that it absolutely commands all the other parts of government." It would be unrestrained were it not for crown patronage influencing the election of members. Offices and pensions at the King's disposal offset the crown's otherwise debilitating dependence on parliament for revenue.[24] (It also ensures the independence of representatives from the binding power of instructions from constituents, that is, tempers republicanism.[25]) The settlement's success rested on institutional innovations—"irregular checks," "corruption," or "dependence"—that the parties did not intend and continue to obfuscate. In contemporary terms, the "constitutional regime" comprised informal institutions and practices not openly recognized, or, when recognized, disavowed as pathological.

The argument of a party of constitutional necessity articulated by Hume was an important insight. It was also, of course, the judgment partisans passed on their own activities. Their association was temporary, required by circumstance, a dangerous instrument political men must occasionally employ for the public good. "The necessity of honest combination" to combat sedition fell far short of regularizing parties as permanent institutions or creating a party system. On the other hand, it avoided absolute condemnation. Advocates of the necessity for parties in particular cases took the step of refusing to disavow them altogether.

An exemplary instance, of course, is the justification of the first American parties "as temporary necessities to make the great experiment succeed."[26] Divided over the strength and scope of national government and the meaning of popular sovereignty, Federalists and Republicans played out their opposition in the struggle over the ratification of the Constitution in 1787, then via coalitions in the First Congress, solidifying party identification in the Second and Third. Until the peaceful transfer of presidential power to Jefferson in 1801, the possibility of violence was real. For Federalists and Republicans contested one another's legitimacy. The Federalists did not think of themselves as a party but as "the natural gentry, rulers of society."[27] They identified their administration with the government, the government with the Constitution and "construed criticism ... as an attempt to subvert the Constitution."[28] The Alien and Sedition Acts were designed to eliminate opposition and led to prosecution of leading Republicans. For their part, Republicans charged that their opponents' real aim was to restore monarchy; Federalists were antirepublican and had no place in a government of the people; Republicans were fighting on behalf of the people as a whole and intended to defeat the political enemy.[29] Jefferson's assessment of the constitutional necessity of partisanship followed:

Were parties here divided by a greediness for office, as in England, to take a part with either would be unworthy of a reasonable or moral man, but where the principle of difference is as substantial and as strongly pronounced as between the republicans and Monocrats of our country, I hold it as honorable to take a firm and decided part, and as immoral to pursue a idle line, as between the parties of Honest men and Rogues.[30]

These exceptional parties of necessity developed the standard apparatus of ordinary parties. Jeffersonians in opposition "sought to coordinate their legislative plans, control the agenda, and seek votes and victories on the floor."[31] State elites were mobilized, and in some states local elections followed the national divide. Jefferson took a historic step when he sought to capture a legislative majority by popular election, and reluctantly called the Republicans a party.[32] ("It was one thing for Jefferson to organize a political party to serve as a springboard into the executive mansion; quite another for him to use it as a reliable instrument of government."[33]) Still, he saw political parties as baneful. He hoped the victory of his party, the successful stand against "the Federalists' slouch toward monarchy," would bring "the complete suppression of party."[34] Antipartyism was the dominant strain of thought, and "the natural desire was not to dignify the struggle but to win it."[35] One commentator describes this exception as "the revolutionary proviso";[36] in Hume's terms, Americans formed parties of constitutional necessity.

Party conflict in the United States became acute during the French Revolution and seemed to threaten civil war. Accusations of foreign loyalty, conspiracy, and treason were traded. Jefferson was charged with "Jacobinism, atheism, fanaticism, unscrupulousness, wanton folly, incompetence, personal treachery, and political treason."[37] He responded, calling the Federalists a faction that "has entered in a conspiracy with the enemies of our country to chain down the legislature at the feet of both." One historian reflected on this period's peaceful denouement in Humean terms:

> Between them the Jeffersonian leaders on one side and John Adams and his supporters on the other created a situation in which this uncomfortable union could survive, and in which the two parties had to continue the effort to accommodate each other—Adams by eschewing a formal

declaration of war . . . and eventually seeking peace with France; the Jeffersonians by ruling out separation or force and keeping their protests and threats on a strictly verbal and legal level.[38]

A good case has been made that during the early, critical decades of the American government, it was nascent political parties that "facilitated their acceptance of the system and its laws. The rudimentary parties that emerged by 1800 by no means guaranteed stability to the young republic" but "they channeled discontent back into the system."[39] Hence Clinton Rossiter's classic assertion: "No America without democracy, no democracy without politics, no politics without parties, no parties without compromise and moderation."[40]

Decades later when the second Republican Party formed in the United States and performed the dramatic act of fighting a civil war to preserve the Union, its spokesmen proclaimed it, too, to be a party of necessity. Republicans set out to save the Constitution from perversion by the slave oligarchy, "a lordly caste." Charles Sumner's great 1860 speech—"if bad men conspire for slavery, good men must combine for Freedom"—"vindicates at once [the party's] origin and necessity." The Party must not be a fugitive organization merely for an election, but "an irresistible necessity." The Union Party hobbled together for the war effort was transient, but the Republican Party would have to remain vigilant in its resistance to constitutional usurpation. ("Prostrated, exposed, and permanently expelled from ill-gotten power, the Oligarchy will soon cease to exist as a political combination," he promised.) Put succinctly: "The first requirement for a justification of party activity among men with a general antipathy to party is this understanding that nothing less than the regime itself is at stake."[41] The party "cannot be less permanent than the hostile influence which it is formed to counteract," Sumner wrote.[42] The ideal remained what it had been. An ally of William Seward, a stanch Whig partisan, wrote admiringly to Seward's son: "Your father knows no party except his country and its constitution and Laws."[43]

The halfway house party of necessity with its disclaimers of partisanship is still with us. Its virulent form is the party of virtue or one-partyism. We recognize its democratic incarnations, too: an honorable combination of Independents to rectify the corruption of established parties and the imbalance of partisan extremism; a nonpartisan party, uniting people of all views in defense of some neglected national interest; an independent presidential candidate who, as one observer remarked of Ross Perot, "had held no public office, was all but unknown seven months before the election, did almost no campaigning in the traditional sense, and spoke a harshly antiparty message."[44] A party to resist and transcend parties.

Returning to Hume, even when it came to parties of constitutional necessity, he set the bar high, allowing just one case to vault over. His clear-eyed account of accommodating party practices did not amount to a considered defense of parties. It merely acknowledged that parties are occasionally moderate and useful. Whether writing "of parties in general" or "of the parties of Great Britain," Hume confessed that "to determine the nature of these parties is perhaps one of the most difficult problems that can be met with."[45] The terms inherited from studying ancient parties and the lens of British constitutional struggle accounted for some of the difficulty. Even in England, it was no easy matter to unravel parties from estates or from the organs of mixed government. Yet court and country did not correspond to nobles and plebs, and parties were intracameral; they divided commons and lords. Hume was not alone in tentatively suggesting but ultimately remaining uncertain whether the parties represented estates or some new, functional equivalent: ministries supported by a party and an opposition.[46] Parties did more than balance; "place seeking" and "influence" could not be explained that way. Hume was sensitive to the use of influence and places to control opposition, but it proved difficult to move from parties of principle and constitutional necessity to this new framework of government and opposition. His puzzlement owed in part to the fact that regular party organization and purposes were just emerging.

Again, it owed in part to the fact that tying parties to British constitutional struggles was not an adequate lens through which to understand the development of parties in Britain, much less parties more generally. "Constitutional necessity" was an obstacle to understanding. As Burke observed, "it rarely happens to a party to have the opportunity of a clear, authentic, recorded declaration of their political tenets upon the subject of a great constitutional event like that of the Revolution."[47] The argument from constitutional necessity opens the possibility of justifiable parties of principle. It keeps the possibility of constructive parties alive, while assuming that these occasions are rare. It does not conduce to appreciation of the regular organization and operation of parties, though. What does?

Burke's Moment of Appreciation: Regulated Rivalry

Three initial moments of appreciation provide conceptual unity for otherwise diffuse observations about party practices and effects. They give partisans terms with which to speak with one another. They are resources for a political theory of parties, refreshing what we ought to know but has been eclipsed by other concerns or taken for granted. At a minimum, they are antidotes to wholesale, reflexive antipartyism. The three moments of appreciation I turn to now are hesitant and grudging. But they open out, as constitutional necessity does not, to viewing parties as not only occasionally necessary but ordinarily acceptable, useful, even morally desireable features of political life. The first of these moments recognizes parties as a form of regulated rivalry, and belongs to Burke.

In the antiparty tradition that sees parties as dangerously divisive, the dreaded endpoint is violent rebellion or civil war culminating in tyranny. Rome is the archetype. Along the way are the other evils Hume laid out: "Factions subvert government, render laws impotent, and beget the fiercest animosities ... and what should render the founders of parties more odious is the difficulty of extirpating these weeds when once they have taken root in any state."[48] Hume viewed even moderated party conflict with suspicion; parties were always just a step from violence. Outside the extraordinary instance of mutual restraint he called a "coalition of parties"; regulated rivalry was a chimera; and partisans themselves were unbelieving. Madison, for example, was convinced that parties acquiesced in electoral defeat only because they lacked military force.[49]

Once alerted to the "fatal" in fatal divisiveness, we notice that military language is ubiquitous in talk by and about parties, even today. It shapes the discourse of partisans and antiparty critics alike. Candidates wage "campaigns" and accumulate "war chests." Voters are "mobilized." Party opposition is assimilated to a battle in which organization, strategy, and generalship are factors in success. The architect of American mass parties in the nineteenth century, Martin Van Buren, conceived of them as combat organizations that demanded "discipline of an almost military severity."[50]

I mention this because it introduces the first moment of appreciation: when militarism *is* just rhetorical and when, despite the accusatory "warring factions," party conflict is not war, not even war by other means. Militarism is replaced by militancy. Conflict is managed. Permanent opposition without violent disorder is not yet a norm, but it is conceivable. The key move was to distinguish party opposition from sedition, treason, and a prelude to civil war. The first moment of appreciation sees partisanship as regulated rivalry, and Burke is its interpreter and advocate, the first to formulate this positive argument in general terms.

"Every good political institution must have a preventive operation as well as a remedial," Burke wrote. Revolution and impeachment are the recognized remedies for tyranny and threats to constitutional order. Party conflict is the preventative that makes these remedies unnecessary.[51] Recall Machiavelli's speculations on the uses of faction and his observation that the Romans were able to set the parties against one another for a long time before division became violent and fatal to the republic. Recall, too, early American partisans who described themselves as "watchdogs" against the opposition's aristocratic or extreme democratic leanings. In the context of British parliamentary politics, Burke solidified and organized these reflections. The spirit of party is a "vigilant watchman over those in power." "The Parties who are Out, are always a Curb, and a Bridle to those which are In, and the Parties which are In, are always a Terror and a Stirrer up to Vigilance in those which are Out."[52] In other words, parties expose one another's crimes and failures.[53] So it is not the case that the "country party" has no reason for being if "the court" upholds the constitution and acts responsibly. "The spirit of party" is permanently useful.

In retrospect, Burke's acceptance of parties as regulated rivalry was both enormously innovative and modest. It recognized organized parties as a political development that might mitigate rather than aggravate the evils that lead to violent political strife. It introduced another form of institutional distrust into political life, a supplement to the mixed constitution, to what one scholar described as Montesquieu's view that "fully developed moderation is a political form of intelligence because political power offers every opportunity and temptation to cast off one's inhibitions[;] moderation can be instilled only by rules and restraints."[54] Burke's "spirit of party" supplemented what came to be the standard view of separation of powers as a checking apparatus designed "to encourage good behavior in the absence of good character."[55] Parties serve Burke's preventative function in ways that other forms of opposition could not. "Rotation in office" institutionalizes suspicion and wards off conspiracy. (It is also some insurance that the effects of decisions on the opposition would be prudently considered for the time when the opposition would govern.) The innovation of regulated rivalry, in practice and conceptually, was to safely add organized opposition *within government* to political criticism and opposition outside government.

This claim for parties lifted them above political associations and secretive societies excoriated as seditious cabals, nurseries of rebellion. Parties were regular, institutional substitutes for private intrigue as well as open rebellion. A modicum of political liberty makes many forms of disagreement and dissent lawful—instigated by individual statesmen, pamphleteers, political clubs, and the press. Party rivalry is distinct from these types of opposition, too, and party opposition in government is potentially conciliatory as often enough outside opposition is not. Avowed partisans, organized and operating in public, had another advantage: they proclaimed their legitimacy and the legitimacy of ongoing, managed, institutionalized conflict. Only parties bring opposition into the frame of government, regularize it, eventually legalize it, and make it politically mundane, a bid for office not power simply.[56]

Burke cast partisans in a new light. They are not normally bent on mutual destruction. They do not see rivals as public enemies. They concede that opposition per se should not be criminalized and admit the distinction between disagreement and punishment. Hence the editor's perceptive title for a collection of eighteenth-century English pamphlets: "Factions No More."[57] The consolidation of this view would be signaled by Lord Brougham's 1826 phrase: "His Majesty's Opposition." The endpoint of this emergent appreciation of parties would be acceptance of periodic party contests, a party "system" in which party rivalry is iterative. For now, appreciation points to something less: Hume's "coalition of parties" in which partisans give up the idea that "the controversy may appear so momentous as to justify even an opposition by arms."[58] They regulate rivalry.

I said a moment ago that parties were organized and began to manage rather than enflame political conflict independent of any very clear understanding of party structures or processes of party contestation. To repeat: "great achievements are accomplished in the mental fog of practical experience."[59] Experience precedes understanding and justification. Among the conditions for the emergence of regulated rivalry in America, one stands out: the experience of political leaders with conventions and constitution making: they "had learned to do business with each other through discussion and concession."[60] In the thought that "the management of political conflict . . . relies on devices culturally acquired and precariously maintained,"[61] "devices" is apt, suggesting institutions and practices put in place by partisans themselves with only tentative understanding.[62] Early moments of appreciation were often ex post justifications; not surprisingly and sometimes correctly, contemporaries viewed them as rationalizations. Experience with party activity is the necessary basis for this first moment of recognition, then.

But insight into the nature of parties is crucial if appreciation of regulated rivalry is to be more than a tentative observation or fragile practice, and if it is to be expressed in general terms. Burke was offering not an explanation for the rise of parties but rather a generalizable argument about their positive uses, and this articulated moment of appreciation is crucial. What is gained when practices are supplemented by recognition and reasoned appreciation? Again, "certain guideposts for future remembrance, and even for sheer reference, arise out of it."[63] By characterizing parties as institutions that conduct regulated rivalry, ideas reinforce practices. In a sense it codifies party politics. It gives partisans terms with which to speak with one another and with the opposition. When Hamilton wrote, "If the Antifederalists who prevailed in the election are left to take their own man, they remain responsible, and the Federalists remain *free and united* and without *stain*, in a situation to resist with effect pernicious measures," we see the glimmer of acknowledgment that parties are engaged in regulated rivalry and that "the Federalists would be in a better position to *return to power* if they voluntarily *gave it up* in the immediate future."[64] Regulated rivalry becomes an element in strategic political calculation. This and the two other moments of appreciation to which I turn become public terms of justification that interrupt the pattern of aversion.

Not many thinkers shared Burke's appreciation for regulated rivalry. Madison, for example, warned that the expedience of creating parties to function as mutual checks on each other is as absurd as promoting new vices to counteract existing ones.[65] Burke's defense was beyond the ken of political thinkers so long as each party expected to end all parties: "The ethic of limited strife, the only scheme consistent with a functioning party system, is accepted only with difficulty—a difficulty more emotional than intellectual. To partisans it offers so little since it withholds complete success."[66] Regulated rivalry underscores every party's status as just a part in a permanently pluralist politics.

Both experience of partisanship and this articulated moment of appreciation are important because Burke's regulated rivalry is demanding. When he insisted that partisans are not necessarily bent on mutual destruction or see rivals as public enemies, we should not imagine that he relied solely on a balance of forces or on prudent retreat, the realist's commitment not to resort to arms, giving up office without a fight as the best chance for reciprocity. Nonviolence— the move from militarism to militancy, from private armies to verbal attack (as when Democrats called Newt Gingrich's "Contract with

America" a Contract on America[67])—is only part of the story. Regulated party rivalry entails political self-restraint, and the true discipline is rightly described as mental and emotional. Political aspirants channel their ambitions and goals through this collective, constraining, typically unheroic, institution. They endure the "terror" of the opposition's vigilance and exposure. Partisans see themselves as firmly on the side of the angels, but regulated rivalry demands acknowledging their partiality, that they do not and cannot speak for the whole, and that their exercise of power is provisional (as is their status as losers, relegated to opposition). Partisans need not view the opposition in Burke's own elevated terms as parties of conviction linked by "common opinions, common affections, and common interests" and dedicated to promoting the national interest. Simply, the discipline consists of conceding each party's status as just one part in a permanently pluralist politics. And with it, acknowledging the provisional nature of being the governing party, the charade of pretending to represent the whole. Tocqueville framed this in the American context in American terms; not only do parties in America moderate the violence of political association; in addition, parties know, and everyone knows, that no party represents the nation. "This results from the very fact of their existence."[68]

All this mutual self-restraint, institutionalizing, and taming of conflict is not to say that extremism and polarization are defined out of parties and partisanship, as I show in Part III. Some parties are correctly judged conspiracies aimed at overthrowing constitutional order and eliminating political opposition. On the other side, regulated rivalry does not presume comity of the sort that makes coalition or unity government possible, what one eighteenth-century commentator described as "a Kind of Methodism in Politicks, whereby a Pretence is made to a higher degree of State-Purity, than can be reasonably expected."[69]

Above all, this is not to say, as many have, that parties operate within an agreed-on constitutional framework. True, if defense of constitutional order is their sole justification, partisans are bound to launch mutual accusations of subversion and illegitimacy. But I see no reason to take the reverse tack and say that by definition parties operate within a settled constitutional framework or constitutional consensus and that interpreting and challenging constitutional bounds or the character of the regime is no business of parties.[70] Often enough parties are organized over or against it, advocate and effect constitutional change, sometimes radical. "Party of principle," before it came to indicate just any ideology or firm commitment to program or doctrine, referred to the ambition to make or restore constitutional order. It is less the substance of normal politics by "small" parties, on the one hand, or the character of hoped-for radical change by "great" parties, on the other, that illuminates this moment of appreciation but regulated rivalry itself. In this respect parties are "content independent."[71] I turn to antisystem parties in the final chapter. My point here is that regulated rivalry extends to profound matters of social character and constitutional organization; party politics can be radical and transformative.

Party conflict entails political self-discipline—institutionalized, eventually legalized, internalized, and made moral habit—and I return to the ethics of partisanship in Part III. Of course, the discipline of regulated rivalry can fail. Unreconstructed partisans of holism, opportunistic parties, and parties such as early Federalists and Republicans set on mutual elimination signal the presence of hostile antipartyism. Regulated rivalry simply says that parties can serve this basic good of nonviolent, institutionalized conflict and political change.

Burke's preventative function *requires* political conflict among parties, clearly, and is subverted by "barons dividing up fiefdoms," collusion, or one-party dominance. His moment of appreciation is echoed in one political scientist's exclamation: "The miracle of democracy is that conflicting political forces obey the results of voting" and create a condition of social peace by means of conflict rather than harmony.[72] The lapse in this otherwise welcome observation is that "the miracle" preceded democracy and was the work of parties.

Burke's formulation of regulated rivalry makes no appearance in democratic theory today. We have only to think of deliberative democratic theory, where often enough conflict is tamed, renamed "disagreement," and ideally transformed into consensus, and where parties are ignored and partisanship is contrasted unfavorably with political independence. In political science, where parties are a premier object of study, scholars of American politics in particular argue that various, contingent factors—deep party polarization, for example, or collusion among parties and a party cartel—give the lie to regulated rivalry. This is hyperbole; regulated rivalry is commonplace here and taken for granted. We are brought face to face with this achievement of parties when it is truly absent or when it fails. We recognize this achievement when deeply entrenched or hegemonic parties weaken the "bridle" and "terror" of ins and outs, for example. We see Burke's moment of appreciation implicit in studies showing that the conditions for achieving parties' "preventative function" are not just material, a matter of rational incentives, but also moral disposition. Burke's moment is the heart of the matter when parties do not accept their status as parts but claim to be the sole voice of the nation, and when parties are just too weak or inexperienced to govern.

Hegel's Moment of Appreciation: Governing

This last point alerts us that in one respect Burke's moment of appreciation is modest. Regulated rivalry is preventative, "exposing one another's crimes and failures." We hear nothing of the positive purposes and responsibilities of parties. Regulated rivalry and the framework of checks by "outs" of "ins" has a distinctive downside: the possibility that "it is more the interest of the opposition to stop the ordinary movement of government, than to prevent its abuse."[73] As in any formulation of checks, it can mean "lying down in the traces" or deadlock.[74]

The second moment of appreciation is, finally, constructive rather than defensive. By bringing opposition within the frame of government, parties do more than manage political conflict; they organize the business of government. This moment belongs—perhaps surprisingly—to Hegel. Hegel, the metaphysician, logician, and philosopher of right, turned his attention to this least abstract of institutions. We can catch at least a glimmer of the characteristically

Hegelian in his moment of appreciation—a typically transformative vision of actuality. Where others saw irrationality or errant self-
serving, Hegel saw parties as requirements of the modern state, "the
rose of reason in the cross of the present."

Hegel's insight about parties is less familiar than Burke's or Hume's
but was just as perspicacious. Like Hume and Burke, Hegel came to his
understanding by reflecting on concrete constitutional arrangements.
As we saw in chapter 2, Hegel viewed political representation in the
German Constitution as a mess of historical property rights "which
the parts have wrested from the whole," the epitome of "privilege
unredeemed by function." The constitutions of the individual German states could not reasonably be described as mixed or balanced,
either; he called Wurtenberg "an anarchy made into a constitution."[75]
He proposed a reformed version of corporate representation. Hegel's
concern was more than just rationalized representation, though. He
explained: the issue in representation is not the *right* of enfranchisement and therefore of who were to be the constituents but the *result*,
the creation of a legislative assembly. Hegel shared this concern with
his nemesis on constitutionalism, Sieyes, for whom activity in the
assembly was the heart of representative government, with the difference that Sieyes despised parties. For Hegel, an assembly—whether
an assembly of estates or corporations or formed through democratic
elections—is not properly constituted without parties.[76]

> Whoever has reflected a little on the nature of an Assembly . . . cannot
> fail to see that without an opposition such an assembly is without outer
> and inner life. It is precisely this antagonism within it that forms its es-
> sence and justification. . . . Without it it has the appearance of only one
> party or of just a clump.[77]

By bringing organized opposition within the frame of government parties achieve more than checking and moderating. Political
men must form parties in order to govern. "However much [the British Parliament] is divided into parties and however great the passion
with which they confront one another, still equally so little are they
factions. They stand within the same general interest," Hegel wrote.
There was no better evidence of France's lack of appreciation for

governing, to his mind, than the fact that every change of Ministry in which the opposition came into power and acted with maxims not very different from those of their predecessors was greeted with surprise.[78] Hegel assumes Burke's regulated rivalry. His own contribution was to elevate an idea implicit in accounts of regulated rivalry into a thesis: parties are organizations aimed at governing. That is their point. He explained, "It is a mark of the uneducated to regard the English opposition as a party against the government or against the Ministry as such, but the fight is only against this single Ministry. . . . What it is often charged with, as if with something bad, namely all it wants is to form a Ministry itself, is in fact its greatest justification."[79]

With this emphasis on governing, Hegel sounds the second moment of appreciation. Parties in opposition do more than check. They contest for office. Parties alone among political associations are "responsible." Responsibility was Hegel's theme. "Responsible" did not mean democratic accountability, as it would later. It meant "responsible for" rather than "to"; responsibility for the business of state. A party is an organized group capable of assuming office and authority and willing to do so, offering credible measures and presumably competent governors. Hegel knew that this was not well understood, and I repeat this key observation: "What it [the opposition] is often charged with, as if with something bad, namely all it wants is to form a Ministry itself, is in fact its greatest justification."[80] On this point Hegel was an Anglophile: only the English have "an idea of what government and governing is."[81] I do not mean to tie this moment of appreciation too tightly to British parliamentarism. Hegel studied the English but did not argue specifically for the Westminster model of party government. Parties in government are consistent with a variety of arrangements for the relation among legislative parties, for forming working majorities, and for the relation between these parties and executives.[82] The point is that parties not only operate within government and hold officials and one another to account, beyond that parties actually govern or stand ready to. Tocqueville saw the governing ambition and capacity of parties in America clearly: evolving from small political associations to national parties, they "form almost a separate nation inside the nation, a government inside the government. . . . [I]t is true that they do not have . . . the right to make law; but they have the power to attack the one that exists and to formulate in advance the one that should exist."[83]

Part and parcel of this moment of appreciation is Hegel's recognition that parties are organizations for selecting and training political leaders. "Political consciousness," by which he means experience in government, is acquired through habitual preoccupation with public affairs.[84] "The business routine" of party *hommes d'état*, which Hegel applauded, stood in contrast to the agenda of *les hommes à principes*, which is "more or less exhausted by the droits de l'homme et du citoyen" and which he disdained.[85] Men of principle are inattentive to the business of the state. Partisans are professional political types. They are the corrective to men attuned to abstraction, to sheer dilettantism. Hegel anticipates Weber in distinguishing them from the "occasional" politicians who cast ballots or deliver speeches, from the "avocation" of heads of associations "who, as a rule, are politically active only in case of need and for whom politics is, neither materially nor ideally, 'their life.' "[86] (We are reminded of contemporary political science designations of "activists" and "amateurs.") Looking back, Weber would remark at "the development of politics which demanded training in the struggle for power, and in the methods of this struggle as developed by modern party policies."[87] Hegel was writing in the midst of this change. He was less interested in electoral politics than in governing. That is why he objected to the halfway concession that would restrict party opposition to "measures, not men." "Measures, not men" suggests disregard for political types and political competence, for getting the business done. It does not adequately suggest responsibility for governing. Collective governing has its requirements. Parties recruit and train political leaders; they regulate access to office; they create organizations and alliances capable of taking responsibility for government.

Concern for the business of government also goes some way to explaining Hegel's opposition to electoral reform. He saw the mass electorate as devoid of "political consciousness." "There was no sustained and organized party activity among the electorate to stimulate the latter's interest, to clarify political issues, and to simplify political decisions."[88] He feared that the English Reform Bill would bring into government *novi homines*, doctrinaire middle-class radicals devoid of commitment to partisanship, unprepared for governing responsibly, a plague of incompetence.[89] The "universal interest" Hegel identified as a condition for effective government refers to political acculturation,[90] cultivated through practice with these institutions.

This also explains why Hegel was sympathetic to "influence" on appointment to parliamentary seats.[91] He did not see it in British terms as a question of constitutional balance or as corruption. Many members of parliament are incompetent and ignorant, Hegel observed, and everything rests on "a number of brilliant men wholly devoted to political activity and the interest of the state." Some of them are assured a parliamentary seat by their own wealth or by the influence their families have in a borough, city, or county. But places for competent men are also ensured through "the influence of the Ministry and then through their party friends."[92] Earlier, Burke had objected to the standard view that "all political connections are in their nature factious," arguing that "connections in politics are essentially necessary for the full performance of our public duty."[93] Hegel gave this idea central place.

The background condition for the rise of parties in government, of course, is active government, regular legislative business. It is no accident that the two great theorists of the modern state, Bentham and Hegel, writing from very different philosophical perspectives, both cast aspersion on customary law and advocated public policy making on matters ranging from trade to police to welfare. Both assigned a critical role to a professional civil service. Both grasped the demanding *business* of government. But where Bentham prized impartial calculators of utility, Hegel perceived the need for parties. Parties promote governmental functions, seize opportunities to exercise governmental power, develop or respond to initiatives, provide rationales for them, and coordinate political action in legislatures to achieve these ends.[94]

Looking back, Hume explained the development of sustained parties in just these terms. Until the seventeenth century, he observed, parties were rare because parliamentary sessions were short, and the members had no leisure to get acquainted either with each other or with the public business.[95] The origin of parties in England stemmed from divisions *within* the Commons, and owed to the need to organize business within this body. Parties arose from "intra-estate" proceedings.[96] This is the parliamentary origin of parties Weber later surveyed; it is in the hands "of those who handle the work continuously."[97] It is one of the paths Duverger would later describe;[98] parliamentary caucuses first, followed by the creation of local electoral committees.

Formal analysis of the origin and purpose of parties in America reinforces this account. Parties are created in response to politicians' need for collective action, to further the aims of ambitious office seekers, whose political goals can be realized only through them.[99] Governing requires more than temporary cooperation or coalition, and parties provide institutional bases for commitment. Party norms, procedures, and incentives allow partisans to hold together over the relatively long term, to organize leadership, to create structures like caucuses and committees, and to govern. No clear distinction was worked out in advance of experience between temporary alliances, piece-meal compromises, vote trades, and other forms of political cooperation, on the one hand, and commitment to cooperation in advance in the form of organized parties, on the other.

Hegel articulated what had been this un-theorized, serendipitous course. Clearly, his moment of appreciation of governing parties assumes and goes beyond appreciation of parties as a means of managing political conflict. It fleshes out the notion of a "loyal opposition" as an organized group capable of assuming responsibility for governing and willing to do so. Hegel put in general terms what others had occasionally observed. Governing would become an explicit recommendation for partisanship. Experience led Disraeli to advise: "You cannot choose between party government and Parliamentary government. I say you can have no Parliamentary government if you have no party government," and he reminded his colleagues, "It is not becoming in any Minister to decry party who has risen by party. If we were not PARTISANS we should not be Ministers."[100] The definitive statement, I believe, is Bagehot's. The House of Commons can do its work "because it is an organized body" with party leadership; the penalty of failure of partisanship is impotence. Party is inherent in the House of Commons, "bone of its bone, breath of its breath."[101]

An example from American political history may be helpful; it indicates that party government is not limited to parliamentary systems and its drama drives this moment of appreciation home. During the Civil War, the governments of the North and the South had similar formal structures, but differed fundamentally in that one was organized by party and one not. They amount to a natural experiment in the uses of parties. Newly created in the mid-nineteenth century in opposition to the leading Democratic and struggling Whig parties, the Republican Party had a coherent political ideology and electoral success, but it assumed responsibility for governing the nation with difficulty. Party turned out to be significant: Lincoln's leadership was enhanced by political partisanship, and the Republican Party gave the North advantages in waging war. Eric L. McKitrick's study details these advantages. The party brought political talent to the fore; party loyalty kept Republican factions from fatally opposing policy; the radical wing of the party supported the president in prosecuting the war with vigor; cabinet choices strengthened party alliances; patronage preserved unity; governors of northern states were party men; and, finally, the Democratic opposition served as a rallying point for tightening Republican organization. Jefferson Davis's leadership of the Confederacy was hampered on every count by the absence of parties. There was no "party platform or party morality" in his congress; the interference of contentious, disorganized men was constant and toxic, with no way to segregate or define them; elections were held without parties to refine the issues; there were no party ties to connect states to the confederate government, and governors obstructed Davis in crucial areas, including the control and recruitment of troops.[102] The contrast underscores Hegel's moment of appreciation.

Appreciation for parties as a way of organizing government predated broad-based democratic elections. It was perfectly possible to be skeptical about the rise of electoral politics and "responsibility to" the people and at the same time to defend party "responsibility for" governing. That changed. Preference for parliamentary-style party government is a recurrent feature of American political thought; Woodrow Wilson's writings at the end of the nineteenth century, E. E. Schattschneider's *Party Government* in the 1940s, and the 1950 American Political Science Association committee report, *Toward a More Responsible Two-Party System*. This familiar example is worth noting here because it was motivated by the perception of a lack of political accountability in the United States. It came in response to what was seen as the blamable ideological and programmatic incoherence of political parties, which made popular control of government impossible.[103] So the whole focus of this defense of parties in government rests on securing accountability to the electorate. Expectations for parties in terms of "representativeness" and accountability overshadow governing.

I propose that the value of governing parties deserves its own moment of appreciation, and for that reason it is worth just listing some of the circumstances that prod us to recognize it as an achievement. One circumstance is when weak, inexperienced, disorganized parties incapable of governing (or unwilling to assume responsibility for governing) create an opening for holist parties, for fascist regimes, or populist presidents wielding emergency powers or governing by decree. Or when the sheer proliferation of parties is immobilizing, an inhibition on coalition and governance. Another circumstance likely to stir this moment of appreciation occurs in fluid pluralist societies when interest and opinion groups multiply and seek to influence government directly. Arrant interest group pluralism is not just chaotic and an obstacle to coherent policy; the result can be "ungovernability." Burke and Hegel provide reasons to challenge the supremacy, at least the monopoly, of the "representative" and "accountability" thesis. It is no small matter to say that parties regulate rivalry and provide resources of organization and leadership for active government.

Both regulated rivalry and governing are forgiving when it comes to the character of parties so long as partisans attend to their "preventive" function, accept their partiality and do not cast the opposition as a public enemy, have political objectives they can defend, and govern reasonably effectively. The tradition of antipartyism that sees parties as dangerously divisive was fearful of great parties. But as we have seen, detractors despised small parties too. Do regulated rivalry and governing require or rule out one or the other, great parties or small, parties of principle or interest?

Implicit in Hegel's moment, and in Burke's, I believe, is the thought that neither regulated rivalry nor governing depends on great parties that reflect deep natural or social cleavages or are founded on partisans' sharing a philosophy. True, Burke defined parties as "promoting by joint endeavors the national interest, upon some particular principle in which they are all agreed."[104] But his preventative function does not require that national interest rises to the level of constitutional necessity or rests on a rigorous notion of "principle."

Does the same latitude extend to small parties? If so, how small? What if parties are undifferentiated? Or "centrist"? Or more bent on conciliation than on "making trouble"? Disparagement of small parties was almost as common as fear of great ones. As this eighteenth-century observer remarked in disgust: "all the parties in the kingdom were broken and frittered into insignificance," and "deserters from every denomination and description" formed promiscuous coalitions.[105] A similar attitude toward small parties is commonplace today, patent in the charge that the party system is "organised imposture," with "sham battles" in which "not the savour of a real distinction remains."[106] "The impression that it is the parties imposing cleavages on society," cleavages deplored as "artificial,"[107] is intended as damning criticism. The designation "catch-all party" is not neutral description, but accusation.

If only implicitly, disparagement of small parties is a way of diminishing the achievements of regulated rivalry and governing. To make this point, consider that historians judge Martin Van Buren harshly. In forming the Democratic Party, the first national electoral party in America, his goal was to erect an institution to win the presidency and to make the presidency intersectional.[108] His only principle was setting aside the issue of slavery. Unless, that is, we count what Van Buren called "the party principle": the value of a national party for achieving office and governing, and partisanship as a path to office for "restless young men from all regions" that trumps social standing, family connections, local attachments, natural aristocracy. (It is no accident that Van Buren was the country's first "ethnic" president, "without a trace of Anglo Saxon bloodlines."[109]) If we accept regulated rivalry and governing as achievements, Burke's and Hegel's moments of appreciation invite us to question the assumption that parties must be great to serve valuable purposes or that partisanship must be a matter of identification with critical social or ideological divisions or entail adherence to identifying principles to be justified. Small parties can do the work of regulated rivalry and governing, so long as they are competitive and competent. (And they can serve as templates for great transformative parties. Hence Webster's quip about Van Buren that the leader of the Free Spoil Party should so suddenly become the leader of the Free Soil Party.) Neither regulated rivalry nor conducting the business of government is necessarily undercut if party differences do not appear to be significant to outsiders, if they fail to create stable partisan loyalty among voters, or if we cannot locate a party's place on the ideological spectrum.

Before parties were accepted, only the claim to be a great party—a party of high principle or constitutional necessity—could justify divisiveness, and then only as a prelude to putting an end to partisanship. Greatness or quasi-greatness would become a standard again in the context of mass parties and democratic elections. Partisans would describe themselves ideologically and parties would be judged by their representativeness, which was taken to mean whether the divisions they drew reflected critical social cleavages or were grounded in foundational principles or a comprehensive set of political preferences. Moreover, once partisanship was extended and became a matter of personal identity for ordinary voters, it is not hard to see that "party ID" could be cast as degrading if it were anything less than a matter of conviction and identification with like-minded citizens on the side of the angels.

This should give us pause if we think these moments of appreciation—regulating rivalry and governing—have independent value and should be viewed as achievements today. For regulated rivalry

and governing seem to be forgiving. They depend on party organization but not on a particular kind of party identity.[110]

This is not the end of the story. A third moment of appreciation
did depend on the character of the lines of division distinguishing
parties from one another. Party identity is vital to philosophical defenses of parties. The view from outside, the "impartial observer's"
perspective, brings to bear moral and philosophical reasons for judging that parties in opposition can operate for the good. The view
from outside also begins to suggest a severe ethic of partisanship.

The Impartial Observer's Moment: Hume's Ethic of Partisanship

Like regulated rivalry and governing, this moment of appreciation derives the advantages of parties from the very divisiveness that appalls
antiparty theorists. Only here, the positive potential of party conflict
extends beyond political institutions, and parties take on a kind of
moral glow. Neither regulated rivalry nor organizing government
were purely pragmatic claims. Still, the value of managed conflict—
nonviolent succession of governments, checking and exposing, competent governing—did not need to be cut from whole cloth. It was
enough to observe and acknowledge parties' capacity to serve these
purposes. The philosophical moment of appreciation goes beyond
the theory of practice. It is not the partisans' view, not even partisans' tutored understanding, guided by articulated insights into
regulated rivalry and party government. It is rather the perspective
from outside. In this section and the next I identify two versions of
the philosophical moment, one with greater expectations for parties
than the other. Neither has a secure place in political theory today,
and like regulated rivalry and governing, this moment of appreciation is worth recovering.

Not surprisingly, an outsider's view of parties is rare, or was until
contemporary political science turned its attention there. As Duverger wrote in the Introduction to his "general theory of parties,"
the subject is one where "high feeling and special pleading are the
rule."[111] In the antiparty tradition whose theme is "fatal divisiveness,"

thinkers do take half a step back from actual party strife to create typologies of parties. As we saw, they propose general categories intended to apply to all parties: men are natural Whigs or Tories, republican or antirepublican, parties great and small, and so on. This was only half a step back from participation in actual party strife, because classification was meant to indicate degrees of dangerousness and because these classifications were typically applied with partisan intent; Madison's accusatory republican/antirepublican divide applied to the first American parties is one example.

The genuine claimant to a philosophy of parties from outside is Hume. Here, as in ethics, he assumed the pose of "impartial observer." We have seen his stern judgment of parties of constitutional necessity. From a perspective of reflective detachment, Hume assessed the actions and claims of Whigs and Tories. Both were able to moderate their positions to affect a "coalition of parties" and achieve the revolution settlement; both were errant outside that singular moment. Hume demonstrates what it means to be an "impartial observer" and what understanding of parties results.

In one respect the meaning of impartial is relative to the parties: nonpartisan. The impartial observer promises to assess parties from a position detached from them all, a standpoint independent of connections. Hume claims something more, though. The position of impartial observer has its own center and ballast, what he calls "the proper medium." "Extremes of all are to be avoided," the impartial observer refrains from excessive praise or blame. In considering parties, this means: "Though no one will ever please either faction by moderate opinions, it is there we are most likely to meet with truth and certainty."[112]

The puzzle is why impartiality and the moderation it recommends should translate into an equitable assessment of parties, an evenhanded distribution of praise and blame for Tories and Whigs, as Hume claimed for his *History* and modeled in his political essays. Why is no one party on the side of the angels? Mill called Hume "the profoundest negative thinker on record";[113] he was thinking of Hume's epistemology, but the point extends to political judgment. Hume explained why no party can have a corner on right.

From the standpoint of the Humean impartial observer, the parties partition laudable political purposes and good sense (and nefarious purposes and bad judgment, too) between them. That, and not just tempering divisiveness, is why a "coalition of parties" is desirable.[114] Parties check and moderate one another in the sense of containing abuses. Beyond that, they complement one another. Substantively, parties "add up." Hume made this point in the context of a mixed constitution: the structure generates parties that advocate for equally necessary constitutional powers: crown prerogatives and parliamentary remonstrance. "The chief support of the British government is the opposition of interest,"[115] and Hume was sensitive that threats to moderation come from an assembly's "combination" as well as from "division."[116] (In "Idea for a Perfect Commonwealth" he speculated on institutional innovations like a "Council of Competitors" with powers of accusation and appeals to the people that would do some of the work of parties.) We are made to see that insofar as there is any party, parties arise in response to one another, and from the impartial observer's standpoint of moderation they are each or all necessary.

Complementarity is the insight the impartial observer brings to parties. Hume posits a distinctive relation between or among parties, then, one that is generalizable beyond the parties of Britain. We encounter versions of this thought today in the view that parties are carriers of the interests of social groups (labor and capital) or ideologies (left and right) that are seen as counterparts, and the view from outside assigns some reason to each.[117] Clearly, this is not the partisans' own view, to which I turn in a moment.[118] The impartial observer also discerns that parties are seldom as they present themselves: sharply dichotomous, sectarian, with positions fixed and irreconcilable. The impartial observer sees that often enough partisan values and positions are continuous with one another, matters of degree.[119] He or she assigns to each party its "proper poise and influence." The impartial observer like Hume himself is a critic, unveiling the partisan "frame" of arguments (Whig history), discerning when a party deviates to the extreme, loses its poise, overreaches for influence, so that the parties are not fruitful complements and do not add up.

Parties represent rationally comprehensible poses, then. Hume did not imagine that parties add up to a philosophically comprehensive whole, however. He saw parties as historically contingent, and this moment of appreciation is compatible with the view that parties themselves identify or create rather than reflect pre-existing lines of division. It suffices that parties are defined in relation to one another and make sense only with regard to one another. From this perspective it is possible to conceive of a constructive dynamic to party conflict. As I show in the next section, it is compatible with a full-blown dialectic of party conflict as progressive, though nothing in the impartial observer's moment of appreciation entails that much. It did not for Hume. Simply, the parties not only check and moderate one another but also complement and correct one another. If parties' rival purposes can be understood as justified in some measure, their conflict (and accommodation) is justified.

The striking thing here is that Hume would impress the impartial observer's view on partisans themselves. We know that he saw partisanship as a social relationship rooted in impulses of affection, and, like all other social relationships, bounded by "limited generosity." It is not that party men are uniquely selfish or self-interested, personally and individually. Or that partisans are uniquely inclined to emotional identification with their own group over the community at large. But Hume did observe that partisan sympathies tended to be more circumscribed than those of members of other groups. More than other bonds, partisanship weakens sensitivity to the judgment of the generality of others, dissolves the restraints of general opinion, and fixes attention single-mindedly on the audience of fellow partisans. "Popular sedition, party zeal, a devoted obedience to factious leaders; these are some of the most visible, though less laudable effects of this social sympathy in human nature."[120] He spelled this out: "Honour is a check on mankind: But where a considerable body of men act together, this check is, in a great measure, removed; since a man is sure to be approved of by his own party, for what promotes the common interest; and he soon learns to despise the clamours of adversaries."[121] As a result, in terms familiar from the antiparty tradition of fatal divisiveness, partisans are passionate, zealots, extremists, exaggerators of merit and demerit. Partisans suffer "madness of heart."[122] They are no more rational calculators of self-interest than parties are simple interest groups. "Moderation is not to be expected in party-men of any kind."[123] That is why Hume wrote that faction is "next to Fanaticism . . . of all passions, the most destructive of Morality."[124]

That was not his last word, however. Hume reflected that with all their defects, partisans might nonetheless be injected with "a small tincture of Pyrrhonism" and hesitation.[125] Political moderation depends on the capacity to adopt the standpoint of the impartial observer, if only episodically. For Hume, political moderation is grounded in philosophic insight, not just pragmatic accommodation and the checking function of opposition. It demands that partisans are sometimes in the frame of mind to assume the impartial observer's perspective and to adjust their self-understanding and conduct, to temper their zeal, accordingly. But how is this compatible with partisanship? Recall Hume's description of the perspective of the impartial observer: "though no one will ever please either faction by moderate opinions, it is there we are most likely to meet with truth and certainty."[126]

He could imagine partisans infused with a dash of skepticism. It is possible to "persuade each that its antagonist may possibly be sometimes in the right[,] . . . that neither side are . . . so fully supported by reason as they endeavor to flatter themselves," and that "there are on both sides wise men who meant well to their country."[127] This expectation is demanding. It demands a sense of fallibility and accompanying humility, for one thing (not "so fully supported by reason as they endeavor to flatter themselves"). It demands a generous estimate of the opposition's intentions, for another ("there are on both sides wise men who meant well to their country"). Hume escalates his demand even further: partisans must also "persuade each that its antagonist may possibly be sometimes in the right."

Hume's *History*, and his essays with their artfully crafted dialogues in which Tory and Whig divide the truth about the English constitution between them, are designed to demonstrate how this might work. They detail what each party should appreciate in the other, their complementary politics. Partisans should be consumers of philosophical history. More, partisans should come to this moment of appreciation on their own. Hume insists partisans acknowledge that no one party is in the complete interest of the nation or even of those who advance it. In short, he proposes an ethic of partisanship equivalent to moderation grounded in philosophic insight into political complementarity. That is the sound basis for political moderation of the sort that preserves regulated rivalry. It is the perspective from which Hume says: "I would only persuade men not to contend, as if they were fighting *pro aris et focis*, and change a good constitution into a bad one, by the violence of their factions."[128]

I can perhaps sharpen the contours of Hume's thought that partisans can take on the impartial observer's perspective by juxtaposing it to Aristotle's discussion of factions in the *Politics*. We have seen Aristotle's argument that in mixed regimes, the public good arises from a combination of parts. He also thought that the polity is vulnerable to parts demanding more than their share, which is why a share in offices by itself is not sufficient for stability. Stability depends on democrats and oligarchs recognizing their partiality and the need for reciprocity. The polity is well ordered if no party wants to alter the constitution because they appreciate the limitations of their own claim to rule. Mutual understanding and a degree of political reciprocity make sharing in rule more than a modus vivendi or accommodation. It is grounded in a sense of justice, in appreciation of each part's contribution to the polity and a distribution of offices and rewards in accord with merit or contribution. Moderation and stability are a matter of objective appreciation of the complementarity of parts.[129]

Let me try to illustrate Hume's ethic of partisanship with an example from contemporary political philosophy. Take John Rawls. He characterized "political liberalism" as a broad category that contains a family of related political conceptions, of which his own justice as fairness is one.[130] So, the principle of equal opportunity is essential, but the conception of "fair equality of opportunity" that he favors is not. Some social minimum is essential, but the "difference principle" he sets out in his theory of justice is not. "These matters," he wrote, "are nearly always open to wide differences of reasonable opinion."[131]

So far, so Humean. Rawls even acknowledges that justice as fairness will be viewed in partisan terms: "As with any political conception, readers are likely to see it as having a location on the political spectrum" as "left-liberal" or "social democratic."[132] But as a partisan of justice as fairness Rawls did not represent it as a theory for the left complemented by a theory of justice from the right. He firmly identified justice as fairness with "the idea of equality most appropriate to citizens viewed as free and equal."[133] At one moment Rawls is a partisan on the side of the angels proposing the best account of what needs to be done. At another moment, he is injecting himself with "a small tincture of Pyrrhonism" and conceding that the opposition may sometimes be in the right.

Hume, we see, could conceive of partisans sharing the insights of the impartial observer. That means a sense of one's own fallibility and a concession that "the antagonist may sometimes be in the right." Both are strong resources for moderation. ("As Trotsky justly reminded the democrat Kautsky, the awareness of relative truths never gives one the courage to use force and to spill blood."[134]) Hume also required partisans to take on the perspective from which the parties are seen to add up. This imperative goes against the grain of actual partisanship, as he knew. The exemplary Rawls aside, the conviction of being on the side of the angels is common enough, and reserve rare. Partisans are not impartial observers; as a political and psychological matter, this is not a posture partisans can assume, much less sustain. Mildness and moderation stand in contrast to enthusiasm. The attitude of "hesitation" is antithetical to much political action. Generous assumptions about the opposition's intentions ("wise men who mean well") are episodic at best. Only sometimes, and only some partisans, stand back from their rightness. And when they do, it does not usually entail (as Hume would have it) unforced appreciation that other parties share in being right. Hume's pose is phenomenologically alien. Is the pose of impartial observer necessary? Partisans do not have to accept Hume's provisos, I argue, only that they are parts and will always be seen as partial.

A less demanding ethic of partisanship might look like this. Partisans do not have to assent to the view that parties share the truth between them, that taken together with the opposition they "add up" to a fully realized political whole. They do not have to see that parties are often continuous and share values or purposes in different degrees. Partisans can, and on a certain normative view of democracy should, speak to everyone and propose what is to them a fully satisfactory account of justice and what needs to be done. Partisans can admit their own fallibility without conceding that their antagonist is sometimes in the right. All that is necessary is acknowledging that organized political disagreement is ineliminable and party conflict its form. No particular reason for reconciling themselves to the status of being just a part, one among others, seems necessary. Partisans need not admit that republican and antirepublican forces, say, are complementary rather than purely antagonistic. They can embrace regulated rivalry and party government without accepting the merits of the opposition and without thinking that parties divide political truth or utility between them. As long as partisans accept regulated rivalry, do not aim at eliminating the opposition, and concede that political authority is partisan and contestable, there is no moral imperative for them to assume the view from outside, the perspective of impartial observer. It suffices that parties reject identifiable elements of the others' projects and promises, create politically relevant divisions, and accept regulated rivalry as the form in which they are played out.

The ethics of partisanship I propose in chapter 7 is not Humean. Its virtues derive not from the leavening of the impartial observer's philosophical moderation but from political dispositions and structures. For Hume, however, and the odd thinker of Humean disposition today, the ethics of partisanship as well as appreciation of parties depends on the impartial observer's detached perspective, judgment of parties' complementarity, and moderation of a kind "likely to bring truth and certainty."

Antagonism and Improvement: A Proto-Millian Philosophy of Parties

The most influential philosophical moment of appreciation shares Hume's assumption that parties are complementary parts that add

143

up. Parties of order and parties of progress, Mill proposed, are both necessary elements of a healthy state of political life, each "deriving its utility from the deficiencies of the other," the opposition of the other keeping each within the limits of reason and sanity.[135] The distinctive thought here is that the relation of parties is dialectical. Their conflict is corrective, improving, progressive. The philosophy of parties, which I call proto-Millian for reasons that will become clear, is ambitious, politically immodest. The expectation is that party conflict not only keeps the other side "within the limits of reason" but produces better political decisions—better at least in the sense of decisions faithful to the public interest and based on reasoned justifications. Neither the checking function of parties I considered earlier nor Hume's thought that parties make distinct and complementary contributions goes this step. Neither proposes that the dynamic of party antagonism is a constructive force by itself. Via Burke and Hume, I surveyed the moves from party divisiveness to parties' checking/preventative function, and beyond to complementarity and moderation. These moments are topped up by the proto-Millian philosophy of parties as agents of improvement, of fruitful synthesis. One more thing: in this version of the philosophical moment of appreciation, the benefits of opposition do not depend on partisans' stepping back to become impartial observers. Less stringently, more hopefully, the dynamic of party antagonism does the work.

The general argument is familiar enough. It should be, because it has a firm footing outside politics in arguments for liberty of thought and discussion as condition for the advance of useful knowledge. The claim that the opposition of contesting views corrects error, heightens awareness of arguments for and against propositions, stimulates both self-reflection and knowledge of the opposition, and produces better decisions and more legitimate ones was Enlightenment orthodoxy applied inside and outside politics and to a host of arguing agents. The case for the collective benefits of antagonism is amplified if we add Mill's signature proposition that on any great question or any of the great practical concerns of life, progress does not "superadd" but substitutes one partial and incomplete truth or prevailing opinion—inevitably blended with error and confusion—for another fragment more adapted to the needs of the time than the one it displaces.[136] Truth, Mill wrote, "is so much a question of the reconciling and combining of opposites, that very few have minds sufficiently capacious and impartial to make the adjustment with an approach to correctness, and it has to be made by the rough process of a struggle between combatants fighting under hostile banners." He called this "the social function of antagonism" without which any government suffers "infallible degeneracy and decay."[137]

My concern is to separate out general arguments for opposition and trial by discussion from this moment of appreciation for political parties specifically. One thing is clear: in this moment of appreciation, assemblies are the generally agreed-on locus of constructive political antagonism. In political bodies, definite proposals are made and specific evidence and arguments are leveled for and against. Condorcet's "Constitutional Plan," for example, was a design for legislative proceedings that would ensure conditions under which representatives could "enlighten themselves as to the grounds and consequences of the decision proposed to them."[138] "Deliberation" meant structured occasions for discussion, for built-in delays for gathering evidence, for reports and publicity. Condorcet's plan was to enable the search for the best possible solution. Mill too allowed that publicity and discussion are "a natural accompaniment of any, even nominal, representation." He referred to "The great council of the nation; the place where the opinions which divide the public on great subjects of national interest, meet in a common arena, do battle, and are victorious and vanquished."[139] "Representative assemblies are often taunted by their enemies with being places of mere talk and *bavardage*," Mill acknowledged, and he pushed back: "There has seldom been more misplaced derision. I know not how a representative assembly can more usefully employ itself than in talk, when the subject of talk is the great public interests of the country."[140] The view became commonplace. In Cavour's concise summary: "The worst chamber is still preferable to the best ante-chamber."[141] Or Bernard Crick's: "Palace politics is private politics, almost a contradiction in terms."[142]

Notice, though, that constructive antagonism is perfectly compatible with aversion to parties and partisanship. When John Adams wrote, "an opposition in parliament, in a house of assembly, in a council, in Congress, is highly useful and necessary to balance individuals, and bodies, and interests against one another, and bring the truth to light and justice to prevail,"[143] neither he nor others in this vein saw *parties* as agents of light and justice. Indisputably the most ardent voice of enlightenment, William Godwin tied social improvement to "communicative politics" (his term) while firmly disassociating the process from parties. The "shibboleth of party," Godwin wrote, "has a more powerful tendency, than perhaps any other circumstance in human affairs, to render the mind quiescent and stationery." In parties "the acrimonious, the intemperate, and the artful" will be most forward; the "prudent, the sober, the skeptical, and the contemplative" will be "overborne and lost."[144] One last example is Bentham, who saw parties as unredeemingly corrupt but insisted that debate "gives off sparks and leads to evidence." The exception, we have seen, is Hegel. Parties make a positive appearance in assemblies; I quoted this passage earlier:

> Whoever has reflected a little on the nature of an Assembly of Estates . . . cannot fail to see that without an opposition such an assembly is without outer and inner life. It is precisely this antagonism within it that forms its *essence* and *justification*, and it is only when it has engendered an opposition within itself that it is properly constituted.[145]

To my mind the exemplary advocate of political opposition is Benjamin Constant: "It is representative assemblies alone that can infuse life into the political body," he argued. "Representative assemblies must be free, imposing and lively." Put sharply: "The misfortune of a republic is when there is no intrigue."[146] Constant made the case for the representation of partial interests simply and sensibly. A hundred deputies elected by a hundred different parts of the country bring individual interests and local preferences into the assembly. "*Forced to debate together*, they soon notice respective sacrifices which are indispensable. They strive to keep these at a minimum. . . . Necessity always ends by uniting them in common negotiation." The general interest is "the representation of all the partial interests which must negotiate on matters common to them."[147]

We cannot help but notice that from the standpoint of contemporary deliberative theory, Constant's view is latitudinarian. Deliberation is not an animal different from negotiation and compromise. Representatives bring interests and opinions to the table, and in open assembly special pleading can be mitigated by the need to negotiate on matters of common interest; perfectly defensible partial interests can be tempered by the necessity for sacrifices; and from these interactions a notion of public good may emerge. Interests and the public interest are in this limited and provisional way reconcilable. There is nothing here of self-abnegating impartiality. Simply, "necessity" forces legislators to debate together.

Contemporary deliberative democratic theories are more refined than Constant's, and deliberation is radically severed from political rivalry. Only a certain form of "reasoning together" counts as deliberation in political philosophy today. "Argumentative scrutiny" is not enough. Often stringent criteria govern what counts as a legitimate argument in reaching decisions, and "epistemic abstinence" dictates that certain considerations be excluded as reasons. (Those who argue on the basis of "illegitimate particularisms" are unreasonable.[148]) Insofar as "the internal telos of deliberation is consensus,"[149] partisanship is anathema by definition. Even deliberative theorists who do not aim at overcoming disagreement yield nothing to parties, which they identify with "coercion, negotiation, or, in its most discursive form, rhetorical manipulation." Disqualification of parties is explicit: "Deliberation aims at judgments about the common good; partisanship advances the interests of a sector of society."[150] In one confident statement: "That deliberation and partisanship are mutually exclusive does not seem particularly controversial. Deliberation is a process of weighing alternative courses of action. Partisanship is the exercise of power on behalf of a chosen course of action."[151] Deliberation is represented as a balm and corrective of party antagonism.

It follows that in contemporary theory, the assembly is not the locus of deliberation in practice.[152] Legislatures are disreputably antideliberative (a recent philosophical defense of legislatures does not mention parties).[153] In fact, the actual setting for deliberation is left ambiguous; the often invoked "public sphere" is everywhere and nowhere.[154] When deliberation is identified with actual institutions where decisions are made, the model sites are courts in which judicial conferences produce reasoned opinions, or the controlled experiments of "deliberative polls" and "citizens' juries." With rare exceptions, then, contemporary political theory distances deliberation from party rivalry. Theorists do not afford parties a moment of appreciation, and I return to contemporary democratic theory's disparagement of parties in chapter 6.

I mention it here because Mill shares more with these severe advocates of deliberation than he does with Benjamin Constant. Constant's "necessity always ends by uniting them in common negotiation"[155] is not sufficient for the fruitful antagonism Mill has in mind. Mill agreed with Constant that the public interest was not "there" to be discovered, but for Mill it was the outcome of the force of the better argument. It turned on a "serious conflict of opposing reasons."[156] Gladstone called Mill "the Saint of Rationalism."[157] He abhorred a politics of interest, that is, ordinary deal making or logrolling in which interests are disconnected from some larger view of the public good.[158] Simply "closing the distance between the initial positions of adversaries" had no particular merit. Most important for purposes of exploring this philosophical moment of appreciation is this: where Constant thought that representation of partisan interests "forces" trial by discussion, Mill, as I will show, reversed the order of priority: trial by discussion depends on the presence of independent representatives, nonpartisans.

I want to take a closer look at the role of parties in Mill's account of "the social function of antagonism." Mill erected the philosophical framework of corrective, progressive antagonism, located the contest of ideas in government, and—this point is critical—insisted that this process requires actual advocates, not devil's advocates or impartial observers, or philosophers reflecting on examples from the past and pointing the way forward. He explained in *On Liberty* that objections have force when they come "from persons who actually believe them, who defend them in earnest, and do their utmost for them."[159] He looked for progress from "the rough process of a struggle between combatants fighting under hostile banners."[160] The question is whether Mill's "trial by discussion" and "social function of antago-nism" is a defense of parties. Is it a genuine moment of appreciation? When Mill speaks of "the great council of the nation; the place where the opinions which divide the public on great subjects of national interest, meet in a common arena, do battle, and are victorious and vanquished," does he intend a brief for parties?[161] If we think in terms of organizing opposition, identifying or creating divisions, directing attention to specific challenges to specific proposals, the "concert" among like-minded advocates that makes trial by discussion a force, parties seem to be candidates.

Nonetheless, there are good reasons to think that in the context in which Mill wrote about "party of order or stability" and "party of progress or reform," each of which "derives its utility from the deficiencies of the other,"[162] he was pointing not to actual political associations but to "modes of thinking." Mill had in mind the jux-taposition of subversive thinkers, on the one side, and those who look at received opinion "with the eyes of a believer," on the other.[163] He had in mind Bentham and Coleridge. It is a leap to apply his declaration of tolerance for "one-eyed men, provided their one eye is a penetrating one," which was a bow to two seminal minds in philosophy, to political partisanship.[164] These "parties" were not ac-tual political organizations. The difficulty in parsing Mill's intentions regarding parties increases if we take into account his observation that for antagonism to work, there must be actual advocates to "do battle."[165] Mill was skeptical that coherent legislation could emerge from "a miscellaneous assembly." He approved of "concert and co-operation."[166] Still, "party of order" and "party of progress" were ab-stractions, not actual, and he did not see parties as promising forces for political correction or improvement.

I call this view from outside, this moment of appreciation of par-ties, proto-Millian because Mill did not dependably share it. Despite invoking parties of order and progress, Mill is clear: "In the present situation of Great Britain, and of all countries in Europe," parties have proved to be incapable of performing the "function of antago-nism" and of serving as the nation's "Committee of Grievances and its Congress of Opinion."[167] Parties could not serve because they were too rarely principled, too little connected to important public interests. They do not provide the "serious conflict of opposing reasons" Mill prescribes. In the Preface to *Representative Government* he spoke witheringly of both "Conservatives and Liberals (if I may continue to call them what they still call themselves)" who have "lost confidence in the political creeds which they nominally profess":[168]

> Without presuming to require from political parties such an amount of virtue and discernment as that they should comprehend and know when to apply the principles of their opponents, we may yet say that it would be a great improvement if each party understood and acted upon its own. Well would it be for England if Conservatives voted consistently for everything conservative and Liberals for everything liberal.[169]

Instead, parties engaged in mock fighting, Mill scolded. In what we recognize as a long-standing antiparty accusation, they are populated by "a people of place hunters"; their struggles are "to decide whether the power of meddling in everything shall belong to one class or another."[170] Partisanship drags down able men "to the level of the meanest animal who can give a vote." Partisans are "pressed into the service of every abuse."[171] Mill's description of Sir Robert Peel is an expression of utter disdain:

> He knows the House of Commons, and the sort of men of whom it is composed. He knows what will act upon their minds and is able to strike the right chord upon that instrument. He has, besides, all that the mere routine of office-experience can give to a man who brought to it no principles drawn from a higher philosophy, and no desire for any.[172]

So it is no inconsistency that Mill levels twin accusations. On the one hand, partisans are unreasonably intransigent, and Mill accused partisans of attacking the adversary in matters that "to a neutral spectator" are indifferent or tolerable enough. On the other hand, partisans exhibit weakness and vacillation. By the "bad morality of party" Mill meant "yielding in small things" but not for the sake of great ones. In a brutal dissection, Mill analyzed the partisan and ostensibly

"Opposition" *Edinburgh Review*'s "pandering to leading opinions," its "habitual see-saw," its "practice of chiming in with existing prejudices." His name for this was "the immorality of omission," by which he meant willingness to accept "miserable palliatives" instead of "manly" effectual improvements.[173] Parties compromise everything, and adherence to party is compromising.

Mill excoriated parties, inveighed against partisanship, and refused to canvass, electioneer, or spend money on his own stand for election to parliament in 1865. He avowed that he would not be a spokesman for local interests and insisted on complete freedom to act.[174] Thomas Hardy described candidate Mill as a picture of "personified earnestness."[175] He seems to embody "the prudery of liberals about politics."[176] Mill confessed that in parliament he raised and defended his favorite principled reforms, his "single visions"—the secret ballot, capital punishment, women's suffrage, proportional representation—in some cases without even pressing for a vote. "I ... in general reserved myself for work which no others were likely to do," and therefore "a great proportion of my appearances were on points on which the bulk of the Liberal party, even the advanced portion of it, were of a different opinion from mine, or were comparatively indifferent."[177] Yet Mill also reported that he was "conversant with the difficulties of moving bodies of men, the necessities of compromise, the art of sacrificing the non essential to preserve the essential."[178] And Gladstone's characterization of Mill as "the saint of rationalism" continues: "though ... a philosopher, he was not, I think, a man of crotchets. ... [T]ogether with the high independent thought of a recluse, he had, I think, the good sense and practical tact of politics."[179]

Does Mill make concessions to partisanship, then? Dennis Thompson shows that Mill had worked out a thoughtful acceptance of political compromise consistent with principled reasons as part of his general theory of liberty and government before he entered politics.[180] Thompson identifies Mill's criteria for justifiable compromise. "The time is not yet ripe" for the best, principled measure is one—but only if the measure would "form the best foundation of a complete measure" in the future. Another criterion for justified compromise is that it produces a better law than proposals by adversaries on either side.

Mill also allows for compromise to protect progress already made against "the current towards the worse" or to correct "the worst features of the existing system." More generally, Mill advocated political gradualism and experimentation, and the intrinsic value of the process itself—the "mutual give and take" of democratic institutions and the anticipation that men of different principles can come to agree on a policy.[181] None of this is dependent on the dynamic that "substitutes one partial and incomplete truth or prevailing opinion—inevitably blended with error and confusion—for another fragment more adapted to the needs of the time." Nor does it seem to be dependent on party organization.

Mill was not adverse to compromise during his brief term in Parliament, and the question, again, is whether his concessions were connected to party. What should we make of Mill's support for Gladstone's reform bill, despite the fact that his signature concerns were not addressed: apportionment of seats and the inclusion of an educational qualification? This is especially telling in light of the fact that Mill opposed a similar measure coming from Disraeli and the Conservatives a year later, even chastising fellow radicals for supporting Disraeli's bill, which turned out to be a significant advance in expanding the franchise. Was this partisanship? Does it put in doubt his insistence that representatives owed nothing to parties as they existed, his insistence on independence? It seems that Mill's support was for Gladstone personally, because he saw the leader as "the one politician of national stature capable of placing principle at the center of political discussion." If anyone could restore the Liberal Party as a party of progressive principles, it was Gladstone.

This indicates that at most Mill did not entirely abandon the possibility of a party of principle. A realignment that would produce a robust conservative and a "really advanced" liberal party, each a carrier of ideas that are partially right and each arguing on the basis of public reasons, was imaginable. Simply, Mill did not see that change happening. Parties could be depended on to defeat that possibility themselves.

This is the background to Mill's work advocating institutional guarantees for antagonism *without* parties. "The constitution does not exist for the benefit of parties," he scoffed.[182] Most important was his long campaign on behalf of Hare's scheme of representation, which Mill presented as enabling opposition without partisanship. Mill offered the standard arguments in favor of proportional representation: untethering representatives from localities, saving otherwise "wasted votes," correcting for "the slavery of the majority," and giving voice to "the scattered elements" who are not bound to great political or little sectarian divisions.[183] But his spectacular enthusiasm for proportional representation—his exclamation that the day when such a trial would be sanctioned by parliament "will, I believe, inaugurate a new era ... destined to give to Representative Government a shape fitted to its mature and triumphant period"[184]—owes to the expectation that proportional representation would divorce representation and deliberation from parties and partisanship.

Mill identified Hare's electoral scheme with "independence." He imagined the plan (a single transferable vote arrangement) as relief from the imperative that "all the opinions, feelings, and interests of all members of the community should be merged into the single consideration of which party shall predominate."[185] Hare's scheme would allow people to be represented "by the man who has most of his confidence in all things, and not merely on the single point of fidelity to a party."[186] Electoral reform would permit candidates to emerge who were not recruited by parties. It would be a stimulus to a new breed of political men. Honorable, distinguished men, "though devoid of local influence, and having sworn allegiance to no political party," would offer themselves in undreamed numbers. "Hundreds of able men of independent thought" would enter the field and be voted into government.[187] Mill called this ideal "personal representation." In place of party he fantasized a "personal merit ticket."[188] His enthusiasm was boundless: the change of electoral system would be a prodigious gain "to our policy, to our morality, to our civilization itself."[189]

The label "personal representation" is also apt because it points to Mill's complaint that partisanship undermines personal responsibility. Parties are irresponsible collectives, and he quoted Bentham: "Boards are screens"; what a board does is the act of nobody, and nobody can be made to answer for it.[190] We recognize Mill's position as the antithesis of "responsible party government," which argues for collective responsibility made possible by cohesive and ideologically distinct governing parties and by majoritarianism.[191] For Mill, the only meaningful responsibility is individual, and that is conditional on nonpartisan independence.

Mill's contemporaries thought his confidence in proportional representation to produce independence was patently misplaced. Bagehot criticized Mill's crusade for "voluntary constituencies" on precisely this point. The notion that representatives would be more independent in their deliberations than those attached to traditional party and to locality was simply wrong. On the contrary, proportional representation would fragment the electorate. The "voluntary constituencies" would be rigid and polarized. Instead of producing independent representatives, Hare's plan would produce parties like churches, with doctrinaire tenets.[192] It would make subservience to party more exacting. Bagehot approved of the party basis of effective government, but only because parties had "no collective earnestness."

To return to the philosophical moment of appreciation, the question is, could this scheme of personal representation, insofar as it was successful in dampening partisanship and bringing into government "hundreds of able men of independent thought," drive improvement on Mill's own terms? Mill did not see proportional representation as an act of "only declaratory significance";[193] it was the condition for deliberation and improvement. Are Independents adequate to the adversarial task? True, Mill's nonpartisan men of merit are not Humean impartial observers. But is his "honorable distinguished" man who swears no allegiance to party a real (not devil's) advocate? Does independence ensure "a serious conflict of opposing reasons" or describe a real struggle between combatants fighting under hostile banners?[194] Why should we think that Independents would spontaneously fall into complementary camps, partisans of order or progress, say, rather than promiscuous coalitions or none at all?

Independent, nonpartisan representatives capable of advancing the cause of improvement was not Mill's only hope for proportional representation. He also thought these independent representatives were the key to creating independent voters. In practice, voters are prone to indifference or sell their votes; they vote under the influence of "someone who has control over them or whom for private reasons they desire to propitiate"; or they vote on the basis of their own "sinister interests or discreditable feelings." Mill commended English voters on just one score: at least they have distaste for "any mere struggle for office by political parties or individuals."[195] But by itself this is not independence and is hardly a signal of engaged public opinion. That is where Mill's distinctive standard—"what [government] makes of citizens and what it does with them,"[196] the potential to promote the virtue and intelligence of enfranchised citizens, including women[197]—connects to proportional representation and independence. Electors take on the moral tone of representatives, and independent candidates detached from locality and partisan interests, who insist on "full freedom to act" with a view to the public good, model political duty. The secret ballot might protect against "undue influence," but it also shields narrow self-interest and conformism. Open balloting would provide the venue for voters to justify their decisions, to demonstrate their own independence.

Despite his retreat from actual parties and celebration of nonpartisanship, Mill was aware that his "new breed" of political men, his Independents, could be a "miscellaneous" group. He was right to be skeptical that coherent legislation could emerge from "a miscellaneous assembly." He was right to approve of "concert and cooperation."[198] To echo Hegel, representation per se is not deliberation any more than it is governing. Yet Mill leaves us to imagine Independents doing the work. A party of Independents, I argue in chapter 7, is nonsense.

I conclude that on balance, Mill was unfaithful to the proto-Millian philosophic defense of parties. When he formulated his deliberative idea for politics—for correction and improvement resulting from antagonism—he invoked parties of order/progress and could imagine them as real. Simply, every look at actual parties appalled him. Still, Mill helped to erect the framework for this moment of appreciation of parties as agents of "social antagonism." And once it is built, we see that partisans are necessary to realize the value of parties. Even if partisans do not display the "small tincture of Pyr-rhonism" Hume proposed and even if they surrender the indepen-dence Mill idealized, the collectivity acquires something of value. Personally, partisans may give up admirable qualities of thought and character, but ordinary citizens and knowledgeable elites benefit. I will argue that partisans are worthy in themselves; the point here is that they are indispensible. Surely, the mix must include partisans with a modicum of "give," nonextremists willing to compromise with factions of their own party and on occasion with the opposition. But Independents, impartial observers, even-handed outsiders have little to work with or on in the absence of partisanship and the lines of division parties draw.

Assessing the Philosophic Moment of Appreciation

As I have reconstructed it here, the outsider's moment of apprecia-tion takes more than one form. Hume's "impartial observer" em-phasizes moderation founded on insight into the complementary contributions of parties. The proto-Millian philosophical position rests on constructive dialectic. Both views from outside share the thought that parties in some sense "add up." They correct for one another's deficiencies. They keep one another "within the limits of reason and sanity." The outcome of their antagonism is better—more reasoned, more likely to be in the public interest—than other ways of reach-ing political decisions. Almost without exception, whenever political theory gingerly approaches an appreciation of parties, we hear echoes of the need for opposition and "trial by discussion" in which parties conceivably provide "the social function of antagonism."

What weight should we give this moment of appreciation? There is reason to be wary, if only because it threatens to eclipse Burke's insight and Hegel's. A great deal is lost if intellectual boredom blinds us to the value of regulated rivalry and responsibility for governing, if these moments of appreciation are taken for granted or overshad-owed by the drama of progressive antagonism. These sober political achievements are liable to be eclipsed by the promise of philoso-phy. For from the Humean and proto-Millian perspectives, regulated rivalry and governing do not suffice. The potential value of parties is to to provide comprehensive, rationally justified programs that, in competition, not only provide "choices" but alter and advance understanding of interests and the common good.[199] There is no compensation for the failure of parties to live up to the standard of correction and progress. This moment of appreciation is an invitation to disappointment.

Historically, political theory harbored no great moral promise parties could disappoint. There was no initial enthusiasm for the promise of parties followed by unusual depravity or the more mundane but inevitable dashing of hopes. But the philosophical moment of appreciation raises expectations. As we doubtless know from personal experience, exasperation can seize even those friendly to trial by discussion. Partisans disappoint when they are unremittingly enthusiastic and resistant to "a small tincture of Pyrrhonism," hesitancy and humility. Parties disappoint when "men, not measures" dominate, when party antagonisms are trivial (Hume's "the colours of their livery"), or when the justifications for measures are not sufficiently grounded in right reasons. They disappoint when contest leads to what seems to be arrant compromise or to paralysis.

Indeed, the failed promise of deliberation can fuel ferocious attacks on parties, most famously Carl Schmitt's *The Crisis of Parliamentary Democracy*. Parties in government stand or fall on the strength of the proposition Schmitt traces to Burke, Bentham, Guizot, and of course Mill: confrontation of differences is aimed at persuading one's opponent through argument of its truth or justice. "Laws arise out of a conflict of opinions (not a struggle of interests)," and "all specifically parliamentary arrangements and norms receive their meaning first through discussion and openness." The essence is "a dynamic-dialectic," Schmitt wrote; he called this "the metaphysic of the two-party system." Without the principle of public discussion "these arrangements would be unintelligible."[200] That is what happens when Millian deliberation devolves into a conflict of interests, a Constantian negotiation. There is no justification for legislative assemblies once it is no longer "a question of persuading one's opponent of the truth or justice of an opinion but rather of winning a majority in order

157

to govern with it." Government by discussion, Schmitt concluded, "counts as moldy."[201] Schmitt is disgusted by the taint of interest in parliamentarism and by discussion without end. Mill had predicted this sort of derision.

Of course, the real thrust of Schmitt's argument is not that assemblies are insufficiently Millian but that deliberation and reasonableness are a sham. They are certainly a radical misunderstanding of "the concept of the political." Existential threats to survival required Hobbism, Schmitt insisted. What was needed was command, "decisionism."[202] The presumptive inability to deal with crisis explained his revulsions: "the dominance of parties, their unprofessional politics of personalities, the government of amateurs, continuing governmental crises, the purposelessness and banality of parliamentary debate[,] . . . the destructive methods of parliamentary obstruction"—the list goes on.[203] This is more than disillusion with "trial by discussion" and party politics. It is wholesale anti-Enlightenment and antipolitics, my subject in chapter 1. Schmitt paired parties and deliberation, but would have opposed the first even if the limitations of the second had not provided an excuse.

The disappointed expectation of "trial by discussion" is a recipe for antidemocratic rancor, then.[204] It invites judicial, bureaucratic, and above all executive substitutes for partisan politics. Exasperation could seize even the most committed democrats. Franklin Roosevelt pronounced that democracy has failed throughout the world because people had "become so fed up with futile debate and party bickerings."[205] The history of representative government is full of this sentiment. Here is Madison writing to Jefferson:

> I say parties and factions will not suffer improvements to be made. As soon as one man hints at an improvement, his rival opposes it. No sooner has one party discovered or invented any amelioration of the condition of man, or the order of society than the opposite party belies it, misconstrues it, misrepresents it, ridicules it, insults it, and persecutes it.[206]

A final caveat. From Humean and proto-Millian perspectives, parties have value as carriers of complementary positions, reciprocally corrective forces. They are indefensible if they fail to divide along dimensions necessary for improvement. We see this clearly in Jurgen Habermas and Jacques Derrida's manifesto for a new European identity that will preserve key elements from the political tradition, among them great parties locked in a battle that results in public enlightenment:

> The party system which emerged from the French revolution was often copied. But only in Europe has it also served as a form of ideological competition, which submits the social-pathological consequences of capitalistic modernization to continued political evaluation. This promotes its citizens' sensitivity to the paradoxes of progress.[207]

In their narrative, great parties explore "the paradoxes of progress": conservative, liberal, and socialist interpretations of the losses of traditional ways of life versus "creative destruction," "chimerical progress" versus real profits. I do not deny the episodic rise of great parties, but appreciation should not depend wholly on their appearance or fruitful antagonism. To rest a defense of parties on a dynamic of correction and improvement resulting from fundamental but complementary differences is to rest it on undoubtedly alluring but unsteady, contingent grounds.

So, one more recommendation for tempering the proto-Millian moment of appreciation is the fact that principles or values or interests do not arise in antagonistic pairs. Often enough parties stand for disparate, unmatched positions. Or important values are assumed, taken for granted, unopposed. Or parties collude and agree to leave things out of politics, ducking problems, or suffering jointly a failure of political imagination. There are of course times when parties take on the character of principled antagonists Mill imagined for conservatives and liberals—though it is not obvious that the most important, creative moments of partisanship are these. In any case, often enough, parties simply do not "add up" and their antagonism is neither enlightening nor progressive.

I believe the proto-Millian moment of appreciation can be rescued by restating it more modestly. Parties do not add up to a comprehensive, philosophically defensible whole. They are not complements whose antagonism is dependably countervailing, much less progressive.

But parties *do* draw politically relevant lines of division, reject elements of the others' accounts of projects and promises, and accept regulated rivalry as the form in which they are played out. Tempered, this moment of appreciation says that parties articulate positions, define divisions, and that their antagonism is the engine of "trial by discussion." It is enough that party antagonism focuses attention on problems; information and interpretations are brought out; stakes are delineated; points of conflict and commonality are located; the range of possibilities winnowed. Truly, "an issue does not become an issue merely because someone says it is,"[208] and parties make that happen. Without parties, deliberation is disorganized and impossible within legislatures, much less on a public, national scale. Indeed, factions within parties, with their ties to specific interest and advocacy groups, ensure that discussion on major questions is not just lofty abstraction but includes the normal political questions of means and apportioning costs. Parties not only organize debate within government; they can organize debate among activist citizens and can force those into argument who would rather evade it. In later chapters I show how antagonism can be taken to "the party in the electorate" to produce "mobilized deliberation."[209]

I would redraw the proto-Millian position in cooler shades. Parties create lines of division and define themselves in relation to one another. For, caveats in view, it is still the case that politically salient values, preferences, programs, interests, and principles are unlikely to be cast in terms of Mill's "serious conflict of opposing reasons" unless partisans do the work of articulating lines of division and advocating on the side of the angels. That is the main point to retain from a pared-down proto-Millian position: without party rivalry, "trial by discussion" cannot be meaningful. It will not be if interests and opinions are disorganized and are not brought into opposition, their consequences are not drawn out, and argument is evaded. Nor can it be fruitful if the inclusion of interests and opinions is exhaustive and chaotic; parties are about selection and exclusion. Shaping conflict is what parties and partisans do and what will not be done, certainly not regularly, without them.[210] I do not intend a rosy view of parties; simply one that mimics Hegel in seeing them as a rose in the cross of the present.

Antipartyism Looking Forward

Disarming and regulating political rivalry and responsibility for governing are the two initial and enduring moments of appreciation of parties. The third philosophical moment of appreciation centers on the combinative nature of parties and the progressive dynamic of party conflict. Except for Mill's, these moments of appreciation arose as reflections on parties in government before government could be described as democratic and before their electoral face was predominant. Partisans did sometimes appeal beyond government to constituencies, but these moments of appreciation preceded the extension of suffrage to most citizens, the rise of electoral parties organized to incorporate people into the political process, the expectation that parties link civil society and government. Even the proto-Millian moment arose before elected officials thought of themselves as dependent on "grass roots," wanting and needing the security of this base in order to justify their place in the structure of what could finally be called representative democracy.[211]

My exercise in retrieval of "certain guideposts for future remembrance, and even for sheer reference" has value if it reminds us that parties need not be entirely identified as they are today with the activities of popular campaigns and elections and political mobilization, and need not be judged solely by standards of representativeness and accountability. That is, my exercise has value if we think that these moments of appreciation—regulated rivalry, governing, and the creation of lines of division—identify enduring achievements, are resources for assessing parties, and challenge contemporary attempts, even in democratic theory, to embrace political pluralism without parties.

By roughly the mid-nineteenth century, the glorious traditions of antipartyism—parties as parts and partisans as divisive—were invoked less often. Today, holist antiparty sentiment based on some vision of unity or anticipation of a consensus society is the occasional property of those on the far left or right, of one-party nationalists or theocrats. Periodic appeals for a unity government or bipartisanship, for centrism or consensus on specific issues, are distinct from the political theories of holism that opposed parties so ferociously. Echoes of the second tradition are more common: the pronounced fear that parties are sinister factions, senselessly, selfishly divisive, magnifiers or irresponsible inventors of cleavages. The rhetoric of divisiveness is still with us. The phrase "ridden with factions" is there in ostensibly objective contemporary social science discussions of political division; the tinge of disrepute is unmistakable.[212] The *Oxford English Dictionary* defines party as "a league, confederacy; a conspiracy, plot" and faction as "always with opprobrious sense, conveying the imputation of selfish or mischievous ends or turbulent or unscrupulous methods."[213] The charge of divisiveness is sometimes leveled promiscuously at parties wholesale. It is pronounced at any sign of political polarization. It is guaranteed to be leveled at "extremist" parties, to which I turn in Part 3.

Abatement of these glorious traditions of antipartyism has not meant general adoption of these moments of appreciation. Nor has it meant that fresh salutary purposes of parties and partisanship have been uncovered and gained a foothold in political theory. Insofar as James Monroe's claim that "the existence of parties is not necessary to free government" has been superceded,[214] recognition of the instrumental uses of parties has not been accompanied by a vigorous defense of them. Rather, the types of antipartyism have multiplied. The glorious traditions of antipartyism have been supplemented with aversions shaped by the experience of mass electorates and institutionalized party systems, adding new high points to the landscape of antipartyism.

Democratization came earlier to America, with electoral parties as well as parties in government before 1800. But that did not mean precocious justifications for parties or partisanship on this side of the ocean. Even the moments of appreciation I have discussed were rare in America. But American parties' "open, conscious appeal to the body of the citizens"[215] did bring advances in aversion. "Progressive antipartyism" is my subject in Part II. It takes aim at mass parties, called "the "organization" before the label "machine" stuck, parties entrenched in what was aptly called "the system." Parties are reviled as corrupt and corrupting, perverters of the democratic spirit. I call this "post-party depression," and virtually every element of contemporary antipartyism and every contemporary scheme for correcting the system by eliminating or circumventing or containing parties has its roots there.

PART II

Post-Party Depression

CHAPTER 4

———⟫•◆•⟪———

Progressive Antipartyism

Crisis of Confidence

Max Weber traced the change from parties as "an association of notables" within government to modern forms he called "the children of democracy." "In order to win the masses it became necessary to call into being a tremendous apparatus of apparently democratic associations" of which the American party organization was "an especially early and especially pure expression."[1] This "apparently democratic" party system, well established in the United States by the 1860s, did not stanch antipartyism.[2] The terms of attack changed, though, creating a third high point on the terrain I am mapping.

"Glorious traditions" of antipartyism focused on division and divisiveness, antitheses of holism and harmony. Modern mass parties were institutions of representative democracy, which accepted political conflict, electoral politics as a premier arena of conflict, and the readiness of politicians to join parties and voters to support them. In the 1850s William Seward affirmed, "What though the elements of political strife remain? They are necessary for the life of free states. What though there still are parties, and the din and turmoil of their contests are ceaselessly heard? . . . Such parties are dangerous only in the decline, not in the vigor of Republics."[3] James Bryce, a British observer of American politics, remarked favorably on a party system that "stimulates the political interest of the people, which is kept alive by this perpetual agitation."[4] In short, "There was here, a particular kind of political world growing out of a mass, sprawling, untidy, competitive society. Political conflict was normal and expected. It needed articulation, shaping, and direction. Parties were necessary."[5]

Progressive critics recognized that these parties were novel political organizations. Even detractors viewed them as extraordinary inventions. Some were as awestruck by political machines as Marx was of the tremendous technological power of capitalism. In *The American Commonwealth*, Bryce describes parties as the great moving forces in America, and he was puzzled by the failure to study them. We need treatises to comprehend the "vast and intricate political machine" that lies outside the Constitution, he insisted.[6] His 1888 work was the first to analyze parties in the United States. His was the first analytic work, that is; in 1842 Jabez Hammond published "The History of Political Parties in the State of New York," "the story of democracy's journey from idea to thing," with Van Buren as hero of the new system.[7] Van Buren published his own *Inquiry into the Origin and Course of Political Parties in the United States* in 1867. One critic urged fellow foes of parties to admit "that it is as original and distinct from all that has gone before as anything political can be." We revere the Constitution, but "of all our political institutions, not one is so new, so entirely made, as it were, out of whole cloth as the American party system."[8]

Under these conditions, aversion to parties is not driven by holistic ideals or dread of divisiveness.[9] The fear is different. If parties are central to elections and elections are integral to representative democracy, and if parties are only "apparently democratic associations," antipartyism raises a desperately troubling question: "Is democracy a failure?"[10] One progressive critic put it sharply: the party system fails in everything it professes to do: it is a device for the prevention of the expression of the common will; it misleads and obscures public opinion; it is simply another form of despotism.[11] Despair of parties is accompanied by mean and disparaging accounts of the sort of people who are partisans—in effect, most voters. Some antiparty writers bravely allowed that the affliction might lie in the people. "The boss is not a political, he is an American institution, the product of a freed people that have not the spirit to be free. . . . [I]t's all a moral weakness; a weakness right where we think we are strongest." And, "We are responsible, not our leaders. . . . We let them divert our loyalty from the United States to some 'party'; we let them boss the party and turn our municipal democracies into autocracies and our republican nation into a plutocracy. . . . [W]e let them wheedle and bribe our sovereignty from us."[12] No amount of populist boosting— "We Americans have on the whole a right to be optimists"[13]—erases this suspicion. The question, "Is democracy a failure?" is the dark heart of "post-party depression." Its "purest expression" and the specifics I detail may be American, but this troubling thought is familiar wherever electoral parties exist.

The urge, of course, was to pull back from charging perversion to the people: "It is idle to argue that for the flaws of representative democracy the people are themselves in the last resort to blame. As a syllogism of political science that is true enough; but as a matter of fact it is no more true than the maxim of practical politics that the voters will never blame themselves for a failure to get what they desire."[14] Moral indignation is redirected at parties. It ushered in innumerable panaceas designed to tame or abolish parties, and riffs anticipating a democracy purified of parties (and of obdurate partisans). Consider this telling statement by Lincoln Steffens: "Political corruption, then, is a force by which a representative democracy is transformed into an oligarchy representative of special interests, and the medium of revolution is the party."[15] "Medium of revolution" is a double entendre. Parties are the agents of corruption, true. But "medium of revolution" suggests the possibility of a uniquely progressive party that would transform democracy from an oligarchy to the real thing. Ostrogorski wrote encouragingly that "through the progress of enlightenment" party ties are being relaxed[16] and imagined a purified party of "Independents." Still, confident, assertive progressive attacks on corruption and hopeful proposals for reform are strained, accompanied by self-reflective anxiety.

Alan Dugan captures this wavering in "Portrait of a Local Politician":

It's like being a winner at an all-night poker game.
I know I can't leave winning without getting beaten up,
so I go on playing, trying to lose a little, but not too much,
hoping that mutual exhaustion will stop the game in the morning. . . .
Then, I can take my winnings and walk away, carefully,
after giving a cut to the loser who follows me
and wants to break my arm,
and go home to sleep like death and dream
that my patience and expertise and money and winning
makes me a hero. No way. They know I have their money.
They know I'm a winner. They can get me if they can.
I know I have to play in the next game
for safety's sake, and try to lose a little.
It's difficult, they're such a bunch of dopes, but they're my boys.[17]

Dugan's metaphor of politics as a game of luck and guile, an adversarial contest between politician and people, is caustic, and his insight into the moral psychology of democratic politics achingly true. The politician wants to be a hero, a "winner," to survive to "play in the next game." And the "bunch of dopes," the voters, are not such dopes. They know he has their money (read: interests / future of the planet) and they want a fair deal. So Dugan's politician is uneasy, looking over his shoulder at the people. "They can get me if they can" is a taunt that covers many doubts. Can they get him? Can we? What would that mean?

As I did in synthesizing "holist antipartyism" and "fatal division," my purpose is to collect a distinctive set of aversions and trace a steady stream of claims about the pathology of parties under the label "progressive antipartyism." The Progressive Era of American politics proper is the extended period coming on the heels of what has been called the "Golden Age" of American parties in the last decades of the nineteenth century and culminating in the years following the First World War. In this chapter I draw mainly on material from this period, which set the terms of this form of antipartyism. I apply the label broadly, though, to indicate a recurrent critical impulse. From a historical standpoint, my use of the label is lax (though historians too give themselves latitude), but for good reason.[18] A set of aversions creates the unity of progressive antipartyism, as they do other antiparty traditions, and these are as pronounced in contemporary political life and political thought as they were during the Progressive Era proper. It is not surprising that Progressivism is the tradition of many intellectuals in America, with their distaste for compromising party politics, wariness of large-scale political organization, and confidence in responsible (nonpartisan) political elites or in an educated, deliberative (nonpartisan) people.[19] Robert La Follette, a hero to those whose political imagination conjures up a progressive party transcending ordinary partisanship, is said to have replaced the lobby with the University of Wisconsin faculty,[20] and the same jibe could be directed at contemporary theorists of deliberative democracy. The temperamental distance between political theorists and partisans owes less to the distance between philosophy and political practice than to distinctive antipathies and hopeful expectations worked out virtually in full in the initial decades of Progressivism. I do not point out every parallel and present incarnation of progressive antipartyism. A few examples suffice. Anything more would be heavy-handed. This form of antipartyism is peculiarly but not uniquely American, and its lively presence is an element in the "post-party depression" of democratic theorists elsewhere.

Interpreting Corruption and Reform

Like "democracy," "progressive" is a morally loaded term; it signals enlightenment, future-looking improvement, if not perfectibility. In its original and every subsequent incarnation, progressivism is moralistic. Its mantra is reform. In politics it is paired with "good government" and "clean elections." The sunny side—the political optimism, the scope of progressive ambitions, the sheer energy of reformist impulses—is familiar. Richard Hofstadter summed it up in a single sentence: "It is hardly an accident that the generation that wanted to bring about direct popular rule, break up the political machines, and circumvent representative government was the same generation that imposed Prohibition on the country and proposed to make the world safe for democracy."[21] A better formulation is that progressivism proposed to make democracy safe for the world. As I show here and in the following chapters, that entails eliminating or purifying parties and replacing partisans with Independents.

Two words capture progressive antipartyism: "corruption" and "reform." Before looking at these more closely, I want to be sure to indicate that progressive notions of corruption are *sui generis*. Corruption is not firmly embedded in some earlier intellectual tradition of public virtue.[22] I bother to make this point because of recent attempts to identify progressivism with republicanism.[23] The story of the seventeenth-century British roots of the ideology of American colonial resistance to a corrupt crown and his ministers is now standard academic history. In this republican account, a designing ministry used monied interests—merchants, banks, debt, and credit—as tools in a conspiracy to effect tyranny and "enslavement."[24] Even at the time of the revolution, republicanism was just one thread among others, not as dominant as academic orthodoxy suggests.[25] Occasionally, progressive discourse does seem to echo these eighteenth-century republican strains, but we should not make too much of this. "Corruption" does not point to the vicious effect of luxury, for example, or signal morally blamable elevation of private over civic life. The modern party institution of rotation in office, which brought large numbers of citizens into public employment and then back into private life, was not seen in republican terms as conducive to liberty and bulwark against an aristocracy of officeholders, much less as an opportunity for cultivating virtue. On the contrary, progressives attacked rotation in administrative terms as inefficient, a plague of incompetence, and as the foundation of scoundrel party and spoils.

Naturally, civic pieties do pop up in the progressive mix. The cant of the greatness of the people is standard electioneering, and when they were not descrying actual voters, progressives indulged in it. When Lincoln Steffens wrote that "Jersey was the head waters of the main stream of corruption against which the reformers everywhere were trying to swim back—back to Jeffersonian democracy," this is not republicanism, and Steffens, immersed in the politics of large

American cities, knew it: "my democracy was a conviction, not a theory."[26] Not every concern with character, civic values, and enlightened public opinion is republican, after all. It may be that "the prime problem of our nation is to get the right type of good citizenship," but if good citizenship means honesty and common sense, is this republican?[27] If "the new patriotism" is "not one which charges into the deadly breach but one which smashes the 'machine,'"[28] is this republican? If "civic renaissance" means government run "honestly, efficiently, and economically," is this republican?[29] If so, the concept has become so elastic as to contain opposition to everything remotely morally or politically disagreeable. Hence the vacuity of the observation: "Progressives retained the formative ambition of the republican tradition and sought new ways to elevate the moral and civic character of citizens."[30] Insofar as the term had concrete meaning, "corruption" fastened not on republican vices but on American sins: slavery, intemperance, and organized greed, and on their connection to party politics. Susan B. Anthony rolled these themes together in patently unrepublican outrage: the parties are controlled by "the liquor interests," which are "positively, unanimously, and unalterably opposed to woman suffrage."[31]

Other characterizations of progressive obsession with corruption and reform are truer to the mark. Historians describe the struggle against parties not in terms of republican virtue and vice, or in progressives' own terms as Independents versus supporters of the machine, but as the struggle between community leaders who shared ethnicity and culture with the grass roots, and those detached from community.[32] In the end, however, the once-standard moralistic reading of progressivism is closest to the bone. The dominant resonance is evangelical and the references biblical—chasing moneylenders from the temple, the mob choosing Barabbas over Jesus, applying the Golden Rule to political corruption, "awakening."[33] One progressive's list of inspiring leaders consists of Savonarola, Luther, and Parkhurst.[34] The response to the wash of corruption was a "social gospel." Veblen called progressives "the people of the uplift." We can discern "the dramatics of Protestant morality" in contemporary antipartyism, too.[35]

Pried from republican political thought, the terms "corruption" and "reform" can be seen for what they are—protean and expressive. "Reform," with its connotation of return to original principles, and "progressive," with its patently un-republican forward-looking perfectibility, float outside the bounds of any very articulated moral or political theory. "A troubled mind groping to find names to fit its discontent" captures progressive preoccupation with "corruption."[36] There is one constant, however, one secure footing: politics is at the heart of the problem and parties are confidently cast as *the* agents of corruption. They are the principal objects in need of reform or, better, abolition.

"The Organization"

Excoriation—"ambition, avarice, and vindictiveness" and more—was the common lot of political types.[37] It would be enough to make it anathema to say that "the major political party is the creature of the politicians, the ambitious office seeker and officeholder."[38] The sentiment that politics is too dirty a business for any decent person to mix with was not unique to modern parties.[39] What gives progressive antipartyism its distinctive themes is *organization*. Where corruption was previously haphazard, unorganized, irregular, occasional, charged to personal flaws or the machinations of a particular group, it is now a "system."[40] Corruption is not limited to illegal behavior that could be addressed through the criminal prosecution of scoundrels.[41] Rather, it extends to a vast field of improper political influence and irresponsibility that needs to be addressed by "reform." It is institutional as well as personal corruption.

Another way of putting this is to say that progressive antipartyism is inseparable from muckraking—that is, uncovering a specific scandal—railroad, insurance, banking—and representing it as a systemic problem for which there is social science evidence of patterns and processes. Before it was given its name, "muckraking" was called sociology.[42] Periodic muckraking is a highlight of American history: strong during the Jacksonian era, repeated by labor parties, Mugwumps, Populists, and progressives to the present—the "discovery" is repeated. Contemporary campaign finance legislation takes aim at "corruption or the appearance of corruption," and the latest federal bill, the Bipartisan Campaign Reform Act, wears the label "reform" in its official title. The term "reform" appears so often in progressivism it is as if it had discernible content.

Two features of parties as large-scale organizations invite distinctive, progressive attacks. First, the party in government is no longer its only face. Urban political machines and state and national parties are organizations with their own managers and entrenched leadership. Teddy Roosevelt could not help admiring the plan of organization itself—the central committees, the delegates from districts, the caucuses, the captains and subordinates who run elections.[43] A remarkable feature of the American political structure is the sheer number of officials who reach office via party organization. There are always nominations and elections to something, always candidates, workers, and campaigns. "Politics never stops," in the specific sense of partisan elections. "The getting of public office, under our present system, by our present processes of nomination and popular election, generally requires either the doing of a large amount of dirty work, or the payment of large amounts of money for the doing of it by other men."[44] Even after progressive reformers succeeded in establishing meritocratic appointed positions and state control of the machinery of elections, parties remained the principal agents of this incessant democratic business.

The party is also "in the electorate." Parties create partisans, shape political participation, color public opinion. They make "an open, conscious appeal to the body of the citizens."[45] These parties are intertwined with the main elements of civil society, from churches to labor organizations, business groups to advocacy groups. All this means that arrant corruption is not restricted to elected officials and party leaders but infects society generally. "The party Organization enabled the citizens to discharge their duty in an automatic way, and thus kept the government machine constantly going."[46] "Constant" is the telling term; organization and ceaseless political business ensures "the ramification of party into all the nooks and corners."[47]

The second feature of mass parties that invites this form of antipartyism is that they are not just devices for choosing governors;

they run government. I discussed the early moment of appreciation of party government in the last chapter. It is one thing to take responsibility for the traditional, limited business of governing and another to push to extend and control government activity. Parties respond to new opportunities to exercise governmental power.[48] They expand the range of public business and raise expectations for public policy and regulation, government-created jobs, contracts, and benefits. As distributions multiply, the channels and points of contact with party and government multiply, and as they do, antipartyism is predictably inflamed.

Tocqueville remarked on the "small party" character of American party politics, meaning that parties are not ideological. Bryce speculated on the basis of opposition between the major American parties (was it federalism vs. local community? liberty vs. authority?) only to conclude that the objects of American parties were transient and that the parties had no deeper meaning, no claim to historical continuity. He could not discern principles even when it came to the matters he judged of great interest, such as liquor traffic, tariffs, and regulation.[49] In Weber's unflattering characterization, "they are purely organizations of job hunters."[50] The distributive politics of small parties draws attention to this parceling out, and spurs preoccupation with whether a particular interest is a special interest, a sinister interest, or a genuine public interest. It gives rise to incessant contests over patronage and over the policy equivalent of patronage.[51] "Pork barrel politics" is the fertile ground of progressive antipartyism. "As an extractive enterprise for the extortion of patronage and plunder from the government, the party acts with great precision."[52]

American parties normally act like small parties.[53] They are institutions of conscious national purpose only episodically: the proto-parties of the revolutionary period based on divergent constitutional interpretation, the Civil War Republican Party, later the intense partisanship of the New Deal. There are innumerable examples of the creativity of small parties and their partisans, and these deserve recognition. The point here is that progressives abhor small parties without longing for "great" parties rooted in deep social cleavages, ideology, or clashes of principle.[54] Their chief ambition was riddance.

New, then, in progressive antipartyism is a "system" of politics with "small parties" amplified by organization, by the scale and scope of activity both electoral and governmental. "The Organization" was the term for parties until "machine" caught on. Progressives gave the term a twist, turning "organization" into a term of abuse by analogy to other sinister institutions. Organized crime was one, and from the progressive perspective the similarity is not hard to see: an organization aimed at territorial political power for the purpose of enriching leaders and advantaging supporters. The analogy could be taken further: like the Mafia, party machines sell protection, police, resolve disputes, and provide a limitless array of jobs, services, and favors. Another counterpart was invoked to cast aspersion on parties: big business. The opprobrium attached to machines, Roosevelt explains in "Machine Politics in New York City," comes from the fact that they are operated largely as business concerns to benefit leaders and their followers. (Ostrogorski felt compelled to refine the point, distinguishing between the machine men who look out only for themselves and the Organization set on the interests of the party.[55]) Commonalities between the behavior of parties and business cartels is a thesis of contemporary progressive theory, which I assess in the next chapter.

"Corrupt and Contented"

The picture of organized corruption is imprinted on our political consciousness; it colors every mention of party even today. Truly, "the negative image of the self-serving political manipulator is as common in American political literature and amid commentators as any image we hold."[56] If as it seems accounts of fraud were overstated, nonetheless the picture is not so distorted as to be meaningless.[57] Local parties were identified with bossism and a system of "spoils," with exploitation of public office for patronage and graft, with "the bribe as a convention of political life and the vote as a commodity for sale."[58] Parties were said to engage in extortion and election fraud—padding the lists with the names of dead dogs, children, and nonexistent persons and the "colonization" of vagabonds who were imported into the city to vote.[59] "Reality was the bribe, the rebate, the bought franchise, the sale of adulterated food," and, of course, co-operation with "commercialized vice."[60] Weber struggled to explain "corruption and wastefulness second to none"; it "could be tolerated only by a country with as yet unlimited economic opportunities," he concluded.[61] His source, Ostrogorski, reported:

> Organization reached its climax; from a broker in offices it rose to be a trafficker in political influence; along with elective posts it sold the power residing in them, beginning with the adjudication of contracts, government orders, and public works, and ending with a wholesale and retail trade in legislation and "protection."[62]

The urban boss was the favorite target of progressive antipartyism. He is "an unofficial leader who exercises irresponsible power primarily to extract patronage,"[63] "a dealer in public privileges who could also command public support."[64] Weber invoked the type in his essay, "Class, Status, and Party": "The typical American Boss, as well as the typical big speculator, deliberately relinquishes social honor."[65] Van Buren had a similar thought:

> There is no one in whose pockets the people are so prone to pour lead, as a man who pursues politics for a living. They soon come to regard him as a wanton upon Providence, and are constantly disposed to show him the cold shoulder. Although many make their living by it, they get it by hook or crook, and no public honors sit well upon them.[66]

Again, parties were corrupt and corrupting, and the organization was everywhere.

> Boss Magee's idea was not to corrupt the city government, but to be it; not to hire votes in councils, but to own councilmen; and so, having seized control of his organization, he nominated cheap or dependent men for the select and common councils. Relatives and friends were his first recourse, then came bartenders, saloonkeepers, liquor dealers, and others allied to the vices, who were subject to police regulation and dependent in a business way upon the maladministration of law. For the rest he preferred men who had no visible means of support, and to maintain them he used the usual means—patronage.[67]

Jane Addams, the peerless reformer, had a less punishing view of political parties than most progressives, and understood "Why the Ward Boss Rules." She was sensitive to the services they provide: "protection and kindness." Of course, partisans were stuck in a lower stage of moral evolution than reformers, but to Addams's mind, concern for the well-being of those close to us makes corruption comprehensible, even palatable:

> A man stands by his friend when he gets too drunk to take care of himself, when he loses his wife or child, when he is evicted for non-payment of rent, when he is arrested for a petty crime. It seems to such a man entirely fitting that his Alderman should do the same thing on a larger scale—that he should help a constituent out of trouble just because he is in trouble, irrespective of the justice involved. . . . The Alderman, therefore, bails out his constituents when they are arrested . . . uses his "pull" with the magistrate when they are likely to be fined for a civil misdemeanor . . . gives presents at weddings and christenings . . . procures passes from the railroads when his constituents wish to visit friends or attend the funerals of distant relatives. . . . Many a man at such a time has formulated a lenient judgment of political corruption. . . . He is good to the widow and the fatherless.[68]

Addams saw parties as webs of mutual obligation on the order of friendship. It is striking how often friendship is invoked in connection with partisanship—and not just the usual idea that parties reward friends and punish enemies. Friendship points to mutual assistance and a fair degree of respect in mundane dealings, to the democracy of everyday life.[69] Addams's assessment mirrored politicians' own self-understanding: "there's got to be in every ward somebody that any bloke can come to—no matter what he's done—and get help. Help, you understand; none of your law and your justice, but help."[70] That is the "enigmatic truthfulness" in Roosevelt's report that "there are no politics in politics."[71]

Most progressives did not have an iota of Jane Addams's sympathy. They were unrelenting. Bernard Crick traces what he calls "the prudery of liberals about politics" "to failure to understand the needs of the less respectable elements of society."[72] We recognize something of that attitude here: the boss may be "chief among neighborhood philanthropists," but "judged by the motives that prompt his acts, he is a serpent spreading the slime of political debauchery over whole sections of the community."[73]

"It would require a Swift or a Carlyle to find words to describe . . . the abuse of the representative principle," wrote one progressive.[74] America had Mark Twain. There is no more acerbic commentary than *The Gilded Age*, with its tales of wanton contracts, spoils, and schemes to get rich. "Laissez faire" could not have been more misleading, and Samuel Clemens as Twain observed the "parallel ascent" of corporations in the economy and the Senate and reported on the wild political activism and political favors that built the railroads.[75] The novel was written in 1863 "as the barbecue was getting underway." "The smallest minds and the selfishest souls and the cowardliest hearts that God makes" serve in Congress,[76] Twain wrote, and his account of the election of a Mr. Simon to the legislature was barely fiction:

> Were there no combinations, no railroad jobs, no mining schemes put through in connection with the election?
>
> Not that I know, said Bigler, shaking his head in disgust. In fact it was openly said, that there was no money in the election. It's perfectly unheard of. . . .
>
> It was melancholy, but Mr. Bigler was not a man to be crushed by one misfortune, or to lose his confidence in human nature, on one exhibition of apparent honesty.

Twain allowed that some elected officials were not as ridiculous as venal "parvenus" and snobbish "antiques." His name for quasi-respectable partisans was the "Middle Ground": "These gentlemen were unostentatious people . . . they were people who were beyond reproach, and that was sufficient." When Twain called elected representatives political "aristocracies," he intended a sarcastic slam at electors, because what riled him was the resemblance of representatives to the people, not any notable difference. "By and by the newspapers came out with exposures and called Weed and O'Riley thieves . . . whereupon the people rose as one man (voting repeatedly) and elected the two gentlemen to their proper theatre of action, the New York legislature." "The country is a fool," he wrote.[77]

This was Lincoln Steffens's assessment, too. As often as possible, progressives maintained hope for democracy by characterizing the people as dupes and victims, and he began his work thinking that muckraking would reveal how the people were deceived and betrayed. Steffens's *Autobiography* recounts his personal education into the true dynamics of corruption. "The people are not innocent. That is the only 'news' in all the journalism of these articles." The "shame of the cities" was that people were shameless, without civic pride. "The misgovernment of the American people," he wrote grimly, "is misgovernment by the American people." Steffens was clear that "the exposition of what the people know and stand is the purpose of these articles, not the exposure of corruption." He called his piece on Philadelphia "Corrupt and Contented."[78]

I want to underscore the significance of this observation for progressive antipartyism. Exploitation of public office is worse than organized crime or fraud in business because it is democratic corruption of and by ordinary people. In contrast to the stern requirements of republican virtue, ordinary private morality is the standard for public conduct here. The thing can be readily grasped. "There can be no question that a great many men do deteriorate very much morally when they go to Albany."[79] Concern about corruption in government turns on the assumption that "our public roles carry greater moral responsibilities than our private ones. We expect to behave better as citizens and public officials than as actors in the private sphere."[80] Better, perhaps, but not substantially differently. Moral congruence explains why "modern sin is not superficially repulsive," why there is no vivid villainy, and why "the hurt of the modern sinner passes into the vague mass, the public, and is there lost to view."[81] Few were ready to proclaim with Steffens that bribery is "no ordinary felony, but treason."[82] The state of mind of the average citizen is one of lassitude, Bryce observed.[83] Indeed, for some, disgust is mingled with amusement. The progressive frustration was "that many do not realize the evil who ought to realize it, and be alarmed, and those who do realize it are not sufficiently alarmed."[84] With the benefit of retrospection, we know that over time, popular indignation rises and falls and that progressive moralism is episodic. Like revolutionary spirit, it is difficult to maintain for long.

Progressives look at the party organization of politics and government and see appalling corruption in which large numbers of ordinary people are complicit and few are indignant. This is chastening. Steffens imagined that Americans might be shamed into antipartyism, and in dedicating *The Struggle for Democracy* to the Russian Czar Nicholas he meant to be provocative. He compared American voters to subjects and advised the czar that he could grant suffrage without fear of revolution because people do not know how to use their voting power. He also compared American voters with disenfranchised African Americans: "the honest citizens of Philadelphia have no more rights at the polls than the negroes down South,"[85] but not because they are disenfranchised and powerless; that is the shame.

Partisans

More fateful for democracy than party politicians exploiting office for gain, then, is the corruption of citizens turned partisans. Citizenship is degraded if individuals do not vote as they see fit, if votes are bought or beholden, cast in anticipation of favors or out of personal obligation. By the early twentieth century, revulsion at the sort of people who were partisans—dishonest, craven, ignorant—had gone on for decades and lost any pretense of civility and constraint. Moreover, the dynamic of corruption was perfectly plain. Parties deformed citizens by creating an entrenched system of dependence. Partisans are beholden. "The clientelist politics of the machines, grounded in ethnic loyalty and the exchange of favors for votes, appeared to be a plague, incubated in immigrant neighborhoods and infecting the entire body politic."[86] From Alexander Hamilton on, political scientists "have thought little of the intelligence or knowledge of the voters."[87] Progressive assessments stand out for their identification of partisanship with dependence and for preoccupation with the types vulnerable to degradation.

This statement is typical: "There is a large element which . . . embodies in a special degree this venality, this narrow morality, and this ignorance, *and for that reason*, supplies the Machine with most of its supporters."[88] Indeed, the party boss was accused of deliberately keeping intelligent and informed voters and candidates out of politics.[89] "An ideal machine has for its officers men of marked force, cunning, and unscrupulous, and for its common soldiers men who . . . must be of low intelligence . . . recruited from the lower grades of the foreign population."[90] This was doubtless fueled by the rough experience of some polling places, which comes down to us in the record of cases involving contested votes; one standard employed by courts was whether "a man of ordinary courage" was able to make his way to the voting window.[91] The premise of Taft's lectures *Liberty under Law* was the need to protect democracy from heedless and corrupt voters, criminal elements, "declasses of every kind."[92] "Compelling evidence of their unfitness was the support that poor, foreign-born voters gave to political machines."[93] Overt declarations of the "unfitness" of partisans would not be repeated today, but we can easily imagine hearing that the "subtle and silent . . . tyranny" of party mirrors the despotism of the "selfish appetites of the unredeemed American individualist."[94] Or this: "the 'good people' are herded into parties and stupefied with convictions and a name, Republican or Democrat."[95]

If parties are corrupt and corrupting and voters incorrigible partisans, then democracy should be defended against them, and many reformers "unabashedly welcomed the prospect of weeding such voters out of the electorate."[96] If party machines depend on mass political engagement, if whole constituencies are a "political slum,"[97] the goal is to keep the party base away from the polls.[98] Male suffrage meant "an invasion of peasants . . . an ignorant proletariat" and "a nightmare of domination by Irish, black, and Chinese immigrants."[99] Reformers gave up on initial attempts to repeal universal male suffrage but pursued other measures effectively, among them tightened naturalization laws, registration requirements, poll taxes, and literacy tests. The secret ballot has been described as a de facto literacy test.[100] Progressives took aim at parties indirectly by legally demobilizing segments of the voting population, in effect redefining the electorate. The practical consequences of these obstacles to participation varied depending on how wide the window of voter registration was, the documentation or number of witnesses required to vouch for eligibility, the size of the precinct (so that a change of residence of just a few blocks could require re-registration), and so on. The capacity of parties to adapt varied, too: some organizations had the resources to underwrite large-scale registration drives, to pay voters' poll taxes, and to hire lawyers to appeal contested votes in the courts. Overall, the effect was to disenfranchise millions of eligible voters: poor, immigrants, and African Americans in the South. A historian of "the decline of popular politics" concludes that reformers (variously named "liberals," "educated men," "independents," "Scratchers," "Mugwumps") assisted in the decline.[101]

In addition to restricting suffrage, antiparty progressives looked for sources of regeneration, ways to transform partisans into independent citizens. Some anticipated that the enfranchisement of women in 1920 would purify democracy of partisanship.[102] Feminists were ardent on this score: Frances Gilman described political parties as institutional expressions of "inextricable masculinity" and anticipated that with women's participation "a flourishing democratic government [could] be carried on *without any parties at all.*"[103] Others thought that "the better element" could leaven the electorate and provide active leadership—or could if these men were politically rejuvenated. Educated men have been blamably apathetic (disinterested citizens may be uninterested). Progressives urged them to give up their preoccupation with money and to throw off timorous conservatism for reform. With abolitionists in mind as exemplars, James Russell Lowell wrote hopefully: "They emancipated the negro; and we mean to emancipate the respectable white man."[104]

We catch a whiff of progressive *noblesse oblige,* and the scent of fear. The dark underside of progressivism is rationalization of antipartisanship with ideologies of nativism, racism, and religious bigotry. One strain of progressivism was associated with social darwinism and eugenics. *The New Republic* editorialized in 1915 in favor of the Committee on Provision for the Feeble-Minded, a group that urged public authorities to take on the problem of "freeing the racial stock from the taint of mental deficiency."[105] The buttress of science was not necessary, though; it was quite enough to see party supporters as lackeys, dupes, and unadulterated self-servers and to identify them with foreigners, the poor, and the inassimilable—criminals, idiots, paupers, anarchists. Historians have brought this background of simmering hostility into the foreground, and no longer unanimously praise progressivism: its title is insincere rhetoric, a cloak for elitism. Progressivism has acquired a "sour reputation."[106]

An Apology for "the Organization"

Historian Joel Silbey praised Lincoln as a "middle level party worker, a devoted Whig, and a hesitant convert to the party of freedom" and urged us

> to separate ourselves from a century-long negative vision of parties and politicians as corrupt, impotent, and meaninglessly engaged in loathsome activities in aid of nothing except their own petty concerns. An attitude toward politics that might have been appropriate amid the excesses of partisan zeal and political corruption of the Progressive period, and which has so shaped many of our attitudes since, gravely misunderstands the world in which Lincoln lived and the role that politics and politicians played in it.[107]

Silbey underscored a particular moment of party greatness by conceding that progressive antipathy was warranted. How can we object to the progressive imperative—"breaking allegiance to party"—if independence means "the voters persuaded not the voters bought"?[108] Can partisanship and support for "the Organization" be defended?

For starters, so long as party organizations distribute benefits—to say nothing of necessities such as jobs—party loyalty serves mundane and not especially venal self-interest.[109] Van Buren knew and rebutted the scorn heaped on "a man who pursues politics for a living"; patronage extends a living to ordinary citizens. In a patronage system, partisanship is rational calculation and partisans' interests are reasonable, stable, and not aptly compared with the short-term payoff of a bribe, say. This is not a robust apology, though, and the dominant appreciative note in the rational choice register points to parties as agents of democratization.[110] Parties offset enough of the costs (including the information costs) of participation to alter the "calculus of voting" and make it worthwhile.[111]

Parties made democracy tangible for millions in substantial non-material terms, and that is the important point. The business of parties was not buying votes, simply, but *partisanship*, an enduring political identity. "He's one of the boys, and I'm for him."[112] Put more soberly, "In the arena in which they functioned, commitment, loyalty, devotion, belonging—being a party member—had a meaning beyond the electoral."[113] Its substance was commitment to political participation of a kind that entailed public work and activity,[114] a form of participation we know needs tending and organization, and that did not survive anonymity.

Urban parties brought immigrants and others into electoral politics, then. They created a political identity, a basis of belonging and respect, a "we." To say that "casting a ballot expressed group solidarity and affirmed the shared values of one's community"[115] may sound like sheer sentimentalism. In fact, parties *did* invest localities and states with a sense of place, and the community roots of political parties were real enough: erecting "the shared patterns of values and the social organization of the local community as a fundamental and persistent force in political life."[116] There is an element of emotional truth in seeing parties as membership groups. And partisanship provided the impetus and basis for other voluntary associations: social clubs based on shops and trades (Workingmen's Free Labor Club; Republican Mechanics' Club), the uniformed marching companies, and many more that historians describe.[117]

The democratizing, assimilating business of parties, the political identity and iota of respect, the "protection and kindness" were evident:

> The Machine does not relieve their material wretchedness only, it also
> relieves their moral wretchedness. The leaders of the Machine have

a kindly word for the humblest inhabitants of their district . . . they shed a ray of human brotherhood on the most miserable creatures. They do it automatically, in the way of business, to everybody without distinction; but they none the less appear as ministers of the cult of fraternity in a higher degree than the priests of the churches and the professional philanthropists; they are nearer to the people, they come in friendly contact with them every day, and the people have confidence in them.[118]

Partisanship was not a purely local affair, however, which brings me to another element in this sketch of an apology for "the Organization." Parties brought ambitious men within the political fold and offered advancement. Patronage created a "national network of public sector Horatio Algers."[119] This was Van Buren's guiding social vision. He saw the need for "a great party, built around a New York–Virginia axis, but open to restless young men from all regions, that would harness their energy" to politics.[120] He invented "the party caucus, the nominating convention, the patronage system, the publicity network, and the Democratic Party itself." Ultimately, the party system and spoils "offered a counterbalance to the centrifugal strains on American society," shoring up "the popular support and authority of the federal establishment."[121] The case for parties as a possible means of weaving together a federal government of separated powers is familiar. ("*These* parties were made to work through *this* Constitution."[122]) Less familiar is the argument that parties operated as the "political safeguard" of federalism by making national officials politically dependent on state and local organizations. Parties created a political culture "in which members of the local, state, and national networks are encouraged, indeed expected, to work for the election of candidates at every level." "The whole process is one of elaborate, if diffuse, reciprocity; of mutual dependency."[123] The major parties were and remain instruments of nationalism, and we recognize the sheer silliness of claiming that the current ideology of the Republican Party, its push for privatization, "does not confidently presume the existence of a national state."[124]

Independents

Political participation is an abstraction apart from specific institutional forms and modes of opposition. Partisanship is one form of participation.[125] This was apparent to antiparty critics, and aversion to partisanship had a life of its own in progressive antipartyism. "Faith in the independent voter was thus closely linked to an opposition of intellectuals to political machines—and, indeed, to parties as such. . . . Since the thoughtless ones were the supporters of the corrupt party machines, then almost by definition the thinking members of society had to become independent."[126] Progressives invented "independent" as a political identity. Once a reference to social condition and general virtue, independence came to refer to political status. *Dependence* is an effect of parties, and partisanship *just is* political dependence. Independence is captured not by nonpartisanship but by antipartisanship. I return to this theme and argue for the "moral distinctiveness of party ID" in chapter 7.

Progressives imagined that "independence is the great purifying agency of politics." They urged: "No person ought to sustain a party or a representative of a party when either of them, as he has reason to believe, will advocate any positively wrong measure."[127] This banal proposition (for nuance think of Mill's discussion of compromise) is meaningful only if partisanship is represented as blind and inertial, if partisans do not exercise judgment of the rightness and wrongness of *any* man or measure. That was precisely the antiparty, antipartisan charge. They looked ahead to a fatal blow to party machines from "a body of independent men pledged to vote for honest candidates irrespective of party."[128] Ostrogorski was encouraged that "public morality has advanced . . . [and] public opinion is beginning to extricate itself from the narrow and deadly groove of parties."[129]

> Our leaders, partly for convenience and partly to keep down expenses, divide us into what they call parties. To these parties they give attractive names like "Republican" and "Democratic." . . . But really both of them represent graft and grafters. . . . Just now we are growing tired of

this sentiment . . . and an "independent vote" is disturbing our political situation.

"The good citizen," Steffens wrote in a temporary, uncharacteristic lapse into hopefulness, "is only just learning . . . to vote independently."[130]

Two lines of argument intermingled in progressive attempts to pry voters away from parties. Not surprisingly, they are inversions of the elements of my "apology" for the Organization. One progressive tack was to insist that voters' real interests would be served by "clean government." In sheer monetary terms, graft and favors are costly. Party government is inefficient. ("Redesigning government" to get rid of fraud and waste and appeals to citizens as taxpayers and recipients of services is nothing new.) If the people would create a steady demand for good government, then "political merchants" would supply it.[131] The other line of argument was a straightforwardly moralistic attack on partisan political identity. Partisanship is shameful degradation, and progressives elevated independence not just as political behavior but as an alternative political identity. Interestingly, the same pair of arguments marked progressive approaches to business. "If the business community could be brought to realize that peace with political buccaneers at their own price is not only bad politics but bad business, the whole system of virtual blackmail would soon pass out of existence."[132] Alongside this case against the expense of corruption, progressives held up the image of an exemplary identity: "Instead of telling business men not to be greedy, we should tell them to be industrial statesmen, applied scientists, and members of a craft."[133]

Teddy Roosevelt was typical in the way he moved back and forth between appeals to people's interest and their pride:

A thoroughly pure, upright, and capable administration of the affairs of New York City results in a very appreciable increase of comfort to each citizen. We should have better systems of transportation; we should have cleaner streets, better sewers, and the like. . . . [But] I do not think it is always worth while to show that this will always be the case. The citizen should be appealed to primarily on the ground that it is his plain duty.

Roosevelt ended on a characteristically aggressive note: if a citizen wishes to deserve the name of freeman, he must prove himself. Otherwise he is only "fit to live under a government where he will be plundered and bullied because he deserves to be plundered and bullied on account of his selfish timidity and short-sightedness."[134]

"Independence" was something more robust than nonpartisanship; it was antipartanship. It had another strong resonance as well. The independent demands to be "recognized as a unique individual who could express herself significantly in public and in private."[135] Detached from machines and from collective labels, political independence was supposed to express *individuality,* not party, policy, or ideology, "a complete individual wholly divorced from particular economic as well as class interests."[136] John Dewey famously projected "the emancipation of personal capacities . . . securing to each individual an effective right to count in the order and movement of society as a whole."[137] The best illustration of the temperamental mix of expressive individualism and idealized political participation is Mary Parker Follett's *The New State.* Her ferocious attack on parties and partisanship adds this individualistic note to the standard fare: "The domination of the party gives no real opportunity to the individual: originality is crushed; the aim of all party organization is to turn out a well-running voting machine. The party is not interested in men but in voters—an entirely different matter." The basic weakness of parties, she continues, "is that the individual gets his significance only through majorities." "Democracy has one task only," she enthuses, "to free the creative spirit of man." "The state must be no external authority which restrains and regulates me, but it must be myself, acting as the state in the smallest detail."[138] Expressive individualism is not quite romanticism—alienation from a world that submerges the individual in impersonal arrangements—but it comes close.

There is reason to question whether independence is compatible with any regular, disciplined, collective activity. Independence raises questions about the shape of democratic participation altogether: partisanship is anathema, but is organized Independence a contradiction? Progressives attempting to organize civic groups or a progressive party often despaired that Independents "recoil from the effort, and aim at creating a sentiment."[139] In chapter 6 I show that progressive cures are at the center of contemporary democratic theory's own proposals for reform. The antiparty moves I detail below—a party of Independents, reforming and circumventing parties, and abolition of parties—are alive today. Even Follett's "group organization as the solution of popular government" makes an appearance.

Voluntary Association and a Party of Independents

"The so-called evils of democracy—favoritism, bribery, graft, boss-ism—are evils of our lack of democracy, of our party system and of the abuses that system has brought," Follett wrote. To her eyes none of the familiar progressive proposals for direct primaries or initiative and referenda, to which I turn shortly, had much merit; the political machines know how to exploit them all. A new method is necessary: the association of citizens in nonpartisan groups for "the produc-tion of common ideas and a collective purpose." Real democracy is not social policies created for the people but policies created by the people, based on "that fundamental intermingling with others which is democracy."[140]

Follett's is the most eloquent voice, but not a lone one, in the exhor-tation to voluntary association. The progressive's preferred combina-tion is voluntary associations of "citizens," "taxpayers," "consumers," and "reformers." These groups would act as a counterweight to "in-visible government," meaning party machines and big business that operate behind "ostensible government."[141] The Civic Federation or its replacement, the Municipal Voters' League, or Good Government Clubs were intended to be "persistently, consistently, and impartially anti-bad-city-government, and nothing else."[142] Progressives pros-elytized for nonpartisan vigilance committees, investigative commit-tees, law enforcement societies, people's lobbies, and voters' leagues, often based on Christian principles.[143] The citizens' leagues formed sub-committees: Garbage Disposal, Improvement of the Waterfront, Civil Service, Small Parks, Investigation of Payrolls. This is volun-tary association spurred by self-selected, unauthorized organizers.[144]

Like Tocqueville before him, Bryce was struck by voluntarism in America: "Where the object is to promote some particular cause, associations are formed and federated to one another, funds are collected, the press is set to work, lectures are delivered . . . deputations proceed to Washington or to the State capital, and lay siege to individual legislators."[145] Sympathetic historians give this explosion of voluntary association their honorific designation: a "movement,"[146] and sympathetic political scientists contrast these associations favorably with professionally run, nonparticipatory advocacy groups today. (Though some observers at the time described them as committees run top-down by a small group of professionals.[147])

This feature of progressive antipartyism, like many others, had an effect on political life beyond what was intended. It did result in associational forms to challenge and circumvent parties. But where progressives had in mind citizen lobbies and small business groups formed in opposition to large combinations, the result was the activation of interest group politics *tout court*.[148] Pressure groups—interest groups, special interest groups, advocacy groups, self-styled public interest groups—turned out to be protean. The favor showered on voluntary association gave them moral imprimatur, and progressives provided what amounted to political instruction in direct channels to government. Voluntary association for reformist ends ushered in the wholesale practice of lobbying groups seeking access and pressing their demands on legislators and the executive, and raised expectations that government officials would be responsive to organized advocacy. As Schattschneider argued, voluntarism introduced organizations to influence government outcomes without the need to create a general opinion in favor of the action. Some groups did (and do still) aim at educating and drawing on public opinion, but many neither have the will nor feel the need to persuade a majority; they do not test their strength in an election; they can make "vast, unverifiable claims" as to their influence, the size and resolution and unanimity of membership.[149] "The result was a fairly drastic transformation of the rules of political participation: who could compete, the kinds of resources required, and the rewards of participation all changed."[150] The ambition, common to a host of progressive reforms and correctives, is to loosen the identification of participation with voting, elections, and parties. I return to echoes of this, too, in the context of contemporary antipartyism in chapter 6.

Antiparty reformers organized outside electoral politics in voluntary associations, then and now. But not all progressives were sanguine that voluntary association was an effective circumvention or counter to parties. So they also prescribed electoral strategies: independent lists of nominations, "citizens' tickets." They advocated "scratching" the name of party nominees from ballots.[151] Fusion efforts and "entangling alliances" were tried, too. Roosevelt started the City Reform Club in 1882 to advance elected officials "irrespective of party."[152] The "Citizens' Union" in New York appealed directly to voters in 1894 with a platform proclaiming the principle of nonpartisanship and a purely municipal program. (It failed to elect its candidate for mayor.)

Progressives also urged "bolting." This political maneuver had already been tried at the local or county level, where party factions would nominate their own candidates for some offices. As a progressive strategy bolting was something else: sheer punishment of parties, hopefully on a massive scale. This was "a new Revolutionary War against the party system"; scratching ballots was like minutemen fighting from behind walls and trees.[153] Progressives prescribed regular defection—punishing the "ins" by voting in the "outs" or leaving parties to the politicians and bolting altogether. Burke's regulated rivalry—"The Parties who are Out, are always a Curb, and a Bridle to those which are In, and the Parties which are In, are always a Terror and a Stirrer up to Vigilance in those which are Out"—was not automatic.[154] The benefits of rivalry needed a boost. "Our old habit of turning out the party in power and electing the other party, which was good enough in national elections, would not do in the exceptionally bad city of New York."[155] Nor would it do in other places if one set of grafters was like another. There were high hopes: Henry Adams viewed Independents as "the party of the centre" that would use defection to bend parties to its will: "Let it be understood that he, with his friends, has once bolted . . . and he will have his full share of influence in the party councils."[156]

Maintaining a "steady war against the professionals" by means of "organized independency" proved difficult and often produced little more than moral pandering to Independents by party regulars. Steffens was blunt: "the Civic Federation, a respectable but inefficient universal reforming association, met without plans in 1895."[157] In Ostrogorski's assessment,

> the heroic character of these efforts soon wore out the zeal of the Reformers, and filled them with a conceit which made them complacently celebrate a triumph on the occasion of the slightest success. To checkmate the Machine, or at all events to cope with it, it was necessary to display a less heroic, but more methodical and more steady, activity.[158]

The refusal to be sufficiently political resulted naturally enough in political impotence. Roosevelt was blunt, too: "It has been wisely said that while martyrdom is often right for the individual, what society needs is victory."[159]

Alert progressives saw the problem: Independents are not partisans. They will not cohere. Complaints about the major parties come mainly "from outsiders, and largely from the men of intellectual cultivation and comparatively high social standing," and very few of these men take an active part in politics, however interested they may be in public affairs. In 1914 Roosevelt wrote to William Allen White that progressives could keep "only the men of high principle and good reasoning power and the cranks. The men in between left us."[160] Independence was an excuse for self-indulgence and inconstancy. Joint action required sacrificing something of one's own opinions— compromise. Disinterestedness and honesty are not enough. Uncovering corruption is not enough. Citing Bunyan's *Pilgrim's Progress*, Roosevelt warned that "the man with the muckrake could look no way but downward . . . to rake to himself the filth of the floor."[161]

> The mass of our good citizens, even after the victories which they had assisted in winning, understood nothing about how they were won. Many of them actually objected to organizing, apparently having a confused idea that we could always win by what one of their number

called a "spontaneous uprising." . . . [I]t may be accepted as a fact, however unpleasant, that if steady work and much attention to detail are required, ordinary citizens, to whom participation in politics is merely a disagreeable duty, will always be beaten by the organized army of politicians to whom it is both duty, business, and pleasure.[162]

The contrast between partisans and the antiparty enthusiasts of citizens' leagues and "bolting" was sharp, then. Voluntarism could be a liability if members feel free to shift involvements and are likely to do so.[163] One progressive noted that "the unity of malcontents is precarious"; the programs proposed are often "an odd mosaic of individual fads"; specific reforms become a "hobby." "Reformers are primarily protestants, and it is the nature of protestants to be insubordinate."[164] Party machines, on the other hand, produced a cadre of people who understood the techniques of government.[165] Ostrogorski reflected, "The study of politics is not the study of the 'Politics' of Aristotle, nor even that of Columbia College" but of the machinery of party organization. Party organizers were "great managers and crack wire-pullers."[166] Reform needed a leader who was "a first-class executive mind and a natural manager of men."[167] Croly hoped that a strong, independent executive would function as a boss who could destroy the "sham Bosses."[168] If progressivism is to be more than a crusade, reformers had to combine as a party against

the unholy alliance between corrupt business and corrupt politics . . . . The deliberate betrayal of this trust by the Republican party, the fatal incapacity of the Democratic party . . . have compelled the people to forge a new instrument of government through which to give effect to their will in laws and institutions. The new party offers itself as the instrument of the people to sweep away old abuses, to build a new and nobler commonwealth.[169]

Dependably, then, some element of antiparty progressives will raise the prospect of a new party. The most histrionic advocate was Lincoln Steffens. He imagined a party on the model of the Bolsheviks:

We cannot do [the job] as Upton Sinclair proposes. We cannot any of us go out as "one good man for governor" and do it individually. We must do it as the American Communist Party, taught, fortunately, by the Russian Pioneers, proposes to do it, by the building of a trained, highly disciplined party, all of whose members—all—want at any cost—to do the same one, agreed-upon, fundamental thing.[170]

To Steffens, Lenin "expressed the patience, determination, and wisdom, practical and ideal, of the small minority which won finally in October." In short: "They had a dictator and the dictator had a plan." Steffens described La Follette wishfully in these terms; "he was a dictator, dictating democracy."[171] The Bolsheviks were a bizarre template for an association of Independents. Steffens's appeal is startling. It is a demonstration of progressivism on the verge of slipping into romanticism.

The claims made by advocates of reform parties (the "Liberal Republican" selection of Horace Greeley to oppose the re-election of Republican President Grant generally counts as the first experiment) are dependably similar. We hear them repeated today. First, "the old parties are husks, with no real soul within either,"[172] so that "it made no difference which side won, the people lost."[173] Next, new Independents, who had bolted from parties, present their reform party as unique: "composed altogether of men who had already had the self-discipline of giving up party for the sake of principle."[174] Finally, the party of Independents professes to represent only universal, civic interests. The 1912 Progressive Party Platform is typically grandiose: "the new party offers itself as the instrument of the people to sweep away old abuses, to build a new and nobler commonwealth."[175]

This is the unmistakable constant in antiparty partisanship. The party of Independents casts itself as the voice of the public interest, unwilling to organize on the basis of divisive interests. Every reform party could authentically adopt the People's Party declaration: "while our organization is political it can not be partisan or sectional in its action."[176] The professions are always the same: the party represents "the entire State"; it aims at the equal advantage of all sections and classes;[177] it comprises Independents who vote not for party or men but for the city, and the State, and the nation.[178] "Vote for the United States, is my cry, neither for the best party nor for the best man."[179]

It would be a mistake to see a party of Independents as a retreat from antipartyism. A party of progressives is partisan only because at present good government is a sectarian goal. It is needed because the popular will is not only thwarted but tainted. Progressive antipartyism arose initially in the context of "small" parties devoted to parceling out offices and tangible goods and favors, but it is no less opposed to oppositional parties rooted in social cleavages or ideology. We do not find many progressives, even today, expressing the thought that "the ideal political system should consist of a conservative party modeled on the British Tories under Benjamin Disraeli, and a liberal one based on the social democratic idea brought to fruition in postwar Europe."[180] Progressivism is rightly associated with sincerity rather than ideology.[181] "Clean government" is not a permanent organizing principle, however. The short-lived Reform Party of the late 1990s, the epitome of a progressive party, is rightly described as a reaction rather than a sustained effort to build a nationwide organization capable of governing. The judgment of regular partisans is that these candidates "are spoilers, and what they try to spoil is the possibility of majority government." (Hence the accusation against Ralph Nader: "what he views as an evil system of politics takes priority over his outrage at the unjust policies of either of the two dominant parties."[182]) Veblen surveyed the field and concluded that progressivism was "well-meaning but unmeaning."[183] It did have one lasting meaning, however. Progressivism "narrowed the cultural authority of partisanship."[184] It created a political identity: the Independent as antipartisan.

Party Reform and Circumvention

This dispiriting account of a party of Independents should not eclipse how much *has* been done by antiparty reformers. Like Whig history in Britain, the progressive account of political reform is standard national fare in the United States, and historians note the "blaze" of political innovation begun and completed during the first fifteen years of the twentieth century.[185] Except for the Seventeenth Amendment designed to weaken state parties by providing for direct election of U.S. senators, a one-time constitutional change, progressive reforms have live, contemporary counterparts. True, bribery, bossism, patronage, and fraud —the original context of progressive antipartyism—are relative rarities today.[186] After the 2000 presidential election "machine politics" refers to the technology used to cast and tabulate votes, not Huey Long. Coalitions of local and state organizations no longer control national presidential nominations. (Though for some scholars this remains the touchstone, and the "traditional party organization" is a benchmark for assessing whether contemporary parties are strong or weak.[187]) Absent graft and spoils, and loosed from the mobilization of partisans by "the Organization," still, American political life is punctuated by an indignant public mood. The signature progressive measures then and now aim at weakening or circumventing parties or, more boldly, at abolitionism. Behind these reforms, then and now, is the conviction that "Party organization and Party machinery are not needed to maintain a republican form of government."[188]

The several sets of progressive reforms are well known, and I survey them only briefly, through the lens of antipartyism. President Garfield's assassination in 1881 gave one reform a dramatic leg up. The assassin was a disappointed office seeker who wrote, "The men that did the business last fall are the ones to be remembered."[189] Civil service reform, first at the federal and then the state level, was designed to starve the machine. "The boss lives by bad administration."[190] "Men of a trashy sort . . . fill our councils"; officials are ignorant, untrained, inefficient, and as always corrupt.[191] Patronage discouraged the most qualified from public office, and rotation was not conducive to competence, much less expertise. Meritocracy and "the purely technical irrefragable needs of administration"[192] required insulation from the "guillotine of the party." "We had bipartisan boards and they had either winked at the corrupt practices of the Democrats or divided the graft. We are now for non-partisan boards, mayors, and a civil service reform modeled upon the British permanent officials."[193] The aim was to suppress opportunities for party corruption. The corollary was to promote good government. Opposition to machines and corruption is separable from opposition to parties per se, of course, but for progressives they were so intertwined as to be indistinguishable: "The Merit System . . . will help to abolish partisanship."[194] It did not. But merit exams and professionalization of career public service have altered the types (and class) of people in government, and civil service reform has been extended to promotion and firing as well as hiring and now encompasses all but the top policy-making positions.

Circumscribing patronage has had consequences for parties. Still, as some politically perspicacious progressives knew well, "the offices that must be taken 'out of politics' are the offices at the head."[195] A second set of reforms sought to circumvent and ultimately undermine parties by mandating nonpartisan at-large local elections.[196] Better yet, the number of elected officials could be reduced altogether, replacing mayors and ward-based aldermen with city management structured on a corporate model, or by government by commission, or by deliberately creating strong executives, counterparts to bosses—"municipal dictators."[197] The whole idea behind reducing the number of elective offices was to eliminate partisan politics at least from city business: "whoever heard of a Republican playground, a Democratic swimming bath"?[198] The city was "the hope of democracy," as it is for some progressives today.[199] Home rule would divorce local affairs from the sordid affairs of the state and the nation. "Divorce" was a persistent theme: the city could be "emancipated from the tyranny of the national and State political parties, and from that of the Legislature—the tool of the party."[200] The mix of ideology, or perhaps just rhetoric, in support of municipal reform is worth noting. "Home rule would create a city republic, a new sort of sovereignty like unto those of Athens, Rome, and the medieval Italian cities" was one formulation.[201] And, in decidedly unrepublican terms, city government "is in the region of business . . . and must be conducted on business methods."[202] A third, domestic formulation has it that municipal administration is "housekeeping," and there, at the "back of the settlement, the small park, the kindergarten, the schools, and the libraries," the salutary influence of women is strongest.[203]

Beginning in the 1880s, progressives produced a third set of reforms: regulation of elections. State by state, decentralized elections organized by parties were remade into governmental functions. Among the key measures were state mandated time of elections, rules for party conventions, prohibition of fusion parties,[204] campaign finance laws, and legally mandated changes in the internal organization of parties, including state party committees with set duties and terms ("to permit the voters to construct the organization from the bottom upward, instead of permitting leaders to construct it from the top downwards"[205]). Perhaps most important were reforms that replaced the partisan ballot: the secret ballot, state control of ballot access, and state control of the structure of the ballot. This was considered vital because the party ticket was "a virtual currency of corruption."[206]

I said progressive reformers produced these changes. Recent historical work shows that party regulars in many states went along with the Australian ballot. They had an interest in disassociating themselves from vote fraud and intimidation, for one thing, and legal reform did that neatly, in a way that leaders of decentralized parties would have found difficult to do on their own. The frequency of elections also made it difficult and expensive to produce ballots for every race; transferring the business to government relieved parties of this burden. Above all, the Australian ballot gave a privileged place to the two major parties in nominating candidates; they had automatic places whereas minor parties had to run petition drives and file nominating papers. The ballot became a "government-subsidized forum that accords selective benefits to major parties."[207] This was not a logical necessity, of course; it was the result of the power of parties on the one hand, and reformers' fears of ballot confusion, on the other, a subject I discuss in more detail in chapter 6.[208]

All three sets of measures—civil service reform, nonpartisan municipal elections and management-style city government, and state-run elections—aimed at cutting off party sustenance, limiting decisions reached via partisan elections, severing the electorate from parties, and regulating parties. But the grimmest antiparty types saw them all as panaceas, patches, mere contrivances. Like the Australian ballot (disparaged as "an attempt to protect the individual citizen from influence . . . to put the citizen himself in a box"[209]), they were disproportionate to the massive perversion of democracy by parties. Conventional wisdom "held that the parties' main source of strength lay in patronage and material control of elections," but the sharpest critics argued that "real party power lay in political control of nominations and elections."[210] That required a different approach.

"The Most Radical Party Reform in American History"

American parties exist "practically for the sake of filling certain offices."[211] This is overstatement, of course; parties serve other purposes. Still, there is truth to the assertion that "he who can make the nominations is the owner of the party." As an opinion of the Oregon Supreme Court put it, "once the stream is polluted at its source, access to its waters, however free, will not serve to purify it."[212] The specific mechanism for nomination (by caucus, delegate convention, mass meeting, or cabal) is less important than whether it is binding, that is, whether all other candidates within the party are denied support, and the party is able to concentrate its strength behind the nominee.[213] So progressives turned their attention to nominations. Bryce recognized that selection of party candidates was the "mainspring of the machine." But when he looked at methods used in other countries he judged designation by the party organization a comparatively "bottom up" process and a mark of popular sovereignty. To antiparty progressives, however, the thing looked very different. The choice of candidates was not "the genius of democratic institutions" but its perversion. Party control of nominations was "a travesty of popular choice." Power was in the hands of professionals who packed meetings and prearranged outcomes. Albert Stickney was the most adamant: "What he [the voter] has is the right of desertion. He has, and can have, under our present system of government, no substantial voice in the selection of his generals. . . . [W]hichever army the citizen may join, or abandon, his right of desertion gives him no substantial control of either men or measures."[214] Bryce did not back down from his judgment that the process was, relatively speaking, democratic and worked. Elective offices are so numerous; conventions come so often that ordinary citizens cannot watch them;

and minor offices are so unattractive that able men do not stand for them. He was right to fasten on the importance of recruitment and nomination by parties and to attempt a thoughtful defense.

In any case, we arrive at progressive attempts to attenuate party control of nominations and elections. The most important was to replace extra-legal "backroom" party caucuses (often a preliminary step that selected delegates to party conventions) with legally mandated direct state primaries in the "open air." Reformers overthrew processes that had not been subject to fixed party rules, much less law, and "turned a process that, unquestionably, had been that of a private association into something resembling a public election."[215] As we would expect, the direct primary was advocated in antiparty terms. "The people have no more control over the selection of the man who is to be President than the subjects of kings have over the birth of the child who is to be their ruler."[216] The direct primary "takes away the power of the party leader or boss and places responsibility for control upon the individual."[217]

"Responsibility for control upon the individual" begs the question. For reformers were divided about who exactly they hoped would gain influence as a result. For some, the purpose of the direct primary was simply to increase popular participation. Caucuses could be more easily manipulated than elections and deterred participation; primary elections would encourage it. The thought was: more voters, hopefully more Independents, ergo more influence on candidate selection. So antiparty progressives pushed specifically for nonpartisan or blanket primaries, which allow voters to choose, office by office, in which party's primary they wish to vote. They pushed for "free nomination" by petition put forward by any group of citizens without reference to parties. For other reformers, as we have seen, the aim was nominations that were selective, so long as the right sort of people were doing the selection. Both maximum participation and selective participation were compatible with doing away with nomination as the prerogative of a closed political organization and with producing candidates who owe as little as possible to party. Progressives continue to hope with Croly that "by popularizing the mechanism of partisan government the state has thrust a sword into the vitals of its former master."[218]

Party regulars had various reasons for resisting these reforms, but they also had reasons not to resist, and in some states the introduction of primary elections was consensual, approved by state legislators. Regulars could favor increased participation in candidate selection provided the voters were partisans. They could support closed primaries.[219] The effect of closed primary elections was most dramatic in the South, where the monopoly of the Democratic Party effectively eliminated black political competition.[220] The effect of direct primaries in other areas was more gradual and turned in part on the emerging reality that a "closed primary" restricted to party adherents was not practicable given the informal and diffuse nature of party "membership" and the difficulty of ascertaining party loyalty. Today, still, the preferred form of primary—closed, open, blanket—is a strategic question for both party leaders and contemporary antiparty progressives and I look at ongoing battles over the primary form in chapter 6.

The direct primary may have been the most radical of party reforms in the course of American history, as Austin Ranney claims, but its main impact came later, on presidential races. It did not fulfill progressive expectations as a force against party selection of candidates.[221] Writing in 1922, Taft anticipated the failings of primary election reform. He argued that the adoption of "purer" democracy has not been a success as measured by low turnout, the absence of discussion, the filtering of fit candidates by party leadership, and the ability of small factions within a party to hijack a primary election. Doing away with caucuses and conventions "has not destroyed, it has strengthened the control of the machine; but it has taken from it an obligation of responsibility."[222] This point was reiterated by party reformers in the 1960s. In *Farewell to Reform*, journalist John Chamberlain concurred:

> The pet political solutions of the Progressives, designed to make government more responsible to the will of the electorate, have notoriously been weak reeds.... Direct primaries have proved not even a palliative.... [N]ominations are made by local nuclei of party workers who know what they want. The direct primary ... creates the illusion,

that an inert "people," spasmodically led, can be aroused to holding the machine politician in line by the threat that they may turn on him at the primary polls. The result is . . . the people are let down. [223]

For many antiparty thinkers, the problem runs deeper than ballot and electoral reforms, then. As long as public officials are selected by elections, and as long as there are frequent elections and large constituencies so that the work is "so vast, so regular, and has so large prizes," parties will run them[224] and candidates will continue to be partisans. The compulsion to carry the next election and with it the fate of their political lives and fortunes pressures representatives to serve the party's "professional election brokers." This is a simplified view, that exaggerates party "brokers." But it too is a commonplace today.

Abolishing Parties: Direct and Deliberative Democracy

A final set of progressive reforms was at the opposite pole from professional civil service and city management: self-government. There is no contradiction between faith in expertise, on the one hand, and direct democracy, on the other, and nothing surprising about progressive cycling—pushing democracy back on the people and then snatching it safely away to the expert.[225] Both are antiparty. Both rest on the assumption that there is one objectively discernible public interest that can be identified and promoted by disinterested public servants and an untainted, nonpartisan popular will.

Famously, progressives championed mechanisms of direct democracy: the recall, the periodic attempts to write term-limit proposals into law, and, most important, the popular initiative and referendum. The "citizens' initiative" was "the key to all progress. It will open the door to all other reforms." It allows Independents to affect the political agenda directly, by bringing measures to the ballot for a vote. "The referendal voting is largely *independent* of party ties or the vote on men."[226] This was a serious onslaught not just against parties, of course, but also against representative democracy. Referenda

would address the peril of "unguarded representation." In an elaborate metaphor:

> Direct Legislation will give the people the power of voluntary move-
> ment; it will bring the public mind into connection with the motor
> muscles of the body politic; it will gear the power of public sentiment
> directly and effectively to the machinery of legislation, with no slip-
> ping belts, switched off currents, or broken circuits.[227]

The not-very-well formulated idea of the popular will takes its
meaning in progressive thought from unorganized nonpartisan decision making. Direct democracy emancipates the people, who are
both "more wisely conservative as well as more wisely progressive"
than the ordinary congress. An additional expectation for direct democracy was that "the ignorant voter and the bigoted partisan who
constitute the curse of the ballot . . . are the very ones who ordinarily care least about a referendum vote." That is, they will not turn
out. The initiative will be in the hands of Independents. Labeled the
"Swiss principle," direct legislation was lauded as "the rising tide of
thought."[228] The Swiss pointed the way to removing "the curse of
partisanship."[229] We see here the height of progressive ambition: to
circumvent representative government and party politics altogether.
The favorite terms for grasping it were evolutionary: in this progressive universal history, parties were a temporary moment in the slow
evolution from despotism to democracy and will ultimately be dis-
pensed with.

As was the case with proposals for voluntary associations of Independents advocating for "clean government," efficacy proved doubtful
and some progressives had second thoughts about placing confidence
in unorganized, popular participation. An uninfluenced, disorganized, uncorrupted vote is inconceivable. One doubter acknowledged that representation and direct legislation merely use different
machinery to touch the pockets or prejudices of some element in the
community, and predicted that the organized portion will trounce
the unaffiliated citizen.[230] Recent experience with referenda and
initiatives confirms this suspicion. In the decades since California's

1978 Proposition 13 capped property taxes, referenda have been used to circumvent elected representatives from both parties on anti-immigrant legislation, term limits, taxes, and more. Studies show that initiatives and referenda are organized and funded by interest groups or affluent political entrepreneurs, by parties (the recall petition promoted by conservative Republicans against the Democratic governor of California in 2003 is an egregious instance), or by factions within parties, often under cover of so-called citizens' groups created for the purpose. A "referenda industry" has grown up, employing professional petition collectors and publicists to do the work of mobilizing voters. Moreover, the complexity of legislative initiatives makes the beneficiaries hard to identify and the likely impact difficult to understand. These are not spontaneous popular efforts, but they do lack party labels to cue voters. In short, direct democracy has many of the faults of partisan politics without the institutional constraints. I will show that contemporary political theorists have tried to address some of the lessons of these false hopes and false starts. In their proposal for "Deliberation Day," for example, Bruce Ackerman and James Fishkin invoke the progressive citizens' initiative but criticize it for its legal formalism, its confidence in civic spontaneity, and its unconcern for political education. "We are proposing something more far-reaching: not a new legal form but a new social context."[231]

There was one move left for antiparty progressives: what I call "party abolitionism." To get rid of parties it was necessary to give up the entire system of tenure by election. In a reversal of proposals for term limits and recall, abolitionists argued that increasing the occasions for stricter popular control would only multiply opportunities for party organization. Instead, Albert Stickney advocated counterintuitively for *unlimited* terms of office. A review of Stickney's "The True Republic" in *The Nation* in 1879 agreed that "the perversion of party has, as every one knows, reached the dimensions of a plague," with offices as prizes for party success at the polls. The reviewer acknowledges that "the changes Mr. Stickney suggests will probably be considered startling," but they would make elections rare and put an end to electioneering![232] In Stickney's scheme, the president would be elected through a series of caucuses and would serve indefinitely, with popular power of removal at all times. (This was not impeachment, but removal for failure to serve satisfactorily in any respect.) Legislators, too, would remain in office during good behavior, and recall would be the prerogative of fellow members of the legislature. Popular elections would take place only to fill vacancies. The great democratic power of calling elections would be returned to the people from the two- and four-year cycles constitutionally prescribed. Vacancies would be rare, and elections few. As important, filling offices would take the novel form of nonpartisan assemblies modeled after the Constitutional Convention. The name "convention" has been hijacked by parties to describe meetings of party delegates, Stickney objected, and it should be restored to designate gatherings of citizens.[233] Local assemblies of 500 people would consider policy questions and select a representative, who would in turn gather with other representatives to select representatives for higher offices, and so on. The result would be the fittest men, chosen for their expertise and public devotion rather than party connections.[234] Stickney's proposal for a "true republic" is reminiscent in some respects of Condorcet's citizens' assemblies in his Constitutional Plan; I mention this to indicate that antiparty progressives were not reluctant to propose radical constitutional change. "We Americans are, of all things a nation of 'political theorizers,'"[235] Stickney wrote. Constitutional revision of "the old machinery of 1787" would be necessary.

A principal motivation for election by popular convention was the desirability of public meeting and deliberation, and in this respect too, as I will show, the resonance to contemporary democratic theory is resounding. "Little thought has been given, in our political past, to the question how a people is to think—as a people—to form and utter a judgment—as a people . . . as regards selection of governors," Stickney observed.[236] In general elections "the citizen is restricted to the right to utter his own separate individual present preference between two or more special men or measures proposed beforehand by single men or single factions. The very essence of democratic free thought is wanting." Perennial election campaigns are not "processes of thought"; they are contests among persons for places.[237] As expected, parties are charged with responsibility for the absence of deliberation. Parties must respond to a multitude of impulses, must compromise to secure majority support, and must reward friends and defeat enemies.[238] Parties obstruct deliberation because, in order to divide the electorate, they select some "issue," some question of a moral or sentimental aspect, to serve as a battle-cry. Above all, Stickney argued, parties obstruct deliberation because separate and antagonistic organizations cannot possibly represent the division of judgment on all public questions. And even if citizens could be divided that way, "public interests demand, not that these two classes of individuals . . . should be separated into two hostile political camps, but that they should be brought together into one common organization, in order that they may be led to co-operate, to confer, and agree—as to the course that is most wise, which is presumably not an extreme view of either class, but a mean between the two extremes."[239] The condition for independence is not just non-partisanship, then, but an end to the system of elections altogether, to be replaced by deliberative "conventions."[240]

We recognize party abolitionist arguments as precursors of contemporary theories of deliberative democracy with their proposals for "deliberative opinion polls," a "minipopulus," neighborhood assemblies, "e-democracy." Some democratic theorists today are similarly intransigent about the incompatibility between deliberation and competitive elections under the aegis of parties. "Our central task," write the authors of "Deliberation Day," "is to convince you that the existing system is broke. Without giving ordinary citizens new tools to challenge sound-bite politics, we confront a clear and present danger."[241] We hear echoes of progressive antipartyism in one political scientist's profession: "Everything about democracy is experimental, and after two hundred years we are still not able to say that the experiment has passed the test."[242]

The Logic of Progressive Antipartyism

Herbert Croly spoke of antiparty reforms such as the initiative and direct primary as "institutionalizing a mood," a mood he described as defensive, rigidly self-protective. Direct democracy and good government by experts were promoted as necessities "to prevent the people from being betrayed—from being imposed upon." "To indoctrinate and organize one's life chiefly for the purpose of avoiding betrayal is to invite sterility and disintegration,"[243] Croly objected. We understand why, when it comes to parties, dour defensiveness edges out optimism, and why hope is brittle. Progressive antipartyism rests on a moral certainty: "there is no doubt that there is at present deep discontent with the actual working of our political institutions."[244] And as I have shown, the blame may settle on the people themselves. The Britisher Bryce brought readers "face to face with the cardinal problem of American politics": "Where political life is all-pervading, can practical politics be on a lower level than public opinion?"[245] Steffens's puzzle expresses this perfectly: "What was the matter? . . . I asked that question many a time, without finding or framing an answer to it. . . . What was this system? . . . [W]e knew the answer, but we didn't want to face it—not clearly."[246] Indignation and accusation, agitated stirring, rebuking and proposing reforms reflect the back and forth between shaming citizens and righteous self-defense against a corrupt and corrupting system.

I do not mean to detract from constructive progressive reforms in saying that the logic of progressive antipartyism is a psychological logic.[247] The "steps" of this logic are not sequential, obviously; progressive antipartyism is a halting alternation between blaming the people or the parties, between enthusiasm and despair of specific reforms. Still, by reconstructing "steps" in the psychological logic of antipartyism, the elements of "post-party depression" I have discussed here come into focus.

First, progressive antipartyism opposes corrupt parties and corrupted partisans. There is enthusiasm for reform. The "honest politician" is always to be hoped for, but progressivism understands that corruption is institutional as well as personal.[248] So uplift is a matter of eliminating opportunities for corruption—sensible reforms of the mechanics of elections and ballots, municipal government, campaign finance laws, and so on. Progressivism arouses people to support these changes alternately through shame and flattery. Thus, Steffens dedicated his great muckraking book, *The Shame of the Cities*, "in all good faith, to the accused—to all the citizens of all the cities in the United States:

> Democracy with us may be impossible and corruption inevitable, but these articles, if they have proved nothing else, have demonstrated beyond doubt that we can stand the truth; that there is pride in the character of American citizenship; and that this pride may be a power in the land.[249]

The second step is taken when it appears that major parties are incorrigible and it seems impossible to separate parties from politics. Even so, representative democracy can be self-correcting. If citizens could transcend partisanship, if they were Independents, this time organized, the apparatus of representative democracy could be reclaimed. Antipartyism could inspire voluntary association or it could ride the dragon of a party of Independents capable of serving as the "medium of revolution."

But experience demonstrated that commitment to a party of Independents is undependable. The effort is not undertaken seriously or nation-wide and is difficult to sustain. Recall Steffens ironically assuring Czar Nicholas that if he instituted elections they would not be unsettling:

> Of course, if [these independent voters] should keep this up for a number of elections they would make both parties represent them, and then the government would come to represent them. But they won't keep it up; at least my people don't. A "landslide" as we call such uprisings, simply has the effect of letting off the feelings of the people; they go back to their business and things remain as bad—I mean as good—as before. . . . [W]e, the people, give up in despair.[250]

"The fundamental trouble," Roosevelt wrote, "was that the country was sick and tired of reform." "The average man was tired of decency in politics," and "the dog returned to its vomit."[251]

The third step is a reflective backing off from shame and blame, from prodding and doubting the people. There is the possibility that the Constitution itself is flawed. It is one thing to say that "the Organization" subverts the Constitution, and another to speculate that democracy cannot work on the American model at all. It gives central place to representation and therefore to elections, which invite parties and partisanship. Good men are helpless in a bad system. As Taft put it, a key feature of the U.S. Constitution was "its purely representative character,"[252] and progressives fasten on the "Swiss" model of referenda and initiative, direct democracy—as if the mechanisms of self-government are spontaneous or invulnerable to partisanship and undue influence.

Admission that the whole American form is a failure, that the grip of the party system and the "Organization" means starting over, turns out to be unabidable, though. Progressivism reverts to a reluctant acceptance of elections and parties, and resignation to permanent, indignant, antipartyism. Steffens again: "It was useless—it was almost wrong—to fight for the right under our system. . . . Either we should all labor to change the foundation of society . . . or go along with the resultant civilization we were part of, taking care only to save our minds by seeing it all straight and thinking about it clearly."[253] This is not cynicism. It reflects an "odd sort of fatalism in their view of democracy. If a thing exists in a free society, it has a right to exist, for it exists by the leave of the people."[254]

Even resignation is not stable, though, and progressives return to the start, to the hopeful prosecution of reform. Making democracy safe for the world by ridding democracy of corrupt and corrupting parties and of partisanship is the enduring progressive ambition.

Post-party depression is a recurrent political mood. In the next chapter I look more closely at the conviction that parties are perverters of the democratic spirit. If progressivism is "a troubled mind groping to find names to fit its discontent," the search for the source is ended: it is "undue influence." The confounding question that remains and that divides antiparty thinkers is whether parties are autonomous, advancing their own special interests, extortionists involved in their own "elaborate influence-peddling scheme."[255] Or are parties instruments of other powerful social forces, captured by outside "sinister interests"? Are parties principals or agents of "undue influence"? I turn next to current incarnations of this element of antipartyism, to "the anxiety of influence" and proposals for reform.

CHAPTER 5

═━▶◆◀━═

The Anxiety of Influence

Today, as in the past, progressive antipartyism and reformism are indignant responses to real political grievances, though typically untempered by appreciation of the positive achievements, actual and possible, of parties and partisanship. In the preceding chapter I traced the threads of loathing. Parties are "perverters of the democratic spirit."[1] Parties are corrupt and corrupting, rooted in the root of all evil: money. Parties exercise undue influence, doling out contracts, favors, and benefits. Parties call public opinion into being, and shape it. They make partisanship a meaningful political identity and undermine independence. Parties are the active agents of what is wrong with representative democracy. They are more than tools of other powerful social forces. Progressive antipartyism maintains the relative autonomy of parties acting in their own special interests. That is why the point of interruption in the system of corruption is *political* reform: to disarm, circumvent, or abolish parties, and, where that is impossible, at least to loosen the hold of partisanship. We have seen that progressive doubts about democracy, and blame as well, were safely transposed wherever possible from the people generally to "the organization."

Testing the limits of progressive confidence in cleansing morals, voluntary association, and the transformation of partisans into Independents is the shadow of the "system." The size and scope of "the Organization" is a preoccupation by itself, and beyond any single party organization there is the "system." As I am about to show, anti-party thinkers argued that the distortions that parties create are systemic. Even the evasion of regulated rivalry is quite regular: a matter of party convergence, collusion, and cartel. Voters are right to harbor "an intangible suspicion that they are in some way the victims of a conspiracy" of one close, oligarchic corporation.[2] Unraveling this system is difficult enough.

In addition, there are recurrent worries about where the true source of undemocratic influence lies. Is the "invisible government" behind the "ostensible government" run by parties or by powers working through them? What if the party system is just part of a larger system of forces inimical to democracy which cannot be corrected by political reform? Are parties actors or pawns, principals or agents, in this democratic charade? Does this "system" have a mover at all? I call this the "anxiety of influence."[3] It is bound up with the perennial democratic fear of real and imagined aristocracies and conspiratorial combinations. The justification for popular parties before parties were justified was to champion "the democracy" against the encroachments of "aristocrats" or "monocrats," "the money power," or a power elite or "establishment," all exercising undue influence. "Although the physical and institutional life of America has been transformed since John Adams first uttered his cry, 'I fear the few,'" writes one political theorist, "the ideas born in the first fifty years of its independent political life remain relatively unaltered and are as vigorous as ever."[4] President Jackson defined aristocracy as wealth that "exercises more than its just proportion of influence in public affairs."[5] The people may not wish to alter the economic order; the majority consents to property and wealth. But had the people consented to the political power of the rich?[6] The use of government to promote the interests of the rich "was not merely unjust, it was 'aristocratic.'"[7] Moreover, the various elites—the bankers, the "money-power," the professionally privileged—coalesce to form a "national power elite" able to control access to political office.

Often enough, fear of "the few" is transferred wholesale to parties. Parties are predators, not a defense against them. But pure antipartyism does not always eclipse troubling thoughts about the source and the direction in which undue influence flows. How could it? Mary Parker Follett does not solve the puzzle, she simply strikes out: "Individuals have not been to blame, but our whole system. It is the system which must be changed," and she rails against big business and corrupt party politics in equal measure.[8] Parties are corrupt all on their own, and politics can create economic elites. But parties can also be taken over and exploited by other special interests. Who captures whom?

In this chapter I analyze the anxiety of influence and assess the phases of anxiety. Not surprisingly, antiparty progressives are unsettled and move back and forth from one target of "undue influence" to another. For example, it was a point in favor of the referendum that "it works both ways; it keeps the corporations from using the legislature for their private gain, and it also keeps the legislators from blackmailing the corporations."[9] We see this ambiguity in contemporary descriptions of "corrupt" and "corrosive" party practices and attempts to regulate them. One judge, puzzling over a recent partisan redistricting case, expressed the anxiety of influence exactly: "Isn't it a fact that when you start doing things in politics you can't ever tell what can happen in terms of influence? Over time it is hard to predict who is going to influence whom in politics."[10] In fact, judicial opinions in the area of campaign finance law are near perfect expressions of cycling, as I will show. To be fair, the thing is hard to grasp. Corruption shifts "from the stark land of bribery, extortion, and simple personal gain to the shadowy world of implicit understandings, ambiguous favors, and political advantage."[11] Put simply, are parties agents or principals? Is the system impenetrable?

Forces of Nature

As we have seen, one progressive addition to older traditions of antipartyism is preoccupation with "organization," with party size, discipline, reach, and scope. Corruption and organization were allied. Size and stranglehold went together. Progressives (again as a broad label) mistrust powerful organizations "clotting society into large aggregates . . . able to act in concert and shut out those men for whom organization was difficult or impossible."[12] The major parties are clots.

Some early progressives adopted the conceptual framework of social darwinism to explain these combinations. The language of "competition" and survival of the fittest were mutually reinforcing and applied to both big parties and big business. An imperative law of combination seemed to be at work. Here again Lincoln Steffens provides a marker. Bigness is a natural drive. Fitness is related to size. "We can't abolish business, we cannot regulate big business, and we are finding that we cannot limit bigness in business, which must grow." The American political machine too is a "natural growth." It owes not to human nature but to uncurbed, undirected natural forces, Steffens went on, somewhat obscurely, though his point becomes clear: "Our purposes and Nature's get crossed; our ethics run counter to her physical laws, and so our bubbles break."[13] The corollary was a fresh set of terms to characterize party leaders. Parties are the work of the best men, meaning not the morally best but the "biologically best."[14] Ostrogorski wrote in this vein: party activists "are recruited by natural selection and not by a formal process" and represent the virtues of firmness, energy, and audacity.[15] Less politely, another advised that the ward boss is usually of low birth, little education, dubious habits, and more or less slovenly appearance, but rather than trying to regenerate him, it is better to acknowledge "that the evolution of the boss follows the law of natural selection." He has the advantage of resourcefulness, industry, perseverance, and no end of shrewd tactfulness.[16] This thinking lay behind Steffens's reflection, "if the process of corruption was so universal, wasn't it natural, inevitable, and, in the scientific historical evolutionary sense, right?" Maybe bribery and corruption are acts of God and muckrakers the agents of the Devil.[17]

Evolution was a specialized and, it turns out, ephemeral framework for picturing the dynamic of organization and scale. In any case, it did not address the relation among different species of big, "fit" organizations. It could not resolve the question of the direction of influence. It may be that business and other economic interests are the most powerful predators. Or it may be that corporations and other money interests are artifacts of favorable laws and financial privileges, and not natural forces. What is clear is that in business and in politics big organizations combined in a "system." I turn to the larger "system" question shortly—to the second phase of the cycle of anxiety of influence in which parties are seen as agents of "unseen brokers," "authors and sponsors of their political being." In the first phase, parties bear the onus all by themselves, and "system" refers, in the American context, to the two-party system where parties undermine democracy by their convergence, collusion, and cartel. These early progressive categories are standard terms of critical analysis of the party system today.

Anxiety of Influence, Phase 1: The Two-Party System

In 1922 Charles E. Merriam advertised the phrase in the title, of his book, *The American Party System*. In political science, "party system" is a neutral description of the structure of party competition. But the American two-party system was contrasted with multiparty systems from the first appearance of democratic parties in Europe, and the contrasts drawn favored two-partyism. "Two-party system is more than a point of reference. It is a synonym for the United States political system and an organizing principle for textbook knowledge of electoral democracy."[18] There are competing explanations for dominant two-partyism in the United States (leaving aside the notion that the British and by extension American two-party system is a reflection of the nation's "sporting instincts"[19]). Probably the most common is single-member winner-take-all districts. So it is worth noting that the district-based system in both England and the United States preceded regular elections, much less partisan elections, and that tying representatives to constituents via geographically defined districts has nothing to do with the number of parties.[20] The 1842 congressional mandate for a national system of single-member districted elections for federal office was a post-party development whose aim was to increase political competition, not to restrict it to two parties.[21] Other explanations for two-partyism include the "median voter" thesis, regulatory obstacles to minor parties, and, closely related, collusive strategies by the major parties to ward off challengers. Its authority owes, too, to half a century and more of dedicated political science analysis of the American two-party system—Duverger's "law" and Anthony Downs's work on voting are classic examples.[22]

As a description of American parties, two-partyism is historically misleading and defies common knowledge. It discounts a lot: one-partyism in the solid South and in specific states, like the long-standing Democratic Party monopoly in Hawaii, the addition and transmutation of parties in this system of two (the Republicans from the Whigs in the 1860s), third parties at the regional (Minnesota's Farmer-Labor Party) and national levels (the Free Soil Party, the People's Party, Roosevelt's Progressives), fusion parties, and so-called third parties today (so-called because they are better described as campaign organizations for independent candidates).[23] There have also been six significant third presidential candidates in this century: Theodore Roosevelt, Robert La Follette, George Wallace, John Anderson, Ross Perot, and Ralph Nader, but except for the first two it is a stretch to count their organizations as political parties rather than ad hoc vehicles of aspirants to office. When third parties emerge they are not lasting. They fall apart, are absorbed by a major party (the Progressives by the Democrats, for example), or, as in the case of the second Republican Party, they supplant an existing party, maintaining systemic duopoly. A current Web site of American parties lists forty-four in addition to the Democratic and Republican Parties, though many exist as parties in name only. They do not have organizations to speak of and do not field candidates in any election at any level.[24] In short, "in no other large democracy (and only a few smaller ones), do third parties have so slight a representation in national politics as in the United States."[25] The actual history of third parties and fusion parties has not altered the authority and norm, the virtual "civic religion," of two-partyism here. Its positive cast derives, appropriately enough, from two suppositions. One is clarity for citizens: cuing. The simplicity of choice between two parties can be handled by voters who know little about candidates besides party affiliation, on this view. The other is "political stability," typically defined in circular fashion as two-partyism, the idea being that two strong parties minimize the unsettling proliferation of intra-party factions and spin-offs.

Within this family of justification, defenders differ about what sort of parties serve simplicity and stability. One view has it that the two parties should speak for defined and differentiated interests or ideologies, enabling the proto-Millian philosophy of dueling parties as agents of improvement. The responsible party government thesis requires distinct party identities and cohesive programs as a condition of accountability. The contrary view has it that parties are better conceived as "umbrellas" or "big tents." Two broad parties absorb various group interests and opinions, the argument goes. In government, they provide incentives to compromise. They prevent the formation of a permanent majority or minority, as Madison hoped. "Madison," one historian explains, "did not initially explore the possibility that a way might be found to join diverse factions in a private, national organization . . . that a coalition of factions could preserve a high level of commitment to political action, yet be forced in some measure to speak the language of general welfare."[26]

From the antiparty perspective, "party system" was never a neutral much less positive phrase, and these rationales were unpersuasive, as they are to critics today. It signified, as "system" does, complexity and circularity, feedback within a powerful structure difficult to permeate and alter. "The system" was bipartisan, and propositions in support of two-partyism struck antiparty critics as proof of the need for counterweights. *Of course* two-partyism is stable—the parties collude to ensure their dominance by prohibiting fusion candidacies and write-in voting, and by legislating costly and time-consuming ballot access restrictions like signature requirements and filing deadlines.[27] There is no electoral state of nature; "the parties are regulating themselves."[28] Whether the framework for understanding two-partyism was evolutionary survival, market behavior, or a regulatory structure imposed by dominant parties in state legislatures, the "party system" was an alarm, alerting antiparty progressives to party convergence, collusion, and party cartel.

Convergence

Parties are "only combinations for the purpose of getting place and power," "battle-cries to elect certain men."[29] Party is the name for a political association aimed at "catching prizes" or "private revenge," personal ambition or venality. We saw in "glorious traditions of antipartyism" that well before they were elements of representative democracy, parties were disparaged as small in contrast to great, and as self-serving rather than principled, as "little more than a Conspiracy of Self-Seekers" or "unscrupulous power groups" bent on spoils.[30] Progressive antipartyism raised the pitch; after all, the observable behavior of large-scale party organizations is more striking than the machinations of a parliamentary caucus. A common reductionist statement is this: "the man who is in politics for the office might just as well be in politics for the money he can get for his vote, so far as the general good is concerned."[31] In simple, jaundiced terms, the parties represent different grafters. Or even the same ones. Anticipating contemporary accusations, progressives noted that private interests contributed to the funds of both major parties. Jay Gould explained: "In a Republican district, I was a Republican; in a Democratic district I was a Democrat; in a doubtful district I was doubtful; but I was always for Erie."[32] (The Supreme Court in a 2003 campaign finance case points out that donors gave substantial sums to both major national parties, "leaving room for no other conclusion that that these donors were seeking influence, or avoiding retaliation, rather than promoting any particular ideology."[33])

I want to be careful to distinguish convergence in terms of the behavioral and organizational characteristics of parties from party "centrism," my subject in chapter 8. Centrism is a sweeping thesis about the convergence of parties at the middle of the ideological spectrum, and the generally diffuse, comparatively nonideological nature of American parties. Outside political science, "centrist" typically indicates blamably amorphous and indistinct. Consider Henry Adams's searing attack on parties in the 1872 election: "Estimated by their professions merely, there would seem to be absolutely no ground of choice between the parties. . . . [T]he two declarations of principle are so curiously identical . . . that they might just as well be exchanged and each party accept the other."[34] Pundits repeat Roosevelt's "tweedledum and tweedledee" to deprecate campaigns as issueless and elections as substantively uncompetitive. "The two parties have morphed together into one corporate party with two heads wearing different make-up,"[35] and literature put out by Ralph Nader's Green Party referred in standard fashion to the "hybrid Democratic-Republican Party."[36] This summing up is classic: "One of the best kept secrets of American politics is that the two-party system has long been brain-dead—kept alive by support systems like state electoral laws . . . public subsidies and so-called campaign reform."[37]

The convergence that is key to this variety of antipartyism, however, is not a matter of positioning on the political spectrum (centrism) or lack of distinct party identity but of purpose and organization. The objective is to get and keep office, apart from any other purpose. E. E. Schattschneider defined party as "an organized attempt to get power . . . here defined as control of the government."[38] This encyclopedia entry is strange but to the point: "Ironically, political parties are not political organizations, because their primary purpose is to elect candidates to public office and only incidentally to press for specific policy agendas."[39] Parties are "flexible strategic instruments that political leaders have designed and can adapt to suit their changing objectives." They are "endogenous" institutions.[40] In this system, it is in a party's interest to be one of the two major parties and in candidates' interests to affiliate with one or the other.[41] Obstacles put in the path of new parties challenging the duopoly are a determining factor in the decision to direct political energy to joining or attempting to "take over" one of the existing major parties.[42] Moreover, once parties exist, politicians must be partisans. Given legislative caucuses, committees, and party leadership, a congressman denied admission (or professing independence) "wandered like a poor ghost, until after one session the Republican caucus considered that his penance had been sufficient."[43] John Aldrich's *Why Parties?* models the common observation that ambitious politicians need parties to achieve their goals—to gain power, govern, and ensure their political survival.

The great convergent goal is not graft or other criminal versions of corruption, then, but political self-preservation. Members of Congress are "single-minded seekers of reelection."[44] Self-dealing by individual officials is not the point, self-perpetuation of the party in government is.[45] Rational choice theory reinforces the convergence view by drawing attention to the common strategies employed to enhance electoral prospects: satisfying constituents in targeted fashion, for example, and distributing benefits with a view to perpetuating political control. It should be clear that despite the propensity to charge partisans with personal ambition and venality, political self-preservation need not be self-serving. Motives are typically mixed. The motive for maintaining the individual in office or party dominance may be to effect policies in the best interest of constituents, supporters, or the public interest. Under some circumstances re-election can be understood as an institutional good. Nonetheless, for critics the goal of political survival casts under suspicion everything from votes in the legislature to constituent services. Behavior is convergent, bipartisan, dictated by "the system."

Party organization is convergent too. A great deal of analysis and normative debate surrounds the question whether and in what respect parties should be seen as private voluntary associations and membership groups. In the United States this takes the form of a doctrinal question about party rights of association protected by the First Amendment. The predominant view is that today "the party in the electorate" is "largely a categorical group" with no interaction, no structured relationships, no organizational life.[46] (This also describes many parties in European democracies today, despite their beginnings as membership organizations—socialist parties, for example, or Christian Democrats.[47]) I will have occasion to dispute this bloodless account and to point out where the idea of parties understood as voluntary associations and carriers of partisanship enters a defense of them. The point for now is that the standard description paints major parties as "an elaborate insider industry"[48] made up of candidates, professional organizers, and hired consultants who provide expertise, polling data, advice on election law compliance, research on opponents, and advertising to "consumers" of messages. Parties have congealed into a permanent political class, connected "only nominally, and vestigially" to outsiders.[49] That is, to voters. This assessment was standard progressive fare, even in the machine era. Ostrogorski observed: "Up to this point not much has been seen of the people, although it has been talked of a good deal; everybody quoted its authority, acted in its name, took pledges on its behalf, but this everybody was made up almost exclusively of the class of professional politicians."[50] Steffens perfected the big party/big business parallel. Proxy votes handed over by stockholders to corporate management are like partisan ballots. Managers immune from oversight are like party leaders immune from popular control. Progressive critics of parties today adopt this analogy and portray "elected officials and dominant parties as a managerial class, imperfectly accountable through periodic review to a diffuse body of equity holders known as the electorate."[51] Schattschneider's division of parties into "an organized group of insiders who have effective control of the party" and a mass of passive "members" who have little say tells the same story. Except that Schattschneider is accepting: the unfortunate result of the fantasy of a party as a large association of voters

> is that it blackens the name of parties by making them appear to be undemocratic oligarchies—which they are, but they were never supposed to be otherwise. The relations of the party and the partisans are not oppressive. The hospitality of the parties has been practically unlimited. . . . [I]n what sense is a partisan injured if he is deprived of the right to control an organization toward which he has no duties? The whole theory is chaotic.[52]

Schattschneider was categorical: "Whatever else parties may be they are not associations of the voters who support candidates."[53]

From the perspective that sees party purposes and organization as convergent, there is one characterization that seems to avoid the worst negatives: "public utility."[54] This representation of party organization and management is comparatively benign. As Schumpeter said, parties are "convenient vehicles for conducting" elections. The designation "utility" assigns them to the service sector. It casts parties in instrumental terms as state-subsidized entities supplying voters with "brand names" and low-cost information about candidates, mechanisms for "reducing the transaction costs" of democracy. There is something to be said for the "public utility" view: it provides a potential reason for resigned acceptance of a party system as a necessary, rudimentary apparatus for running elections. But all this is a stretch. "Public utility" has some purchase where parties receive the bulk of their funding from government; direct public support may go some way toward transforming them into semi-public entities. In the United States, where state subsidy does not exist to any significant extent and parties are privately funded, the "public utility" analogy is more misleading than helpful. Precisely because of private money, parties appear as sites of corruption. Whether they are the extorters or the objects of bribes, campaign financing is said to be the principal way "undue influence" operates.

"Public utility" is prescriptive; indeed, that is the analogy's main thrust. As the name suggests, citizens have a special interest in public utilities, and the major parties should be subject to regulation in return for legal privileges.[55] The progressive accusation is precisely that these so-called public utilities regulate themselves. There is no better illustration than partisan districting, a practice that "leads to a system in which the representatives choose their constituents rather than vice versa."[56]

Strategic Convergence: Partisan Gerrymandering

The convergence of major parties, each "an elaborate insiders' industry," is perfectly compatible with ferocious party competition and parallel efforts to curtail the competitiveness of the opposition. Where predominance in state legislatures permits, each party manipulates electoral rules to harm the chances of the opposition and to secure and enhance its own majority. The purpose may not be to promote interests adverse to the public interest–that is a separate question (though hardly an open question for antiparty progressives). The purpose is to get and keep office. The most studied mechanism is partisan gerrymandering, which has been described as "a paradigmatic instance of the structural pathology" of the system. What is partisan gerrymandering, and why does it pervert democracy?

Gerrymandering is the mechanism by which the party in control of the state legislature draws district lines to exaggerate its voting strength or to entrench its status as majority party for the rest of the census decade.[57] Today, technology and sophisticated information about groups of voters make partisan manipulation exact. Among the tactics: lines are drawn to protect incumbents or to pit incumbents of the opposition party against one another; opposition party strength is concentrated in one area to reduce competition in other districts ("packing") or the opponent's strength is dissipated by distributing it among adjacent districts ("cracking"). Legislative redistricting has been described as "one of the most conflictual forms of regular politics in the United States short of violence."[58] I cannot resist mention of one much-publicized example from Texas. The story in short is that in 2003 the Republicans in the state legislature, long sufferers of districting by a majority Democratic Party, saw a chance to increase their delegation to the U.S. House. The case is unusual because it was a mid-census maneuver, and unusual too for the capers that ensued. To prevent a vote on the redistricting bill that they were sure to lose, a coterie of Democratic legislators escaped the state on buses to Oklahoma. The Republican speaker of the House issued civil warrants for their arrest and set Texas Rangers and forces from the Department of Public Safety after them. The vicissitudes of a vote on the new districts stretched out for months. The intensity of the fight is explained in part by the stakes: not only the political survival of senior incumbent congressmen but also the party's control of Congress. That is the potential power of the partisan gerrymander: an additional party seat in one state could result in a change of party balance in the House of Representatives. At a moment when national political power was narrowly divided between the parties, the Texas districting scheme added five Republican members to the House.[59]

When he wrote, "the increasing efficiency of partisan redistricting has damaged the democratic process to a degree that our predecessors only began to imagine," Justice Souter expressed the orthodox progressive judgment of this common partisan practice.[60] What is the damage? The Texas drama does not tell us whether partisan redistricting was unfair to voters or to the Democratic Party; nothing in the political battle spoke to what fairness (or any other standard) requires.

Progressive legal scholars look to the courts for a diagnosis and remedy. But at this writing the Supreme Court has never invalidated a redistricting plan as "too partisan" and declined to invalidate partisan gerrymandering in 2005 in *Vieth*. By contrast, it is settled constitutional law that political equality requires "one person, one vote," a principle backed up by statistical standards for when deviation from strict population formulas is permissible. Courts have also found it possible to detail the "qualitative unfairness" of racial gerrymandering that dilutes the votes of minority groups, and judicial standards are in place that strike a balance between political equality and commitments to minorities.[61] Should there be limits to the free hand parties have in drawing lines to advantage themselves, and if so, why?

The Justices in *Vieth* could not agree on the harm of partisan gerrymandering, and those who could name a constitutionally recognizable harm could not agree on a standard the Court might impose to correct it; the dissenters offered four different remedial proposals.[62] Justice Stevens's measure of unconstitutional practice, for example, is gerrymanders "devoid of any rational justification . . . when partisanship is the legislature's sole motivation—when the pretense of neutrality is forsaken unabashedly and all traditional districting criteria are subverted for partisan advantage."[63] But neither the other Justices nor commentators have rallied to this view. Redistricting done for no reason other than partisan gain *is* an expected part of the system. Partisan gerrymandering is as old as the republic, older in fact, and Justice Scalia summarized the history of the practice beginning with colonial Pennsylvania and pointing up highlights like Patrick Henry's attempt to gerrymander James Madison out of the First Congress.[64] Justice Stevens's outrage notwithstanding, as a matter of practice there are few "traditional standards of neutrality" to forsake, and gerrymandering is not "devoid of any rational justification" if partisanship suffices.

Judges and legal commentators may be baffled or divided about whether there are grounds to say there is "too much" partisan gain, and whether it is possible to fashion remedies, but academic political scientists have pronounced a consensus on a principle for identifying when partisan gerrymandering is objectionable. "The symmetry standard"

> compares how similarly-situated political groups would fare hypothetically if they each (in turn) receive the same given percentage of the vote. The difference in how parties would fare in terms of legislative seats is the "partisan bias" of the electoral system.[65]

Partisan gerrymandering is not unjustifiable per se, on this view, but a districting plan that does not treat parties symmetrically is.[66] "Both parties [should] have the *opportunity* to capture the same amount of seats, if they receive a particular percentage of the statewide vote."[67] The extent to which they do not is "partisan bias." Even if "symmetry" were adopted as a standard by the Court, it does not tell us when as a normative or constitutional matter partisan bias is "excessive." The justices who favor ruling some partisan gerrymanders unconstitutional use elusive terms such as "egregious" to single out impermissible patterns, but deviation for objective "symmetry," without more, is just as indeterminate. Gary King and others suggest several possibilities for implementation: one is a rule requiring states to make a good-faith effort to engage in as little partisan bias as possible; another is a rule that prevents a party from manipulating districting to gain control of one or more seats than it otherwise would be entitled to; another is a rule prohibiting egregious gerrymanders, that is, ones that show a bias above a certain percentage.[68]

In *Vieth* Justice Breyer invoked "serious democratic harm" from partisan gerrymandering. But nothing in my discussion so far indicates what the harm is. One answer is unfairness. The symmetry standard gets its imprimatur there; "partisan bias" means that "one party has stacked the deck to such a degree that the plan burdens the other party's 'rights of fair and effective representation.'"[69] Advocates of symmetry carefully distinguish this from a separate democratic concern: "electoral responsiveness," which refers to the extent to which the division of seats between parties responds to changes in voter preferences.[70] Electoral responsiveness looks for proportionality between a party's electoral strength and its legislative representation.

The most responsive arrangement, of course, is proportional representation, some version of Mill's "self-constituting constituencies."[71] But in a winner-take-all district system the winner is always favored with a bonus in seats; that is a given. So to be useful, electoral responsiveness must say more about when the distribution of political representation is "distorted," when a "representational harm" is inflicted. Here, concern is for majorities. Partisan gerrymandering violates "fair representation" when it thwarts the translation of majority votes into a majority of seats. "Because majoritarian ideas are so deeply engrained in our political system," it "somehow seems more heinous to prevent a majority from exercising its mandate, than merely to exaggerate the size of a majority."[72]

A blunter account of the harm of partisan gerrymandering exists. Consistent with the first defense of parties in chapter 3, the political harm of partisan gerrymandering is to obstruct Burkean regulated rivalry. The issue is not fairness or electoral responsiveness but deliberate interference with the rudimentary check of party competition. Justice Breyer's opinion in *Vieth* expresses this concern: "parties play a role in allowing voters to support the status quo or 'throw the rascals out' and only a party-based political system that satisfies this minimal condition encourages democratic responsibility."[73] On its own terms, "to qualify as a two-party system it is not enough that the dominant parties lock third-party competitors out of public office; they must be genuinely competitive with one another."[74] The charge that partisan gerrymandering fatally undermines regulated rivalry is advertised widely today, with appeals to data such as these: congressional elections after the 2000 census districting were the least competitive in U.S. history.[75] In 2004, sixty-five House races were uncontested and another 359 were won by a margin of victory political scientists describe as "no contest" or "landslide." Fifty-three were won by "comfortable" margins of victory. Only twenty-three races were competitive or tight.[76] These outcomes cannot be charged to partisan gerrymandering alone, of course, but to the extent that they are, does this amount to obstruction of the basic rationale for parties? It would if uncompetitiveness were durable, if rivalry were weakened not for just one or a few elections, and if one-party dominance were entrenched. If, for example, it were reasonable for the opposition party to decline to contest certain elections at all, so that voters would have no opportunity to throw the "ins" out. How much competitiveness, where, how many "uncontested" races, "landslides," "comfortable margins of victory" over how many election cycles amounts to "structural pathology"? At moments the number of uncontested and uncompetitive elections is certainly startling. But politics changes quickly as a result of events, popular candidates, and party organization, and what looked like secure party seats change hands. Indeed there are dramatic shifts, altering party control of government. As a sweeping description of long-term uncompetitiveness over a significant range of state and national elections, "structural pathology" does not hold up well; at least the idea needs refinement.

Political theorists and legal scholars adopt fairness, electoral responsiveness, or maximum competitiveness as principled grounds for opposing partisan gerrymandering. But severe antiparty thinkers are not enthusiastic about any of these. Partisan gerrymandering per se is the harm. And it is not a "structural pathology" of the system; it *is* the system. It is one demonstration of the convergent two-party system in action, evidence of the dominance of the two major parties serving their own political interests. It is objectionable quite apart from its consequences for fairness or electoral responsiveness or maximal competitiveness. The business itself is loathsome. Identifying and enforcing a standard of permissible partisan districting—symmetry, for example—has little appeal. The only corrective or, rather, the palliative because it does not reform "the system," is just what we would expect: nonpartisan districting commissions. Commissions appeal to progressives because partisan manipulation is muted; ideally, commissions would be "interest blind," employing only neutral standards like contiguity and compactness, as Justice Stevens prescribed. In practice, districting commissions composed of experts and respected citizens are not politically impartial; commissions too use criteria that take account of group interests and the prospects of electoral success—including the interests of the major parties.[77] Moreover, even advocates of commissions concede that these bodies are less accountable to voters than the gerrymandered, gerrymandering state legislature, and this is one impetus behind proposals (especially in the case of minority districting) to give community groups a central role in implementing the Voting Rights Act.[78] In any case, for anti-party thinkers commissions are palliatives; they do not undermine or eliminate the dominance of parties in shaping elections; at best they succeed in the minimal objective: partisan "legislators should not have final authority over the electoral process."[79]

There *is* one characteristic, antiparty imperative that heightens opposition to partisan gerrymandering. To the extent that partisan gerrymandering reduces the competitiveness of elections, it reduces participation. "Election effects" posits a positive relation—how much is unclear—between competitiveness and turnout.[80] A further (un-proven) claim is that higher turnout means more participation by Independents. As we have seen, a perennial hope is that participa-tion by nonpartisan, independent voters will reform "the system." If progressives must resign themselves to a party system, at least the aim should be activating Independents. Competitive elections mobi-lize them. Independents stay home if they think the system is rigged, more so if party convergence in organization, purpose, and strategy are compounded by collusion and districting "appears to be done by barons dividing up fiefdoms."[81]

Party Collusion

The conviction that parties are in league with one another is not unique to American progressive antipartyism: here is a turn-of-the-century British howl at the Governing Group and the Opposition: "the latter are less anxious to overthrow their rivals than to preserve the system which, in due course, and by the connivance of those ri-vals, will bring to them also the opportunities and emoluments of of-fice." The parties "have long been accustomed to working and trading together, in great harmony," Albert Stickney observed.[82] This comic description could have been written today: "The advocates of an un-necessary insane asylum at Goshen combine with the champions of a superfluous normal school at Podunk, and with the help of the friends of a useless reformatory at Wayback, a legislative majority is secured for a combined raid on the State Treasury."[83] Political science adds systematic institutional analysis of the conditions that enable or inhibit various forms of logrolling and inter-party deal making. (Of course, not all bipartisan measures are aptly described as collusion; some compromise may be necessary to get any public business done and may result in perfectly justifiable, universal programs.)

Party collusion around policy is second-order business; collusion in shaping electoral rules is first-order. Once again, districting is front and center in the United States. Partisan gerrymandering is the rule, but another strategy has parties in state legislatures agreeing on a plan for partisan balance and "safe districts." Steffens reported on the "rough working agreements" in Illinois by which the Democrats took the city and the Republicans Cook County and each governed "for the good of the party."[84] Put simply, "In the perfect bipartisan gerrymander, every incumbent is placed in a safe district; the 'ideal' would be no competitive elections on general election day."[85]

Without necessarily subscribing to Schattschneider's definition—"democracy is not to be found *in* the parties but *between* the parties"[86]—a sine qua non is contested elections. Consider this expression of confidence by Martin Van Buren's biographer: the Democratic Party organized by "Old Kinderhook" has survived two centuries, and despite "the acrimony, gridlock, and corruption that taint the process more than we care to admit . . . there is a fundamental balance at its core—an internal gyroscope, based on brute competition—that has allowed this system to continue, with only a few modifications, from 1828 to the present."[87] The point is clear: "brute competition" is the saving grace of a party system. With major parties colluding, the essential faith is shaken.

Party Cartel

"Cartel" looks beyond convergence in the overall shared purposes, organization, and behavior of parties, and beyond mutually advantageous collusion between the major parties on matters of districting policy (the reformatory at Wayback) and the day-to-day conduct of government business. Cartel focuses specifically on the legal barriers to political competition from minor parties, fusion parties, or Independents.[88] "Incumbent politicians of the two major parties generally can agree on at least one thing—the desirability of keeping new parties and independent candidates off the ballot through burdensome access restrictions."[89] Early progressive sensibilities suspicious of bigness ("clotting society into large aggregates ... able to act in concert and shut out those men for whom organization was difficult or impossible"[90]) and exquisitely attuned to corporate trusts not surprisingly portrayed the dominant parties in analogous terms. We quickly grasp the evocative power of "cartel." It is viscerally negative. The very thought that parties mimic anticompetitive business practices is a reason for invoking it. It looks at the system, not particular people or parties—at the background of electoral law and at who makes the regulations. "Cartel" draws attention to principal pieces of the regulatory regime put in place during the Progressive Era as part of its antiparty reforms. Again, these measures were initiated by antiparty activists, but some were enacted with the complicity of the major parties looking to eliminate third-party competition. Legislation made third-party and independent places on the ballot difficult. In most states "fusion" parties (or "cross endorsement," in which the candidate of a major party is also listed on the ballot as the candidate of a minor party) were outlawed.

In progressive antiparty writing today, economic terminology generally, and recourse to cartel as a type of business combination specifically, is commonplace.[91] The cartel analogy depends for its force on the norm of "politics as akin to a robustly competitive market—a market whose vitality depends on both clear rules of engagement and upon the ritual cleansing born of competition." It signals that "politics shares with all markets a vulnerability to anticompetitive behavior." Party leaders are said to employ a maneuver of corporate management called "lockup,"[92] creating barriers to competition from both other parties and their own internal factions.[93] For those who see "cartel" as a useful characterization, the United States does not have a two-party system simply in which there are two dominant parties with minor parties agitating, nudging, and altering the major parties, and occasionally winning office for their candidates.

Rather, "the system" is a permanent duopoly. Skepticism toward self-serving managerial practices in the corporate domain should apply even more vigorously to the political domain where, after all, "shareholders" have no "exit options."[94] In the cartel analogy, voters are not the only victims; so are third parties and Independents and factions within major parties, actual or potential.

The payoff of "cartel" for legal progressives is diagnosis of the anticompetitive effects of election law, and the analogy points to corporate law as a guide for correction. Early legal measures to ensure that business managers perform their fiduciary duties to shareholders now take a backseat to competitive structures within which managers make decisions, and that can be used to discipline them. By analogy, in electoral law, the judicial focus is on the rights of individual voters and the associational rights of parties, and attention should turn instead to the electoral framework. The objective should be to ensure competitive political markets that will discipline party managers to act in the interest of shareholders, voters.[95] Under the sway of this analogy, contemporary progressives propose that courts should intervene to optimize if not maximize competition, and should apply antitrust law to the major parties.

I do not mean to endorse the party cartel thesis. After all, competitiveness is a norm in democratic party politics apart from any economic analogy. So what is gained and what lost by "cartel," besides the explicit invitation to courts to break up these combinations? "Cartel" does not provide insight into the normative reasons for political competition generally, or the perfectly justifiable purposes of party competition specifically. "Political market" is no better. In the "party cartel" literature, both the historical time frame and the baseline for appropriate competition are unrefined, and scholars admit that "it is far easier to identify dramatically anticompetitive practices than it is to specify precisely what optimal competition would look like."[96]

A more important reason to step back from the cartel analogy is that it delivers the message that electoral politics is a market with parties in the business of selling candidates. An unfortunate implication is that voters behave like consumers in search of choice and price (and quality?). The analogy fails, too, because voters (or the worth of their vote) should be equal, not unequal as they are as consumers,[97] and political philosophers are rightly adamant to challenge economic perspectives on these grounds. "Cartel" is better employed as part of an antiparty critique that indicates the *inapplicability* of markets to politics. The main point holds in any case. "The structural cancer" of party self-entrenchment[98] is abominable because democracy can exist "only when effective political competition generates genuine political choices."[99] This original "moment of appreciation," regulated rivalry, is at work in challenges to collusion between the major parties to create "safe seats." The point of agreement is the pathology of uncontested races when it is the result of self-dealing legal maneuvers, such as collusive partisan gerrymandering. The imperative of competition holds whether the norm is choice among sharply, substantively differentiated parties or simply a contest to fulfill the Burkean prescription that "outs" curb the "ins," to ensure rudimentary electoral accountability. A contemporary historian echoes orthodox progressive terms when he says that "the 'corruption' here is that the system loses an essential counterbalance."[100]

I belabor this point because, obvious as it may seem, it is not the main concern of antiparty progressives, and it is not the sole motivating concern behind charges that the major parties constitute a cartel. For antiparty thinkers, "the tyranny of the two-party system" is no less a tyranny for being competitive.[101] The objective behind calls for political trust-busting is not more competitive parties but challenges to the major parties both from within and from outside. The two are related; most third-party and independent challenges are the work of disaffected partisans, spillovers from rivalry within a major party. The two-party system stifles both interparty and intraparty competition—and may aim as much at the second as the first.[102] Party leaders use devices to entrench their incumbent position.[103] (Thus, legal challenges to regulations that are represented in terms of a contest between the state and the party's right of freedom of association are sometimes better understood as contests brought by factions within a major party.) "Cartel" is shorthand, pointing to the characteristic objective of antiparty progressives—ensuring not two robust competitive parties but incentives for bolters and space for independent challengers.

All the reasons for wanting multiple parties or fusion parties (referred to as "proportional representation by other means"[104]) or independent candidacies or a party of Independents are brought to bear against the cartel. Critics remind us of the historical contributions of third parties and their participatory potential. Third parties are extra-constitutional means for agitating and cleansing politics. (Progressive inattention to antisystem parties hostile to democracy is striking, and I discuss extremist parties in chapter 9.) Issues and opinions ignored by the major parties deserve a hearing, and bolting from the two-party system is more than symbolic protest; it is a specific way of making demands heard. At a minimum, the possibility of choosing a minor party or fusion party candidate or Independent makes voting something other than a ritual of consent. Successful candidates, much less successful minor parties, are rare, it is true, even regionally, but that does not undermine their importance or justify seeing them as purely expressive.

Of particular interest here is the reason antiparty critics have for opposing two-party entrenchment even if the parties are competitive or, better, the reasons that are *not* on offer. Neither voter choice nor the representativeness of parties is the heart of antiparty arguments, and this deserves notice. Generally, proportional representation and multiple parties are prescribed when voter choice is a primary value and is closely tied to a theory of representation. Whatever the theory (mirroring or "presence," trustee versions, and so on), representation is not satisfied by a two-party system; it is tyrannical to identify popular sovereignty with voter choice, and then limit the choice to two.[105] That is the usual argument against two-partyism. In contrast, the severe, antiparty position resists two-party entrenchment because it strengthens the undue influence of the major parties. They are "clots." They wield inordinate power. They are self-perpetuating and self-entrenching and advance their own special interests. They comprise an aristocracy or oligarchy or power elite. It is not that multiple parties are desirable in themselves because they offer voters more choice or are better representative of diverse interests and opinions. Simply, a flush of minor parties and "organized independency" might undermine this duopoly and parties overall.

Correctives for the "structural pathology" of party entrenchment are based on a mix of empirical assumptions, historical interpretations, and, we see, normative ideals of democratic representation.[106] For those sympathetic to parties in theory, the chief goal is to set parties against each other, to force them to be competitive, to enact Burke's regulated rivalry, which could involve either multiplying the number of competitive parties or ensuring competition between the two major parties. However, to the extent that "cartel" and "political market" reflect the values of competitiveness and voter choice, they do not adequately address deeper antiparty concerns. For antiparty thinkers, regulated rivalry is not a priority. Striking down obstacles to new entrants is key, and the chief reason is to undermine "the system." If parties are ineliminable, then at least they should be multiplied, that much is clear. The measure of regulation and reform is whether it strengthens independence and undercuts parties and partisanship.

Anxiety of Influence, Phase 2

Convergence, collusion, and cartel capture one phase of the anxiety of influence. A crucial theoretical point emerges from this unholy trio, namely, recognition of the independent political purposes of parties, and appreciation, if that is the right word, of their relative autonomy. Progressive antiparty thinkers acknowledge the quasi-autonomy of political parties as institutions capable of generating political space, shaping electoral rules, and accumulating resources for self-determined action, endowed with the energy of organization and willing to govern. Parties embrace, play off, and exploit powerful social and economic forces in their own special interests. Of course, for antiparty progressives, autonomy means that parties are not responsive to the people or bound by the public interest. But party autonomy also suggests independence from the control of other organized interests. In this first phase, they are not agents for special interests or brokers negotiating for private individuals and groups. That is the defining dread of the second phase of the anxiety of influence, where fears about the direction of influence are unrepressed. Convergence, collusion, and cartel—"an elaborate insider industry"—can be descriptively correct without getting at the real perversion: parties captured by stronger social and economic forces. Parties are "brokers of unseen principals."[107] Is it true that parties enjoy a "natural superiority" in democracy and that they allow themselves to be harried by pressure groups "as a timid whale might be pursued by a school of minnows"?[108] Or is the party system a piece of another larger system? Social science's great purpose—to identify the "power elite" and measure its influence—is obviously outside my purview, which is the wavering (but I argue compelling) perception of the relative autonomy of parties in this progressive version of antipartyism.

This phase of anxiety, in which parties are agents of powerful principals, is almost too familiar to belabor. Lincoln Steffens's charge is standard: "You will find business men back of the politicians. They are usually."[109] Steffens spoke of "the living System of our actual government":

> It flowed out of politics into vice and crime; out of business into politics, and back into business; from the boss, down through the police to the prostitute, and up through the practice of law into the courts.[110]

And,

> there were political parties, but the organizations were controlled by rings, which in turn were parts of State rings, which in turn were backed and used by leading business interests through which this corrupt and corrupting system reached with its ramifications far and high and low into the social organization.[111]

Polk's 1890 address on the power of capital, which "has levied tribute on the great political parties . . . which must be paid in servile party subserviency to its greedy demands"[112] is emphatic. This account could have been written by supporters of rigorous campaign finance laws today:

> Private individuals who have business affairs that require . . . action on the part of public officials, therefore make it a regular practice to

contribute large sums of money for what are termed "political purposes"; that is, for bands of music, political meetings, and the many and
large lawful expenses of a political campaign as now conducted . . . .
[M]en do not call that bribery. There is no direct agreement for any
payment of money, for a specific vote or act, or for any vote or act. . . .
The ordinary idea of corruption is one of mere pecuniary corruption.
But what difference does it make, in results, whether you buy official
action with private money or with a public office?[113]

Despite the sometimes simplistic rhetoric of enemy big business and
doubt about whether parties are perverters of democracy all on their
own, progressives do not trace a straight causal line from "the money
power" to political corruption. Steffens conceded that the words "big
business" are "a blind phrase that leads nowhere."[114] "Big money" is
more political trigger than social analysis.

This stands in plain contrast to radical political critiques of representative democracy in which it is ridiculous to see political parties
as anything but tools of economic elites. Social theorists from Marxists to democratic socialists ascribe primacy to economic forces. The
answer to the question, "who makes the decisions that are ostensibly made by the people?" is the ruling class, capital, those vested in
the economic status quo.[115] Insofar as electoral politics figures at all,
these forces capture parties, buy candidates, and sell them to voters.
Radical critics have no particular antipathy toward parties and do
not spend their ammunition firing at them. Parties are epiphenomenal. Political conflict is something comparatively trivial. "Political
action might pervert human affairs; at its best, it could only register
social reality."[116]

Progressive suspicion of arrant business interests simply does not
rise to the level (or plumb the depths) of a Marxist analysis or any
other comprehensive social theory. To do away with "everything as to
which there can ever be a question of privilege or blackmail" is Teddy
Roosevelt's definition of socialism. He dismissed it with breathtaking
casualness in a letter to Steffens: "socialism, incidentally, wouldn't
work."[117] Predatory poverty is as bad as predatory wealth; "the rich
must be fair and the poor must be contented—or, if not contented,

at least they must be orderly."[118] Radical designs for economic and social restructuring, whether significant redistributive policies or schemes of public ownership ("the only permanent check upon the enslavement of the people by the most amazing plutocracy the world has ever seen"[119]), were not a signature of historical progressivism, nor are they today. Indeed, some progressives contemplated socialism through their own lens and were sympathetic mainly on the bizarre ground that socialism would eliminate corrupt and corrupting parties: "That it would substitute public for private ownership of the agencies of production has overshadowed in general consideration its necessary effect upon political parties," Roosevelt complained.[120] The positions I lump together promiscuously as "radical" critiques of representative democracy charged early progressives with conservatism, and still do. They want both wealth and democracy (with good reason, given their connection).[121]

Whatever hold "the money power" has, progressives never entirely abandon the notion of parties as principals. Politics shapes the creation and distribution of wealth. Political favors and policy create economic elites and corporate "clots." The three-volume turn-of-the-century *History of the Great American Fortunes*, like its counterpart published at the next turn of the century, *Wealth and Democracy*, are snarling *political* histories of plunder and pre-emption, driven by policy, not self-directing markets or economic laws.[122] When progressives say economics creates and controls men's activities, they mean, as Frederick Howe did, economic institutions traceable to political privileges and concessions[123] and to the "expert political minority" that manages party affairs.[124] One self-professed heir of historical progressivism blasts "the reductionist tendency to trivialize the entire domain of politics by looking upon it as a reflex of more fundamental things going on elsewhere in society."[125] For undue influence, parties are *primus inter pares*, even if they do not operate alone.

It also helps to understand progressive antipartyism to see that it is not egalitarian. Indignation is aroused by privilege and by specific, blatant political inequalities. Both terms are significant. *Political* institutions and influence, not background social and economic structures, matter most. And *inequality* has sufficient meaning by itself for political purposes, without an account of equality. This is worth a pause. Consider the contrast to political philosophy's characteristic attentiveness to the complex conceptual facets of political equality. "Justice requires that individuals be treated equally with regard to their interests," and "each citizen ought to have equal resources to affect the outcomes of the collective decision-making procedure."[126] In Rawls's terms, the regulative principle is "approximately equal . . . opportunities to influence the outcome of political decisions."[127] Political philosophers assign an expressive value to political equality as well. Political equality is valuable as a mark of citizen status, not only as a means to other ends. Participation demonstrates one's standing as a citizen, and equal participatory opportunities are a concrete expression of respect. "One could hardly take seriously one's status as an equal citizen . . . if owing to a lack of resources one was precluded from advancing one's views effectively in the public forum."[128] In the language of contemporary theory, political equality is a principal form of "recognition" as an equal; it is the public status assigned by democratic institutions. We will be disappointed if we look for even a pale reflection of systematic analysis of the elements of political equality in progressive political thought, much less interest in the foundations of political equality.[129] Here is the noticeably divergent sound of progressivism: "Wealth disparity introduces massive political inequality skewed to a predictable set of self-interested positions" and permits "wholly unjustifiable differences in political power to emerge. . . . The obvious inequalities introduced . . . cause many persons to lose faith in the system."[130] Progressive arguments against partisan gerrymandering, say, or the party cartel are about political entrenchment and undue influence, not political equality.

One illustration underscores this contrast and progressive attention to particular inequalities rather than equality. Political philosophers make equality the centerpiece of their analyses of just elections. The dominant view holds that money is the equivalent of votes (not the analogue of speech) and, of course, that votes should have equal weight. Personal and corporate wealth should not be allowed to translate into unequal political influence, or unequal opportunities to attempt to persuade. This norm of political equality is reflected in schemes for an "equal-dollars-per-voter" campaign finance scheme or vouchers that citizens can use to support candidates or election-oriented organizations.[131] Little of this makes its way into progressive accounts. Strategies focus on insulating elections specifically from powerful economic forces. Progressives recommend restrictions and cabining to correct for sinister interest, not to equalize opportunities to influence political outcomes. "The integrity of the political process"[132] is harmed by special interests. It is antiplutocratic, not egalitarian. The compensation for theoretical wispiness is an acute sense of the practical locus and effects of undue influence.

Simply, inequality, not equality, is the touchstone, and inequality is defined by concrete instances of "undue influence" by "the few." "Do the people rule?" is a way of pointing to those others who actually rule, and draws on the cumulative experience of things that go wrong. The perversion of democracy is adequately captured by the charge of privilege—somebody trying to get a tariff, subsidy, franchise, or benefit from government.[133] The familiar antiparty language is appropriately negative: "distortion of the political process," "corrosion," or "undue influence" are the dominant terms; oligarchy, aristocracy, elites, and "special interests" are the targets. Progressive antiparty critics, attuned to the larger system, as they are in the second phase of anxiety of influence, are democrats but not egalitarians or social radicals.

Cycling Through the Phases of Anxiety

The anxiety of influence makes antipartyism interesting and renewable. The concept of "system" admits circularity, feedback of influence, and with it the elusiveness of cause and blame. Who is agent and who principal? When is the connection between big money and big parties bribery and when is it extortion? The "system" is resonant of a Foucauldian world. Steffens observed:

> everything I looked into in organized society was really a dictatorship, in this sense, that it was an organization of the privileged for the control of privileges, of the sources of privilege, and of the thoughts

and acts of the unprivileged, and that neither the privileged nor the unprivileged, neither the bosses nor the bossed, understood this or mean it.[134]

Teddy Roosevelt confessed to the anxiety: "The affair dragged on for an indefinite time; no one was able actually to determine whether it was a case of blackmail on the one hand, or of bribery on the other." In "Phases of State Legislation," he described taking charge of a bill: "I had stipulated that not a penny should be paid to insure its passage. It therefore became necessary to see what pressure could be brought to bear on the recalcitrant members; and, accordingly, we had to find out who were the authors and sponsors of their political being."[135] The "authors and sponsors of their political being" could be national corporations, businesses in the district, constituents united by some interest, or groups outside the district whose interests and values conform to the representative's (or party's) own or to party managers'. And the direction is not clear: "While it is true that the parties compete for the support of the interests, it is also true that the interests compete for the support of the parties."[136] The direction is left ambiguous in this statement, for example, that parties' historic traffic in places and honors is supplanted by a more insidious "traffic in policies."[137]

Senator John McCain, co-sponsor of the 2002 campaign finance reform bill, laid the blame on parties when he referred to "an elaborate influence-peddling scheme by which both parties conspire to stay in office by selling the country to the highest bidder."[138] Former senator and presidential candidate Bill Bradley's account is less clear:

> Money not only determines who is elected, it determines who runs for office. Ultimately it determines what government accomplishes—or fails to accomplish. . . . Real reform of democracy, reform as radical as those of the Progressive era and deep enough to get government moving again, must begin by completely breaking the connection between money and politics.[139]

There is no indication of direction of influence here; "breaking the connection" covers all possibilities. "The basic problem was, and is, that in our democratic system, government and policy is developed through ongoing contact and cooperation with legislators, most of whom are candidates most of the time, executive officials serving the President and Vice-President who often are candidates, and political party representatives."[140]

Taft's formulation captured the ambiguity better than any other, and resonates today: Congress, legislatures, city councils, and local authorities, he wrote, are all "under suspicion of yielding unduly to corporate influence."[141] "Yielding unduly" does not mean quite the same thing as "undue influence." "Undue influence" is a bolder causal assertion—the direction of corruption is one-way, from business interests and private wealth to parties, or vice versa. "Yielding unduly" is more nuanced, and parcels out some blame to each side. Both formulations use the phrase "influence," which suggests some mechanism of covert pressure. Both are plagued by the elusiveness of "undue," which suggests that influence and yielding can be fitting, respectable, justifiable. It must be, if representation is to have any meaning, if not all interests and influences are sinister.

There is little new in charges of corruption or in the interventions proposed to "break the connection between money and politics," to which I turn in a moment, or in anxiety about which way influence operates and whether "the system" can be unraveled. Many reformers and democratic theorists today are progressives in the latitudinarian sense I have employed. Their aim is not to attack social inequality or to effect economic restructuring but to insulate government from corruption or the appearance of corruption or "undue influence" or, in the recent variation, "privileged access." Since the early 1970s, observes one political theorist, government has "responded to public demands for new rules to limit campaign contributions, require disclosure of financial interests, restrict the gifts officials may accept, and regulate the types of jobs they may take after they leave office."[142] These rules may not have been a response to "public demands," in fact, but it is a quick summary of the elements of a strategy of containment. Insulation begins with elections,[143] and the chief target of institutional reform has been campaign financing.[144] The imperative is to cordon off elections, whether the target is the influence of "the money power" on parties or the influence of parties themselves through their funding of candidates. "The root of all evil" cannot be uprooted, but it can be cabined.

One motivation for reform stands out brightly as distinctively antiparty: the charge that the perception of "undue influence" depresses political participation. It is one thing to speak of "the actual corruption threatened by large financial contributions and the eroding of public confidence in the electoral process through the appearance of corruption";[145] to say that the perception of the "undue influence" of contributions on elections makes ordinary citizens "cynical and discouraged";[146] or to affirm that "massive circumvention of the federal campaign finance laws had produced a profound public cynicism about the very integrity of our political system."[147] These descriptions of public attitudes are ascertainable, if not exactly measurable. It is another thing altogether to assert a causal connection to nonparticipation such that "money squeezes out" participation, except for participation by blind partisans. The effect of this stronger claim is not just to add force to the conclusion that "nothing would do more to restore faith in democracy, as well as democracy's competence to address real problems, than radical campaign finance reform." Beyond that, in saying "money talks louder than votes and voters increasingly stay home,"[148] the suggestion in context is that the ordinary voters who stay home are not partisans but Independents. The aim of reform is to return confidence and influence to them, to excite their participation, and I assess these proposals in the next chapter.

The Anxiety of Influence: *FEC v. Colorado Republican Federal Campaign Committee*

I will use *FEC* as a window onto the currency of the anxiety of influence.[149] All the points are covered: the progressive move to cabin elections from the "undue influence" of money on politics, of money on parties, and, for some hopefuls, of parties per se. The chief mechanism of containment in the United States is campaign finance laws curtailing contributions to candidates and parties: the Tillman Act of 1907, the 1947 legislation, the Federal Election Campaign Act

241

Amendment of 1974 and the 2002 Bipartisan Campaign Reform Act. Opinions in Supreme Court rulings in cases challenging campaign finance legislation are near perfect expressions of what I have called the anxiety of influence. One case, the 2001 Supreme Court decision *FEC v. Colorado Republican Federal Campaign Committee*, repays attention because it makes the phases of anxiety vivid. The case is about party expenditures specifically, and we see that parties appear both as agents of corporate predators and other special interests and as autonomous actors pursuing their own special interests. My perspective is the antiparty tenor of opinions in this case, and given this I set aside discussion of First Amendment doctrine. I also set aside debates about the effect of spending on the quality of campaigns: whether restricting contributions and expenditures "reduces the quantity of expression by restricting the number of issues discussed, the depth of their explanation, and the size of the audience reached"[150] or whether restrictions are a way to limit the distortion of information and upgrade deliberation.

FEC v. Colorado upheld a federal law that put a wedge between parties and candidates. The law limits the contributions a national or state party organization can make to its own congressional candidates' campaigns.[151] The ruling in this case tracks the 1976 decision in *Buckley v. Valeo*, the modern constitutional baseline.[152] There, the Court upheld legally mandated limits on direct contributions to candidates, in order to combat corruption or the appearance of corruption. It also ruled that expenditures by individuals and groups "in coordination" with candidates had the same potential for corruption as direct contributions.[153] But the Court struck down limits on "independent expenditures" by interest and advocacy groups in support of candidates. They judged these to be poor sources of leverage and unlikely to be corrupting on the theory that from a candidate's point of view they might be unwelcome, duplicative, or counterproductive. Against this background, the issue raised in *FEC* is "whether a party is otherwise in a different position from other political speakers."[154] Following the reasoning in *Buckley*, the Court held parties to the same constraints, for the same reasons, as other groups, and it required parties' unregulated expenditures be made without consultation or coordination with candidates. The law at issue in *FEC* therefore restricted parties' ability to fund their own candidates. As the Colorado Republican Party's brief explains, under the statute, the Republican Campaign Committee "would face serious criminal penalties if, in cooperation or consultation with its own candidate for Congress, it were to pay for a single letter to each eligible Colorado voter, or even to . . . each registered Colorado Republican, explaining how electing that candidate would advance the Party's platform and values."[155]

A parsing of *FEC* briefs and opinions reveals three main positions. The dissenting justices defend parties as institutions crucial to democracy. They characterize parties as voluntary associations that run candidates who share the party's policy goals. (Without their candidates, parties would be just another political interest group.[156]) The dissenters go on to defend coordinated expenditures on behalf of candidates.[157]

> [A party expenditure] not only reflects its members' views about the philosophical and governmental matters that bind them together, it also seeks to convince others to join those members in a practical democratic task, the task of creating a government that voters can instruct and hold responsible for subsequent success or failure.[158]

The dissent rehearses the obvious. "Voters know parties by their candidates and know candidates by their party affiliations. Mutual attribution is unavoidable. Without broaching the metaphysical question of identity, it is clear that parties have a "natural, strong, preexisting tie" to candidates. Put simply, "forcing a party to engage in campaign speech independent of its candidate is an 'unnatural act.'"[159] On this view, prohibiting party expenditures in coordination with candidates is a serious not just incidental curtailment of party activity. The predicted effect of treating parties under the law as if they were just another rich individual or interest group is, as a later dissent in *McConnell* worried, to "dilut[e] the central role that political parties traditionally have played in our democratic process."[160]

The opposing position set out in the *FEC* brief and adopted by the Court is that parties should not be treated differently from other wealthy individuals or groups seeking to influence candidates and policies. "Rich political activists crop up, and the United States has known its Citizens Kane. Their money speaks loudly too, and they are therefore burdened by restrictions on its use just as parties are."[161] Parties should be in the same position vis-à-vis limits on campaign funding as wealthy political activists, media executives, and political action committees. Parties should not be permitted any financial influence denied other participants in public dialogue.[162] The brief and the majority opinion are both noticeably, aggressively antiparty. Petitioner's brief offers an extended narrative of the Framers' distrust of parties in support of the position that parties have no favored constitutional status. Despite parallels between parties and Citizens Kane, parties are *not* just wielders of "undue influence" among others. Rather, the majority opinion casts parties as significantly different and more dangerous than other groups.

When it comes to explaining their dangerousness, we see the Court cycling through the phases of the anxiety of influence I have described. The majority's hostile response to the dissent's characterization of parties as associations formed to run a candidate who shares its policy goals expresses the view that parties are captured: "It would ignore reality to think that the party role is adequately described by speaking generally of electing particular candidates."[163] The majority redescribes parties as funnels from donors to candidates. Parties serve as conduits for the "special interest" money that candidates are prohibited from receiving directly. They are "matchmakers."[164] Coordinated expenditures are "pass throughs" from donors:

> Parties are necessarily the instruments of some contributors, such as PACs, whose object is not to support the party's message or to elect party candidates, but rather to support a specific candidate for the sake of a position on one, narrow issue, or even to support any candidate who will be obliged to contributors. Parties thus perform functions more complex than simply electing candidates: they act *as agents* for spending on behalf of those who seek to produce obligated officeholders. It is this party role, which functionally unites parties with other self-interested political actors, that the Party Expenditure Provision targets.[165]

It makes no difference that the party expenditures at issue in *FEC* come from "hard money" raised in small regulated amounts and not large "soft money" donations. In either case, coordinated expenditures are nothing but "disguised contributions" given "as a quid pro quo for improper commitments from the candidates."[166] It is blamable "myopia" to refuse to see "how the power of money actually works in the political structure."[167]

Expenditures coordinated between candidates and parties at issue in this case were judged the functional equivalent of direct contributions to candidates, corrupting and therefore regulable. In 2003 in *McConnell*, the centerpiece of the Court's ruling on the Bipartisan Campaign Reform Act was a similarly stern position vis-à-vis "soft money"—previously unregulated donations from corporations, unions, and rich individuals to the parties rather than to individual candidates. The funds were principally used for general party activities like voter identification and registration, "get out the vote" drives, and generic party advertising. Defenders of this restriction argued that in fact, the funds were funneled through state parties (described as "outposts of the national parties"[168]) back to federal candidates, hence the phrase "soft money loophole" and characterizing soft money as the equivalent of money laundering. Soft money donated to parties, the *McConnell* Court agreed, is simply a way of eviscerating the restrictions upheld in *FEC*.

We recognize the majority opinions in *FEC* and *McConnell* as one phase of the anxiety of influence. Coordinated expenditures, like campaign contributions from individuals or corporations, "buy influence." The original formulation in *Buckley v. Valeo* that these funds are a source of "corruption and appearance of corruption" has been amplified by judges and legal and political theorists piling on other descriptions of harm: "undue influence" and "corrosive effect." In a perfect echo of "corruption and the appearance of corruption," the *McConnell* Court says the public interest in regulation "extend[s] to 'undue influence on an officeholder's judgment, and the appearance of such influence.' "[169] *McConnell* names an additional species of harm: contributions and expenditures buy "special access" to officeholders. We see the concern shift from quid pro quo, cash-for-votes

245

exchanges (covered by criminal law and difficult to detect) to actual influence on political decisions ("to claim that such actions do not change legislative outcomes surely misunderstands the legislative process"[170]) to "access" in an effort to influence officials' judgment. Nothing is more elusive than influence (except "undue"), and the *McConnell* majority concedes that "mere political favoritism or opportunity for influence alone is insufficient to justify regulation."[171] Yet the Court turns inconclusiveness into a justification for upholding restrictions: "Unlike straight cash-for-votes transactions, such corruption is neither easily detected nor practical to criminalize,"[172] so it is reasonable to cordon off party money.

In the passages of the majority opinion I have cited, parties are cast as agents for special interests, "unseen principals." There is the thought that parties are captured, manipulated: "Whether they like it or not," they act as agents for spending of those who seek to produce "obligated officeholders."[173] Parties are open "to exploitation as channels for circumventing contribution and coordinated spending limits binding on other political players."[174] This takes us through one phase of the anxiety of influence.

There is the usual uncertainty, though, as "anxiety" predicts. The second phase acknowledges party autonomy and casts parties as principals, not funnels, channels, instruments, or agents. We find this, too, in the majority opinion in *FEC v. Colorado*, where the Justices concede that outside contributions to parties and candidates do not necessarily imply that parties are controlled by donors. Parties are self-serving actors "peddling access." Parties—that is, their organizational leadership and chief officeholders—exercise undue influence on their own, for their own political reasons, and candidates must be insulated from them too. Parties are counterparts, not agents, of "big money." Indeed, they are in an even better position to exercise undue influence on candidates than are private donors. The Court concedes that it is natural for parties and candidates to work together ("financial support of candidates is essential to the nature of political parties as we know them"[175]) and that breaking the connection can inhibit promotion of the party's message. But finally the public interest in constraining if not severing this connection is decisive.

What undue influence do parties exert on their own candidates? The answer is simple and startling. "Effective use of party resources in support of party candidates may encourage candidate loyalty and responsiveness to the party."[176] Why is the "effective use of party resources" to encourage loyalty and responsiveness a democratic harm? Discipline is central to the responsible party government view of representative democracy, for example. Why shouldn't parties condition financial support for candidates on adherence to the platform or cooperation with leadership? As the dissent in *FEC* points out: "The very aim of a political party is to influence its candidate's stance on issues and, if the candidate takes office or is reelected, his votes."[177] The Court majority paints a different picture: of candidates vulnerable to the tyranny of party.[178] Parties produce "obligated officeholders" and "indebtedness." We hear echoes of the early progressive claim that the party is corrupt and corrupting because it creates dependents. Dependent on party and obligated to leadership, candidates are not only unresponsive to electors, they are inhibited from exercising the virtue of independence.

Evidence suggests that direct party contributions to campaigns accounts for a small percentage of candidates' funding, and that "less than one percent of party money is contributed to federal candidates and only about ten percent is spent on their behalf."[179] Moreover, for better or worse, parties do not distribute funds to candidates to ensure faithfulness to the party program or leadership, but for strategic reasons. "Maintaining party control over seats is paramount."[180] The object of funding is to win close races in an effort to control legislatures, and "the primary consideration in allocating funds is which races are marginal."[181] The Democratic Senatorial Campaign Committee, for example, allocates money on the basis of a candidate's poll numbers, the financial health of the campaign, and which party candidates have the best chance of winning. A Court majority in a later case accepted studies showing that political parties "target" their contributions to candidates in competitive races and that this represents a significant amount of total candidate funding in these races.[182] From a progressive antiparty perspective, however, the fact that the Democratic Senatorial Campaign Committee or Vermont

Democratic Party allocates money strategically, that it is "not acting as a mere conduit, allowing donors to contribute money in excess of the legal limits," is no comfort.[183] It is proof of parties' undue influence: representatives who are financially indebted to the party as a whole or to individual party leaders with their own political interests and agendas. Insulating campaigns and elections from the influence of the major parties is as important for democracy as cabining off the direct influence of "the money power."

Competitiveness

If progressives were not so intent on insulating elections from the undue influence of parties, one consideration weighing against elements of campaign finance legislation might have purchase. The contention (around which empirical disputes swirl) is that soft money contributions to parties and party expenditures on behalf of candidates increase competition. The bulk of party support goes to nonincumbents, and party funding is the chief resource for most challengers. (Little political action committee money flows to nonincumbents.[184]) Restricting party spending hurts challengers. It depresses the regulated rivalry of major parties. Moreover, the Bipartisan Campaign Reform Act (BCRA) is said to disadvantage minor parties and independent candidates. It applies the same restraints on fundraising and party spending to minor parties, on grounds that even one minor party candidate managing to get elected can be corrupted or suffer the appearance of corruption.[185] "Everyone knows, this is an area in which evenhandedness is not fairness."[186]

This consideration was central in a case challenging Vermont's "extreme" restrictions on contributions to candidates for state office and on party expenditures—including limits on volunteer expenses. In 2006 in *Randall v. Sorrell* the Court struck down a Vermont law for setting limits judged impermissibly low. The restrictions inhibited "an appropriately competitive, accountable, and fair democratic electoral process." Extremely low limits "implicate the integrity of the electoral process."[187] As Justice Breyer's majority opinion explained, stringent restrictions can "harm the electoral process by preventing challengers from mounting effective campaigns against incumbent officeholders, thereby reducing democratic accountability."[188] The interesting aspect of this decision is that it did not rest on voters' individual rights to contribute or parties' First Amendment rights to effective political association. True, the Court was concerned that the limits "would reduce the voice of political parties" in Vermont to a "whisper."[189] "Mute" and "hamper" pop up in the opinion. The focus, however, was candidates' ability to mount a campaign: the law "prevents the candidates from amassing the resources necessary for effective advocacy." Taken together, the constraints Vermont would impose add up. Justice Breyer lists them:

> substantial restrictions on the ability of candidates to raise the funds necessary to run a competitive election, on the ability of political parties to help their candidates get elected, and on the ability of individual citizens to volunteer their time to campaigns.

The *Randall* Court takes on the role prescribed by progressive legal scholars it had declined to assume in partisan gerrymandering cases, where one party or parties in collusion undermined competition. Here, the Court acted to protect "the structural integrity of the democratic process"—meaning "competitive elections." This is welcome to those concerned above all with competitiveness, regulated rivalry. But as we have seen, stern antiparty progressives do not accept competitive two-partyism as the right correction for what is wrong with the system.

A commentator on campaign finance reform cautions: "Crucial to understanding of American public funding is that it has not been developed primarily to help parties,"[190] and in *Randall* the Court came to the parties' rescue by striking down "extreme" limits. But skeptics question this analysis. After all, the principal piece of federal legislation (BCRA) was, as its name indicates, "bipartisan." One explanation for the bill is collusion by incumbent partisans, and Justice Scalia argues the point in *McConnell*: any restriction on the flow of money is anticompetitive. The majority logic that struck down a particular set of contribution and expenditure limits as "extreme" should apply to all limits on this account. BCRA is an incumbent protection bill. "We are governed by Congress and this legislation prohibits the criticism of Members of Congress by those entities most capable of giving such criticism loud voice: national political parties and corporations, both of the commercial and the not-for-profit kind."[191] The same concern has been raised about the basic provisions for public financing of campaigns, which favor major party candidates over Independents and new party candidates. The *Buckley* Court upheld these provisions, judging that Congress (i.e., the major parties ensconced there) has a legitimate interest in not funding hopeless candidates and in not promoting factionalism.[192] In response, the opposition characterizes the Federal Election Campaign Act of 1974 as "a major party protection act."[193] Justice Souter, who would have upheld all limitations on contributions and spending, objects: suspicion that "incumbents cannot be trusted to set fair limits, because facially neutral limits do not in fact give challengers an even break . . . is itself a proper subject of suspicion."[194]

Predictions that BCRA would have fatal consequences for parties have not been borne out in the short run, and the *McConnell* Court appears at this writing to be more accurate than party declinists if only because the history of campaign finance regulation proves that political parties are extraordinarily flexible in adapting to new restrictions on their fundraising abilities."[195] There are always fresh proposals because of the "hydraulic" nature of the flow of money and because of parties' adaptability and capacity to compensate for obstacles.[196]

That said, if the only unregulated money in elections is independent expenditures (principally advertising) uncoordinated with campaign organizations, the legal framework invites the creation of entities dedicated to raising and spending unlimited amounts on behalf of issues and indirectly (because the law sets limits on electioneering ads) on behalf of candidates.[197] Some of these groups are ideological and policy groups whose core mission is political advocacy. But often these are "stealth" committees whose names conceal their political orientation and interests, much less their donors. Justice Kennedy spoke in these terms of political action committees that "attract their own elite power brokers, who operate in ways obscure to the ordinary citizen."[198] Party money comes in part from interest groups, true, but it is also an antidote to interest group advocacy and electioneering. The point is that antiparty progressives are disinclined to worry that reforms might weaken parties relative to other political groups, and that committees invented with the sole purpose of influencing election outcomes might drown out the voices of partisans.

For antiparty advocates of regulation, contribution and expenditure limits are not the best way to cordon off democratic politics from big money operating on and through parties. The preferred progressive correction, of course, is public financing of elections, with ceilings on spending and the provision of floors for all candidates. "Clean elections" (the phrase is pure progressivism) would eliminate all private money from campaigns, including a candidate's own. It is perfectly consistent with antipartyism that public financing of election campaigns, where it exists, sends money to individual candidates directly, not via the party organization or elected leadership. A proposal to provide public campaign funds in presidential elections to political parties rather than to candidates was changed to ensure that "a national committee of a political party will not be able to use and control a large Federal payment as a weapon to dictate party policies and strategies . . . to candidates and potential candidates."[199] There is also the progressive hope that rightly designed and made mandatory, public financing might increase the number of challengers, third parties, and Independents.

Not even public financing can assuage progressive concerns about the undue influence of party, though. "The system" is robust. Candidates are dependent on parties, even apart from funding. For example, they need the support of party insiders, whose convergence on a favored presidential candidate as been called the "invisible primary." The requirement that candidates run primaries in fifty states means that none has the staff or know-how to conduct in effect hundreds of campaigns around the country. Nonmaterial resources are scarce, and party leaders allot them. The process remains party-centered.[200] Progressive antipartyism remains resistant.

All Interests Are Sinister Interests

At the limit, in the grimmest accounts, "undue influence" is global. It refers to all promises and deals, services and pressures that are part of politics generally and party politics specifically. "In a rough sense," Robert Dahl wrote, "the essence of all competitive politics is bribery of the electorate by the politicians. . . . The farmer . . . supports a candidate committed to high support prices, the businessman . . . supports an advocate of low corporation taxes . . . the consumer . . . votes for candidates opposed to a sales tax."[201] For those who seriously adhere to this dour perspective, elections are under the permanent shadow of quid pro quo. Worse, elections aside, corruption is intrinsic to the whole system of constituency representation and service. It produces "obligated officeholders." The relation *is* confounding. "Isn't our corrupt government, after all, representative?" Steffens asked.[202] He records a Philadelphia politician's puzzled confession: "I'm loyal to my ward and to my—own, and yet—Well, there's something wrong with me, and I'd like to know: what is it?"[203]

The implication here is not just that self-interested behavior that does not take account of the interests of others skews democratic outcomes, but also that self-interest is somehow illegitimate. "Deeper corruption" is no help in distinguishing self-interest (always tainted) from public interest, though. It is no help in explaining why conflicting views of the public interest—over social security or national security—are any less likely to be tainted by partisan pandering or promises. It does not allow the presumably equally noxious possibility that parties identify and even create interests and opinions rather than reflect or exploit them: the view that "the Member first transmits his Notions to his Creatures, and they, under the name of his Constituents, instruct him, as he first instructed them."[204] "Deeper corruption" simply expresses the anxiety of influence taken to a purist pitch. The identification of responsiveness to constituent interests with bribery and of service with pandering does more than dilute the notion of vote trafficking. Those who identify "deeper corruption" with "the politics of self interest itself" level a wholesale attack on democracy understood in part as a matter of aggregating interests (and judgments about legitimate interests) and translating them into policy—no matter that interests are well-thought-out, deliberated, and fairly negotiated. The author of "deeper corruption" rejects Justice Brennan's claim that "our tradition of political pluralism" assumes "voters will pursue their individual good through the political process." Stringent progressives imagine something like the reverse of proportional representation, which ties officeholders closely to a self-identified constituency. This position aims at common agreement about the public interest. It imagines democracy as "soulcraft." Its ideal is independence of the sort we recall from the keynote speaker at the 1912 Progressive convention: "I would like to be an American Congressman."[205]

For the most part, however, the anxiety of influence does not rest on suspicion of all private interests or a particular normative account of the public interest. Its lodestars are negative: aristocracy and privilege, "undue influence" and "yielding unduly." And in this cycle of anxiety, the onus is on parties. The negative implications are clear, then, and the positive prescriptions are guided by antipartyism. What would it take to correct the system?

CHAPTER 6

―――≫•◇•≪―――

Correcting the System: Association, Participation, and Deliberation

Two Interventions

"Anxiety of influence" encompasses nothing less than the question "who rules"? In the framework of progressive antipartyism, the question is truncated, concentrated on undue influence that makes itself felt through parties and electoral politics. What can break the cycle of democratic perversion by parties or their "unseen principals"? Can the system be corrected? It must be, if we accept the notion fundamental to progressivism and echoed in contemporary democratic theory, that "the function of democracy has been to provide the public with a second power system, an alternative power system, which can be used to counterbalance the economic power."[1] It must be if the regulative ideal of democracy is "empowering the common, recognizable interests of ordinary people, and nothing more."[2]

The correctives proposed do not have social or economic restructuring as their goal. They are rooted in neither a particular theory of justice nor a systematic account of fair terms of participation. The preoccupation, now familiar, is countering "undue influence." "The common recognized interests of ordinary people" is defined in contrast to "the money power" or "special interests." Its principal content is oppositional. Its positive content is minimal but not negligible: a connection between people and government loosely described as "responsiveness."[3]

I've surveyed the spate of progressive reforms aimed at curtailing parties—initiative and referenda, civil service reform, and others, including the very-much-alive business of primary election reform and campaign finance reform. Two other interventions are more substantial than legislative "fixes." They are rooted in democratic theory and are a persistent part of political life and thought today, and both are driven by the steady drumbeat of antipartyism. Both correctives aim at the failings that alarmed Lincoln Steffens when he wrote: the party system is a device for the prevention of the expression of the common will; it misleads and obscures public opinion; it is simply another form of despotism.[4]

One corrective is voluntarism, first put into self-conscious use as a counter to party organization during the Progressive Era. Voluntarism as a principle rests on confidence in the people's ability to form groups and advocate collectively in the public interest in opposition to special interests. In today's terms, the voluntary associations of civil society provide motivation and resources for civic engagement, counterweights to assignable special interests, and in the aggregate a democratic alternative to "the system." In the first half of this chapter I focus on the aspirations of "good civil society" theorists to escape the dominance of parties and elections. I am critical of these sometimes fanciful expectations. But I am aware that there is nothing fanciful about the actual explosion of groups—advocacy groups, interest groups, self-styled public interest groups—and the challenge they pose to parties. Moreover, if there is a "moral distinctiveness" to partisanship, as I argue in chapter 7, then insofar as the purpose and effect of these groups is to idealize a plurality of memberships and political identities that stand opposed to partisanship, they are troubling and need deflating.

The second corrective is popular participation in elections. Voters can unsettle "the system" if their participation is deliberative and nonpartisan. Recall Albert Stickney's objection: "Little thought has been given, in our political past, to the question how a people is to think—as a people—to form and utter a judgment—as a people . . . as regards selection of governors."[5] One challenge for those rehabilitating participation is to make electoral decisions deliberative. Parties, on this account, are obstacles to thoughtful, independent consideration of men and measures. A parallel concern, repeated ceaselessly, is that the major parties not only create a class of inestimable partisans, but, in addition, they depress participation by nonpartisans. Parties *demobilize* citizens. The question is, how to revive electoral participation and refashion it to give influence to Independents? In the second half of this chapter I look at deliberative democratic theory with a view to theorists' attempt to divorce participation from parties in order to improve the quality of popular decisions and amplify the influence of Independents.

Versions of interventions in the "system" by means of voluntary association and improved and improving popular participation are at the heart of democratic theory today. We recognize these theorists as heirs of early Progressives in disposition and political imagination, and plainly in their persistent antipartyism. I continue to apply the "progressive" label because it fits. I attend in some detail to their ambitions for civil society and electoral reform, mapping this antiparty territory and marking where theorists go astray. I note "contemporary political theory's silence and myopia about the place of party and partisanship in democratic politics"[6] and show that on their own terms, democratic theorists are wrong to revile or disregard them.

As a prelude to my discussion of these strains of contemporary democratic theory, notice that there appears at first to be little trace of the once-standard categorization of democratic theory. One account was minimalist democracy (Schumpeter's competitive struggle among party elites for the people's votes); a second was interest group or pluralist democracy; a third was participatory democracy. The types were analytic tools, but they also stood in dynamic normative relation to one another. Minimal, electoral democracy inspired the sociological realism and aspiration to democratic inclusiveness of interest group pluralism. In turn, the contingencies and inequalities of pluralism provided the impetus for participatory democratic theory. In political theory today, new taxonomies like aggregative versus deliberative democracy or market versus forum or liberal democracy versus republicanism appear to have supplanted the older structure. But a closer look suggests that it only appears to have been superceded. Actually, the older categories have been refreshed and renamed. Elite democracy corresponds to progressive characterizations of a system dominated by entrenched parties where, at best, voting works "simply as a random shock whose virtue is to check the elite's authoritarian tendencies."[7] Pluralism and participatory theory correspond to the two types of progressive intervention to correct the party system. Civil society theory is the refined and moralized counterpart of interest group pluralism, and deliberative democracy is the philosophically mature counterpart of participatory theory. Advocates see them, as advocates did their precursors, as counters to competition or collusion between party organizations and as countervailing forces to the undue influences that operate on and through them.

Pluralist Theory

Taking up the thread from chapter 5, campaign finance measures are a signature progressive response to "corruption," "undue influence," and "privileged access" by special interests. The suspicion that insulating elections from unlimited private funding is little more than a provocation to rearrange the channels of influence is irrepressible because both parties and special interests are endlessly resourceful. The dispiriting "hydraulics" of campaign funding is just part of the grim picture. Money directed to party organizations and campaigns is not the only "way in" to official decision making, after all, and no reform focused exclusively on "clean elections" blocks other avenues of influence. Progressive interest in voluntary association is motivated in part by skepticism about the possibilities of electoral success for "the democracy" in the face of entrenched parties and their "unseen principals." An added impetus to voluntary association is recognition that even electoral success may not translate into political success.[8] Achieving representation in government may not be enough to outweigh the influence of special interests that operate on parties and officials outside and around the electoral process.

Thanks in part to the initial, formidable wave of association building by early progressives, the "group principle" has been well learned. In chapter 4 I looked briefly at progressive proselytizing for nonpartisan vigilance committees, investigative committees, law enforcement societies, people's lobbies, and voters' leagues. But where progressives had in mind citizen lobbies and small business groups as counterweights to large combinations, the actual result was wholesale activation of interest group politics. Pressure groups, advocacy groups, and self-styled public interest groups turned out to be protean. Progressives gave voluntary association moral imprimatur and provided what amounted to political instruction in direct channels to government. There is a bit of irony in the fact that early progressive associations were the model of how to create and wield organizational resources for groups of all persuasions.

Studies analyze the avenues of political influence these groups paved: direct lobbying, agenda setting, providing information to legislative committees, bill writing, formulating arguments persuasive to particular constituencies (or framing appeals to the common good).[9] Studies of what used to be aptly called "pressure groups" point to innovations like issue advertising, which is not limited to election campaigns[10] and has become a regular mechanism for supporting and opposing legislative proposals, foreign policy, presidential initiatives, and judicial appointments. Schattschneider's thesis in *Party Government* that "the distinguishing mark of pressure tactics is not merely that it does not seek to win elections, but that in addition it does not attempt to persuade a majority" may apply to persuading an electoral majority. But interest and advocacy groups today *do* mobilize voters (think AARP); they target slices of the public and propel organized campaigns of congressional letter writing, phone calls, and e-mails. Lobbying used to be defined in contrast to grass-roots mobilization, and certainly personal contacts and professional networking remain potent. The defining contrast no longer holds, though. Grass-roots lobbying techniques for contacting and influencing decision makers, first invented by citizen groups and consumer-based groups, have been adopted by all sorts of associations. In short, Schattschneider's description of pressure group "guerrilla tactics" is confounded by the attention that interest and advocacy groups, including corporations, pay to public image and public opinion.[11] All demand to be heard, pursue access, and seek influence both publicly and in the chambers of power.

From its inception, pluralist democratic theory was sensitive to the range of politically salient interests (or values or identities), and recognized that any discussion of interest "becomes inevitably a discussion of associations, for the association is the visible body of something of which the interest is the invisible motive."[12] Interest group pluralism was never simply descriptive. It was justified by the need for self-generated independent organizations as protection against elites, counters to domination and abuse of power by parties or their unseen principals. Pluralism reflected a democratic norm of inclusiveness: everyone has interests to defend and opinions to advance about his or her own good, or the group's good, or the public good, and every interest was at least potentially a political interest group. Pluralism was associated from the start with democratization.

Granted, the world of associations was never egalitarian—background social and economic resources prevent that. Well-organized and well-funded associations with staffs and legal counsel can take advantage of tax exemptions for nonprofits, for example, or create separate corporate entities for political advocacy. They negotiate the pluralist universe as disadvantaged groups cannot. Famously, "the inequality of civic engagement is unambiguous."[13] Of course, voluntary associations are no more of a piece than they are equal. Like the original progressive citizen groups, many are formed with the sole aim of political advocacy, access, and countervailing influence. Political science documents the ever growing number of nonprofit organizations supported by patrons, corporations, or foundations as well as membership dues, professionally led and dedicated to legislative lobbying and media relations: groups like NAARP or NRA or NOW.[14] Political influence is their mission. For other groups political engagement is an indirect, often unanticipated consequence of their defining activities. Nonpolitical associations from fraternal groups like the Boy Scouts to churches and mosques to business corporations take up specific political issues and nudge them into public consciousness and onto political agendas. American separation of church and state does not prohibit political advocacy by religious associations or political mobilization by clergy.[15]

Despite unequal resources, interest group pluralism was not exclusive or exclusionary, and an ever-expanding universe of private and quasi-public associations add their voices and pressure to this alternative system. Material and "post-material" organizations jockey for influence: philanthropy against philanthropy, organized gun owners against gun controllers. Association is seen as the corrective to association, just as more speech is seen as the antidote to dangerous or offensive speech.

It is not surprising that in a recent study, more people said that interest groups represent them than political parties.[16] This is significant because the two forms of political organization are not fungible. Interest and advocacy groups are typically "single-issue" pressure groups. They target beneficiaries, gun owners, say, or retirees. Their adherents are voluntarists whose "membership" has no binding character, unlike the vote. (Parties alone among associations are "strong publics," meaning their activity culminates in binding decisions and electoral success may translate into legislation.[17]) Nor are there standards for assessing the claims of often self-selected spokespersons of organized groups to represent particular people, interests, and opinions. The criteria governing authorization and accountability in formal representative institutions, loose though they may be, have not been accommodated to "lay citizens" speaking on behalf of others.[18]

These groups are committed to making *government* work—for themselves or on behalf of their notion of the public interest. Despite progressive expectations, their objective is not necessarily making democracy work.[19] Associations are under no imperative to be broadly responsive to or responsible for the electorate as a whole. Schattschneider's contrast has purchase: "The major parties must do what pressure groups need not do at all; they must consider the balance of relations among the interests."[20] This is crucial. To the extent that voluntary associations succeed in circumventing or capturing parties, to the extent that parties are cast as "umbrellas" that cover the jockeying of groups, the unique purposes of parties are lost sight of. The result is an alternate, pluralist version of competitive democracy. Interest and advocacy groups do not have to pretend to consider "the balance of relations among the interests." Certainly, in pluralist democracy, inclusiveness and counterbalancing are unplanned. They are also competitive with parties for the political attention and support of citizens and undermine "the moral distinctiveness of partisanship" that is my subject in the next chapter.[21] Yet in the rejuvenated version of pluralism I am about to describe, democratic theorists look to them for moral and political improvement, and invest the universe of voluntary associations with responsibility for circumventing or supplanting the party system.

"Good Civil Society" versus Political Parties

The ideal of voluntary association as a corrective to entrenched parties harks back to Progressive Era citizens' groups. Perhaps the most ardent account of "group organization [as] the solution of popular government" was Mary Parker Follett's *The New State*. If we leave aside both her vision of local and work-based organizations combined in a new federal system and the philosophical Idealism that gives a peculiar spiritual tenor to her work, and just focus on the "group principle," we see the aspirational face of association plainly. "The so-called evils of democracy," Follett writes, "favoritism, bribery, graft, bossism—are the evils of our lack of democracy, of our party system, and of the abuses which that system has brought."[22] Standard progressive reforms like the direct primary and the popular initiative and referendum cannot break the power of parties; the party organization is quite capable of using "direct government" for its own ends, she warned. As long as the vote is cast by isolated individuals, it cannot be progressive. Follett went on to point out the limitations of other progressive reforms directed against the party machine—what she called the "fetish" of campaigns to elect "good" men to office and the misguided preoccupation with voters. This was all just "patching, mending, restraining," not real, constructive work. Democratic reform requires a new method: the organization of men and women in nonpartisan groups for the production of common ideas and a collective purpose. "It is only through group organization that the individual learns . . . to be an effective political member." Follett predicted an evolution of self-understanding: from individual rights to individual duties to society to the culminating idea of the individual as an "activity of society," meaning group formation. "The chief need of society today is an enlightened, progressive and organized public opinion, and the first step towards enlightened and organized public opinion is an enlightened and organized group opinion."[23]

In democratic theory today, pluralism has been injected with a fresh, powerful positive valence and takes the name "civil society." It bears a moral load that "interest group pluralism" did not. Civil society is the progeny of Follett rather than David Truman. Civil society is defined by its theorists as a realm of "concrete and authentic solidarities"[24] that counter isolation, temper materialism, and create webs of connection. Associational life is the source of "trust" and "social capital," which spill over from religious groups, book clubs, and athletic teams as well as advocacy groups to public life. A point of agreement among civil society theorists is that a categorical distinction can be drawn between associations organized around ideas, values, and identity, on the one hand, and interest groups proper, on the other. For example: "public interest groups and special interest groups may be distinguished on the basis of the claims that the former advance *judgments* about the common good whereas the latter advance *interests* of a sector of the society."[25] (Of course, theorists sometimes differ in whether they judge a particular association a special interest, sinister interest, or public interest group.)

It is fair to say that pluralism has received a progressive face-lift and reappears in this moralized guise. The contributions associations are expected to make to democracy are faithful to Follett's spirit; the chief positive effect is "the group principle" itself. There is nothing natural about civic engagement, and the ordinary associations of civil society serve as boot camps of citizenship.[26] Hope for democracy rests on "dispersing [sovereignty], exploring the unrealized possibilities in . . . institutions such as schools, workplaces, churches and synagogues, trade unions and social movements."[27]

With this expectation, civil society theorists embrace voluntary associations formed for almost every conceivable purpose: religious associations, cultural and ethnic groups, quasi-civic membership groups like rotary clubs, but not political parties, which are left off every catalogue of associations.[28] This is another indication that the parameters of civil society are carefully drawn and normatively charged. Other groups besides parties are beyond the civil society pale: business corporations and in some accounts unions fall outside, again by definition. The associations of "good civil society" are not Hegelian estates, either, and members do not have fixed corporate identities. Civil society is not a segmented society and excludes groups that balkanize, enclaves mistrustful of outsiders, associations with vicious purposes and parochial norms. Naturally, judgments differ as to whether a group's internal life and organization are incongruent with liberal democracy, so that it is a "greedy" totalistic association and not an element of civil society.

The crux of what I'll call "good civil society" is that associations operate within the charmed circle of the "civil." For the most part, "participation" is a synonym for voluntary association and volunteerism broadly; it is identified with "efforts to start a hospital or help the homeless." The label "activist" attaches to community service, not specifically political participation.[29] Exemplary associations include "faith-based" groups and neighborhood organizations, philanthropic and social service groups that have a direct and immediate improving impact on their members and their beneficiaries. The justification is not only that "if you want to make a difference, you should do it face-to-face," but also that politics as it exists is disreputable, and "disillusionment," "cynicism," and "distrust" warranted.[30] Democracy is understood in informal, social terms, in Tocquevillian terms. A striking demonstration of this occurs at the basic level of definition. Consider this definition of democracy from contemporary political philosophy: "Democracy is not simply a form of politics but a framework of social and institutional conditions that facilitates free discussion among equal citizens—by providing favorable conditions for participation, association, and expression."[31] Observe its negative—"not simply a form of politics"—and its deviation from the standard political science definition of democracy as government "chosen periodically by means of popular elections in which two or more parties compete for the votes of all adults."[32] "Not simply a form of politics" is the democratic mantra of civil society theory. Associational life promises to socialize, decentralize, pluralize public functions. Parties fall outside this circle; after all, they seek to "control the levers of government." They "routinely, pervasively, and legitimately exercise influence from *within* government."[33]

Where do parties stand in all this? I have said that no list of civil society groups includes parties, and parties are often expressly excluded. A moral hierarchy of modes of civic activism sets members of voluntary associations on top and partisans on the bottom. A segment of partisans, disparagingly called "hyperactivists,"[34] is singled out and identified as quintessentially, self-servingly "interested." They constitute a "new breed of benefit seeker,"[35] "new" because the advantage sought is not patronage, because their connection to a party does not entail loyalty or discipline, and because they do not perform the drudgery of party organization. Instead, activists promise parties the support of their connections, and like the interested advocates they are, they look for specific policy outcomes.[36]

More generally, civil society theory distinguishes parties from voluntary associations and partisanship from membership. Thus, "party identification" (party ID) does not require enrollment and entails no obligation (not even voting for the party candidate); it has been described as a fiction created by primary registration laws. True, voter registration as a partisan "imposes absolutely no affirmative party obligations on the voter, in terms of time or money, and it does not even obligate him to vote for the party's positions or candidates or to vote at all."[37] Small individual contributions to parties are described as something other and less than membership dues, as one-time support for a candidate, lacking civic significance. At best, it is on a par with membership in professionally led groups where the main activity is check writing or the "Astroturf" participation of a letter-writing campaign. (Electronic mail is not dialogic, clearly, but it is churlish to deny that this is participation on a large scale.[38]) I take failure to acknowledge the volunteerism of partisanship as myopic and claims that the party has no existence for partisans in the electorate as manifestly wrong. Party organizations remain decentralized associations; federalism and the organization of elections by districts have guaranteed that. "Fifty states and innumerable districts and localities have created thousands of partisan elected officials, party leaders, and organizations with their own constituencies and supporters."[39] One estimate is 490,000 offices are filled through elections.[40] The delegate selection process in presidential campaigns requires an active campaign in fifty states at local levels—in effect hundreds of campaigns around the country. "This is a vast, vast undertaking."[41] It has been estimated that a fully staffed two-party system assumes the participation of at least 200,000 activists.

> The party organization is a grouping of people, most of them contributing their time and energy on a purely voluntary basis. Even paid professional party workers ... share many of the attributes of volunteers. [Legal definitions] ignore these men and women of the party, their goals and ambitions, their interactions and relationships. ... Yet, the activity and motivations of those men and women are closer to the real world of party politics than all the statutory paragraphs put together.[42]

It is also a blinkered perspective that fails to recognize how much the motivations of active partisans closely mirror those valued by "good civil society" theorists. The material rewards of party activism have been diminished and incentives are personal solidarity rewards, issue or ideological goals, social gratification, identification with the group, and recognition in the community. "Scholars who have questioned party workers about their motives for service ... know the familiar answers. They were asked to serve, and they assented because it was their civic duty."[43] Similarly, there is an answer to those who distinguish the "group principle" from party. Party building looks very much like lauded voluntary association. Recruiting partisans is on a continuum with cultivating voters, but it is not identical. *Candidates* may build ad hoc enclaves of activists devoted to their interests, constituencies that last for the life cycle of a campaign. But major parties are not of the moment. To be effective, parties must have long-run organizational and political goals. They have to establish and maintain local presence, build cadres of supporters, coordinate the support of social leaders, and in the case of major parties seek membership from every salient group.[44]

In certain respects it is true that parties are not voluntary associations and partisanship is not membership. In arguing in chapter 7 that partisanship is "morally distinctive," I point out the respects in which partisanship is *not* just another form of membership.[45] But a sharp analytic distinction between party identification and voluntary association in membership groups is untrue to the continuum that is partisanship, certainly to the experience of many who devote a part of their lives to party goals. The two are not mutually exclusive, but they are not fungible, either.

Civil society groups may have direct links to parties themselves, of course. All sorts of associations provide organizational resources, volunteers, and funds for political campaigns; churches, unions, and neighborhood associations are fertile grounds for recruiting voters. Group interests and opinions can be converted into programs and policies, though the translation is not direct; typically, parties refashion and generalize groups' highly particular claims. (Put more strongly in standard pluralist terms, parties have been *defined* as coalitions of interest groups, social movements, sectional interests, and citizen activists.[46]) Importantly, however, for civil society theorists, associations' connection to parties does not signify partisanship. From the perspective of "good civil society," if there is anything redeeming about a relation to parties in pursuit of their own goals, it is that they remain untainted by partisan commitment. Civil society groups are loathe to be cast as pillars or elements of "umbrella parties," and the exceptions (unions, for example) are castigated as entrenched parts of the entrenched system.[47] Often enough, preoccupied as they are with specific outcomes, groups act like Jay Gould for Erie, and support candidates from either party who they hope will be in a position to advance their aims. From the standpoint of civil society theory, their beneficial influence is conditional on independence. They cannot operate as a corrective to the system if they are captured by parties or dependent on officials for public funding and other support. Only reluctantly, temporarily, and instrumentally do civil society theorists see parties as an intermediary between groups and government; this is strange, because a guiding concern of civil society theory is mediation, and parties are the bridge between the "background culture" of civil society and the "public political forum."[48] But civil society theorists do not attend to parties in these terms, nor do they conceptualize parties on a continuum between social groups and representative government. The energy and focus are on the internal life of groups and on the effects of membership on men and women personally and individually.

"Good" versus Combative Civil Society

In "good civil society" theory, associations are valued above all for the dispositions and practices they cultivate. Theorists cast certain groups, including political parties, out of the charmed circle and attend to whether the internal life of associations promotes specific capacities:—reciprocity, reasoning together, reaching agreement, "trust," tolerance, care for the common good. Civil society theorists are geared up and at their morally persuasive best in countering apathy, silence, resignation, and detachment and presenting association membership as a means to the suitably reticent goal of civic "engagement". Follett's "group principle" posits: "It is only through group organization that the individual learns . . . to be an effective political member."[49] But civic education is not political education. Indeed Follett's prescription for education in being "an effective *political* member" is satisfied indirectly, and in some accounts of civil society it is nearly eclipsed. So it is worth observing a tension between the laudatory civic dispositions association membership promises, on the one hand, and voluntary association as an effective corrective to a system dominated by parties and their "unseen principals," on the other. What is wanted from "the group principle," then, civic identity or political identity?

High on the list of capacities "good civil society" theorists would like to see cultivated in voluntary association is deliberation, and they draw an explicit distinction between a group's deliberative aspect and its "pressure function."[50] Deliberation is about giving reasons. It is rational discussion among respectful equals governed by norms of reciprocity, and the importance of cultivating this capacity is tied, of course, to deliberative democracy as a political ideal. Very briefly, in deliberative democracy, the process of reaching decisions is generally contrasted to decision making by means of negotiation or bargaining, which depend on the relative power of the parties.[51] It is contrasted with aggregation and majoritarianism; if a vote is not preceded by deliberation, it has nothing to commend it but the force of numbers. The guiding idea is to eliminate the relevance of all inequalities except the advantage of better reasons. ("If the deliberations of democratic citizens are crucial in the legitimation of market inequality, we cannot allow market inequalities to have an overwhelming impact on deliberations."[52]) Deliberation offers citizens justifications for political outcomes based on reasons that everyone can reasonably accept. In this sense, proponents claim, only deliberative democracy is faithful to fundamental democratic notions of fairness and equal respect.[53] (Indeed, for some theorists democracy *just is* deliberative democracy; deliberation is the defining characteristic of any democratic regime.[54]) The promise is that deliberation broadens perspectives by exposure to political views unlike one's own, encourages the production of good reasons, cultivates tolerance, and expresses the mutual respect of justification.[55] The promise for the collectivity is Follett's "enlightened group opinion." Not least, deliberation is balm for the distemper of partisanship.

One relevant point of interest here, and the connection to associations, is democratic theorists' promise that "the deliberative model of democracy does not represent a counterfactual thought experiment."[56] It is not utopian. They identify the institutions that make deliberation a regular practice, or could.[57] Historically, as we have seen, attention is focused in Millian fashion on legislatures—on actual political sites of collective decision making—and the structures that invite informed and reasoned argument there (committees, conference procedures, caucuses, rules requiring minority input into agenda setting, closure, and transparency). In "moments of appreciation," we glimpsed the thought that parties might carry the banners and provide the "serious conflict of opposing reasons" that meets a latitudinarian definition of deliberation, or "trial by discussion" (not deliberation at all, on stringent views of the criteria of deliberation, but not reducible to just political talk, either). Today, advocates of the marriage of "good civil society" and deliberative democracy point to different venues for deliberation. These thinkers are concerned with ordinary citizens, not officials, and want to assign deliberation a place of its own. The "public sphere" is the name for these arenas. It is severed from parties and elections and official arenas of political decision making (Jurgen Habermas prescribes "a clear and enduring demarcation between this [public] sphere and the formal political system"[58]). Later in this chapter I look at deliberation in the context of parties and elections. For civil society theorists, however, deliberation is vested in the voluntary associations of civil society: in "meetings of grass roots organizations, professional associations, shareholders meetings, and citizens' committees in hospitals and other similar institutions."[59] One enthusiastic statement of this position—"the primary function of these secondary associations ought to be to promote discussion"[60]—is perverse unless civic education is a principal goal of membership and deliberation is a principal goal of civic education; after all, in most groups, deliberation, if it occurs, is in the service of the activities members pursue, and is not their primary function.

This marriage of civil society and deliberative democracy, with its promise of improved citizens, has problems on its own terms. It is not attuned to the conditions under which deliberation might work. Voluntary associations join like-minded people with shared purposes. Members reinforce one another's views. Their activity is solidaristic. Voluntary associations avoid internal dissent. As a result of social pressure, reputational concerns, and the sorts of arguments likely to arise spontaneously in relatively homogeneous voluntary associations, the process typically inclines members to a common position more extreme than the starting point, rather than to illuminated disagreement. In any event, deliberation is unlikely in most of the associations lauded by civil society theorists. The disagreements that arise over activities, leadership, and internal organization do not normally rise to the level of conflict or moral conflict that is the occasion for prescribing the rigor of deliberation. Empirical work confirms this point. "Those highest in voluntary association memberships are least likely to report cross-cutting political conversations."[61] Social network theory and political psychology combine to show that people are most likely to confront political conflict in contexts with "weak ties" and "loose connections" and in sites more heterogeneous than membership groups,[62] chiefly in the workplace.[63] (And, of course, in partisan politics.)

The problem is not only that civil society groups are unlikely loci of deliberation. Beyond that, we do have to wonder whether voluntary associations as described by the civic ideal are capable of challenging the system dominated by parties and their "unseen principals." Empirical work reveals a trade-off between deliberation, on the one hand, and political advocacy and influence, on the other: "it is doubtful than an extremely activist political culture can also be a heavily deliberative one."[64] Political activity demands "passion, commitment, solidarity," conviction that we are "on the side of the angels." Michael Walzer reminds us that no organization that sets itself against "established hierarchies of power and wealth . . . will ever succeed unless it arouses the affiliative and combative passions of the people at the lower ends of the hierarchies. The passions that it arouses are certain to include envy, resentment, and hatred."[65] It does not bode well for the ability of voluntary associations to cultivate "effective political members" if group norms and members' dispositions spurn rhetoric, demonstration of sheer numbers, proselytizing, militancy—standard elements of political activity. Or if associations prize reciprocity when political organizing is learning to act "in accordance with a script they don't write themselves."[66]

A secondary strain of civil society theory is combative. "Empowerment" is the avowed goal of association and group solidarity here, as "trust" or "social capital" is to the benign strain. High-minded insistence on distinguishing civic-oriented voluntary associations from interest groups of the sort I quoted above abates.[67] Education through group membership is forthrightly political.[68] Association itself is a political resource, and that central fact of pluralism is at the heart of combative civil society theory whose advocates typically focus on those who are chronically unorganized and disassociated: the poor, members of certain racial or cultural groups.[69] These people need what Walzer calls the "meat and potatoes"[70] resources of civil society—newspapers, cultural societies, schools, social service networks, and above all political advocacy groups. Oddly, some proponents of combative civil society propose public subsidies for organization.[71] Walzer, for example, looks to government: "Only the state can guarantee that no group or coalition is permanently excluded from realistic contention; state officials can't simply hold the ring; they have to intervene on behalf of the weakest groups."[72] This assumes what was in doubt, the possibility of nonpartisan support for voluntary associations, and agreement on which associations deserve underwriting. It is like squaring the circle. Public assistance aside, the thrust of "combative civil society" is clear. Associations should not be expected to mirror the restrictive standards of deliberation advocated by "good civil society theorists." Dispensation should extend to weak, disfavored groups in the world of ordinary politics where imbalances of power are plain. Under these conditions, the countervailing remedy is to attract attention with something other than the merits of the argument: with show of numbers, emotional display, disruptive activity, sharp language, anger, and denuniciation.

The division between "good" and "combative" civil society is not just temper ("civic engagement" vs. "political empowerment") or the sort of association touted as exemplary (religious groups providing social services vs. organized workers or African Americans). More important, the democratic failing that combative group theorists address extends beyond entrenched parties, "special" interests, and "big money" to include the very groups prized by theorists of "good civil society." From the combative standpoint, the civic universe itself is "remarkably oligarchical; its political leadership a 'cartel of elites.' "[73] Associations claiming to speak for the public interest, the moral majority, or a common cause exercise "undue influence" themselves. Public interest groups can seem as remote from (even antagonistic toward) the concerns of disadvantaged minorities, say, as they are from the powerful interests they expressly oppose. Again, the ground for self-designated groups with self-selected spokespersons to represent particular people, interests, and values is often uncertain—more so when they designate themselves defenders of the common good. These groups and their leaders are formally irresponsible. And it is these leaders who have political influence in the corridors of power. The idea of a pluralistic "public sphere" as antidote to "the system" is undiscriminating. It is one thing to favor associations that are oppositional and democratically self-protective—demanding government transparency, for example, or investigating, publicizing, censuring, or pressing for political inclusion. It is another thing to put democratic hopes on the unstoppable array of groups, even if they claim to pressure in the public interest and not some special interest. For the reasons indicated, I am skeptical that civil society theorists make a compelling case for groups as a corrective to "the system" on their own terms.

Moreover, to the extent that "the group principle" does result in effective political influence, pluralism constitutes a challenge to the democratic promise of "empowering the common, recognizable interests of ordinary people, and nothing more."[74] Schattschneider's response to antiparty pluralists is the strongest we have. It rests on the theoretically important insight that a "conflict system" shapes political conflict and that when *parties* "stage the battle," the scope of conflict is more open and democratic than a system based primarily on interest groups, even if many are "good" voluntary associations pressing their view of the public interest and if the "cartel of civil society elites" is not narrowly self-serving. Programmatic parties with strong national leadership are more defensible than the appalling "hypertrophy of pressure politics," the "undemocratic and dangerous" government by interest group. For Schattschneider, the choice is between a party system and a system of "irresponsible organized minorities and special interests." The choice as posed is too stark; the objective should be a reciprocal relation between civil society groups and parties, and the right mix is contextual and variable.

Schattschneider was also confident in his assertion that parties have a "natural superiority" in democracy.[75] Obviously, antiparty progressives do not share that view. But neither do they acknowledge the threat posed by the sorcerer's apprentice of pluralism, or that the "group principle" when it aims at circumventing parties and elections actually underscores their value. Parties and electoral politics are not easily dismissed, then, not if "the associations of civil society are ruled by elites of various sorts, who also aim at permanence"[76]—that is, if a system of interest group politics competes with parties (or if parties just are coalitions of powerful groups). And not if there is an iota of sense in the thought that "the big game is the party game because in the last analysis there is no political substitute for victory in an election."[77]

The antiparty theorists I have just discussed—advocates of civil society as an alternative democratic system—are pluralists. Often their concern is compensatory resources for powerless minorities, disorganized groups and unarticulated interests. Progressivism's most devastating charge, however, has always been that political parties are routinely unresponsive to the "common, recognized interests of ordinary people." The concern is powerful not powerless minorities and the failure of parties to respond to majorities. This directs us to a second category of corrective to the party system, one attuned to majoritarianism as the primary reality of electoral politics in the United States.[78] On this view, revitalization of participation as a force against undue influence cannot happen in a partisan fashion (a notion I will argue against), but it cannot happen entirely apart from electoral politics either.[79]

Parties versus Participation

Look to participation for democracy? How not? "The simple act of voting is the ground upon which the edifice of elective government rests ultimately."[80] Moreover, an operative assumption of democratic theory is that as decision making goes, elections are relatively egalitarian.[81] So this corrective looks to the people as voters. It is often pointed out that voters individually are impotent and that if the expectation of enfranchisement is effective political action, the result is bound to be frustration. Voters in combination, however, can use the ballot as a tool to unsettle self-serving, entrenched parties and the undue influence of interest and advocacy groups operating on and through them. But only if voters are Independents, not partisans, and if the electoral system is made responsive to them. Democracy can be self-correcting if electoral competition is not stymied by a party cartel, if citizens are not thoughtless, undiscriminating partisans, and if the people actually turn out to vote.

273

It would be going too far to say, "Democracy cannot endure without elections. They are not the only method of maintaining popular control of government, but they are the essential one."[82] Democracy *is* conceivable without elections, as progressive proposals for direct democracy demonstrate. Popular control is an overstatement, too.[83] A better formulation is "responsiveness" to constituents, to the interests and opinions of like-minded groups outside the constituency, and to popular expressions of opinion on specific issues.

> Public dissatisfaction with politics and government is connected more closely to popular perceptions on the input side than the output side of the equation. In fully operative democracy, people are likely to have developed the firm expectation that they have the right to be heard, that officials should listen when they speak, and that government actions should therefore be primarily a response to the voice of the people.[84]

But responsiveness to anything like "the voice of the people" requires universal turnout (or nearly) as well as universal suffrage, and progressive intervention begins there.[85]

> [If citizens are] denied, or if they deny themselves the right to do these things [to vote, to join this or that party or movement, to form a caucus or oppositional faction], then democracy is replaced by the rule of some people over others. It may be that anyway, much of the time, but the possibility of citizen activism . . . at least imposes some restraint on the rulers.[86]

With a few exceptions, data for European democracies shows declining participation and declining party membership;[87] the United States is no longer a dramatic outlier. In the 2004 U.S. presidential race 60 percent of the eligible population voted, the most since 1980.[88] That means an estimated 80.4 million eligible adults declined to vote. The turnout is lower in local, state, and off-year congressional elections—roughly 25 to 35 percent.[89] Harvard University's Joan Shorenstein Center's "Vanishing Voter Project" divides nonvoters into categories: apathetic, disconnected, alienated, or disenchanted.[90] This is not to insist that nonvoters (wryly described as "the largest political party") are all politically anomic, because in any election some portion of nonvoting is circumstantial. A neutral description has it that nonvoters constitute a reservoir or slack in the system. No one contemplating this "reservoir" can fail to wonder whether these 80 million would, if mobilized, swamp the existing majority in any election or on any issue or add to the majority's authority by replicating the voting patterns of those who do turn out. Schattschneider was confident that the effect would be explosive: "The unused political potential is sufficient to blow the United States off the face of the earth."[91] This is hyperbole. The bias of participation is not speculation—patterns of turnout reveal chronic nonparticipation by socially and economically disadvantaged groups[92]—but the potential impact of universal turnout is.

Rational choice theory poses the participatory quandary differently, of course: what explains the large percentage of the population that *does* vote? Even in uncontested elections! (A tongue-in-cheek suggestion, "as Downs goes up, U.S. turnout goes down," meaning patterns of change in turnout—especially among economists and political scientists—correlates with citations to Anthony Downs's work on the irrationality of participation.[93]) Contemplating the English Reform Bill of 1830, Hegel accurately described voting as "the exercise of a wholly occasional calling," and he anticipated "the paradox of participation":

> From this indifference to the franchise we can easily draw an indictment against a people on the score of political obtuseness or corruption. . . . Yet this harsh judgment must be softened if we ponder what must obviously contribute to such lukewarmness: namely, the sense that amongst the many thousand of votes cast at an election, a single vote is actually insignificant . . . [The voter] has a definite inkling of this quantitative insignificance of his vote. Of course, the qualitatively high considerations of freedom, duty, exercise of sovereign rights, participation in general affairs of state, may be emphasized against indolence. But sound common sense is glad to stop at what is effective.[94]

As Hegel suggested, duty operates too. Put simply, "difference-making is only one of the ways in which we can have moral reasons to do something."[95] Civic-mindedness is a counterweight to "indolence" and "common sense," and studies emphasize social and civic gratifications of participation. Elections are expressive rituals as well as mechanisms for making decisions. Another characterization says that voting demonstrates support for democracy itself, which can be understood as a contribution and therefore not simply expressive.[96]

In any case, Hegel's summary alerts us to the moral disapproval leveled at nonvoters. From the progressive antiparty standpoint, nonparticipation is as dangerous as obtuse partisanship. Even if passivity signals acquiescence in election outcomes, it is not the same as active support for "clean government" and the public interest. Nonparticipation is license and encouragement to the "undue influence" of organized interests. It abets self-dealing and self-perpetuating parties. Nonparticipation is charged to the personal deficiencies of individual citizens—a lack of self-protective behavior and "a shortfall in civic virtue."[97] It is explained by "the ignorance, indifference and shiftlessness of the people."[98] Political scientists are less likely to make overt moral judgments and point to institutional inhibitions on participation. Exercising the right to vote can be difficult if places and hours of polling are restrictive. There are onerous obstacles like registration requirements. There is voter fatigue in the United States, with its frequent elections for every level of office, to say nothing of referenda. Intimidation and barriers deliberately imposed by parties themselves for partisan advantage are additional deterrents. Political scientists generate proposals for institutional remedies: fewer elections, liberal registration rules, absentee ballots, weekend voting, compulsory voting, and so on.[99] However, one comprehensive comparative study eliminates most institutional factors as determinants of high or low turnout, including compulsory voting, proportional systems, and measures to simplify the act of voting and lower its costs.[100]

All of these explanations for nonparticipation—personal culpability and institutional inhibitions—pale next to the furious assignment of responsibility to parties. "Demobilization" is seen as both willful strategy and the unintended but predictable result of the conduct of the major parties. Parties are depressors. In a sense, this is the final blow. Before mass parties, Hegel had worried about suffrage: "There was no sustained and organized party activity among the electorate to stimulate the latter's interest, to clarify political issues, and to simplify political decisions."[101] With the emergence of parties attuned to the electorate, that changed. I cite James Bryce again: the party system "stimulates the political interest of the people, which is kept alive by this perpetual agitation."[102] Historians point out that the first American party organizations pushed to expand participation. As early as the 1820s, mobilization was the business of party organizations armed with messages designed to generate high turnout. They had "a previously unexploited field, no competition, a relatively small electorate"; it was "like fishing in a pond that has never been fished before."[103] The attempt by parties to include more citizens by liberalizing the franchise, and to get the largest possible number of citizens to vote, were real democratic achievements. Party competition rather than dramatic seizures of power by the people is credited with accomplishing enfranchisement and mobilization.[104]

Today, we see a *volte face*, and progressive antipartyism introduces this grim addition to its standard charges of party corruption, convergence, collusion, and cartel. *Parties depress participation.* The catalogue of ways parties alienate voters includes egregious cultivation of rich donors, inattention to issues that matter to ordinary people, the incivility of partisan discourse. Recall Schattschneider's thesis: "The role of the people in the political system is determined largely by the conflict system, for it is conflict that involves the people in politics and the nature of conflict determines the nature of the public involvement."[105] On the antiparty view, the conflict system forged by parties produces uninvolvement. As one typical summary puts it: "if free elections leave so many in the electorate dissatisfied with where they have to stand, and *push large numbers out of the electorate entirely*, then it is fair to conclude that the political process is badly defective."[106] Proven or not—and there is no compelling empirical evidence I am aware of—the presumed connection between major party conduct and abstention has become a commonplace of political science and political punditry. It is widely accepted that "negative views of political parties are a general feature of contemporary public opinion," and the critical next step linking negativity to nonparticipation—"one potential consequence . . . may be declining involvement in elections and other aspects of partisan politics"—is presumed to follow.[107] The negative attitude toward parties as ascertained by surveys may be accurate, but it does not speak convincingly to the cause of nonparticipation.

Nonetheless, "parties depress participation" is a ubiquitous lament and a justification offered for virtually every proposed regulation and reform. It is the constant refrain of supporters of campaign finance legislation, for example.[108] The "cynical assumption that large donors call the tune" and the alleged capture of parties by "unseen principals" or by very visible ones result in disaffection and withdrawal. The claim is made over and over. Unregulated contributions "jeopardize the willingness of voters to take part in democratic governance."[109]

> The ability of the average person to have a meaningful impact on elections will diminish as the electoral weight of the largest donors increases.... [H]ard money increases would make their vote less meaningful, and they would therefore be discouraged from forms of electoral participation such as volunteering, making small contributions, and even voting itself.[110]

The most disturbing charge in this vein is that nonvoting is an *effect* of party mobilization, not its antithesis.[111] Literal demobilization is seen as a credible party strategy today.[112] The rare, startling example is vote suppression: in one instance paying church ministers (or supporting their favored projects) in return not for delivering votes but for keeping voters at home.[113] Nothing this blatant is necessary to generate the "depressor" accusation, though. It is enough to point out that electoral strategy does not dependably incline parties to get out the maximum number of voters. We are accustomed to the view of candidates and officeholders as "political entrepreneurs" intent on attracting the votes of consumers, but even in contested elections winning does not require cornering the market. It is "unnecessary and wasteful" to win 100 percent of the vote.[114] This is particularly true for incumbents whose goal is re-election, not maximum vote share. A good description of this conduct is "strategic activation." The parties' goal is to induce "particular, finely targeted portions of the public to become active," which involves "identifying and activating the small segments of citizens most likely to 'get their message' and vote or lobby government."[115] The idea is not to shape or change voters' opinions but "to channel and strengthen latent opinions and to provide information to support preexisting attitudes." The standard is efficiency: "hitting the right target with limited resources."[116] John Aldrich observed that parties have long relied on "cost reduction techniques as the centerpieces of their turnout drives," but traditionally these were in the service of generating enthusiasm for the contest and maximizing participation by potential partisans. Today, critics assert, the strategy has changed: "Expending scarce resources in an area of opposition strength is obviously unwise, but so too is mobilizing the party's own supporters where they are not needed."[117] Targeting is a finely tuned, professionally managed operation, research-driven by demographics, polling, focus groups, and the voting history of a district. Put sharply, where once the issue for parties was voters' information about candidates, now it is candidates' information about voters. Replicating marketing data on consumers, parties target individualized messages and turnout efforts, so that "the very, very personal is political."[118]

Targeted activation ignores the nonvoting public. It ignores voters unlikely to be supporters. One chapter of campaign strategist Dick Morris's advice book for candidates, *The New Prince*, is titled "The Irrelevance of the Undecided Voter."[119] Competition is narrowly focused, and so is mobilization. So long as there are popular elections, voters are not dispensable and will never fall from view. But even if they do not depress participation parties do demonstrate enormous tolerance for abstention,[120] and we know that disinterest in mobilizing voters is relevant to the disproportionate number of nonvoters who are poor. In effect, the parties are content to allow a major segment of the nation to remain outside. Verba, Schlozman, and Brady propose a trio of causes for why people don't take part in politics—because they can't, because they don't want to, because nobody asked.[121] The point here is that parties don't ask. In fact, there is sound evidence that national parties spend a good portion of their funds on state and local party organization, voter registration, and grass-roots campaign activities to increase voter turnout. But as we saw, this is not the prevalent perception of party spending, and it has not deterred regulation of "soft money" contributions to party organizations for these purposes. The accusation that parties depress participation is too broad and goes too far. A different explanation for failure to mobilize voters lays the blame on candidate-centered campaigns and constraints on party funding and support. Candidates who organize supporters are newsworthy: an article on the campaign of Senator Paul Wellstone, which committed 30 percent of its resources to volunteer "footsoldiers" in contrast to the normal 3 percent, is titled: "Politics with People, Reinvented."[122] For most candidates, however, strategic targeting is attractive. The doleful result is that lower income voters are "disenfranchised so to speak by a growth of politics less and less linked to parties."[123]

Participation by partisans is at higher rates and more dependable than other voters', and I return to this in the next chapter. Nevertheless, even here parties are said to slough off the democratic task of mobilization.[124]

> In few party systems has the separation between the party organization and the party's faithful voters been as great as it is in the American party system. American parties largely have failed to integrate the party's most loyal supporters into the party organization. . . . Nor have the American parties mounted any substantial program to educate their loyal electorates into the principles and traditions of the party. They view even the most sympathetic voters as a separate clientele to be reinforced anew at each election.[125]

Progressives are plainly concerned about eligible nonvoters and positively dote on nonpartisans. At the same time, they do not praise partisans for participating (nor do they extend sympathy to partisans for their political leaders' lack of solicitude). Rather, partisans are reviled as a contributing cause of the participatory deficit.

This is no mere footnote to the story that parties depress participation. Much of the blame for nonparticipation falls on party activists and identifiers. One scholar hypothesizes that progressive expectations for advances in participatory democracy like primary elections have had the opposite effect, because partisan participation—agitated, conflictual, intense—causes other voters to stay away. Primaries bring out "extremist voices" and "turn Americans off."[126] This, at least, is the claim, and as I show in the next section, it is used to justify prescriptions for reform. The progressive answer to the question, "What kind of offers do we have to make to get the abstainers into the system?"[127] does not involve party mobilization. On the contrary, it is a matter of disempowering parties and defanging partisans.

California Democratic Party v. Jones

The belief that parties are responsible for nonparticipation and cause eligible voters to stay home and the hope that maximum participation by nonpartisans is the corrective for the party system lay behind California's Proposition 198. The initiative was advanced as a reform measure aimed at the major parties. It called for a "nonpartisan" or "blanket" primary, which would require the state to list candidates randomly on a single ballot and would allow voters regardless of their party affiliation to vote for any candidate from any party for any office. It passed with strong popular support. The initiative was enthusiastically characterized as "a classic example of party regulation justified as an attempt to shape the character of politics for the better by democratizing the way that parties conduct their affairs."[128] In effect, in a blanket primary votes are cast for individual candidates, not parties, and if enough nonpartisans participate, the selection of candidates is taken out of the hands of partisans and party organizations.

The thought was that by giving voters more choices in primary elections (any candidate, from any party, for any office, regardless of the voter's affiliation), more people would turn out. At least this was the nominal claim, because, again, there is no good evidence that the structure of primary elections or dissatisfaction with candidates offered in party primaries explain nonvoting.[129] There is little reason to think that the arrangement would actually expand the active electorate by bringing out habitual nonvoters. The reasoning might apply a bit better to partisans insofar as the blanket primary might give them an incentive to vote even if their own party's primary were uncontested or candidates unappealing, but we know that the impetus to cross-over voting is weak.[130] In any event, the main objective was to increase turnout by nonpartisans and by their participation to decrease the undue influence of party activists and wrest control of nominations from party hard-liners.

I spoke in chapter 5 about the dreaded undue influence of party leaders, managers, and activists, and we see it writ large here: party insiders control nominations and are biased toward candidates who appeal to the "base" of fervid partisans. (In fact, studies are inconclusive about whether party managers and activists incline to factional candidates, to those who they think can unite the factions of the party, or to those who can beat the opposition in the general election,[131] or whether as is likely they are divided on this point.) In any case, the argument goes, party activists incline to "candidates who are more partisan and who take positions on the policy issues of the day that are not representative of the majority of the electorate." California's traditional closed primary system "favors the election of party hard-liners . . . and stacks the deck against more moderate problem-solvers." It produces candidates with "extreme positions."[132] The California initiative was put to voters by one faction in an internal party conflict. Self-declared moderate Republican Tom Campbell's Senate primary defeat by Bruce Herschensohn and Christian Right elements spurred Campbell and his supporters to place the blanket primary on the ballot. They portrayed it as "an attempt to take power from Democratic and Republican party leaders."[133] Advocates promised that a blanket primary would lead to the election of candidates "less beholden to party officials," candidates who "better represent the electorate" because they "stand closer to the median policy positions of their districts." This is my subject in chapter 8.

The California initiative exhibited more than a whiff of aversion to partisanship, clearly. It charged parties with turning off voters. It identified active partisans who are the most regular voters in primary elections with extremists. It would have used electoral law to lock in the norm of maximum participation and it associated participation with a particular theory of party competition—"centrism."[134] For voters, antipartisanship seems to have been a motivating factor: "While

political scientists may disagree on the question of whether the political system is benefited when parties are more or less distinct or polarized, it is apparent that the voters have sided with less partisanship
in adopting Proposition 198."[135] The proposition was aptly described
as "a rebellion of the electorate against the rights claims of the party
institutional apparatus and the party-in-government to condition
the terms under which the party presents itself to voters."[136]

A closer look at the decision in *California Democratic Party
v. Jones* underscores these points and raises the question, who should
decide? The District Court had upheld the blanket primary as a legitimate "experiment in democratic government." The Supreme Court
reversed. There was no quarrel among the justices over the proposition that the aim of drawing more voters into the electoral process
by making the primary nonpartisan was a public good. (Only Justice
Scalia objected that there was no compelling interest in "curry[ing]
favor with persons whose views are more "centrist" than those of
the party base.[137]) But it is not hard to see that by itself the abstract
prescription "more participation" (still less, "more participation by
nonpartisan voters") cannot by itself determine what electoral rules
should be or who should make them.[138] There is no right to vote in
primary elections. Indeed, within the limits of nondiscrimination,
"there is no basic right to participate that exists independently of the
institutional framework; entitlements to participate in electoral competition are creatures of this framework."[139] The *meaning* of electoral
laws is what matters.[140]

The progressive view has it that democracy just means maximum
inclusion at every point in the electoral process. That is the way to
empower "the common, recognizable interests of ordinary people,
and nothing more."[141] As we see, the rationale for mandating blanket
primaries is that they draw more citizens into the political process at
this crucial stage. "A consideration of freedom of association ought
not to operate as a bar to state regulation of internal party processes"
if regulation is necessary to ensure "fair access to the political arena"[142]
But there is little reason to think that "fair access" translates into
blanket primaries specifically. Assuming what is unproven, that the
nonpartisan primary would maximize participation—even assuming

what was actually wanted, participation by nonpartisans—is that the only democratic value in play? Certainly, that is the implication of the question "Do the parties or the people own the electoral process?"[143]

The question for the Court was whether "the state's" (or, more accurately, California voters') asserted interest in maximizing voter turnout outweighed the parties' objection to blanket primaries as a violation of their First Amendment freedom of association.[144] I want to consider the argument for party autonomy not in constitutional terms but in terms of making elections "more democratic." If the worth of the right to vote does not exist apart from the institutional framework in which it is exercised, then the nature and quality of political competition matter. On a strictly minimal, Burkean view of the checking function of parties, parties' substantive identities may not loom large, and from this standpoint there may be no objection to a nonpartisan primary.[145] But apart from that bare position, the meaningfulness of the vote is dependent on the political identity of parties and candidates, which is typically refined and tested at the primary stage of elections when partisans select their candidates and driving issues. Even more than "open primaries," the aptly named "nonpartisan primary" assigns this "basic function" of parties to "persons wholly unaffiliated with the party, who may have different views from the party."[146] It allows Independents and cross-over voters from rival parties to cast potentially decisive votes. Maximizing voting by Independents, habitual nonvoters, and cross-over partisans weakens partisans' control over "its most precious possession, the right to bear its label."[147] The nonpartisan primary has been likened to "letting UCLA's football team choose USC's head coach."[148] If party identity is significant, it argues for allowing "the party"—its organizational leadership, partisan officials, activists, partisan voters, and voters willing to align with the party at least for this purpose (as in "open primaries")—to select its candidates, issues, and campaigns. True, strategic voting in primaries by cross-over voters from the opposition party calculated to produce a weak candidate is rare; it is unlikely that supporters of the opposition could "hijack" the process, nullifying the preferences of partisans. But nonpartisan voters, Independents, and habitual nonvoters could dilute or alter the party's political identity in a particular election or over time. That was the point of the proposed reform, after all. It is also true that rules designed to satisfy the "median voter" may work against minority groups that have gained a foothold in a major party but would be rendered less competitive as a result of the influence of nonpartisan voters.[149] At the limit, "a candidacy determined by the votes of non-party members is arguably a fraudulent candidacy."[150]

From this standpoint, democratic values—institutional and systemic values, not just the associational rights of parties—favor closed primary elections or party caucuses and conventions. Whether party competition "absolutely requires that parties define their own membership for the purpose of nominating candidates" is an open question in practice; the assertion that expanding the right of participation "could be enough to destroy the party"[151] is open to doubt. It depends on who votes, to what purpose in any given election. That uncertainty is a reason for accepting the principle that the parties should decide on the nominating process. For example, a state-mandated closed primary prevents parties from testing which candidates and issues appeal to nonpartisan and cross-over voters. In 2003 the California Democratic Party voted to allow political Independents to vote in the next presidential primary; the California GOP proceeded with its closed primary.[152] The parties' claim to have a right to reject a blanket primary seems to extend to the right to withdraw from state-mandated open primaries altogether (an argument the Court rejected in the 2005 case, *Clingman v. Beaver*[153]) on the view that "there must be some protection of their [parties'] core partisan quality."[154] The Court's ruling in *Jones* seems to offer some protection. Justice O'Connor acknowledged that the primary is "precisely the point at which the associational interest of the party is at its zenith. . . . What's left of any associational rights if this can stand?"[155] Eliminating effective party association was of course the objective behind the blanket primary proposal.

Legal scholars who see the present party system as pathological direct attention away from the Court's conventional balancing of the individual rights of voters to participate in (all) elections against the associational rights of parties. Their concern is not protecting parties' associational rights or advocating that partisan activists concerned about the party's political identity should set the procedures for determining who should choose candidates.[156] They interpret *Jones* using a "functional" approach to the law of democracy.[157] A "democracy-reinforcing" standard should apply, meaning what will "best help realize the appropriate systematic aims of elections."[158] But as we see, there is more than one systemic aim. There is maximizing participation (here, with an eye to increasing the influence of nonpartisans specifically). There is substantive competition among parties and candidates and the plausible thought that differentiation is ensured by partisan control of nominees and issues. There is the minimal Burkean standpoint of parties' checking function.

There is also more than one view of who should decide among electoral rules that foster one aim over others. If we think that critical first-order institutional questions should be subject to careful deliberation, we have reason enough to question the California proposal. Deliberation is alien to the initiative process as it stands. Even maximum-participation loyalists who supported the blanket primary question whether electoral structures should be decided this way. "Whatever the overall talents of the rank and file, political change in the realm of process should not be as sensitive to the public's wishes as political change in the realm of policy."[159] We have reason to challenge the dominant progressive answer that a voting majority should choose how governors are chosen, and that they should have recourse against the regulatory regime erected by entrenched partisan state legislatures. The consequences of the California initiative for participation and its effect on the major parties could not have been clear to voters (they are not evident to political scientists dedicated to the subject.) Proposition 198 was "a low-visibility issue with very little surrounding campaign."[160] This initiative had all the deficiencies of initiatives and referenda generally, in terms of how they are written (citizens have no voice in this) and public information about their likely consequences. Recall Follett's caution to her fellow progressives about the popular initiative and referendum. Ballot questions are not democratically inspired, she warned; they are the work of parties, or factions of parties, or political entrepreneurs. Today, they are promoted through privately funded campaigns organized by professionals employing targeted mailing, market testing, and paid signature gatherers.

Nonetheless, "let the voters decide" is the orthodox progressive position, and it suggests a standard for judicial intervention: "courts should distinguish between democracy-regulating laws that are vehicles for incumbent or partisan self-entrenchment and those that reflect permissible choices (wise or not) about how to structure democracy."[161] On this view, the *Jones* Court should have upheld the blanket primary:

> Primaries are not internal party affairs. Rather, primaries are a means for voters to structure the electoral process by winnowing down candidates to a list of finalists to run in the general election. Voters through the initiative process or the state legislature should be allowed to dictate the form of that winnowing process.[162]

There is yet another progressive perspective on the California proposal for reforming the primary system. The line of thought is a bit convoluted; it argues that the Court should have upheld the referendum result because it invites intra-party contests, which in turn stimulate political participation. As we saw, certain leaders of the Republican Party organization outside government initiated the popular vote on the blanket primary. Elected officials in the California state legislature from all parties opposed it. The proposition was not the result of popular upsurge against the major parties but a bid by one faction of the Republican Party for electoral advantage. If we see the California proposition as a contest among party leaders on matters of ideology, internal procedures, message, and strategy, we can understand why some progressive legal scholars conclude: "The only way to discern the true voice of 'the party' is to permit the political process to work itself out."[163] The Court should have upheld the results of the initiative, on this view, but not because the proposition was passed by popular vote, or because "the party" has no associational immunity from regulation.[164] Rather, because contests over regulating party activity are intra-party contests among party leaders,[165] and intra-party as well as inter-party rivalry creates competition and inhibits self-entrenchment. Finally, competition, including internal party factionalism, is a spur to turnout. We have come full circle. The reasoning is indirect, but we understand the thrust of the argument. Political contests over electoral rules are stimulants to participation. In the absence of certainty about which form of primary increases participation, the one certainty is that internal and inter-party contests excite interest. Ideally, that excitement spurs participation by nonpartisans. Concern for competition as a provocation to participation is a constant theme in the progressive repertoire of reform. We see it here, and again in enthusiasm for reforms that invite minor parties and independent challenges to the "duopoly."

Against Duopoly: Competition and Participation Again

The blanket primary promised, unconvincingly, to correct the system by increasing overall participation and somewhat more plausibly by increasing the influence of nonpartisan voters and defusing the influence of active partisans. Other proposals for reform hinge on counterweights to the major parties: minor parties, independent candidacies, and fusion parties. Advocates argue that the major parties are indifferent to the concerns of ordinary citizens and to the public interest. As we saw in "Progressive Antipartyism," a recurrent dream is the rise of a party of Independents: an "anti-party party."[166] Failing that, or preparatory to that, is the effort to challenge the major party cartel and self-entrenchment, at least to unsettle parties' powerful duopoly. Minor parties are understood to arise as a result of major party failures "to do what the electorate expects of them—reflect the issue preferences of voters, manage the economy, select attractive and acceptable candidates, and build voter loyalty to the parties and the party system."[167] The existence of ballot alternatives provides an outlet for dissatisfaction, on this view, and minor parties attract voters "who are particularly concerned about issue dimensions that are suppressed by the existing party alignment."[168] More generally, minor parties counter the presumptive demobilizing effects of duopoly by motivating interest in elections. (Of course, minor party candidates and independent candidates do occasionally affect the outcome of elections by drawing voters away from one of the major parties; Green Party candidate Ralph Nader won only 2.7 percent of the national vote but he "almost certainly cost [Democratic presidential candidate Al Gore] a clean win."[169])

As described in my earlier discussion of the party cartel, state laws endorsed by the major parties make third-party and independent places on the ballot difficult; for this reason and others minor parties and independent candidacies are costly and notoriously difficult to organize, even at the local or regional level. A more promising route is "fusion" or "cross endorsement." In the nineteenth century it was common for a major and minor party to jointly nominate the same candidate, who appeared twice on the ballot. Fusion allowed voters to choose between party lines in voting for that candidate. The benefits to the minor party are clear. Fusion is a way a minor party can communicate its message in the context of an election, gain credibility with voters, and avoid asking voters to "waste" their vote for a candidate that cannot win. If procedures call for the fusion candidate's votes to be disaggregated, the minor party has evidence of the dimensions of its support, giving it influence with the winning candidate and the capacity to demand alterations in the major party's agenda. Fusion can change the balance of power within a major party—a role of minor parties generally. In a signal example of major party collusion, many state legislatures banned fusion parties at the turn of the century.

Renewed dissatisfaction with major parties spurred recent litigation to overturn these bans. The case brought by Minnesota's "New Party," *Timmons v. Twin Cities Area New Party*, involved a model progressive corrective to the system. A unanimous court of appeals had ruled the state's antifusion law unconstitutional:

> consensual multiple party nomination may invigorate [democracy] by fostering more competition, participation, and representation in American politics. As James Madison observed, when the variety and number of political parties increases, the chance for oppression, factionalism, and nonskeptical acceptance of ideas decreases.[170]

Writing in a similar vein, Justice Stevens dissented from the Supreme Court majority in *Timmons*: "The fact that the law was both intended to disadvantage minor parties and has had that effect is a matter that should weigh against, rather than in favor of, its constitutionality."[171] But a majority of the Supreme Court took a narrow view and upheld the fusion ban. The Court's harsh characterization of the fusion party's motivation is striking: by aligning itself with a major party for the purposes of garnering sufficient votes to qualify for ballot status and perhaps offering its own candidate in the next election, the minor party "exploits" the electoral process. Just why fusion deserves the epithet "exploitative" is not obvious. It emerges that the Court is disparaging because fusion does not increase choices among *candidates*, only among parties. To the extent the minor party does not seem to be offering anything of its own except the party label and organization (and ideological or programmatic challenge to the major parties), there is nothing to be said for the practice. The Court even denies that the ban imposes heavy costs on the fusion party, because it remains free to ally itself with the major party, to participate in the campaign, to urge its supporters to vote, and so on. In short, there is no reason to protect fusion if choosing an individual to hold office is the sole point of the electoral process, as the Court repeatedly insists. It is worth noting that although he would have struck down the ban on fusion, Justice Stevens's understanding of voting is the same as the one invoked by the majority to uphold the ban: elections are about choosing an individual to hold public office, not choosing a party to control office.[172] Both sides in the case depreciate parties. Ballot access for candidates is germane. Voter choice is germane. But parties are weightless.

In fact, the Court has demonstrated little solicitude even for voters in this connection. From the standpoint of critics of the two-party system, and not critics only, the expressive aspects of fusion—the message voters deliver—is one reason for defending the practice. But Courts denigrate expression as an element of the individual right to vote. Voting for a fusion candidate who is already on the ballot under the aegis of a major party is just a way of expressing political views or registering protest, and does not deserve protection. Dismissing out of hand any use of the ballot to "optimize the expressive content of the vote cast"[173] exhibits a constricted view of participation. It is one thing to distinguish voting from a generalized right to speech, and another thing to quash specific messages about voters' preferences in assigning offices—messages that only balloting can deliver to candidates, parties, and the public as a whole. Occasionally courts concede that "the election campaign is a means of disseminating ideas as well as attaining political office," but that is dictum.[174] The *Timmons* Court dismissed this goal flatly as an illegitimate effort to transform the ballot into "a billboard for political advertising."[175]

The Supreme Court took the same pinched position when it upheld Hawaii's law prohibiting write-in candidacies in *Burdick v. Takushi*. As long as candidates had "reasonable" ballot access, voters had no separate interest in opportunities to express their preferences by adding a name that does not appear on the official ballot. Again, the act of voting is to determine an officeholder, not send messages, the majority insisted, and the sole purpose served by organized write-in efforts was "giving vent to short-range political goals, pique, or personal quarrels."[176] In practice, the Democratic Party's dominance in Hawaii meant that the ban deprived many voters of *any* substantial voice in selecting candidates for the entire range of offices. The *Burdick* dissent was fiercely accusatory, and rightly so:

> the majority's approval of Hawaii's ban is ironic at a time when the new democracies in foreign countries strive to emerge from an era of sham elections in which the name of the ruling party candidate was the only one on the ballot. Hawaii does not impose as severe a restriction on the right to vote, but it imposes a restriction that has a haunting similarity in its tendency to exact severe penalties for one who does anything but vote the dominant party ballot.[177]

What consideration outweighed political expression and competitiveness and provided the Court's decisive argument against fusion in *Timmons*? The argument that won the day was Minnesota's interest in warding off "political stability" and avoiding "voter confusion." Justice Stevens raised appropriate doubts about the factual basis of these interests, beginning with skepticism about "ballot manipulation" and "imaginative theoretical sources of voter confusion."[178] After all, fusion does not transform the ballot into an open forum with unlimited choices; it does not provide ballot access to just any advocacy group. Avoiding voter confusion is an objectionable, unsustainable claim in any case; as an assumption about the capacity of the typical voter it could as easily apply to complex ballot initiatives and to the choices presented in a blanket primary.

"Stability" is the main thrust of the *Timmons* decision, then, and the Court ruled that Minnesota could reasonably conclude that "political stability is best served through a healthy two-party system."[179] States must be permitted to "temper the destabilizing effects of party splintering and excessive factionalism."[180] The theme is repeated over and over: electoral regulations legitimately aim at avoiding "unrestrained factionalism," intra-party discord, splintering. Instead of relegating political competition safely to the internal dynamics of the major parties, fusion invites it to spill over into multiple parties, and the same logic applies to minor parties and independent candidacies. Justice Stevens dissented from the majority on this point about stability, too, but not in the terms we might expect. He argued that the ban on fusion was unjustified because there is no evidence that the two-party system is at risk. Minor parties do their work of increasing competition and voter choice without unsettling the system. "It demeans the strength of the two party system to assume that the major parties need to rely on laws that discriminate against independent voters and minor parties in order to preserve their positions of power," he wrote.[181] He would have protected two-partyism without also protecting these particular parties and their present leadership from challenge. "Factionalism" can "destabilize" a major party without destabilizing the two-party system, after all. "The question is not whether American politics will continue to be organized around two dominant parties; it is whether, given that . . . those parties will face sufficient competitive pressures to keep them appropriately responsive to diverse interests."[182]

In decisions like *Timmons* whose effect was to uphold the advantages of the two major parties, the Court did not expressly justify a major party cartel. But the justices were so focused on the state interest in warding off factionalism and the multiplication of parties as threats to political "stability" that the result was to condone entrenchment. For progressive critics, "stability-enhancing" regulation is just another name for duopoly. In the last chapter I discussed the theory of party cartel, and legal scholars' invitation to courts to intervene and bust the party "trust" in matters of districting. They are similarly adamant in urging courts to resist rather than abet major party entrenchment in cases like *Timmons* where the stakes are key points of potential popular influence like ballot access for minor parties and selection of candidates.[183]

Competition for the two major parties and challenges to self-entrenchment are progressive goals; Justice Stevens deemed robust competition "the core of our electoral process." The Supreme Court's demonstrable unconcern for facilitating electoral competition by antisystem parties and its truncated view of the motivation and justification for voting roils progressives, and should. But the real payoff for progressives is that competition inspires voter interest and increases participation. They laud Stevens because he "would make the entire structure of constitutional analysis turn on whether regulations of politics expand or constrict voter participation."[184] We encountered this plausible but speculative link between competition and participation in the context of the blanket primary and now again in the expectation that fusion encourages voting by those disaffected from the major parties because they are able to avoid a wasted vote. Stevens's dissent in a later case drives the linkage home: "states do not have a valid interest in . . . protecting the major parties from competition or in stunting the growth of new parties," but states do have a valid interest "in encouraging the maximum participation of voters."[185]

That a more competitive arrangement will inspire turnout is an article of faith: challenges to two-partyism will bring out habitual nonvoters, or at least nonpartisans and declared Independents. That, rather than, say, a change in party programs or candidates or greater commitment to voter mobilization by major parties is the hoped-for lever. Moreover, and this is key, under arrangements like the blanket primary or fusion, these voters will behave differently, certainly differently than partisan voters in the thrall of the major parties. The imperative is to assure ordinary people more of a say than elections normally allow—more of a say, that is, if decisions are made under conditions that alter the character of that say. I turn to this deliberative corrective now.

Making Voters Deliberative

Blanket primaries and antisystem parties raise hopes for popular influence by means of electoral politics rather than directly via initiatives and referenda or via interest and advocacy groups operating outside the electoral system. But renewed attention to participation in elections does not speak to the quality of participation—whether decision making by voters is informed, independent, and directed to the public interest. That is the onus of democratic theorists who are not resigned to the thought that "democracy is made for the people, not the people for democracy" and that preoccupation with the quality of participation is "pedantic."[186] Citizenship entails deliberative responsibility. Participatory democratic theorists insist that suitably designed electoral institutions and new arrangements oriented to elections can perform the task of "organizing and stimulating public deliberation" and providing "a framework that facilitates well-informed and adequately reflective judgment."[187] We saw that civil society theorists were preoccupied with deliberation, too, but they would cultivate deliberative dispositions in voluntary associations severed from the formal political process. Here, I turn to democratic theorists who see elections as a potential, deliberative "public sphere." These theorists do not accept a formal or moral division between deliberation and election as a process of reaching decision; the two are intertwined. They do not sever deliberation from majoritarianism; both are defining aspects of democracy.[188] These theorists have in mind for voters some cognitive, informational, and moral threshold, if not high standard. They are unwilling to accede to a "competence insensitive" account of democracy[189] (or to a morally insensitive one). They argue that political judgment and behavior are affected by the institutional structures within which citizens consider political questions, and the question is what can improve them.

If we ask which systems "either elicit or submerge ideological or programmatic dispute . . . . encourage or discourage popular participation in substantive disagreement about the course of state policy,"[190] the antiparty answer is that partisan elections submerge and discourage. If the aim is to "refine and enlarge the public view," parties are seen as obstacles: "The rise of political parties—more interested in competing for office than deliberating about policy—interfered with this vision."[191] Indeed, parties favor loyal partisanship, and the implication is that they also favor unenlightened, self-interested voters:

> Earlier generations of politicians might have wished to exploit the ignorance and selfishness of voters, but they labored under technical disadvantages. . . . [W]ithout scientific random sampling and the modern art of survey design . . . they could not penetrate the hearts and minds of ordinary Americans to learn precisely which combinations of myth and greed might work to generate support.[192]

The progressive ambition, then, is to interest citizens in elections and the policy issues at stake in elections, to enhance the quality of their attention and thinking, to alter voters' political behavior and with it political outcomes. For every theorist of deliberation the expectation is twofold: first, a better rendering and understanding of both particular and common interests enlightens voters personally and individually, so that they make better decisions when they participate politically. Second, the overall process of deliberation has a broader systemic influence on decision making by officials. Enlightened participation is a corrective to "the system" because it can change the balance of influences on partisan officials. Antiparty thinkers move from the negative—offsetting undue influences—to the minimal positive content I pointed to earlier: an institutional connection between people and government marked by "responsiveness." Moral confidence is plain in the expected connection between more and better participation—thoughtful, independent decisions—and influencing elected officials to attend to public rather than special interests. The hope for popular influence has to do with the moral authority of decisions justified by public discussion and good reasons and with the quality of these decisions. Schemes like "Deliberation Day," to which I turn in a moment, are based on "the Law of Anticipated Reaction."[193] If preferences, opinions, and positions are arrived at deliberatively, they

have a claim on officials that they lack if they were arrived at by voters in isolation or under the thrall of partisanship. Informed views,
clarified and refined through a deliberative process, are more worthy
of respect.

Behind schemes for improving the quality of participation is a
wholesale rejection not just of an unresponsive party duopoly in favor
of more party competition but also of market analogies overall. The
core idea behind the market model, and its deficiency for democratic
theorists, is the questionable status of unjustified preferences. Deliberative democratic theorists (and not just they) question the meaning and value of "pre-existing" individual preferences. Voting on the
strength of pallid or uninformed preferences or attitudes or blind
partisanship is the poor material of "minimal" or "elitist" democracy.
For starters, "the authority of existing preferences, as criteria of salience, is tainted by their causal history."[194] That alone underscores the
limitations of "more choice," simply. Moreover, on many matters individuals do not have preferences at all; they are uncertain, confused,
ambivalent, cross-pressured. There is no complete set of preferences,
no plain congruence with bare electoral choices, no firm understanding of consequences. Finally, the connections voters draw between
their preferences and political choices are typically ill-informed. At
a minimum, deliberation is a process of sharpening preferences and
forging better connections among interests and opinions and political objectives.[195] In certain respects this contrast between market and
political decisions is obviously overdrawn: individuals may not know
what they want or need materially as consumers any more than they
do politically, hence arguments for product regulations and a degree
of paternalism in consumer choices. Both producers and parties create as well as meet needs, offer up the necessarily restricted range of
matters to be chosen/decided. So the market model of responding to
consumer demands is itself stylized. In any case, the idea is that the
actually existing range of preferences should not exhaust the range of
political alternatives or determine outcomes.[196]

This underlies the basic claims made for deliberation, which
shapes and alters voters' considerations. The claims are both epistemic and moral. Citizens need a clearer conception of their own

interests and values; deliberation creates informed preferences. They also need a clearer conception of the interests and values of others and of the public interest. The process should provide critical, undistorted (nonpartisan) information. (Consistent with this are proposals for denying voters certain kinds of information; "filters to insulate them from information that might distort their decisions."[197] For example, experiments with "deliberative polls" insulate participants from the media-driven emphasis on the "horse race" and on candidate personalities.) Campaign finance reform and other measures to block "undue influence" do little to assure that valuable information is presented; silencing big donors who "drown out" other voices could just mean softer voices or more noise. A pluralism of sources by itself is not a corrective. So other measures focus on citizens and candidates having equal access to adequate information and reasons. Persuasive arguments on all sides of a question must be laid out, so that no case escapes notice. The process should produce estimates of costs and consequences so that the likely effects of policy for citizens personally and individually, for the groups with which they identify, and for the nation as a whole are clarified. "The conditions of public deliberation should be favorable to the thoughtful consideration and comparative assessment of all the positions represented. Citizens should be enabled to reach political judgments on the basis of an adequately informed and reflective comparison of the merits of contending positions."[198] Deliberative democratic theorists replace moral philosophy's "anorexic tendency"[199] to exclude many kinds of arguments, and typically propose only that arguments be "accessible." All this is standard.

Deliberative theorists are divided on whether or not the aim is consensus on some aspect of the common good.[200] They are divided on whether deliberation fails if it does not focus participants disinterestedly on the public interest and produce impartial judgments of what conduces to the public interest. Public spiritedness and disinterestedness are not always the aim; reasoned agreement (or disagreement) can be justifiably based on considerations of interest.[201] For some deliberative democratic theorists, clarifying and correcting for particular interests and opinions is a necessary prelude to deliberation, which then considers only the common good. For others, deliberation serves important democratic purposes simply by clarifying self-interests, the justifications for them, and thus the reasons for conflict even if the result is sharper divergence than before deliberation. Jane Mansbridge has proposed a composite, three-stage understanding of deliberation: a "pre-deliberative" stage in which like-minded individuals come to an understanding of their particular interests, a stage of "full deliberation" in which individuals enter into discussion with one another to clarify areas of conflict and commonality and ideally arrive at agreement about what serves the common good, and a final stage of "negotiation," which ensues if disagreement cannot be reconciled and consensus cannot be reached. (Only if that fails should voters simply vote in what they understand to be their self-interests.)[202]

The constant in all this is unyielding antipartyism. Party leaders and candidates are not deliberating agents. Party competition is not a forum for "trial by discussion." Party organizations are not settings for deliberation among partisans. Partisanship among voters is absolutely antithetical to considered reflection; "party ID" as a "shortcut" to electoral choice is nondeliberative by definition. As one critic puts it, "Party identification under certain conditions may be a serviceable cue for many voters, but . . . the collective results produced by voters using these shortcuts are [not] as satisfactory as the results realized by well-informed voters."[203] Even if they are not indifferent to the value of "trial by discussion" and present positions with reasons and articulated pros and cons, parties cannot be counted on to satisfy the requirements of "completeness, coherence, and range of alternatives."[204]

> Even a well-ordered regime of programmatic competition may not satisfy the aim of placing before the voters a sufficiently broad range of alternatives. In spite of competitive incentives, organizational inertia and historical practice might leave salient positions unrepresented by any established party. There is no general reason to suppose that openness of party governance to participation by the rank and file would change this.[205]

I defend parties and partisanship on these points below and in the next chapter.

298

In chapter 3 I discussed deliberation in representative assemblies (which sometimes, if only ambivalently, entertained parties as the bearers of "a serious conflict of opposing reasons"), that is, "deliberation across the aisle." At a minimum, "It is the collective and diverse character of the representative organ, and not any prior or independently established belief in the virtues of debate, that explains the role conferred on discussion."[206] In contrast, in the democratic theory I am considering here, deliberation is for "lay citizens." For most deliberative democrats it is not sufficient that voters hear or read competing arguments, pros and cons, as attentive voters do in the course of party politics. Exposure is not enough, nor is better information, better reasons. People must take active part in deliberation about policies and candidates. They must deliberate in person and collectively, under conditions of equality. They must offer justifications for men and measures. The *experience* of deliberation, "inclusive, judgmental, and dialogic,"[207] is personally and collectively improving.

There is another reason for insisting on actually deliberating citizens. Theorists insist that democratic decisions made in a way and in a context that "acknowledges their collective authority"[208] are the only truly democratic ones. Aggregation by means of markets and, by extension, by means of unreconstructed elections is the registration of the preferences of voter-consumers. Voting is necessarily an isolated and individualist act, at least so long as the secret ballot is preserved. (Some democratic theorists would unveil the vote precisely to encourage voters to feel they might be held accountable and made to justify their choice. For these advocates, any danger that the open ballot would make voters more vulnerable to influences other than the better argument is outweighed by the expectation that at least they would be protected against the unique pressure of party: "A thousand voices would take the place of this single intervention."[209]) Voting is not a deliberative act. But the process preceding voting in elections or preceding other participatory activities, such as voting on an initiative or expressing political preferences in response to polls, should be. Deliberation and majoritarianism are both necessary. Contemporary theorists (joined now by social scientists) throw up a steady stream of proposals for deliberative democracy reminiscent of the Progressive era proper.

Nonpartisan Deliberation

The most discussed correctives to the electoral and party system are experiments with "deliberative polls" and "citizens' juries," sometimes described as "mini-publics."[210] These are controlled settings of randomly chosen citizens who meet in person in groups small enough to allow for participation in deliberation (two to three hundred for a long weekend, in the typical "deliberative poll") or through online replications of face-to-face meetings. Most of these deliberative experiments take up a single policy issue, such as genetically modified food or proposals for changes in electoral rules, and discussion is divorced from elections. The goal is to create a "counterfactually enhanced information environment."[211] Participants are insulated from the usual sources of information and persuasion and the usual conditions under which they respond to polls about their preferences. They are provided with selected, unbiased information and with balanced panels of experts. Trained moderators guide discussion (a deviation from the egalitarian standards applied by other theorists). The emphasis is on arguments for and against competing proposals. These settings have been shown to alter participants' understanding and opinion of the question at hand; the information and expertise provided and absorbed have measurable effect (more, it is suggested, than actual discussion among participants.[212]) Deliberative experiments conducted in the context of presidential primary elections have a different outcome. Participants do not necessarily change their preferences for particular candidates or their perceptions of candidates, though they *do* give greater weight to policy issues in their evaluation of candidates. It seems that the surest measures of outcome have to do with the impact of deliberation on participants themselves: an improved sense of political efficacy, the likelihood they will participate in the future, even general engagement in public affairs of a sort that makes them "more interesting" to their spouses.

Deliberative experiments are seldom binding.[213] They normally lack any formal political status or authority. Sometimes they are commissioned by public agencies in order to get a sense of public opinion on some issue. Knowing that decisions count can alter the character of the collective decision, if not the quality of deliberation. Nevertheless, the deliberative process promises more than argument for argument's sake or self-improvement. In many cases, political influence is the goal. The intention is for the results to become part, hopefully a well-publicized and persuasive part, of the mix of voices from interest groups, media, and parties, informing public debate and official decision making. The informed public opinion produced through deliberation can be persuasive to policy makers (though Goodin and Dryzek point out that "market testing" of proposals may have more weight in legitimizing a policy or troubleshooting likely opposition if they reflect "raw" public opinion and large numbers rather than the views of a selective slice of deliberatively educated voters[214]). Another hope is influence on public discussion and public opinion.

That helps to explain one constant in deliberative experiments and in the theory of deliberative democracy. The citizen gatherings are not supposed to be arenas of partisan contestation, replicating and refining the political universe outside. Deliberation and the authority of its results require a predominance of Independents, nonpartisans, and nonvoters. Deliberation is above all for those who are usually averse to political discussion and conflicting views.[215] Whether participants are chosen randomly or selectively to ensure diversity or whether participation is as nearly universal as possible, the aim is a representative group. The parameters of "representativeness" are not spelled out, though the idea is to include "the diversity of social characteristics and plurality of initial points of view in the larger society."[216] Most experiments do not claim statistical representativeness, and we know that localism does not produce a cross-section of citizens or voters generally. The plain thrust of "representative" is to ensure that the group is not principally comprised of partisan voters or activists. Politicians are excluded, and self-selection is suspicious precisely because it produces a group in which partisans or stakeholders hold sway. The requirement is a group in which "lay citizens and nonpartisans" predominate.[217] We recognize the same considerations at work here as in the proposed blanket primary—diluting the undue influence of partisans. Deliberative decisions are persuasive to other voters, their outcomes trustworthy, precisely to the extent that they are the decisions of "ordinary citizens," not partisans.[218]

For deliberative democratic theorists, the expectation goes beyond the fact that decisions are informed and participants are representative. The influence of outcomes on political officials is supposed to come from the moral authority that attaches to the process of deliberation. The results of deliberation provide incentives for officeholders to attend to the public business because they claim the authority of care and relative disinterest over other voices and influences. (Some deliberative democrats also think that these decisions enjoy epistemic superiority.) This moral authority does not translate directly into political authority, and deliberation is not an instrument of popular control of officials. Again, the promise is that if voters are deliberative and independent, representatives will be responsive. The hope is that the spread of deliberative forums, the iteration of experiments in popular deliberation of policy and institutional design, the cumulative impact of participation in deliberative schemes, creates standards and expectations for authoritative political reasoning.

One ambitious scheme is "Deliberation Day," a design for a nationwide deliberative forum dedicated to discussion of issues in anticipation of elections. The local "citizens' assemblies" that Bruce Ackerman and James Fishkin propose differ from experiments with "deliberative polls" and "citizens' juries." Deliberation Day calls for discussion without moderators and assigned materials, for one thing. Deliberation is not restricted to a single issue, for another.[219] Most important, Deliberation Day is publicly mandated for a "critical mass" of citizens, not a sample. Participation would be encouraged by paying attendees a stipend, providing transportation, and declaring Deliberation Day a national holiday. The aim is to maximize participation. Maximum participation is valuable for its educational potential, of course, and to ensure that overall (if not in every local assembly) every perspective relevant to the issues discussed is brought to bear. Not least, to repeat, maximum participation is important because success depends on convening a group that is not predominantly partisan. This is accomplished if the assemblies mirror not local *voters* but local citizens broadly, including the mass of habitual nonvoters.

Apart from repressing or diluting partisanship, deliberative theorists are not always clear about the meaning and methods of nonpartisan or impartial deliberation. Thinking back to my earlier discussion of deliberative assemblies in chapter 3, do deliberative experiments aim at reconstructing either citizen Hume or citizen Mill? This deserves consideration; it can clarify the often unclear expectations for deliberation.

The simplest way of thinking about the objective of deliberation is avoiding the obvious shoals of partisanship. That would mean attention to "framing," the cognitive device well studied by political psychologists.[220] We know that expressions of attitudes are context-dependent. For example, voters will respond differently to being asked whether they want to ban "preferential treatment" (yes) than whether they wish specifically to ban affirmative action in city contracting and hiring (no).[221] Put strongly, "the opinions expressed by the public on political issues should be understood not as the revelation of fixed inner states but as the result of a question-answering process, one that mimics the dialogue surrounding controversial political issues."[222] Nonpartisan consideration of men and measures would have as its aim exposing the partisan purposes and effects of policies themselves and of partisan framing ("death tax"/estate tax). This exercise is obviously difficult and like other forms of ideological unmasking bound to be contested. Still, the goal of exposing partisan objectives and how they are presented in order to be persuasive has the advantage of bearing a perceptible connection to politics as it exists outside the precious deliberative arena. The danger, as proponents of deliberation recognize, is that unveiling performed in the spirit of exposing cynical partisan strategies might produce general mistrust and withdrawal rather than excited participation.

To the authors' credit, Deliberation Day does assign at least the major parties a role. Each party selects issues to be discussed (there is also opportunity for citizens to bring up other matters). The initial debate is between party representatives, and local party leaders answer questions. Discussion then takes place in small groups of fifteen where people take turns speaking for ninety seconds each (a valiant effort to have both official participation in deliberation and equal participation). The structure is designed for dialogue between candidates or party leaders and citizens, with time for parties "to explain their reasoning and to be educated in turn."[223] Deliberation Day is in anticipation of elections, so beginning from the standpoint of partisan orientations makes sense.

Still, it is not clear that nonpartisanship as described is simply a matter of unveiling partisan positions and clarifying the grounds of opposition. Rather, even in this proposal the desired outcome may be achieving a balance of partisan positions. One way of putting this question is to ask whether the Humean ambition, the pose of the "impartial observer" I discussed in chapter 3, applies to Deliberation Day and allied proposals. Hume imagined that the parties divided the constitutional field, that each represented a rationally comprehensible, complementary part, that each had a share in being right. That is why his ideal was moderation and assigning to each its "proper poise and influence." This does not fit well with most deliberative experiments, which do not take partisan positions and arguments for and against as their starting point and are unconcerned to demonstrate the continuity or counterpoise of these positions. Even Deliberation Day does not assume the party positions that form the basis of discussion are complementary or that from the participant standpoint, a balance of partisan positions is discernible. The more modest goal seems to be discussion of issues in a context that exposes partisan objectives and arguments and is even-handed, without aiming at a constructive amalgam—what Hume might call "a coalition of parties" that deliberators should be able to appreciate. Ideally, partisan positions are well stated, without zealousness or "madness of heart," and are set in sharper relief and relation to one another than occurs in the ordinary course of elections. As Mill allowed, the exchange of ideas might not change views or alter participants' view of their interests and values or of the public interest. But those holding them would enjoy the rational assurance of being right.

Deliberative schemes may rest on regulative ideals other than nonpartisanship, however. The implication of experiments focused on the preparation of balanced materials, experts, and orchestrated presentation of pros and cons is that it is possible to achieve not just nonpartisanship but impartiality. That is, proposals, reasons, and arguments could be presented in a way that is not attentive to the partisan orientation of a policy and to exposing partisan framing but rather constructs a full and coherent menu of alternative proposals, standpoints, and arguments for and against. Here, Humean assumptions are even less apt. Party positions cannot be the starting point if we assume that parties do not provide "completeness and coherence," standing as they often do for disparate, unmatched positions, taking important arguments for granted so that they are unarticulated and unopposed, or suffering jointly failures of imagination. In these deliberative schemes, the aim is not a rehabilitation of partisan positions and clarification of reasons for and against but a substitute agenda. The aim is disinterested, dispassionate give and take over policy proposals removed from politics and stakeholders, with the ultimate goal of having citizens find and settle on the best solution.

The problem with impartiality as a regulative ideal of deliberation is that we do not have standards for the relevant universe of alternative programs and reasons, any more than we have democratic standards for what makes one "frame" more acceptable than another for deliberative purposes. We recognize the same set of problems endemic to critiques of media "gatekeepers." It is one thing to expose media bias. This does not necessarily undermine justifications for a partisan press, television station, or Web sites; it leaves segmented media in tact while identifying it as such. It is another thing to demand balance. And it is still another to insist that the imperative is to transmit information impartially, as in this stringent imperative: "Nothing should be noticed or absorbed except the information. Nothing else should be memorable."[224] The imperative obviously leaves out the determination of which information is relevant to deliberation; it is insensitive to the impossibility and sterility of "information" per se.

If we think back to my discussion of Mill in chapter 3, we recall his commendation of "a serious conflict of opposing reasons" and the thought that deliberation is progressive when it takes the form of "the rough process of a struggle between combatants fighting under hostile banners" by "persons who actually believe them, who defend them in earnest, and do their utmost for them."[225] Deliberation Day and its cousin experiments lower the hostile banners. Mill too put hopes in nonpartisan deliberators and looked ahead to "hundreds of able men of independent thought." He had lost faith in actual parties, which is why I called the philosophical defense of parties "proto-Millian." Even so, he gave consideration to combatants. They are indispensible to deliberation. Even if *their* minds are not changed by good arguments, others' are, and at the collective level, outcomes are improved. The two Millian ingredients—hostile banners and Independents—are consistent if the expectation is enlightened Independents and better decisions. This is a strong response on their own terms to political theorists who because of their "deep-rooted rationalist approach to deliberation" fail to appreciate the role of partisanship in democratic politics.[226] It is one example of how even stern regulative principles of deliberation might justify nondeliberative or quasi-deliberative practices. It is not the whole story, however, and stands as a caution to deliberative theorists, for reasons I spell out now.

Deliberation and Parties

Is reconstructed participation, enlightened and imbued with moral authority by deliberation, a corrective to "the system"? Some important things are missing—cast out or simply left out by designers of these proposals. On my view of deliberation, partisanship is desirable as well as unavoidable. For one thing, dread parties and partisans provoke one another to take up opposing positions and offer reasons. If their political talk does not rise to the standard of deliberation, still, parties provide the material for others to supplement and correct. They provide the fuel for more refined deliberation by others, including favored Independents. Even if partisans surrender the independence deliberative theorists value, the collectivity acquires something of value. Even if (what I don't admit) partisans give up admirable qualities of thought and character, ordinary citizens and knowledgeable elites benefit. The benefits of party conflict can be the un-aimed-for result of what partisans do half-thinkingly, and what will not be done without them. Parties are integral to democratic deliberation, and deliberation elucidates their significance. Put simply, the framework for political deliberation requires the rough process of a struggle among combatants fighting under hostile banners. Once the framework is built, we see that partisans are necessary to realize the value of parties.

Perhaps the clearest need for parties from the standpoint of deliberation is that the universe of considerations and perspectives is infinitely expandable, and, contrary to antiparty critics, the best positions and arguments parties can produce are a reasonable slice at it. Parties do the work philosophy cannot: determine the range of matters for discussion and decision. Theories of democratic deliberation prize a "variety of perspectives," but democratic politics cannot proceed on the basis of arrant pluralism, without distillation. *Partisans* generate conflicting positions and advance opposing arguments within a framework designed for adversarial show. They have to.[227] Parties draw politically relevant lines of division, reject elements of the others' account of projects and promises, and articulate positions, and their antagonism is the engine of "trial by discussion." Party antagonism focuses attention on problems, information and interpretations are brought out, stakes are delineated, points of conflict and commonality are located, the range of possibilities winnowed. Truly, "an issue does not become an issue merely because someone says it is."[228] Again: "What starts as a relatively unstructured mass of diverse opinions with countless cleavages within the electorate is transformed . . . disagreements are reduced, simplified, and generalized."[229]

Moreover, parties construct both available choices and how they appear in ways that are not simply responsive to the constellation of interests or preferences that may have existed before campaigns. "Parties are as much engaged in prioritizing choices, and therefore suppressing some of them, as they are in expressing alternatives that may exist in the minds of ordinary citizens."[230] When Schumpeter spoke of the "absence of effective volition" on the part of voters, he meant that there is no political demand independent of supply. The authors of the classic text *The Changing American Voter* emphasized one "simple but important theme": "the public responds to the political stimuli offered it."[231]

Without parties, public opinion is (or is even more) amorphous and episodic. Habermas acknowledged that voters "can perceive their own interests only in light of pregeneralized interest positions" offered by parties.[232] And "It is only when more-well-defined issues are proposed for its deliberation that the influence of the people on the government of their society can be real and effective."[233] Parties work to persuade voters that something is in their interest rightly understood and in the public interest, or not adverse to it. They work to show not only that their proposals are beneficial but also that the electorate or some part of it already desires them. Finally, the "who" of partisanship matters in political decision making. Where deliberation is partisan, partisans are identified, and so are their antagonists, the beneficiaries of their plans, and those who bear the costs. Indeed, "the fact that a policy adopted by one party is actually inimical to the interests of some minority . . . gives rival parties a reason to draw attention to that fact."[234]

The rare, strong assertion that parties are "essential for deliberation"[235] is welcome. Militating against it in practice is the fact that parties may fail to present "more-well-defined issues." More important, well-defined issues are not always the heart of democratic deliberation and decision. One purpose party competition uniquely serves is setting out general aims and orientations. Parties are in the business of ideals as well as policies; they are enduring associations that look to the future. If we extend deliberation beyond policy issues, parties are even more essential as both deliberative forums and deliberating agents, and I enlarge on this argument below and at greater length in Part III.

In most accounts of democratic deliberation, policy proposals are the subject, and the process is untethered from parties and elections. In the artifactual setting of Deliberation Day, partisan positions are considered at one remove from actual politics. If deliberation aims not only at enlightenment but also at influence, it must be connected to political participation.[236] That is another reason for adding parties and partisanship in a robust manner to deliberative forums and for appreciating and enhancing the quasi-deliberative business of actual party politics. Parties are the engines of "mobilized deliberation."[237] I say this in the face of accusations that parties depress participation, both strategically and as a sour consequence of their ordinary activities. Again, the presumed connection between major party conduct and electoral detachment has become a commonplace. Antiparty progressives argue both that the major parties are depressants and that political competition apart from and against the major parties excites participation. One rationale offered for nonpartisan deliberative schemes is that they would attract citizens who are turned off by party politics (echoing the claim that a nonpartisan primary election would bring out habitual nonvoters). But there is little reason to think that artifactual deliberative settings translates into a taste or tolerance for political participation by the great mass of citizens, including nonvoters.

Notice that deliberative schemes propose incentives for participation in their exercises, but they do not address the quandary of the relation between deliberation and actual political participation I introduced earlier. On the one hand, deliberative schemes temper contestation and restrict it to measures, not men. They are not obvious settings for cultivating tolerance for political conflict among the many voters and nonvoters who want pragmatic solutions to problems and see political argument as unnecessary and partisan combat in particular as diversion from getting the business done.[238] On the other hand, even tempered deliberation, the "serious conflict of opposing reasons" deliberative experiments promise, may be enough to confirm nonvoters in their aversion. Deliberation is uncomfortable for people who avoid political conflict, however focused on specific policy issues and however mannerly. Studies indicate that exposure to conflicting views produces greater understanding of these views and the rationales for them, but depresses political participation. There are a number of reasons for this: deliberators become aware of arguments against their own position and become doubtful, ambivalent, politically paralyzed nonparticipants. Or dispositionally inclined and culturally habituated to social harmony, they recoil from participating in politics where the conflicting views learned in the deliberative setting are brought to life.[239] Deliberative settings may be endured; participants may even be enlightened. But it is not clear that they will be politically energized.

Earlier, I observed tension between two strains of civil society theory. Deliberation Day and proposals like it are closer to the "good" civic strain than the combative. In citizen assemblies, people are encouraged to think in terms of reciprocity and the general good. There is dispassionate education and exchange, not popular mobilization. Deliberative polls and citizen juries are oriented to informed preferences about issues and knowledgeable voting, not angry, oppositional organizing. Deliberation is not directed against particular hierarchies and "undue influences," "big money" or entrenched party elites. At least, there is little evidence that deliberative settings dependably finger these forces and challenge them directly. "In the real world, the theory of deliberative democracy seems to devalue the only kind of politics that could ever establish a practical egalitarianism."[240] Though deliberative designs may improve the quality of information and discussion, that is, its enlightening features are plain, there is nothing in these schemes that speak to "effective organized opposition to the established hierarchies of wealth and power."[241] They are resolutely antiparty, and it is hard to imagine any democratic theorist today subscribing to Walter Dean Burnham's assertion:

> Political parties, with all their well-known human and structural shortcomings, are the only devices thus far invented by the wit of Western man which with some effectiveness can generate countervailing collective power on behalf of the many individually powerless against the relatively few who are individually—or organizationally—powerful.[242]

Partisans drive deliberation. Not some abstract ideal of impartiality or good citizenship but partisanship and its challenges is activating, even if it is aversive to some. Deliberation is likely to be interesting and urgent only when it is about choosing sides. By their regular participation and exhibition of emotional commitment, partisans demonstrate that making decisions and choosing sides is a value. I could say, contrary to the spirit of deliberative theorists, that the objective of deliberation is improved partisanship and that improved partisanship is more important for democracy than independence, and I argue as much in the next chapter.

Men, Not Measures

One limitation of deliberation from the standpoint of what parties do is captured by the confession: "It would . . . be normatively pleasing if deliberation reduced the role of candidate personality in vote choice."[243] What advocate of deliberation does not share the rueful observation that "judging a candidate's political character from his or her personal character, having first judged personal character from media character, is far more inaccurate than judging a book by its cover"?[244] Perhaps deliberative forums could improve judgment of character so that assessments are not altogether subjective, lucky, or dead wrong. They could provide at least some basis for trust in what voters and potential supporters and endorsers think they see. But personality seems to be the limit case: all the correctives imagined and implemented can be undone by this ultimate vicissitude of politics. Deliberative democratic theorists want measures, not men. This is impossible. Rescuing party politics from the unreasonable and from everything willful is unreasonable. More important, it is unfaithful to representative democracy.

Bernard Manin reminds us that representative government is not self-government and that elections introduce what he calls an "aristocratic" element into democracy. He means that unlike the ancients' democratic mechanism of filling offices by lot, elections are explicitly opposed to government by the people. From this standpoint, modern democracies are really mixed constitutions, and individual candidates standing for election are antidemocratic. Apart from the historical contrast Manin constructs, however, the term "aristocratic" is misleading because the men and women who are recruited and come up through party politics do not comprise a social or economic elite. They are not a Madisonian natural aristocracy, either, dependably refining and enlarging the public view. There is nothing outstanding about the quality of their moral reasoning. Nor are candidates as a class exceptional along some dimension of political mechanics—superb "organization" types or exemplary placatory professional politicians. Manin's contribution is to draw theoretical attention to the individual candidate, to personality and the audience for it.

Parties care about candidates' personalities, of course. Personalities raise money and excite turnout. Candidates suffer from drab. At the same time, the presence of "traits" adds a gigantic indeterminacy to party politics—it is the ultimate vicissitude. It is the obvious element of luck, along with the weather on election day. Periodic public hand-wringing about the elusive, irrational, pull of personality comes from candidates themselves—at least from the unlucky, earnest ones, programmatic types, who find self-display jarring and resist the powerful pressure to describe their campaigns as a personal odyssey. Personality is also regrettable to those who want to calibrate, strategize, make election a matter of skill.[245] Indeterminacy accounts for the maddening trials of political strategists charged with creating and projecting a candidate's "image." Parties themselves are at sea when it comes to the dimensions of "aristocracy," buffeted and sometimes submerged by the waves of personality that often seem to turn the tides of selection.

For the personal qualities that are valued or just engaging and seductive (I do not want to overstate the matter with "charismatic") and win over voters are varied and unpredictably variable. The attractive political personality may have the appeal of stolidity, of gravitas; a candidate should "appear presidential." But the contrary appearance of being ungrounded seems to have magneticism for voters too. There is no predicting whether or not voters want someone they can "trust"; the risky, slightly undependable personality, on the edge of corruption, immorality, grasping for power also has allure so long as he or she is able to stir people up, pinch them, and make them feel politically alive and active. There is no predicting whether voters *identify with* personalities and recognize some likeness (self-flattery) or want a personality *unlike* themselves. Do voters respond to heroic self-inflation, ambitiousness, the unconcealed desire to have all eyes focused on him or herself? Or to humility? Solemnity or irreverence? Or simply to the person who seems "built for winning"? Only one thing is clear: personality has nothing to do with merit—though it is not incompatible with merit, either.

From the deliberative standpoint the intrusion of personality is abhorrent; there is nothing to be said for it except perhaps for a sober estimate of character in some politically relevant respect, a trait that strikes impartial observers as a "fit" with the needs of the moment. Since Burke and Bolingbroke, we have heard that if we must have parties, they should be about "measures, not men." Subordinating personality to ideology is a key justification for party-list proportional representation systems. So, what can be said for personality, which can be decisive in party politics?

Personality brings us face to face with the *face* of political agency, of political men and women. Individuality is showcased in elections as at few other moments. The salience of personality also makes the sovereignty of the electorate vivid. It reminds us that voting is antideferential, performing what Kateb calls "a radical chastening" of political authority.[246] It is a way of thumbing one's nose at acceptable political elites and sober issue activists. It is relief from the onus of fairness, accepting of sheer willfulness. Henry Adams's heroine Mrs. Lightfoot Lee was enthralled by men who want not only to exercise power but to step up onto the stage where we can watch them at it. The personal contest and the drama are plain: as Adams wrote, "not one of them who had aimed at high purpose but had been thwarted, beaten, and habitually insulted; what varied expression of defeat and unsatisfied desire; what a sense of self-importance . . . what a craving for flattery; what despair at the sentence of fate!"[247] At the same time, parties contain the effects; personality is not let loose entirely; it is not everything. Attraction to personality and its characteristic flaws is compatible with good reasons for judging its importance or unimportance.[248] In stable party politics the weight of personality is tempered so that personal ambition does not rise to demagoguery or foment purely personal factionalism.[249] Individual candidates almost always run on a party label and depend on party support, and the personal narratives that are the inevitable accompaniment of contemporary candidacies are linked to party, policy, and shared visions of the future. Independent candidates appealing to nonpartisan voters, individual to individuals, come closest to subjectivity run wild, unconstrained by the "ethics of partisanship" I describe in Part III. In his great novel *All the King's Men*, Robert Penn Warren describes Willie Stark, the fictional candidate for Louisiana governor in 1930, mesmerizing crowds: "There wasn't any Democratic party. There was just Willie, with his hair in his eyes and his shirt sticking to his stomach with sweat. And he had a meat ax in his hand and was screaming for blood."[250] Of course there wasn't just Willie Stark "screaming for blood," there was the party.

Elections are a ritualized contest, not violent combat or anarchic melée. But neither are they ordered sites of dialogue. It is possible to add opportunities for deliberative experiments and to improve the give and take of partisans on issues and visions, but irreverence and disorderliness and fractiousness in electoral contests are ineliminable and warranted. Party "competition" does not capture these elements. When the adversarial ritual of contesting individuals is subdued or elections are uncontested, more is lost than "trial by discussion" and voter choice. Along with these, political engagement evaporates. Robert Penn Warren puts these words in Willie Stark's stump speech: "I don't expect all of you to vote for me. My God, if all of you went and voted for Willie, what the hell would you find to argue about? There wouldn't be anything left but the weather, and you can't vote on that." Both men and women to run for office and voters to select them require the stimulation of contest—the vicarious aggression. We do not know with certainty the reasons for voter turnout. But the familiar proposition that engaging "alienated" or "disenchanted" nonvoters is a matter of centrism or extremism or sharper ideological identity or more substantive and adroitly presented party programs or "cleaner elections" are all partial explanations. A serious list of reasons for voter disaffection surely includes the plain fact that cognitive and moral demands take a "hedonic toll," and politics without personality contributes to what Robert Lane has called the "unhappy polity." Agonistic contest is the "primal drama" of politics, including representative democracy, which cannot stay alive without it. We can conceive of democracy without parties but not parties without the clash of personality that is one aspect of regulated rivalry. Parties invite and temper both.

The progressive "but" is familiar by now. Parties are entrenched and self-serving, unreconstructed partisans are the bane of democracy, and ordinary voters need saving from both. The antiparty poses I have analyzed up to now—glorious traditions emphasizing division and divisiveness, progressive concern with corruption, convergence, collusion, and cartel—are just that, antiparty. All along we have had glimpses of another element: antipartisanship. This additional high point of the terrain has its own force, and partisanship stands out as a target in a lurid spotlight of its own. Parties may be grudgingly accepted as convenient vehicles for holding elections, but partisanship is reviled as morally and politically degrading. It is deformed citizenship. Individual voters move to the center of attention, and as this discussion of interventions to correct the system suggests, the aim is to convert partisans into Independents.

Every partisan claims to be "on the side of the angels." Independents do too. Neither is justified, but at least partisans have their feet on the ground. I will turn the usual understanding of partisanship on its head: of course, partisans support parties, but the reverse is of interest, too—parties are carriers of partisanship. Partisanship is a distinct and valuable political identity and should be seen as an achievement. I turn now to my own moment of appreciation of partisans "on the side of the angels." I argue for the moral distinctiveness of "party identification" and suggest elements of an ethics of partisanship.

PART III

The Moral Distinctiveness of "Party ID"

CHAPTER 7

——⟫·◇·⟪——

Partisanship and Independence

All political partisans think they are "on the side of the angels," and political Independents think no partisan is. Partisan voters are mistrusted as lackeys or craven hacks, blind loyalists or rational calculators out for spoils. At moments of party polarization like the one in which I write, in contests over the nomination of a Supreme Court Justice or the competence of a political appointee to head the Federal Emergency Management Agency, the barb "partisan" comes out of improbable mouths, a virtual reflex. It is no virtue to cultivate the sentiment that your party is "on the side of the angels." We recognize "partisan" as invective. Partisans' undisputed moral superiors are "Independents." I am going to take sides—not between opposing partisans but between partisanship and independence. I argue here for the moral distinctiveness of partisanship as *the* political identity in representative democracy.[1]

The "party in the electorate" had its heyday in the era of machine politics and enthusiastic popular mobilization, with solidarity inscribed on the mastheads of the partisan press: "Democratic at all times and under all Circumstances" is the banner of a Wisconsin paper; "Republican in everything, independent in nothing," the message of one Chicago paper.[2] Ardent antiparty progressives glumly conceded that if we must have parties, at least voters should be nonpartisan. They proselytized for "the divine right to bolt" from parties, and gave being a political "Independent" honorific status. Independence was a key element of antiparty strategy, a potential counter to the "undue influence" of party managers and their principals, "the money power." Progressive enthusiasm was rooted in conviction that partisanship was degrading, and confidence that independence was both a laudatory disposition and responsible political behavior. Independents were voters persuaded, partisans were voters bought. Independents were the hope for "good government" and "clean elections." "Independence is the great purifying agency of politics."[3] Long an American civic ideal of economic and social self-reliance, independence was replanted in the soil of electoral politics and fertilized by progressive antipartyism. In this chapter I use American materials, but once again substantial parts of my account of partisanship and independence apply to other advanced democracies, with one difference I will note.

Progressive faith in independence is with us in force. Today, the term "independent" continues to have resonance, and at the same time its specific political sense has solidified. "Independent" is comfortably ensconced alongside Democrat and Republican in everyday political talk. Few things are more touted than their importance in elections—fuelled by incessant polling and media fixation on "swing voters." Independents are the object of tender solicitude—made vivid in the 2004 "town meeting" presidential debate between George Bush and John Kerry to which only "undecideds" and Independents were invited. They can be forgiven the illusion of efficacy and a hint of smugness.[4] I have discussed one instance of the favor in which Independents are held: the 1996 California ballot initiative to change from closed party primaries in which only registered party members could select candidates for the general election to a "nonpartisan" or blanket primary in which any voter, including Independents and voters registered with another party, can vote for any candidate. The selling point of the proposal was blatantly antipartisan: it would increase participation by non-party-identified voters, wrest control from party leaders, dilute the undue influence of party activists, and ease the way for the election of "moderate problem solvers" over "party hard-liners."[5] The California initiative identified partisan primary voters with extremists and would commit these elections to nonpartisans.

Even among early antiparty Progressives, a few sober observers noted that enthusiasm for independence might be misplaced. One writer sensibly refused to praise independence indiscriminately:

> It is obvious that men sometimes act independent of parties from good motives, sometimes from bad motives, sometimes from public interests, sometimes from personal and selfish interests; sometimes for a noble cause, sometimes for an ignoble cause. Recognizing party as a necessary or beneficial agency in popular government, if it be asked whether bolting is justifiable, it must be answered that it is not if the bolting is prompted by reasons that are trivial, petty, spiteful, selfish, ignoble; but that it is justifiable if the reasons given are good and sufficient. Who is to judge the reasons that are given? Manifestly the only reply is that every man must answer for himself to his own individual conscience and judgment.[6]

This quote gets at something important. It sees partisanship as the typical or default position, and independence as a deliberate choice, requiring justification.

My purpose in this chapter is to complete the map of the terrain of antipartyism. Articulated antipartisanship is a new feature on the landscape. Contemporary Independents and their advocates are creative in their loathing. They are unattuned to the glorious traditions of antipartyism. As we have seen, one tradition abhors parties as "unwholesome parts" that disfigure what should be a perfectly unified political community. The other tradition accepts political pluralism but abhors divisive parties that upset balance and enflame conflict. Independence today does not spring from some ideal of national unity transcending adversarial politics or anticipation of a classless, seamless, consensual society. Nor do Independents express fear that parties are fatally divisive. They are as likely to describe parties as frustratingly indistinct or to view them with an attitude of "dismissive neutrality."[7] Despite appearances, then, independence is not antipartyism but a different thing: antipartisanship. Antipartyism and antipartisanship are separable, of course. We can concede the usefulness of political parties and still despise partisanship, just as we can appreciate partisanship in the general sense of "partisans of a cause" yet despise parties as vehicles.

My further purpose is to defend partisanship, and implicit in this defense is a positive assessment of political parties. It may seem like an unsettling reversal of the common-sense view that partisanship supports parties as political institutions to argue, as I do here, that one value of parties is to serve as "carriers" of partisanship. I do not mean that parties reflect partisans' political preferences or attitudes—they are creators as well as reflectors. My point is that if representative democracy has good reasons for valuing partisanship as a political identity, then there is additional justification for parties beyond the ones I have discussed so far.

Independence is a distinctive political identity, too, defined as the antithesis of partisanship. The "independent" label is more than just an artifact of polling—a response of "no preference" to a survey. Plainly, the resonance of "independent" is positive. Its antonym, after all, is dependence or subordination. The label is a point of pride. The self-designation (by the proper noun Independent) and the adjectival description (independent) go hand in hand. My goal is to chip away at the moral high ground claimed by Independents and to provide partisanship with at least an iota of dignity. I argue against the notion that an "intelligently and progressively democratic" system depends on the ability of its supporters to attain a nonpartisan spirit.[8] This seems to me exactly wrong.

Political Science and Party ID

Orphans of political philosophy, parties are *the darlings* of political science. I noted in the Introduction that the disjuncture between political science and political theory is striking. Parties are built into the standard definition of democracy as government "chosen periodically by means of popular elections in which two or more parties compete for the votes of all adults."[9] Contrast, once more, this definition from political theory—"Democracy is not simply a form of politics but a framework of social and institutional conditions that facilitates free discussion among equal citizens"—or the even sharper contrast we find in the notion of democracy as "a way of life."[10] I concoct a conversation between political science and political theory, and exploit resources from both to construct my case for the moral distinctiveness of party ID.

Political science deserves the first word, for the modern discipline's empirical research and statistical methods were developed studying parties and elections, and its terms and concepts dominate the literature.[11] From the start, voting behavior has been associated with the concept of "party identification." The phrase "party ID" is a standard item in the political science lexicon. Party ID refers to an individual voter's avowed affiliation with a political party and has both cognitive and affective elements. It is a matter of personal identification, not legal status or membership, ascertained principally through survey research. It is "antecedent to, distinct from, and influential on individual voting decisions."[12] It is a stable predisposition, acquired early. It is strongly associated with the motivation to vote and a key predictor of the voter's choice. That, of course, explains its interest for political scientists. In fact, "party identifiers have seemed so great a social reality in the United States that they command more scholarly attention than party organization."[13] Party ID has been described as "arguably the most successful explanatory construct in political science."[14] (Small surprise that as political psychologists turn to neuroscience research, the first thing they test is the portion of the brain in Democrats and Republicans that respond to partisan cues. "Cold reasoning" sections of the cortex are quiet, it seems; "the process is almost entirely emotional and unconscious, with flares of activity in the brain's pleasure centers when unwelcome information is being rejected."[15])

We can understand, then, why political scientists became preoccupied with the apparent waning of partisanship in the American electorate and in other established democracies.[16] There are fewer avowed partisans and their commitment to their party is less intense.[17] The numbers are rough and contested, though overall growth in the "independent" category is clear. The count of Independents is estimated to have risen from 23 percent of voters in 1952 to 33 percent in 1996.[18] In 2004 self-identified Independents amounted to an estimated quarter of voters; in some states the figure is closer to 40 or even 50 percent.[19] Rarely does the percentage of self-identified partisans rise to over 50 percent of voters.[20]

Analyses of party ID in political science are bound up with methodological choices and measurement ambiguities. Nothing is as intricate or exhaustively examined as the wording and sequencing of "stem" and "branch" questions on voter surveys ("it is difficult to identify a word ... that has not been a source of controversy"[21]); nothing more laboriously examined than the pitfalls of comparing or combining the results of surveys whose questions and time frames are dissimilar. Interpretations of the data are as nuanced as sophisticated hermeneutics. "Party ID" is a testament to the remarkable, untiring efforts, the hothouse discipline, of political science. Assessing partisan trends is a delicate business, clearly, and political scientists scrupulously caution that the decline of party ID can be exaggerated or misconstrued. They employ strict rules for coding and interpreting survey responses and invent ever more refined subcategories: strong and weak party identifiers, strong and weak party "leaners," "pure" Independents and "leaning" Independents, independent partisan supporters, unattached voters, and so on.[22] I try to keep up. Authors of *The Myth of the Independent Voter* refer skeptically to the "putative growth in independence." Disaggregating and exhaustively analyzing, they conclude that most Independents are "closet Democrats and Republicans."[23] Not only do most voters most of the time remain partisan in their voting behavior,[24] the growth in the category of "independent" is mainly in the "leaning" categories, those who behave as partisans, "quasi-loyalists."[25] ("Ask yourself: do you know anyone who really vacillates between the two political parties with each election?"[26]) It is consistent with the growth of independence to say, too, that the effect of partisanship on voting behavior has grown since 1972 and that recently the American voting public has become more partisan. That is, more partisans are strong partisans, and more Independents confess party leanings.[27]

Again, the behavioral consequences of these measures of party ID interest political scientists and political strategists. As one student of the subject put it, as long as Independents behave like partisans, it does not matter what we call them.[28] Another sees differently "the true lesson" of the finding that two-thirds of those calling themselves Independents are as regular in their support of one party in national elections as so-called weak party identifiers: "Not that most declared independents are closet partisans, but rather that many who nominally identify with a party are in fact behavioral independents."[29] Finally, political scientists agree on just two unremarkable points. One is unexceptional: "although the outcome of each election reflects the idiosyncracies of personality, campaign events, and policy stances, it remains the case that candidates tend to fare better at the polls when their fellow partisans constitute a larger share of the electorate."[30] Analysts also agree that there is no end to the strategic challenges posed by partisanship or its lack. Even if the relative proportions of Democrats and Republicans is stable, if most voters describe themselves as Democrats, Republicans, or "strong leaners," if many Independents are closet partisans, and if few voters cross party lines, still, enough voters are "undecideds" or "persuadable leaners" or "swing voters" and enough partisans are moved in the short term by political events or character that candidates and parties (and political consultants) must decide whether to frame issues in ways that reinforce partisanship, or that capture voters who have no party anchor, or that persuade voters of the opposition party who are personally sensitive to a "wedge issue" to come over.[31]

In 1876 Henry Adams described the Republican Party as "an army whose term of enlistment has expired. . . . [T]he field is full of stragglers." The military metaphor was more resonant after the Civil War than today, but it still works. The phenomenon is not adequately captured by numbers. The data do not reveal the hopeful spirit in which so many contemplate independence, the puzzlement of those for whom "the wonder rather is that the majority still cling to the ruts,"[32] or the fact that no contemporary democratic theorist advocates rounding up the stragglers.

Independence as Antipartisanship

What explains these Independents? The orthodoxy is that independence is an expression of antipartyism. Indeed, a familiar assumption is that independence is *the result of* negative appraisals of parties. It is associated with "exit," economists' name for a direct way of expressing unfavorable views of an organization.[33] If the "tyranny of the two-party system" "allows no protest to be counted within its terms," independence is plausibly seen as an attempt to get out of the double bind of voting that makes consent almost impossible to withdraw.[34] One thesis points to party polarization specifically as a provocation to independence. (We saw the same claim made about nonvoters: party polarization depresses participation.) This explanation has been refuted by authors who reached this conclusion regretfully, for they had hoped to confirm that independence was the result of antipathy toward party polarization.[35]

Independents are not alone in criticizing parties, after all. Partisans on the one hand and nonvoters on the other may agree with items on the list of the pathologies of parties. Critics from every quarter sign onto the basic elements I have surveyed: parties are too responsive to powerful minorities; they are insufficiently responsive to powerless minorities; they are routinely unresponsive to majorities. There is little evidence that Independents are more motivated by progressive convictions about party corruption, capture, or cartel than either partisan voters or nonvoters, or that they are more critical than others of parties on grounds of doctrinal inadequacy or candidate selection, performance or organization.[36] Independents *do* articulate criticisms of parties, of course. They may see current parties as creating the wrong kind of divisions, not those that in their individual judgment are politically important. They may simply view the political field as "godless and forsaken." But this is not a consistent rejection of parties. Nor does it distinguish Independents from nonvoters or even disaffected partisans. Some "fundamentalist" Independents see party divisions as inherently too rigid to allow personal judgment to be exercised over time.[37] This is an important element of Independents' self-perception, and I return to it below, but it does not satisfactorily equate independence with antipartyism.

Analysts report that for the electorate as a whole, parties are less objects of dissatisfaction than insignificant: "The parties are currently perceived with almost complete indifference by a large proportion of the population."[38] According to the chief proponent of this thesis, nonpartisanship owes not to dissatisfaction with parties nor, as is often conjectured, to the thought that parties do not offer meaning-ful choices, but rather to the fact that their salience for much of the electorate is weak. Voters see parties as irrelevant for solving prob-lems and inconsequential for government outcomes.[39] Roughly one-third of survey respondents agree with the proposition "The truth is we probably don't need political parties in America anymore," and a third of voters prefers that "candidates run as individuals without party labels."[40] This is compounded by the view we saw expressed in Supreme Court decisions on election law that "the function of an election in the United States is to choose an individual to hold public office, not to choose a political party to control the office."[41] Pre-sumably, Independents share these attitudes along with other voters. Even if Independents were measurably *more* dismissive of parties than other voters and nonvoters, and more convinced of their ir-relevance, indifference is less trenchant than antipartyism. Research fails to support antipartyism as a cause or defining characteristic of independence, in short. Independents are not "partisan antiparty" thinkers. Henry Adams observed that opponents of parties "agree only in negatives."[42] Among Independents today not even the nega-tives are consistent. There is no "company of Independents," only an earnest nongroup of individual voters.

What animates self-identification as an Independent if not an-tipartyism? The self-designation "Independent" attests that a voter does not think of him- or herself as a Democrat or Republican. It is an avowal of detachment. Now, for some who respond "no prefer-ence" on surveys, independence is not a meaningful category and has no particular significance. These nonpartisans are aptly described as "bystanders," "undecideds," or unattached "floaters."[43] They are sim-ply puzzled or cross-pressured or deeply ambivalent nonpartisans. Independence is different. It is an elected status. It goes beyond nonpartisanship—not being either a Democrat or Republican—to stake out distinct political ground: disavowal of partisanship. A useful analogy is to those who responded to the 2001 American Religious Identification Survey that they are "without faith." The nonbeliever population numbers 29.4 million, or 14 percent, of Americans, up from 8 percent in 1990. (Interestingly, the "no religion" cohort has one of the highest percentage of political "Independents": 43 percent.) This large, amorphous group includes a distinct sub-group who profess that they are agnostics, atheists, or "secular."[44] Similarly, we have all heard (or offered) nostrums like "the good citizen votes his or her conscience." In surveys, fewer than 10 percent of respondents disagree with the statement "The best rule in voting is to pick the best candidate, regardless of party label."[45] But only some of these are Independents, who elevate this widespread profession—"I always vote for the person who I think is best, regardless of what party they belong to"[46]—into a positive political identity, into Lincoln Steffens's "I am a mugwump or independent."[47]

In practice, Independents choose a party candidate when they vote, and there is no reason to think that they view this as a forced choice, a repulsive obligation to which they are resigned, or a default position for lack of anything better. Simply, their vote for a party candidate is not to be taken as a mark of partisanship. Hence the suggestion that many Independents are "closet partisans." With its implication of covertness rooted in shame, "closet partisan" is apt. Even if they are behavioral partisans, Independents do not want to be thought of that way. They do not think of themselves in those terms. We begin to comprehend that self-styled independence is expressive. It has to do with a voter's self-understanding and self-presentation—with his or her political identity—rather than with a sustained critique of parties. The real shared negative is not antipartyism, then, but *antipartisanship*, now transformed into a distinct political identity. The negative is turned positive with the help of the inimitably positive, unmistakably normative "independence."

Independence: From Civic Ideal to Political Identity

Plainly, independence is an evocative term. The label itself is inviting. The decline of party identification is a general phenomenon in advanced democracies; nonpartisan is a growing category. But "Independent" does not appear to have a counterpart in other places. It is not an avowed status and lacks strong moral resonance.[48] Why is independent antipartisanship a vaunted political identity in the

United States? The luster of independence, its positive valence, borrows from a broader civic ideal with roots in American political ideology, replanted in the soil of electoral politics.

A principal element of the American civic ideal is social and economic self-reliance. It is not enough to be represented, to have one's interests and opinions taken into account. People must be electors and exercise that right freely, intelligently, and responsibly. Citizenship requires "men who have been accustomed to independence of action and that breadth of view which only the responsibility of directing their own affairs can produce."[49] Judith Shklar has shown that American citizenship is not only a matter of formal rights but also of civil standing tied to self-reliance. It is the capacity to "care for and take responsibility for oneself, and to avoid becoming needlessly dependent on others."[50] As a matter of intellectual history this ideal is overdetermined: it can be traced to both republicanism and to liberal individualism, and it has indigenous sources as well. The ideology of self-reliance was heightened in America in response to slavery, the ultimate subjection. Slavery, made potent by racism, colored political perceptions. It made disenfranchisement a mark of slavery, an insult as well as an injustice. "The consequences of having the vote were insignificant," Shklar argued, but it was "ardently desired" because without the vote, "men who have no property are put in the situation of the slaves of Virginia; they ought to be saved from the degrading feeling."[51] Social distinctions, already flattened in America, collapsed into this one overriding distinction: dependent/independent, with voting as the mark of civic standing. Citizens must "be independent persons in both their political and civil roles, who give and withdraw their votes from their representatives and political parties as they see fit, and who sell their labor but not themselves."[52] Voting became *the* ritual act of citizenship, and disenfranchisement on the basis of race or gender was seen as an insufferable exclusion.

At the same time, independence as self-reliance was seen as compatible with social "influence." Historically, independence and deference were not contradictory. It was not servility or subordination to defer to the lead of those more educated, capable, and virtuous, to social superiors who offered a personal bond, a favor, a greeting, influence. Federalist No. 35 is a classic nod to "the great chords of sympathy": mechanics and manufacturers "know that the merchant is their natural patron and friend," and "their votes will fall upon those in whom they have most confidence."[53] With the expansion of suffrage and creation of mass parties deference was replaced by the accusatory dependence. The stereotype of the partisan was born: ignorant, inertial, deferring to party leaders who are *not* their moral betters but typically worse, in Weber's description, to men willing to relinquish social honor, not a natural aristocracy but winners in the bloody contest of natural selection, the "biologically best."[54] Partisanship was seen as a form of abject subordination, rooted in dependence. Whatever the tie—clientelism, capture, sheer gullibility—the partisan is not politically self-reliant. As we saw, the heart of the Progressive charge was that parties corrupt supporters by creating an entrenched system of dependence sustained by need or by the desire for favors. This mating of partisan and servile was commonplace; Horace Greeley touted that the *New York Herald* broke free of the "servile partisanship" of other papers, "partisan mouthpieces" dependent on patronage.[55] Dependence is the reason for partisanship and submission the degrading antidemocratic effect. Partisanship is willing subjection. (Edmund Morgan pointed out something similar for opposition to a standing army in favor of local militias: "contempt for the persons who would subject themselves to the tyranny of military discipline." "Regular soldiers were 'a species of animals, wholly at the disposal of government,'" in blind submission.[56])

A long-standing element of American ideology, then, "independence" was refocused from a general civic ideal of self-reliance to political identity as antipartisan. Progressive antipartisanship is exemplary, but there is no end of examples of this opposition between partisanship and civic self-reliance. One dramatic case involves feminists and Mormons. The religious disgust that lay behind legislation outlawing plural marriage is better known than the equally important connection Congress and the Supreme Court drew between polygamy and undemocratic patriarchy, subversive of secular democracy. Congressional debates rang with charges that "the government of Utah today has no semblance to republican government."

"Laws must be enacted which will take from the Mormon Church its temporal power," President Hayes wrote; "Mormonism as a sectarian idea is nothing, but as a system of government it is our duty to deal with it as an enemy of our institutions and its supporters and leaders as criminals."[57]

Women in Utah were among the first in the United States to vote and had the backing of Susan B. Anthony and Elizabeth Cady Stanton. The 1870 congressional bill enfranchising women in the territories was passed in part with the thought that Mormon women would use their political rights to overturn polygamy. Utah's non-Mormons opposed female suffrage, but the Mormon-dominated Utah legislature implemented it, and women voted solidly for the Mormon candidate in the elections of 1872. Plainly, political participation by women was an extension of domestic relations, and their main political activity turned out to be a defense of plural marriage. "I have often seen one solitary man driving into the city a whole wagon load of women of all ages and sizes. They were going to the polls and their vote would be one."[58] Seventeen years later, feminists joined with antipolygamy groups, and Congress disenfranchised Mormon women.

The Mormon case combined the economic dependence of women on men generally with polygamy and deference to the hierarchy of a church-based political party—the perfect storm. Nothing as pointed as the exercise of patriarchal authority over women's vote is at issue for Independents today, and bribery, bossism, patronage, and fraud—the sources of dependence that Progressives railed against—are the exception. Nonetheless, the perception of an indissoluble connection between party loyalty and material benefits persists. We see the view that the motivation for partisanship is short-term personal advantage in Justice Scalia's dissent in the 1990 Supreme Court case *Rutan v. Republican Party of Illinois*. The case was one of a series of rulings that continued the progressive tradition of narrowing the range of public jobs in which partisanship was a permissible factor in hiring, firing, promotion, and transfer. Justice Scalia objected to the majority's elimination of these vestiges of patronage. He was not approving of patronage, exactly; his judgment reflected what he saw as grudging realism. In the absence of concrete material and political advantages, partisanship would fall off dangerously, he warned. "The vast underpinnings of both major parties is made up of men who seek practical rewards. Tangible advantages constitute the unifying thread of most successful political practitioners." Without patronage, Justice Scalia wrote, "even the most enthusiastic supporter of a party's program will shrink before such drudgery."[59]

One facet of the progressive stereotype of partisanship predominates today. Even without the subordination that comes from material or social dependence, partisans do not make up their own minds. The charge is sometimes alienated judgment, sometimes sheer absence of judgment. "A lifedom of leading strings had wholly unfitted [partisans] for independent political action."[60] William Dean Howells observed that his father's partisan weekly could be safely late in getting to subscribers: "They could wait; their knowledge of the event would not change it, or add or take away one vote either way."[61] Partisan reasoning is skewed, set in some "deadly groove" or inertial under the thrall of attachment to a party. Ostrogorski characterized partisanship as prejudice: "After all, the name of the party is its own justification in the eyes of millions of electors. They say, 'I am a Democrat' or 'I am a Republican,' as the case may be, just as a believer says, to explain and justify his faith, 'I am a Christian.' . . . [H]e will vote even for a yellow dog."[62] "The "good people" are herded into parties and stupefied with convictions and a name, Republican or Democrat."[63] "Stupefied" is key. This is not the occasional triumph of loyalty over principle or self-interest; simply, partisans are thoughtless. Of course, any voter might exhibit poor judgment of character or policy or be "unduly influenced." Partisans face the specific accusation of sheer infantilism, absence of judgment.

A picture emerges of partisans ceding judgment or unwilling to exercise their capacity for political judgment. Partisanship is the antithesis of the civic ideal that "every man must answer for himself to his own individual conscience and judgment."[64] Notice the premium put on reasoning, and on a certain characterization of unreason. The complaint is not what we might expect: that partisans are too passionate, their emotional intensity overwhelming their better judgment. It is not that partisans are blinded by strongly held beliefs. They are simply manipulated or led, or they are prejudiced, fixed in grooves set early in life. Partisan reasoning is disturbed not by the unruly passions of great parties and causes, of conviction and ideology, but by lack of energy or motivation or integrity to trouble to come to an independent judgment. We recognize an interesting switch from the glorious tradition of antipartyism that saw partisans as ferociously divisive. The stereotype is duller: the partisan is dependent, thoughtless, judgment-impaired if not seduced or bought. Steffens put it bluntly: "I don't see how any intelligent man can be a partisan."[65]

The stereotype of the Independent is the reverse. The Independent is a free agent, neither a "cog in the machine" without judgment nor a client whose judgment is bought. He or she is the kind of person who assesses men and measures uninfluenced by party loyalty, history, ideology, or favors. Independents are proud of their resistance to the sway of passion and of compromising commitments but prouder still of being alert, deliberate, intelligent. Britisher James Bryce has praise for "an exceptionally thoughtful and unprejudiced element in the population, an element which judges for itself, rejecting party dictation, and desires to cast its vote for the best man."[66] Characterizations of Independents today are similarly flattering, adding well-informed to self-reliant. The Independent is a nimble "positive empiricist whose process of consideration of electoral choices . . . requires the collection of relevant information from the election campaign."[67] Which is why, in contrast to unreflective partisans, *their* votes are said to be a window into their minds. Here is another rosy portrait:

> Millions of citizens are still voting, even if they are not relying on party cues or early-learned partisanship to the degree they once did. . . . [T]his might encourage the public to judge candidates and parties on their policies and governmental performance—producing a deliberative public that more closely approximates the classic democratic ideal. This development may be more likely because the new independents tend to be young, better educated, and cognitively mobilized.[68]

"Cognitively mobilized" strikes the right contemporary note. It gives independence a cast a bit less moralistic than "unbiased estimate of the public good"[69] and a bit more intellectual than the progressive preoccupation with personal dependence and corruption. "Cognitively mobilized" also contrasts with sheer passivity before the onslaught of political marketers. Nothing is more common than the analogy between elections and markets in which parties "sell candidates" to passive voter-consumers by means of political advertising. Breezy descriptions of parties plying voters with "brand names" and low-cost information about candidates are widely repeated, and in this analogy, independent voters are like savvy consumers. Their vote is not a reflex response to what they superficially absorb from advertising and punditry or a reflection of "nonattitudes" created on the spot in response to the latest polling question. It is "cognitively mobilized."

Independence is more than a point of "no preference" on a survey of political attitudes, but narrower than the general civic ideal of self-reliance. It is a political identity whose core is contrastive: antipartisan. It would go too far to say that Independents see themselves as an elite of honesty, good sense, and freedom. (Though claims made on behalf of the quality of reasoning and motivation of Independents echo arguments for women's suffrage: the presumptive education, respectability, and civic-mindedness of middle-class women—in contrast to immigrants and to black males enfranchised by the Fifteenth Amendment.) Independents are free-standing citizens, their status uncompromised by attachments. When my students describe themselves as "Independents" the positive valence is plain.

In fact, there may be an affinity between independence and youth. William Howard Taft reflected: "In my college days, I was wont to think of parties and partisanship as a necessary evil and something which ought to be abolished, if possible, and of the man who held himself aloof from party as the model to be followed."[70] We can speculate about the connection between independence and the life-cycle project of breaking away from family ties. Parents' political behavior and affiliation is the best predictor of children's partisanship, or lack of it,[71] though "socialization" in the family is something of a black box. It is enough to say: "Many men inherit their political organizations from their fathers, die in them, and transmit the same valuable political inheritance to their sons. That is human nature."[72] From the perspective of those young people for whom independence is a global psychological goal, voting as an enactment of ascriptive identity is liable to be seen as personal weakness, as immaturity. If party ID is inherited, then independence is not the original position; it must be claimed, and declarations of independence are personally meaningful.

This raises a question prompted by the literature on identity politics. If inherited "party ID" is akin to ethnicity or religion, why is liberation seen as a personal accomplishment, a positive good? When it comes to other social identities, young people may walk away from or tear themselves off from family affiliations and group ties, but more often they affirm them. Why, in this era of identity politics, is *this* identity ignominious and the partisan from youth something of a reprobate? We have seen part of the answer. Disapproval borrows from the stereotype of partisanship as dependence and "cognitive demobilization," made stronger by passive inheritance. Is the perspective from political science different? What is "party ID"?

Political Science and Party ID

The idea of party identification made its appearance in early work on elections. The locus classicus is *The American Voter*, in which Campbell, Converse, Miller, and Stokes characterized party ID as "an enduring attachment" and "psychological orientation." It was conceived as both cognitive and affective connection to a party. Their main thesis was that identification is not a name for favorable political assessments of the programs or performance of a party. On the contrary, "the influence of party identification on attitudes toward the perceived elements of politics has been far more important than the influence of these attitudes on party identification itself."[73] In the authors' words:

> Partisans are partisan because they think they are partisan. They are
> not necessarily partisan because they vote like a partisan, or think like
> a partisan, or register as a partisan, or because somebody else thinks
> they are a partisan. In a strict sense they are not even partisan because
> they like one party more than another. Partisanship as party identifica-
> tion is entirely a matter of self-definition.[74]

This characterization, combined with the fact that party ID is stable and responds "very slowly to voters' impressions of party leaders, their policies, and their success or failure in handling government," was not a welcome finding.[75] It confirmed the stereotype of partisanship as "blind" and the partisan as devoid of judgment—as "more of a rationalizing voter than a rational one."[76] "The literature of the time," one political scientist summed up, "maintained that ordinary Americans ... were poorly informed, that their issue attitudes—if they had any at all—were unstable, disorganized, and polluted by selective perception and partisan bias, and that ultimately their votes were largely driven by an apolitical party identification."[77]

In industrial-scale feats of production, political science "revisionists" have challenged the classic account of partisanship as "the unmoved mover." The common revisionist thrust is that attitudes do shape party ID and that changing political attitudes alter political orientation. Partisanship is active, alive to the connection between preferences or attitudes and party positions. On this common ground, revisionists spar with one another armed with different accounts of partisans' relation to parties. One formulation is that party ID is an expression of proximity between voters' political attitudes and their perceptions of parties. The substantive baseline in assessing "proximity" or "congruence" is disputed, but the basic point is clear: party ID is the result of evaluating party platforms and leaders based on one's prior preferences or attitudes (or, more rarely, ideology:[78] "The decisions of the American electorate appear almost wholly free of ideological coloration"[79]). Party ID is a short-hand or information-saving device for "congruence." In other revisionist formulations, congruence takes a back seat to voters' concern for party competence. "Retrospective voting" is the key to political behavior on this view, and partisanship is a sort of "running tally" based on the results of party promises and performance for a voter's own welfare[80] (or based on prospective expectations of party competence as a result of past performance[81]). Uniting revisionist accounts is the claim that voters "actually do reason about parties, candidates, and issues."[82] They are absolved of the arbitrariness of "partisans are partisan because they think they are partisan."

336

This is not spectacularly encouraging if only because assessments of the distribution of political information and the quality of political reasoning, the way voters connect information to specific judgments about policies and government performance, though variable, are grim.[83] For one thing, if "issues" and party positions are eclipsed in electoral politics, as the media-driven focus on the "horse-race" suggests, then congruence and tallying are not well informed. Moreover, the events that influence voters may be superficial, "skin-deep," vulnerable to scandal and short-term economic events. As one political scientist sums up: voters are "perversely resilient" to information and moved by "unenlightened self-interest."[84]

In addition, to the extent that "voters vote on actions they equate with results,"[85] candidates are at the mercy of their capacity to understand who is responsible for political outcomes. The difficulty of assigning responsibility is endemic wherever decision making is collective.[86] But it is compounded in the context of elections. Assigning responsibility entails evaluating the reasons given for political decisions—reasons that may or may not be coherent or offered publicly at all. Voters must be able to tell whether or not the consequences of a decision were predictable—consequences that may not emerge conveniently in sync with election cycles and that can be deliberately obfuscated by policy design. All this is bound to make the rational basis for "pocketbook voting," for example, "murky at best."[87] Beyond these objective difficulties, voters' attribution of praise and blame does not seem to conform to any observable standard of responsibility, hence the title: "Blind Retrospection: Electoral Responses to Drought, Flu, and Shark Attacks."[88]

We can trace a steady devolution in political science from the model of the rational voter to the reasonable voter to the minimally "reasoning voter" and can follow fascinating demonstrations of how much the mind can do with how little, and how "low information rationality" operates. (If Churchill had known what social scientists now know, he might not have said that "the best argument against democracy is a five-minute conversation with the average voter"; he might have known just how much is compacted into support for a candidate because "he's a good man."[89]) These considerations—along

337

with moral concern that voters reason about the public interest, influenced solely by the best argument—were the negative inspirations for deliberative democratic theory; they underscore antipartisanship and the proposals for citizen deliberation I discussed in the last chapter.

Whatever deficiencies political scientists uncover, the appeal, indeed triumphalism, of revisionism is to tie party ID to reflection on experience and responsiveness to events, to undercut "blind partisanship." Moreover, the deficiencies revealed do not confirm the worst negative stereotype of partisans. Empirically, there is little evidence that partisanship today is a form of dependence or subordination. Nor is there evidence that partisanship is a kind of blocked judgment or dumb inertia. These studies should, however, affect the stereotype of Independents. For if voters generally emerge as minimally reasoning and less than enlightened, Independents fare worse. Political science has long noted the disjuncture between independence as a civic ideal and descriptions of nonpartisan voters in practice. "In the era before survey research, independence was the mark of the ideal citizen," but election analysts have altered its positive valence.[90] "Far from being more attentive, interested, and informed, Independents tend as a group to have somewhat poorer knowledge of the issues, their image of the candidates is fainter, their interest in the campaign is less, their concern over the outcome is relatively slight."[91] This forty-year-old assessment still holds. "Pure Independents" are the least interested in politics, the most politically ignorant, the lightest voters.[92] Independence loses its luster if it is synonymous with "no preference" and characterized by patent political indifference and more than the usual political ignorance.

We would expect Independents to be at a comparative disadvantage vis-à-vis partisans if we take account of the costs of information and the ways in which voters acquire it inexpensively. Learning about politics in everyday life and through social networking is more likely for those who have partisan attachments.[93] Partisans spend *more*, not less time attending to politics. They have more hooks for taking in new information, and we know that adding new information to old is easier than initial acquisition. Partisans are more motivated, take more interest in electoral competition, and care more about who wins. Independents' comparatively diminished grasp is plausible. The independent category in survey research includes a subgroup of voters that *are* relatively politically interested and informed, with high "issue concern" and turnout. (The satirical online journal *The Onion* describes politically engaged Independent David Haas, 25, as a "big democracy geek" who even votes in primaries.[94]) Still, this presumably attentive subgroup of Independents ("leaning Independents") is no different or better than partisans.

We might be tempted to say that case-by-case political assessment means that Independents perform the rational calculations many political scientists would like to be able to attribute to voters generally, that they are "nimble empiricists." Yet we cannot say that the perspective from which "issue voting and partisan identification are best conceived as the opposite ends of a continuum" applies to them or that Independents are distinguished by a concern for issues over personality, say. Independents do not appear to have or use more, different, or better information than partisans or to be more "cognitively mobilized" or more deliberative. Independents are not clammering for forums in which they receive information free of advocacy or drama; they are not ambitious for the sort of learning that rejects even "a tough question . . . if it deflects even a blink of attention from the information."[95] Simply, political science provides no warrant for the conclusion that voting without reliance on party cues or early-learned partisanship produces a deliberative public that "more closely approximates the classic democratic ideal."[96] Precisely to the extent that they are relatively free to ignore partisan arguments and reference points in their own thinking, Independents' considerations are likely to be more chaotic and ad hoc than more coherent.[97] In the last chapter I discussed deliberative experiments designed to achieve something more robust than "cognitive mobilization," and I proposed that instead of suppressing them or diminishing their salience, partisan perspectives rather should be identified and better stated, partisan positions and arguments should be set in sharper juxtaposition, and, perhaps most important, overall partisan orientations should be more dramatically demonstrated than occurs in the day-to-day course of politics. The beneficiaries would be independents as well as partisans.

In political science, the debate over party ID has traced a pendular arc, with a strong swing back in the direction of the original pole staked out by *The American Voter*'s characterization of party ID as an "enduring attachment" and "psychological orientation." As we saw, revisionists portrayed partisanship as susceptible to an unpredictable array of events and contingent information such that on some accounts party ID exists "only as a political attitude that is the product of contemporary short-term factors with no more durability or centrality than other political attitudes such as preferences on questions of public policy."[98] Researchers return from this to the classic understanding of party ID as "enduring attachment" with one important difference: attachment to the party as an organization, that is, "identification with a party," is not the apt characterization but rather "identification as" a partisan. Party ID is a social identity. It is based on a voter's mental image of who partisans are, of the party as a social group, and whether or not a voter thinks of him- or herself in terms of this image of Democrats or Republicans. Put simply, "partisan self-conceptions much more closely resemble ethnic or religious self-conceptions than they do evaluations of political leaders, opinions about party platforms, or voter intentions."[99] The psychological process of identification as a Catholic or Democrat, and not the draw of theological doctrine or party platform, is decisive.[100]

What follows from this understanding of party ID? For one thing, partisanship is more than an "information-saving device" for directing voting behavior. The "cognitive short-cut" approach to partisanship may accurately describe psychological mechanisms, but it is misleading insofar as *identification* is not obviously an efficient or necessary way to save cognitive resources.[101] For another, the parallel between partisanship and social identity points to the durability of party ID. If it is identification as a member of the social group of partisans, then only gradual, long-term alterations in the character of that group—who partisans are and whether a voter sees him- or herself as one of them—gives rise to a significant new cast of partisans or the fading of partisan identity. Seldom "do political events alter the stereotypes of partisan groups, and that is why most reversals of political fortune—scandals, diplomatic crises, economic news, legislative outcomes—leave little imprint on the partisan attachments of the adult electorate."[102] Again, evaluations of policies, candidates, "wedge issues," and so on may affect voting behavior; some partisans too are "persuadable voters" and can be moved to vote for an opposition candidate if campaigns effectively attract them with targeted messages on an issue or policy that is particularly personally relevant to them.[103] But these responses to the political environment are ordinarily transitory. On this point, analysts of countries with diverse party systems agree: party ID is "separate from immediate vote choice."[104] This is not the modest stability that rides out day-to-day political vicissitudes, either. "Recessions, wars, and dramatic swings in the political fortunes of the parties tend to leave a shallow imprint on the partisan affiliations of adults, just as doctrinal and organizational disputes within Christian sects typically have little effect on the religious affiliations of churchgoers."[105]

Partisanship understood as political identity also illuminates the difficulty of initiating and maintaining new parties. In addition to the organizational challenges and the obstacles deliberately thrown up by entrenched parties to quash competition I discussed earlier, new parties must breach the formidable wall of party ID. Failed attempts in the United States to create a new party from the top down—something the recent emphasis on money, media, and professionalism as the driving force of electoral politics misled would-be party builders to think was possible—make the point. Political entrepreneurs and independent candidates may erect a campaign apparatus, achieve ballot access, garner a showing of votes, and even win an election, but these achievements are tenuous absent voters who identify as partisans. That is not surprising if party ID has to do with deeply rooted images of "the sort of people who are partisans" of party X.

The most important gain from seeing party ID as political identity is a refinement of the phenomenology of partisanship. Like other identities, party ID entails "loyalty to particular people, the sense of being at home with these people, the richness of a received tradition, and the longing for generational continuity."[106] Quite apart from the

341

extent of any single partisans' network or political activity, partisans know there is a "we" out there. They vote with allies, not as sole individuals. Partisanship is about who "we" are, a mix of personal and political history, memories of political defeats and triumphs, and why "we" are "on the side of the angels" and deserve to govern, and "they" do not. Although individuals may stop identifying as Democrat or Republican, they rarely *switch* partisan identity.[107] This makes sense if conversion signals a significant change in self-definition. Similarly, independence is not a "halfway house" from one party to another,[108] again not surprising if independence is self-identification as antipartisan. The difference of course is that the core element of partisanship—identification with others—does not hold for Independents. The driving force behind independent identity is antipartisanship, that is, self-definition in opposition to a stereotype of partisanship. These points will be important to my argument for "the moral distinctiveness of party ID."

The return to an understanding of party ID as political identity incorporates some basic revisionist findings. Like revisionists, theorists of partisan identity absolve partisans of inattention and mindless inertia. Partisans *do* absorb information and revise opinions and *do not* reflexively view party leaders or programs in a positive light. The "biased learning" hypothesis is rejected. Democrats and Republicans are not ordinarily polarized in response to new information; their responses move in the same direction; there is "parallel learning."[109] The upshot of the twin facts of attachment and learning is "we can expect a disjuncture between what voters think of parties and the degree to which they identify with partisan groups." As some readers will doubtless recognize from their own experience, partisan hearts and minds are not always in sync.[110]

Partisanship as Identity Politics

If partisanship is a political identity, it may be helpful to think of partisan participation as a form of "identity politics." I do not mean to say that partisanship is a political expression of some other, primary social identity—that African Americans ally themselves qua African

Americans with the Democratic Party. My stronger point is that partisanship is a distinct identity, and participation as a partisan is a form of identity politics. By following this thread, I hope to provide a fresh vantage point onto partisanship and independence.

"Identity politics" is now a familiar category in political theory. It begins with mutual identification of people around recognizable social attributes—usually ethnicity, race, or the catch-all "culture." The markers of social identity may be positive or negative, self-designated or imposed from outside, and the group may be cast as superior or stigmatized.[111] Unless identity politics is *defined* in terms of ascriptive race or ethnicity, there is no reason to exclude partisanship any more than religion.

A seeming obstacle to understanding partisanship as identity politics confronts us from the start, however, when a distinction is drawn between identity groups on the one side and interest and advocacy groups on the other. If partisanship *just is* the alignment of a voter's preferences with party, and if ideological proximity to party is seen as short-hand for interest, then to say that partisanship is not reducible to interest is counterintuitive, or simply wrong. So let me spell this out. Theorists of identity politics argue that "the defining feature of an interest group is the coalescing of individuals around a shared instrumental goal that *preceded* the group's formation."[112] Organized interest groups like the NRA obviously fit this description. In contrast, identity groups are not defined by instrumental goals. Indeed, the business of identity politics is often to specify widely shared and politically salient interests flowing from the group's experience: "for historical personal reasons of the particularity of our experience, our interests are causally associated with our group's interest."[113] The possibility that members of an identity group may have divergent or conflicting interests is sometimes offered as explanation for the prominence of the "politics of recognition." The goals of enhanced public standing for the group, respect for members, and appreciation for the group's culture and value transcend the potentially divisive business of specifying a common set of policy goals.[114] The relevant theoretical point is simply that identity-based politics is not reducible to interest.

343

Partisanship is congruent with this account of identity politics. Partisan identity is avowed connection to what "people like me" value, think, and do politically. Of course, partisans promote specific interests and programs that support them. But the partisan "we" is not reducible to these or motivated exclusively by them. Another way of making this point is to say that identification as Democrat or Republican is misdescribed as a choice, if choice means that an individual could compare what is offered by the parties and could elect to identify by calculating which would serve his or her interests better. It would be misleading to speak of the individual "decision" to appropriate the group label Democrat, if decision suggests that alternative partisanship was equally available, psychologically. That helps to explain why individuals may fall off from their identification as Democrat or Republican but rarely *switch* party ID.

The parallel I am proposing between partisanship and identity politics is revealing in another respect. The identity politics of race or ethnicity is often associated with "the politics of presence"— representation in formal and informal arenas by "people like me." The politics of presence allows African Americans who are not in districts that elect a black representative to consider members of the Black Congressional Caucus as their "surrogate representatives."[115] We know of course that identity groups are porous and that there are few standards for identification as a feminist or evangelical Christian, African American, or Democrat. No advocacy group can claim to represent all African Americans, and no party leader or candidate can claim to represent all Democrats. Nonetheless, within these limits, the politics of presence holds for many members of a social identity group and for partisans. The politics of presence has been criticized for favoring "likeness" over efficacious representation, but this charge is overly broad. Representatives of all stripes may fail to fulfill their constituents' trust, and the sound motivation for a "politics of presence" is precisely trust: trust in those "like me" to be responsive to our group and to make decisions to which we are likely to respond positively. This dynamic is helpful for understanding partisanship. Given the unknowns surrounding decisions that must be taken in the course of a term in office, along with the fact that representatives are not delegates with mandates, specific preferences for policy are less important over time than general attitudes or orientations. Partisans trust officials of their own party more than others. Republicans in a Democratic district or state are happy to have Republicans as a majority in the legislature. And trust is two-way: officials trust that partisans will turn out to vote and will generally support even decisions that entail compromise and costs. In economists' terms, "The larger the trust, the lower the transaction costs and the more continuous the political exchange process."[116] If partisanship were solely a matter of "congruence" of preferences or a "running tally" of performance and not political identity (partisan hearts as well as minds), the dynamic would be inexplicable.

I have proposed that partisan politics is a form of identity politics, and not reducible to the identity politics of other, prior social groups. This runs up against the orthodoxy that individuals become partisans by way of their membership in social, religious, or cultural groups.[117] The early Republican Party, for example, grew out of abolitionist and temperance groups and Bible tract societies. From this standpoint, contemporary parties are diffuse versions of societal-based parties in the nineteenth and first half of the twentieth centuries that originated as arms of trade unions or denominational religious groups. This warrants attention. Even for parties whose historical origins are inseparable from a specific social group like the Christian Democrats, there is a propensity to gloss over the steps from religious identity to general political identity, and the additional steps that lead from political identity to organized identity politics, sometimes but not necessarily in the form of partisanship.[118] The formation of Christian Democratic parties in Europe illustrates the complicated contours of this development, and a nuanced and decidedly nondeterministic historical narrative has replaced the early view that party organization is just an extension of the church in politics, that religious groups "place their demands, and a political party transmits them" to the political system. Instead, lay political leaders took a religious identity that in respect to democratic politics was neutral or hostile, and characterized the religious community in a way that came to include political identity conducive to democratic participation via the confessional party.[119] Party activists were shapers, not beneficiaries of religious political identity, inventors of partisanship.[120] This tells us that social identity is not always and certainly not automatically translated into political identity, much less partisanship,[121] and of course that the partisan identification of a social group is not necessarily of a piece.

We cannot assume that parties are segmented or that an "umbrella" or "catch-all" party comprises social groups jockeying internally for influence and position. Nor should we assume that parties are adequately understood as coalitions of groups. This is not to deny alliances forged by intense policy-oriented groups with parties, or that specific party organizations have been appropriately described as coalitions, the sum of their separately organized constituencies (the New Deal Democratic Party, most famously[122]). In chapter 6 I discussed the avenues that organized social groups use to influence officials; the relationship between government and society is reciprocal, and often parties are the mediating institution. In terms of campaigning, candidates and parties may identify and "microtarget" specific voting coalitions—increasingly differentiated elements of the population or "issue publics." But both "influence" and short-term vote-getting strategies are separable from partisanship. Certainly, party builders are "rational prospectors" who mine the organized groups of civil society for leaders and voters. African Americans are drawn into the Democratic Party via black churches, and white conservative evangelicals into the Republican Party via congregations. (The motto of Campus Crusade for Christ is—"get 'em saved; get 'em baptized; get 'em registered.") "We don't want no body no body sent" is too strong, but being sent (or recruited) is the usual route to political participation.[123] None of this undermines partisanship as identity politics in a register different from other social identities and as something more than their immediate political expression.

My way into partisanship may begin with "my own sort of person" in social terms, but the transitional steps from social identity group to partisan political identity involve loosening, eclipsing, or transformation of this prior identity for political purposes.[124] Understanding partisanship as epiphenomenal, an instrumental association in political service of some other social identity, may describe some activists focused on specific policy goals, but it is unfaithful to a common personal experience of partisanship. Partisans avow identification with others in a political group some of whose members also belong to narrower identity and interest groups—environmentalist and lesbian and gay groups, Christian conservatives and sectoral business associations. But partisanship alters these, often transcends them, and for many it has the character and force of an original, self-standing political identity. An exclusive focus on the social beginnings or foundings of parties is liable to misrepresent the nature of partisanship, its relative autonomy.

That is perhaps the key point to emerge from the proposition that "partisan self-conceptions much more closely resemble ethnic or religious self-conceptions than they do evaluations of political leaders, opinions about party platforms, or vote intentions."[125] Political scientists drew this analogy for the purpose of showing that like ethnicity or religion, partisanship is a stable identity.[126] We can now see that the analogy does other work. It says that partisans comprise a political identity group that cannot be adequately understood as a direct expression of some deeper or prior social identity. Partisanship today should not be seen as subordinate to class or religion, ethnicity or ideology. This may explain votes in the short run, but not partisan identity. The identity politics framework suggests that people become Democratic partisans if they see Democrats as the sort of people who are like them, and the "likeness" that is attractive, the elective affinity, is variable. (The process works in reverse: "If *they* are supporting him, how can he be good for *me*?"[127])

This is consistent with the findings of Verba et al. that group consciousness does not act as an independent force in political participation in the United States today.[128] "Partisan attachments become highly influential, whereas more fundamental social identities, such as sex, religion, or social class, tend to have less predictive power," and this study concludes: "Because American parties do not reflect the deep seated divisions that beset other countries, they represent a *more* psychologically salient and penetrating form of identification."[129] Naturally, this does not hold for divided societies where parties just are arms of social groups in conflict; this is my subject in chapter 9. Even then, party systems can provide institutional pressures as well as moral ones for inclusiveness, and social scientists propose that depending on electoral design, parties and partisanship can serve as an antidote to ethnic or religious differences in segmented societies. In the United States and other established democracies today, partisanship cannot be understood simply as a vehicle or expression of some anterior social identity. Partisanship is not epiphenomenal. Once partisan political identity is formed, it has independent life and force. It is a political identity like no other, and I will make this argument in a moment. Before I turn there, I want to look at what partisanship as identity politics says about Independents.

The Weightlessness of Independence

The ingredients are at hand to reconsider independence. The kind of person who judges men and measures unbiased by partisanship, indeed determinedly aloof and unobligated, is the proud self-definition. My own assessment is summed up in the thought that Independents are "not self-reliant, but weightless."[130] Independents are as detached from one another as they are from parties. There is no "company of Independents," only earnest individuals (my students personify the type). If, as Ignazio Silone says, the crucial political judgment is "the choice of comrades," Independents do not make it.[131] "Atomism" is an overworked metaphor, but it applies to Independents: atoms of the unorganized public bouncing off the structures of a party system.

Because political self-reliance is part of its appeal, it is well to dispose of two heroic representations of independence. Independence evokes personal political freedom ("the only obligation which I have a right to assume is to do at any time what I think right"), but the Independent is not bravely Thoreauian. In the context of the national parties' support for slavery and the Mexican War, Transcendentalists insisted that it was a moral disgrace to associate with any party. In contrast, independent antipartisanship is a permanent status. It is not that current party positions are in their individual judgment morally abhorrent or politically unimportant. More likely, they view party divisions as inherently too rigid to allow for the exercise of personal judgment. But we cannot conclude that antipartisanship owes to wounded conscience or to offenses against principle entailed by party loyalty. Thoreau disparaged not just parties but voting as a sort of gaming in which character is not at stake.[132] Independents vote, and we have no reason to think that despite the vicissitudes of their political conduct, they are constant at some deeper level, their votes grounded in moral principle or enacting ideological consistency. Why assume anything other than: "To change parties or convictions . . . may merely involve changes of mind"?[133] Independents who are "closet partisans" may be consistent, but they are *avowedly* politically unreliable, invulnerable to demands of consistency and loyalty, though unreliability is not portrayed as querulousness or fickleness or an excuse for self-indulgence. The self-image and the favorable image advocates construct of Independents is the very opposite of this nineteenth-century judgment: independence is "[a mask] for political vacillation, weakness, inconsistency of temperament or self-interest."[134] The attribution of moral or political integrity to Independents is a gift.

Nor is there warrant for casting Independents as Humean impartial observers, judicious umpires between parties, inclining victory to this side or that side "as they think the interests of the country demand,"[135] or for casting them as Millians sensitive to "half-truths," as if *they* bring appreciation of the limitations of each side and balanced information to bear and take responsibility for providing corrective arguments for and against party positions. (It is partisans who "bring the counter-argument into sharper relief."[136]) There is no reason to see Independents as centrists out to rectify too much partisan extremism, either—as if they are the agents of moderation in a political process in which it is too rare. Taft's affirmation of independence is wrong in both its specifics: "I do not wish to deprecate the course of those broad-minded citizens of intelligent discrimination and patriotic purpose who, on grounds of general welfare, sometimes support one party and sometimes the other. They are essential in our system."[137] Why assume Independents are "broad-minded citizens" especially motivated or equipped to judge what is in the "general welfare"?

After all, independence is perfectly consistent with self-interested voting as well as public interest voting. Contemporary independence does not fault partiality per se but partisanship specifically. Although the term "independent" is resonant of the civil ideal of the disinterested citizen mindful of the public good, it is consistent with either of the two views of voting that compete for supremacy in political theory: preference-based decision making as analyzed in the boundless literature on social choice, and public-interested decision making, favored by most strands of normative democratic theory and pronounced uncompromisingly by John Stuart Mill: "His vote is not a thing in which he has an option; it has no more to do with his personal wishes than the verdict of a juryman. It is strictly a matter of duty; he is bound to give it according to his best and most conscientious opinion of the public good."[138]

Have I focused on real life voters and not grappled with independence as a regulative ideal? What if Independents *were* disinterested deliberators of the public interest or intrepid citizens offering themselves as counterweights to partisan extremism? Or what if independence described actual voters in the deliberative contexts I have described, settings contrived to suppress partisanship, provide balanced information, and facilitate carefully reasoned decisions? I do not think independence stands up in any case, for reasons I am about to stress. Even the most admirable Independent in a hypothetically reformed system of full information and deliberation lacks the moral distinctiveness of party ID.

For now, my point is that independence is not an adequate democratic ideal because it is weightless. Ostrogorski reflected on the fact that Americans live "morally in the vagueness of space . . . as it were, suspended in the air."[139] He thought partisanship filled a portion of the moral void, meeting an emotional need. The "vagueness of space," "suspended in the air" describes an existential condition. The insubstantiality that concerns me is political. Influence is not a defining purpose of independence. Antipartisanship is. Exhibition of self-reliance is. So is political self-expression: disavowing party

ID, the Independent demands to be "recognized as a unique individual who could express herself significantly in public and in private."[140] Independence is not quite romanticism. It lacks the drama of radical individualism with its global rejection of association and membership—Thoreau's alienation from society and revulsion at the thought of joining. But it comes close to romanticism in regard to politics: aversion to being seen as a partisan, a cog in a machine. "*Individualism* is of course *against* parties."[141] The weightlessness of independence flows from its barely suppressed antipathy to being a part of political organization. No "third party" should come between the independent elector and his or her vote. The relation of Independent to candidate is perceived as individual to individual.

The corollary of detachment is unconcern with power. Despite claims for the salience of independent voters in specific elections, Independents are not antipartisan because they imagine they will be more effective. In plain contrast to partisanship, considerations of acting with others for effect is no part of Independent identity. It is not about "ends to be achieved in concert."[142] Independents are not sending a coordinated message, even if analysts are in the business of interpreting what their votes meant. True, others want Independents to constitute a collective force. A "real temptation" for political strategists is "created wherever a few thousand voters become detached from the regular parties and are placed in a condition to be manipulated and thrown from one party to the other."[143] On occasion nonpartisan voters (including but not restricted to Independents) may decide an election, but to say that they "throw the election" one way or the other is misleading because there is no "they" there. Simply, the vicissitudes of the votes of nonpartisans have that unplanned effect.

Independents' political adequacy has been a long-standing worry for those who hoped they would be effective agents of democratic reform. Teddy Roosevelt warned against "the deification of independence." The Independent "must try to accomplish things; he must not vote in the air," he cautioned, otherwise independence is a politics of "mere windy anarchy."[144] Albert Stickney was an antiparty Progressive who nonetheless conceded: "Whichever army the citizen may join, or abandon, his right of desertion gives him no substantial control of either men or measures, and is far from being the right of free deliberate action that he has been commonly supposed to possess."[145] Nonetheless, as we have seen, a potential army of Independents is seductive to the political imagination of antipartisan thinkers. In his long campaign on behalf of Hare's scheme of representation, Mill imagined "a personal merit ticket" made up of candidates unaffiliated with parties, supported by independent voters. Lincoln Steffens found independents "captious and irritating" but still imagined they could be a decisive force in politics—if only they were dependably progressive[146] (that is, partisan). Critics of the major American parties today periodically imagine organizing Independents as Theodore Lowi did, for example, when he commended a third party with the specific intent of "parliamentarizing the presidency."[147] These are fantasies projected onto Independents, not the pose of Independents themselves.

In the end, Independents are parasitic on the issues and positions struck by parties. They are reduced to choosing between courses arranged by others.[148] From the perspective of defenders of party politics, the Independent's unconcern for parties as institutions and dispositional incapacity for partisanship is a form of free-riding. They do not assume responsibility *for* the institutions that organize elections and government or responsibility *to* other like-minded citizens. They are not recruiting others to a position. Neither persuading nor joining is a mark of this status. It is not his or her business "to formulate and to set before the whole electorate opinions that are held in common by a portion of it, to impress the merit of these opinions by concerted effort upon the whole body of voters."[149] I will give the last word on this subject to Edmund Burke, who said it first: justifying a political position requires "not only that in his construction of these public acts and monuments he conforms himself to the rules of fair, legal, and logical interpretation," but also that his construction is in harmony with a party. Though even Burke considered it perhaps "to overstrain the principle" to make "neutrality in party a crime against the state."[150]

In fairness, influence is not a feature of this political identity. Nor is being "on the side of the angels" inasmuch as taking sides is precisely what partisans do. I imagine that few Independents would chaff at the observation of weightlessness or be disturbed by the thought that "a detached man may be virtuous but he is weak."[151] For all these reasons, the notion that an "intelligently and progressively democratic" system depends on the ability of its supporters to attain a nonpartisan spirit is exactly wrong.[152] So, let me make the positive case for the moral distinctiveness of party ID.

Partisanship and the System: Participation and Stability

In an earlier chapter I identified three historical "moments of appreciation" of parties: Burke's regulated rivalry, Hegel's organization for governing, and the proto-Millian dynamic of a "serious conflict of opposing reasons" carried on under hostile banners by "persons who actually believe them, who defend them in earnest, and do their utmost for them."[153] Political science details other reasons to value parties specific to contemporary representative democracy. With the serious caveats of "Progressive antipartyism" and "anxiety of influence" in view, parties can enhance representatives' accountability to voters.[154] There is the argument that interdependence among national, state, and local party organizations is the "political safeguard" of federalism in the United States.[155] Political science surveys the role of parties in forming majorities capable of governing[156] and in the United States overcoming the potentially paralyzing effects of formal separation of powers. There is the proposition that only parties can offset arrant interest group politics. Most basic, parties mobilize voters. A rare defender of parties points out these functions:

> To formulate and to set before the whole electorate opinions that are held in common by a portion of it, to impress the merit of these opinions by concerted effort upon the whole body of voters, to afford a means whereby responsibility for a policy shall be borne in common by all who advocate it—these appear to be the true functions of a political party. . . . So long . . . as there are opinions to be formulated, ends to be achieved in concert, and responsibilities to be effectively shouldered, we are not likely to get rid of the best agencies yet devised for accomplishing these results.[157]

These systemic apologies for parties may be conceded without conceding the value of partisanship in the electorate, however. We have seen Independents and nonpartisan elections commended. So it is not repetitious to reflect on the systemic value of *partisanship*. One thing stands out: participation. Like other political identities, partisanship belongs to a particular institutional framework, and voter turnout is best understood not as one manifestation of political participation in general but as specific to elections.[158] If "the simple act of voting is the ground upon which the edifice of elective government rests ultimately,"[159] its significance is beyond dispute. Party ID is demonstrably related to high levels of participation.[160] Party ID makes voting habitual. It creates a unique form of "interest" in participation.[161] Those who profess no attachment to a political party are less likely to participate, and studies of nonvoters indicate that nearly half called themselves Independents.[162] It is hardly surprising that when the percentage of nonvoters is high enough to raise the alarm of large-scale democratic failing, party ID—with its regular participation—looks good. (Outside my subject, but demanding mention: steady high levels of participation "unaffected by crises and charismatic leaders" looks good, too, for example, against the sudden mobilization associated with the catastrophic democratic breakdown of Weimar.[163])

Moreover, partisan participation exhibits a certain animation. Electoral competition in America and other advanced democracies has been disparaged as "audience" democracy with voters as spectators.[164] (A cynical formulation has it that elections have replaced religious controversy as a species of entertainment,[165] which would make recent elections in the United States, given the prominence of professions of faith, a combined spectacular—though even so not all citizens seem drawn to the spectacle.) Partisans cannot be described as idle spectators of contending sides who tune in and out. In contrast to baffling nonvoters and baffled "undecideds," partisans return to the contest with interest and some energy, for good reason. They "feel happier about having their allies in charge."[166] This is not the sheer vicariousness of Red Sox fans "high-fiveing" their team's victory; a Republican victory really is Republicans' doing. Partisans sustain and affect the play. They want the rest of us to take sides. They are motivated to participate and spur others to turn out in order to give their candidate the widest margin or a mandate, not a mere win. "More" of us, even temporary supporters, make the victory more significant and more gratifying. Similarly, partisans want to send a message of the extent to which a losing candidate has support.[167] Party ID is an impetus to participation even when elections are uncontested. Voting by partisans has characteristics of a collective act. Partisans are not voting alone.

Continuing in systemic terms, partisanship is linked to several aspects of political stability. It extends the horizon of political expectations, for one thing. Partisanship allows parties to carry on in the long run, despite political vicissitudes and electoral defeats; they are necessary for survival and recovery.[168] In a similar vein, partisans are carriers of a more extended story about the party than may be told by the candidates of the moment. Memories of past elections (and governance) and anticipation of future ones act as a constraint on the contingencies of party policy and candidates. Partisan identity, with its incorporation of party history and character, however small, is a touchstone and a check on short-term, arrant, political considerations. "We don't do that" is no insurance of political integrity or continuity, but it is a brake on discontinuity. Finally, party ID contributes to democratic stability by providing what has been called a "surplus of politics" beyond the choice of the moment.[169] Relative to unanchored voters and nonvoters, partisans' interest persists in nonelection years, outside the cycles of campaigns. This is increasingly important as the distinction between campaigns and governing is elided. Campaigning is continual, governing is campaigning, and partisans are more likely to sustain attention.

This point is worth a pause. Civil society theorists ignore parties, and as a result do not help us recognize the elements of parties that mirror voluntary association. I spoke of this in chapter 6. Here, I repeat that candidates and activists may live their political lives in the short run, motivated to win *this* election and implement *this* policy. Partisans live their lives in the long run. It is not just that parties must have long-run organizational and political goals. It is that partisans do; they are forces for integrity in that sense. Their history sustains their future as partisans.

In short, partisanship rather than voting simply is a significant underpinning of democratic participation and stability. These systemic benefits are normative if we think that participation and stability are valuable goods. They are largely unintended consequences of partisanship, however, not any partisan's purpose. My defense of partisanship is rooted in the qualities that make it a unique political identity and that partisans recognize about themselves. Invoking ideas introduced in earlier chapters, I propose three preliminary articles in defense of partisanship and end with one categorical defense of the moral distinctiveness of party ID.

Preliminary Articles in Defense of Partisanship: Inclusiveness, Comprehensiveness, and Disposition to Compromise

The first preliminary article points to the *inclusive* character of party ID in the United States. Party ID is identification with other partisans. Where it is an original identity, or at least not reducible to prior social identities, the "we" of partisanship is more inclusive than other political identities. To repeat, this is less true for partisans of extremist parties or segmented ones where social identity *just is* partisanship and participation is compelled. The inclusiveness of partisanship is apparent though not exclusive to partisanship in a system of "catch-all parties."[170] The implication of the name is that despite their names (Christian Democrat or Social Democrat, for example), parties no longer represent and do not even represent themselves as representing specific groups. They are not exclusive. At its most basic, inclusive partisanship is identification with Democrats from Florida to California and at every level of government. Moreover, no other political identity is shared by so many segments of the population as measured by socioeconomic status or religion.[171] "With few exceptions, the parties draw votes in significant numbers from every stratum of the population."[172] One exception is African American identification as Democrats, which began with the presidential election of 1964. In the past few U.S. presidential elections voting has

356

divided along lines based on stringency of religious observance as measured by patterns of church-going.[173] (The persistence of this divide and whether it is a partisan divide remains to be seen.) These patterns do not undermine the larger point: "the sort of people" who are Democrats or Republicans and are perceived as fellow partisans cuts a wide swath. Finally, without conceding that the major parties are undifferentiated or indistinct, they are internally heterogeneous ideologically as well as socially. Partisans are not clumped tightly together on an ideological spectrum.[174] No one ideological spectrum applies to party positions, either. Along the dual dimensions of social liberalism/conservatism and economic liberalism/conservatism, for example, the major parties have been described histrionically as "coalitions of enemies."[175] Partisans of the major parties are manifestly heterogeneous when it comes to issues and their priority; some actively disagree with elements of their own party's platform and prefer one or another position taken by the opposition.

This is not to say that partisans have an especially deep moral commitment to inclusiveness, only that the disposition to tolerate or welcome diversity is characteristic of partisanship wherever partisans are ambitious to be in the majority.[176] Importantly, this ambition is not just for reasons of political necessity. Partisans want to win, but even in a winner-take-all system a plurality can suffice. They want to have a particular policy enacted, but other forms of association can influence outcomes. Rather, partisans want the moral ascendancy that comes from earning the approval of "the great body of the people." As we saw, Tocqueville recognized that majoritarianism signified more than a procedural requirement for political victory when he wrote: "The parties have a great interest in determining the election in their favor, not so much to make their doctrines triumph with the aid of the president-elect as to show by his election that those doctrines have acquired a majority." He anticipated overeager appeals to a silent majority. "When they lack it among those who have voted, they place it among those who have abstained from voting, and when it still happens to escape them there, they find it among those who did not have the right to vote."[177] Persuading a majority of the people is a triumph. The potential moral force of majoritarianism (and of a majority "plus") is its resonance with "the great body of the people." If it cannot claim to be the voice of God, it can claim a majority "on the side of the angels."

Inclusiveness becomes a conscious partisan value, in short. Particular candidates may have short-term strategic interests (or safe seats) that allow them to activate only "the base," the party's most committed and intense supporters. Candidates and party officials may take groups for granted. One consultant confessed: "No Democratic candidate for whom I have ever worked has ever asked me, in a general election, 'How can I win the black vote?'"[178] Particular sets of activists—intense and policy-oriented—may focus on a single policy or salient value and on the supporters who will advance that goal. They may join with others in a coalition within the party and compromise over the selection of candidates, and to that extent their disposition, too, is somewhat inclusive—but only insofar as these accommodations serve their goals, not the party or partisans overall. They are labeled "extremist" when they prefer to be a majority in a minority party instead of a minority in a majority party, and I return to this in the next chapter. Ordinary partisans, in contrast, expect mobilization—exposing, educating, arousing as many as possible to support the party. They have a broad view of "the sort of people we are" and aspire to inclusiveness. The audience for their story of what must be done for the nation does not embrace everyone, of course. For the partisan "we" comprises a mix of political and personal history, appeals to events and crises, why "we" deserve to govern, and *why "they" do not*—their folly, injustice, incompetence, disregard for worthy interests, betrayal of common values, unfaithfulness to the Constitution. Party ID is in part negative association. Unlike other political identities, party ID is mutually exclusive; one cannot be both Democrat and Republican. The partisan "we" aspires to be as inclusive as possible, casting the partisan "other" as sectarian, narrow, and few.

The second preliminary article in defense of party ID is related: identification with others in a group with responsibility for telling a comprehensive public story about the economic, social, and moral changes of the time[179] and about national security. This is not just a matter of being "forced in some measure to speak the language of general welfare," though that constraint is real enough.[180] There is something more at stake here, a democratic obligation that partisans assume. John Rawls observed that to gain enough support to win office, parties must advance some conception of the public good, adding: ideally, we should not only offer arguments that one can "reasonably expect other reasonable people" to accept, but also these should not be ad hoc,[181] marshaled willy-nilly as electoral strategy or changing circumstances dictate. We should situate them in what we consider the most reasonable and "complete" conception of political justice we can advance. And we should speak to *all* citizens as citizens and not view them only as situated in some interest group or social class.[182] This would be a forbidding standard were it not for parties. It is why normative accounts of agenda setting that apply standards of completeness, coherence, and range of alternatives acknowledge the importance of parties.[183]

It would be foolish to say that party ID *entails* a systematic conception of justice or even a complete and coherent story of national direction.[184] Often enough partisans, like candidates, seize on an ad hoc issue or event and their party's competence to deal with it (in contrast to the untrustworthy, oblivious, incompetent opposition). All that said, partisans are not single-issue voters (though any particular vote can be swayed when partisan "hearts and minds" are not in sync).[185] Partisans are sincere in proposing their allies as decision makers for the nation as a whole across a broad set of problems in terms that can appeal to "the great body of the people." Party ID is bound up above all with a general orientation,[186] with the *longue durée* of who we are,[187] with "traditional party values" invoked by candidates and officials, to which partisans are responsive; with reasons why we point the country in the right direction, the one required by justice or national security; reasons why they do not. (In proportional representation systems the comprehensive story is more likely to be developed, if it is developed, by a governing coalition of parties, hence less accessible to ordinary partisans and voters. Fewer parties enables coherent and comprehensive narratives.)

Party ID differs from identification with other groups that seek political influence in part on account of the aspiration to tell a comprehensive story.

> What starts as a relatively unstructured mass of diverse opinions with countless cleavages within the electorate is transformed into, or at least represented by, a single basic cleavage between the two sets of partisans. . . . [D]isagreements are reduced, simplified, and generalized into one big residual difference of opinion.[188]

I use this quote again because the dynamic is right, though "a single basic cleavage" and "one big residual difference of opinion" is hyperbole. It is enough to say that partisanship entails a story of what the nation requires that weaves a constellation of elements in general terms that appeal to citizens in general and that alternative political identities to partisanship push forcefully in the other direction of contraction and fragmentation. This simple point follows from my discussion of "civil society" correctives to democratic failings in chapter 6. Supporters of interest and advocacy groups, whether self-styled public interest groups or special interest lobbies, are preoccupied with specific policies, issues, or values—that is their "red meat." One reason why ordinary, civilian partisans are typically not extremist is that single-mindedness—the appeal of adhering to just one single policy that dominates all other issues and reasons, seeing it as not just urgent but uniquely imperative—is not strong.

Remember, I am speaking here of partisan voters—not a surge of activists or those who ally with a party as a temporary vehicle for exercising influence. Election campaigns target small groups of voters including opposition partisans who have specific disagreements with their party's position on some matter, and whose votes may be won. The "wedge issue" is effective strategy. It garners votes. But it does not alter the character of partisanship. The vicissitudes of targeted messages and slivered audiences and divisive issues of the moment could eclipse or obliterate entirely the more general story of "who we are" and what the nation needs now. But partisans, more than some candidates and typically more than election strategists, resist fragmentation. Partisanship has a looseness, a buoyancy that comes from attachment to a comprehensive story about the times for the nation as a whole.

Inclusiveness and a comprehensive account of what needs to be done are only possible if partisans demonstrate the disposition to compromise. My third preliminary article speaks to the disposition to compromise *with fellow partisans*. Before I speak to this, consider the observation introduced in chapter 6 that men and women seek out like-minded networks and are rarely exposed to conflicting views. It is true that partisanship entails solidarity. Partisans are militants at least for the duration of campaigns. Partisan networks are networks of the like-minded. Nonetheless, I half dissent from the characterization of partisans as like-minded and protected from conflict because intra-party dissension flares all the time, unsuppressed. Hofstadter wrote: "this business [deliberation] goes on not merely in the legislative process, where Madison expected it would, but also in the internal processes of the great political parties."[189] Partisans conflict over the direction the party or its candidates will take in elections and in the course of governing, or the proper stance in opposition. Which interests and issues are the crucial lines of division? Which positions are necessary to win, where? Which candidate can appeal to the base without alienating the general electorate? Which ideas or candidates fall outside the bounds and are unfaithful to "the soul of the party"?

This makes parties not only agents in public political discussion but also arenas of political discussion internally—deliberative "public spaces." Deliberation among partisans fails to rise to the level political philosophers model or democratic theorists organize in actual experiments. But it conforms to a latitudinarian view of argument and evidence employed in the process of negotiating and compromising. Compromise entails a tolerance of small gains, getting less than we want in order to get something, settling for less in order to prevent even worse. Compromise extends to tolerating the fact that in the politics of the moment measures we approve of are justified or "sold" in terms we do not. Of course, some accommodations will be intolerable; partisans will refuse to vote for the party candidate or will bolt.[190] Infinite flexibility can be abject, evidence of pandering or raw opportunism. But learning to act "in accordance with a script they

361

don't write themselves"[191] is a requirement of political organizing, and what Independents cannot abide. And unyielding commitment to principle or policy that disdains compromise is described even by fellow partisans as extremist. Partisans assume the responsibility of compromise not only to to secure enough support to put plans into effect but also to preserve the partisan "we" into the future. In turn, compromise is possible because of the continuity of party ID.[192] Partisans for a cause, group, or policy exist within parties, and compromise acknowledges the overarching collective "we."[193]

Inclusiveness, comprehensiveness, and the disposition to compromise—elements of party ID—are congruent with standard democratic virtues. They evoke a semblance of mutual respect, minimal concern for the interests and opinions of others, provisionality, and resolving disputes through argument.[194] They do not characterize partisanship at every point in the history of major parties. They do not characterize partisans of minor parties or supporters of extremist parties who are sectarian and exclusionary, tell a story that is narrow and piecemeal, and are fiercely uncompromising, as I show in chapter 9. Perhaps I should retreat and say that these features of party ID are valuable only sometimes and within a particular party system. But I want to say more. Partisanship as political identity is sui generis. Among political identities, only partisanship has this *potential* for inclusiveness, comprehensiveness, and disposition to compromise. These preliminary articles set the contours for the best possible partisanship. They provide grounds for criticism of actual partisanship. They lend authority to the characterization of partisanship as "patriotism of the second degree."[195]

The Moral Distinctiveness of Party ID

We learn from early moments of appreciation of parties what Schattschneider would later restate: a party system creates a system of conflict, gives it form and scope. It "stages the battle." Partisanship is identification with others in this system of regulated rivalry that defines representative democracy, and its moral distinctiveness revolves around identification with others in this.[196]

Regulated rivalry as an alternative or preventative to civil war was the initial moment of recognition: parties could exist conditionally within a rule-bound system, today, a system governed by election law. Partisans situate themselves in this system of political opposition. They identify as a participating "we." That means at its most basic that partisans do not look to liquidate, erase, or permanently disorganize the opposition or represent them as public enemies. Partisans are not bent on mutual destruction. An opposition seen as mistaken, corrupt, unfair, or unjust does not rise to illegitimacy. It is not outlawed. That some will be dead wrong and take sides against the angels is perfectly normal, and here "error has the same rights as truth."[197]

The system of regulated rivalry also means that unlike minorities in other arenas of majority decision making, partisans do not see minority status as irreversible. In other social and political contexts the term of power is not periodic and fixed by rules; the conflict is not iterative; the future may disappear from view. Partisans do not secede or revolt, go underground or withdraw in defeat. "Elections are not followed by waves of suicide."[198] Partisans keep the losing side alive, in public view, on the ready not just to alter a particular outcome but to have their party take responsibility for governing. This bears a resemblance to the general normative argument in favor of consent to a rule to be bound by a majority decision, only it is more specific and for partisans it entails personal identification with the bounded system of regulated rivalry.

Partisans in the majority, too, recognize that their standing is partial and temporary. That is, partisanship entails commitment to the provisional nature of political authority, its periodic recreation. We might think that the vicissitudes of fortune and the limits of human volition make this existentially true, a felt experience. Or we might say that all citizens in democracy, or at least all voters, have a part in this. They do, structurally. But partisans are expressly identified with it. They are the active, avowed, intentional agents of what George Kateb has called the "radical chastening" of political authority.[199] This is the distinguishing feature of representative democracy, and the moral distinctiveness of partisanship.

I do not want to let the personal aspect of regulated rivalry slip by unnoticed. Earlier, I quoted Teddy Roosevelt's caution against being too delicate, his advice to "show them that one is able to give and to receive heavy punishment." It is easy to disparage this as political bravado or to see punishers as political brutes. Partisanship brings the knocks of compromise and defeat home to ordinary voters. How not, given personal identification, and the stakes? Persistence in the regulated rivalry, overcoming the inclination to withdraw or bolt, detach and declare independence is the achievement of partisans.

I want to be clear that the political constraints imposed by a system of regulated party rivalry, the Burkean checking power of parties that put partisans on good behavior, are just a piece of the picture. The moral distinctiveness of party ID turns on the fact that partisans do not imagine that their party could speak for the whole. True, inclusiveness, comprehensiveness, and disposition to compromise contribute to partisans' claim to be offering a satisfactory account of justice and what needs to be done for the nation as a whole. True, partisans want the opposition to be defeated (or enlightened). But they do not want or expect the elimination of political lines of division. They do not claim that their party speaks for the whole. They are always partial, and however ardent and devoid of skepticism there is a limit and reticence to partisan claims. Even in power, they are not the nation. "If a party actually rules, it acts for the public; but so long as it calls itself a party, it does not quite identify itself with the public, and remains in a sense private."[200] That is the categorical moral distinctiveness of party ID: partisans do not imagine that their party speaks for the whole. Their party is just a part. Tocqueville observed that parties in America know, and everyone knows, that no party represents everyone. "This results from the very fact of their existence."[201]

Partisans recognize that their standing is partial and temporary. Why do partisans accept being just a part? For prudential reasons: the long-term view commends it, the prospect of being in the minority. There is the agonistic drama, the sheer excitement of opposition. (Willie Stark's "I don't expect all of you to vote for me. My God, if all of you went and voted for Willie, what the hell would you find to argue about? There wouldn't be anything left but the weather, and you can't vote on that.") Partisan identity is defined in terms of "the other." All that said, the moral distinctiveness of party ID is that partisans do not think they could or should speak *for* the whole while still thinking they should speak *to* everyone. Partisanship is the political identity that does not see political pluralism and conflict as a bow to necessity, a pragmatic recognition of the inevitability of political disagreement, a philosopher's glum concession to the ineradicable "circumstances of politics."

The moral discipline of partisanship is clear if we review the less taxing philosophical resources for accepting pluralism and the status of being just one part. Partisans are not accepting on purely logical grounds, because they are Millians attuned to "half truths" and the dynamic by which every position derives its utility from the deficiencies of the other. They accept their status as parts whether or not they imagine that the lines of division are ineradicable because they mirror some fundamental dualism in human nature (Jefferson's conviction that "the terms whig and tory belong to natural as well as to civil history") or that the parties summed add up to some political or philosophically grounded whole. Nothing in partisanship particularly commends the view that parties are based on human disposition (party of order/party of progress) or some "overriding philosophical dualism in American politics" (Democrats with their concern for justice as distribution and Republicans with their concern for justice as the conditions for producing wealth are each partly right; "left *and* right" are more apt to get it right.[202]) Appreciating the status of part is the discipline of partisanship, not the achievement of impartial observers.

When partisans do invoke foundational lines of division, it is often incantation, a sign of failure of political creativity. For there is no fixed set or range of possibilities for opposition. There are always new lines of division. The corollary of the categorical "partisans do not imagine that their party speaks for the whole" is taking up the challenge of fluid pluralism. Pluralism without foundations brings us to the final element of the moral distinctiveness of party ID in representative democracy. By now it is familiar. Parties are not reflections of cleavages "there" in society or expressions of pre-existing interests or opinions. Great or small, parties do not adopt fully developed conceptions of justice that exist antecedent to political activity. Parties are creative agents, and active partisans "are persons who take the initiative in proposing a line of division"[203] and bringing it to public awareness, and with that introducing a "power into the political world." That is the achievement of partisanship.

Democratic theory is particularly withholding when it comes to acknowledging the creativity of partisanship. Contemporary theorists prize the political inclusion of a "variety of perspectives," but pluralism per se, "according positions a hearing," is not democratic politics. "The clash of political beliefs, and of the interests and attitudes that are likely to influence them," which Rawls and other philosophers concede is "a normal condition of human life,"[204] do not spontaneously assume a form amenable to democratic debate and decision. Someone must organize Mill's "serious conflict of opposing reasons." Creativity in politics is rarely a subject of political theory. For good reason theorists often fix their attention on war and destruction, instability and loss. When they do turn with relief to political creation, they identify it with founding moments, constitutional design, transformative social movements. Only rarely do theorists acknowledge that the lines of division created by parties and voters' response to them may amount to "a surrogate constitutional convention."[205] In any case, political creativity is recognized in its most dramatic incarnations, not with "normal politics." Partisanship is the ordinary not (ordinarily) extraordinary locus of political creativity.

The expectation that partiality is ineliminable, that parties do not speak for the whole, together with the political creativity of parties—all these connect partisans intimately to the practices of representative democracy. Partisanship is avowed attachment, publicly enacted, to the form of political partiality and opposition characteristic of representative democracy. A distinctive political identity that is self-consciously partial and accepts its status as a part is significant, of course, because partisans alone among social groups are prepared for their own to assume responsibility for governing.

366

For political scientists, the significance of partisanship for predicting the vote is plain. I have tried to work out its significance for democratic theory—its value such that we can flip the common-sense view that partisans support parties. The normal orientation is the one taken in moments of appreciation of parties: regulated rivalry, governing, and a stripped-down philosophical defense in which parties are deliberating agents and deliberative arenas. From this standpoint, partisanship is necessary to realize the value of parties. We may not admire partisans, but representative democracy benefits from parties and hence needs partisans. In this chapter I reversed perspectives and proposed a moment of appreciation for parties as "carriers" of partisanship. I have offered a defense of partisanship as a political identity set off from others. Inclusiveness, comprehensiveness, disposition to compromise are vital to political pluralism. The expectation that parties are always just parts and the task of shaping a system of conflict make party ID *the* political identity of representative democracy.

I began this book by pointing out that parties and partisanship are indisputably the orphans of political philosophy. Why aren't political theorists busy connecting the practice of democratic citizenship with partisanship, or the virtues of citizenship with the qualities of partisanship? Why don't theorists connect deliberation with party conflict? A decline of partisanship with less engagement and less deliberation? If antipartisanship were simply of the moment, it might be forgiven just now. In 2007, provoked in part by fervid linkage between politics and religious observance, partisans seem to take being "on the side of the angels" literally. Antipartisans have ammunition when they charge that party officials and activists diverge from each element of the moral distinctiveness of party ID: they seem to want to destroy the other as an effective and legitimate opposition; they seem to view themselves as the nation, not a part; compromise even with fellow partisans is not in their repertoire; intransigence is a virtue that trumps getting the public business done. Without conceding these points, they do not apply to ordinary, civilian partisans. Nor do they make my characterization an idealization, because the articles I have proposed are actual, not just conceivable. In any case, extremism and polarization are not grounds for repressing, eliminating, or circumventing parties and partisanship and prizing independence—that *would* be a hopeless idealization and a misguided abandonment of the distinctive political identity of representative democracy. What is needed is not more independence but more and better partisanship. I turn now to "centrism and extremism," to the way partisans relate to the opposition, and to the ethics of partisanship applied to those in power.

CHAPTER 8

———⟫•◆•⟨———

Centrism and Extremism
and an Ethic of Partisanship

In chapter 7 I made a case for the moral distinctiveness of "party ID."* My subject was the political identity of civilians, partisan voters. Here, I turn to the regulated rivalry of party officials, activists, and partisan representatives. I have said all along that parties create lines of division. They define themselves in terms of opposition. Besides this simple fact that parties are rivalrous and at least minimally divergent, how do we think about parties and partisans in relation to one another?

Social scientists measure parties' relative electoral strength and capacity to govern: parties are hegemonic or dominant, weak or ineffectual. Another standard framework is in terms of positioning on an ideological continuum: parties are left or right, far left or far right. Neither of these characterizations has a strong hold on analysis of partisanship in the United States, where the two major parties enjoy relative parity, and ideological labels and positioning are not entrenched in our political vocabulary. Instead, major American parties are generally said to be centrist. When they stray off-center, the reflexive description is "extremist," and when partisans are consistent and disciplined in their opposition, they are said to be polarized.

These terms pose the puzzle for this chapter. I introduce it with a few observations:

The President is viewed as the quintessential political pragmatist, standing before an ideological buffet, picking some from this tray and some from that. . . . "the bubble in the carpenter's level."[1]

In this race, it's the center against the middle.[2]

The election of 2004 left our country deeply divided over whether the country is deeply divided.[3]

Today's governing Republican majority can justly claim that it has defied . . . normal laws of political gravity. . . . It has strayed dramatically from the moderate middle of public opinion."[4]

The puzzle is this: why are "centrist" and "extremist" such accessible, apparently meaningful terms for characterizing the relation of parties and partisans to one another? "Centrism" is only in part sound electoral strategy, and "extremism" is only in part a predictor of electoral defeat, an admonition not to defy "normal laws of political gravity" if partisans want to win and govern. This is only in part, because extremist is not a neutral term of political analysis. It is leveled by partisans against opponents and by political pundits selecting the strongest possible negative label. It is a radical intensification of "partisan" as a term of attack, the *ultimate* political opprobrium. Why should off-center be accusatory? Why isn't political taste like the restaurant patron's who sent his steak back to the kitchen because it was "too medium"? These questions are amplified if we consider the disjuncture between steady accusations of extremism in day-to-day politics, on the one hand, and what is often described as the characteristic centrism of the major American parties, on the other, or the disjuncture between perceptions of party polarization and the common mantra that American parties lack distinct political identities.[5]

As I write in 2007, a political analysis with the title "Off Center" comes as no surprise.[6] The major American parties are seen as sharply differentiated, disciplined at the federal level, and one or both are said to be extremist, their relation polarized. The surprise is how swiftly this headline supplanted titles like "Dead Center: The Perils of Moderation," and the disgusted observation: "there's nothing in the middle of the road but yellow stripes and dead armadillos."[7] Parties, it seems, can also be *too* centrist, overly convergent, failing to create identifiable lines of division, or what are judged the right lines. President Clinton's "third way" has been unflatteringly called an "unabashedly mongrel politics,"[8] "audacious in its centrism,"[9] making Clinton a "party-killer who undermined the Democratic Party's identification with the progressive achievements of Roosevelt and Johnson."[10] The turnabout to parties "off center" is notable.

Indeed, to say that one supplanted the other is misleading, and temporary at best. For off-center and dead center are simultaneously live descriptions. They are proof that we cannot be confident that accounts of parties as centrist or extremist, convergent or polarized, are the product of sober analysis of political trends rather than advocacy or, as I will argue, short-hand for a set of normative assumptions. I recall introducing conservative political organizer Ralph Reed to a predominantly hostile audience at Brown University, where students and faculty were vocal in calling him an "extremist." Common sense, I reminded them, suggests that the spokesperson for a large voting bloc capable of building political alliances and firmly entrenched in one of the major parties cannot be far outside the mainstream—at least not without sober analysis of the term and the context. At a minimum, whether the Christian Right is extreme depends on what the politically active citizenry looks like overall. If "extremist" is more than a sheer epithet, and if it is not a matter of ideological positioning, what does it signify?

Plainly, centrism and extremism are political salvos, not just terms of political analyses. They also contain normative judgments that comprise an implicit ethic of partisanship. By bringing these judgments into the foreground for examination, I hope to show that centrism and extremism are a window onto democratic norms and expectations for parties specific though not unique to American politics. Centrism carries a moral load. It is intended to provide "a strong dose of reassurance."[11] And extremism signals deviation less from some putative political center than from the ethics of partisanship.

Specifically, extremism refers to failure to take responsibility for mobilizing voters. It signals unresponsiveness and inattention to the range of concerns facing the nation. And it points to boasted intransigence, an avowed rejection of norms of compromise necessary to get the public business done. Each of these deviations from the ethics of partisanship is the result of a kind of single-mindedness that takes one idea or aim to its limit, thereby upending the democratic purposes of parties. Extremism as a normative accusatory refers not or not only to party positioning but to the disposition and conduct of partisans in opposition. Centrism, understood as a rejection of extremism, sets parameters to the temper and scope of regulated rivalry. I will show why.

Extremist Rhetoric

What does it mean to say that one or both major parties is extremist? The first thing to note is that in the context of American party politics the term does not refer to antidemocratic parties—fascist or communist, for example. "Militant democracy" is on guard against antisystem parties that do not respect the terms of regulated rivalry, opportunistic groups that exploit the electoral system for holist or fatally divisive ends. These "typological extremists" look to disrupt constitutional order, oppose democratic institutions and legal processes of change, threaten violence against or on behalf of policies, and believe political opponents should be destroyed (often on the view that "we" are the real citizens and "they" are alien).[12] In the United States "extremist" seldom refers to these threats. There have been exceptions, the Communist Party USA, for example. This resonance is useful to pundits, as when a prominent Democratic columnist describes the Republican House majority whip as a "card-carrying extremist" and as "hard-right."[13] For the most part, though, radical parties here are nonviolent and unintimidating and are engaged instead in what Hofstadter usefully called a "nonresponsible critique of government."[14] I take up the subject of "militant democracy" and justifications for excluding and banning parties in the final chapter.

In pointing to partisan extremism I do not just mean incivility, either, the demonization of political adversaries, or raw language, verbal violence. Rather, what interests me is the literal accusation "extremist" leveled at parties, party activists, candidates, and the conduct of partisan officials. Although my chief concern is with "extremist" as analysis and norm, it is helpful to begin with a look at rhetoric overall. We are familiar with if not inured to negative hyperbole and inflammatory terms, poisonous talk about perfectly ordinary partisans. Democrats called Newt Gingrich's Republican "Contract with America" a "Contract *on* America."[15] A columnist calls the House whip and Senate Majority leader "mad dogs" and then criticizes *their* "ballistic language."[16] It is hard to ignore the deliberate evocation of violence. In the course of a federal budget dispute Democrats accuse a Republican Congress of holding the whole country hostage, threatening to basically blow up the government, of blackmail and bomb throwing; Republicans accuse Democrats of terrorist tactics. A political pundit describes politics in 2006 as "Sunni-Shiite style of politics," aggressive tribalism and, mixing war metaphors, as "trench warfare."[17] Even political scientists committed to analytic rigor can get carried away, as in this description of party polarization: "The bulk of the American citizenry is somewhat in the position of the unfortunate citizens of some third-world countries who try to stay out of the cross fire whilst Maoist guerillas and right-wing death squads shoot at each other."[18]

An anthropologist might see this as the residue of pre-party eras in which political opposition was considered illegitimate and conflict was settled with bloodshed. In chapter 2 I looked at the long history in which parties were seen as fatally divisive and on the verge of civil war, secession, or revolution. We can also understand the rhetorical assimilation of party opposition to a battle on a view of party politics that no longer prevails. Van Buren used the terminology of war because he conceived of parties as combat organizations that demanded "discipline of an almost military severity."[19] Of course, we can make sense of extremist rhetoric in periods of sharp division between parties on fundamental moral issues that wrack the country, slavery, for example, or war, or matters believed to define national identity. At their inception, American political parties, Federalists and Republicans, declared themselves parties of principle, defenders of the Constitution. As we saw in chapter 2, each saw the opposition as intractably subversive; each accused the other of alliance with foreign powers bordering on treason. In early party contests, Jefferson was charged with "Jacobinism, atheism, fanaticism, unscrupulousness, wanton folly, incompetence, personal treachery, and political treason."[20] Great parties are expected to clash in dramatic fashion, their opposition expressed in heightened terms.

Extreme rhetoric is not tied to a particular conception of parties as disciplined troops and is not restricted to moments of extraordinary principled or existential opposition, however. The heated atmosphere of the 2000 counting of electoral votes for the presidency may account for the Republican suggestion that Mr. Gore had "staged a coup" and the Democratic suggestion that Mr. Bush was stealing the election.[21] But virulent language is hardly limited to close electoral contests; it resounds in day-to-day politics and in ordinary campaigns.

This is worth reflection. One suggestion is that extremist rhetoric is a response to the requirements of the media—to a press possessed by "conflict, scandal, polls, process and gaffes." To get coverage a speech must include attack lines and exhibit malice. Television programs feature paired partisans squaring off against each other—incarnations of the thought that there are just two dueling positions on every issue, to say nothing of the overtly partisan shows with screamers who aim at "stoking the passions of true believers."[22] Media explanations assume that rhetoric has escalated as well as spread, though evidence suggests that incivility in party politics is something of a historical constant. In any case, the daily diet of media-fueled rhetorical extremism—the language of crisis, conspiracy, fools, and public enemies—begs the question of public receptivity to this fare.

Rhetorical extremism suggests a cultural habit of casting political opposition in the darkest light—as conspiracy and emergency. It suggests familiarity with "prompters of paranoia."[23] Extremist rhetoric from the dark underside of "uncivil society"—from hate groups, private militia, secret societies, and radical organizations— is not surprising; they routinely resort to threatening language to show that they should be taken seriously, that they are poised for incendiary action. We normally assume that there is a clear difference between the extremist rhetoric of ordinary politicians and the grim intentionality—the "clear and present danger"—we attribute to groups that normally stay away from the electoral arena and public office. We tolerate extremist rhetoric in partisan politics precisely because we see it as dissimilar in kind and objective from these groups' vicious talk. This distinction can be falsely self-congratulatory, as if hate-spewing, violence-talking groups are sui generis. As one insightful commentator wrote of a self-styled militiaman: "He is a stranger *of* a strange land, warped not against his culture but by it, and the curve of his warp follows the curve of the culture; it is only steeper and continues farther, off the edge of the graph."[24] We should allow that rhetorically at least, mainstream political talk and the virulence of groups in uncivil society are in dynamic contact:

> Any suggestion of conspiratorial evil against a prominent politician, no matter how extreme the charge or how scanty the evidence, glides from the margins of politics to the center, on a sort of media conveyor belt that carries it from the rantings of the fringe groups of the right and the left into the respectable zone of public discourse.[25]

This makes it hard to tell whether political actors mean what they say. When is extremist talk just incivility? When is it political rhetoric calculated to exploit popular feelings, the exaggerated pose of partisans charging one another with disregard for the common good? When does it reflect the deep beliefs and subversive intent of hostile associations for whom militancy is latent militarism?

We generally understand and accept the ordinary purpose of extremist rhetoric in the context of party politics: to generate enthusiasm for the contest. Language is calculated to excite political action by evoking palpable threats and naming enemies. From the point of view of political activation, nothing is as hazardous as drab. Exaggeration of the stakes and demonization of opponents are standard electoral fare. So is activation using scare tactics. Direct mailings raise alarms and point to immediate peril. Specific political conditions make extremist rhetoric tactically sound. It is reinforced by both voter apathy and voter independence. The less conventional political activity appears to be satisfying, the more strenuously partisans insist on high stakes. A depressed political mood seems to require some electric participatory jolt. So partisans pronounce grievances, exaggerate danger, arouse resentment. They declare war against this or that partisan opponent as well as problem. Similarly, where parties are close in an electoral race or in polls, one way to try to "escape the purgatory of parity" is to resort to rhetorical extremism.[26]

Like any regime, representative democracy must reinforce the values on which it is based and the sentiments that undergird them. Hence alongside extremist language we have the rhetorically benign: the incantations, the bromides, "important not because they are true but because their performance is so consistent, so popularly sanctioned." "In a way ... rhetoric of this sort asks citizens to vote for themselves."[27] Bernard Manin shed light on this indirectly when he observed that the standards for candidates to elected office are not defined or announced in advance. Candidates attempting to distinguish themselves have to guess what voters want, which characteristics they value. "Nothing in the elective method requires that voters be fair to candidates ... this is the corollary of freedom of choice."[28] Small wonder we see bromides but also the opposite: exaggerated charges that the opposition candidate has stepped outside the circle of *any* reasonable set of standards and is "extremist."

Centrism/extremism has a place in electoral strategy, then, anticipating the discussion I come to in a moment. When the center is the place to be electorally, and when the center is indistinct, we hear both kinds of rhetoric. On the one hand, textual analysis of partisan speeches and campaign rhetoric describes them as lacking in definition, marked by "low insistence" scores, "the unsteady search for something agreeable to say, the impertinent amalgamations and transmogrifications." Politicians "negotiate the intellectual terrain moment by moment" because of "difficult pluralism," trying to follow a political road map to avoid offense.[29] On the other hand, if centrist positions are not clearly marked, the territory may be hard to navigate and defend except by recourse to the charge of extremism. To the extent that the major parties both claim to appeal to the moderate middle, to ordinary citizens, "extremist" is a plausible way to say that the opposition is out of touch with consensus or political reality. A report assessing the Democrats' chance of winning a Senate majority in the 2000 elections explained: "Democrats have realistic chances to beat incumbent Republicans only in swing states, and even then . . . only where they can make a reasonable case that the Republican is an extremist, a buffoon, or both."[30] In Ohio's Sixth Congressional District, the challenger attacks the incumbent for being "too extreme."[31] So this is a standard partisan tactic: "argue that the Democrats/Republicans are going too far . . . be the voice of moderation against the extremist Democrats/Republicans. 'I'm for that, but not so much.'"[32] "Extremist" suggests that however fuzzy the location and boundaries of the moderate middle, the opposition is beyond the pale. We recognize this as the dynamic of "the other."

Rhetoric and tactics do not exhaust explanations for why the accusatory label "extremist" has political appeal, however.[33] It does not help us understand why objections to partisan extremism coexist with objections to party centrism, complaints about party polarization with complaints that the parties are diffuse and lack definition. Political scientists try to apply these concepts with some care, and I attend to this work in the following three sections. These findings hold considerable interest for students of parties and partisanship, but they have limitations. In the end, political science does not capture why "extremist" is such a readily available, seemingly all-purpose accusatory. Nor why, though centrism is generally a norm, partisans can be too middle-of-the-road, extreme in their centrism. Political science does not take us all the way to explaining the deeply rooted antiextremist impulse as it applies to parties and partisanship. To complete the picture, I turn to political theory.

The Spatial Model and Mongrel Parties

The dominant political science approach to the relation among parties employs a spatial model. "Extreme" is an indication of relative political positioning, of political geography.[34] It indicates a point along a given spectrum typically labeled left/right or liberal/conservative.

The spatial model posits a single continuum and assumes that all politically salient issues, conflicts, and actors can be positioned along it. The extremes are located at each end of a continuum; hence "far left" and "far right" or "fringe." Implied by this spatial model is the existence of a center, and the designation "extremist" is the view from the middle. The political spectrum enjoys impressive absorptive power.[35] It "serves the function of organizing and simplifying a complex political reality, providing an overall orientation toward a potentially limitless number of issues."[36]

Marcel Gauchet recounts the origin of this approach to the relation of parties in the history of French political geography. A range of points ideologically designated from left to right permitted an exquisitely mapped terrain capable of capturing both major divisions and fine, internal variegation: "right" and "left," "extreme right" and "extreme left," "center right" and "center left," and so on. It provided an infinitely subdividable field, which was useful in a political system marked by multiple parties, the continual emergence of new parties, and shifting coalitions, a system in which political identity, even in elections, was in terms of orientation, not party label. The French topography highlighted division; to occupy the middle was to give up indispensible identifying terms of political belief and to opt out of the real political contest.[37]

In the United States, by contrast, the party contest has been largely a two-party affair and political identification is more often in terms of party label than positioning. Democrat and Republican have not been consistently associated with left/right or liberal/conservative. The U.S. spatial model has few points. The common indicators are center and off-center positions, called extremes (not necessarily two symmetrical extremes and, despite the terminology, not necessarily far from the center). Major parties typically vie to claim a position at the center, often converging there. It is said that the spatial model is politically important because it preserves positional references, which become stereotypes fixed in the public mind. But in the United States political geography does not serve as a strong "memory notion" of the sort that Gauchet describes for right/left in France. The spatial model has few points and few historical echoes. It is truncated and resoundingly presentist.[38]

Why are there so few points on the United States spectrum, and why is locating major parties on a continuum comparatively unenlightening? Heading the list of institutional factors is the electoral system, specifically, the absence of proportional representation. Proportional representation encourages small parties and enables them to have a presence in decision-making bodies. The greater the opportunity to divide up offices, the more differentiated parties will be. "The adoption of [proportional representation] strengthened articulation everywhere," Duverger concluded.[39] Minor parties rarely lack distinct identities. Their raison d'être is to differentiate themselves socially or programmatically. (There are exceptions, like the 1993 upstart German party in Hamburg that called itself, simply, the "Instead Party."[40]) Lipset observed that American third parties almost never campaign from the center,[41] and Alexander Bickel wrote in the same vein: "Again and again minor parties have led from a flank, while the major parties still followed opinion down the middle. In time, the middle has moved, and one of the major parties or both occupy the ground reconnoitered by the minor party."[42] Third parties are a factor behind the moving center, then, but do not establish fixed extremes or identify intermediate points on the spatial model. Moreover, third parties and candidates may be chiefly concerned with process or good government or the powerful personalities of their nominee rather than programs and positioning; Ross Perot's presidential candidacy is an example.

Single-member districts and plurality-based elections may inhibit multiple parties but do not mandate party duopoly. I have discussed the formidable organizational obstacles to third-party formation and legal barriers to ballot access in the United States designed to inhibit new party entrants, prohibitions on fusion candidacies, and the difficulty of altering party identification. The result is that it is in a party's interest to be one of the two major parties and in candidates' interests to affiliate with one or the other.[43] If there are ideologically positioned "wings," they are generally located within the major parties. Thus, there was no thought in the 1970s and '80s that Christian social and cultural opposition would form an independent Christian Party. Instead, the religious right trained activists to make their voices heard in the Republican Party at local and state levels and, by enrolling voters, was able to "infiltrate" the party organization, gaining visibility and clout.[44]

The characteristics of major parties are the decisive reason why pinpointing the ideological location of candidates and parties is difficult and why even general, global positioning may not have much significance. We saw in the last chapter that partisans of the major parties are heterogeneous. "The great accomplishment of the American party system has been that it created agreement in the face of great diversity. By their cross-sectional and non-ideological character, the parties were able to encompass all groups, or at least some of every group."[45] (The Democratic Party of the time embraced both George Wallace and George McGovern.) Again: "Each major party has become a hodgepodge of various and conflicting interests." One more repetition: The parties are "great, bland, enveloping coalitions, eschewing the assertion of firm principles and ideologies, embracing and muffling the struggles of special interests."[46] The implication is that major parties are mutually indistinct, "mongrel," and undifferentiated. Candidates from outside the major parties dependably accuse them of indistinctness: Barry Goldwater's jibe party "me-too-ism" and George Wallace's assertion that there wasn't "a dime's worth of difference" between the Democrats and Republicans, for example. In 2000, Ralph Nader's literature on behalf of his Green Party presidential bid refers to the "hybrid Democratic-Republican Party," which the *New York Times* echoed in a headline reading "Here Comes the Donkephant."[47] Lack of definition exposes parties to "the hazards of all purveyors of nondurable consumer goods: competition with a more attractively packaged brand of a nearly identical merchandise."[48]

"Tweedledum and tweedledee" is stern criticism. It casts in doubt parties' ability to cue voters and to offer meaningful programmatic choice.[49] The normative implication is that distinct, stable, and disciplined lines of division are necessary elements of healthy democratic politics and political representation. Academic advocates of the ideal of responsible party government articulate this thesis: only differentiated parties can make consistent promises to the electorate, govern well, produce nontrivial outcomes, and be held accountable for performance in office.[50] On this view, "centrism is nonpartisan or bipartisan or antipartisan."[51]

We recognize, however, that the alternative to "mongrel" is not necessarily ideologically distinct parties with comprehensive pro-grammatic differences. The rationale for party positioning vis-à-vis one another may be contingent: "a scandal, a fancy, a blunder, a de-pression, or a world war.[52] The lines of division between parties may not be spectral but drawn in terms of competence or management, or a prescription for national identity related to immigration, say, or the public role of religion. In the literature on "critical elections," a defining characteristic is the displacement of one conflict by a new polarizing issue,[53] but polarization need not be marked by ideologi-cal differences.[54] Even if the distinction between parties can be de-scribed ideologically or in terms of general left/right orientation, this can occur near the middle if the whole ideological spectrum is truncated relative to parties historically or to the location of parties in other democracies.[55] In short, there are few active points on the truncated political spectrum in the United States, and locating par-ties on it may not be especially meaningful.

The major parties are commonly characterized as mongrels. A pointed expression of the "hodgepodge" thesis came in a dissent in the United States Supreme Court case *Democratic Party of U.S. v. Wisconsin*. The case concerned the national party's preference for closed primaries and its refusal to seat convention delegates bound to vote in accord with the results of Wisconsin's legally mandated open presidential primary. The Court upheld the Democratic Party's right to set its own rules for seating delegates on grounds that the law interfered substantially with the party's First Amendment right of association. Justice Powell dissented; his reasoning is to the point and crushing from the perspective of the spatial model:

> If appellant National Party were an organization with a particular ide-ological orientation or political mission ... the state law might well open the organization to participation by persons with incompatible beliefs and interfere with the associational fights of its founders. The

Democratic Party, however, is not organized around the achievement of defined ideological goals. Instead, the major parties in this country "have been characterized by a fluidity and overlap of philosophy and membership." . . . It can hardly be denied that this Party generally has been composed of various elements reflecting most of the American political spectrum. The Party does take positions on public issues, but these positions vary from time to time, and there never has been a serious effort to establish for the Party a monolithic ideological identity by excluding all those with differing views. As a result, it is hard to see what the Democratic Party has to fear from an open primary plan.[56]

Legal scholars who supported California's blanket primary law, which would have opened primary elections to Independents and registered voters of opposition parties, justified state interference in precisely these terms. The parties' First Amendment right of association would not be seriously burdened or the character of the party endangered because "the major political parties lack the unity of purpose and cohesive membership characteristic of most private organizations."[57]

Centrism and Extremism

Mongrel parties, ideologically indistinct smorgasbords of values and programs, tell us that ideological positioning is not a sustained part of the major parties' self-definition, or partisans'. Centrism/extremism is a *substitute* for a defined political spectrum. Moreover, political geography of left / right does not correspond in a stable fashion to party identification as Democrat and Republican. This is not to say that voters are unable to place themselves, policies, or parties on a truncated spectrum, if prompted, only that ideological positioning is not the common mode of political orientation. One study reports, "people were eager to express their thoughts on political parties, interest groups, and elected officials but rarely did we hear sentiments suggesting that policies were too liberal or too conservative."[58] To a greater extent than thirty years ago, the major American parties have tilted in liberal and conservative directions, surveys reveal, both at the level of individual members of Congress and among many partisans.[59] Still, "people are not particularly comfortable with an ideological spectrum even though it tends to fascinate elite observers."[60]

The spatial model was designed to direct attention to party positioning where ideological orientation vis-à-vis other parties was significant;[61] it provided a short-hand for signaling political belief. But in the United States the truncated spectrum's principal use is not ideological discrimination. Instead, it is to indicate the danger of being "mispositioned" for garnering votes. Certainly, groups self-identified as centrist claim to represent a majority, and majorities describe themselves as moderate centrists. Small parties and elements within the major parties that diverge from the center tend to represent themselves as an aggrieved and embattled minority. The assumption in American politics is that the center is dominant. If competition for office defines parties, and if candidates must win a majority or plurality of votes, then the centripetal force of party competition in the United States pushes parties to the center. James MacGregor Burns explained: "No major party can cater to the demands of any extremist group because to do so would antagonize the great 'middle groups' that hold the political balance of power. . . . The majority party—and the opposition that hopes to supplant it—must be competitive; if either one forsakes victory in order to stick to principle . . . it threatens the whole mechanism of majority rule."[62] Successful positioning is toward the center, and those at the extreme are "seriously out of touch with reality."[63]

Technical explanations for party centrism and convergence owe to Anthony Downs. The theory of the "median voter" assumes that each voter has a "single-peaked" preference and that there is a center of gravity in voter distribution. The ideal point of the median voter is the equilibrium point, and parties attempting to maximize votes target it.[64] Candidates who take positions closer to the median will tend to defeat those who do not, and party leaders with an eye on winning have incentives "to deliberately change their platforms so that they resemble one another."[65] The median voter thesis was dominant during the initial wave of electoral studies in the 1950s and '60s, and remains something of an article of faith in political science, despite both formal and empirical studies demonstrating that there is no "median voter." There is no shape for the distribution of voter preferences because voters do not have "single peaked preferences." There is no unidimensional spatial spectrum, hence no equilibrium point for vote maximizers.[66]

Nonetheless, political scientists continue to predict party convergence in the middle. They also accept the premium this thesis puts on issue voting rather than other explanations for choice and other tools at parties' disposal besides policy positions, candidate's character, for example. Without subscribing to the median voter thesis, they propose other reasons for centrism. One is uncertainty; lack of information about where voters stand commends vagueness and diffuseness.[67] Given an array of salient issues, with no one issue dominant, many voters are cross-pressured or ambivalent. With sufficient information about voters, parties can opt for strategic targeting of the sort I have described, true, but cross-pressured voters also commends a strategy of safe centrism. Add to this the notion that close elections are said to be decided by Independents or "undecideds" and the assumption that they hold centrist views. (This reasoning can be circular on the improbable logic that voters are undecided because they cannot choose between parties already situated close together.[68])

More simply still, the centrist thesis finds support in research showing that the political attitudes of the electorate just are centrist. "Ordinary people are by and large moderate in their views."[69] Study after study suggests that a strong plurality of the overall population identifies with the moderate middle.[70] Leading supporters of the view that American parties are now polarized agree that "political leaders . . . are at daggers' point while the general population is generally not."[71] One researcher reports this remark as characteristic: "I'm just morally frustrated. . . . Everyone is polled today. . . . It's polled by certain questions you ask. They are asked in such a way that you have to give them one extreme or another and nothing in the middle. I think America wants to be in the middle more than anything."[72] (I cannot resist noting the resonance to social status and the self-designation "middle class" by almost all Americans. "By the second decade of

the nineteenth century Americans were already referring to themselves as a society dominated by the 'middling' sort," Gordon Wood
observes. They did not mean a stratum of people lying between an
aristocracy and a working class; in America, "it seemed as if the
middle class was all there was."[73]) To illustrate: "in the middle" describes this counterpoise of attitudes toward an activist national government: "we have come rather decidedly to reject the idea that more
government is progress," but "Americans have not come to see less
government as progress."[74] Popular centrism makes political sense
of President Clinton's call to rally the "vital center" and his "third
way"—signaling his outright rejection of the liberal label.[75] Clinton
successfully "coopted the center by consensus positions on balancing
the budget, education, and welfare."[76] (Having signed the welfare reform bill, Clinton "could tell critics that its very harshness made his
reelection more necessary to 'fix' the law or to keep it from getting
worse, turning his apostasy into a commendation."[77]) The corollary
of electoral centrism is that people want to be governed today "from
the center, incrementally, and through consensus."[78]

In light of this surfeit of accounts of mongrel parties advised to be
centrist, what explains extremism and polarization, insofar as they
describe party positioning (and not the confrontation of "great parties" of principle)? Specific political shifts have been heralded as necessary conditions for extremism and polarization in the United States,
chiefly the end to the split within the Democratic Party between its
conservative southern and liberal northern factions. This may have
been enabling, but what do political scientists see as the motivation
and *dynamic* of extremism?

The leading explanation can be summed up as "preaching to the
choir," an addendum to the centrist thesis so weighty that if it described a fixed state of affairs it would come close to toppling the
thesis altogether. This account of the dynamic of extremism accepts
the electorate's preponderant centrism and the parties' imperative to
maximize votes but sees a countervailing force in the two-stage election process. In three quick steps: primary elections get low turnouts
even by the low standard of American elections; these primary election voters are "more ideologically extreme" than general election

voters; and they are more ideological than thirty years ago (political scientists report that on average strong Republicans are more conservative and strong Democrats have grown more liberal[79]). Staking out centrist positions is a working strategy for general elections, the argument goes, but not in competitive races with primary challenges. Hence Nixon's famous advice to Bob Dole about winning the GOP presidential nomination: "run like hell to the right," and once nominated, "run like hell back to the center."[80] Safe seats intensify the invitation to extremism posed by party primaries: when one party has a lock on victory, contests between parties are less important than primary contests among those vying for the dominant party nomination.[81]

This systemic explanation is unsatisfying; something more is necessary to explain why candidates looking ahead to the general election would stake out "extremist" positions, and to explain why political scientists find parties positioning off-center today. The heart of the analysis is the proposition that at present new candidates and their activist supporters "come disproportionately from the ranks of those with intensely held extreme views."[82] Their preferences are "more extreme and more intensely held" than in the past [83] and revolve around a limited set of issues.[84] They are only a part of "the base" that dependably turns out for primaries, and an even smaller part of all party identifiers much less voters generally.[85] These activists are labeled "purists" or "hyperactivists"[86] and are described as a "new breed of benefit seeker."[87] "New" because, as I said earlier, the advantage sought is not patronage; their connection to a party does not entail loyalty or discipline; and they do not perform the drudgery of party organization. Instead, like the advocates they are, they enter party politics opportunistically, to advance specific policy outcomes or to promote sectarian values.[88] "Activists today may not always demand extreme purity, but they are more likely to have strong policy motivations rather than to be oriented toward winning elections just for the spoils of victory."[89] "Whatever the sample studied—state convention delegates, national convention delegates, financial contributors, campaign activists, or candidates themselves—those so motivated come disproportionately from the extremes of the opinion distribution."[90]

The voluntarist nature of political activism gives them an opening.[91] They are self-selected and enter party politics with a background of experience in social movements, interest groups, or "good civil society" advocacy groups. These "hyperactivists" have added to the repertoire available to members of interest groups and civil society associations that I discussed in chapter 6. They have abandoned the thought that the way to correct the system is to remain within the charmed circle of the "civil" untainted by partisan attachments or via advocacy groups that operate outside parties. Instead of circumventing parties, they set out to capture them. They do not come up mainly through party organizations, then.[92] They do not share ordinary partisans' political identity, their inclusiveness, their comprehensive story of "who we are," their disposition to compromise. These activists seem to confirm the picture of partisan like-mindedness and homogeneity. ("Polarization entrepreneurs" "have as one of their goals the creation of spheres in which like-minded people can hear a particular point of view from one or more articulate people, and also participate, actually or vicariously, in a deliberative discussion in which that point of view becomes entrenched and strengthened."[93]) Finally, they are *motivated by* sharp policy cleavages. They are attracted to activity "because of the relative stances of the two parties."[94]

True, these activists are an antidote to apathy, and comprise constituencies whose voices are not necessarily heard in general elections. On the other hand, like Independents (though in reverse), they can dilute ordinary partisanship and, as I show shortly, subvert the ethics of partisanship. We recognize this state of affairs as a new version of the challenge that interest group pluralism poses to the democratic promise of "empowering the common, recognizable interests of ordinary people, and nothing more."[95] It is reason to reissue Schattschneider's warning against the "hypertrophy of pressure politics," now within parties.[96] Like pressure groups, these activists are single-minded in their aims and intractable.[97] That is their strength.

"Reining in the ideological extremists" was the argument used by supporters of the California initiative for blanket primaries, which was instigated by a moderate Republican candidate who lost in a party primary.[98] By inviting Independents and voters registered with the opposition party to participate in the election, candidates would be encouraged to solicit the support of these moderate cross-over votes by taking centrist positions. On this argument, candidates would not be able to win the election by appealing only to rarified activists and placating the hard core. But "reigning in" is properly the business of party leaders. For in these accounts of extremism, deviation from the center is principally the work of individual candidates and coteries of activists, not party organizations or partisans wholesale. Party leadership typically wants to avoid primary contests, does not endorse primary candidates, and wants to push nominees back to the center.[99] The original median voter thesis was criticized for assuming that parties and candidates are able to reposition themselves to appeal to voters when in practice their "spatial mobility" is constrained by party history and partisan identity. Activist "extremists" are either oblivious or frankly indifferent to this problem. That weighty consideration is the business of party leadership responsive to ordinary partisans and to the story of who "we" are. Hence there are moves such as the Democratic Party leadership's attempt to leaven representation of minorities at nominating conventions with guaranteed representation for "super-delegates," state and local party officials presumably closer to a wider range of partisans. Democratic Party reformers, avowed centrists, drummed the point home in the title to their recent report to party leadership: "The Third Way Middle Class Project."[100] Of course, the distinction between self-selected activists and party officials breaks down to the extent that officeholders and party organizers are themselves products of this selection process,[101] now in position to pressure wavering moderates by threatening to organize primary challenges against the laggards.[102] "Abandoning the center" is the work of activists who do not speak for or to ordinary partisans, and in this respect, "extremism" brings us back to the "anxiety of influence." It evokes the anxiety that major parties are "an elaborate insider industry"[103] managed by a self-perpetuating elite.

Political science analysis of party extremism and polarization in the United States is of the moment.[104] Explanations rooted in the two-stage primary and other long-term structural elements of the electoral system are not entirely satisfying. The primary system has been in place for a long time and much of its history coincided with party centrism. And party leaders could work assiduously to recruit candidates from other venues besides movement and advocacy groups. So systemic explanations are rivaled by contingent ones. Students of contemporary parties reasonably ask, why extremism now? They answer that specific political events have provoked the dynamic just described. In fact, for some analysts, the term "polarization" is inapt insofar as it suggests parallel movement by both major parties when moves away from the center and disciplined divergence are largely the work of one party (Republicans). In this analysis, the impeachment process against President Clinton was the start. The 2000 undecided election compounded the intensity of party division: the closeness of the race and the move by a divided Supreme Court to decide the outcome fueled partisan animus. President Bush's decision to go to war in Iraq and other decisions that would have long-term institutional consequences like filling Court vacancies contributed to polarization. In short, extremism and polarization are deliberate political choices by activists of one party.[105] This can have an effect on the opposition, of course: "Many moderates, radicalized by President Bush, now define themselves as liberals."[106]

Abandoning the Center

"In the middle of the twentieth century, the Democrats and the Republicans danced almost cheek to cheek in their courtship of the political middle. Over the past thirty years, the parties have deserted the center of the floor in favor of the wings."[107] "Abandoning the center" is censorious. It assumes a certain positioning of voters and the responsibility of major parties to locate there. The logic of centrism is both a predictor of electoral success and normative—it is where parties should be positioned. If the standard of representativeness is congruence with the preferences, attitudes, or interests of ordinary people, and if they occupy the moderate center, then off-center parties are unrepresentative. That is the charge: "The extremes are overrepresented in the political arena and the center is underrepresented."[108] Political scientists speak of the "artificial polarization" of today's civic universe.[109] Activists' "hatreds and battles are not shared by the great mass of the American people." "The political order that now exists in the United States creates unnecessary conflicts and indulges itself in conflicts that are the concern of relatively small numbers of unrepresentative people." To drive the point home: "There is little evidence that Americans' ideological or policy positions are more polarized today than they were two or three decades ago, although their choices often seem to be. . . . A polarized political class makes the citizenry appear polarized, but it is only that—an appearance."[110]

The challenge is to assess the meaning of "abandonment" and the charge that extremists are overrepresented without drowning in an ocean of theories of representation and a sea of empirical studies.

Few things in political science have consumed more attention than electoral system design: the translation of votes into offices and seats. Judging the way particular electoral systems allow for or discourage congruence between voter preferences and party positions is difficult enough. It is compounded by the trade-offs between successful electoral congruence and effective governing. For even with a defined standard of proportionality, translation into governing coalitions and political outcomes is elusive: "party-strength proportionality will have the same legislative effects as interest proportionality only if it mimics it, but it will mimic it only if the rank-ordered political interests of a party's voters are accurately reflected in the party's program (and if every voter is a member of a party)."[111] Given this difficulty, the result may be that "election under a proportional system . . . is no longer a vital and political action . . . but simply a calculable act of only declaratory significance . . . in its essence, only a statistical or census function."[112] By evoking proportional representation, we see immediately the limitations of incongruence for understanding the accusatory charge "extremism."

For their part, theorists who insist that representative congruence requires multipartyism or proportionate representation rarely use terms like "centrist" or "extremist," which are too blunt for their purpose.[113] They see a two-party system as inherently unable to reflect adequately the range of voters' interests and opinions. The classic statement is Mill's in *Representative Government*:

> not only the general opinion of the nation but that of every section of it, and as far as possible every eminent individual whom it contains . . . can count upon finding somebody who speaks his mind, as well or better than he could speak it himself . . . where very interest and shade of opinion in the country can have its cause even passionately pleaded.[114]

Mill's case for proportional representation was actually part and parcel of his criticism of parties. He argued for the single transferable vote applied to independent candidates, for "personal representation." A similar concern for "every section" motivates advocates of proportional representation today. They imagine a political spectrum rich with points. For example, they may encourage not only particularist parties representing African Americans, but also a multiplicity of parties sufficient to "break white voters down into enough subsegments that racial division would no longer influence party competition."[115] As this example shows, theorists of representation may eschew ideological and positional analysis and look instead for representation for specific minority groups, immigrants in recent writings.[116] In any case, the concern of these theorists is *not* "abandoning the center" or the underrepresentation of majority views.[117]

For their part, critics for whom extremism does mean "abandoning the center" do not appeal to proportionality and choice. The framework of centrism/extremism is disconnected from the standard of congruence built into theories of proportional representation. The idea is not that candidates and parties should span a spectrum of ideological positions or give a wider range of salient interests and opinions voice and influence. Antiextremists want centrism. At issue for them is the overrepresentation of intense minorities and the underrepresentation of majorities. It is "undue influence" by "hyperactivist" partisans. "Extremist" points to deliberate and gross unconcern for the moderate middle, as when parties "do not provide a natural home for the plurality of Americans who define themselves as moderate."[118]

Against this background, how do we know whether centrist voters are "abandoned"? If congruence refers to a single issue, policy position, or social value, it is likely to be of little help in assessing the alleged distance between voters and partisan candidates or officials. Once again, candidates and parties normally lay out a plethora of issues and positions—ideally, they address a comprehensive vision to the nation as a whole. Once again, voters do not have "single-peaked preferences." No one-to-one correspondence is possible. Their interests are not of a piece. ("Christians do not completely ignore their economic interests. . . . Certainly they feel cross-pressures between their Bible and their pocketbook."[119]) "Voting groups that do care intensely about just one or a very few matters are called "issue publics,"[120] and identifying the distance between their preferences and the positions taken by partisan candidates or officials is more practicable. For the most part, however, "issue publics" correspond to the activist advocates whom political scientists charge with skewing party positions in the first place. Clearly, "issue publics" are not the objects of solicitude; they are not the abandoned population of centrists, orphans of extremist parties. This is not to say that "abandoning the center" is unmeasurable or meaningless, only that it is as difficult as identifying the center. In the Senate, for example, if senators from the same state vote their separate party's increasingly differentiated policy goals, presumably one or both has deviated from the moderate middle.[121]

A final difficulty with grasping the meaning of "extremist" as off-center arises if voting is not predominantly issue-based, much less ideologically positioned. We know that many voters look instead for the way parties identify problems or major national goals. They respond to cues of other partisans—"the sort of people we are." They are drawn to or repulsed by personality ("personal information drives out policy information") or competence. Overall, the "policy space" concept is not always as consequential for voters as attention to the spatial model suggests.[122] Take just one example of the difficulty of ascertaining whether "extremist" defined as incongruent with the view of the centrist majority holds: survey research on popular attitudes toward the tax cuts imposed by George Bush and the

Republican-dominated Congress during the president's first term.[123] Critics who called these tax policies "extremist" saw them as the work of ideologues and special interests able to effect a policy in direct opposition to the preferences of ordinary Americans. Despite applying their formidable tools to this question, political scientists have been unable to come to agreement on whether this account is accurate. One researcher who finds remarkable public support for tax cuts goes on to point out that many respondents admitted that the tax cut was something they "haven't thought about." Voters in income classes that should be expected to oppose tax cuts for the rich were not for the tax cuts, but neither were they opposed to them. People appeared to weigh attitudes about their own tax burdens more heavily than attitudes about the tax burdens of the rich—that is, they displayed "unenlightened self-interest."[124]

So it is not surprising to see some political scientists shift ground. "Extremist" refers to a disjuncture between party positions and objectively determinable interests, or some independent judgment of salient interests, rather than voter preferences as reported in survey research. To be meaningful, "abandoning the center" is not a matter of unresponsiveness to the preferences of the moderate middle or the majority. Instead, the focus is on some independent standard. Political scientists focus on income, for example, and note the polarization of parties around questions of redistribution such that the "median income family" (vs. voter) is not adequately considered. Political theorists can appreciate this move. If preferences are "tainted by their causal history,"[125] then mirroring them has no privileged status, and "abandoning" the center may or may not be a failing. As we have seen, democratic theorists look instead to the standard of justifiable preferences, which emerge from deliberative polls or other settings that ensure improved information and exposure to balanced pros and cons of policy positions. Or they employ independent standards of equality, say, and show that parties do not hold inequality in check.

If we take the creative role of parties seriously, parties are responsible for creating lines of division, not simply reflecting voter positions. This too alters the status we assign to congruence. Parties "forge collective identities, instill commitments, define the interests on behalf of which collective actions become possible, offer choices to individuals, and deny them . . . . They create opinion as much as they represent it."[126] Parties create the center and imbue partisans with the expectation that leaders will be attentive to it. Thus, Clinton's electoral centrism was expected to be solidified in "a coordinated policy program that would make of his centrism . . . a vital center of change."[127] To take another example, there is no consensus on immigration in the United States today, or in other Western democracies; public sentiment is enflamed and divided. It is the business of parties to draw the lines of division and, on an issue so close to the bone of national identity, national security, and labor, to try to fashion intra-party consensus or sufficient compromise across the aisle to produce policy. "Abandoning the center" is significant, I will show, not when it reflects a clear middling position but when public business as defined by parties is not getting done.

Here is the point to which I have come. "Extremism" as incongruence, as "abandoning the center" may be demonstrable as a bit of analysis on a particular issue, candidate, or party in a particular campaign or election cycle or in the short-term beyond that. But it is not a sound route to understanding steady, unrelenting recourse to the accusatory "extremist" in American politics. One partial explanation is the way the spatial model is truncated when there are just two major parties and a dominant self-defined moderate middle. To the extent that parties do not converge there, the default description of positioning is "extreme." I have also said something about why partisans resort to rhetorical accusations of "extremist."[128] Voter apathy and the fact that the center, the presumptive place to be, is difficult to identify give "extremist" its punch. All this goes some way toward understanding the resonance of "extremist" in the course of normal politics even if party positions are not far removed from the center and not particularly polarized. But the ground covered so far fails to capture the moral tenor of the accusation that a party or partisan is "extremist."

When political scientists point to divergence between the overall electorate or ordinary partisans and "the thin stratum of . . . party and issue activists" (or the not-so-slim strata of political representatives in Congress whose positions have become more widely separated on partisan lines[129]), their tone is critical. One exorcized academic called partisan activists "extremists" against the middle, "fanatics," "clowns," jokers."[130] Vehemence of this sort falls outside the bounds of sober academic analysis, of course, and the temper of this criticism is telling. "Extremists against the middle" evokes the political accusation that parties are "abandoning the center," but the accusatory "extremist" is not always a reference to positioning. "Fanatics" points to something else: single-mindedness. The moderate middle is not single-minded, nor are ordinary partisans. They are of several minds, and their partisan hearts and minds are not always in sync. By itself the range of issues and judgments of character and competence at stake in party competition makes single-mindedness impossible, as critiques of the median voter explained. Rather, partisan identity is tied to a general orientation and a comprehensive story about the state of the nation, about who "we partisans" are. "Fanatic" anticipates my argument that the charge of "extremism" is a normative judgment that can be divorced from positioning. "Fanatic" rejects persistent, uncompromising preoccupation with a single right position, resting on a single value, with regard to a singular issue as deviation from an implicit ethic of partisanship.

The full significance of "extremism" requires untethering it from positioning and rhetoric. Then we see that even if "centrist" is *not* laudatory—if the centrist pose is characterized as indistinct, placatory, or antipartisan—still, "extremist" is not laudatory either. Indeed, partisans can be extreme in their centrism. "Extremism" has a normative thrust; that explains its power as abandoning the center does not, for reasons I have shown. "Extremist" is better understood as a violation of the ethics of partisanship.

Antiextremism: Defending Democratic Norms

"Extremist" is convenient short-hand for three ways in which partisan officials are unfaithful to democratic expectations for parties and partisanship. "Extremist" signals abdication of responsibility for mobilizing voters. It signals inattentiveness to articulating a comprehensive story about the state of the nation, addressed to the nation as a whole. And it signals the adoption of intransigence as a value at the expense of getting the public business done. These echo the elements of "the moral distinctiveness of party ID" I discussed earlier: inclusiveness, comprehensiveness, and disposition to compromise. They take on a somewhat different aspect applied to the regulated rivalry of candidates, party officials, and representatives, but the outlines are familiar. When extremism is something more than a reference to ideological positioning, an electoral strategy, or a favorite term of political abuse, one or more of these facets of the ethics of partisanship is implicitly at stake.

Why are these failings labeled "extremist"? Falling off from inclusiveness, comprehensiveness, and compromisingness is rooted in what I take to be the unifying characteristic of extremism: single-mindedness. Failure to mobilize voters, to be responsible for identifying a comprehensive range of public concerns, and to compromise are each the result (the justifiable result in extremists' eyes) of preoccupation with a single value or issue, policy or cause. One reason ordinary partisan voters and officials are not extremist is that for them single-mindedness has no appeal. It is not that personally and individually they may have the capacity to endure or even enjoy the jockeying of pluralism or that philosophically they are Millians appreciative of the overall benefits of the trial of ideas. Rather, it inheres in the expectation that in party politics single-mindedness is out of place. It arouses moral aversion and earns the label extremist. The extremist is one-eyed, monotonic, unwavering, to repeat, single-minded. He or she is not just right, but right on a particular matter of such singular urgency that it eclipses all competing matters, suppresses all cautions, and rationalizes unfortunate consequences.

The values or positions advanced single-mindedly are not necessarily outside the mainstream or off-center, as the spatial model would suggest. Extremism is a matter of modality. "Extremism" says that values and programs are advanced in a temper, at a register, and in a mode that is unyielding. With this in mind Duverger recommended supplementing the conventional distinction of radical/conservative

396

with moderate/extremist temperaments, which can be found in all parties.[131] There are illustrations of the accusation of extremism in this sense over time and across the political spectrum. President Taft warned against advocates of the progressive program: "such extremists are not progressives—they are emotionalists or neurotics—who have lost the sense of proportion."[132] The accusation is captured in a recent description of the transformation of the Republican Party "from a motley collection of go-slow conservatives and traditional antistatists into a formidable juggernaut of committed right-wing true believers."[133] As a matter of disposition and political conduct, extremism can accompany centrist views; Burns and Sorenson speak of "immoderate centrism."[134]

I will look at the three elements of an ethic of partisanship in turn, beginning with exclusiveness.

Uninclusive Extremism

"Extremist" charges partisans with deviating from the democratic norm of inclusiveness. From the first mass parties, democratic hopes attached to political participation, and one role of parties—perhaps their most heroic achievement—was (and continues to be, must noticeably in new democracies) popular political integration and mobilization. Inclusiveness is a democratic value and parties bear primary responsibility for participation. Extremism charges partisans with failing to try to maximize participation, indeed with *causing* apathy and withdrawal. The point here is not that positional extremism has "turned Americans off"[135] but that by virtue of their single-mindedness, extremist parties are not in the business of mobilization.

The presumptive connection between public perceptions of off-center partisan extremism in terms of either positioning or rhetoric, on the one hand, and lack of participation in elections, on the other, is a commonplace in political science and political punditry today, as we saw in chapter 6. The assertion is familiar: "extremist voices" frustrate and alienate voters. Piling up these assertions does not alter the fact that the causal connection between turnout and partisan extremism has little empirical support. (Some studies show that close elections between polarized parties with negative campaigning increase turnout.[136]) Assertions that positional extremism depresses participation are not only unproved, they have to be weighed against other contributing causes, from registration rules to the quality of candidates and the competitiveness of particular races. "Rational indifference" is another reason commonly offered for voter apathy. So is the fact that for many people political conflict per se is aversive, and exposure to party rivalry—no matter what their relative positioning or intensity—is unsettling.[137] More to the point, the same assertion that parties depress participation has been leveled at centrist, convergent parties. The 1950 American Political Science Association report, for example, warned parties to develop sharply differentiated programs in order to ease voter frustration with "tweedledum, tweedledee."[138] No matter what their positioning, it seems, parties are periodically faulted for offering unviable choices and engaging in conduct that causes voters to turn away from politics.

To be clear: the claim that there is no difference between the parties is consistent with popular perceptions that both parties are "out of touch" with the people.[139] "Out of touch" has no necessary connection to extreme as a point on the political spectrum. It reflects the view that candidates and officials are inattentive to ordinary voters and assume positions that serve their own special interests. Moreover, parties and partisans of all stripes may restrict their persuasive attention and mobilizing efforts to the dependable partisans necessary to win,[140] disregarding certain groups entirely.[141] Centrist parties and moderate candidates may choose calculated avoidance of uncertainty. Put bluntly, parties "hunt where the ducks are."[142] As we have seen, "get out the vote" can be technically sophisticated, efficient, and selective. Under certain electoral conditions the parties' goal is to induce "particular, finely targeted portions of the public to become active," which involves "identifying and activating the small segments of citizens most likely to 'get their message' and vote or lobby government."[143] "Who cares what every adult thinks," one Republican Party strategist said; "It's totally not germane to this election."[144] So parties step back from the cost and energy of mass mobilization; even deliberate "demobilization" is a tool in the electoral tool-kit.

From the standpoint of an ethics of partisanship, with its standard of inclusiveness and responsibility for mobilizing voters, this is always shirking. It is a failing. Only sometimes, however, does inattention or demobilization provoke the accusatory "extremist," and rightly so. "Extremism" is earned when indifference toward masses of voters, uncertain voters, even fellow partisan voters is not a short-term electoral strategy, an efficient use of resources, but the result of single-minded focus on one issue or value. The extremist is seized by this singular concern and has a narrow view of the right-minded voters who warrant political attention. There is a litmus test for supporters. Extremists label likely opposition voters lost souls, uncertain voters unworthy, and partisan voters who are not sufficiently ardent traitors. Extremists think in terms of orthodoxy; even fellow partisans are heretics if they are unenthusiastic in support of the item of faith. Single-minded attention to a particular value or policy and to a faithful population of partisans supercedes the responsibility to persuade and attract as many voters as possible. This is the result not of sober strategy but of enthusiasm. Winning by just enough with the support of a right-minded "base" or sacrificing victory for purity altogether is the preferred course. We can understand denunciation of partisans' disinterest in inclusiveness and reliance in hunkered-down fashion on pockets of proven loyalists, right-minded elements. The extremist is impervious, dismissive, or hostile toward the rest. This is undemocratic disdain for inclusiveness.

Uncomprehensive Extremism

Single-minded preoccupation with a certain issue or value offends against the norm of comprehensiveness too. One thing distinguishing parties from other political groups is the comprehensiveness of their concerns. Ordinary partisans tell a story about who "we are." They want their party to identify a whole range of matters relevant to governing. They want to speak to the nation as a whole. Extremists are monotonic. This accusation differs from the charge that extremists "abandon the center." After all, partisans can address a wide variety of concerns from the fringe; off-center is not single-minded. The extremist properly understood is simply, unacceptably, inattentive to this range, and abandons responsibility for comprehensiveness. I said that most ordinary partisans are not extremists because adhering to just one single value or issue has no appeal. We see why. Partisans just are interested in politics broadly and responsive to political concerns as they arise.

One place we find this norm of comprehensiveness expressed is in expectations about the conduct of political representatives. Once elected in the United States district-based system, representatives are expected to be responsive to and work on behalf of all their constituents, not just their partisan supporters. This is not prudent reciprocity, as in the caution, "the winner will represent the losers because the losers are not permanent; the winner may be the loser in the next election."[145] The partisan official should have a comprehensive view of matters of public concern, at least matters that concern *her* public, and should be responsive to all citizens, to consult widely, to hear people out. The imperative is ethical, and no theoretical account of representation (resemblance, talent, or natural aristocracy, etc.) makes much of a dent in this belief that the elected official ought to attend to his or her entire district or state. Lani Guinier and Gerald Torres point out that this norm underlies the Supreme Court's "representational theology, premised on the claim that whoever wins an election represents everyone." In Justice O'Connor's words, a "representational harm" is inflicted if representatives "believe that their primary obligation is to represent only the members of [a] group, rather than their constituency as a whole." The idea that only a part is represented rather than the whole sends "a wrong message," O'Connor continues; it is "altogether antithetical to our system of representative democracy."[146] Representation is not just about who prevails in an election. It entails an ongoing relationship between governors and governed. A decision process of majority or plurality rule may govern choice, but the outvoted minority has as much claim to the winner's concern as the majority.

We recognize this as the inverse of proportional representation; indeed, this "representational theology" provokes reaction in support of proportional representation. Taken literally, it provokes the accusation that this notion of representation is oblivious to partisanship and partiality and that representing everyone is illusory. The norm of attention to the comprehensive concerns of citizens is not a sham, however, once we understand that the stake here is less political *outcomes* than consideration. ("In fully operative democracy, people are likely to have developed the firm expectation that they have the right to be heard, that officials should listen when they speak."[147]) It is about consultation, not instruction. "Extremism" is an accusation of willful deafness and disinterest, the unresponsiveness of a one-eyed activist for whom any matter besides his or her singular concern is a distraction, indeed a betrayal of core beliefs. The extremist is unresponsive, a point captured by the observation "he is not a receiver, he is a transmitter."[148] Extremist singularity violates expectations of the role of even intensely partisan representatives. People expect partisan representatives to listen, to demonstrate "information-based moderation."[149]

Of course, parties are incessantly accused of being unresponsive to a specific range of concerns, of being attuned only to special interests, the wealthy, campaign contributors, lobbyists. They are "hijacked" by powerful groups, "unduly influenced." Or they are preoccupied with their own electoral interests. If we ask, again, when does unresponsiveness become "extremist," the answer is: when the candidate or representative is not "hijacked" but self-sequestered, and when narrowing from a comprehensive set of concerns to one sole preoccupation, known to be partial or tangential to constituents, is elective. When falling off from comprehensiveness is a deliberate and celebrated expression of single-mindedness. Righteous harping on a single principle, value, policy, or cause and willful inattention to the all the rest is a deviation from the ethics of partisanship.

Uncompromising Extremism: Getting Public Business Done

The third facet of partisan extremism is disinclination to compromise. In chapter 7 I discussed the disposition to compromise among ordinary partisans; my focus here extends to compromise "across the aisle."[150] Uncompromising partisans are called "purists" and "true believers," "wingnuts." The extremist label signifies intensity and a harsh and unconciliatory stand. "Hard-core" is a metaphor for rigid. Extremists see accommodation as perverse or futile, and compromise as capitulation. So, for example, even subscribers to Republican policies may complain about unyielding partisanship: "I did not become a conservative in order to become a radical."[151]

Implied by intransigence as an avowed good is lack of commitment to getting the public business done. It is abdication of responsibility for governing. Uncompromising extremism violates the ethics of partisanship with its disregard for the consequences of single-mindedness for addressing problems, finding solutions, moving forward. Put starkly, the extremist takes "a middle finger approach to governing."[152] We see this at work when representatives say that the partisan opposition "holds the House hostage," meaning the opposition has given up on discussion and negotiation and is sabotaging regular business. When members of Congress label one another extremist, they mean to say that a representative "refuses to play the game." There is no back and forth, no movement. This is the implication of the statement by Senate Majority Leader Robert Dole's chief of staff: "He instinctively believes in reaching across the aisles. He is reluctant to look at extremes."[153] One strategist advises, "An elected official must strengthen his ties with the opposition party to avoid capture by his own. The ability to cross the aisle for votes makes the extremists in one's own party impotent."[154] Robert Dahl *defined* extremist politics as a politics unalloyed by procedures for negotiating and deciding.[155]

The extremist regards "compromise as opportunism, as something dishonest, as something sneaky and shady, as a mark of lack of integrity. Not in my vocabulary."[156] He or she reneges on the implied mutual obligation of partisans to work within this system and to make the system work. The accusatory "extremist" recalls Hegel's argument that parties are institutions for governing. Single-minded intransigence fouls this purpose. It prefers paralysis or loss (or victory at any cost) to compromise. The phrase that captures this best is "embracing intransigence as a public value."

Antiextremism is entrenched in American political thought, and disposition to compromise is often cast as an American cultural trait.

Several variations on this theme are worth noting. The origin of the party system, as Hofstadter and others explain, was made possible in part by the Constitution makers' experience doing business—their experience with discussion and concession; they were "justifiably proud of their flair for compromise." Jefferson thought the public temper required avoiding anything "rash and threatening"; "these are the observations not only of a statesman who thinks he divines a popular preference for moderation," Hofstadter notes, "but also of a party leader who seeks to strike the right note to build a coalition of opposition interests."[157] The disposition to compromise has also been explained as a constituent element of liberal consensus. The "moral ecology" Alan Wolfe records in his study of American culture is ordinary, step-by-step, quiet, and exercised in reasonable ways, with a faith in balance and a propensity to acknowledge fallibility. The political counterpart of this moral "bricolage" is political accommodation. Politicians act in sharp contrast to expectations when they "overpromise . . . speak in loud rather than soft tones, and substitute ideology for common sense."[158] An even more sweeping account by Gordon Wood regards compromise as a feature of the United States as a commercial society: "all those innumerable petty transactions . . . in which all parties gain—that was commerce." Habits of "interminable succession of exchanges" translate into expectations for political negotiating, reciprocity, and inter-party compromise.[159]

Other social scientists represent uncompromising extremism as the result of a cultural shift common across advanced industrial societies and linked to changes in the issues confronting political decision makers. "Post-material values,"[160] the argument goes, are not amenable to compromise. At the same time decisions about economic distributions, which are said to be more amenable to negotiation, have receded, converted into permanent entitlements or automatic spending programs, consigned to administration or to bipartisan commissions. Taken together, these changes make for a partisan agenda dominated by the concerns of people whose attachment to "quality against quantity, people against profits, health against wealth," is intractable.[161] As an explanation for uncompromising extremism, post-materialism is not compelling. For one thing, the wholesale characterization of economic issues as amenable to compromise is doubtful; "deep preferences" attach to questions of economics and welfare.[162] Moreover, "In politics, economic questions are not narrowly material; our reactions are affected by loyalties and memories and by culture generally, and the crucial issue is less dollars than dignity."[163] Just think of partisan debates over the estate or death tax. Post-materialism fails, too, insofar as opposing partisans *are* able to stake out some common ground on "values issues." To say nothing of the difficulty of classifying issues as post-material, consider, for example, the coexistence of two perspectives on civil rights claims: as an affirmation of American culture and values and as compensation for a targeted group of beneficiaries.[164] Or consider immigration: is it an issue of national political identity or jobs?

In politics, habits of compromise owe a lot to institutional design. Parties are not supposed to advance their claims as if they could "rule the regime" alone.[165] They are just parts. Political scientists study the internal rules of legislatures that encourage or inhibit negotiation "across the aisle." Rules for agenda setting, committee assignments and the degree of independence of committee chairs, the possibility of amending bills, cloture, and so on make it more or less likely that the dominant party will be able to avoid hearing out the minority (or factions within its own ranks), much less make concessions. There are good reasons on both sides of the question for electoral winners in a majoritarian system to be forced to take into account and accommodate minority views in governing.[166] For a variety of reasons, American institutions "do not ordinarily endow the candidates or parties who receive a majority of votes in an election with enough power to carry out their policies over the opposition of the defeated minority."[167] Most legislation requires more than a simple majority. It is not surprising, that a party system in which effective opposition is an essential, institutionalized element of government acknowledges that the legitimacy of *both* minority rule and majority rule is ambiguous. Extremism is a disposition that rejects this ambiguity and exploits institutional design—cloture rules, filibusters—in the service of disinclination to compromise, self-righteously avowing and justifying intransigence as a regular diet, and exploits agenda setting to bring to the fore the most divisive issues, preferring show to achievement.

It should go without saying that some things are not appropriate for compromise and that single-minded disinclination to compromise can be put in the service of noble ends—"extremism in the cause of liberty is no vice." There should be no opprobrium attached to substantive positions that are off-center, are ardently advocated, and polarize politics; that goes with being a great party, and our judgment rests on political morality, which cannot be reduced to an ethics of partisanship. Parties deeply divided on a question of justice or the existential character of the nation are my subject in the next chapter. The ethics of partisanship does not always favor compromise, much less doing just anything to produce results. Moderation and accommodation can indicate complacency in the face of remediable injustice. Flexibility may be humiliating evidence of cravenness, deference, or concern for reputation or may be wantonly self-serving. We can understand disparaging the sort of disposition to compromise that "plays particularly well to the talents of expedient, entrepreneurial politicians ... looking for targets of opportunity."[168] Opposition to uncompromising extremism does not entail lauding raw opportunism. Partisans need not be professionally placatory.

Whether a politician of principle is acting too politically or not politically enough is tangential to the question of extremism.[169] Suffice to say that among the criteria of sound compromise are: the time is not ripe for the preferred alternative; the agreement could facilitate future cooperation; concessions would not set back progress already made. These guidelines are abstracted from J. S. Mill's writings on compromise, which he offers as someone "practically conversant with the difficulties of moving bodies of men, the necessities of compromise, the art of sacrificing the non essential to preserve the essential."[170] Mill's discussion is the best there is (though his own reputation on this score was something else, as we see from the public's objection to candidate Mill on account of "his extremism ... his unwillingness to compromise, his single vision."[171])

Attempts like these to locate the parameters of justifiable compromise is the domain of politics as usual. Partisan politics as usual includes tactical refusal to compromise—specific exhibitions of intransigence on the part of leadership to demonstrate party discipline and undermine opposition. The permanent disposition of uncompromising extremism is something else. Ordinary, moderate partisans are not always models of flexibility. But they do not subscribe as extremists do to intransigence as a public value.

An example of extremism in action is the 1995 budget showdown between President Clinton and Republicans in Congress. In a move symbolic of their mission to revolutionize government by curtailing its size and activities, and believing that they could capitalize on polls indicating diffuse public mistrust of government, Republicans were willing to starve it and shut down offices. Their "intransigence was seen as just this side of nutty,"[172] meaning that they lacked the ability to judge the limits of public tolerance for dramatic poses over people's interest in getting business done (a pledge Republicans repeated in pursuing President Clinton's impeachment). One analyst describes Republicans acting "too rashly extremist for the moderate sensibilities of most Americans," including many who voted for them.[173] The example fits the mold: "Party activists are not merely more extreme than average Americans, *they are also less likely to compromise* (they might say 'betray') core beliefs."[174]

Extremists disdain coordination, compromise, or assurances. As examples indicate, extremism is unconcerned with effective outcomes. Extremists "cant about principles," "hunger after loaves and fishes," but are often unable to formulate a policy or conduct a responsible opposition. Disinclined to critically examine their own stance, "practical acquaintance with the difficulties of the position" they assume eludes them. They pledge themselves to ignore facts.[175] "No allowance is made for social learning or for incremental, corrective policy-making."[176] Extremists might be identified by resistance to Benjamin Franklin's confession: "For having lived long, I have experienced many instances of being obliged by better information, or fuller consideration, to change opinions even on important subjects, which I once thought right, but found to be otherwise."[177] As a result, extremists do not do what they can to improve the prospects of success even for their *own* programs and policies. They do not find failure ignominious. The unyielding pose can also be seen as sheer political stupidity, of course, as lacking in the ability to judge the limits of public tolerance for symbolic gestures and heroic poses over realistic alternatives, hence the claim that extremism "distorts reality."

From the standpoint of the ethics of partisanship, decisions must be taken, business done. "Our need for effective government is decisive. . . . Americans have adopted an essentially Machiavellian idea of political virtue: what matters in a leader is the ability to get results."[178] This is an overstatement. Opposition to disinclination to compromise is hardly an invitation to use any means for any end. It is part of an ethic of partisanship. "What matters is getting results" alerts us that one of the baleful consequences of partisan extremism is a climate of political disgust and antipartyism. It is generally true that "compromise may be a dirty word in Washington [today], but out among the public it is a very positive term."[179] Nevertheless, when ordinary partisans' resistance to extremism is prolonged and frustrated, and unremitting extremism on the one side and calls for compromise in response do not move things forward, the result can be aversion to partisan politics altogether and to *both* compromise and intransigence as distasteful and unjustifiable. Ordinary people come to abhor what on their view from outside is aptly termed "partisan bickering." They come to insist that there are common-sense solutions to most problems, that partisanship is obstructionist, and that government is rightly conceived as a management problem. "They imagine that anybody not connected with biased special interests and self-serving elected officials would basically arrive at the same place." "Just fix it" is the mantra. Analysts attribute support for Ross Perot's independent candidacy to this attitude. His attractiveness was not his positions, which were an indecipherable "mish-mash," but his process claims: "pry government out of the hands of elites, get under the hood and just fix it, electronic town meetings, kick all the incumbents out." In short, "What people want government to do and how they want government to do it are, more often than not, two entirely different things."[180] This antipolitical posture opposes extremism without favoring inclusive, comprehensive, compromising partisanship. These antipolitical types, the "just fix it" pragmatists, are correct in only one thing: asserting the public interest in getting public business done.

There is one more corrupting effect of extremist deviation from the ethics of partisanship. When single-mindedness prevails and the public business is not getting done, it can have the effect of reducing partisan politics to cycles of mutual unmasking.

Extremism and the Politics of Hypocrisy

Ordinary partisans do not concede that the uncompromising extremist is a principled moralist or that intransigence signals noble fidelity to ideals. Zeal and censoriousness, self-proclaimed moral rigor and self-sacrifice are vulnerable to deflation. Of course, the accusation that self-serving behavior masquerades as passionate dedication to the public interest is endemic to partisanship. Henry Adams took this world-weary position: "Declarations of principles adopted by Presidential conventions are not intended by those who frame them to express intentions, and should not be so construed."[181] Politics regularly gives rise to post hoc justifications for decisions, rationalizations for both accommodation and intransigence. Partisan politics positively invites exposure, beginning with Bolingbroke's advisory: "A man who has not seen the inside of parties, nor had opportunities to examine nearly their secret motives, can hardly conceive how little a share principle of any sort, tho principle of some sort or other be always pretended, has in the determination of their conduct."[182] Uncompromising extremism adds fresh provocation to this steady state. It raises the pitch of political unmasking. That is because the extremist's zealous claim of sincerity in a higher cause provokes moral aggression. Hypocrisy, Judith Shklar observed, "is a form of coercion . . . it is the sheer unfairness of being forced to esteem someone more highly than he deserves that is so infuriating."[183]

So in keeping with extremists' own censoriousness, opponents hold them to an absolute adherence to their professions. They unearth inconsistent stands and contrary votes. Changes over time are represented as cynical dishonesty. Failure to live up to professed ideals is vulnerable to attack from two directions: as moral weakness on the one side and as proof that appeals to principle were pandering, designed to deceive, on the other. Uncompromising extremism is a magnet for this sort of attack because partisans justify their inflexibility self-righteously as faithfulness to a dominant issue, a singular value, a pressing cause. Extremists tend to be indignant and inquisitorial and to brand opponents as abject, stupid, or traitors to ideals. We recognize the charge "extremist" as an accusation not only of rigidity but also of complacency rooted in fundamental certainty and self-righteousness.

Once again, institutional incentives to despised conduct, in this case political hypocrisy, exist that have no particular connection to extremism.[184] Overreaching by successful candidates who win by slim margins is one example. Instead of seeing this as a sign of voter moderation, winners improbably claim a "mandate" and govern as if they had one, "to spin the straw of slim majorities and popular skepticism into the gold of electoral and policy victories."[185] Or partisans claim to have the support of a silent majority. Or in particular instances partisans exploit the procedural rules of an institution to avoid having to accommodate the opposition.

"Extremist" speaks less to expected conduct of this sort than to an underlying violation of a core democratic disposition. Extremists exhibit a moral failing best described as hubris. With its single-mindedness, its violation of inclusiveness, comprehensiveness, and disposition to compromise, extremism is tyrannical, despotic. It expresses a morally reprehensible, undemocratic superiority. It violates the basic tenet of partisanship—that being "on the side of the angels" does not obscure the fact that a party is still a part. That explains the moral indignation behind the accusatory "extremist." For ordinary partisans—voters, activists, candidates, and officials—political clashes are not struggles between good and evil. Nor are they clashes between right and right—the tragic struggle of equally convincing claims. The foundation of parties and partisanship is acceptance of pluralism, an iota of tolerance if not "a sense, a shade, of relativism."[186] This is less than Hume's "small tincture of Pyrrhonism," which is a permanently skeptical pose; antiextremism does not demand rationalist moderation. Most often what is at work is simply the sobering lessons of experience. "Extremist" is a democratic accusatory when it refers not to positioning or rhetoric but to deviation from the ethics of partisanship. The extremist is not off-center but too adamantly, proudly, and totally right.

I have examined the prevailing centrism/extremism schema from a number of angles. Recourse to "extremist" is overdetermined, and we see why it is a reflexive term of opprobrium, part of the daily political diet. The spatial model invites it when there are two major parties, a dominant center, and few other points. This contributes also to rhetorical accusations of "extremist." My main concern has been to understand the moral tenor of the accusation that a party or partisan is "extremist." That meant untethering it from party positioning and tying it instead to an ethic of partisanship.

Throughout this book I have identified moments of appreciation in the glorious traditions of antipartyism and progressive challenges, and I have defended partisanship against its nemesis, the vaunted "independence." Not all parties are defensible, of course. "Militant democracy" is the name for self-protection against parties that would exploit regulated rivalry in order to undo it. It is democracy's response to parties that do not accept that they are parts. Justifiable violations of democratic principles and practices, including exclusion of parties and criminalization of partisanship, are my final subject.

If we cast an eye at established democracies broadly, we see changes in the threats parties pose and the reasons offered for outlawing parties in self-defense. Antidemocratic ideologies, communism and fascism, gave rise to the original theory of militant democracy. Today these are eclipsed by ethnic and religious parties, parties based on particularist social identities, parties that receive support from outside the country—émigrés or an ethnic or religious diaspora. We hear in some of the arguments for exclusion echoes of holist defenses of national identity or fear that parties enflame differences and are fatally divisive. With this, my study comes full circle. With the establishment of stable party systems, the two glorious traditions of antipartyism—holism and the fear of violent divisions—gave way to other concerns. "Progressive antipartyism" was thorough-going, clearly, but it identified comparatively benign failings, presumably corrigible. Holism and fear that parties are fatally divisive never disappeared as critical perspectives, though, and they are alive today. Like the glorious traditions of antipartyism with which I began, the purpose of bans on parties is to deny full, unfettered sway to politicized pluralism. When is this justifiable?

CHAPTER 9

―――⟫⋅◆⋅⟪―――

Militant Democracy: Banning Parties

Justifying Antipartyism

When Gus Hall died in October 2000, the *New York Times* obituary described him as "the zealous lifelong Communist who led the American branch of the party from the cold war through political oblivion in the post-Soviet era."[1] The cold war's virulent anticommunism with its repressive federal and state legislation forced members underground and left the party in hopeless disarray. When vestigial branches began to run candidates again in state elections, and Indiana refused to allow the Communist Party (CP) to enter the 1972 race (for failure to submit a loyalty oath affirming that the party does not advocate the overthrow of government by force), the Supreme Court unanimously declared Indiana's exclusion of the party from the ballot unconstitutional and described its earlier rulings to the contrary "thoroughly discredited."[2] Gus Hall ran for president four times between 1972 and 1984, to "yawning indifference."[3] Indeed, adherence to the party is viewed as politically insignificant, a personal idiosyncrasy, reflected, for example, in Harvard President Bok's casual observation that the faculty was mostly Democrats and Republicans but that "we do have some faculty members who fall outside the spectrum being either libertarians or Communists or goodness knows what."[4] It recalls Justice Holmes's dismissal of subversives in *Abrams* as puny anonymities, or Justice Douglas's diminishment of American communists as "miserable merchants of unwanted ideas."[5]

The Communist Party is saved from oblivion by the memoirs of warring intellectuals and as complainant in court cases interpreting the First Amendment.[6] Doctrines related to freedom of speech and association enunciated by the Supreme Court in the line of cases from *Gitlow* and *Whitney* to *Dennis* and *Scales* are standard academic fare: advocating versus inciting unlawful conduct; parsing the terms of Holmes's "clear and present danger" test; the intricacies of the Fifth Amendment applied to disclosure of membership in an officially designated subversive organization. The Supreme Court's version of the party's history in *Scales*, important not for its accuracy but as perception, provides a concrete reminder of the sense of peril that seemed to have justified singling the CP out for exposure and control, warranted making party membership grounds for deportation and denial of public employment, and inspired now incredible state laws authorizing twenty-year prison sentences (Texas), life imprisonment (Michigan), or the death penalty (Tennessee) for membership.[7] In 1945, the Court explained, the party was changed from an independent political party to a constituent element of the worldwide Communist movement controlled by foreign agents.[8] The CP everywhere was only "pretending to be but another political party."[9]

The Communist Party is a touchstone for thinking about the parameters of permissible parties and the grounds for banning parties and disqualifying candidates running for office. Up to now I have said little about the content of parties, except that they create lines of division. My appreciation of parties and partisanship is not rooted in a substantive account of just political aims or a particular set of democratic principles to which parties must subscribe. (Inclusiveness, comprehensiveness, and disposition to compromise are second-order norms that I use to outline an ethic of partisanship.) It should be clear that neither "extremism" as a violation of the ethics of partisanship nor "extremism" as ideological positioning justifies the suppression of parties or partisans. I have said little about the political aims of parties that credibly place them "on the side of the angels," in short. I can at least offer reasons for substantive *antipartyism* and say something about the parameters of permissible, that is, lawful parties. My examination of antipartyism requires this final piece.

The "paradox of democracy"—restricting rights of political association of groups that threaten democracy—is generally said to be no paradox at all.[10] "A constitution is not a prescription for suicide, and civil rights are not an altar for national destruction."[11] Hans Kelsen observed that "when the constitutions of democratic republics . . . deny political parties legal recognition, they no longer inhibit the implementation of democracy, as constitutional monarchies did; they only close their eyes to the facts."[12] Sometimes, however, the facts justify banning.[13]

In chapter 3, I traced the early acceptance of parties that acquiesced in political pluralism and acknowledged their irreducible partiality, that is, parties committed to Burke's and our regulated rivalry. Political parties just are congruent with democracy if they are committed to operating within the electoral system by appealing publicly to voters for a chance to enter and control government; if they do not aim at destroying opposition parties as enemies; and if, on losing an election, they give up office without a fight. This is a fairly simple standard that justifies excluding parties that threaten civil war or violent hostilities, parties that do not accept their status as parts but pretend to be the sole representative of the nation.[14] Add to this parties whose substantive objectives violate a fundamental democratic principle such as denying civil or political rights to part of the population—whether a minority or majority group. I will show that parties are also banned when they pose existential challenges to an established ideal of national identity. With this, my study comes full circle. In chapters 1 and 2 I discussed two glorious traditions of antipartyism: holism, which finds parts and partiality intolerable, and the fear that parties are fatally divisive, which accepts partiality but sees parties as exacerbating divisions, provoking violence. We recognize traces of the longing for holism and the fear that parties are fatally divisive in bans on parties that spread hate and advocate exclusion and on parties that would alter the settled idea of national unity and political identity.

My objective in this chapter is to outline the justificatory resources democratic theorists and legal scholars have at hand for banning parties, outlawing political practices, and disqualifying certain partisans from participation in elections and government. In the sections below, I identify and discuss four principal reasons for substantive antipartyism and for banning parties: violence, incitement to hate, existential challenges to national identity, and outside support or control. The reasons as applied and the criteria used to determine whether parties or partisans support violence, say, are difficult matters of political judgment, not always made in good faith. I provide materials to indicate why "as applied" is terribly difficult, and I offer my judgment on particular cases. The Communist Party USA is my touchstone for the United States, but in this final chapter I cast the net widely and look at cases from across established democracies. My categories are an attempt to bring some order to substantive antipartyism and to legal prohibitions on parties. But on reflection, for reasons that will become clear, I doubt that this subject is amenable to a sharp analytic framework or stable regulative principles except in the broadest sense. As a result I will leave the matter close to where I found it: an underdescribed and undertheorized region of the democratic landscape, a corner of the terrain of antipartyism that is rarely visited.[15]

The Changing Terms of "Militant Democracy"

When Duverger wrote that party membership takes on a "truly religious form" and that "the term party includes veritable churches with their clergy, their faithful, their belief, their orthodoxy, their intolerance," he was referring to "political religions"—Jacobins, Bolsheviks, by extension Maoists.[16] Today, the force of the analogy is reversed, and political religion refers to religion proper. In a turn of the screw, fundamentalist Islam has been called "the new Marxism."[17] The thread I develop in this chapter is that thinking about the justifiable limits on the sort of parties allowed to participate in democratic elections has shifted away from the antidemocratic parties Duverger and others had in mind.

That an electoral majority might choose an antidemocratic government is the classic "paradox of democracy," which political theorists have addressed in familiar terms: we cannot consent to foreclose the possibility of consent and democratic decision making in the future. (The value of democracy and electoral institutions is assumed; its ground is a prior and separate philosophic question.) This dictates the once standard reason for excluding and criminalizing any party that sees the opposition as an enemy to be denied rights of political participation—that is, any party with the intention of eliminating or closing off open access to elections in the future. Historical experience warns that once in office, certain parties will destroy democratic institutions. The CP USA, for example, was decried as the antidemocratic party par excellence, working for the violent overthrow of the government, even if in some nebulous future. The U.S. Supreme Court put the matter simply: "it is fraudulent for a group seeking violent revolution to . . . disguise itself as a political party and use the very forms of the democracy it seeks to subvert in order to gain support and carry on its nefarious ends."[18] Democratic self-defense was the principal reason for outlawing parties in countries haunted by the European interwar experience and the catastrophe of National Socialism, compounded by Bolshevism. After World War II, democracy required protection in nations where it had not been unequivocally embraced by voters. Karl Loewenstein's 1937 phrase "militant democracy" became a constitutionally enshrined response to fascist and communist parties whose political ideologies reject the democratic core of open regulated rivalry.[19] In a shift of tone but to the same purpose, Aharon Barak of the Israeli high court calls this pose "defensive democracy."[20]

There is virtually no full-blown antidemocratic political theory today. The exceptions are theocratic or integralist ethnic claims, and Islamist parties raise some of the questions presented by radical secular parties in the last century. Are they opportunistic, exploiting elections in order to supplant pluralist politics with the rule of the party of virtue? Is moderation strategic, to avoid criminalization ("a theocrat in a necktie"[21])? Or does electoral activity signal accommodation to constitutional constraints and institutional counterbalances, among them the regulated rivalry of multiple parties?

The orthodox view of "militant democracy" is not the whole story today, and my typology of reasons for banning parties reflects this shift. The standard terms of democratic self-defense apply only with difficulty or anachronistically to xenophobic anti-immigrant parties, say, or to sectarian parties that oppose a strict principle of secularism in public life. Justifications for banning overtly antidemocratic parties cannot be neatly applied to parties banned for inciting hatred against an ethnic or regional group, to parties with separatist programs, or to parties that pose existential challenges to national identity.[22] These parties have only a loose identification with twentieth-century political ideologies, if any.

We understand why these questions arise in some form in every established democracy, though they are less directly and immediately relevant in the United States than other places. The challenge arises everywhere because when the struggle for empowerment is "waged within the world of democratic politics," it is waged through parties.[23] With political organization, the fact of pluralism, including religious and ethnic pluralism, is made concrete for democratic purposes. Religious and ethnic parties aim at organizing and mobilizing social groups—or claim to speak in their name.[24] They appeal to voters as the champion of the interests of one group, sometimes to the exclusion of others.[25] Religious and ethnic parties, among others, compete for office to win their share (or more than their share) of public benefits and support. They organize to have a new pillar added. Or they insist that some other group's claim to public recognition or public funding (national minorities, immigrants, refugees, guest workers) should be denied. These parties do not satisfy an ethics of partisanship, which prizes inclusiveness, comprehensiveness, and disposition to compromise. But the parties do fall within the acceptable terrain of democratic politics. Particularist parties and bloc voting should not be uniformly depreciated. They are key instruments of political conflict but also of political integration.

When do these parties step outside the bounds and arouse the justifiable resistance of "militant democracy"? Parties are said to exploit electoral politics impermissibly not only when they fail to abide by the terms of regulated rivalry but also when they incite hatred against other groups or aim at altering the secular or religious, the civic or ethnic character of the nation (reminding us that "un-American" supplements undemocratic in accounts of the hatefulness of the Communist Party and that "godless" was as aversive as state ownership of the means of production).

The timeline of constitution writing and constitutional interpretation reflects the changes I have begun to describe: the general shift from defense against parties wielding antidemocratic political ideologies to particularist religious and ethnic parties that challenge national unity (or the existing pluralist mix) and identity. The older standpoint is reflected in Article 21 of the German Constitution: "Parties which, by reason of their aims or the behavior of their adherents, seek to impair or destroy the free democratic basic order or to endanger the existence of the Federal Republic of Germany shall be unconstitutional." Newer constitutions, amendments to older constitutions, and statutory law incorporate religious, ethnic, racial, and linguistic constraints on party organizing. Israel's Amendment 7A to the Basic Law passed in 1985, for example, prohibits parties from participation in elections if they have as their central objective denial of the State of Israel as the state of the Jewish people. India's "corrupt practices" law bans campaign practices that employ "the promotion of, or attempt to promote, feelings of enmity or hatred between classes of citizens of India on grounds of religion, race, caste, community or language by a candidate" and proscribes the use of religious symbols in elections.[26] In Portugal: "political parties shall not employ names that contain expressions which are directly related to any religion or church, or emblems that can be confused with national or religious symbols" nor may they employ "a name or manifesto that possesses a regional nature or scope." Turkey's Constitution and Political Parties Act of 1983 are wielded against parties that aim to alter the unitary state and against parties that challenge a specific, stringent understanding of secularism.[27] Banning these parties has a significance that suppression of revolutionary ideological parties of the left and right did not: it is liable to close off the central political method of accommodating ethnic and religious pluralism, and can amount to the political exclusion of a whole sector of society. A self-declared expert on "comparative fanaticism" points out that fascism and antifascism were relatively simple conflicts compared with those underlying the exclusion of religious or ethnic parties.[28]

Militant Democracy and Freedom of Political Association

Before taking up justifications for banning parties and disqualifying partisans, it is useful to try to mark a baseline of freedom of political association. Party building in democracies occurs against the background of freedom of speech and association. Democratic theorists propose several moral and political grounds for freedom of association and extend the liberty to all kinds of groups. These philosophical catalogues of reasons and protections share one theme: the significance and for democratic theorists the priority of *political* speech and association. Outlawing political groups requires strong justification, and the bar is presumably higher when political association takes the form of electoral parties. International covenants and human rights treaties proclaim universal suffrage and rights of speech and political association; the European Court of Human Rights, for example, has stated that "political parties are a form of association essential to the proper functioning of democracy."[29] Anchoring political parties in national constitutions is commonplace,[30] with statutory party law supplementing or substituting for constitutional guarantees. The German constitution reads: "The political parties participate in the forming of the political will of the people. They may be freely established." In France: "Political parties and groups shall contribute to the exercise of suffrage. They shall be formed and carry on their activities freely." Italy's constitution mandates that "all citizens have the right freely to organize themselves in parties in order to cooperate in a democratic way in determining national policy." Turkey's reads: "Citizens have the right to form political parties and in accordance with the established procedure to join and withdraw from them," and "political parties are indispensable elements of the democratic political life." Israel's Basic Law refers to "candidate lists."[31] Spain's constitution specifies two grounds for recognizing parties: the individual right to establish and participate in parties and "the existence of the party system as the essential platform for the exercise of political pluralism."[32] Written before electoral parties were legitimate, the U.S. Constitution mentions neither parties nor a general right of political association, though protections have been secured under the First Amendment as subsidiary to freedom of speech.[33]

Indeed, parties are sometimes assigned a distinct legal status rather than afforded protection as just one member of the general class of voluntary associations. Thus, the International Covenant on Civil and Political Rights distinguishes the "civil rights" of association from the "political rights" of standing for election.[34] The German constitution sets parties off from other political groups; Article 21 sees parties as "integral elements of the constitutional state" in what has been called the "party state" designed to create a stable democratic system based on parties. Note that the distinct legal status of parties in contrast to other protected groups is not always protective; it is sometimes designed to work against certain parties. The Bulgarian constitution recognizes the "right to identity"—ethnic, cultural, religious, and linguistic—and with it the right of association to pursue these interests. But the constitution prohibits these associations from pursuing objectives or engaging in activity that is the domain of political parties, and it prohibits political parties organized on ethnic, racial, or religious lines. Similarly, separate articles of the Turkish constitution refer to freedom of association and to the right to form parties in an effort to prevent the politicization of religious and cultural differences, above all to prevent claims on behalf of minority rights from becoming the program of a party.[35]

Nowhere is political speech and association absolute, of course, and neither is protection for parties. International covenants and courts articulate general standards of "reasonableness": rights of speech and association are subject "to such reasonable limits prescribed by law as can be demonstrably justified in a free and democratic society." The Council of Europe and European Court of Human Rights have held that banning parties is compatible with human rights if there are convincing and compelling reasons to justify restrictions, as was the case with "totalitarian groups."[36] In a 1984 decision the U.N. Human Rights Committee held that organizing a fascist party in Italy was an act "removed from the protection of the Covenant by Article 5" in order to defend against erosion of democracy from within. The U.N. has approved electoral standards that permit "the exclusion of violent or anti-democratic groups from the electoral process." To anticipate my argument about changed threats, the U.N. monitored (and implicitly condoned) elections in Mozambique in which the only parties allowed to participate were those whose objectives are "non-regional, non-tribal, non-separatist, non-racial, non-ethnic, and non-religious."[37]

The categories of justification for exclusion I propose below bring some order to the subject, but they are not good predictors of banning if only because the meaning and application of these standards are closely tied to a nation's political history. Their significance and priority follow less from abstract political reasoning than from experience. Party bans are "a demarcation from the past," aimed at correcting the "paradigmatic wrongs of the old regime."[38] Thus, justifications for banning reflect the vicissitudes of politics at the moment of constitution writing. Postwar Germany's Basic Law was written to outlaw "extremism,"[39] and the term was chosen for its inclusiveness. That is, provisions were written to encompass both Nazism (outlawing the National Socialist Party) and, as important, the Allied administration's emergent Cold War confrontation with the Bolsheviks (outlawing the German Communist Party). In Italy, by contrast, the postwar constitution aimed specifically at preventing the reorganization of the Fascist Party, and the Italian communist and socialist parties and others joined in support of this singular ban. The idea was to proscribe this exception, not to compass "antisystem" or "extremism" broadly. In the United States, preoccupation with secretive, conspiratorial political groups masquerading as benign generated the broad category "subversive" organizations. Everywhere, in short, laws aim at "our extremists."[40]

A baseline of freedom of association and reasons for exclusion are not only tied to particular historical experiences; also contributing to the elusiveness of standards is the range of considerations that enter into the judgment of danger. Democratic self-defense and "reasonable limits" do not indicate what evidence is required to assess the danger specific parties pose: the party's express aims as set out in platforms or speeches by party leaders? The party's internal organization? Association with armed militia or violent groups by some party members? There is the difficulty of estimating the likelihood of electoral victory, too, and the probability that the party in office will enact antidemocratic policies. Judgments are even more difficult if the concern is that a party's activities erode democratic institutions over the long term or, more elusive still, corrupt democratic attitudes, so that the damage comes from the party's participation in elections per se.

Normative standards provide a basis for applying limits on political association, but finally, these judgments are political, made by judges, legislators, or executives, vulnerable to partisanship and partiality, sometimes pretexts for repressing opposition. Often enough banning is motivated by prejudice or an exclusionary national ideal, a unitary political identity hostile to ideological, religious, or ethnic pluralism. Especially during wartime, conditions are ripe for repressive overreaction.[41] Judgments are vulnerable to popular exaggerations of danger; they are political responses (or provocations) to hysteria. George Kennan's prediction that legislation enacted to suppress the Communist Party would turn the country into "the very power we are trying to combat: intolerant, secretive, suspicious, cruel, and terrified of internal dissension" was borne out.[42] Restrictions on parties, regulation, exclusion, disqualification, and criminalization are matters of judgment often performed in the haze of danger.[43] The fear factor is typically exacerbated by animosity toward the party's supporters. We know that suppression of "subversive organizations" in the United States has been aimed at groups identified with religious and ethnic minorities (Jews and immigrants from outside Western Europe), spurred by nativist fear of aliens as revolutionaries or by fear as a pretext for racism or anti-Semitism. The first of the trio of anticommunist acts was the Alien Registration Act, known as the Smith Act, passed in 1940, with its requirements of registration (ultimately 5 million people were registered) and mechanisms for deportation. Parties may be accommodated as a result of contingent calculations of danger as well—as a "safety valve" to ward off civil war, to prevent driving a political organization underground, or to keep supporters from affiliating with mainstream parties where their influence might be camouflaged.

The Simple Ground: Violence

The first seemingly simple, paradigmatic reason for banning parties is violence. Threats of violent political opposition and revolutionary overthrow are outlawed by every regime, by open and closed societies alike. Laws dealing with conspiracy, criminal activity, and threats to political stability extend to associations generally rather than parties specifically, but distinct considerations enter when democratic self-defense is marshaled against threats of violent upset from political parties. A defining characteristic of parties is assurance that in situations of deep political division, conflict is restricted to the regulated rivalry of obtaining political office and influencing laws and policy by peaceful, electoral means. Unlike secret, conspiratorial groups, parties are presumptively committed to persuasion in public competition. Unlike revolutionary groups or private militia, political parties are not armed. Their objective is to mobilize voters, not armies. Simply put, "A political party cannot bear arms; this exists in no democracy."[44] Hamas's participation in Palestinian elections was supported by Prime Minister Mahmoud Abbas for pragmatic reasons, but his public statements reflect the basic standard: "A political party plus a militia is unacceptable."[45] Parties are defined to exclude resort to violence. The terms of militant democracy justifiably proscribe "fundamentalism in power and chauvinism with an army."[46]

Parties structured along military lines and internal authoritarianism are often taken as evidence of actual capacity and probable intent to resort to violence, hence laws requiring that the organization of parties be democratic, and demands for transparency and accountability.[47] Spain and Italy outlaw "secret and para-military associations" and "those associations that, even indirectly, pursue political ends by means of organizations having a military character." French law proscribes any group or movement "that resembles, in its form and military organization, a combat group or private militia." Germany dictates that parties' "internal organization must conform to democratic principles."[48] Clandestine meetings, secret membership lists, and front organizations are antithetical to party politics where public avowal of mass membership is the norm for participation in political life. I will expand on this point using the Communist Party USA in the next section.

European politics between the world wars was marked by paramilitary, mass parties of the left and right. Today, the principal examples are parties claiming to represent ethnic or religious minorities or, in some cases, excluded majorities. Thus, Turkey banned the only legal pro-Kurdish political party HADEP (People's Democracy Party) for purported ties to the militant separatist PKK (Kurdistan Workers' Party), which the government views as a terrorist organization. This points to the fact that violence today typically takes the form of insurgency, terrorism, or hostilities between antagonistic religious or ethnic groups. It is close and immediate, unlike advocacy of revolution in some indeterminate future. Parties are charged with actual "association" with violent groups and "support" for their activities, or, less often, the party itself is a political wing of an organization hoping to win broader popular sympathy by entering elections. Surveys suggest that elements within parties take the initiative in forming or promoting violent groups more often than than the reverse.[49] (An example of this exception is the Israeli IRGUN, transformed by Menahim Begin into the Herut Party.) Not only do party members engage in violence ("Know-Nothings" preventing immigrants from getting to the polls, to use a historical example), but the party qua organization may engage in it.

Sinn Fein was the political embodiment of the Irish Republican Army, and Hamas, which does not maintain an organizational division between its political and military branches, engages in both "popular" Intifada-related violence on the street and activities by its military-terrorist arm.[50] The considerations entering into the judgment that a party is associated with violent activity or supports armed groups are typically more ambiguous than these examples suggest. Consider Spain's ban of Batasuna, the Basque independence party. Rowdy demonstrations and "incidents" at a municipal hall by Batasuna party members could not justify disqualifying the party as a whole. The formal charge against the party was that by its refusal to condemn acts of violence by the armed ETA ("Basque Fatherland and Liberty"), a separatist movement linked to bombings and assassinations, the party legitimized terrorist actions.[51] This justification for banning the party is insupportable, too, on my view. It makes silence the equivalent of legitimization, and legitimization the equivalent of active support. Apparently, refusal to condemn ETA was insufficient for the Spanish court as well, for the General Counsel stepped up charges and argued that Batasuna offered financial and logistical support to ETA. The charge had it that ETA used Batasuna "for one sole purpose: to take advantage of the benefits accorded by the democratic system (subsidies, public funding . . . access to free electoral campaign slots . . .) in order to sustain, support, spread and multiply the effects of terrorist violence as well as the fear and intimidation it generates."[52] According to the charge, ETA and Batasuna constituted a single legal-political network that coordinated terrorist and political action over many years. The international press and Amnesty International protested the 2002 ban, arguing that association between individual members of the party and the ETA did not amount to party advocacy or material support for terrorism. The decision seemed to rest on guilt by association. The case points up the question constitutional courts and the European Commission on Human Rights have to grapple with: who speaks for the party? When are members' actions representative and imputable to the party, and what is the party's responsibility to discipline or expel leaders or members whose actions violate the law?[53]

A second example fleshes out these difficulties and points up the obvious: principles of freedom of political association and reasons for banning are meaningful as applied, in context, typically in the haze of danger. In 2002 a revision of Amendment 7A of Israeli law added to its list of disqualifications parties or candidates whose "goals or actions, expressly or by implication, include . . . support for armed struggle by a hostile state or terrorist organization against the state of Israel."[54] This was the basis of the effort to disqualify the candidacies of two members of the Knesset, Azmi Bishara and Ahmad Tibi, prominent Arab politicians and chairmen of two parties. Both defended the Palestinian uprising in the Second Intifada as justified resistance to occupation. Because the Second Intifada was accompanied by suicide bombings, the MKs were accused of supporting terrorism against civilians. Bishara also avowed support for Hezbollah in its war against Israel, calling it "a brave organization that has taught Israel a lesson—it can have occupation or it can have peace."[55] In 2001 he attended a ceremony sponsored by the Syrian government in memory of President Hafez al-Assad and called on the Arab world "to unite against the warmongering Sharon government."[56] The Knesset stripped Bishara of his parliamentary immunity after a speech made on Palestinian Authority television expressing belief that the Palestinians would be victorious in their uprising. He was accused of "identifying with a terrorist organization" and "expressing verbal praise, sympathy, and encouragement for violent actions which could lead to death or injury." For his part, Ahmad Tibi, who served as an adviser on Israeli affairs to Yasir Arafat, was charged with calling participation in the Intifada a "duty" and praising Palestinian resistance in Jenin, a home of Palestinian suicide bombers. Tibi resisted his disqualification: "I was elected to be an authentic representative of the Arab public . . . individuals, also from the Jewish public, supporting my views and the views of the party. . . . You are negating for us the right to be part of the consensus, of the discussion."[57]

The Israeli Court unanimously ruled against disqualifying Tibi; by itself his defense of resistance to occupation did not constitute support for terrorism. A divided Court voted 7–4 against disqualifying Bishara. One dissenting justice argued that Bishara's endorsement of Hezbollah constituted impermissible support for a terrorist organization ("Regarding the question of whether Hezbollah is a terrorist organization, it is sufficient that the government of Israel declared that it is a terrorist organization according to its authority under the law to decide"). Another dissenter emphasized that Bishara's public appearance in an enemy state constituted impermissible support.[58] But the majority interpreted Amendment 7A to mean that verbal and symbolic support were insufficient. Active engagement at high levels was necessary; meetings with Hezbollah or members of Palestinian terrorist groups must be for the explicit purpose of organizing or encouraging attacks. One MK wondered, "Would there ever be a member of the American Senate who was an adviser to Saddam Hussein"?[59] The rhetorical question succeeds in emphasizing the unusual latitude Israel grants party lists, but taken literally the remark misses the mark. A pro-Saddam candidate would be unable to get the signatures necessary for ballot access in the United States, and first past the post elections would make the candidacy purely expressive, but it would be lawful. On the view expounded here, "association" with and "support" for violent groups entail more than advocacy of violence. Banning requires a verifiable connection to actual riots, bombings, sabotage, assassination.[60]

More often, however, violence as a ground for banning parties is applied to parties that advance "fighting faiths" without threatening concrete undertakings or imminent violence. In American law the line is drawn *within* the category of speech: advocacy versus incitement. Strong liberal and democratic norms favor unconstrained advocacy of abstract doctrine including verbal support for resistance against government as long as it does not rise to the level of incitement. The distinction is hardly crystalline. Briefly, incitement entails a close connection between speech and action; it requires intent to call for a violent or criminal act *now;* and the immediate violation must be likely to occur.[61] (Government need not "wait until the putsch is about to be executed, the plans have been laid and the signal is awaited."[62]) Criteria like "clear and present danger" attempt to capture the standard, which is echoed in court decisions outside the United States and has philosophical imprimatur.[63] The clear and present danger test is more often invoked than applied, however, or applied in a way that does not afford dependable protection to political speech and association. In practice, "incitement" works mainly to preclude banning participation in elections solely on the basis of party platform and goals. As Justice Douglas argued in his *Dennis* dissent from the conviction of leaders of the Communist Party under the Smith Act, the defendants were charged not with "conspiracy to overthrow" the government but with conspiracy to form groups and assemblies of people who teach and advocate the overthrow of the government by force.[64]

Many legal bans do not make the advocacy/incitement distinction at all, of course. It is not necessary to show the intent to incite an action, or the imminence of action, or that advocacy increases the likelihood of violence or illegal activity, or that the speech or program directly caused others to act. No actual danger is necessary to warrant exclusion. Instead, content-based restrictions apply to party doctrine, platform, and positions taken by party leaders, and violation of these restrictions is sufficient grounds for exclusion or criminalization.[65] One of the first decisions of the postwar German Constitutional Court in 1952 was to ban the German Communist Party, holding that the official doctrine of communism excluded any form of legal opposition and was therefore antidemocratic and presumptively violent.[66] The ban was upheld by the European Commission of Human Rights.[67] Categorical proscriptions eliminate the need to draw lines between advocacy and incitement; they obviate the need to estimate the probability and proximity of danger.

We see that the tests for support of violence are variable and that variation owes to the particulars of political history as well as political and legal theory. They apply to all political associations, not parties only. When it comes to parties, the terms of "militant democracy" alter somewhat. In addition to advocating or supporting violence, we have the accusation that the group is "not really" a party. I detail this move by looking at treatment of the Communist Party USA.

Not Really a Party: The CP USA

In its early years, the CP was democratic, indigenous (born in 1919 from a schism in the American Socialist Party), and operated as a political party, running candidates in open elections.[68] When ballot access laws permitted, the party pursued electoral organizing in an effort to reach potential sympathizers and recruit members. (The CP was alone in early efforts to recruit southern blacks; in 1932 the party chose James Ford as its vice-presidential candidate, the first African American to be nominated for national office.) Of course, there were always communists who thought that "parliamentary activity" undercut the party's self-proclaimed role as the leading edge of a world revolutionary movement. Still, the CP USA was oriented to elections. Strategic decisions had to do with working with or within other third parties such as the Farmer-Labor Party or La Follette's Progressive Party, forming or joining a united front labor party, or going it alone. In 1936 the decision was whether to support Roosevelt and the New Deal; in 1947 whether to endorse Henry Wallace's third-party candidacy.

Until the Cold War, the CP was not singled out as *the* organized threat to democracy. The 1917 Espionage Act generated the first judicial tests of the First Amendment and aroused the first serious national discussion of antidemocratic groups since the Alien and Sedition Act of 1798. The act was passed and enforced before the CP USA was formed, and the 1920 "Red scare" with its arrests and deportations swept up socialists and anarchists, populist reform movements, and organized labor as a whole.[69] During World War II it was possible to "fuse American and Russian patriotism." (Cold War anticommunists had a short memory: the "most infamous question of the next two decades—'Are you now or have you ever been . . . ?' encompassed the past."[70]) In 1944 Earl Browder dismantled the party as such, replacing it with a nonpartisan "political-education association," in effect a left-wing lobby. Recruits were not supposed to be revolutionists.[71] During the Cold War, the CP did become the chief target of aggressive enforcement of older standing laws[72] and new repressive legislation: "loyalty programs, emergency detention plans, undercover surveillance, legislative investigations, and criminal prosecutions of Communists."[73] Title I of the the McCarran Act created the Subversive Activities Control Board and required the identification of party officers and registration of "communist action" and "communist front" organizations substantially directed, dominated, disciplined, or controlled by the "world Communist movement."[74] One observer explained the stringency of the law: "The McCarran Act does not require Communists to register as Communists; the Act requires Communists to register, under oath, their agreement with its definition of 'Communist,' that is, to register as deceivers, criminal conspirators, traitors, and then says that if a Communist does not sign a sworn statement so defining himself he will be liable to imprisonment for five years *for every day* he fails to so label himself."[75] The Subversive Activities Control Act, Justice Black wrote, "makes it extremely difficult for a member of the Communist Party to live in this country and, at the same time, makes it a crime for him to try to get a passport to get out." The CP's electoral history was exploited; names collected to secure ballot access were used for official and unofficial black-lists. Humiliation, fines, forfeitures, and lengthy imprisonment made it impossible for the party to function as either a radical organization or a political party. It was decimated as a result of "blows, desertions, defeats, and persecutions"; its resources were spent in legal defense, which had become its principal business.[76] Justice Black's dissent in *Communist Party v. Control Board* in 1961 calls the finding that the Communist Party of the United States was a "Communist-action or-ganization" within the meaning of the Subversive Activities Control Act a "fateful moment in the history of a free country," "the first ban-ning of an association because it advocates hated ideas—whether that association be called a political party or not."[77]

Treatment of CP USA alerts us to a crucial but underappreciated point: few cases turned solely on subversive activity or on advocacy or incitement alone. Findings of antidemocratic and violent intent hinged to a significant extent on the party's organization. Organiza-tion was the best evidence that the CP was only pretending to be a party. It linked "not really a party" and "un-American."

The pretense is not hard to uncover if the baseline is the conduct and organization of mainstream American electoral parties mainly concerned with campaigns and short-term political issues. (I have ar-gued against this as an adequate description and norm throughout.) In contrast, the Communist Party's objective was not electoral suc-cess but propaganda and organizing. CP candidates were party func-tionaries, not individual personalities.[78] The CP had "card-carrying" and dues-paying members, whereas in the United States voter reg-istration in primary elections was a loose, noncommittal stand-in for membership. Moreover, unlike electoral parties, the CP sought strength not in numbers but in "selected, dedicated, indoctrinated, and rigidly disciplined members." This provoked the otherwise odd charge that while purporting to be a political party the CP was a "highly disciplined organization."[79]

Of the organizational signs that the CP was not really a party, the most important was secrecy. Public avowal of partisanship character-izes political life,[80] and secrecy is not only a vice to most Americans but also undemocratic. That a large percentage of CP members kept their membership secret is only partly explained by anticommunist repression. The party's parallel underground had other objectives besides efforts to evade indictments and prison sentences. Cadres in "deep, deep freeze" were sent abroad and remained inactive. Others, the "operative but unavailable" leadership, assembled underground "for the express purpose of giving emergency leadership in the expectation that the country faced world war and military dictatorship."[81] Secrecy was a mark of the professional revolutionary. Similarly antithetical to American parties was the CP's front organizations. Parties have often had roots in the associations of civil society. "Front organization" reverses that relation: the association is a creature of the party; its connection camouflaged. "Front organization" became an official designation in 1954; the 1961 edition of Congress's *Guide to Subversive Organizations and Publications* lists 663 front organizations and offers bizarre formulas for detecting these apparently innocent groups. "The first requisite for front organizations is an idealistic sounding title," the guide explains; "does the organization present itself as nonpartisan yet engage in political activities and consistently advocate causes favored by the Communists"?[82] Among the examples of idealistic camouflage: peace, civil rights, protection of the foreign-born, support for Smith Act "victims," abolition of H-bomb tests, exploitation of national and minority groups.[83]

The determinative element defining the CP as something other than a political party responsive to its members and voters, of course, was that policy and leadership were directed from Moscow. The "control" component of the Internal Security Act was as important as the antidemocratic components. It was the literal proof of un-American. At the time, there was little firm evidence of foreign control.[84] Historians have since documented changes in and by leadership in response to power struggles inside the Soviet party and the twists and turns of Soviet policy. Whether this amounted to acting as the "agent" of a foreign power is a separate question; at least it appears to have been unclear to American leaders themselves what Moscow demanded of them except to "keep in step." What is clear is that alignment with the Kremlin was the decisive proof that the party was

431

poised for violent overthrow. "The Communists have no scruples against sabotage, terrorism, assassination, or mob disorder."[85]

Learned Hand wrote in *Dennis*: "The American Communist Party . . . is a highly articulated, well contrived . . . organization, numbering thousands of adherents, rigidly and ruthlessly disciplined. . . . We hold that it is a danger 'clear and present.'"[86] Legal historian Geoffrey Stone explains, "Prosecution under the Smith Act was not about the Communist Party as a 'political' force. . . . No one feared that the party was about to 'overthrow' the U.S. government by winning elections. The fear was that the party, as an agent of the Soviet Union, would subvert American government . . . by instigating labor, class, and racial conflict and discontent."[87]

Centralization and rigid authoritarian bans on factions and internal discussion are not mechanisms of effective organization. Irving Howe and Lewis Coser argued convincingly that the party's organization was fatal to its political capacity in the United States precisely because of its unresponsiveness—its domestic leaders' ignorance of the actualities of American political life and temper.[88] The party did not represent the views of its members or American workers. It is not surprising that recruits cycled in and dropped out within a year or two—too short a time to be instructed in Stalinist doctrine, much less transformed into committed conspirators.[89] "The only truly safe generalization that can be made about American Communists is that most of them became ex-Communists."[90]

The CP USA illustrates reasons for attending to parties' internal organization. Germany's Basic Law requires internal democracy and "transparency," for example. It is not hard to understand certain restrictions as a defense against secret parties or parties organized in cells or paramilitary units. Nor is it hard to grasp demands for congruence between the requirements of nondiscrimination in public life and internal party rules (the U.S. *White Primary* cases speak to this point). Reasonable legal mandates for the particulars of democratic organization are not well worked out, though.[91] Should parties be required to give members the ability to elect party leadership? What about party nominees? Rules for arriving at the party platform? The parameters of permissible internal dissent?

Inciting Hate

The core of "militant democracy" is preserving regulated rivalry, and the irreducible justification for outlawing parties is violence. Subsequent justifications are progressively more distant from this straightforward reason for banning parties and disqualifying partisans. Inciting hate is the second category. It aims at suppressing parties that appeal to and excite racial, religious, or ethnic animosity. In fact, "inciting hate" is misleading as a description of this justification for political exclusion. It is too narrow. In many cases proscriptions apply regardless of intent to incite hostility; it is enough that parties mobilize in the name of ethnicity or religion. In some countries *any* reference to race, religion, or ethnicity in the course of electoral activity, any appeals for or against parties and candidates on the basis of race or religion, is ground for exclusion from the electoral process.

In certain respects these restrictions can be easily assimilated to "militant democracy." "Inciting hate" is sometimes linked to violence. Derogatory references to race, religion, or ethnicity just are proven triggers of violent hostility between sects or ethnic groups. This is one rationale for Israel's ban on the Kach Party.[92] The party platform called for the forced "transfer" of Arabs from Israel. Meier Kahane described Arabs as "cancer in the midst of us . . . . Let me become defense minister for two months and you will not have a single cockroach around here! I promise you a *clean* Eretz Yisrael." These appeals were made against the background of Kahane's proposals for prohibiting Arab-Jewish intermarriage, which recalled Nuremberg laws for the Protection of German Blood. The party and its successor, Kahane Is Alive, were outlawed following an attack on Arabs in Hebron in 1994.

Inciting hate has another direct connection to democratic self-defense if hateful partisans create a climate of fear. Aggressive political demonstrations, disorder during election campaigns, and general marauding and hate mongering are intimidating. Intimidation depresses political participation by victim groups, normally minorities, but other citizens as well. The "silencing" effect attributed to hate speech generally amounts in this case to inhibiting participation in electoral politics. This raises the vexing question whether parties should be afforded more or less liberty than other civil and political groups. We encountered the problem in the context of campaign finance law in the United States in the form of restrictions on financial support for candidates that were applied to private and corporate donors and—over the protest of the major parties—to parties themselves. The same question arises more dramatically here: is prohibition of hate speech more or less justified as applied to parties than hate speech codes in other contexts? On the one hand, public attention turns to politics during campaigns and elections, and censoring and exclusion from the electoral arena can be the effective equivalent of silencing a partisan position. On the other hand, the predominant argument has it that the public role of parties and government involvement (in effect, licensing parties, setting ballot requirements, and funding campaigns) combine to make them more amenable to regulation than other political associations. On this view, intimidation by parties, which inhibits democratic participation by fearful voters, is the decisive consideration.

At issue too is the threat that if a hateful party is successful in its electoral bid to control or influence government decision making, it would implement discriminatory policies or worse: strip opposition religious or ethnic groups of civil or political rights, discriminate against national minorities (or majorities), deport despised elements of the population. "Antidemocratic" refers to violating basic norms of civil liberty and political equality. In Likud MK Dan Meridor's words, "The establishment of democracy . . . is not just a mechanism for elections . . . .perhaps it is primarily the equal worth of all people."[93] The idea is that parties should not be licensed if they publicly exploit hate to win, and if they would propose exclusionary or discriminatory legislation if they do. These restrictions do not depend on the likelihood of victory, though. They apply to parties that are incapable of winning elections or of implementing antidemocratic policies if they attain office; they apply when parties do not pose an identifiable danger.

The reason for banning parties that incite hate does not necessarily turn on anticipated violence or intimidation or the consequences for policy if the party is victorious, then. It may turn on predicted effects on individuals as a result of the party's electoral activity per se. The ground for exclusion has to do with undermining democratic attitudes. The assumption is that hateful electoral speech and programs are corrosive of the moral culture of democracy. The deep harm is undermining conditions for the reproduction of democracy. Thus, Canada's Court ruled it permissible to criminalize hate speech because it "erodes the tolerance and open-mindedness that must flourish in a multicultural society which is committed to the idea of equality."[94] We are reminded of the U.S. Court's early, unprotective "bad tendency" doctrine, which appealed to the "natural tendency" of words, the reasonably probable effect of words, to produce bad outcomes over the long term.

Thus, the U.N. General Assembly designated 1971 "International Year for Action to Combat Racism *and* Racial Discrimination"; the two wrongs are separable. The chief accusation against parties is spreading racism apart from racist conduct or any direct harm to victims. (Indeed, incitement to racial hatred may be more severely prosecuted than acts of racial discrimination—the reverse of the priority in the United States, which permits hate speech but enforces laws against discrimination in both public and private arenas.[95]) In short, incitement to hate is less a matter of provoking specific behavior or effecting policy in the short term than eroding democratic habits. German criminalization of neo-Nazi groups has been explained as necessary to protect young people from Nazism rather than to protect society from Nazi youth.[96] Undermining democratic dispositions may have been the reasoning behind Belgium's ban of Vlaams Blok, which portrayed foreigners as "criminals who take bread from the mouths of Flemish workers" and advocated repatriation of non-European immigrants; the Court found the party guilty of "permanent incitement to segregation and racism."[97]

The typical defense against disqualification is to deny the party has racist attitudes by attempting to distinguish anti-immigrant arguments based on a policy of protecting jobs, say, from ethnic or racist loathing. Meier Kahane's Kach Party was banned from Israeli elections under both the racist parties clause of Amendment 7A and the antidemocratic parties clause.[98] The two are difficult to unravel, as we see. Kach's lawyer protested both. The defense itemized the attributes of democracy—freedom of the press, of the vote, and so on—and argued that Kach had not acted against any of these rights. Against the racism charge the defense protested that Kach called for the forcible mass expulsion of Arabs not because of their religion or ethnicity but because they were members of a nation at war with Israel (though Kach was explicitly opposed to civic equality, and would make being Jewish a qualification of citizenship).[99]

Preserving and promoting a political culture of civic and political equality is seen as the positive obligation of democratic government and as justification for imposing constraints on parties. Still, positive affirmation of democratic values—an oath or ritual egalitarian language—is not required for parties to compete in elections. Qualification does not depend on demonstrations of respect, on avowed commitment to civic and political equality, or on willingness to accommodate religious or ethnic differences. Rather, certain forms and expressions are categorically disallowed.

"Inciting hate" can be compassed within the parameters of democratic self-defense by connecting it to violence, to policies that deny civil and political rights to hated groups, or to the corruption of democratic dispositions. But when partisan appeals to religion and ethnicity do not entail hate speech, when proscription extends to *any* electoral appeal for or against parties on the basis of ascriptive characteristics, militant democracy fails to capture the stakes or the justification for banning. The Indian Supreme Court has enforced a 1951 electoral law criminalizing "corrupt practices" by parties. The law, as mentioned above, forbids "the promotion of, or attempt to promote, feelings of enmity or hatred between classes of citizens of India on grounds of religion, race, caste, community or language by a candidate,"[100] and goes on to outlaw "the appeal by a candidate or his agent . . . to vote or refrain from voting for any person on ground of his religion, race, caste, community or language or the use of or appeal to religious symbols." The idea is not that derogatory language triggers violence or provokes hatred; that is captured by the first prohibition. Instead, this clause makes any appeal to religion, race, caste, or language ground for banning.

Why? Is the prohibition a matter of preserving the secular character of the Indian state as pronounced in its constitution? In support of this interpretation Gary Jacobsohn shows that the courts have distinguished between parties invoking Hindu as religion (impermissible) from Hindu as a way of life of the people of the subcontinent (permissible). This may be a partial explanation for the ban in Indian law, where the historical lesson of the fatal divisiveness of religious parties is fresh, and recurrence a live possibility. But it does not fit well within the rubric of militant democracy if only because strict secularism is not universally seen as a defining characteristic of democracy. Certainly, public appeals to religious particularism are generally thought to be consistent with democracy, at least outside stern philosophies of public reason. Jacobsohn offers a second explanation for the Indian law by saying that "corrupt practices" undermine the *aspirational* principles of the Indian constitution. The national goal is the regulation of social and economic inequality, a problem historically inscribed in a hierarchical social order and correlated to religion. Invoking racial and religious divisions in the context of elections violates the principle of equality—which explains why the law is named "corrupt practices." Corruption is used in the theoretical sense of undermining this foundational value.

An alternative interpretation of this regulation is this: particularist appeals in the electoral context are impermissible because they are taken to deny that all citizens are Indian. That is, whether or not religious or ethnic appeals imply hatred or inequality, they fracture an ideally inclusive national identity. Electoral particularism is impermissible if parties are seen as standing in effect for different societies. Separatist parties are the most egregious but not the only challenge to national integrity and unity. One society understood as a fair system of cooperation among free and equal persons is incompatible with parties based on presumptively permanent religious or ethnic or status divisions. Recall the historical argument for the mixed regime: unity and stability secured by the political recognition of entrenched classes or social groups. When particularist parties structure democratic elections and group identity is built into the framework of government we have something like a mixed regime, at best a balanced complement of potentially hostile forces. One reason for India's parties law is the political judgment that given the nation's history, unrestricted particularism contributes to instability rather than equilibrium. But the reasoning is aspirational as well as pragmatic. Banning electoral appeals to "religion, race, caste, community or language or the use of or appeal to religious symbols" aims to preclude politically entrenched divisions. The problem with this justification for restriction of particularist parties is that the distribution of rights and benefits in democratic states is sometimes tied to group membership, as is the case in India. When multicultural democracies prescribe differential civil rights, it is understandable that the struggle for empowerment to preserve or alter these arrangements is waged through parties seeking political representation.[101] Because India officially organizes whole areas of life in terms of group membership, censorship of parties on grounds of institutionalizing difference in democratic politics is jarring. We can understand the proscription as a judgment of the requirements of civil peace and stability. But only a unitary civic view of democracy would justify outlawing partisan appeals to race or religion or ethnicity as undemocratic.

We recognize in the Indian law and other countries' proscriptions of parties based on religion or ethnicity the contours of the antiparty tradition that saw parties as fatally divisive. Certain parties and partisan activities exploit divisions. They are sinister engines of destructive partiality. They are "associated with painfully deep and unbridgeable differences in national politics, with religious bigotry and clerical animus, with treason and the threat of foreign invasion, with instability and dangers to liberty."[102] We recall the hierarchy of dangerousness that early antiparty thinkers worked up: Hume on the miseries caused by sectarian parties: "in modern times, parties of religion are more furious and enraged than the most cruel factions that ever arose from interest and ambition."[103] Legally inscribed regulations guard against these fatally divisive grounds of partisanship.

The Indian "corrupt practices" example is of particular interest because of its ambiguity. The antidemocratic nature of appeals to race or religion and fear of violence are not the only grounds for prohibition.

Justification also turns on the implications of particularist parties for the integrity and aspirational character of the Indian state. This directs attention to a third ground for banning parties, one that is even less aptly accommodated by orthodox "militant democracy": parties that challenge national identity.

Existential Danger

This category of justification for banning parties rests on existential threats to the state's identity. The concern to preserve political identity and integrity is older than contemporary multicultural challenges, of course; it is older than democracy, and not unique to democratic states either. From Aristotle's *Politics* (when is a city no longer the same city?) to the present, the character of a nation, some bedrock principle or practice, defining institution or unalterable constitutional core (the taboo against a constitutional amendment to erase the Bill of Rights, for example) is said to make it *this* state and is inviolable. Concerted advocacy or attempts via elections to alter these laws, constitution, treatment of groups, or national unity (secession or proposals for federalism) are equated with threats to identity and integrity, as existential threats to national survival. To be clear, identity need not be constitutionally defined as it was in Germany after the Second World War when the country set out political principles that could not be altered or amended. Simply, some boundary line, albeit a not-so-bright line, divides the aims of opposition parties from advocacy of what is taken to be a rival society *tout court*. The "survival" or "existence" at issue is not a matter of external conquest or violent overthrow of government from within, but using the electoral process to transform political identity. Even if parties conform to the norms of regulated rivalry and do not have antidemocratic objectives or agitate hatefully, they can be suppressed for threatening the identity of *this* democracy, this nation.

National identity has elements not encompassed by democracy, and in tension with it: the Jewish character of Israel, for example. ("Every Palestinian refugee who is homeless, and jobless, and countryless should be provided with a home, a job, a passport. Israel cannot admit these people, at least in vast numbers. If it does, it will no longer be Israel."[104]) Presumptively, at stake is the state's ethnic, racial, religious, or secular character. The standard "paradox of democracy" poses this question: if the unalterable character of the nation is democratic (as in the U.S. constitutional guarantee of a republican form of government), does a party's program or conduct threaten to subvert it? Here, the question is: if the constitution upholds secularism, what is the standard for distinguishing a party that wants to change the terms of the relation between state and mosque, for example, from a party that is "in the pocket of various Islamic brotherhoods . . . a gang of fundamentalists aiming to create an Islamic state"?[105] The perilously uncertain judgments of "reason of state" (when the state must violate its own principles in self-defense against enemies) and the equally uncertain judgments about when advocacy of radical political change is likely to result in violence or electoral victory with resultant intolerable policies are amplified here. Occasionally, the threatened element of identity is concrete: maintaining Jewish demographic superiority in Israel, for example. For the most part "identity" is more diffuse and not captured by subverting core democratic institutions.

Defending the identity of the state against parties that would alter it is an invitation to discrimination and exclusion. For one thing, the status quo is the baseline, precisely what parties organize to contest publicly. Preservation conflicts with interpretation and reinterpretation of political identity as part of the business of democracy. Existential threat as a justification for banning is an opening for essentialism. It bears traces of holist antipartyism. Though these party bans do not reflect wholesale opposition to pluralism and partisanship, still some notion of wholeness or integrity—territorial, ethnic, religious, secular—is inviolable.

It may be helpful to look at this category of political identity as a scaling up of a set of questions familiar to political theorists from the literature on multiculturalism and to legal scholars from constitutional law on religious free exercise. In assessing a group's demand for accommodation and exemption from general laws, courts typically inquire whether a practice is central to the group's identity.

When would obedience to civil law threaten the group's viability? Or if the viability standard is deemed too stringent, how substantial must the burden on the group be to mandate exemption or accommodation?[106] What aspect of authority, law, practice, or tenet is defining? Must the claim for religious exemption be theologically required, doctrinally compelled, the fulfillment of a religious duty, or is it sufficient that an act is dictated by religious belief? My point in repeating this set of questions posed by judges and decisive in opinions on religious freedom and accommodation is that the desire of nations to preserve their political identity in perpetuity and to ban parties that would alter it raises an analogous set of questions.

Another parallel to religious exemption and accommodation follows: should courts or legislatures defer to the group's own account of the centrality of the burden public policy imposes on faith? There is sound reluctance to base the judgment entirely on the group's (religious leaders') view of what is necessary for religious identity and community to survive and flourish. Similarly, who should define the inviolable elements of national political identity that serve as the ground for outlawing parties? Where the state is identified with a religious establishment or with a version of secularism, who speaks for the requirements of faith or separation? Where the state is an ethnic or multiethnic state, who decides whether partisanship on behalf of a particularist group undermines integrity, or the settled pluralist equilibrium? Normally, the interpreters are courts, and generally the legislature (partisans with seats) or executive is the prosecutor. It is typically a case of established authorities, a majority or entrenched minority, interpreting political identity and resisting democratic transformation by outlawing political challengers.[107]

This rationale for banning can apply not only to fringe parties or ferociously unpopular minorities but also to majorities. In France, the ban on head scarves in public schools affected Muslim minorities; in Turkey the ban (and a similar prohibition of beards in universities and other public institutions) touched religiously sensitive elements of most of the population. The Turkish Constitutional Court's defense of the principle of secularism is a prime example of an existential justification for banning parties. Article 2 of the

Constitution refers to the Republic of Turkey as a "democratic, secular and social State." Turkish law forbids using religious symbols for political ends, and to take one case, Recep Tayyip Erdogan, currently head of the Turkish government, served a prison term after reading a poem with religious imagery at a political campaign rally.[108] Laws defining secularism have been used to dissolve Islamic parties. In 1995 Welfare became the largest party in Turkey with 158 seats in the National Assembly and was dissolved in 1998 while the party was in power as part of a coalition government and Erbakan served as the first Islamic Prime Minister. Turkey also banned the Virtue Party in 2001, expelling several but not all of the more than one hundred Virtue MPs, one for supporting a female deputy who attempted to be sworn into the National Assembly while wearing a head scarf. The AKP ("Justice and Development Party") is the heir of Welfare and Virtue. The party challenged the constitutional principle of secularism in place since 1982. The Turkish example repays attention.

Turkey's Constitutional Preamble reads in part: "As required by the principles of secularism, there shall be no interference whatsoever by sacred religious feelings in state affairs and politics." The reference to "religious *feelings*" signals a stringently secular disposition with regard to politics. It expresses determination to eliminate religion from public political life.[109] Turkish separation of state and religion is one-directional, though; government is protected from religion but not vice versa. The Directorate of Religious Affairs operating under the authority of the prime minister's office was an essential part of the state structure, and the Political Parties Act of 1983 prohibited parties from campaigning to alter or eliminate it. Government was vested with the role of "guiding and controlling the organization of religious services" and religious personnel hired, paid, and controlled by the state. "Secularism" meant transcending the multiple Islamic identities and penetrating Islamic groups, including parties.[110] It did not mean no state interference in religious practice, leaving religious affairs and services to the communities, or leaving women alone to wear head scarves in universities and government offices—the issue that figured in the legal challenge to AKP. Parties that campaign to change this balance are subject to dissolution.[111] Interpreting and enforcing secularism lay with specific ruling groups, "we secularists."[112] Turkish secularism, it is fair to say, had the result of provoking the politicization of religion.

The national constitutional court's decision to uphold the ban on the Welfare Party in the late 1990s turned on the established interpretation of secularism. The party was dissolved on grounds that its leaders advocated wearing head scarves in state schools and buildings, and this position in the debate over head scarves was seen as advocacy of Shari'a (Islamic law) provisions and as a wedge for other legal changes in criminal law and the status of women.[113] "Democracy is the antithesis of sharia. . . . With adherence to the principle of secularism, values based on reason and science replaced dogmatic values. . . . Within a secular State, religious feelings simply cannot be associated with politics, public affairs and legislative provisions."[114] The European Court of Human Rights agreed that the party's claim to interpret secularism differently from official secularism was a pretext and that the party intended to introduce Shari'a law; the court affirmed the dissolution of the Welfare Party.[115] But with a difference: where the Turkish Court appealed chiefly to secularism as a core element of national identity, the European Court on Human Rights used the orthodox standard of incompatibility with democracy and human rights. Secularism, the ECHR wrote, is "in harmony with" democracy (stopping short of affirming secularism as a defining characteristic of democracy). Instead, the European Court focused on the Welfare Party's intent to set up a plurality of legal systems which on the Court's view would lead to discrimination based on religion and would threaten national legislative and judicial unity: the party "would do away with the State's role as the guarantor of individual rights and freedoms and the impartial organizer of the practice of the various beliefs and religions in a democratic society."[116] Under pressure from the ECHR, the Turkish Court did modify its position to the extent of ruling that advocating removal of the Department of Religious Affairs is not sufficient reason to dissolve a party. It began in this way to disentangle stringent secularism from Turkey's political identity as a democracy.[117] But in a 2004 case involving religious symbols, the ECHR again agreed with Turkey's Constitutional Court that the ban on head scarves in universities was consistent with its defining historical experience and even in the absence of disturbance of public order did not "breach the principle of pluralism."[118]

The Turkish Court has also banned Kurdish parties, again to pre-serve national identity. Here, the constitutional anchor is "territorial integrity of the state and unity of the nation." "Territorial integrity" outlaws separatist parties, and "unity of the nation" outlaws parties advocating federalism or autonomous rule. In practice, it outlaws parties based on minority identity. The HEP party was indicted for aiming to destroy the "inseparable unity" existing between the Turk-ish state and the Turkish people. According to this argument, the Kurds were part of the Turkish nation, and the party's claim to rep-resentation on ethnic grounds amounted to separatism. HEP had the confounding task of demanding the right to represent a specific ethnic group in elections while challenging the idea that assertions of cultural and linguistic distinction were per se attempts to create a politicized minority with separatist aims. The Court upheld the ban, ruling that groups could follow their traditions but insisted these could not become a basis for claiming minority status or political representation; the domain of politics must exclude cultural "partic-ularities." HEP impermissibly "expressed a desire to establish a new social order based on race."[119] It defied unitary political identity. In 2005 the ECHR heard an appeal from the Democracy and Change Party (DEP), which had been dissolved on grounds that behind its stated aim of promoting the Kurdish language was the real aim of subverting Turkish territorial integrity and national unity. The Euro-pean Court ruled that the DEP's program was not contrary to fun-damental principles of democracy and that there was no "pressing social need" for the ban, holding Turkey in violation of Article 11 of the Convention, freedom of association.

The best known examples of the existential justification for ban-ning parties are cases from Israel. The Declaration of Independence calls for Israel to be both a Jewish state and a democracy, and the delicate balance between these two reasons for banning—denying Israel as a democracy and as a Jewish state—has been described as "deliberate irresolution."[120] In 1964 two Arab parties, El Ard and the

Socialists List, were disqualified for negating Israel's existence by espousing pan-Arab nationalism and solutions to the Palestinian issue based on "the will of the Palestinian people." This was seen as aiming at the destruction of the state of Israel.[121] The high court upheld the ban, ruling that the state of Israel is coincident with its Jewish character. A concurring opinion in *Yeridor* in 1965 laid out the argument in full. The internal order of government is not sacred and its alteration is not a crime, but Israel's Jewish character *is* unalterable. Arab citizens must participate within the framework of the state, and "state" entails Israel's uniquely Jewish identity.[122] The parties' platforms justified restricting participation in elections.

In 1984, challenges to the Arab-Jewish PLP ("Progressive List for Peace") led to Amendment 7A of the Basic Law, which set out three criteria for disqualifying party lists: denying the existence of the State of Israel as the state of the Jewish people, denying the democratic character of the state, and inciting racism. PLP protested the Jewish character requirement and called for Israel to become "a state of all its citizens," a binational state. (Yoav Peled insists, "The PLP was the mirror image of Kach. Both agreed that Israel could not be both Jewish and democratic. Kach said that Israel had to be a Jewish state and not democratic; PLP said that Israel had to be democratic and not Jewish."[123]) Those urging disqualification argued that avowal of Israel's Jewish character was a prerequisite for serving in the Knesset; loyalty to the state meant loyalty to the Zionist state. In the earlier case, El Ard's platform had called for establishing an Arab state in Israel; here, the PLP called for an ethnically neutral one ("Israel is the state of its Jewish and Arab citizens"). In a 3–2 decision in *Neiman,* the Israeli Court upheld participation by the PLP, but without resolving the tension between democratic and Jewish identity. The Court did not distinguish negating Israel's Jewish character from negating its existence. But the Court did interpret negation of the state's Jewish character narrowly so as to protect the party. Statements by PLP leaders did not amount to a clear intent or unambiguous program or a sufficiently central or dominant aim, the Court ruled; they do not rise to the level of threat posed by El Ard's pan-nationalism and what was judged its determination to erase Israel's existence. As one concurring

Justice wrote, the PLP represented another viewpoint within Israeli politics and did not present "a clear or immediate" threat.[124]

My point is that existential justifications for banning parties are an independent standard and cannot be assimilated to democratic self-protection. Attempts to justify banning parties by arguing that a majority group has a right to self-determination do not hold up. It may be that a democratic majority or coalition elects to protect essentialist characteristics such as Israel's identity as a Jewish state. But it does so democratically only when it is the result of democratic decisions and not by banning parties that challenge it. There may be good moral and political reasons to defend the Jewish character of Israel even at the expense of the fundamental right to political participation by parties whose goal is a multinational or purely secular state. The preservation of national identity may take priority over liberal or democratic elements. But to cast defense of identity or integrity as democratic self-defense regardless of its costs to democratic participation is sheer confusion. It ignores Isaiah Berlin's admonition that not all values are complementary; that politics may require tragic choices.

No "moment of appreciation" intervenes to temper suppression and exclusion of parties that pose existential challenges. There is no impartial observer's standpoint, discerning the useful complementarity between secular and religious parties; no Millian dialectic of mutual correction and improvement from the parties of nationalists and separatists. In pluralist democracies the coexistence of parties proposing and defending against alterations in the dominant understanding of political identity is even more inescapable than the unnerving "paradox of democracy." Banning parties in defense of identity, integrity, unity stirs whispers of the glorious tradition of antiparty holism and still stronger echoes of fear of fatal divisiveness.

Democratic Self-Determination: Outside Support and Control

Control by a foreign government was the weightiest factor in the judgment that the CP USA was "not really a party." Parties are supposed to be organized democratically, or at least in a nonauthoritarian, nondictatorial manner. They are supposed to be responsive to their members and supporters, to contributors, or to the public interest, not to foreign governments and outside political groups. Outside support and control is the fourth justification for banning parties. This category does not have the same status in law or political theory as violence, hate, and political identity. Rules prohibiting campaign contributions and expenditures by noncitizens are taken for granted, and punishment for violation falls far short of banning or exclusion. But this justification for banning is not as obvious or mundane as campaign funding law might suggest, and outside support for parties is a serious matter today. For partisanship does not respect national boundaries. As much or more than in the era of international socialism (though typically without formal organizations), parties and partisans look outside. Multiculturalism, the movements of peoples, and globalization lead to parties supported, managed, or controlled by leaders abroad. Even a small party can loom large if it is identified with a foreign government, a vocal alien population, or a wealthy and politically energized émigré group. The question comes to a head when parties profess that their primary loyalties are to the group, not the nation, made more potent when the group extends outside national borders, and reaching its acme when a party identifies with enemies of the state. Less dramatic conditions suffice for weak parties or those denied public funding to appeal to international networks for money, materials, and organizational support.

The straightforward rationale for restrictions on outside support is that it is impermissible interference in domestic political affairs by a foreign government, a political party in a foreign country, or an international political organization. The scope of democratic representation is national (or based on sub-national political units), and outside control violates self-rule. Political parties are supposed to be responsive to their supporters at home and to the electorate as a whole, not to foreigners. There is also the simple fear of corruption of elected representatives indebted to outsiders, their votes on specific issues bought. Any foreign influence is "undue influence," though

447

we recognize that the situation is more complicated when support comes from émigrés or an ethnic or religious diaspora. International law on the right of self-determination sets limits on interference in domestic politics by other states. Matters are acute when parties receive support from foreign governments, and clandestine assistance is most egregious. The Soviet Union provided financial assistance to CP USA, and a consistent theme of judicial decisions focused on the fact that the party was not an independent political party but a constituent element of the worldwide Communist movement controlled by foreign agents.[125] There are myriad examples of foreign support, most obviously when the CIA channeled money to pro-American and anticommunist parties in Europe and Latin America.

The argument against interference in domestic political affairs can be turned on its head, however. Countries that are signatories to international conventions have an obligation to maintain democratic elections and arguably to enact self-protective legislation against antidemocratic parties.[126] This raises the question whether international enforcement of democracy is justified, and whether it includes outside support—governmental or nongovernmental—for democratic political parties or for efforts to undermine antidemocratic ones. U.S. Secretary of State Condoleezza Rice declined to interfere with Hamas' participation in Palestinian elections in 2006: "This is going to be a Palestinian process, and I think we have to give the Palestinians some room for the evolution of their political process."[127] But the normative question remains: what incentives can outsiders justifiably offer to encourage Hamas to give up arms; what punitive measures? Is there a positive mandate for outside support (or opposition) for certain parties as a fulfillment of international obligations?

Justifications for banning parties or prohibiting outside support rooted in the general principle of sovereignty or democratic self-determination specifically come up against the real world of democracy where outside/inside is not as sharp morally or politically as it is legally. (Not even legally, as the EU demonstrates, where the call for transnational parties for election to the EU Parliament is growing, and the absence of European parties contributes to the view that the constitutional regime suffers a democratic deficit.) As a matter of political theory, certainly, proscriptions against outside support cannot be resolved by appealing to self-determination without further argument. For these prohibitions respect a strict domestic/foreign divide that cuts against the grain of contemporary political theories where the moral arbitrariness of state boundaries is a frequent theme.

Take the moral claim that democratic participation is owed all those whose interests are "affected" by decisions, not just those with formal rights of citizenship and suffrage. At a minimum it opens up arguments for the potential extension of political rights to resident nationals from other states—immigrants, guest workers, refugees. Some of the reasons for differential civil and political rights extend beyond those who are not naturalized citizens or residents to cover émigrés or neighboring populations. The movement of peoples challenges formal civic- and state-centered participation. Indeed, on the "affected interest" standard, the reach is potentially boundless.[128] Reflecting on the meaning of citizenship and on the demands of distributive justice, political theorists raise questions and propose principles for the allocation of political rights to participation. But parties and outside support for them pose a separate question from the franchise. Individuals and groups do not need to vote in order to "associate" with and "support" parties by providing funding, materials, organizational expertise, leadership, or publicity. When is prohibition of outside support for parties justifiable? Émigrés or ethnic groups in neighboring countries or diaspora have reasons for political engagement different from those of other interested outsiders. One way of formulating the question for political theory is whether partisanship is derivative of citizenship. Or is partisanship the larger, umbrella category and citizens' rights of political association are one but not the only framework for party organization and contestation?

I do not mean to endorse outside support or transnational parties. I raise the matter here to suggest that outside support and control, once an unchallenged justification for regulating or disqualifying parties, merits reconsideration. A sympathetic literature in social science and in political theory applauds the creation of transnational civil society organizations on matters ranging from building dams to human rights groups. In most writing on the subject, these social and political associations are applauded. Not parties. Here too, the subject of political parties is pretty much ignored, despite the fact that common political sympathies among religious and ethnic groups do not respect borders, that parties support groups and causes outside their country, and that domestic party leaders and organizations receive support from outside as well.

Faith in Politics

Every move to ban parties is infused with a mix of elements—the appetite to get or keep power, fear of subversion or social and political instability, sheer abhorrence. Political self-defense against violence, incitement to hate, existential challenges to national identity, and external interference in elections are subject to interpretation and vulnerable to discriminatory application. Moreover, justifications for proscription are typically framed in terms of "necessity," always ambiguous. The similarity between orthodox "militant democracy" and preserving political identity is that "identity," like "subversive" and "antidemocratic," invokes "necessity," even if the likelihood and proximity of harm are radically uncertain. These judgments are bound to be a mix of principle, prudential considerations, and fear and loathing. The questions of how much electoral support are religious or ethnicity-based parties likely to have and would a place in government have the feared results are addressed in the haze of felt danger.

As "necessity" suggests, the considerations for disqualifying parties are generally immediate, the perspective short-term. Longer term considerations like the "bad tendency" to erode democratic dispositions and the positive conditions for democratic reproduction are invoked in the context of bans on political hate speech by parties and candidates, for example, but in practice immediate political concerns dominate. Social science studies of the long-term implications of party organization are valuable because they extend the time-frame. Using the experience of European fascist regimes as a baseline, social scientists have attempted to explain why the nations of Western Europe became democratic between 1848 and 1921, why so many survived the crisis of the interwar period, and why Germany, Italy, Portugal, and Spain were spectacular failures.[129] The party system and the character of parties is one important element. Studies draw parallels between this bit of European history and parties in democracies outside Europe today, with the shift in focus I have emphasized away from antidemocratic political ideologies and toward parties based on ethnic and religious cleavages with the potential to change a nation radically from secular to religious, from civic to ethnic, and vice versa. (These questions resonate today in Europe too, of course, and to a lesser extent in the United States, with the politicization of ethnic and religious groups and the potential for particularist parties or religious wings of major parties and intense, targeted electoral mobilization.)

My point is that these studies address not only democratic failure but also the democratizing potential of parties. The consensus among historians is that in Europe (and something similar holds for the United States, as we have seen) "the politicization of religion had beneficial effects for democratic development. By integrating newly enfranchised groups and by turning them from opponents into supporters of parliamentary democracy, confessional parties contributed to the consolidation of democratic regimes." Indeed, on this view, "the CDU [Christian Democratic Union], not the more thoroughly studied Social Democratic Party, integrated those who needed to be integrated—the cultural and political conservatives—into a durable liberal order."[130] Studies explore the conditions that move a group organized as a party from "radical rejectionism to mainstream politics."[131] Islamic parties in Turkey are cast as a possible parallel. From Welfare to Virtue to the AKP Party, the challenge of religious parties whose agendas include changing the religious policies of the state has moderated in ways that recall European Christian Democracy. Unlike Islamists "with their visions of rule by shari'a (Islamic law) or even a restored caliphate," Muslim party leaders in Turkey are described today as having the mundane goal "of crafting viable electoral platforms and stable governing coalitions to serve individual and collective interests—Islamic as well as secular."[132] The dominant Islamic party has expanded its constituency beyond its religious supporters

and brought new groups into electoral politics. Democratic integration, the argument goes, has been encouraged in Turkey by institutional constraints on these parties (including the cautionary history
of bans imposed by the Turkish Court, the European Court, and the
military). In political science terms, political entrepreneurs come to
judge that their ambitions are better served by effectively signaling
moderation than by maintaining oppositional poses, spurred above
all by the iteration of elections and political learning. This does not
ensure that particularist parties have a deep ideological commitment
to every element of democracy or to the established regime of secularism (or establishment) or unity, only that electoral political competition, like any strong institutional practice, is formative. Social scientists speak of a "virtuous cycle" in this connection. The imperatives
of regulated rivalry are the force for political integration. "Muslim
Democrats are in the streets looking for votes and in the process are
changing Islam's relation to politics."[133]

Political science brings out other factors that speak to long-term
political incorporation and acculturation through parties and partisanship. In numerous contexts, lay organizers of religious parties
challenge the exclusive authority of clerics. Shaping and activating
religious political identity, they do not frontally wrest interpretive
authority from religious leaders or claim to be *the* voice of faith, but
political entrepreneurs do interpret the political significance of faith
(only sometimes on theological grounds), and as a result, churches
and clerics lose their "monopoly over the definition" of the faith and
the representation of the faithful.[134]

In democracies "faith in politics" has the potential for democratic
acculturation. At a minimum, religious and ethnic parties reflect the
logic of denominationalism applied to politics; that is, they accept
that they are not the one or universal faith. Entry into electoral politics often entails the need to argue that what is good for the group is
also a public good (or no public harm). Religious and ethnic groups
are induced to cast their demands in terms that apply beyond themselves. These assertions are aspirational, of course. It assumes a long-
term view, which courts and legislators with the task of permitting
or banning parties often do not take, and claim they cannot. These

final thoughts on democratic integration via party organization do not speak to the particulars of any given party. They do not tell us how national election laws should be written, nor when the imperatives of "militant democracy" and defense against hate, changes to national identity, and outside intervention are justifiably invoked. I offer this brief consideration and the double entendre "faith in politics" simply as a counterweight and to say that the subject is ripe for attention by democratic theorists.

"Orphans of Political Philosophy" Again

The subject of substantive antipartyism and justifiable bans on parties and disqualification of partisans has been neglected by political theorists, one final instance of the observation that political parties are the "orphans" of political philosophy. Political commentary flourishes, but the academic literature on the subject is slight. I do not know of any comprehensive collection of cases or comprehensive discussion in political or legal theory of substantive antipartyism and prohibition.[135] Where discussion exists, it is stagnant, fixed on the orthodox terms of "militant democracy." Except for invoking democratic principles, theorists have little to say about justifiable antipartyism and exclusion. Why has political theory not addressed the changed threats and the new limits governments place on political parties today? Why has political theory not addressed how pluralism has altered or eclipsed the classic "paradox of democracy"?

In other places I have written about the "cold shoulder" contemporary liberal democratic theory turns toward particularist parties based on religion, race, and ethnicity, especially.[136] Philosophically, the aversion owes to the fact that these parties combine two things theorists finds normatively challenging if not disqualifying as grounds for democratic decision making. I refer to the arguments advanced by theorists of public reason and deliberative democracy who scrupulously consider whether political justification should or should not accommodate either religious and ethnic appeals or appeals to partisanship, much less the two combined.[137] Parties are "mere interest groups, petitioning the government on their own behalf,"[138] and

453

partisanship is identified with resistance to the changes of mind and heart via rational discussion that deliberative democracy encourages. "Much political debate," John Rawls laments, "betrays the marks of warfare ... rallying the troops and intimidating the other side."[139] Even apart from stern public reason and deliberation, heightened aversion toward particularist parties expressed by virtually the whole company of democratic theorists is not hard to explain given the glorious tradition that saw parties as fatally divisive. Today, too, it rests on fear that religious and ethnic party conflict will escape the bounds of regulated rivalry. Hume's caution that religious parties bring madness, fury, fatal divisions, misery, and devastation is with us.[140]

The implicit assumption in democratic theory, implicit because the subject is seldom pursued, is that parties based on religious, ethnic, racial, or cultural identity are uniquely dangerous. Among the grim assumptions: religious and ethnic parties are not "real parties"; they are opportunistic and not committed to electoral democracy. They are intransigent, uncompromising, militant if not militaristic. Religious political claims aim at bending law and policy to the imperatives of a single faith, and ethnic parties at imposing a single ethnic identity on public life. These parties are authoritarian in their organization and goals; the religious party's hold on members owes to coercion of the faithful by clerical authorities and the ethnic party's on an ascriptive rather than voluntary identity politics imposed by self-selected leaders.

These are empirical claims. Each is rebuttable. On the one hand, parties of all kinds may be unyielding, "extremist"; to them, justice demands meeting their demands; they may be holist and opportunistic and do not acknowledge their own partiality. On the other hand, all kinds of parties concede that they are parts and learn that compromise yields benefits. Similar charges have been leveled against ideological parties and parties based on economic and class cleavages, as we know.[141] Political science has a lot to say about credible incentives for moderation and political accommodation, that is, for participation in regulated rivalry. Nonetheless, in democratic theory, the assumption of fatal divisiveness sets these parties apart from the larger field of unpalatable parties, and often enough outside the pale.

Political theorists do speculate, however, about how to make decisions under conditions of disagreement based on religion or ethnicity. Typically, their prescriptions avoid partisan mobilization and are (comparatively) depoliticized, at least removed from parties and electoral politics. As Robert Dahl put it, "conflicts involving subcultures . . . are too explosive to be managed by ordinary parliamentary opposition, bargaining, campaigning, and winning elections."[142] Instead, theorists look to "pillarization," "consociationalism," or some sort of equilibrium based on informal understandings among political elites able "to forge tactical agreements and tension-relieving compromises."[143] A common theme in democratic political theory is group representation without parties, and antipartyism is the default position of even the most sympathetic theorists of identity politics. One philosopher of multiculturalism, for example, recommends public forums for cultivating a "dialogically constituted multicultural society" and prescribes institutional venues such as an "interreligious consultative council" to make representations to government. He insists, however, that "the national parliament is not such a place for it is divided along party lines, unused to debating large questions, might not include minority representatives, and so forth."[144] Most often, democratic theorists favor delegating judgments to independent courts in hope of removing them from political arenas.[145]

This chapter is a promissory note, then. It constitutes an appeal to political theorists to turn attention to the reasons for substantive antipartyism and justifications for banning parties (and, of course, to the larger subject of parties and partisanship). Parties associated with violence, with hate, with challenges to the identity of the nation, with ties to outside groups that undermine the relevance of borders for partisan politics require at least as much careful thought from political theory as they do empirical study from political science. They provoke the sort of antiparty arguments and justifications for banning I have laid out. They recall the glorious traditions of antipartyism. When for good reasons parties are protected and allowed to organize lines of division and mobilize partisans, they revive moments of appreciation as well.

Conclusion: "We Partisans"

Contemporary antipartyism is easy to document: parties depress participation; parties "turn voters off;" parties are captured by special interest groups or rich donors; party positions are too centrist or too extremist; parties do not contribute to public understanding of men or measures; they are unresponsive to public opinion or to the public interest. These (and many other) discontents with parties and partisans are expressed by pundits, on the one hand, by philosophers, on the other, and often enough by partisans themselves. "We partisans" are always on the side of the angels, but not even partisans defend parties or partisanship beyond their own.

I have retrieved rare moments of appreciation from the long history of antipartyism and proposed my own: regulated rivalry, governing, and a stripped-down philosophical defense in which parties are deliberating agents and arenas. I have cast parties as a principal source of political creativity—a role acknowledged implicitly in disparaging descriptions of parties inventing "artificial and nominal" divisions and in the thought that "the smallest appearance of real difference" suffices as an excuse for contesting for power. This criticism should not be damning. For creating lines of division is the achievement of partisanship, and the heart of introducing a "power into the political world." Without it "trial by discussion" cannot hope to shape political decisions. Through parties interests and opinions are organized and brought into opposition, their consequences are drawn out. "The clash of political beliefs, and of the interests and attitudes that are likely to influence them"[1] do not spontaneously assume a form amenable to democratic debate and decision. Someone must organize Mill's serious conflict of opposing reasons. Someone must create the lines of division over social aims, security, and justice. Party rivalry is constitutive. It "stages the battle."

Partisans are necessary to realize the value of parties. Parties require "the rough process of a struggle between combatants fighting under hostile banners." The challenges parties pose to one another's principles and policies have force when they come "from persons who actually believe them, who defend them in earnest, and do their utmost for them."[2]

I have also flipped perspectives, arguing that parties are necessary to realize the value of partisanship. The virtues I assign partisanship—inclusiveness, comprehensiveness, and a disposition to compromise—are crucial for politics in pluralist societies. They distinguish partisanship from other political identities, and give the lie to the notion that an intelligent and progressive democratic system depends on the ability of citizens to attain a nonpartisan spirit. Above all, partisans are personally, positively identified with the ongoing business of regulated rivalry. Partisanship is the political identity that does not see pluralism and political conflict as a bow to necessity. This commitment entails political self-restraint, mental and emotional discipline, for partisans see themselves as firmly on the side of the angels, but acknowledge their partiality. Partisans do not imagine that their party speaks for the whole. They concede their party's status as just a part in a permanently pluralist politics, and with it the provisional nature of being the governing (or losing) party. They do not withdraw, detach, and passively or cynically leave democracy to others; the "we" of party ID is sustaining. All this makes partisanship *the* political identity distinctive of representative democracy, and connects partisanship with the practice of democratic citizenship.

On the Side of the Angels is a first look at parties and partisanship. I have left a lot undone. For one thing, I have only skimmed the surface of historical antipartyism. I have identified some of the canonical arguments about the danger of parties and some of the reasons why the logic of pluralism does not always lead to parties. Still, the status of political pluralism in the work of our greatest writers and its often explicit severance from partisanship remains underexplored. Approached with this theme in mind, both individual texts and the course of modern political thought could be illuminated, the heroes of pluralism given their due.

My discussion of contemporary democratic theory also left remainders. I have said something about "elite" theory, interest group pluralism, and deliberative democracy, but future work could explore in greater detail their particular reasons for depreciating partisanship. Moreover, the contemporary materials I have introduced are mainly American. I believe that comparative politics especially of multiparty systems will confirm both the critiques and the measures of appreciation I have laid out. It would take another essay to demonstrate that "the moral distinctiveness of party ID"—inclusiveness, comprehensiveness, and disposition to compromise—applies to these systems. Further study would also underscore the fact that Independence has a special place in American political life and thought. Chapter 9 on "militant democracy" is also a promissory note: in a first pass at comparison I identified the set of standards by which a wide range of democratic systems judge certain parties unlawful. They demonstrate the commonalities of permissible pluralism, and what sort of parties are beyond the democratic pale.

Finally, there is a lot to say about how institutional arrangements and normative expectations could shape the work parties do, and I have said little about prescriptions. My appreciation of regulated rivalry led me to approve of correctives to party entrenchment and to reject proposals that aim to circumvent or eliminate parties or starve them of resources. I have been critical of civil society theory when enthusiasm for membership in voluntary associations and advocacy groups comes at the cost of diminishing partisanship. But it remains to set out a better account of the positive relation between civil society groups and parties. Prescriptions for improving parties' role in political education and mobilization, the quality of participation, communicating information, delineating stakes, assisting deliberation by identifying points of conflict and commonality are a separate sub-ject, which I intend to pursue. Readers should not take my appre-ciation of parties and partisanship for complacency. As I said in my introduction, it is one thing to show why democratic theorists should adopt these orphans of philosophy and take them in. Rehabilitation of parties in practice is another matter, deserving of whatever scrap of utopianism is in us.

In retrospect, I see this book as an act of reparation. In *Member-ship and Morals: The Personal Uses of Pluralism in America,* I talked about freedom of association for groups of all kinds, but gave parties short shrift. My neglect provided impetus for assessing the absence of discussion of parties in contemporary democratic theory, and the bad scent of parties in political theory broadly. Antipartyism was my original subject, and remained an organizing principle for much of this book. But early on, I came to see parties as the distinctive, defin-ing voluntary associations of representative democracy. Thinking my way to the achievements of parties and the virtues of partisanship was an unexpected detour that became an unanticipated homecoming.

NOTES

Introduction: An Appreciation of Parties and Partisanship

1. E. E. Schattschneider, *Party Government* (New York: Holt, Rinehart, 1942), 10.

2. Hannah Pitkin, *The Concept of Representation* (Berkeley: University of California Press, 1967).

3. Why on its own terms is the politics of difference antipartisan? For one thing, difference demands the politics of presence vs. representation. The distinct perspective or voice must be preserved, not incorporated within an umbrella party. Of course, the politics of difference might conduce to a system of multiple parties and proportional representation. But characteristically, the politics of difference favors nonelectoral groups—advocacy groups and movements—with presumptively stronger and more meaningful connections to supporters than political parties. Compared with interest, advocacy, and identity groups, parties are seen as "too blunt to serve as a link" with the functional powerholders of society. Otto Kirchheimer, "The Transformation of the Western European Party System," in *Political Parties and Political Development*, ed. Joseph LaPalombara and Myron Weiner (Princeton: Princeton University Press, 1966), 177–200.

4. Nancy L. Rosenblum, "Political Parties as Membership Groups," *Columbia Law Review* 100, no. 3 (April 2000): 813–44. For a full discussion, see Nancy L. Rosenblum, *Membership and Morals: The Personal Uses of Pluralism in America* (Princeton: Princeton University Press, 1998). The quotation is from Amy Gutmann and Dennis F. Thompson, *Democracy and Disagreement* (Cambridge: Harvard University Press, 1996), 12, 359.

5. Robert E. Goodin and John S. Dryzek, "Deliberative Impacts: The Macro-Political Uptake of Mini-Publics," *Politics and Society* 34, no. 2 (2006): 219–44, 221. I discuss exceptions in chapter 6.

6. Anthony Downs, *An Economic Theory of Democracy* (New York: Harper, 1957), 34. In a recent overview of the empirical literature on parties, Susan C. Stokes observes: "positive democratic theorists are more likely to view parties not as a weed

but as a necessary microbe lodged deep in the digestive tract—not pretty, but vital to keeping the body politic in good health." "Political Parties and Democracy," *Annual Review of Political Science* 2 (1999): 243–67, 244.

7. Adam Przeworski proposes that in political science, as in theory, democracy is a positive, evaluative term. He asks whether there is "good reason to think that if rulers are selected through contested elections then political decisions will be rational, governments will be representative, and the distribution of income will be egalitarian." He concludes not. But he points to the "miracle" of peaceful regulation of conflict in "Minimalist Conception of Democracy: A Defense," in *Democracy's Value*, ed. Ian Shapiro and Casiano Hacker-Cordon (Cambridge: Cambridge University Press, 1999), 23–55, 25, 44–45.

8. Schattschneider, quoted in John H. Aldrich, *Why Parties?* (Chicago: University of Chicago Press, 1995), 3. There are exceptions: six small Pacific archipelagos with cultural resistance to contestation have democratic elections without parties: Micronesia, Kiribati, Marshall Islands, Tuvalu, Belau, and Nauru. See Dag Anckar and Carsten Anckar, "Democracy without Parties," *Comparative Political Studies* 33, no. 2 (2000): 225–47.

9. Aristotle's "wisdom of the multitude" was part of an argument for a mixed regime, not democracy. Josiah Ober provides this assessment of Aristotle on democracy: "The 'best possible' regime was designed by the philosopher as an alternative to democracy, which was the 'best corrupt' regime and the default choice for actual regimes 'these days.'" *Political Dissent in Democratic Athens: Intellectual Critics of Popular Rule* (Princeton: Princeton University Press, 1998), 316, 323. Ober notes too that "no real democrat would want to argue from the grounds Aristotle imputes to defenders of democratic justice" (318). Prevailing assumptions about democratic knowledge (and its social construction) dictated the character of philosophical criticism we find, most famously, in Plato. Josiah Ober, "How to Criticize Democracy in Late Fifth and Fourth Century Athens," in *Athenian Political Thought and the Reconstruction of Democracy*, ed. J. Peter Euben, John R. Wallach, and Josiah Ober (Ithaca: Cornell University Press, 1994), 149–71.

10. Wilfried Nippel observes that a historian invited to talk about ancient republicanism faces a fundamental problem: ancient political theory in the fifth and fourth centuries focused on republican cities and their problems maintaining liberty and stability. "Existing monarchies are considered only as survivals from a remote past or as forms of government typical of semi-barbarian areas at the periphery of the Greek world." The city-state of self-governing citizens was considered the only legitimate form of political organization. The threat to city-states was tyranny. "Ancient and Modern Republicanism: 'Mixed Constitution' and 'Ephors,'" in *The Invention of the Modern Republic*, ed. Biancamaria Fontana (Cambridge: Cambridge University Press, 1994), 6–26, 6. It is also the case that "the leading forgers of the antidemocratic tradition which was to dominate western political theory for two millennia not only suffered from class bias, but also had personal axes to grind." Cf. Carl J. Richard, *The*

Founders and the Classics: Greece, Rome, and the American Enlightenment (Cambridge, MA: Harvard University Press, 1994), 124.

11. Richard, *Founders*, 234. Richard points out that the American thinkers who turned to Athens were antebellum southerners in support of slavery (241).

12. Justice Scalia's dissent in *Rutan et al. v. Republican Party of Illinois,* 497 U.S. 62 (1990) at 106.

13. Because political leadership needs to be renewed, and because the ritual of democratic elections as currently understood requires political parties, the state provides (or guarantees) parties. Richard S. Katz and Peter Mair, "Changing Models of Party Organization and Party Democracy: The Emergence of the Cartel Party," *Party Politics* 1, no. 1 (1995): 5–28, 22.

14. Harvey C. Mansfield, Jr., *Statesmanship and Party Government* (Chicago: University of Chicago Press, 1965), 178, citing Burke.

15. Bernard Crick, *In Defense of Politics* (London: Continuum, 2000), 15.

16. Giovanni Sartori, *Parties and Party Systems* (Cambridge: Cambridge University Press, 1976), 77.

17. Hume, "Of Parties in General," in *Hume: Political Essays*, ed. Knud Haakonssen (Cambridge: Cambridge University Press, 1994), 33–34. The quote continues: "factions subvert government, render laws impotent, and beget the fiercest animosities among men of the same nation."

18. Letter 1789, cited in Harvey C. Mansfield, Jr., ed., *Selected Writings of Jefferson* (Arlington Heights, IL: AHM Publishers, 1979), xli.

19. *OED* Online 2004 entry for "party." Available at http://www.oed.com/.

20. Burke, cited in Mansfield, *Statesmanship and Party Government*, 166.

21. Schattschneider, *Party Government*, 37.

22. Mansfield, *Statesmanship and Party Government*, 1.

23. Crick, *In Defense*, 18. In this spirit, Sartori wrote that "parties are correlative to, and dependent upon, the *Weltanschauung* of liberalism." *Parties and Party Systems*, 13.

24. Theodore Lowi and Joseph Romance, *A Republic of Parties? Debating the Two-Party System* (Lanham, MD: Rowman and Littlefield, 1998), 5.

25. John Ferejohn helped me see this point.

26. I do not take up the discouraging theses that deny the efficacy of political agency in any currently imaginable form, especially modern constitutional democracies, vis-à-vis dominant and dominating forces insulated from our wills and purposes. Usually the focus is on "states in the maw of the global economy." John Dunn, *The Cunning of Unreason: Making Sense of Politics* (New York: Basic Books, 2000), 354.

27. Gaetano Mosca, *The Ruling Class* (New York: McGraw-Hill, 1939), 177.

28. Maurice Duverger, *Political Parties: Their Organization and Activity in the Modern State* (New York: John Wiley and Sons, 1954), xv.

29. Cited in Bruce L. Kinzer, "J. S. Mill and the Problem of Party," *Journal of British Studies* 21, no. 1 (1981): 106–22, 111.

30. John Stuart Mill, "On Liberty," in *The Collected Works of John Stuart Mill*, ed. John M. Robson, vol. 18, *Essays on Politics and Society, Part I* (Toronto: University of Toronto Press, 1963–91), 253.

31. John Rawls, *A Theory of Justice*, revised ed. (Cambridge, MA: Harvard University Press, 1999), 195–96; Rawls, *Justice as Fairness: A Restatement* (Cambridge, MA: Harvard University Press, 2001), 118.

32. Theodore Roosevelt, *American Ideals and Other Essays, Social and Political* (New York and London: G. P. Putnam's Sons and Knickerbocker Press, 1897), 38.

33. Henry Adams, *Democracy: An American Novel* (New York: Airmont Publishing, 1968).

34. "On the Side of the Angels" is the title song in the musical *Fiorello* (music by Jerry Bock, lyrics by Sheldon Harnick, book by Jerome Weidman and George Abbott; opened 1959). However, it was coined by Benjamin Disraeli in an 1864 speech at Oxford University against Darwinism ("The question is this: Is man an ape or an angel? Now I am on the side of the angels") but has since come to mean "supporting the good side" (*American Heritage Dictionary of Idioms*, s.v. "on the side of the angels").

35. John Rawls uses the phrase in *Political Liberalism* (New York: Columbia University Press, 2005), 449. Russell Muirhead and Nancy L. Rosenblum, "Political Liberalism vs. 'The Great Game of Politics': The Politics of Political Liberalism," *Perspectives on Politics* 4, no. 1 (2006): 99–108.

36. That is the question with which Sartori opens his work, *Parties and Party Systems*, 40. His answer is that "a modern society cannot be left unchanneled. Modern societies need to be or become 'pervasively politicized society'" (42).

37. Daniel Defoe, "On Government by Parties," in J.A.W. Gunn, *Factions No More: Attitudes to Party in Government and Opposition in Eighteenth-Century England* (London: Frank Cass, 1971), 86.

38. Roosevelt, *American Ideals*, 76.

39. Jesse Macy, *Party Organization and Machinery* (New York: Arno Press, 1974 [1912]), 2.

40. Hillaire Belloc and Cecil Chesterton, *The Party System* (London: Steven Swift, 1911), 110.

41. Theodore Roosevelt, in *History of U.S. Political Parties*, vol. 3: *1910–1945: From Square Deal to New Deal*, ed. Arthur M. Schlesinger Jr. (New York: Chelsea House, 1973), 2604.

42. Lincoln Steffens, *The Autobiography of Lincoln Steffens* (New York: Harcourt, Brace, 1931), 394.

43. Philip Pettit, "Democracy, Electoral and Contestatory," in *Nomos XLII: Designing Democratic Institutions*, ed. Ian Shapiro and Steven Macedo (New York University Press, 2000), 134.

44. A scheme by which both parties conspire to stay in office by selling the country to the highest bidder. Cited in Kevin Phillips, *Wealth and Democracy: A Political History of the American Rich* (New York: Broadway, 2003), 325.

45. For current examples of this application, see Richard Bernstein, "What Is Free Speech, and What Is Terrorism," *New York Times,* August 14, 2005, Week in Review section, p. 14.

46. Thomas Jefferson to John Adams, June 27, 1813, from vol. 13 of *The Writings of Thomas Jefferson* (Washington, DC: Thomas Jefferson Memorial Association, 1907), 279.

47. Larry D. Kramer, "Putting the Politics Back into the Political Safeguards of Federalism," *Columbia Law Review* 100, no. 1 (January 2000): 215–93, 272–73, n. 225.

48. Joseph LaPalombara and Jeffrey Anderson, "Political Parties," in *Encyclopedia of Government and Politics,* vol. 1, ed. Mary Hawkesworth and Maurice Kogan (New York: Routledge, 2004), 381–98, 383.

49. Burke, cited in Mansfield, *Statesmanship and Party Government,* 166.

50. Bernard Manin, *The Principles of Representative Government* (Cambridge: Cambridge University Press, 1997), 219. On the "party in service," see Aldrich, *Why Parties?,* who dates it from the 1960s at 159ff. and 272ff.

51. LaPalombara and Anderson, "Political Parties," 384. Or the Polish Minister who responded to the question of whom he represented: "I represent subjects that do not yet exist." Cited in Ingrid Van Biezen, "On the Theory and Practice of Party Formation and Adaptation in New Democracies," *European Journal of Political Research* 44, no. 1 (January 2005): 147–74, 155. There are innumerable typologies. Richard Gunther and Larry Diamond provide one (which they admit "lacks parsimony") with fifteen species of party divided into genus on the basis of organization, programmatic orientation, and tolerant vs. proto-hegemonic in "Species of Political Parties: A New Typology," *Party Politics* 9, no. 2 (March 2003): 167–99.

52. The contested question in political science is whether the typology and evolutionary story based on West European parties applies today. Do newer European democracies, post-communist states, and others transitioning to democracy follow a similar trajectory and arrive at similar party forms, or diverge from them? Is the pattern of party development contextual and *sui generis*? If there is convergence of party types everywhere, do newer parties anticipate the direction older parties will have to take? "The universality of the scenario whereby parties originate in legislatures and then extend themselves to the electorate has not been established"; other cases include negotiated transition from military rule and "up-from-the-bottom" explanations. Stokes, "Political Parties and Democracy," 246.

53. Schattschneider, *Party Government,* 65. Sartori's summary strikes the right tone: "When 'part' becomes 'party,' we thus have a term subject to two opposite semantic pulls: the derivation from *partire,* to divide, on the one hand, and the association with taking part ... on the other." He concludes by essentially giving up on distinctions: Party "remained a close synonym for faction" (*Parties and Party Systems,* 3–4).

54. Mosca, *Ruling Class*, 201.

55. Max Weber, "Class, Status, and Party," in *From Max Weber: Essays in Sociology*, ed. H. H. Gerth and C. Wright Mills (New York: Oxford University Press, 1946), 194.

56. That is precisely the controversy in historical writing on parties, work on eighteenth-century British parties, for example.

57. One recent study *defines* parties as coalitions of interest groups that create parties to nominate and elect politicians to do their bidding. Marty Cohen, David Karol, Hans Noel, and John Zaller, "Political Parties and Presidential Nominations," unpublished manuscript, p. 24.

58. Richard Hofstadter, *The Idea of a Party System: The Rise of Legitimate Opposition in the United States, 1780–1840* (Berkeley: University of California Press, 1972), 6.

59. Sartori, *Parties and Party Systems*, 63. To cite just one political science definition: "an organization qualifies as a political party if it is expected to endure beyond the lifespan of those who bring it into existence; if, in organizational terms, it is articulated at the local as well as national level; and if it competes in elections with the intention of capturing the major institutions of government, through which, alone or with others, it intends to exercise power in its own name." Joseph LaPalombara, "Reflections on Political Parties and Political Development, Four Decades Later," *Party Politics* 13, no. 2 (2007): 141–54, 143–44. Longevity is relative. The vast majority of parties that contested elections in western democracies did not survive more than a few elections intact and did not join government. Cited in Leonard Weinberg and Ami Pedahzur, *Political Parties and Terrorist Groups* (London: Routledge, 2003), 107.

60. Max Weber, *Economy and Society* (Berkeley: University of California Press, 1968), 938.

Chapter 1. Glorious Traditions of Antipartyism: Holism

1. Ioannis Evrigenis pointed out to me that in Byzantium the symbol of sovereignty is a two-headed eagle. As this caution suggests, I am not making universalistic claims but identifying the main categories of antipartyism in the canon of Western political theory.

2. For an extended discussion of utopianism, see George Kateb, *Utopia and Its Enemies* (London: Free Press of Glencoe, 1963).

3. Jean-Jacques Rousseau, *The Social Contract* (New York: Penguin, 1968), 83.

4. Thomas Hobbes, *Leviathan* (New York: Penguin, 1951), 247, 378, 363. Hobbes is anti-utopian only in his harsh rejection of classical ideals; he too constructs the standards for a perfectly unified state.

5. Rousseau, *Social Contract*, 86, 134.

6. Certain universal and unalterable standards—natural law, natural right—may obtain. They are standards for judging the changing forms of social relations, not for stopping or opposing change.

7. Hobbes, *Leviathan*, 81.

8. Rousseau, *Social Contract*, 61, 81.

9. Hobbes, *Leviathan,* 161, 365.

10. Hobbes conceded that the sovereign did not have to be a natural person, but a sovereign assembly simply compounds the problem of parts and partiality. The logic of sovereignty is unitary.

11. Hobbes, *Leviathan*, 220, 227–28. Hobbes's innovation was to characterize the absolute sovereign as the representative or agent of the people, rather than the people as his agents.

12. Thomas Hobbes, *De Cive: The English Version* (Oxford: Clarendon Press, 1983), 137.

13. E. E. Schattschneider, *Party Government* (New York: Holt, Rinehart and Winston, 1942), 23.

14. Hobbes, *Leviathan*, 372, 279, 274 ff., 375.

15. See Patrick Riley, *The General Will before Rousseau* (Princeton: Princeton University Press, 1986), 244ff.

16. Judith N. Shklar, *Men and Citizens: A Study of Rousseau's Social Theory* (Cambridge: Cambridge University Press, 1985).

17. Rousseau, *Social Contract*, 69, 150, 137, 99, 85.

18. In this discussion I refer to *The Social Contract*. In *Government of Poland* and the *Constitution of Corsica* Rousseau made allowance for the preservation of classes and their political representation; the status of these works vis-à-vis his ideal republic is a matter of contention. This discussion is an attempt to illuminate holist antipartyism and is not an exhaustive interpretation of Rousseau.

19. Rousseau, *Social Contract*, 71. In *Government of Poland* (Indianapolis: Hackett, 1985), where Rousseau allows for classes and representation and a more complex governmental structure, he repeats, "This whole business of drawing of lines— between chambers, between departments—is a modern invention. The ancients, who knew much more than we know about the preserving of freedom, were ignorant of any such expedient. Rome's senate governed half the known world, but the idea of dividing itself into parts never so much as crossed its mind" (34).

20. Rousseau, *Social Contract*, 141. This applies to representation in the sense of awarding public recognition and standing to parts. For a discussion of whether Rousseau intends an elected representative council to initiate legislation for ratification by the general will, see Ethan Putterman, "Rousseau on Agenda-Setting and Majority Rule," *American Political Science Review* 97, no. 3 (2003): 459–69. The relation between *Social Contract* and Rousseau's writings on Corsica and Poland is outside my purview here. I view the latter not as applications of Rousseau's republican

NOTES TO CHAPTER 1

principles but as nonrepublican reflections on the best possible regime for the size and class structure of these societies. Certainly, in *Government of Poland* Rousseau's characterization of law ("the law, which is merely the expression of the general will, is certainly the product of the interplay of all sectional interests, combining with and balancing one another in all their variety," 42) is contrary to the best understanding of the *Social Contract*.

21. Rousseau, *Social Contract*, 81.

22. Bernard Manin, "On Legitimacy and Political Deliberation," trans. Elly Stein and Jane Mansbridge, *Political Theory* 15, no. 3 (1987): 338–68, 345.

23. Ibid., 349.

24. Interpreters disagree about Rousseau's hospitability to civil society and to public discussion outside the decision arena. It is enough for my thesis that prohibition against communication is not literal but aimed at the formation of factions.

25. Hans Kelsen counts Rousseau among the "apologists for popular sovereignty" who, in saying the minority is mistaken about the true content of the general will, broaches a religio-metaphysical hypothesis about the wisdom of the people. "On the Essence and Value of Democracy," in *Weimar: A Jurisprudence of Crisis*, ed. Arthur Jacobson and Bernhard Schlink (Berkeley: University of California Press, 2000), 84–109, 106–7.

26. Kateb, *Utopia*, 94. My representation of Rousseau's republic as a holist utopia does not mean that political theorists are wrong to draw on elements for discussion in democratic theory. He is currently read as both an egalitarian and elitist.

27. Joseph LaPalombara and Jeffrey Anderson, "Political Parties," in *Encyclopedia of Government and Politics*, vol. 1, ed. Mary Hawkesworth and Maurice Kogan (New York: Routledge, 2004), 381–98, 385ff.

28. J.A.W. Gunn, *Factions no More: Attitudes to Party in Government and Opposition in Eighteenth Century England* (London: Frank Cass, 1971), 2.

29. Thus distinguishing antiparty holist parties from the one-party dominance of regions and periods in U.S. history. See Hugh Douglas Price, "One-Party Systems in Anglo-American Experience," in *Authoritarian Politics in Modern Society*, ed. Samuel Huntington and Clement Moore (New York: Basic Books, 1970), 75–98.

30. Maurice Duverger, *Political Parties: Their Organization and Activity in the Modern State* (New York: John Wiley & Sons, 1963), 261.

31. Harvey C. Mansfield, Jr., *Statesmanship and Party Government* (Chicago: Chicago University Press, 1965), 11; Isaac Kramnick, *Bolingbroke and His Circle: The Politics of Nostalgia in the Age of Walpole* (Cambridge, MA: Harvard University Press, 1968).

32. Cited in Richard Hofstadter, *The Idea of a Party System: The Rise of Legitimate Opposition in the United States, 1780–1840* (Berkeley: University of California Press, 1972), 17.

33. Cited in Giovanni Sartori, *Parties and Party Systems* (Cambridge: Cambridge University Press, 1976), 11.

34. Carl Schmitt, *The Crisis of Parliamentary Democracy* (Cambridge, MA: MIT Press), 63, on Marxists.

35. Lily Ross Taylor, *Party Politics in the Age of Caesar* (Berkeley: University of California Press, 1949), 162. Holism does not proceed by "the gentle means of conciliation and absorption." Hofstadter, *Idea of a Party System*, 127.

36. Holist antipartyism was associated with the derogation of Roman institutions and Rome as a mixed polity, spurring the attention of political historians, cf. Taylor, *Party Politics*, 49. The best known work is Carl Schmitt's writings on dictatorship and Caesarism. For a good discussion, see John P. McCormick, "From Constitutional Technique to Caesarist Ploy: Carl Schmitt on Dictatorship, Liberalism, and Emergency Powers," in *Dictatorship in History and Theory: Bonapartism, Caesarism, and Totalitarianism*, ed. Peter Baehr and Melvin Richter (Cambridge: Cambridge University Press, 2004), 197–220.

37. Hannah Arendt, *On Revolution* (New York: Viking, 1963), 271. Arendt sees this repeated in the conquest of the Soviets by the Bolshevik Party.

38. Ibid., 250. Arendt argues both that the Jacobins fought the regular party system, and that they were a product of it; she charges incessant factional strife in the Assembly, and popular disgust and indifference, as a condition for Terror. She describes one-party dictatorship as "only the last stage in the development of the nation-state in general and of the multi-party system in particular," 269. The fascist version is the theme of her *Origins of Totalitarianism* (New York: Harcourt Brace, 1951).

39. Schmitt, *Crisis*, 53.

40. Irving Howe and Lewis Coser argue that the decision to "go legal" as an electoral party was promoted by the Cominterm in the early 1920s. *The American Communist Party: A Critical History* (New York: Praeger, 1962), 102.

41. *Dennis v. United States*, 341 U.S. 494 (1951) at 563 (Jackson, J., concurring).

42. Samuel Huntington, *Political Order in Changing Societies* (New Haven: Yale University Press, 1968), 312.

43. Robert O. Paxton, *The Anatomy of Fascism* (London: Penguin Books, 2004), 85, 124–25.

44. *Dennis* (1951) at 567 (Jackson, J., concurring).

45. C. B. Macpherson, *The Real World of Democracy* (Oxford: Oxford University Press, 1965). Macpherson's standard for one-party rule is whether there is intra-party democracy (20–21, 27).

46. Arendt, *On Revolution*, 277.

47. Cited in Paxton, *Anatomy of Fascism*, 126.

48. Arendt, *On Revolution*, 272.

49. For a review of the recent literature on fascism and parties—under which circumstances democracy with competitive parties was irreversible and which conditions produced fascism during the interwar period, see Thomas Ertman, "Democracy and Dictatorship in Interwar Western Europe Revisited," *World Politics* 50,

no. 3 (1998): 475–505. Ertman argues that the combination of thick civil society and party competition at the center of political life were the mutually reinforcing factors that allowed for democratization and its durability.

50. Fascists and Nazis were radical, innovative successors to the parties earlier in the century that distinguished themselves as a party "above all parties." Those earlier parties of the anti-Semitic right and of the left, reactionary and revolutionary, had to enter the political arena to win political power, but their aim was to rise above parties, indeed above the outmoded nation. The Jews were a transnational force; imperial and anti-Semitic parties needed to be, too; see Arendt, *Origins*, 38ff.

51. Arendt, *Origins*, 315.

52. The current historical view is that inter-war Germany was rife with the associational life of "civil society." Indeed, associational life increased during periods of economic and political strain. Civil society was vulnerable to being infiltrated by National Socialists and associations turned up political projects because of the weakness of regular parties and government institutions. Nazis filled a political vacuum, exploiting networks of civic engagement. See Sheri Berman, "Civil Society and the Collapse of the Weimar Republic," *World Politics* 49, no. 3 (1997): 401–29, 417.

53. For a discussion emphasizing the contributing factor of a semi-presidential constitutional structure, see Cindy Skach, "Constitutional Origins of Dictatorship and Democracy," *Constitutional Political Economy* 16, no. 4 (2005): 347–68.

54. Kelsen, "On the Essence and Value of Democracy," 351 n. 35, 355.

55. For the cite from Friedrich and Brzezinski and a cautious discussion of the success of these parties, see Paxton, *Anatomy of Fascism*, 122 ff.

56. Arendt, *On Revolution*, 274; 336.

57. Cited in Paxton, *Anatomy of Fascism*, 144.

58. Bernard Crick, *In Defense of Politics* (London: Continuum, 2000), 16.

59. Paxton, *Anatomy of Fascism*, 57.

60. The phrase is used in Guillermo A. O'Donnell, Philippe C. Schmitter, and Laurence Whitehead, eds., *Transitions from Authoritarian Rule: Tentative Conclusions about Uncertain Democracies* (Baltimore: Johns Hopkins University Press, 1986), 16.

61. Schmitt, *Crisis*, 58; Gopal Balakrishnan, *The Enemy: An Intellectual Portrait of Carl Schmitt* (New York: Verso, 2000), 73. Schmitt later turned against Russia as the mechanistic, materialist, atheistic antithesis of existential politics of friend/enemy.

62. Pareto cited by Kelsen, "On the Essence and Value of Democracy," 356 n. 35.

63. Schmitt, *Crisis*, 16. "Democracy seems fated then to destroy itself in the problem of the formation of a will" (38). "Bolshevism and Fascism . . . are, like all dictatorships, certainly antiliberal but not necessarily antidemocratic" (16).

64. The negative connotations of party inhibited public embrace of democratic transitions in Germany, Italy, and Japan after World War II. Russell J. Dalton and Steven Weldon, "Partisanship and Party System Institutionalization," *Party Politics* 13, no. 2 (2007): 192.

65. Crick, *In Defense of Politics*, 59.

66. See Gaetano Mosca, *The Ruling Class* (New York: McGraw Hill, 1939), 176.

67. Nancy L. Rosenblum, "Religious Parties, Religious Political Identity, and the Cold Shoulder of Liberal Democratic Thought," *Ethical Theory and Moral Practice* 6, no. 1 (2003): 23–53; Stathis Kalyvas, *The Rise of Christian Democratic Parties in Europe* (Ithaca: Cornell University Press, 1996).

68. Statement by the Turkish Islamic candidate Erdogan, 1996, cited in R. Quinn Mecham, "From the Ashes of Virtue, a Promise of Light: The Transformation of Political Islam in Turkey," unpublished manuscript, p. 13.

69. Vali Nasr, "The Rise of 'Muslim Democracy,'" *Journal of Democracy* 16, no. 2 (2005): 13–27, 23.

70. Giovanni Sartori, *Parties and Party Systems* (Cambridge: Cambridge University Press, 1976), 43.

71. Crick, *In Defense of Politics*, 70.

72. O'Donnell, Schmitter, and Whitehead, *Transitions*, 49.

73. Cited in Lisa Wedeen, *Ambiguities of Domination: Politics, Rhetoric, and Symbols in Contemporary Syria* (Chicago: University of Chicago Press, 1999), 45 (emphasis added)

74. See, e.g., Iliya Harik, "The Single Party as a Subordinate Movement: The Case of Egypt," *World Politics* 26, no. 1 (1973): 80–105.

75. Cited in Wedeen, *Ambiguities*, 42.

76. Rupert Emerson, "Political Modernization: The Single-Party System," in *Political Parties*, ed. Roy C. Macridis (New York: Harper Torchbooks, 1967), 238–66, 261.

77. Chinua Achebe, cited in Claude E. Welch, Jr., "The Single Party Phenomenon in Africa," *Transafrica Forum* 8, no. 3 (1991): 85–94, 87.

78. That is the question with which Sartori opens his work (*Parties and Party Systems*, 40). His answer is that "a modern society cannot be left unchanneled. Modern societies need to be or become "pervasively politicized society" (42). For an extended discussion of one-party states and modernization, see Joseph Lapalombara and Myron Weiner, "The Origin and Development of Political Parties," in Lapalombara and Weiner, *Political Parties and Political Development* (Princeton: Princeton University Press, 1966): "[T]he emergence of political parties is a useful institutional index of a level of political development and its emergence is related to the modernization process" (7). The authors provide a classificatory system for one-party states (37ff.).

79. The phrase is Duverger's describing the Turkish People's Republican Party (*Political Parties*, 277).

80. T. J. Pempel points out that "the vast majority of the nation-states in the world could be characterized as one-party states," by which he means regimes with party systems dominated by a single party. "Introduction," in *Uncommon Democracies: The One-Party Dominant Regimes*, ed. Pempel (Ithaca: Cornell University Press, 1990), 1. Sartori referred to this as a "predominant party system" in which one party outdistances all the others (*Parties and Party Systems*, 192–93). Alan Ware discusses

the reasons dominant parties may have for permitting and even encouraging opposition parties in *Political Parties and Party Systems* (Oxford: Oxford University Press, 1996), 138. Attention has shifted from how monopolistic a single party could be to how nonmonopolistic it could be. "Can the Party Alone Run a One-Party State: A Discussion," in *Political Opposition in One-Party States*, ed. Leonard Schapiro (New York: John Wiley, 1972): 15–32, 15. For standard categories of one-partyism, see Sartori, *Parties and Party Systems*, 39ff, 217ff.

81. For a theoretical discussion of the problematic conflation of legitimacy with compliance, loyalty and belief and dissimulation of loyalty, see Wedeen on "the politics of as if"—stable regimes without legitimacy (*Ambiguities*, 5ff.).

82. In practice, the holist party is the sole regulator of participation and source of legitimacy; in some cases it is more important than the state. The party is a principal means of controlling citizens—an organization for one-way communication from the top down, to spread propaganda or intimidate. Membership is vital for advance (or just survival) in virtually any social context. Add to this the fact that "one party" states, self-styled democracies, came into their own as the principal modern form of authoritarian government, and the grim picture of modern holist parties is rounded out. Samuel Huntington, citing Franz Neumann in "Social and Institutional Dynamics of One-Party Systems," in *Authoritarian Politics in Modern Society*, ed. Huntington and Clement Moore (New York: Basic Books, 1970), 3–47, 8, 4.

83. Emerson, "Political Modernization," 249.

84. A classic statement is Emerson. The "transition" is to political modernization without, as in the current phrase, "transitional regime," a presumptive path to democracy.

85. See O'Donnell, Schmitter, and Whitehead, *Transitions*, where transition refers to the launching of the process of dissolution of an authoritarian regime by the installation of some form of democracy (6). The authors argue that the breakdown of democratic regimes and the transition from authoritarian ones are not symmetrical (19). "Transition" is generally short-hand for this process, really two processes of "liberalization" and "democratization." In fact, the transition for which one party claims responsibility is often economic development.

86. Huntington's discussion of Lenin is in the context of revolutionism; his point about party is more general. *Political Order*, 336ff.

87. Ibid., 342, 315.

88. Ibid., 310.

89. Ibid., 422.

90. Huntington's model for developing nations is Lenin's Bolshevik Party; the stress is on mobilization. An alternative model for one-partyism is the political machine. Harik proposes a "collaboration" model, a synthesis of ideological discipline and control that comes from identifying and organizing "collaborators" at the subnational level.

91. See, e.g., Raymond A. Hinnebusch, "Political Recruitment and Socialization in Syria," *International Journal of Middle East Studies* 11, no. 2 (1980): 143–74.

92. Seymour Martin Lipset, "The Indispensability of Political Parties," *Journal of Democracy* 11, no. 1 (2000): 48–55, 49.

93. Cited in Wedeen, *Ambiguities*, 2. On the economizing of violence through political cults of president and party, see 156ff.

94. E. E. Schattschneider in the context of American parties, *The Semisovereign People* (New York: Holt, Rinehart and Winston, 1960), 12.

95. Crick, *In Defense of Politics*, 73.

96. Ibid., 27.

97. O'Donnell, Schmitter, and Whitehead, *Transitions,* regarding authoritarian regimes generally (9).

98. Ware, *Political Parties*, 137. The phrase is Sartori's, *Parties and Political Systems*, 58.

99. Ali Sabri, cited in Harik, "The Single Party," 99.

100. Cases suggest that the dissolution of authoritarian regimes comes principally from divisions within the party leadership. O'Donnell et al., *Transitions*, 65.

101. Emerson, "Political Modernization," 261.

102. Jeremy Waldron, *The Dignity of Legislation* (Cambridge: Cambridge University Press, 1999), 154.

103. See John Locke, *Second Treatise of Government* (New York: Bobbs Merrill, 1952), 59, §105; 63, §110.

104. Ibid., 55, §97; 56, §98.

105. Manin, "On Legimacy and Deliberation," 342.

106. Benjamin Constant, *Principles of Politics Applicable to All Government,* ed. Etienne Hofmann (Indianapolis: Liberty Fund, 2003), 32. Constant went on to observe that a unanimity rule "did not make all citizens free, but rather subjected them all to one person."

107. Waldron, *Dignity*, 126–27. The very idea of majority decision detracts from the authority, legitimacy, and simple appeal of law conceived as anonymous, neutral, and distanced from politics (24). "Everyone knows that argument in Congress or in Parliament is explicitly and unashamedly political" (25).

108. Emerson, "Political Modernization," 256–57.

109. Hans Kelsen's defense of democratic majoritarianism consists of reframing the principle: a majority/minority principle whose significance is precisely the drive to compromise. "On the Essence and Value of Democracy," 102.

110. Manin, "On Legitimacy and Deliberation," 361.

111. Schattschneider, *Party Government*, 92.

112. John C. Calhoun, *A Disquisition on Government and a Discourse on the Constitution and Government of the United States,* ed. Richard K. Cralle (Union, NJ: Lawbook Exchange).

113. Manin, "On Legitimacy and Deliberation," 343.

114. Adam Przeworski, "Minimalst Conception of Democracy: A Defense," in *Democracy's Value,* ed. Ian Shapiro and Casiano Hacker-Cordon (Cambridge: Cambridge University Press, 1999), 23–55, 48.

115. George Kateb, *The Inner Ocean: Individualism and Democratic Culture* (Ithaca: Cornell University Press, 1992), 59.

116. Gerhard Leibholz, *Politics and Law* (Leyden: A. W. Sythoff, 1965), 27.

117. Waldron, *Dignity*, 126ff. In epistemic terms, first articulated by Aristotle, the "summation argument" lauds the virtue and prudence of the many joined together—begging the question, majority of whom? See Aristotle, *The Politics*, trans. Carnes Lord (Chicago: University of Chicago Press, 1984), bk. 3, chap. 11, pp. 100–101, or more generically, 1281a40–b7. Majoritarianism was rarely defended in American thought in terms of epistemic considerations.

118. Waldron: "the method of majority decision attempts to give each individual's view the greatest weight possible in this process compatible with an equal weight for the views of each of the others. . . . [It] also accords maximum decisiveness to each member" (148).

119. Kateb, *Inner Ocean*, discussing Rousseauian direct democracy (52). American political thought also contains the view that majoritarianism is not an aggregate of individuals standing for the people; it is the voice of an organic whole. For a discussion, see C. Edward Merriam, *A History of American Political Theories* (New York: Macmillan, 1920), 189ff.

120. Manin, "On Legitimacy and Deliberation," 359.

121. Kelsen, "On the Essence and Value of Democracy," 87. Also see Leibholz, *Politics and Law*, on "the largest amount of individual political freedom" (27).

122. Judith N. Shklar, "The American Idea of Aristocracy," in Judith N. Shklar, *Redeeming American Political Thought*, ed. Stanley Hoffmann and Dennis Thompson (Chicago: Chicago University Press, 1998), 146–57, 146.

123. I am indebted for this interpretation to Shklar, ibid.

124. "A Candid State of Parties," in *James Madison: Writings*, ed. Jack Rakove (New York: Library of America, 1999), 530–31 (emphasis added). I make this point tentatively, because although the import of "the great body of the people" is not entirely clear, it is not just a synonym for the numerical majority. Jefferson attacked Hamilton for "daring to call the Republican party *a faction*." Cited in Hofstadter, *Idea of a Party System*, 11.

125. Bruce Ackerman, *The Failure of the Founding Fathers: Jefferson, Marshall, and the Rise of Presidential Democracy* (Cambridge, MA: Harvard University Press, 2005), 17.

126. Alexis de Tocqueville, *Democracy in America*, trans. Harvey C. Mansfield Jr. and Delba Winthrop (Chicago: University of Chicago Press, 2000), 127.

127. Ibid., 230.

128. In Gerald Leonard's account the climax of the story is the election of 1840 when party was integrated into the constitutional system. *The Invention of Party*

Politics: Federalism, Popular Sovereignty, and Constitutional Development in Jacksonian Illinois (Chapel Hill: University of North Carolina Press, 2002), 16.

129. Ibid., 30.

130. Ibid., 239.

131. Ibid., 5. For Leonard's correction of the classic account by Hofstadter, see 6ff.; the battle was not over social and economic positions of Democrats and Whigs but over the question of party itself and its relation to the Constitution. Hence the "constant interpenetrations, and thus the tenuousness of the distinctions among three modern categories: a 'normal' politics of choice among substantive policies, a politics of 'constitutional construction' in which the basic structures and customs of democratic governance—the unwritten constitution—are at stake, and a politics of constitutional interpretation in which the meaning of the constitutional text itself is at issue" (14). Leonard's theme is party as defender of the unwritten Constitution—of the sovereignty of the majority. A party-less Constitution would always be an undemocratic Constitution (18).

132. Ibid., 5, 10–11; 203.

133. Ibid., 155.

134. The emergence of the presidency as a vehicle for the expression of popular sovereignty is Ackerman's theme: "It was now [after 1801] perfectly appropriate to describe presidential elections as contests by rival parties for majority support; and once the winning side had gained a mandate from the People, it was wrong to deprive the victorious party of executive power." *Failure of the Founding Fathers*, 205.

135. The idea of party mandates seems to have originated with the first mobilization of voters by socialist parties in Europe, which associated mandates with radical change. G. Bingham Powell, *Elections as Instruments of Democracy: Majoritarian and Proportional Visions* (New Haven: Yale University Press, 2000), 69.

136. Ordinarily, large victories, majorities and more, are not mandates; only victories over successive election cycles, against mobilized opposition, on a clear line of division are.

137. Kateb, *Inner Ocean*, 38, 40–41.

138. Constant, *Principles of Politics*, 35.

139. Schattschneider, *Party Government*, 84.

140. Schattschneider, *Semisovereign People*, 104, 102. Totalitarian mobilization, which exploited popular disgust at parties and their representative claims, was the precipitant of this observation. Arendt, *Origins of Totalitarianism*, 312.

141. Kelsen, "On the Essence and Value of Democracy," 94. In chapter 7 I discuss the fact that the tendency is not irresistible.

142. Seymour Martin Lipset, "What Are Parties For?" *Journal of Democracy* 7, no. 1 (1996): 169–75, 170.

143. Arendt's grudging acceptance of British and U.S. two-party systems does not allow this. "In this system the opinions of the people are indeed unascertainable for the simple reason that they are non-existent. Opinions are formed in a process

of open discussion and public debate, and where no opportunity for the forming of opinions exists, there may be moods—moods of the masses and moods of individuals, the latter no less fickle and unreliable than the former—but no opinion." *On Revolution*, 272. Arendt goes on to say that interests and welfare can be objectively ascertained and represented, but not opinion. Parties are not popular organs, on this view; they are not public spaces, do not create public spirit, and are not vehicles of political action.

144. Cited in Powell, *Elections*, 263 n. 2.

Chapter 2. Glorious Traditions of Antipartyism: Fatal Divisiveness

1. Richard Hofstadter, *The Idea of a Party System: The Rise of Legitimate Opposition in the United States, 1780–1840* (Berkeley: University of California Press), 12.

2. J.A.W. Gunn, *Factions No More: Attitudes to Party in Government and Opposition in Eighteenth-Century England* (London: Frank Cass, 1971), 16.

3. David Hume, "Of Parties in General," in *Hume: Political Essays*, ed. Knud Haakonssen (Cambridge: Cambridge University Press, 1994), 34.

4. Gunn, *Factions No More*, 7.

5. The phrase is Ronald Symes's, in *A Roman Post-Mortem* (Sydney: Australasian Medical Publishing, 1950), 3.

6. Cited in Bernard Manin, *The Principles of Representative Government* (Cambridge: Cambridge University Press, 1997), 52.

7. Symes, *Roman Post-Mortem*, 4–5.

8. The exception here is Montesquieu, who pointed out that there had always been factual strife in Rome, both among the aristocratic families and between the aristocracy and other groups without it destroying the republican constitution. He explained the fall instead by the too rapid imperial expansion, as discussed in Kurt von Fritz, *The Theory of the Mixed Constitution in Antiquity: An Analysis of Polybius' Political Ideas* (New York: Columbia University Press, 154), 254ff.

9. For a good summary of the debates and the evidence, see Andrew Lintott, *The Constitution of the Roman Republic* (Oxford: Oxford University Press, 1999), 163ff.

10. For several clear reasons apart from the anachronism of mass electoral parties: elections were not normally entered with a view to taking sides on political questions, and there is considerable question whether anything more organized or coherent than family and personal influence had importance for managing elections. see ibid., 169–70. Lintott argues that there is little direct evidence of the motivation even for the very general notion of a political party as a group striving for power and dominance in the state (175). The broad political groupings I refer to below as optimates and populares were, Lintott argues, without political organization as such (174).

11. See P. A. Brunt, "'Amicitia' in the Late Roman Republic," *Proceedings of the Cambridge Philological Society*, no. 191 (1965): 1–20, 17.

12. Lily Ross Taylor, *Party Politics in the Age of Caesar* (Berkeley: University of California Press, 1949), 7. This is not to say that the meaning of friendship was restricted to political ally, of course; it was not purely expedient. But in contrast to modern social life, private friendship and public life were difficult to separate. And even today there is a particular kind of friendship that comes from shared political experience.

13. "Party" and "party feeling," Lintott argues, were used comparatively rarely and "nearly always to refer to political parties created by civil war." *Constitution of the Roman Republic*, 173.

Bernard Manin has explored the fact that republics introduced selection for office by lot rather than choice in order to stave off parties. Manin, *Principles of Representative Government*, 51, 6, 42ff. For a discussion of the mix of election and lot and the way various modes inhibit or promote popular self-defense against oligarchy in Rome and Florence, see John McCormick, "Contain the Wealthy and Patrol the Magistrates: Restoring Elite Accountability to Popular Government," *American Political Science Review* 100, no. 2 (2006): 147–63.

14. Cited in Donald Earl, *The Moral and Political Tradition of Rome* (London: Thames and Hudson, 1967), 55.

15. Taylor, *Party Politics* 8ff., 13. Lintott argues that *factio* had a specific meaning and seems to indicate the concentration of individual influence in a narrow oligarchic group, though personal connections and intrigue. *Constitution of the Roman Republic*, 165.

16. Cited in Earl, *Moral and Political Tradition of Rome*, 55.

17. Ibid., 58.

18. A careful comparison of Machiavelli's *Discourses* and *Florentine Histories* is Gisela Bock, "Civil Discord in Machiavelli's 'Istorie Fiorentine,'" in *Machiavelli and Republicanism*, ed. Gisela Bock, Quentin Skinner, and Maurizio Viroli (Cambridge: Cambridge University Press, 1990), 181–201. For a very different account in which Machiavelli's "parties" are inseparable from religion, and disputes between emperor and pope were the prototype as well as origin of modern parties and tied to foreigners and empire, see Harvey C. Mansfield Jr., "Party and Sect in Machiavelli's 'Florentine Histories,'" in *Machiavelli's Virtue* (Chicago: University of Chicago Press, 1996), 137–75.

19. Bock, "Civil Discord," 182.

20. Cited in ibid., 182.

21. Ibid.

22. Machiavelli, *Discourses on Livy*, trans. Harvey C. Mansfield Jr. and Nathan Tarcov (Chicago: University of Chicago Press, 1996), bk. 1, chap. 49, p. 101; on consuls, bk. 3, chap. 27, p. 274.

23. Chap. 11, "Of Ecclesiastical Principalities." In Machiavelli, *The Prince*, trans. Harvey C. Mansfield Jr. (Chicago: University of Chicago Press, 1998), 46.

24. Machiavelli, *History of Florence and of the Affairs of Italy*, intro. Felix Gilbert (New York: Harper Torchbooks, 1960), vii, 310. Lintott concludes that throughout

Roman republican history political organization was shifting and electoral pressures complex but agrees that there is a powerful argument that in the late Republic "in normal politics one or two powerful factions did not control the political process. When this did in fact happen, it was the result of civil war, as in the seventies . . . or the result of a political crisis, as in the aftermath of Gaius Gracchus' overthrow. In other words, it was created by political and ideological cohesion rather than the normal links of amicitia and officium" (181).

25. Cited in Harvey C. Mansfield Jr., "Whether Party Government Is Inevitable," *Political Science Quarterly* 80, no. 4 (1965): 517–42, 528; Machiavelli, *Discourses*, bk. 1, chaps. 4–5.

26. Machiavelli, *The Prince and the Discourses*, ed. Max Lerner (New York: Modern Liberary, 1940), bk. 1 of *Discourses,* chap. 7, p. 132. Machiavelli prescribed something like this to mitigate instability in Florence.

27. Ioannis Evrigenis, "The Enemy of My Enemy Is My Friend," 20. Unpublished manuscript.

28. Some Englishmen advised the Crown that while factions "are at enmity among themselves, they shall have no aversion to him." Lord Cowper to George I, cited in Caroline Robbins, "Discordant Parties: A Study of the Acceptance of Party by Englishmen," *Political Science Quarterly* 73, no. 4 (1958): 505–29, 514. Benjamin Constant used the chaos of Roman politics as an example of the necessity for a neutral power to mediate between the parties. He was thinking of France and prescribing modern constitutional monarchy. Benjamin Constant, *Political Writings*, ed. Biancamaria Fontana (Cambridge: Cambridge University Press, 1988), 186.

29. Machiavelli, *The Prince and the Discourses*, bk. 3 of *Discourses*, chap. 27, p. 491.

30. I am grateful to conversation with Eric Nelson on this point about armed "*partigione.*" Machiavelli's view of disunity has been read out of his work by some interpreters, including Harrington, who thought that if the material basis of division could be eliminated, there was no ground for parties.

31. This does not mean that Machiavelli did not have a single theory of human nature; grandi and people arise from circumstances. For a discussion of this point, see Evrigenis, "The Enemy," 3 n. 7.

32. Bock, "Civil Discord," 198.

33. George Washington, "Farewell Address to the People of the United States," September 26, 1796. Available at http://earlyamerica.com/earlyamerica/milestones/farewell.

34. Hume, "Of Parties in General," in *Political Essays,* 36.

35. Cited in Mark Spencer, "Hume and Madison on Faction," *William and Mary* Quarterly 59, no. 4 (2002): 869–96.

36. Aristotle, *Politics,* trans. Ernest Barker (Oxford: Oxford University Press, 1995), 182ff. or 1302a34 more generically.

37. Madison letter to Jefferson, October 24, 1787, www.constitution.org/jm/1787/1024.tj.txt.

38. Hume, "Of Parties in General," in *Political Essays*, 35; Alexander Hamilton, James Madison, and John Jay, *The Federalist*, intro. Edward Mead Earle (New York: Modern Library, 1941), No. 10.

39. James Madison, "Parties," in *James Madison: Writings*, ed. Jack Rakove (New York: Library of America, 1999), 504.

40. Mansfield, "Whether Party Government Is Inevitable," 525.

41. Anthony, Lord Shaftesbury, "An Essay on the Freedom of Wit and Humour," cited in Gunn, *Factions No More*, 78–79.

42. Madison, "To Thomas Jefferson," in *Writings*, 150. A main theme of American political history is that the mixed Constitution was succeeded by the notion of separated powers. Madison is the chief theorist of institutional checking and balancing. Very quickly this vision, which is still a central tenet of constitutional law, was amended by parties and the changing dynamic of unified/divided government.

43. Madison, "No. 10," in Hamilton, Madison, and Jay, *The Federalist,* 55, 56.

44. Madison, "No. 50," in ibid.

45. Madison, "Parties," in *Writings*, 504–5. When in Federalist No. 51 Madison declared that the remedy for branches of government encroaching on one another was not to be found in parties, but "ambition must be made to counteract ambition," meaning "the interest of the man must be connected with the constitutional rights of the place" (ibid., 337), he had it wrong. Parties cross the boundaries of separated powers.

46. Madison, "Parties," in *Writings*, 504.

47. Douglas Adair, 'That Politics May Be Reduced to a Science': David Hume, James Madison, and the Tenth Federalist," *Huntington Library Quarterly* 20, no. 4 (1957): 343–60, was the first contribution.

48. Hume thought that an established church would bribe fractious clergy into indolence. See Spencer, "Hume and Madison."

49. Adair, "Political Reduced to Science," 351.

50. Though he did not agree that commercial republics would not go to war against one another. Madison, Federalist nos. 9 and 43.

51. Hamilton, Madison, and Jay, *The Federalist*, 60, 340.

52. Jefferson cited in John Zvesper, *Political Philosophy and Rhetoric* (Cambridge: Cambridge University Press, 1977), 92.

53. Hamilton, Madison, and Jay, *The Federalist*, 58, 61.

54. For a discussion of Madison on the multiple factions at the constitutional convention (not the single divide that produced the great compromise), in contrast to the Pennsylvania case where the "Council of Censors" was "split into two fixed and violent parties," see Paul J. Pollock, "Is the *Federalist* Anti-Party?" *Political Science Reviewer* 12 (Fall 1982): 79–97, 90.

55. Madison cited in Gordon Wood, *The Radicalism of the American Revolution* (New York: Knopf, 1991), 253.

56. Diamond, cited in Bruce Ackerman, *We the People*, vol. 1, *Foundations* (Cambridge, MA: Harvard University Press, 1991), 226.

57. Hume, "That Politics May be Reduced to a Science," in *Political Essays*, 12–13; Hume, "Of the Independency of Parliament," in *Political Essays*, 24.

58. Hume, "Of Parties in General," in *Political Essays*, 39. The foundation of a regular party system in England brought the eclipse of "great," i.e., religious parties.

59. Alexis de Tocqueville, *De La Democratie en Amerique*, ed. Eduardo Nolla (Paris: J. Vrin, 1991), 138 n. d.

60. Alexis de Tocqueville, *Democracy in America*, trans. Harvey C. Mansfield and Delba Winthrop (Chicago: University of Chicago Press, 2000), 166ff., 175.

61. Letter to Eugene Stoffels, January 12, 1833, in Alexis de Tocqueville, *Lettres Choisies Souvenirs: 1814–1859*, ed. Francoise Melonio and Laurence Guellec (Paris: Quarto Gallimard, 2003), 296–97.

62. T. B. Macaulay, *History of England*, cited in Mansfield, "Whether Party Government Is Inevitable," 520.

63. Thomas Jefferson to John Adams, 1813, in vol. 13 of Thomas Jefferson, *The Writings of Thomas Jefferson*, memorial ed. (Washington, DC: Thomas Jefferson Memorial Association), 279.

64. Cited in Robbins, "Discordant Parties," 509.

65. Tocqueville, *Democracy in America*, 167, 170.

66. Judith Shklar, "Democracy and the Past: Jefferson and his Heirs," in Judith N. Shklar, *Redeeming American Political Thought*, ed. Stanley Hoffmann and Dennis F. Thompson (Chicago: University of Chicago Press, 1998), 180.

67. Madison, "A Candid State of Parties," in *Writings*, 530–31.

68. Cited in Hofstadter, *Idea of a Party System*, 83. I make this point tentatively, because the import of "the great body of the people" is not entirely clear. I do not think, however, that it is a synonym for the majority.

69. Madison, "A Candid State of Parties," in *Writings*, 530.

70. James Conniff points out the connection between characterization of parties and the concrete practices of partisans, especially as regards Britain in the eighteenth century, in "Hume on Parties: The Case for Hume as a Whig," *Eighteenth Century Studies* 12, no. 2 (1978): 150–73.

71. Aristotle, *Politics*, trans. Lord, bk. 5, chap. 3, p. 152, or more generically 1303b15.

72. Sartori, *Parties and Party Systems*, 77.

73. Mansfield, "Whether Party Government Is Inevitable," 523–24.

74. Dr. Johnson cited in Crick, *In Defense of Politics*, 112.

75. Edmund S. Morgan, *Inventing the People* (New York: Norton, 1998), 176–77.

76. The set piece is Cosimo de Medici in bk. 4 of Machiavelli, *History of Florence*, 310.

77. Madison, "No. 10," in Hamilton, Madison, and Jay, *The Federalist*, 55.

78. Ibid., 56.

79. Cited in Hofstadter, *Idea of a Party System*, 188.

80. Halifax, "Political Thoughts and Reflections," in Gunn, *Factions No More*, 44.

81. Farewell Address cited in John Kenneth White and Philip John Davies, *Political Parties and the Collapse of the Old Orders* (Albany: SUNY Press, 1998), 7.

82. James Ralph, "A Defence of the People," in Gunn, *Factions No More*, 148.

83. Adam Ferguson, *An Essay on the History of Civil Society*, ed. Fania Oz-Salzberger (Cambridge: Cambridge University Press, 1995), 245.

84. Gunn, *Factions No More*, 9.

85. Halifax, "Political Thoughts and Reflections," in ibid., 45.

86. William Godwin, *Enquiry Concerning Political Justice* (Oxford: Clarendon Press, 1971), 140.

87. Mark A. Kishlansky, *Parliamentary Selection: Social and Political Choice in Early Modern England* (Cambridge: Cambridge University Press, 1986), 16, 17, 73, 75, 226, 190. And "there is almost no evidence . . . that there was a connection between the selection of members to Parliament and the activities of members of Parliament" (16). "Neither candidates nor leaders of the community recognized the possibility than an electoral contest might take place simply because there was a rough equality of support for two or more aspirants" (81). The oligarchic character of election and "deference" lasted well into the eighteenth century.

88. The personal structure of politics, more than legal restrictions on suffrage, kept most people from participating. (I discuss the antiparty attack on dependency and the insistence on economic and political independence in chapter 4.)

89. Morgan, *Inventing the People*, 41.

90. Wood, *Radicalism*, 121, 87, 173, 259, 276.

91. Cited in "Party," in Nicholas Comfort, *Brewer's Politics: A Phrase and Fable Dictionary* (London: Cassell, 1993), 442.

92. Manin, *Principles of Representative Government*, 193.

93. Aristotle, *Politics*, trans. Barker, bk. 4, chap. 7, pp. 149–50. The people/poor was not an inclusive category and fell short of universal suffrage. But "a state in which many poor men are excluded from office will necessarily be full of enemies."

94. Plato, *The Republic*, trans. Allan Bloom (New York: Basic Books, 1991), 30.

95. Aristotle, *Politics* trans. Barker, bk. 2, chap. 2 and 3, pp. 39, 41

96. Bk. 4 of Aristotle's *Politics* ("Methods of Constructing Democracies and Oligarchies") is an exhaustive survey of the types and combinations of "actual regimes." (trans. Barker, bk. 6, chap. 1, 229ff.).

97. Josiah Ober challenges the usual reading of Aristotle as formulating a utopia, a philosophically conceivable polity, separate from the best possible polity, in *Political Dissent in Democratic Athens: Intellectual Critics of Popular Rule* (Princeton: Princeton University Press, 1998).

98. Aristotle, *Politics*, trans. Barker, bk. 4, chap. 11, p. 160.

99. In some versions, the members retain their corporate identity and separate vote and either distribute offices and powers or share with different weights in different governmental functions. Jean Bodin, *On Sovereignty*, ed. Julian H. Franklin (Cambridge: Cambridge University Press, 1992), 303.

100. Aristotle, trans. Barker, bk. 4, chap. 9, pp. 153ff. On polity specifically, see bk. 4, chap. 14, pp. 167ff.

101. Julian H. Franklin, "Sovereignty and the Mixed Constitution," in *The Cambridge History of Political Thought, 1450–1700,* ed. J. H. Burns and Mark Goldie (Cambridge: Cambridge University Press), 298–328, 321. For Aristotle on the modes of fusion, see *Politics,* bk. 4, chap. 9; on nobles and people deliberating together, see bk. 4, chap. 14; on appointments to office, bk. 4, chap. 15; on judging, bk. 4, chap. 16.

102. Aristotle, *Politics,* trans. Barker, bk. 4, chap. 12; bk. 4, chap. 9, pp. 153–55. Faction, the condition Greeks called stasis, occurs when there is no agreement about the vesting of office (bk. 5, chap. 1, p. 179).

103. Andrew Lintott, "The Theory of the Mixed Constitution," in *Philosophia Togata II: Plato and Aristotle at Rome,* ed. Jonathan Barnes and Miriam Griffin (Oxford: Clarendon Press, 1997), 70–85, 72.

104. Consider recent debates about Friedrich Munzer's notion of the essential oligarchy of the Roman Republic with a politics based on a constellation of parties comprising coalitions of clans whose politics had little to do with policies but a struggle for political dominance. This is challenged by Karl-Joachim Holkeskamp, "Fact(ions) or Fiction? Friedrich Munzer and the Aristocracy of the Roman Republic—Then and Now," *International Journal of the Classical Tradition* 8, no. 1 (2001): 92–105. See too Willfried Nippel, "Ancient and Modern Republicanism: 'Mixed Constitution' and 'Ephors,'" in *The Invention of the Modern Republic,* ed. Biancamaria Fontana (Cambridge: Cambridge University Press, 1994), 6–26, 9ff.

105. Montesquieu, *The Spirit of the Laws,* ed. Anne Cohler, Basia Miller, and Harold Stone (Cambridge: Cambridge University Press, 1989), 160.

106. Ibid., 155.

107. Ibid., 16–19.

108. J.A.W. Gunn, "Influence, Parties, and the Constitution: Changing Attitudes, 1783–1832," *Historical Journal* 17, no. 2 (1974): 301–28, 303.

109. Richard Tuck, *Philosophy and Government: 1572–1651* (Cambridge: Cambridge University Press, 1993), 204.

110. Blair Worden, "English Republicanism," in Burns and Goldie, *Cambridge History of Political Thought, 1450–1700,* 447.

111. J.G.A. Pocock argues that Court and Country in eighteenth-century debate were distinguished by constitutional interpretation: country arguing that the balance required independence, court that balance required interdependence. "Machiavelli, Harrington, and English Political Ideologies in the 18th Century," *William and Mary Quarterly* 22, no. 4 (1965): 549–83, 571.

112. Bernard Crick's characterization of feudalism. *In Defense of Politics,* 64.

113. Aristotle, *Politics,* trans. Barker, bk. 3, chap. 11, p. 109.

114. Ober, *Political Dissent,* 321.

115. Aristotle, *Politics,* trans. Barker, bk. 5, chap. 6, p. 194.

116. Ibid., bk. 3, chap. 11, p. 109; bk. 5, chap. 8, p. 163.

117. Cicero, *De re publica, De Legibus* (Cambridge: Harvard University Press, 1928), 105.

118. Montesquieu, *Considerations on the Greatness and Decline of the Romans*, 415 cited in Judith N. Shklar, *Montesquieu* (New York: Oxford University Press, 1987), 59.

119. Tuck argues that from the 1590s in England balance became the key term as politics was seen in terms of interests, 96.

120. Montesquieu, *Spirit of the Laws*, 164.

121. Machiavelli, *Discourses*, bk. 2, chap. 2.

122. The true history of each reveals that at different points in time, power, particularly the power to make law, was not shared and could not be. These regimes were either aristocratic or democratic, and in each the so-called monarch was for show. ("What led Polybius and Contarini astray in Sparta was the title 'kings'.") Bodin, *On Sovereignty*, ed. Julian Franklin (Cambridge: Cambridge University Press, 1992), Book I, Chapter 8, p. 1 and Book II, Chapter 1, pp. 90ff. For Franklin's criticism of Bodin on logical and historical grounds, see xiii–xxv.

123. Z. S. Fink, *The Classical Republicans* (Chicago: Northwestern University Press, 1962), 28–51.

124. Quoted in Nippel, "Ancient and Modern Republicanism," 23.

125. Corinne Comstock Weston, "The Theory of Mixed Monarchy under Charles I and After," *English Historical Review* 75, no. 296 (1960): 426–43, 429. See too M.J.C. Vile, *Constitutionalism and the Separation of Powers* (Indianapolis: Liberty Fund, 1998), 48.

126. Wood, *Radicalism*, 95.

127. In any case, the great change from ancient to modern mixed constitutions (in addition of course to changed social elements) was the idea that the constitution was not just a set of variable institutional arrangements but a fundamental law, a body of law not subject to alteration by ordinary legislation—an idea that came to maturity with American constitutionalism. See the discussion in Nippel, "Ancient and Modern Republicanism," 24.

128. Both mixed government and separation of powers were sometimes complicated by the distinct idea of institutionalized checks and balances, in which each political body—whether it is understood to represent a social force or a function of government—exercises a degree of direct control by playing an authorized part in the others' business. Fink, *Classical Republicans*, 4. The standard study, on which I rely, is Vile, *Constitutionalism*. Howell A. Lloyd, "Constitutionalism," in Burns and Goldie, *Cambridge History of Political Thought*, 254–97; Franklin, "Sovereignty and the Mixed Constitution."

129. See Pasquale Pasquino, "The Constitutional Republicanism of Emmanuel Sieyes," in Fontana, *Invention of the Modern Republic*, 110ff.

130. Carl J. Richard, *The Founders and the Classics* (Cambridge, MA: Harvard University Press, 1995), 235.

131. Though he meant as an object of study, not retrievable model, in *Spirit of the Laws*, 172. Both sides in the constitutional controversy used Montesquieu. The Federalist arguments on separation of powers are more familiar than the Antifederalists' appeal to Montesquieu's sociology—on laws fitting the customs of the people: "The vision of New Hampshire militiamen enforcing the law in Georgia, and vice versa, was frightening"; Shklar, "Positive Liberty, Negative Liberty in the United States," in *Redeeming*, 123.

132. For direct reading, see Richard, *Founders*. Classic pastoralism and the Antifederalists is a central theme of his. The Whig argument is Bernard Bailyn's, *Ideological Origins of the American Revolution* (Cambridge, MA: Harvard University Press, 1967), and J.G.A. Pocock's *The Machiavellian Moment: Florentine Political Thought and the Atlantic Republican Tradition* (Princeton: Princeton University Press, 1975), which juxtaposed the Whig opposition and supporters of monarchy to the Republican-Federalist debate. The view that classical republicanism in its Whig version, with its fear of monarchy on the one hand and democratic anarchy on the other, gave way after the revolution to a peculiarly American concern with majority tyranny is Gordon Wood's, in *The Creation of the American Republic, 1776–1787* (Chapel Hill: University of North Carolina Press, 1969).

133. The ancient synthesis was mainly struck by Pocock in *The Machiavellian Moment*; the anti-Lockean argument for the ancients in American political thought and history was formulated by Bernard Bailyn in *Ideological Origins of the American Revolution* and Gordon Wood in *Creation of the American Republic*. For a discussion of the distinctive influence of the Greek tradition in republicanism and in the American Founding in particular, see Eric Nelson, *The Greek Tradition in Republican Thought* (Cambridge: Cambridge University Press, 2004). As Nelson observes, it is one thing to resolve this intellectual conflict by showing the mutual influences of Lockean and classical ideas; it is another to show that the notion of "classical influence" is simplistic and needs to be disaggregated.

134. Hamilton, Madison, and Jay, *The Federalist* 85 (no. 14), 457 (no. 70).

135. Madison, "No. 9," in Hamilton, Madison, and Jay, *The Federalist*, 49–50. Judith N. Shklar, "Montesquieiu and the New Republicanism," in Judith N. Shklar, *Political Thought and Political Thinkers*, ed. Stanley Hoffmann (Chicago: University of Chicago Press, 1998), 255.

136. Letter cited in Shklar, "Democracy and the Past," in *Redeeming*, 174.

137. Charles Pinckney cited in Shklar, "A New Constitution for a New Nation," in *Redeeming*, 160.

138. Though the Republican refrain was that Federalists had a preference for England and monarchy; Hofstadter, *Idea of a Party System*,167ff.

139. Wood, *Creation*, 112, 89.

140. Cited in Correa Moylan Walsh, *The Political Science of John Adams* (New York: Books for Libraries Press, 1969), 292.

141. Bernard Manin, "Checks, Balances, and Boundaries: the Separation of Powers in the Constitutional Debate of 1787," in Fontana, *Invention of the Modern Republic*, 27–62, 34–35, 44.

142. Some constitutional thinkers went a step further. Following Harrington, they retained the notion of aristocracy but substituted "natural aristocracy" (sometimes referred to as an aristocracy of virtue) for birth. Natural aristocracy was not a designated class but a reference to "the right sort" who deserved to govern and who would come to the fore in politics if aristocracy based on entrenched inequalities of wealth were eliminated and if most people had some property (an enlarged, moderate middle class).

143. Arendt, *On Revolution* (New York: Viking, 1963), 229.

144. Gerald Leonard, *The Invention of Party Politics: Federalism, Popular Sovereignty, and Constitutional Development in Jacksonian Illinois* (Chapel Hill: University of North Carolina Press, 2002), 26.

145. Madison, "Parties," in *Writings*, 504. He and others anticipated that laws restricting property and inheritance would do this work: end primogeniture and entails, making for the equal division of estates among heirs, the division of lands of intestates equally among all children; as Jefferson put it, "these laws . . . laid the axe to the root of the Pseudo-aristocracy." Cited in Nelson, *Greek Tradition*, 203.

146. Madison: "Should a state of parties arise founded on geographical boundaries and other physical and permanent distinctions which happen to coincide with them, what is to control these great repulsive Masses from awful shocks against each other"? The object was "to form a new state of parties founded on local instead of political distinctions; thereby dividing the Republicans of the North from those of the South, and making the former instrumental in giving to the opponents of both an ascendancy over the whole." Cited in Hofstadter, *Idea of a Party System*, 202.

147. The checking dynamic pluralism makes possible is an unfortunate expedient only. To infer that this implies that organizing parties is beneficial "is not less absurd than it would be in ethics, to say, that new vices ought to be promoted, where they would counteract each other." Madison, "Parties," in *Writings*, 505. Nor did pluralism prevent the formation of regional parties on the basis of "southern oligarchy," slavery, and states rights—which confirmed the worst fears and led to civil war.

148. Schattschneider, *Party Government*, 7, 8. Schattschneider's argument is that Madison failed to see that parties might be used as beneficent instruments of popular government.

149. Here again we see the tendency to insist on a proper definition of parties where the baseline is some modern electoral organization. Were these organizations of the 1790s parties? They were fledgling parties in the sense that they were both groupings within Congress to organize government and mechanisms for organizing elections.

150. Leonard, *Invention of Party Politics*, 180.

151. This is the thesis of John Aldrich and Ruth Grant, "The Antifederalists, the First Congress, and the First Parties," *Journal of Politics* 55, no. 2 (1993): 295–326.

"Junto" is at 304; "monocrat" at 321. Voting on most matters was chaotic, but on the measures judged continuous with debates about the articles and the Constitution, which put the regime at stake, partisan divides are discernible. See too Larry D. Kramer, "Putting the Politics Back into the Political Safeguards of Federalism," *Columbia Law Review* 100, no. 1 (2000): 215–93, 272ff.

152. Kramer, "Putting the Politics Back," 272ff.

153. See Charles Sumner, "The Republican Party: Its Origins, Necessity and Permanence," speech before the Young Men's Republican Union of New York, 11 July 1860. Reprinted in *Library of the University Pamphlets* II (New York, 1860), 6. This notion of a southern oligarchy was shared by Whigs, Democrats, and antislavery radicals. In this, and in the subsequent history of civil war and reconstruction, the Republican Party saw itself as the party of national unity, opposed to both oligarchy and the breakup of the union.

154. Cited in Hofstadter, *Idea of a Party System*, 8, 17.

155. For a discussion of representative democracy as neither a betrayal nor poor substitute for immediate democracy and of Condorcet as its principal theorist, see Nadia Urbinati, "Condorcet's Democratic Theory of Representative Government," *European Journal of Political Theory* 3, no. 1 (2004): 53–75.

156. Cited by Sartori, *Parties and Party Systems*, 11.

157. Chastened by the Terror, Sieyes would later devise a complex scheme of four constitutional bodies. See William H. Sewell Jr., *A Rhetoric of Bourgeois Revolution: The Abbe Sieyes and What Is the Third Estate* (Durham: Duke University Press, 1994).

158. The Abbe was less clear about the fate of clerical privileges and of priesthood as a public office.

159. Sewell, *Rhetoric*, 45.

160. Emmanuel Joseph Sieyes, *What Is the Third Estate* (New York: Praeger, 1963). He also designed the administrative reorganization of France into uniform departments and disputed the representative character of the parliaments.

161. Murray Forsyth, *Reason and Revolution: The Political Thought of the Abbe Sieyes* (New York: Leicester University Press, 1987), 90.

162. Cited in Pasquino, "Constitutional Republicanism," 115.

163. Cited in Sewell, *Rhetoric* 46.

164. Cited in Arendt, *On Revolution*, 243.

165. Cited in Stephen Holmes, *Benjamin Constant and the Making of Modern Liberalism* (New Haven: Yale University Press, 1984), 91.

166. Constant, cited in George Armstrong Kelly, *The Humane Comedy: Constant, Tocqueville, and French Liberalism* (Cambridge: Cambridge University Press, 1992), 42.

167. On Jefferson and revolutionary spaces, see Arendt, *On Revolution*, 238ff. Sieyes is closer to Benjamin Rush: although "all power is derived from the people, they possess it only on the days of their elections. After this it is the property of their rulers" (239).

168. Murray Forsyth, *Reason and Revolution: The Political Thought of the Abbé Sieyes* (New York: Holmes and Meier, 1987), 136.

169. Quoted in ibid., 78.

170. This idea is recurrent in political theory; consider this twentieth-century definition of Parliamentarism: "formation of the governing will of the state ... through a collegial organ elected by the people." Hans Kelsen, "On the Essence and Value of Democracy," in *Weimar: A Jurisprudence of Crisis*, ed. Arthur Jacobson and Bernard Schlink (Berkeley: University of California Press, 2000): 84–109, 96. Kelsen goes on to describe parliamentarism as a compromise between the democratic demand of freedom and the "principle of the division of labor that is a condition of all socio-technical progress" (96–97). The contrast to Sieyes is Condorcet's proposals for a constitutional apparatus that invited constant interaction between citizen assemblies and government. Urbinati, "Condorcet's Democratic Theory," 59.

171. Quoted in Forsyth, *Reason and Revolution*, 139, 75.

172. Quoted in ibid., 39, 75.

173. See Pasquino, "Constitutional Republicanism," for the argument that Sieyes was a republican and his tolerance of some form of monarchy opportunistic.

174. Sieyes, *What Is the Third Estate*, 133. Sewell argues it signaled the bourgeoisie in a diffuse non-Marxist sense—productive but not all workers. This raised the question whether the aristocracy had to be exiled or could "convert" by word or deed into citizens of the nation. Gary Kates argues that it was the germ of the antidemocratic suffrage laws opposed by radicals, including Paine, in "Tom Paine's Rights of Man," *Journal of the History of Ideas* 50, no. 4 (1989): 569–87, 583.

175. Cited in Sewell, *Rhetoric*, 93.

176. Sieyes, *What Is the Third Estate*, 159.

177. G.W.F. Hegel, "The German Constitution," in *Hegel's Political Writings*, intro. Z. A. Pelczynski (Oxford: Clarendon Press, 1964), 149, 151. Hegel was most tolerant of the Wurtenberg Constitution; see his "Proceedings."

178. Hegel, "The German Constitution," in ibid., 248, 242.

179. Hegel, "The German Constitution," cited in Pelczynski's introduction, in ibid., 35. He argued that Sieyes's homogenization and his emasculation of the monarch opened the way for Napoleon in "The English Reform Bill" (in ibid., 322).

180. Hegel, "Wurtenberg," cited in Pelczynski's essay in *Political Writings*, 74; "Wurtemberg," 264.

181. Hegel, "The English Reform Bill," 318.

182. Hegel, "The German Constitution," 206.

183. G.W.F. Hegel, *Philosophy of Right* (Oxford: Clarendon, 1952), §302, 197.

184. Ibid., §303, 198.

185. Hegel's distinction between civil society and state was not a prescription for institutional separation. Because she confuses philosophical understanding of civil

society and state with political theory, Fania Oz-Salzberger calls Ferguson's influence on Hegel ironic, in "Introduction" to Ferguson, xix.

186. Hegel, *Philosophy of Right*, §273, 176; §272, 175.

187. Ibid., §273, 176; §272, 175.

188. Ibid., §§311, 314, 202–3, 155, 196.

189. Bagehot, *English Constitution*, xxxiv; xxvii.

190. Corporate-like notions of fixed social parts and guaranteed representation (modern mixed government) can lead to a defense of parties. For those who resist the rigidity and separatism built into these mixes and balances, parties have a potential role as agents of cross-cutting cleavages. We know that Calhoun's nullification thesis prompted Madison to shift from opposing an overbearing majority party to a qualified defense of majoritarianism. In this vein, political science studies of divided societies prescribe an electoral system that encourages broad umbrella parties.

191. G.D.H. Cole, "The Social Theory," in *The Pluralist Theory of the State: Selected Writings of G.D.H. Cole, J. N. Figgis, and H. J. Laski*, ed. Paul Q. Hirst (London: Routledge, 1989), 94.

192. Neo-corporatism is viewed variously as survival of old schisms and corporate representation or as a response to crises of capitalism. Philippe C. Schmitter, "The Consolidation of Democracy and Representation of Social Groups," *American Behavioral Scientist* 35, nos. 4–5 (March/June 1992): 422–49, 434.

193. Guillermo O'Donnell, Philippe C. Schmitter, and Laurence Whitehead, eds., *Transitions from Authoritarian Rule: Tentative Conclusions about Uncertain Democracies* (Baltimore: Johns Hopkins University Press, 1986), 37–38. The authors point out the similarity to a cartel of party elites (40).

194. See, e.g., Giandomenico Majone, "Ideas, Interests and Institutional Change: The European Commission Debates the Delegation Problem," unpublished manuscript.

195. Philip Pettit, *Republicanism: A Theory of Freedom and Government* (Oxford: Oxford University Press, 1994); John P. McCormick, "Contain the Wealthy and Patrol the Magistrates: Restoring Elite Accountability to Popular Government," *American Political Science Review* 100, no. 2 (May 2006): 147–63, 157.

196. Hume, "Of Parties in General," in *Political Essays*, 34.

197. Madison, "Parties," in *Writings*, 504.

198. Madison, "No. 10," in Hamilton et al., *The Federalist*.

199. Letter to James Monroe, 1822, in *James Madison's Advice to My Country*, ed. David B. Mattern (Charlottesville: University Press of Virginia, 1997), 76.

200. Tocqueville, *Democracy in America*, 171.

201. Edmund S. Morgan, *Inventing the People*, documents the way in which early "instructions" to representatives and "petitions" to government were often top-down (222ff.).

202. In John H. Aldrich, *Why Parties?* (Chicago: University of Chicago Press, 1995), 4.

203. Eric L. McKitrick, "Party Politics and the Union and Confederate War Efforts," in *The American Party Systems*, ed. William N. Chambers and Walter Dean Burnham (New York: Oxford University Press, 1967), 117–51, 123.

204. Explanations for variations in party systems diverge. One school focuses on the nature of underlying social cleavages; its weakness is "extensive evidence of the non-mobilization of differences." The other focuses on institutional constraints, mainly electoral rules. See Susan C. Stokes, "Political Parties and Democracy," *Annual Review of Political Science* 2 (1999): 243–67, 247–288.

205. Michael F. Holt, *The Political Crisis of the 1850s* (New York: John Wiley & Sons, 1978), 183.

206. Mansfield, *Statesmanship and Party Government*, 14.

207. Schattschneider, *Semisovereign People*, 74.

Chapter 3. Moments of Appreciation

1. Cited in Harvey C. Mansfield Jr., "Whether Party Government Is Inevitable," *Political Science Quarterly* 80, no. 4 (1965): 517–42, 528; Machiavelli, *Discourses on Livy*, trans. Harvey C. Mansfield Jr. and Nathan Tarcov (Chicago: University of Chicago Press, 1996), bk. 1, chaps. 4–5.

2. John Toland, "The State-Anatomy of Great Britain," in J.A.W. Gunn, *Factions No More: Attitudes to Party in Government and Opposition in Eighteenth-Century England* (London: Frank Cass, 1971), 54.

3. Sartori, *Parties and Party Systems*, 18, borrowing from Oakeshott.

4. Hofstadter, *Idea of a Party System*, 39.

5. Aldrich, *Why Parties?*, 69; 29.

6. Arendt, *On Revolution*, 222.

7. In *History of England from the Invasion of Julius Caesar to the Abdication of James the Second, 1688*, 6 vols. (New York: Harper and Brothers, 1879), and his political essays. The relation between the two is outside my subject; see *Hume: Political Essays*, ed. Knud Haakonssen (Cambridge: Cambridge University Press, 1994).

8. Hume, "Of the Parties of Great Britain," in *Political Essays*, 40.

9. Hume, "Excerpts from Hume's *History of England*," in *Political Essays*, 234, discussing Charles I and the Petition of Right; 248, a discussion of Charles I's dissolution of the Short Parliament; 249–50.

10. Ibid., 245. The contest over Hume's partisanship ("thinking Whig" or Tory) can be sampled in James Conniff and Geoffrey Marshall, "David Hume and Political Scepticism," *Philosophical Quarterly* 4, no. 16 (1954): 247–57; Duncan Forbes, *Hume's Philosophical Politics* (Cambridge: Cambridge University Press, 1975), 212ff.

11. Hume, "Excerpts from Hume's *History of England*," 241, 237.

12. Ibid., 240. He constructs a dialogue between Whig and Tory: Whig attachment to the idea of a contract and the priority of statutes vs. partisans of the court

and the priority of experience; the Whig language of abdication and election of a king vs. the Tory "desertion" and advocacy of regency over election.

13. Hume, "Excerpts from Hume's *History of England*," 238; 244.

14. Hume, "Of the Parties of Great Britain," 43.

15. Hume, "Of the Independency of Parliament," in *Political Essays,* 26.

16. Hume, "Of the Coalition of Parties," 93; Morgan, *Inventing the People,* 116ff., 218ff.

17. Hume, "Excerpts from Hume's *History of* England," 244; "Of the Parties of Great Britain," 43.

18. See Forbes's citations of Hume's letters, *Hume's Philosophical Politics,* 128.

19. Cited in David Miller, *Philosophy and Ideology in Hume's Political Thought* (Oxford: Clarendon Press, 1981), 176.

20. "Even that party amongst us, which boasts of the highest regard to liberty, has not possessed sufficient liberty of thought in this particular." Hume, "Excerpts from Hume's *History of England*," 246.

21. Ibid., 247.

22. This is the general argument of Mansfield, "Whether Party Government Is Inevitable."

23. Hume, "Of the Coalition of Parties," 209.

24. Hume's writing on this score was a rebuttal of Bolingbroke; for a full discussion see Forbes, *Hume's Philosophical Politics,* 200ff.

25. Morgan, *Inventing the People,* 219.

26. Aldrich, *Why Parties?*, 28; for an account of the mix of principle, interest, and institutional need that led to the development of these first parties in government, see 70ff., 93ff. On the party politics of the First Congress, see John Aldrich and Ruth Grant, "The Antifederalists, the First Congress, and the First Parties," *Journal of Politics* 55, no. 2 (1993): 295–326.

27. Gordon Wood, *The Radicalism of the American Revolution* (New York: Knopf, 1991), 298.

28. Cited in Hofstadter, *Idea of a Party System,* 107.

29. Aldrich and Grant, "Antifederalists," 298.

30. Cited in Hofstadter, *Idea of a Party System,* 124.

31. Aldrich, *Why Parties?*, 80.

32. Ibid.

33. Bruce Ackerman, *The Failure of the Founding Fathers: Jefferson, Marshall, and the Rise of Presidential Democracy* (Cambridge, MA: Harvard University Press), 143.

34. Ibid., 101; Wood, *Radicalism,* 298; Aldrich, *Why Parties?*, 80.

35. Gunn, *Factions No More,* 2.

36. Ackerman, *Failure of the Founding Fathers,* 24. This is distinct from the argument proposed by legal historians that the guarantor of constitutionalism, protector of the contentious state/national balance was not initially thought to be judicial review but popular political action organized and channeled early on by parties. Larry

D. Kramer, "Putting the Politics Back into the Political Safeguards of Federalism," *Columbia Law Review* 100, no. 1 (2000): 215–93, 272ff.

37. Hofstadter, *Idea of a Party System*, 138.

38. Ibid., 120. Hofstadter cites Madison's conviction that the acquiescence of defeated parties in elections hinged in good part on the absence of available military force to abet usurpation (131 n.).

39. Kramer, "Putting the Politics Back," 273–74.

40. Clinton Rossiter, *Parties and Politics in America* (Ithaca: Cornell University Press, 1960), 1.

41. Aldrich and Grant, "Antifederalists," 310.

42. Sumner, "Republican Party," 2, 14.

43. Michael S. Green, *Freedom, Union, and Power* (New York: Fordham University Press, 2004), 265.

44. John J. Coleman, "Resurgent or Just Busy? Party Organizations in Contemporary America," in *The State of the Parties: The Changing Role of Contemporary American Parties*, 2nd ed., ed. John C. Green and Daniel M. Shea (Lanham, MD: Rowman and Littlefield, 1996), 367–84, 370; Francis Lieber, cited in Hofstadter, *Idea of a Party System*, 259.

45. Hume's account of the real balance, dependent on patronage, was the view from outside, unacknowledged by any party. The added confounding element was the propensity of Tories in particular to move from principled defense of monarchy (indefeasible right) to affection for a particular line of succession. See Hume, "Of the Parties of Great Britain," 280–81 nn.

46. J.A.W. Gunn, "Influence, Parties and the Constitution: Changing Attitudes, 1783–1832," *Historical Journal* 17, no. 2 (1974): 301–28.

47. Edmund Burke, *An Appeal from the New to the Old Whigs* (New York: Library of Liberal Arts, 1962), 54.

48. Hume, "Of Parties in General," in *Political Essays*, 34.

49. Cited in Hofstadter, *Idea of a Party System*, 131 n.

50. Ibid., 244.

51. Cited in Mansfield, *Statesmanship and Party Government*, 174.

52. Daniel Defoe, "On Government by Parties," in Gunn, *Factions No More*, 86.

53. A nineteenth-century Albany newspaper, cited in Hofstadter, *Idea of a Party System*, 251.

54. Shklar, *Montesquieu*, 85.

55. Dennis F. Thompson, "Restoring Distrust," in Thompson, *Restoring Responsibility: Ethics in Government, Business, and Healthcare* (Cambridge: Cambridge University Press, 2005), 249.

56. See Morgan for a discussion of extra-parliamentary associations in Britain and America. They were fewer and more discredited in Britain (232–33). Party government and later party democracy brought them together.

57. Gunn, *Factions No More.*

58. Hume, "Of the Coalition of Parties," 93.

59. Sartori, *Parties and Party Systems*, 18.

60. Hofstadter, *Idea of a Party System*, 74ff., 76.

61. Gunn, *Factions No More*, 1.

62. Sartori takes sides in the structural vs. political contest about the conditions for regulated rivalry. In discussing twopartyism, he writes: "It should not be taken for granted . . . that twopartyism *presupposes* a set of favorable conditions—cultural homogeneity, consensus on fundamentals, and the like. If one reviews the development of the two party countries historically, it appears that twopartyism has largely *nurtured* and molded such favorable conditions" (*Parties and Party System*, 192).

63. Arendt, *On Revolution*, 222.

64. Ackerman, *Failure of the Founding Fathers*, 100.

65. James Madison, "Parties," in Rakove, *James Madison: Writings*, 504.

66. Gunn, *Factions No More*, 2.

67. James MacGregor Burns and Georgia J. Sorenson, *Dead Center: Clinton-Gore Leadership and the Perils of Moderation* (New York: Scribner, 1999), 270.

68. Tocqueville, *Democracy in America*, 185.

69. "The Sentiment of a Tory in Respect to a Late Important Transaction and in Regard to the Present Situation of Affairs," in Gunn, *Factions No More*, 105.

70. On parties that challenge constitutional essentials, see Nancy L. Rosenblum, "Banning Parties: Religious and Ethnic Partisanship in Multicultural Democracies," *Journal of Law and Ethics of Human Rights* 1 (2007): 17–75.

71. I am indebted to John Ferejohn for this point. See too John Aldrich's *Why Parties?* Perhaps his main point is that parties are "endogenous," the creation of political men to address collective action needs specific to historical and institutional situations, different problems; hence, there is no one party form. Aldrich describes this work as "new institutionalist," where structure-induced incentives (rather than preferences) affect outcomes.

72. Przeworski, "Minimalist Conception of Democracy," 23–55, 49.

73. Adam Ferguson, "Remarks on a Pamphlet Lately Published by Dr. Price," in Gunn, *Factions No More*, 214.

74. Franklin Roosevelt's exasperation: The "three horse team of the American system of government" could not function "if one horse lies down in the traces or plunges off in another direction." Cited in Bruce Ackerman, *We the People*, vol. 2, *Transformations* (Cambridge, MA: Harvard University Press, 1998), 325.

75. I leave aside Hegel's philosophy of the state as "a great architectonic edifice, a hieroglyph of reason which becomes manifest in actuality." Hegel, *Philosophy of Right*, addition to §279.

76. Z. A. Pelczynski, introduction to *Hegel's Political Writings*, 91. Pelczynski's introductory essay describes Hegel's reading, correspondence, and experience in the various German states and his persistent interest in politics.

77. Hegel, "Proceedings of the Estates Assembly in the Kingdom of Wurtenberg," cited in the introduction to ibid., 89.

78. Hegel, "The English Reform Bill," in ibid., 329.

79. Hegel, "Proceedings of the Estates Assembly in Wurtenberg," 258.

80. Hegel, "Proceedings of the Estates Assembly in Wurtenberg," 258.

81. Hegel, "English Reform Bill," 330.

82. For a recent discussion of parties and parliamentary/presidential/semi-presidential systems, see Cindy Skach, *Borrowing Constitutional Designs: Constitutional Law in Weimar Germany and the French Fifth Republic* (Princeton: Princeton University Press, 2005). The chief concern of political scientists on this score is party coherence and political stability.

83. Tocqueville, *Democracy in America,* 181–82.

84. That and a civil service; bureaucracy is a principal theme of *Philosophy of Right.* On the similarity to another state theorist, Jeremy Bentham, see Nancy L. Rosenblum, *Bentham's Theory of the Modern State* (Cambridge, MA: Harvard University Press, 1978). One great difference in their accounts of the organization of the state was Bentham's derogation of parties.

85. Hegel, "Proceedings of the Estates Assembly in Wurtenberg," 257–58; "English Reform Bill," 323.

86. Max Weber, "Politics as a Vocation,"in *From Max Weber: Essays in Sociology,* ed. H. H. Gerth and C. Wright Mills (Oxford: Oxford University Press, 1946), 83.

87. Ibid., 90.

88. Pelczynski, introduction to *Hegel's Political Writings,* 80.

89. Hegel, "English Reform Bill," 328. The people understood simply as voters, we have seen, "leave political life hanging, so to speak in the air"; they are severed from "corporations and communal associations, the circles where particular and universal interests come together." Hegel, *Philosophy of Right,* addition to §290.

90. Pelczynski, introduction to *Hegel's Political Writings,* 91.

91. Hegel, "English Reform Bill," 328.

92. Ibid., 323–24.

93. Burke, "Thoughts on the Cause of the Present Discontents," cited in Sartori, *Parties and Party Systems,* 9. See Burke, "Thoughts on the Cause of the Present Discontents," in *Select Works of Edmund Burke: A New Imprint on the Payne Edition,* 4 vols. (Indianapolis: Liberty Fund, 1999), vol. 1, 69–155, 146ff.

94. I have not found evidence that Hegel attended to the role of parties in organizing assemblies in any detail. For a discussion of the advantages parties provide in agenda setting (regulating access to plenary time) in contrast to the "legislative state of nature," see Gary W. Cox, "The Organization of Democratic Legislatures," in *Oxford Handbook of Political Economy,* ed. Barry Weingast and Donald Wittman (Oxford: Oxford University Press, 2006): 141–61.

95. Hume, "Excerpts from Hume's *History of England,*" 248.

96. Gunn, *Factions No More,* 12ff. Contrast this historical view with accounts that define parties as modern electoral parties and see the origin of parties in the need to incorporate unprecedented numbers of people into the political process; cf. Joseph LaPalombara and Jeffrey Anderson, "Political Parties," in *Encyclopedia of Government and Politics*, vol. 1, ed. Mary Hawkesworth and Maurice Kogan (New York: Routledge, 2004), 381–98.

97. Weber, "Politics as a Vocation," in *From Max Weber,* 102ff.

98. Maurice Duverger, *Political Parties: Their Organization and Activity in the Modern State* (New York: John Wiley and Sons, 1963), xxivff.

99. Aldrich, *Why Parties?,* 4. The existence of parties, he argues, creates incentives for their use (24). Of course, Aldrich emphasizes in addition parties as a solution to the electoral problems of ambitious political men.

100. Cited in "Party," in Comfort, *Brewer's Politics,* 442.

101. Walter Bagehot, *The English Constitution* (New York: Garland, 1978), 141–42.

102. Eric L. McKitrick, "Party Politics and the Union and Confederate War Efforts," in *The American Party Systems,* ed. William N. Chambers and Walter Dean Burnham (New York: Oxford University Press, 1967), 117–51.

103. Discussed in Samuel H. Beer, "The Rise and Fall of Party Government in Britain and the United States," in *More Adventures with Britannia,* ed. William Roger Louis (Austin: University of Texas Press, 1998), 281–301, 283.

104. Burke, "Thoughts on the Cause of the Present Discontents."

105. "A Brief and Impartial Review of the State of Great Britain at the Commencement of the Session of 1783," in Gunn, *Factions No More,* 224.

106. Hillaire Belloc and Cecil Chesterton, *The Party System* (London: Steven Swift, 1911), 18, 25, 152.

107. Bernard Manin, *The Principles of Representative Government* (Cambridge: Cambridge University Press, 1997), 193.

108. I am grateful to Jack Rakove for comments on this point in discussion of the Wesson Lectures, Stanford University, 2006.

109. See Wood, *Radicalism,* 299ff; Aldrich, *Why Parties?,* 56. The ethnic theme is worked out in Ted Widmer, *Martin Van Buren* (New York: Henry Holt, 2005), 6.

110. On the sufficiency of moderate differences for party competition, see Schattschneider, *Party Government,* 93.

111. Duverger, *Political Parties,* xv.

112. Hume, "Excerpts from Hume's *History of England,*" 247.

113. John Stuart Mill, "Bentham," in *Collected Works of John Stuart Mill,* vol. 10, ed. John M. Robson (Toronto: University of Toronto Press, 1977), 80.

114. Hume, "Of the Coalition of Parties," 206.

115. Hume, "Idea of a Perfect Commonwealth," in *Political Essays,* 229.

116. Ibid., 228.

117. This view of the relation of parties as dividing a significant and identifiable field is common today, vivid, for example, in (Democratic) preoccupation with justice as distribution vs. (Republican) concern with the production of wealth or, simply, left and right. I take this example from Russell Muirhead, "Left *and* Right: A Defense of Partisanship," unpublished paper for the Dartmouth Politics Colloquium, November 2002.

118. That seems to be the function of the "court of competitors" he proposes in Hume, "Idea of a Perfect Commonwealth," 225.

119. Tories are lovers of monarchy and of liberty; Whigs too, but each exaggerates one element. Hume, "Of the Parties of Great Britain," 44–45 and 278–79 nn.

120. Hume, *Enquiries Concerning the Human Understanding*, cited in Stephen Holmes, *Passions and Constraint: On the Theory of Liberal Democracy* (Chicago: University of Chicago Press, 1995), 49.

121. Hume, "Of the Independency of Parliament," in *Political Essays*, 24.

122. Hume, "That Politics May Be Reduced to a Science," 12–13; Hume, "Of the Independency of Parliament," 24.

123. Hume, "Of the Independency of Parliament," 26.

124. David Hume, *The Letters of David* Hume, ed. J.Y.T. Grieg (Oxford: Clarendon Press, 1932), vol. 2, p. 286, cited in Andrew Sabl, "Hume's Moral Psychology of Party," 3, unpublished manuscript on file with the author. Sabl's whole point is the corruption of partisanship; he does not see in Hume the "moment of appreciation" I detail here.

125. Cited in Frederick Whelan, *Order and Artifice in Hume's Political Philosophy* (Princeton: Princeton University Press, 1985), 330.

126. Hume, "Excerpts from Hume's *History of England*," 247.

127. Hume, "Of the Coalition of Parties," 94.

128. Hume, "That Politics May Be Reduced to a Science," 14.

129. Aristotle had a deeper view of the relation of parties than even this account of justice suggests. His further insight is that no one principle of rule (wealth, freedom) is in the complete interest *even of those who advance it*. Aristotle, *Politics*, trans. Barker, bk. 3, chap. 13, pp. 115–17; Patrick Coby, "Aristotle's Three Cities and the Problem of Faction," *Journal of Politics* 50, no. 4 (1988): 896–919, 908–9. Each taken alone is self-defeating: claims based on wealth open the way to claims to rule by the wealthiest; aristocratic virtue to kingly virtue, and so on. But Aristotle does not seem to require this insight into the internal inconsistencies of parts. Justice is hard enough. A similar argument holds for Polybius and Harrington. Pocock, "Machiavelli, Harrington, and English Political Ideologies in the Eighteenth Century," 549–83.

130. All committed to reciprocity, the priority of basic rights and opportunities, and the means to make effective use of freedoms. John Rawls, *The Law of Peoples; with, The Idea of Public Reason Revisited* (Cambridge, MA: Harvard University

Press, 1999), 140–41. For a full discussion of Rawls on parties, see Russell Muirhead and Nancy L. Rosenblum, "Political Liberalism vs. 'The Great Game of Politics': The Politics of Political Liberalism," *Perspectives on Politics* 4, no. 1 (2006): 99–108.

131. John Rawls, *Political Liberalism* (New York: Columbia University Press, 1993), 235.

132. John Rawls, "Preface for the French Edition of *A Theory of Justice*," in *Collected Papers*, ed. Samuel Freeman (Cambridge, MA: Harvard University Press), 415–16.

133. John Rawls, *Justice as Fairness: A Restatement* (Cambridge, MA: Harvard University Press, 2001), 49.

134. Carl Schmitt, *The Crisis of Parliamentary Democracy* (Cambridge, MA: MIT Press, 1985), 64.

135. Mill, "On Liberty," in *Collected Works,* vol. 18, p. 253.

136. Ibid., 253.

137. Ibid., 252, 254; Mill, "On Liberty," 253; Mill, *Considerations on Representative Government* (New York: Library of Liberal Arts, 1958), 116.

138. Jean-Antoine-Nicolas de Caritat Condorcet, "On the Principles of the Constitutional Plan Presented to the National Convention," in *Condorcet: Selected Writings*, ed. Keith Michael Baker (Indianapolis: Bobbs-Merrill, 1976), 159.

139. Mill, *Considerations on Representative Government*, 58.

140. Ibid., 82.

141. Cited in Schmitt, *Crisis of Parliamentary Democracy*, 7.

142. Bernard Crick, *In Defense of Politics* (London: Continuum, 2000), 20.

143. Cited in Hofstadter, *Idea of a Party System*, 38.

144. William Godwin, *Enquiry Concerning Political Justice* (Oxford: Oxford University Press, 1971), 140.

145. Hegel, "Proceedings of the Estates Assembly in Wurtenberg," cited in Pelczynski's introduction to *Hegel's Political Writings*, 89.

146. Benjamin Constant, *Political Writings*, ed. Biancamaria Fontana (Cambridge: Cambridge University Press, 1988), 197; Constant, *Principles of Politics Applicable to All Governments*, ed. Etienne Hofmann (Indianapolis: Liberty Fund, 2003), 329.

147. Constant, *Principles of Politics*, 327, 328.

148. Joshua Cohen, "Democracy and Liberty," in *Deliberative Democracy*, ed. Jon Elster (Cambridge: Cambridge University Press, 1998), 185–231, 194. When strong, the normative interests that constrain reasons can do all the work of democratic theory—they can leave little space for democratic decisions.

149. Jeremy Waldron, *Law and Disagreement* (New York: Oxford University Press, 1999), 151; Cohen, "Deliberation and Democratic Legitimacy," 22–23. The alternative goal to consensus in deliberative theory is again better decisions or identifying the noncoercive conditions for democratic justification.

150. Thomas Christiano, *The Rule of the Many* (New York: Westview, 1996), 276, though Christiano argues for proportional representation with candidate slates.

151. These quotes are from Adolf G. Gundersen, "Deliberative Democracy and the Limits of Partisan Politics: Between Athens and Philadelphia," in *Political Theory and Partisan Politics*, ed. Edward Portis, Adolf Gundersen, and Ruth Shively (Albany: SUNY Press, 2000), 97–116, 98.

152. David M. Estlund sees the legislature as the deliberative institution that should maximize resemblance to hypothetical model deliberation; he loosens the requirements for the informal political sphere. *Democratic Authority: A Philosophical Framework* (Princeton: Princeton University Press, 2008), 202–3.

153. Waldron, *Law and Disagreement*. One exception is Bruce Ackerman and James Fishkin, *Deliberation Day* (New Haven: Yale University Press, 2004). Deliberation Day assigns major parties a role: see chapter 6, "Correcting the System."

154. Habermas mandates "a clear and enduring demarcation between this sphere and the formal political system." Stephen White, *The Recent Work of Jurgen Habermas* (Cambridge: Cambridge University Press, 1988), 126. For a critical view of deliberative hopes for civil society, see Nancy L. Rosenblum, *Membership and Morals: The Personal Uses of Pluralism in America* (Princeton: Princeton University Press, 1998). Social science converges on the view that most voluntary associations are homogeneous and not ripe sites for "trial by discussion" of conflicting political views (the exception is professional associations). The setting most likely to expose individuals to conversational opposition is the workplace. See Cynthia Estlund, *Working Together: How Workplace Bonds Strengthen a Diverse Democracy* (Oxford: Oxford University Press, 2003).

155. Constant, *Principles of Politics*, 327, 328.

156. Cited in Bruce L. Kinzer, "J. S. Mill and the Problem of Party," *Journal of British Studies* 21, no. 1 (Autumn 1981): 106–22, 111. On Mill and the agora as model, see Nadia Urbinati, *Mill on Democracy: From the Athenian Polis to Representative Government* (Chicago: University of Chicago Press, 2002). It is consistent with stern contemporary deliberative theory that Mill was preoccupied with justification. He did not assign the actual business of governing to representative assemblies. "The only task to which a representative assembly can possibly be competent is not that of doing work, but of causing it to be done; of determining to whom or to what sort of people it should be confided, and giving or withholding the national sanction to it when performed." Mill, *Considerations on Representative Government*, 78–79.

157. Cited in Nicholas Capaldi, *John Stuart Mill: A Biography* (Cambridge: Cambridge University Press, 2004), 324.

158. Defined as support for a measure that serves one member's interests in return for support for yours, where these interests are disconnected from one another and from some larger view of the public good.

159. Mill, "On Liberty," 245.

160. Ibid., 252, 254.

161. Mill, *Considerations on Representative Government*, 58.

162. Mill, "On Liberty," 253.

163. Mill, "Bentham," in *Collected Works*, vol. 10, p. 77; Mill, "Coleridge," in *Collected Works*, vol. 10, p. 119.

164. Mill, "Bentham," vol. 10, p. 94.

165. Mill, "Recent Writings on Reform," cited in Kinzer, "J. S. Mill," 107.

166. The phrase is cited in Jeremy Waldron, *The Dignity of Legislation* (Cambridge: Cambridge University Press, 1999), 33. For the opposing view see Kinzer, "J. S. Mill," 107.

167. Mill, "Edinburgh Review," in *Collected Works*, vol. 1, p. 315; Mill, *Considerations on Representative Government*, 116, 82.

168. Mill, *Considerations on Representative Government*, 2.

169. Ibid., 108.

170. Ibid., 66.

171. Mill, "Edinburgh Review," 315.

172. Cited in Kinzer, "J. S. Mill," 109, n. 15.

173. Mill, "Edinburgh Review," 296, 302, 307, 314, 315.

174. Capaldi, *John Stuart Mill*, 321.

175. Cited in ibid., 323.

176. Crick, *In Defense of Politics*, 125.

177. Cited in Dennis Thompson, "Mill in Parliament: When Should a Philosopher Compromise?" in *J.S. Mill's Political Thought: A Bicentennial Re-assessment*, ed. Nadia Urbinati and Alex Zakaras (Cambridge: Cambridge University Press, 2007), 166–99, 169.

178. Mill, "Autobiography," in *Collected Works*, vol. 1, p. 87, cited in Thompson, "Mill in Parliament," 171.

179. Cited in Thompson, "Mill in Parliament," 171.

180. Mill's representative is an advocate who, in the words of one interpreter, "should *adhere* to its cause but not be driven by it" and whose "nonprejudicial attachments to their convictions" would allow them to change their minds in the course of deliberation about the public good. The first characterization is Urbinati's in "Representation and the Forms of Democratic Participation," unpublished manuscript, 28. The second sympathetic description—previewed in her titles—is Urbinati, *Mill on Democracy*, 83.

181. Thompson, "Mill in Parliament," 173. For a discussion of the concept of compromise as "less than their initial preferences or principles imply," see 36 n. 4; Mill cited in ibid., 177, 175, 176.

182. Mill, "Personal Representation," in *Collected Works*, vol. 28, p. 182.

183. Proportional representation would rescue democracy from failing even in its ostensible object—giving the power of government to the majority, which meant in practice a majority of the majority who are often a minority of the whole. Mill, *Considerations on Representative Government*, 120, 123, 127, 104.

184. Ibid., 126.

185. Mill, "Personal Representation," 182.

186. Ibid., 178.

187. Mill, *Considerations on Representative Government*, 114ff.; Mill, "Personal Representation," 176–86.

188. Mill, *Considerations on Representative Government*, 122ff.

189. Mill, "Personal Representation," 177.

190. Mill, *Considerations on Representative Government*, 196.

191. For a history of the idea and its connection to perceived failures of American parties, see Austin Ramney, "Party Responsibility," in *International Encyclopedia of the Social and Behavioral Sciences*, ed. Neil Smelser and Paul Bates, vol. 16 (Amsterdam: Elsevier, 2001), 11103–6.

192. Bagehot, *English Constitution*, 154ff.

193. The phrase is Gerhard Leibholz's, *Politics and Law* (Leyden: A. W. Sythoff, 1965), 55.

194. Mill, "On Liberty," 254.

195. Mill, *Considerations on Representative Government*, 8, 158, 67.

196. Ibid., 28.

197. It was a doctrine that "in virtue of its superior comprehensiveness might be adopted by either Liberal or Conservative without renouncing anything which he really feels to be valuable in his own creed." Ibid., 2.

198. The phrase is cited in Waldron, *Dignity of Legislation*, 33. On party organization even under Hare's scheme—tickets and a ticket of "national intellect and character" see Mill, *Considerations on Representative Government*, 295.

199. For a philosophical statement of party competition and choice as the defining characteristic of democracy, the condition for "giving laws to ourselves," see Robert Goodin, "The Philosophical Foundation of Party Government," unpublished manuscript.

200. Schmitt, *Crisis of Parlimentary Democracy*, 5, 46, 43, 34, 41, 3.

201. Ibid., 7.

202. "Democracy seems fated then to destroy itself in the problem of the formation of a will" (ibid., 38). See too John P. McCormick, "Irrational Choice and Mortal Combat as Political Destiny: Reconsidering the Essential Carl Schmitt," *Annual Review of Political Science* 10 (2007): 315–39.

203. Schmitt, *Crisis of Parlimentary Democracy*, 19. "In the face of all this," Schmitt concludes, "the belief in a discussing public must suffer a terrible disillusionment" (50).

204. On "the chaos of unrepresented and unpurified opinion," vulnerable to molding by a "strong man," see Arendt, *On Revolution*, 231.

205. Cited in Ackerman, *We the People*, vol. 2, p. 325.

206. Cited in Hofstadter, *Idea of a Party System*, 28.

207. Jurgen Habermas and Jacques Derrida, "February 15, or, What Binds Europeans Together: A Plea for a Common Foreign Policy, Beginning in the Core of Europe," *Constellations* 10, no. 3 (2003): 291–97, 296.

208. Schattschneider, *Semisovereign People*, 74.

209. The phrase is Bruce Ackerman's, *We the People*, vol. 1, 285.

210. "Some one has to politicize events, to define their political relevance in terms of a choice between or among parties." Holt, *Political Crisis of the 1850s*, 183.

211. Shklar, *Redeeming American Political Thought*, 11.

212. J. M. Hansen, "Faction," in Smelser and Bates, *International Encyclopedia of the Social and Behavioral Sciences*, vol. 8, 5234–36, 5236.

213. *OED* Online, 2004. Available at http://www.oed.com.

214. Cited in Wood, *Radicalism*, 299.

215. Jesse Macy, *Party Organization and Machinery* (New York: Arno Press, 1974 [1912]), 2.

Chapter 4. Progressive Antipartyism

1. Max Weber, "Politics as a Vocation," in *From Max Weber*, 102, 105, 107. Weber's 1918 discussion of party organization and "the ascendancy of the plebescitarian form" is from Moisei Ostrogorski, *Democracy and the Organization of Political Parties*, 2 vols., trans. Frederick Clarke (New York: Macmillan, 1922), vol. 1, p. 104.

2. Both American historians and political scientists study the origins of the American "party system." The central debate is whether to stress continuity (and the related question, what is the starting point of the modern party system) or discontinuity— i.e., critical elections, realignment, institutional reform and the existence of three or four or more distinct party systems. A good introduction to the historiography is Richard L. McCormick, *The Party Period and Public Policy* (New York: Oxford University Press, 1986).

3. Cited in Joel Silbey, "Always a Whig in Politics: The Partisan Life of Abraham Lincoln," in *Papers of the Abraham Lincoln Association,* vol. 8 (Springfield: University of Illinois Press), 21–42, 40.

4. James Bryce, *The American Commonwealth* (London: MacMillan, 1889), 51.

5. Silbey, "Always a Whig," 40.

6. Bryce acknowledged the pathologies of parties but finally concluded that "the party did in the end represent the demands of public opinion and when public opinion was aroused it was always obeyed by the party." Merriam's analysis of Bryce cited in Francis Graham Wilson, *The Elements of Modern Politics* (New York: McGraw Hill, 1936), 331.

7. Widmer, *Martin Van Buren*, 39.

8. Macy, *Party Organization and Machinery*, xi–xii.

9. Bryce notes the absence of any treatise on the subject, no author who describes impartially the actual daily working of the "vast and intricate political machine" that

lies outside the Constitution (*American Commonwealth*, 4). Ostrogorski is commended by contemporaries as filling that gap; Jesse Macy calls Ostrogorski's the most important attack on the party system in *Party Organization*, xvii.

10. Lincoln Steffens, *The Autobiography of Lincoln Steffens* (New York: Harcourt Brace, 1931), 394.

11. Lincoln Steffens, *The Shame of the Cities* (New York: Hill and Wang, 1904), 11, 12.

12. Ibid., 11.

13. Theodore Roosevelt, *American Ideals and Other Essays, Social and Political* (New York and London: G. P. Putnam's Sons and Knickerbocker Press, 1897), 7.

14. William Bennett Munro, *The Government of American Cities* (New York: Macmillan, 1913), 332.

15. Lincoln Steffens, *The Struggle for Self-Government: Being an Attempt to Trace American Political Corruption to Its Sources in Six States of the United States with a Dedication to the Czar* (New York: McClure Phillips, 1906), 42.

16. Moisei Ostrogorski, *Democracy and the Party System in the United States* (New York: Arno Press, 1974 [1910]), 420.

17. Alan Dugan, *Poems Seven: New and Complete Poetry* (New York: Seven Stories Press, 2001), winner of the 2001 American National Book Award in Poetry.

18. Richard Hofstadter included populists in his rubric "the age of reform," and this is particularly apt as regards antipartyism. The Golden Age is marked, for one thing, by high levels of voter turnout, which fell below 70% for the first time in 1904 and below 60% eight years later and never returned to its nineteenth-century levels. McCormick, *Party Period*, 222.

19. Hofstadter, *The Age of Reform* (New York: Vintage, 1955), 155, 12.

20. John Chamberlain, *Farewell to Reform: The Rise, Life and Decay of the Progressive Mind in America* (Gloucester, MA: Peter Smith, 1958), 237.

21. Hofstadter, *Age of Reform*, 5, 18. Hofstadter brings together American populism, progressivism, and the New Deal, and my account of progressive antipartyism draws from his detailed analysis of the "mood" of progressivism.

22. Bruce Ackerman's account of minimal civic virtue, which he calls a "Federal economy of virtue" of private citizens, has elements of progressivism but without the religion. *We the People*, vol. 1, 231ff.

23. See, e.g., Michael Sandel, *Democracy's Discontent: American in Search of a Public Philosophy* (Cambridge, MA: Harvard University Press, 1996): "Whether self-government . . . is possible under modern conditions is at best an open question" (202). Sandel contrasts the liberal, voluntarist conception of freedom with "the notion that government should shape the moral and civic character of its citizens" (201), which he identifies with progressivism. "Progressives retained the formative ambition of the republican tradition and sought new ways to elevate the moral and civic character of citizens" (209). A striking example of the amorphousness of republicanism is Robert Kelley, "Ideology and Political Culture from Jefferson to

Nixon,"*American Historical Review* 82, no. 3 (1977): 531–62, in which he speaks of Yankee Republicanism, nationalist republicanism, localistic republicanism, and egalitarian collectivism (549).

24. Kevin Phillips, *Wealth and Democracy: A Political History of the American Rich* (New York: Broadway Books, 2002), 300–301; Phillips's point is that the eighteenth-century radical heritage "took root in the national psyche and bloomed again in the 1790s, 1830s, 1890s, and 1930s."

25. The Whig fear "was fueled by a very diffuse sense of corruption. That is why the suspicion of aristocracy is not set against any great trust in the people, as one might expect. That is one of the odd things about it." Judith N. Shklar, "The American Idea of Aristocracy," in Shklar, *Redeeming American Political Thought*, 148.

26. Steffens, *Autobiography*, 495, 606.

27. Samuel P. Hays, "Political Parties and the Community-Society Continuum," in *The American Party System: Stages of Political Development*, ed. William N. Chambers and Walter Dean Burnham (New York: Oxford University Press, 1967), 152–81.

28. Josiah Strong, *The Twentieth Century City* (New York: Baker and Taylor, 1970), 103.

29. William Howe Tolman, *Municipal Reform Movements in the United States* (New York: Femining Revell, 1895), 33.

30. Sandel, *Democracy's Discontent*, 209.

31. Cited in Eldon Eisenach, *The Lost Promise of Progressivism* (Lawrence: University Press of Kansas, 1994), 116.

32. Hays, "Political Parties," 164. Walter Dean Burnham explains political mobilization in the late nineteenth century in terms of "the re-Christianization of the country through pietistic religious revivals" and "increasingly polarized ethnocultural conflict in which political and religious perspectives became closely fused into a coherent framework." *The Current Crisis in American Politics* (New York: Oxford University Press, 1982), 80.

33. Steffens on the crucifixion of Jesus and the crowd preferring Barabbas to Jesus (*Autobiography*, 526): "He was crucified, just as my leaders of the people were crucified." There is an infusion of Puritanism, too. See Van Wyck Brooks's *The Wine of the Puritans: A Study of Present-Day America* (London: Sisley's Limited, 1908), for example. "The Trust is organized commerce with the Golden Rule excluded and the trustees exempted from the restraint of conscience." People's Party statement cited in Arthur M. Schlesinger Jr., ed., *History of U.S. Political Parties*, vol. 2, *1869–1910: The Gilded Age of Politics* (New York: Chelsea House, 1973), 1774.

34. Tolman, *Municipal Reform*, 39. Another affirmed that "in all progressive States there have been men who corresponded to the Hebrew prophets," preferably prophets who seek to influence political conduct. Macy, *Party Organization*, 10, 42.

35. Chamberlain, *Farewell*, 220–37.

36. Marvin Meyers cited in Morone, *Democratic Wish*, 76.

37. Judith Shklar, citing Hamilton, in "Alexander Hamilton and the Language of Political Science," in *Redeeming*, 7.

38. John H. Aldrich, *Why Parties?*, 4.

39. Chamberlain, *Farewell*, 172.

40. Frederic Howe, *The City, the Hope of Democracy* (New York: Scribner's, 1905), 92.

41. Schattschneider, *Party Government*, 168.

42. Chamberlain, *Farewell*, 130.

43. Roosevelt, *American Ideals*, 112ff.

44. Albert Stickney, *The Political Problem* (New York: Harper and Brothers, 1890), 24.

45. Macy, *Party Organization*, 2.

46. Ostrogorski, *Democracy and the Party System*, 365.

47. Bryce, *American Commonwealth*, 51.

48. This is the theme of Richard McCormick, *Party Period*, 181.

49. Both Democratic and Republican parties have traditions, Bryce conceded, and both "claim to have tendencies," but they lack distinctive principles. In contrast to English parties, whose struggles for office are therefore redeemed from selfishness. Bryce, *American Commomwealth*, 16, 21.

50. Weber, "Politics as a Vocation," 108.

51. McCormick, *Party Period*, 209. Some distributive politics are not divisive but universalistic; see Kenneth Shepsle and Barry Weingast, "Political Preferences for the Pork Barrel," *American Journal of Political Science* 25, no. 1 (1981): 96–111.

52. Schattschneider, *Party Government*, 134.

53. The leaders of small parties can oversee transformation to a party based on a ferocious grievance, or principle; for example, Van Buren left his own Democratic Party to create the Free Soil Party. Ted Widmer, *Martin Van Buren* (New York: Henry Holt, 2005), 154–55.

54. An exception is Elihu Root on "two great political parties [that] oppose each other upon fundamental differences." Cited in Eisenach, *Lost Promise*, 119.

55. Ostrogorski, *Democracy and the Party System*, 229.

56. Silbey, "Always a Whig," 38.

57. The consensus of historians is that election fraud was actually uncommon or, as Roosevelt reported (114), ineffective—"campaign expenses" were simply pocketed and little was actually spent to bribe the voters supposed to be bribed, whether to vote or to abstain from voting. See, e.g., an analysis of "repeaters," "floaters," etc. in Burnham, *Current Crisis*, 78ff.; Alan Ware, *Political Parties and Party Systems* (Oxford: Oxford University Press, 1996), 72, 73.

58. Justin Kaplan, introduction to Mark Twain and Charles Dudley Warner, *The Gilded Age* (New York: Trident Press, 1964), v. Bribing members of Congress was

made illegal in 1853, according to Dennis F. Thompson, *Ethics in Congress* (Washington, DC: Brookings Institution, 1995), 2.

59. Ostrogorski, *Democracy and the Party System,* 177 (though as always corruption had its functionalist defenders—department bureaus and consulates and agencies and contracts are the "honestly earned" rewards of partisanship).

60. Hofstadter, *Age of Reform*, 201, 175.

61. Weber, "Politics as a Vocation," 109.

62. Ostrogorski, *Democracy and the Party System*, 92.

63. Schattschneider, *Party Government*, 162.

64. Hofstadter, *Age of Reform*, 175.

65. Weber, "Class, Status, Party," 180.

66. Cited in Widmer, *Martin Van Buren*, 163.

67. Steffens, *Shame*, 155.

68. Jane Addams, "Why the Ward Boss Rules," *Outlook* (April 2, 1898): 17–28.

69. Rosenblum, *Membership and Morals,* chapter on "The Democracy of Everyday Life."

70. Steffens, *Autobiography*, 618.

71. Roosevelt, *American Ideals*, 122.

72. Bernard Crick, *In Defense of Politics* (New York: Continuum, 2000), 124.

73. Munro, *Government*, 176.

74. Frank Parsons, *The City of the People* (Philadelphia: C. F. Taylor, 1901), 278.

75. Phillips, *Wealth and Democracy*, 239.

76. Cited by Kaplan, introduction to Twain and Warner, *Gilded Age*, xi.

77. Ibid., 237, 213; cited by Kaplan, xx.

78. Steffens, *Shame*, 101, 2, 5, 9, 21.

79. Roosevelt, *American Ideals*, 76.

80. Judith Shklar, *Ordinary Vices* (Cambridge, MA: Harvard University Press, 1984), 78.

81. Cited in Chamberlain, *Farewell*, 131.

82. Steffens, *Shame*, 4, vii.

83. Bryce had a different view of public/official morality: "He comes to think that politicians have a morality of their own, and must be judged by it. It is not his morality; but because it is professional, he does not fear that it will infect other plain citizens like himself." *American Commonwealth*, 232.

84. Ibid., 234, 233.

85. Steffens, *Shame*, 198.

86. Alexander Keyssar, *The Right to Vote* (New York: Basic Books, 2000), 121.

87. Shklar, "Alexander Hamilton and the Language of Political Science," in *Redeeming*, 7.

88. Ostrogorski, *Democracy and the Party System*, 273 (emphasis added).

89. Ware, *Political Parties*, 68.

90. Roosevelt, *American Ideals*, 117.

91. Richard Bensel, "The American Ballot Box: Law, Identity, and the Polling Place in the Mid-Nineteenth Century," *Studies in American Political Development* 17, no. 1 (2003): 1–27, 13.

92. William Howard Taft, *Liberty under Law* (New Haven: Yale University Press, 1922), 7.

93. Keyssar, *Right to Vote*, 121.

94. Cited in Eisenach, *Lost Promise*, 113.

95. Steffens, *Shame*, 236.

96. Keyssar, *Right to Vote*, 159.

97. Parsons, *City of the People*, 276.

98. Benjamin Ginsberg and Martin Shefter, *Politics by Other Means* (New York: W. W. Norton, 1999), 185ff.; Michael McGerr, *The Decline of Popular Politics: The American North, 1865–1928* (New York: Oxford University Press, 1986), 45ff.

99. McGerr, *Decline of Popular Politics*, 46, citing Francis Parkman in 1878.

100. Mark Lawrence Kornbluh, *Why America Stopped Voting: The Decline of Participatory Democracy and the Emergence of Modern American Politics* (New York: New York University Press, 2000), 126. We see a brittle, testy position: one way around parties were democratic reforms such as the direct primary, initiative, and referendum, but could they be advocated unless the eligible electorate was winnowed and redefined?

101. McGerr, *Decline of Popular Politics*, 43. See Ware on reforms in the South that enabled the disenfranchisement or demobilization of black voters (*Political Parties*, 169ff.).

102. On the shifting attitude of parties toward women's suffrage and its relation to electoral competition, see Keyssar, *Right to Vote*, 213ff. Ostrogorski talks about the participation of women, before the franchise, for the purification of municipal life contaminated by party politics. *Democracy and the Party System*, 173.

103. Cited in Eisenach, *Lost Promise*, 116.

104. Cited in McGerr, *Decline of Popular Politics*, 56.

105. Editorial in *New Republic* 9, no. 50 (October 16, 1915): 272. In the 1927 compulsory sterilization case *Buck v. Bell*, Justice Holmes wrote: "The principle that sustains compulsory vaccination is broad enough to cover cutting the Fallopian tubes," ending with the famous punch: "three generations of imbeciles are enough." Daniel J. Kevles, *In the Name of Eugenics* (New York: Knopf, 1985), 111.

106. McCormick, *Party Period*, 264.

107. Silbey, "Always a Whig," 36, 40.

108. Lincoln Steffens, *The Letters of Lincoln Steffens*, 2 vols., ed. Ella Winter and Granville Hicks (New York: Harcourt, Brace, 1938), vol. 1, p. 107.

109. Jane Addams's report that the alderman of her ward had as many as 2600 constituents on the public payroll is often cited. Kornbluh, *Why America Stopped Voting*, 41.

110. Historians document the connection between the creation of parties and enlarging the suffrage: "between 1824 and 1840, the bookends of Van Buren's federal

career, the number of voters increased from 400,000 to 2.4 million." Widmer, *Martin Van Buren*, 7.

111. Aldrich, *Why Parties?*, 101–2.

112. Roosevelt, *American Ideals*, 119.

113. Silbey, "*Always a Whig*," 41.

114. On partisan spectacles, see McGerr, *Decline of Popular Politics*, 36ff. McGerr is particularly useful on the partisan press (14ff.).

115. McCormick, *Party Period*, 164.

116. Hays, "Political Parties," 158.

117. McGerr, *Decline of Popular Politics*, 23ff.

118. Ostrogorski, *Democracy and the Party System*, 271–72.

119. Morone, *Democratic Wish*, 91. For a recent discussion of the relative quality of candidates in the last third of the nineteenth century, when they were chosen by strong party organizations, and the consequences for heightened electoral competition, see Jamie Carson, Erik Engstrom, and Jason Roberts, "Candidate Quality, the Personal Vote, and the Incumbency Advantage in Congress," *American Political Science Review* 101, no. 2 (May 2007): 289–301.

120. Widmer, *Martin Van Buren*, 7, 8.

121. Morone, *Democratic Wish*, 90.

122. This was Woodrow Wilson's signature argument; without parties government will remain checked and balanced, incapable of acting. The quote is from Schattschneider, *Party Government*, 125.

123. Larry D. Kramer, "Putting the Politics Back into the Political Safeguards of Federalism," *Columbia Law Review* 100, no. 1 (2000): 215–93, 278–79. On the "successive waves of reform [that] maimed and nearly killed this system," see 280ff..

124. Sidney Milkis, cited in Alan Wolfe, *Return to Greatness: How America Lost Its Sense of Purpose and What It Needs to Do to Recover It* (Princeton: Princeton University Press, 2005), 85. Progressives did not acknowledge this institutional basis for nationalism. Contemporary progressives acknowledge it only implicitly, if they do. For example, the proposal for "Deliberation Day" is cast as an opportunity to make presidential elections a context for political education at the local level mainly because of the national scope and vertical reach of parties; party representatives are the untouted backbone of this deliberative scheme. Bruce Ackerman and James Fishkin, *Deliberation Day* (New Haven: Yale University Press, 2004), 32ff.

125. Schattschneider discussed in Disch, *Tyranny*, 110.

126. Howard Penniman, *The American Political Process* (Princeton: Van Nostrand, 1962), 38, cited in Bruce E. Keith et al., *The Myth of the Independent Voter* (Berkeley: University of California Press, 1992), 38–39.

127. Cited in McGerr, *Decline of Popular Politics*, 56; 55.

128. Bryce, *American Commonwealth*, 713.

129. Ostrogorski, *Democracy and Organization*, vol. 2, p. 600.

130. Steffens, *Struggle,* xix, 41.

131. Steffens, *Shame,* 8–9.

132. Munro, *Government of American Cities,* 177.

133. Steffens, cited in Chamberlain, *Farewell,* 229.

134. Roosevelt, *American Ideals,* 45.

135. Judith N. Shklar, *American Citizenship: The Quest for Inclusion* (Cambridge, MA: Harvard University Press, 1991), 60.

136. Cited in David B. Danbom, *The World of Hope: Progressives and the Struggle for an Ethical Political Life* (Philadelphia: Temple University Press, 1987), 175.

137. Cited in Eisenach, *Lost Promise,* 133.

138. Mary Parker Follett, *The New State: Group Organization the Solution of Popular Government* (University Park. Pennsylvania State University Press, 1998), 137–38.

139. Bryce, *American Commonwealth,* 47.

140. Follett, *New State,* 159, 178, 226, 180.

141. Progressive Party Platform, 1912, cited in Eisenach, *Lost Promise,* 136–37.

142. Good Government Club statement, 1893, cited in Tolman, *Municipal Reform,* 93.

143. Ostrogorski, *Democracy and the Party System,* 310.

144. The organizational interpretation of progressivism proper by some historians focuses on voluntarism—the drive to form cooperative groups. The other face, of course, is progressive confidence in neutral bureaucracy, more below. McCormick, *Party Period,* 267.

145. Bryce, *American Commonwealth,* 322.

146. Eisenach, *Lost Promise,* 122.

147. See, e.g., Munro on the Municipal Voters' League, in *Government of American Cities,* 368–69.

148. "Instead of leading to a broader commitment to the public interest, progressive efforts . . . had merely whetted appetites for more narrowly based class legislation." Danbom, *World of Hope,* 177.

149. Schattschneider, *Party Government,* 188ff.

150. McCormick, *Party Period,* 348. State building, as historians record in detail, increased the domain of government and the institutions of government, opening avenues for political influence outside of parties. See, too, Jerry Israel, ed., *Building the Organizational Society* (New York: Free Press, 1972). I take this up in chap. 7.

151. Ostrogorski, *Democracy and the Party System,* 307–8.

152. McGerr, *Decline of Popular Politics,* 61.

153. Cited in ibid., 57.

154. Daniel Defoe, "On Government by Parties," in J.A.W. Gunn, *Factions No More: Attitudes to Party in Government and Opposition in Eighteenth-Century England* (London: Frank Cass, 1971), 86.

155. Steffens, *Autobiography,* 250.

156. Cited in McGerr, *Decline of Popular Politics*, 56; Bryce, *American Commonwealth*, 163ff. The New York Mugwump support for Democrat Grover Cleveland is said to be "the highpoint of organized independency." McGerr, *Decline*, 58.

157. Steffens, *Shame*, 239.

158. Ostrogorski, *Democracy and the Party System*, 310.

159. Cited in Schlesinger, *History of U.S. Political Parties*, vol. 3, p. 2606.

160. "The public grew to identify us with all the members of the lunatic fringe of public life." Roosevelt in Schlesinger, *History of U.S. Political Parties*, vol. 3, p. 2604.

161. Cited in Chamberlain, *Farewell*, 140.

162. Roosevelt, *American Ideals*, 131–32.

163. See Rosenblum, *Membership and Morals*.

164. Munro, *Government of American Cities*, 157–58, 383.

165. Thurman Arnold, cited in Hofstadter, *Age of Reform*, 323.

166. Ostrogorski, *Democracy and the Party System*, 225–26, 17.

167. Steffens, *Shame*, 259, on Walter Fisher of Chicago.

168. Disch, *Tyranny*, 166 n. 57.

169. Progressive Party Platform, 1912.

170. Steffens, *Letters*, 1031, 1934.

171. Steffens, *Autobiography*, 761, 762. "The Russian Revolution had abolished all those privileges which, in this country, balked all reforms. Gone! All gone" (Steffens, *Letters*, 1007). And "they had a man, Lenin, who could and who did always, finally, close the debate and demand action, united, and planned." Steffens, *Autobiography*, 762.

172. Roosevelt, "Confession of the Faith" (1912), in Schlesinger, *History of U.S. Political Parties*, vol. 3, p. 2596.

173. Marion Butler, "Keynote Speech, People's Party" (1896), in Schlesinger, *History of U.S. Political Parties*, vol. 2, p. 1790.

174. Henry Demarest Lloyd, "The Populists at St. Louis" (1896), in ibid., 1802.

175. Progressive Party Platform, 1912.

176. Cited in Schlesinger, *History of U.S. Political Parties*, vol. 2, at p. 1753. The People's Party, invoking "the people," meant nonsectional people: "Resolved, That we hail this conference as the consummation of a perfect union of hearts and hands of all sections of our common country. The men who wore the gray and the men who wore the blue meet here to extinguish the last smoldering embers of civil war." St. Louis Platform (1892), cited in ibid., 1765.

177. Macy, *Party Organization*, 7, 13.

178. Steffens, *Shame*, 6. In fact the Progressive Party, which nominated Theodore Roosevelt for president in 1912, was dependent on Roosevelt's personal popularity; the party collapsed four years later when Roosevelt returned to the Republican fold. McCormick, *Party Period*, 178.

179. Steffens, *Letters*, 164.

180. Wolfe, *Return to Greatness*, 169.

181. Chamberlain, *Farewell*, 227.

182. Wolfe, *Return to Greatness*, 142.

183. Cited in Chamberlain, *Farewell*, 307.

184. McGerr, *Decline of Popular Politics*, 66.

185. McCormick, *Party Period*, 332.

186. On the reasons for the decline of machines, see Hofstadter, *Age of Reform*, 270.

187. Marty Cohen, David Karol, Hans Noel, and John Zaller, "Political Parties and Presidential Nominations," 6 ff., unpublished manuscript.

188. McCormick, *Party Period*, 235; citing Stickney and Clark and Brown, 238.

189. Morone, *Democratic Wish*, 104.

190. Schattschneider, *Party Government*, 176.

191. Cited in McCormick, *Party Period*, 238.

192. Weber, "Politics as a Vocation," 88.

193. Steffens, *Autobiography*, 250.

194. Parsons, *City of the People*, 471.

195. Stickney, *Political Problem,* 129.

196. There is one notable exception. Munro defends parties as associations that set before the electorate opinions held in common by some portion, that impress the merit of these opinions, and that afford a means of responsibility for policy, as necessary in local as in state and national politics. Munro also concedes the frequent identity of state and local issues and the need for local politicians to have strong ties to state legislators.

197. One consideration was that by attaching opportunity for genuine community service to offices, they would attract capable and honest men. Historians are ungenerous in assessing the effects of these attacks on the party system: "No issue better illustrates the ideological limits of reform than ... much-heralded innovation of commission government." Not only did it introduce "patrician, upper-class standards" in city decision making, but it actually encouraged extra-legal control by parties, subverting its original purpose. Joel Schwartz and Daniel Prosser, *Cities of the Garden State: Essays in the Urban and Suburban History of New Jersey* (Dubuque, IA: Kendall/Hunt Publishing, 1977), 72.

198. Tolman, *Municipal Reform*, 34.

199. McGerr, *Decline of Popular Politics*, 49.

200. Though records of the Municipal League show skeptics, like Charles Beard, who thought that reforms had not "permanently reduced the power of the expert political minority that manages public affairs." Frank Mann Stewart, *A Half Century of Municipal Reform: The History of the National Municipal League* (Berkeley: University of California Press, 1950), 39, 96.

201. Howe, *The City*, 164.

202. Cited in McGerr, *Decline of Popular Politics*, 65.

203. Howe, *The City*, 175.

204. Reforms included prohibition of fusion parties, and historians suggest that our entrenched two-party system may be partially attributable to the electoral reforms of the turn-of-the-century and state courts that countenanced regulations that, at a time when there was still regional multipartyism, deliberately minimized electoral competition. Adam Winkler, "Voters' Rights and Parties' Wrongs: Early Political Party Regulation in the State Courts, 1886–1915," *Columbia Law Review* 100, no. 3 (January 2000): 873–900, 892. See too Disch, *Tyranny*.

205. Cited in Winkler, "Voters' Rights," 880.

206. Disch, *Tyranny*, 49. For a discussion of ballots and balloting in the nineteenth-century, see Bensel, "American Ballot Box."

207. Disch, *Tyranny*, 27.

208. A long-standing effect of ballot reform was that legal control of the process set the stage for legislation transforming nominations and made a host of questions legally justiciable. Ware, *Political Parties*, 197.

209. Stickney, *Political Problem,* 161.

210. McCormick, *Party Period*, 253–54. "It was of no avail to purify the primaries, to protect by law their proceedings, so long as they led only to a convention, inevitably manipulated by bosses and rings of professional politicians." Ostrogorski, *Democracy and the Party System,* 342.

211. Bryce, *American Commonwealth*, 73, 101. The section title is Austin Ranney's, cited in Ware, *Political Parties*, 246.

212. Cited in Winkler, "Voters, Rights," 882.

213. Schattschneider, *Party Government*, 64.

214. Stickney, *Political Problem*, 32–33.

215. Ware, *Political Parties*, 57.

216. Senator Benton cited in Ostrogorski, *Democracy and the Party System*, 42.

217. Cited in Winkler, "Voters' Rights," 884.

218. Cited in Disch, *Tyranny*, 43.

219. Ware, *Political Parties*, 207. Ware's is the definitive study. For a comparison with European party nomination procedures, see 84ff.

220. This is the finding of V. O. Key, largely confirmed by Ware, ibid., 169ff.

221. Cited in ibid., 246.

222. Taft, *Liberty*, 28–29.

223. Chamberlain, *Farewell*, 308. This was written from a self-declared "radical" or socialist perspective; Chamberlain would later become a libertarian conservative.

224. Stickney, *Political Problem*, 60, 61, 63.

225. Morone, *Democratic Wish*, 118.

226. Parsons, *City of the People*, 303, 275–76.

227. Ibid., 305.

228. Ibid., 288, 275–76, 286.

229. Macy, *Party Organization*, 22.

230. Munro, *Government of American Cities*, 342.

231. Ackerman and Fishkin, *Deliberation Day*, 164.

232. Review of Albert Stickney, *A True Republic* (New York: Harper and Brothers, 1879), in *The Nation* 29, no. 740 (September 4, 1879): 161.

233. "The law fails to provide any organization whereby the people can act together, as one people, in the selection of its highest public servants. Factions are therefore formed outside the law; and the citizens are compelled to act with some faction. Then comes this mass of election work, with its secrecy, its necessary use of large amounts of money, even if the uses are only legitimate, and its employment of dirty men and dirty methods." Stickney, *Political Problem*, 57.

234. Cited in John R. Vile, *Rewriting the United States Constitution: An Examination of Proposals from Reconstruction to the Present* (New York: Praeger, 1991), 29.

235. Stickney, *Political Problem*, 179.

236. McCormick, *Party Period*, 244–50.

237. Stickney, *Political Problem*, 84, 78, 92.

238. Hays, "Political Parties," 177.

239. Stickney, *Political Problem*, 87–8; 87.

240. There is an interesting parallel to Condorcet's constitutional scheme in that both wanted to combine election and deliberation; see Nadia Urbinati's discussion in *Representative Democracy: Principles and Genealogy* (Chicago: University of Chicago Press, 2006).

241. The most elaborate scheme is Ackerman's and Fishkin's for "Deliberation Day" (165).

242. Theodore Lowi, "Toward a More Responsible Three-Party System: Plan or Obituary?," in Green and Shea, *State of the Parties*, 171–89, 189; Theodore Lowi and Joseph Romance, *Republic of Parties: Debating the Two-Party System* (Lanham, MD: Rowman and Littlefield, 1998), 30.

243. Croly was also among the first to predict that the initiative facilitated minority rule—giving the edge to well-organized and -financed groups employing propaganda campaigns. Cited in Hofstadter, *Age of Reform*, 267, 268. Lisa Disch cites early progressives who saw third parties as watchdogs against the corrupt dominant party machines (*Tyranny*, 94–95).

244. Stickney, *Political Problem*, 3.

245. Bryce, *American Commonwealth*, 231.

246. Steffens, *Autobiography*, 397.

247. I am grateful for Joseph Kochanek for suggesting the outlines of this progression.

248. Thompson, *Ethics in Congress*, 4. Institutional corruption is Thompson's main theme. It is built into the fact that representatives must pursue both the public interest and constituent interests, the principle of serving all citizens and serving supporters. See 166 for summary.

249. Steffens, *Shame*, 26.

250. Steffens, *Struggle*, xx.

251. Roosevelt in Schlesinger, *History of U.S. Political Parties*, vol. 3, p. 2604.

252. Taft, *Liberty under Law*, 11, 15.

253. Cited in Chamberlain, *Farewell*, 76–77.

254. Bryce, *American Commonwealth*, 234.

255. John McCain—a scheme by which both parties conspire to stay in office by selling the country to the highest bidder. Cited in Phillips, *Wealth and Democracy*, 325.

Chapter 5. The Anxiety of Influence

1. Frank Sarouf, "Extra-Legal Political Parties in Wisconsin," *American Political Science Review* 48, no. 3 (September 1954): 692–704, 692, discussing American attitudes toward parties.

2. Hillaire Belloc and Cecil Chesterton, *The Party System* (London: Steven Swift, 1911), 9, 23, 33.

3. I take the phrase from the title of Harold Bloom's book about the theory of poetry, *The Anxity of Influence* (New York: Oxford University Press, 1973).

4. Judith N. Shklar, "The American Idea of Aristocracy," in Shklar, *Redeeming American Political Thought*, 157.

5. Cited in Shklar, "Democracy and the Past: Jefferson and His Heirs," in ibid., 180.

6. Shklar, "American Idea of Aristocracy," 156.

7. Shklar, "Democracy and the Past," 181.

8. Mary Parker Follett, *The New State, Group Organization the Solution of Popular Government* (University Park: Pennsylvania State University Press, 1998), 167.

9. Frank Parsons, *The City of the People* (Philadelphia: C. F. Taylor, 1901), 311.

10. Cited in Dennis F. Thompson, *Just Elections: Creating a Fair Electoral Process in the United States* (Chicago: University of Chicago Press, 2002), 47.

11. Thompson, *Ethics in Congress*, 7.

12. Hofstadter, *Age of Reform*, 216.

13. Steffens, *Letters of Lincoln Steffens*, 348.

14. Steffens, *Autobiography*, 492–93.

15. Moisei Ostrogorski, *Democracy and the Party System*, 279.

16. William Bennett Munro, *The Government of American Cities* (New York: Macmillan, 1913), 174–75.

17. Steffens, *Autobiography*, 706, 829.

18. Lisa Jane Disch, *The Tyranny of the Two Party System* (New York: Columbia University Press, 2002), 63. Multipartyism and multimember districts have their American defenders too. The favored form is a proportional representative system with single transferable vote.

19. Cited in Maurice Duverger, *Political Parties: Their Organization and Activity in the Modern State* (New York: John Wiley & Sons, 1963), 217.

20. Edmund S. Morgan, *Inventing the People* (New York: W. W. Norton, 1988), 39ff.

21. Samuel Issacharoff and Richard Pildes, "Politics as Markets: Partisan Lock-ups of the Democratic Process," *Stanford Law Review* 50, no. 3 (February 1998): 643–717, 676–78.

22. See Disch, *Tyranny,* 63, 73ff.

23. Two-partyism also ignores the standard observation that decentralization makes for fifty separate state party systems in the United States and many local arms and internal factions. For an assessment of the variation in third-party support over time, see Shigeo Hirano and James M. Snyder Jr., "The Decline of Third-Party Voting in the United States," *Journal of Politics* 69, no. 1 (February 2007): 1–16.

24. Directory of U.S. Political Parties: www.politics1.com.

25. Robert Dahl, *Pluralist Democracy in the United States: Conflict and Consensus* (New Haven: Yale University Press, 1967), 214. Explaining the duopoly, Dahl adds the factor of "force of habit and tradition" (218). And "rapid growth in third-party votes is a sure sign of an abnormal state of affairs" (214).

26. L. Laurence Moore, *Selling God: American Religion in the Marketplace of Culture* (New York: Oxford University Press, 1994), 82.

27. In 1976 Eugene McCarthy spent 80% of his campaign funds to cope with ballot access requirements; Issacharoff and Pildes, "Politics as Markets," 687.

28. Daniel Hays Lowenstein, "Associational Rights of Major Political Parties: A Skeptical Inquiry," *Texas Law Review* 71, no. 7 (June 1993): 1741–92, 1756–77.

29. Cited in Richard L. McCormick, *The Party Period and Public Policy: American Politics from the Age of Jackson to the Progressive Era* (Oxford: Oxford University Press, 1986), 242.

30. Sartori, *Parties and Party Systems,* 77.

31. Theodore Roosevelt, *American Ideals and Other Essays, Social and Political* (New York and London: G. P. Putnam's Sons, 1897), 134.

32. Cited in Phillips, *Wealth and Democracy,* 322.

33. *McConnell v. Federal Election Commission,* 540 U.S. 92 (2003), opinion of Stevens and O'Connor for the Court, 148.

34. Henry Adams, "The 'Independents' in the Canvass," *North American Review* 123, no. 253 (October 1876): 426–67, 433.

35. Cited in Phillips, *Wealth and Democracy,* 320.

36. Letter to potential contributors, paid for by Nader 2000 General Committee, Inc.

37. Theodore J. Lowi, "Toward a Responsible Three-Party System: Prospects and Obstacles," in Green and Shea, *State of the Parties,* 42.

38. Schattschneider, *Party Government,* 35, 58.

39. David Knoke, "Political Organizations," in *Encyclopedia of Sociology,* 2nd ed., vol. 3, ed. Edgar F. Borgatta and Rhonda J. V. Montgomery (New York: Macmillan, 2000), 2147–62, 2148.

40. Michael S. Kang, "The Hydraulics and Politics of Party Regulation," *Iowa Law Review* 91 (October 2005): 131–88. But contra Kang they are institutions, not "informal coalitions" (9) with "nothing to regulate except a large variegated group of roughly likeminded individuals" (10). For Kang, parties are not themselves essential actors in American politics (15).

41. John H. Aldrich, *Why Parties?* (Chicago: University of Chicago Press, 1995), 54.

42. Studies of the Christian Coalition's strategy vis-à-vis the Republican Party in the 1980s illustrate this. See, e.g., John C. Green, James L. Guth, and Clyde Wilcox, "Less Than Conquerors: The Christian Right in State Republican Parties," in *Social Movements and American Political Institutions*, ed. Anne N. Costain and Andrews S. McFarland (New York: Rowman and Littlefield: 1998), 117–36.

43. Ostrogorski, *Democracy and the Party System,* 285. Issacharoff and Pildes compare German constitutional law, which held that a representative without party affiliation could not be excluded from committees merely because he was not a member of a party; constitutional protection of parliamentary minorities extends to independent representatives ("Politics as Markets," 698).

44. David Mayhew, *Congress: The Electoral Connection* (New Haven: Yale University Press, 1974).

45. Thompson, *Just Elections,* 177.

46. Paul Allen Beck and Frank J. Sarouf, *Party Politics in America*, 7th ed. (New York: HarperCollins, 1992), 141.

47. See Ingrid van Biezen, "On the Theory and Practice of Party Formation and Adaptation in New Democracies," *European Journal of Political Research* 44, no. 1 (January 2005): 147–74, for a review of the literature. In newer democracies, in Southern and Eastern Europe, for example, party organizations were never socially anchored. Besides structural reasons, there is the "negative connotation associated with the institution of the political party" in postcommunist politics.

48. E. J. Dionne Jr., *Why Americans Hate Politics* (New York: Touchstone, 1991), 332.

49. Joan Didion, *Political Fictions* (New York: Knopf, 2001), 21.

50. Ostrogorski, *Democracy and the Party System*, 161.

51. Issacharoff and Pildes, "Politics as Markets," 646.

52. Schattschneider, *Party Government*, 58–59.

53. Ibid., 53.

54. For a good discussion, including the state action doctrine used to say that parties are public, see Daniel Hays Lowenstein, "Associational Rights of Major Political Parties: A Skeptical Inquiry," *Texas Law Review* 71 (June 1993): 1741–92, 1748ff.

55. Public utilities are agencies "performing a service in which the public has a special interest sufficient to justify governmental regulatory control, along with the extension of legal privileges." Leon Epstein, *Political Parties in the American Mold* (Madison: University of Wisconsin Press, 1986), 157. As public utilities, parties' function is not to serve as intermediaries from society to government but to

transmit government services (and propaganda) to the public. Richard S. Katz and Peter Mair put it: "democracy ceases to be seen as a process by which limitations or controls are imposed on the state by civil society, becoming instead a service provided by the state for civil society." "Changing Models of Party Organization and Party Democracy: The Emergence of the Cartel Party," *Party Politics* 1, no. 1 (January, 1995): 5–28, 22. Political parties have been described as "parties-in-states' clothing" (Epstein, *Political Parties*, 155). Mark E. Rush, "Voters' Rights and the Legal Status of American Political Parties," *Journal of Law and Politics* 9, no. 3 (Spring 1993): 487–514.

56. *Session v. Perry*, cited by Stevens in dissent, in *Vieth v. Jubelirer,* 541 U.S. 267 (2004).

57. Justice Kennedy in *Vieth v. Jubelirer*. Hasen points out in "The Political Market" that in some instances analysts use one-partyism to define lockup, in others even robust two-party competition may not be appropriately competitive if third parties are excluded (725). Thompson points out that "incumbency protection is not always undesirable, and may under some conditions promote electoral justice even while serving the [incumbents' self-interest]." Thompson, *Just Elections*, 176.

58. Andrew Gelman and Gary King, "Enhancing Democracy through Legislative Redistricting," *American Political Science Review* 88, no. 3 (September 1994): 541–59, 541.

59. Eventually, the bill was passed and upheld by the Justice Department. See David Kiron, "The Texas Redistricting Caper," in *Ethics and Politics: Cases and Comments*, ed. Dennis F. Thompson (Belmont, CA: Thomson/Wadsworth, 2006), 177–82.

60. *Vieth v. Jubelirer,* Justice Souter dissenting at 345.

61. There is a literature on the trade-off between electing minorities to office and legislation addressed to the interests of minority voters. Districting permits the first but may deter the second. Descriptive representation comes at the cost of minority-sponsored legislation. See Charles Beitz, *Political Equality* (Princeton: Princeton University Press, 1989), 141ff.

62. No justice in *Vieth v. Jubelirer* argued that the Constitution requires districting by nonpartisan, independent commissions.

63. *Vieth v. Jubelirer,* Justice Stevens dissenting at 318.

64. Ibid., Scalia for the Court at 274.

65. Brief of Amici Curiae by Professors Gary King, Bernard Grofman, Andrew Gelman, and Jonathan N. Katz in support of neither party in *Jackson et al. v. Perry* Nos. 05-204, 05-254, 05-276, 05-439, pp. 2–3.

66. Ibid., p 5. Bernard Grofman and Gary King, "The Future of Partisan Symmetry as a Judicial Test for Partisan Gerrymandering after *LULAC v. Perry,*" unpublished manuscript, pp. 4–5. In *LULAC v. Perry* (547 U.S. [2006]), a majority of justices showed some interest in adopting the symmetry standard, though it was not employed in the case.

67. Brief, by King et al., 9.

68. Ibid., 3.

69. Ibid, 11.

70. Ibid., 22–23.

71. Thomas W. Pogge, "Self-Constituting Constituencies to Enhance Freedom, Equality, and Participation in Democratic Procedures." *Theoria* 49, no. 1 (June 2002): 26–54.

72. Brief by King et al., 39.

73. *Vieth v. Jubelirer*, Justice Breyer dissenting at 357. In the last four Congressional elections, 98% of incumbent Congressmen won their way back to Washington, compared with 85% after World War II. See John Friedman and Richard Holden, "Redistricting and Electoral Competition," *New Republic Online* (June 2006) available at http://www.tnr.com, accessed August 17, 2006. In their longer, unpublished paper on the subject, the authors argue against gerrymandering as the cause of incumbent reelection, pointing instead to money in politics, a polarized electorate, paucity of challengers, and constraints on gerrymandering imposed by the Voting Rights Act. They suggest that redistricting may increase electoral responsiveness.

74. Disch, *Tyranny*, 61.

75. Pildes, "Foreword: The Constitutionalization of Democratic Politics," *Harvard Law Review* 118, no. 1 (November 2004): 28–154, 62–63.

76. FairVote/Center for Voting and Democracy (http://www.fairvote.org).

77. So commissions too need a standard, like "symmetry." Thompson's point is not only that districting is an unavoidably political process but also that competing political values are at stake. Thompson, (*Just Elections*, chapter 3).

78. Heather Gerken, "A Third Way for the Voting Rights Act: Section 5 and the Opt In Approach," in *The Future of the Voting Rights Act*, ed. David Epstein, Richard Pildes, Rodolfo De La Garza, and Sharyn O'Halloran (New York: Russell Sage Foundation, 2006).

79. Thompson, *Just Elections*, 175. His three criteria for just elections—worked out for many aspects of election law—are equal respect, popular sovereignty, and free choice.

80. Mark Franklin, *Voter Turnout and the Dynamics of Electoral Competition in Established Democracies since 1945* (Cambridge: Cambridge University Press, 2004), 211, 219.

81. Pildes, "Constitutionalization of Democratic Politics," 63. Pildes argues that judicial creation of a general but necessarily vague constraint is better than none: it would create a credible threat that would cause state legislators to restrain themselves, "a process much like the internalization of *Shaw*" (the racial gerrymander case) (69–70). Pildes implicitly concurs with Stevens's dissent: "What is clear is that it is not the unavailability of judicially manageable standards that drives today's decision. It is, instead, a failure of judicial will to condemn even the most blatant

violations of a state legislature's fundamental duty to govern impartially." *Vieth v. Jubilier,* Justice Stevens dissenting at 341.

82. Albert Stickney, *The Political Problem* (New York: Harper Bros., 1890), 175.

83. Cited in McCormick, *Party Period,* 209.

84. Steffens, *Struggle for Self-Government,* 45.

85. Pildes, "Constitutionalization of Democractic Politics," 60.

86. Schattschneider, *Party Government,* 60.

87. Widmer, *Martin Van Buren,* 57.

88. Issacharoff and Pildes, "Politics as Markets," 708–9.

89. Michael J. Klarman, "Majoritarian Judicial Review: The Entrenchment Problem," *Georgetown Law Journal* 85, no. 3 (February 1997): 491–553, 521.

90. Hofstadter, *Age of Reform,* 216.

91. See, e.g., Heather MacIvor, "Do Canadian Political Parties Form a Cartel?," *Canadian Journal of Political Science* 29, no. 2 (June 1996): 318–33, on regulations allotting media time that effectively exclude third parties and independent candidates, among other measures.

92. For a good definition of how management deals to its own advantage in the case of a bid for the corporation, see Richard L. Hasen, "The 'Political Market' Metaphor and Election Law: A Comment on Issacharoff and Pildes," *Stanford Law Review* 50, no. 3 (February 1998): 719–30, 721.

93. Issacharoff and Pildes, "Politics as Markets," 646.

94. Ibid., 649.

95. Ibid., 647.

96. Ibid., 680.

97. This is John Rawls's point in *Political Liberalism* (New York: Columbia University Press, 2005) about regulating campaign finance (362).

98. Pildes, "Constitutionalization of Democractic Politics," 44.

99. Ibid., 43.

100. Phillips, *Wealth and Democracy,* 340.

101. Disch, *Tyranny,* 7.

102. Kang, "Hydraulics and Politics." See too Lowenstein, "Associational Rights," and Elizabeth Garrett, "Is the Party Over? Courts and the Political Process" *Supreme Court Review* 95 (2002): 95–152, 137.

103. Issacharoff and Pildes, "Political as Markets," 648. The authors argue at length that this—and not racist exclusion of black voters per se—was the strategy of the South's white primary system.

104. Disch, *Tyranny,* 12.

105. Ibid., 7.

106. Richard H. Pildes, "Democracy and Disorder," *University of Chicago Law Review* 68, no. 3 (Summer 2001): 695–718, 696.

107. Howe, *The City,* 6.

108. Schattschneider, *Party Government*, 192ff., 196.

109. Steffens, *Letters*, 190.

110. Steffens, *Struggle*, 3. See too "The Boss, the Party, and the System," in Howe, *The City*, 92.

111. Steffens, *Shame of the Cities*, 236.

112. Leonidas Pol, Presidential Address at Ocala, December 2, 1890, cited in Schlesinger, *History of U.S. Political Parties*, vol. 2, 1747. It was a call for a populist party.

113. Stickney, *Political Problem*, 54–55.

114. Cited in Chamberlain, *Farewell to Reform*, 132.

115. Michael Walzer, *Politics and Passion* (New Haven: Yale University Press, 2003), 23ff.

116. Sheldon Wolin, *Politics and Vision: Continuity and Innovation in Western Political Thought* (Princeton: Princeton University Press, 2004), 415.

117. Steffens, *Letters*, 197.

118. Cited in Chamberlain, *Farewell*, 238.

119. Cited in ibid., 143.

120. Macy, *Party Organization and Machinery*, 268.

121. Political science focuses on conditions for democracy, among them a strong middle class. On the moral effects of declining prosperity and expectation, see Benjamin M. Friedman, "Meltdown: A Case Study," *Atlantic Monthly* 296, no. 1 (July/August 2005): 66, on how a many-year downturn threatens tolerance and citizens' freedoms.

122. Gustavus Myers, *History of the Great American Fortunes*, 3 vols. (Chicago: Kerr and Company, 1909); Phillips, *Wealth and Democracy*.

123. Howe, *The City*.

124. Charles Beard, cited in Frank Mann Stewart, *A Half Century of Municipal Reform: The History of the National Municipal League* (Berkeley: University of California Press, 1950), 96.

125. Ackerman, *We the People*, vol. 1, 228.

126. Christiano, *Rule of the Many*, 59, 70.

127. Rawls, *Political Liberalism*, 327.

128. Beitz, *Political Equality*, 192.

129. Beitz (ibid.) classifies accounts of political equality as "best result," "popular will," and fair procedures. His institutional prescriptions are guided by three regulative interests of citizenship: recognition, equitable treatment, and deliberative responsibility.

130. Cited in *Adams et al v. Federal Election Commission* jurisdictional statement No. 02-1740, p. 21. Available at http://www.supremecourtus.gov/bcra/021740jurisst .pdf, accessed July 28, 2007.

131. Philosophers look at campaign finance in terms of a conflict between liberty—the liberty of individual donors, parties, corporations, and other groups to participate

in the electoral contest through funding candidates and parties—and political equality, usually understood as equal opportunity to influence electoral outcomes, but also candidates' equal opportunity to win support. Beitz, *Political Equality*, 211–12. A different argument has it that if principles of equality were realized in society, there would be no need to limit or equalize the political influence of citizens by restricting campaign contributions. Given background equality, citizens should be able to decide how to spend their resources, including spending to attempt to influence elections and political outcomes.

132. *McConnell v. Federal Election Commission* 540 U.S. 93 (2003), Justice Stevens for the Court at 137.

133. Steffens, *Letters*, 194.

134. Steffens, *Autobiography*, 591.

135. Roosevelt, *American Ideals*, 69, 79.

136. Schattschneider, *Party Government*, 86.

137. Belloc and Chesterton, *Party System*, 110.

138. Cited in Phillips, *Wealth and Democracy*, 325.

139. Cited in ibid., 405.

140. Chamber of Commerce of the United States jurisdictional statement, *Chamber of Commerce, et al. v. Federal Election Commission*. No. 02–1756 (2003). Available at http://supreme.lp.findlaw.com/supreme_court/briefs/02-1756/02-1756.apt.ccus .pdf, accessed August 17, 2006.

141. Taft, *Liberty under Law*, 26.

142. Thompson, *Ethics in Congress*, 4, 109. Institutional corruption is Thompson's main theme.

143. The plurality opinion in *McConnell v. FEC*, 540 U.S. 92 (2003), gives a terse history of reform. See Justice Stevens for the Court, 115–132 (Section I of the opinion).

144. Gary Jacobson, *The 2000 Elections and Beyond* (Washington, DC: CQ Press, 2001), 3.

145. *Federal Election Commission v. National Right to Work Committee* 459 U.S. 197 (1982), Chief Justice Rehnquist for the Court at 208.

146. Dan Clawson, Alan Neustadt, and Denise Scott, *Money Talks: Corporate PACs and Political Influence* (New York: Basic Books, 1992), 126.

147. *McCain et al. v. McConnell et al.*, No. 02-1702 (2003) jurisdictional statement, p. 2. Available at http://supreme.lp.findlaw.com/supreme_court/briefs/02-1702/02-1702.apt.mccain.pdf, accessed July 28, 2007.

148. Robert Kuttner, "One Way to Clean Up Our Government," *San Diego Union-Tribune*, March 24, 1996, p. G3.

149. U.S. Supreme Court rulings on campaign finance legislation are a moving target. As I write this, the Court has issued a decision that alters the standing interpretation of one important element of McCain-Feingold (*Federal Election Commission v. Wisconsin Right to Life*, 551 U.S. [2007]). My discussions here and in the next

chapter focus not on decisions but on justices' reasoning as articulate examples of antipartyism and rare acknowledgement of the uses of parties.

150. *Buckley v. Valeo*, cited in *Randall v. Sorrell*, 548 U.S. (2006).

151. *Federal Election Commission v. Colorado Republican Federal Campaign Committee*, 533 U.S. 431 (2001).

152. The *Randall v. Sorrell* Court, with the exception of Justice Thomas and Scalia, declined to use the case to consider overruling the precedent or stated outright that they would not overrule it.

153. I leave aside the problem of the vagueness and overbreadth of what constitutes coordinated/independent expenditures, of what constitutes "cooperation, consultation, or concert," as well as the standard of "express terms" advocating the election or defeat of an identifiable candidate that is supposed to distinguish issue ads from campaign expenditures.

154. *FEC v. Colorado Republican Federal Campaign Committee*, Justice Souter for the Court at 445.

155. Brief for Respondent, *FEC v. Colorado Republican Federal Campaign Committee*, No. 00-191 at 2. Available at http://supreme.lp.findlaw.com/supreme_court/docket/2000/febdocket.html, accessed July 28, 2007.

156. Ibid., 7.

157. Ibid., 4. Federal election law *defines* a political party as an association that "nominates a candidate for election to any Federal office whose name appears on the election ballot as the candidate of such association."

158. *Colorado Republican Federal Compaign Committee v. Federal Election Commission* 518 U.S. 604 (1996), Justice Breyer (in judgment but not speaking for the Court) at 616.

159. Brief for Respondent, *FEC v. Colorado Republican Federal Campaign Committee*, No. 00–191 at 8.

160. *McCain et al. v. McConnell et al.*, No. 02-1702 (2003) jurisdictional statement, p. 12. Closing the soft money loophole also put a wedge between national and state and local parties, which had acted together to raise and use these previously federally unregulated funds. The California Democratic Party's brief objects to this effort to isolate the various units of the parties and limit their collective activities. *McCain v. McConnell*, jurisdictional statement, 7.

161. *FEC v. Colorado Republican Federal Campaign Committee*, Justice Souter for the Court at 454.

162. Brief for the Petitioner, *FEC v. Colorado Republican Federal Campaign Committee*, available at http://supreme.lp.findlaw.com/supreme_court/briefs/00-191/2000-0191.pet.aa.pdf, accessed August 17, 2006, p. 18.

163. *FEC v. Colorado Republican Federal Campaign Committee*, case syllabus as printed in 150 L. Ed. 2d 461, at 468.

164. Ibid., Justice Souter for the Court at 461.

165. Ibid., Justice Souter for the Court at 452.

166. Ibid., Justice Souter for the Court at 441, quoting from *Buckley v. Valeo.*

167. Ibid., case syllabus as printed in 150 L. Ed. 2d 461, at 468.

168. *McCain et al. v. McConnell et al.*, No. 02-1702 (2003) jurisdictional statement, p. 7. Available at http://supreme.lp.findlaw.com/supreme_court/briefs/02-1702/02-1702.apt.mccain.pdf, accessed July 28, 2007. Ansolabehere and Snyder, in research done before this case, show that national party funds go to state and local parties for voter registration and mobilization. See Stephen Ansolabehere and James M. Snyder Jr., "Soft Money, Hard Money, Strong Parties," *Columbia Law Review* 100, no. 3 (April 2000): 598–619, 608.

169. *FEC v. Colorado Republican Federal Campaign Committee*, at 441.

170. *McConnell v. Federal Election Commission*, 540 U.S. 93, Justices Stevens and O'Connor for the Court at 150.

171. Ibid., Justices Stevens and O'Connor for the Court at 153.

172. Ibid.

173. *FEC v. Colorado Republican Federal Campaign Committee*, Justice Souter for the Court at 452.

174. Ibid., Justice Souter for the Court at 455.

175. Ibid., Justice Souter for the Court at 445.

176. Brief for the Petitioner, *FEC v. Colorado Republican Federal Campaign Committee*, p. 17.

177. *FEC v. Colorado Republican Federal Campaign Committee*, Justice Thomas dissenting at 477.

178. Ibid., Justice Souter for the Court, esp. at 452. On the actual use of money, see Brief for Respondent, *FEC v. Colorado Republican Federal Campaign Committee*, No. 00–191 at 27, n. 17. The intent was to limit the overall amount of election spending, a misconceived and ineffective purpose.

179. Ansolabehere and Snyder, "Soft Money," 603–4.

180. *FEC v. Colorado Republican Federal Campaign Committee*, Justice Thomas dissenting at 478.

181. Appendix to Petitioner's Brief, *FEC v. Colorado Republican Federal Campaign Committee*, No. 00–191, at 66a. Available at http://supreme.lp.findlaw.com/supreme_court/briefs/00-191/2000-0191.pet.app.pdf, accessed July 28, 2007.

182. *Randall v. Sorrell.* Available at http://laws.findlaw.com/us/000/04-1528.html, accessed July 28, 2007.

183. *FEC v. Colorado Republican Federal Campaign Committee*, Justice Thomas dissenting at 478.

184. Ansolabehere and Snyder, "Soft Money," 608–9. The authors do not think the effect of party contributions on challengers is significant simply because parties spend so little on individual races (610).

185. *McConnell v. FEC*, 159.

186. Ibid., Justice Scalia dissenting at 249. He details elements of the reform calculated to favor incumbents, such as raising hard money caps.

187. Ibid., 136, cited in *Randall v. Sorrell*.

188. *Randall v. Sorrell*. The majority offered five criteria for when contribution limits transform a difference in degree of expression into a difference in kind. The dissent challenged what it saw as the majority's unsupported, unruly *impression* of appropriate limits.

189. Justice Breyer, citing the District Court decision (118 F. Supp. 2d at 487) in *Randall v. Sorrell*.

190. Epstein, *Political Parties*, 310.

191. *McConnell v. FEC*, Justice Scalia dissenting at 248. He details elements of the reform calculated to favor incumbents, such as raising hard money caps.

192. Issacharoff and Pildes, "Politics as Markets," 695. See *Buckley v. Valeo*, 424 U.S. 1 (1976)

193. Cited in Issacharoff and Pildes, "Political as Markets," 688. "Protection Act" is from Steven Rosenstone, Roy Behr, and Edward Lazarus, *Third Parties in America: Citizen Response to Major Party Failure* (Princeton: Princeton University Press, 1996), 26.

194. Justice Souter's dissent in *Randall v. Sorrell*.

195. *McConnell v. FEC*, case syllabus as printed in 157 L. Ed. 2d 491, at 519.

196. "Hydraulic" is Samuel Issacharoff and Pamela Karlan's term in "The Hydraulics of Campaign Finance Reform," *Texas Law Review* 77, no. 6 (June 1999): 1705–38. Many propose that the most efficacious check on corruption is publicity, but advocates disagree about which arrangement makes for greater transparency. Should major donors be channeled away from candidates into independent expenditures to ensure optimal public disclosure? Alternatively, transparency recommends channeling money into contributions to candidates to promote accountability by elected officials. This is discussed in Kang, "Hydraulics and Politics," 17 n. 66.

197. In *FEC v. WRTL* a majority of the Court set standards for distinguishing permissible issue advocacy from impermissible electioneering.

198. *Randall v. Sorrell*.

199. Epstein, *Political Parties*, 310. Brief for the Petitioner, *FEC v. Colorado Republican Federal Campaign Committee*, 19 n. 6. For a defense of parties as conduits of public campaign funding, see Daniel Hays Lowenstein, "The Root of All Evil Is Deeply Rooted," *Hofstra Law Review* 18, no. 2 (Fall 1989): 301–67.

200. Marty Cohen, David Karol, Hans Noel, and John Zaller, "Political Parties and Presidential Nominations," unpublished manuscript, 15, 19. The authors emphasize the interpenetration of the career interests of politicians and intense-policy oriented groups (24). They define parties as coalitions of groups and conclude: "some part—we suspect a rather large part—of what is often derogated as 'fat cat' or 'private' money is rather a form of organized party support" (50). Of the four indicators of forces in the "invisible primary"—polls, endorsements, media, and fund raising—the authors argue that the endorsements of political leaders are the most autonomously important influence (chapter 8, pp. 1–2).

201. Cited in Thomas Christiano, *Rule of the Many,* 141.

202. Steffens, *Letters,* 195; *Shame,* 11 .

203. Steffens, *Autobiography,* 414–15.

204. For a historical discussion of instruction, see Edmund Morgan, *Inventing the People* (New York: W. W. Norton, 1988), 221.

205. Cited in James Morone, *The Democratic Wish* (New York: Basic Books, 1990), 113.

Chapter 6. Correcting the System: Association, Participation, and Deliberation

1. Schattschneider, *Semisovereign People,* 121.

2. Philip Pettit, "Democracy, Electoral and Contestatory," in *Nomos XLII: Designing Democratic Institutions,* ed. Ian Shapiro and Steven Macedo (New York: New York University Press, 2000), 105–44, 134.

3. Hannah Pitkin defined representation as "acting in the interest of the represented, in a manner responsive to them." *The Concept of Representation* (Berkeley: University of California Press, 1967), 209.

4. Steffens, *Shame,* 11.

5. McCormick, *Party Period,* 244–50.

6. Urbinati, *Representative Democracy,* 38.

7. Helene Landemore, "Democratic Reason," thesis presentation notes, p. 2.

8. For example, fair procedures or guaranteed places for minority representation do not ensure legislative success.

9. The literature is vast. Frequently cited as a model is Morris Fiorina, *Congress: Keystone of the Washington Establishment* (New Haven: Yale University Press, 1977).

10. This is the subject of the 2007 Supreme Court decision *Federal Election Commission v. Wisconsin Right to Life (WRTL),* 551 U.S. (2007). In widening the window for issue ads, the Court declined to open the window just for nonprofit advocacy and lobbying groups such as WRTL, whose business is political influence, but instead opened the field for business as well.

11. Schattschneider, *Party Government,* 189, 203–4.

12. Ibid., 21.

13. Kay Lehman Schlozman, Sidney Verba, and Henry Brady, "Civic Participation and the Equality Problem," in *Civic Engagement in American Democracy,* ed. Theda Skocpol and Morris P. Fiorina (Washington, DC, and New York: Brookings Institution Press and Russell Sage Foundation, 1999), 445ff., 457. An earlier statement: "The pressure system has an upper-class bias"; Schattschneider, *Semisovereign People,* 32ff.

14. As I indicated in chapter 4, the growth is directly related to the growth of government; organizations attempt to forge links to the political representatives and agencies whose decisions affect them.

15. The number of Washington-based religious advocacy groups (they resist the title "lobby" as sordid) is mushrooming on social agendas like abortion, church-state issues, civil rights and humanitarian legislation, international justice—the list is open-ended and includes considerable political attention to the nitty-gritty business of property and tax legislation, for example.

16. Cited in John Coleman, "Resurgent or Just Busy? Party Organizations in Contemporary America," in Green and Shea, *State of the Parties,* 367–84, 369. Polling in the United States indicates that only a bare majority of respondents, 53%, feels well represented by the two major parties. Jack Dennis and Diana Owen, "Popular Satisfaction with the Party System and Representative Democracy in the United States," Paper Presented at the IPSA Meeting, Quebec City, August 1–5, 2000, pp. 19–20.

17. Jean Cohen, "American Civil Society Talk," in *Civil Society, Democracy, and Civil Renewal,* ed. Robert K. Fullinwider (Oxford: Rowman and Littlefield, 1999), 58.

18. Of course, legal frameworks exist for nonprofit groups, with boards and fiduciary responsibilities; my reference here is to the claim to be representative as an element of influence.

19. Making democracy work is the goal of groups committed to government transparency, for example, or investigating, publicizing, and censuring officials, or pressing for the political inclusion of formally excluded groups.

20. Schattschneider, *Party Government,* 98.

21. This is not an American phenomenon only. See Patrick Seyd and Paul Whitely, "British Party Members: An Overview," on competition between parties and single-issue groups (*Party Politics* 10, no. 4 [2004]); Peter Mair and Ingrid van Biezen, "Party Membership in Twenty European Democracies, 1980–2000," *Party Politics* 7, no. 1 (2001); Russell J. Dalton and Martin P. Wattenberg, eds., *Parties without Partisans: Political Change in Advanced Industrial Democracies* (Oxford: Oxford University Press, 2006).

22. Follett, *New State.*

23. Ibid., 178, 180, 179, 335. She adds a point that would become central to civil society advocates: group organization will throw up "real leaders": "It is only the organization of society which will bring out leadership" (227–28, 231).

24. Michael Walzer, "The Idea of Civil Society: A Path to Social Reconstruction," *Dissent* 39, no. 2 (Spring 1991): 293–304, 298.

25. Christiano, *Rule of the Many,* 276.

26. Rosenblum, *Membership and Morals.*

27. Amy Gutmann and Dennis F. Thompson, *Democracy and Disagreement* (Cambridge, MA: Harvard University Press, 1996), 12, 359.

28. See National Commission on Civic Renewal, *A Nation of Spectators: How Civic Engagement Weakens America and What We Can Do About It,* final report (College Park, MD: National Commission on Civic Renewal, June 24, 1998); *A Call to Civil Society* (New York: Institute for American Values, 1998); Fullinwider, *Civil Society, Democracy, and Civic Renewal.*

29. *A Call to Civil Society*, 14. For data, see Nancy Burns, Kay Lehman Schlozman, and Sidney Verba, *The Private Roots of Public Action* (Cambridge, MA: Harvard University Press, 2001).

30. Elizabeth Crowley, "More Young People Turn Away from Politics and Concentrate Instead on Community Service," *Wall Street Journal*, June 16, 1999, p. A28.

31. Joshua Cohen, "Procedure and Substance in Deliberative Democracy," in *Deliberative Democracy: Essays on Reason and Politics*, ed. James Bohman and William Rehg (Cambridge, MA: MIT Press, 1997), 407–38, 412.

32. Anthony Downs, *The Economic Theory of Democracy* (New York: Harper, 1957), 34.

33. Daniel H. Lowenstein, "Symposium: Regulating the Electoral Process: Associational Rights of Major Political Parties: A Skeptical Inquiry," *Texas Law Review* 71 (1993): 1741–92, 1758.

34. Steven Schier, *By Invitation Only: The Rise of Exclusive Politics in the United States* (Pittsburgh: University of Pittsburgh Press, 2000), 16–17. Hyperactivists comprise "only 5% of the adult population" and are biased toward upper income and education; see Byron E. Shafer and William J. M. Claggett, *The Two Majorities: The Issue Context of Modern American Politics* (Baltimore: Johns Hopkins University Press, 1995), 117.

35. Schier, *By Invitation Only*, 92.

36. Ronald Inglehart describes active political involvement on the part of "cognitively mobilized" people, geared to issue-specific participation and to "elite-directing" rather than "elite-directed" modes of participation in *Culture Shift in Advanced Industrial Societies* (Princeton: Princeton University Press, 1990), chap. 10, esp. 363, 367.

37. *Nader v. Schaffer*, 417 F. Supp. 837 (1976), opinion at 843.

38. Rosenblum, *Membership and Morals*, 234ff.

39. John F. Bibby, *Politics, Parties, and Elections in America* (Chicago: Nelson Hall, 1992), 60.

40. "On election day a voter in California may cast more votes than a voter in the U.K. casts in a lifetime." Stephen Ansolabehere, online reply to comments on his "The Search for New Voting Technology," *Boston Review*, October 2001, available at http://bostonreview.net/BR26.5/ansolabehere2.html.

41. Cohen, Karol, Noel, and Zaller, "Beating Reform, 15. The authors also point out that there are tens of thousands of citizens in the parties' donor pools.

42. Beck and Sarouf, *Party Politics in America*, 113.

43. John F. Bibby, *Politics, Parties, and Elections in America* (Chicago: Nelson Hall, 1992), 113, citing Eldersveld.

44. John P. Frendreis, James L. Gibson, and Laura Vertz, "The Electoral Relevance of Local Party Organizations," *American Political Science Review* 84, no. 1 (June 1990): 225–35, 227.

45. Kay Lehman Schlozman, Sidney Verba, and Henry Brady, "Participation's Not a Paradox: The View from American Activists," *British Journal of Political Science* 25, no. 1 (January 1995): 1–36.

46. "Parties are the creatures of interest groups, ideological activists and others whom we call intense policy demanders. These groups organize the parties to get the government policies they want"; "politicians exist because groups find them useful"; and "groups select politicians who act, in effect, as agents of the groups." Cohen, Karol, Noel, and Zaller, "Political Parties and Presidential Nominations," 24.

47. This is one area in which things may be different in multiparty systems where organized interest groups and advocacy groups can more readily assume the form of minor parties.

48. John Rawls, "The Idea of Public Reason Revisited," in *Collected Papers*, ed. Samuel Freeman (Cambridge, MA: Harvard University Press, 1999), 575.

49. Follett, *New State*, 179.

50. Christiano, *Rule of the Many*, 244, 248. If groups are principally deliberative, their oligarchic character will recede (268).

51. Gutmann and Thompson allow that deliberation is not always the best practice for decision making: voting simply or bargaining and so on may serve. In *Democracy and Disagreement* they say that "deal-making, log-rolling, pork-barreling, coalition-building and the like" are appropriate only for matters that "raise no moral issues" (69, 70, 57–58), "Deliberation is not a substitute for the exercise of other forms of power." *Why Deliberative Democracy* (Princeton: Princeton University Press, 2004), 46. But only deliberation can decide where deliberation is required.

52. Bruce Ackerman and James Fishkin, *Deliberation Day* (New Haven: Yale University Press, 2004), 190.

53. For the several grounds of why deliberation legitimates and of the moral claims for deliberation, see Samuel Freeman, "Deliberative Democracy: A Sympathetic Comment," *Philosophy and Public Affairs* 29, no. 4 (Fall 2000): 371–418 .

54. Urbinati, *Representative Democracy*, 3.

55. The claims made for deliberation are more extensive than I note here. They include epistemic claims about correct or best possible decisions. For a review of the literature on the conceptual criteria of deliberation, the evaluative standards applied to deliberation, and empirical conditions, see Dennis F. Thompson, "Deliberative Democratic Theory and Empirical Political Science," forthcoming, *Annual Review of Political Science* 11 (2008).

56. Seyla Benhabib, "Toward a Deliberative Model of Democratic Legitimacy," in *Democracy and Difference: Contesting Boundaries of the Political*, ed. Benhabib (Princeton: Princeton University Press, 1996), 84.

57. Joshua Cohen, "Deliberation and Democratic Legitimacy," in *Deliberative Democracy: Essays on Reason and Politics*, ed. James Bohman and William Rehg (Cambridge, MA: MIT Press, 1997), 67–92, 73.

58. Stephen White, *The Recent Work of Jürgen Habermas* (Cambridge: Cambridge University Press, 1988), 126.

59. Gutmann and Thompson, *Democracy and Disagreement*, 12, 359.

60. Christiano, *Rule of the Many*, 244, 248.

61. Diana Mutz, *Hearing the Other Side: Deliberative versus Participatory Democracy* (Cambridge: Cambridge University Press, 2006), 35.

62. Ibid., 26.

63. Cynthia Estlund, *Working Together: How Workplace Bonds Strengthen a Diverse Democracy* (Oxford: Oxford University Press, 2003). Mutz adds professional trade and business organizations and school service clubs such as Parent-Teacher Associations (37).

64. "[There is] inherent tension between promoting a society with enthusiastically participative citizens and promoting one imbued with tolerance and respect for differences of opinion" (Mutz, *Hearing the Other Side*, 3). By "deliberation" Mutz means everyday talk that does not meet philosophical criteria but does expose people to conflicting political views. Mutz points out that the most knowledgeable and politically engaged people (partisans) are not the people most exposed to oppositional viewpoints (32). She puts the choice between homogeneity and participation vs. diversity and deliberation sharply, and chooses the latter (148).

65. Walzer, *Politics and Passion*, 130.

66. Ibid., 92, 93.

67. We might say that identity politics proceeds in the framework of interest group pluralism (that is, in countries where there is no formal, institutionalized multiculturalism that allocates public goods and even legal status by group membership).

68. Political scientists sometimes describe these oppositional groups and movements as the functional equivalent of an antisystem party. Jeffrey M. Berry, *The New Liberalism: The Rising Power of Citizens Groups* (Washington, DC: Brookings Institution, 1999), 7.

69. Particularly those concerned about basic human needs, and most particularly recipients of means-tested social services.

70. Walzer, *Politics and Passion*, 32, 39.

71. Joshua Cohen and Joel Rogers, "Secondary Associations and Democratic Governance," in *Associations and Democracy*, ed. Erik Olin Wright (London: Verso, 1995). One proposal would extend the "equal-dollars-per-voter" standard of political equality developed in connection with campaign finance reform to associations.

72. Walzer, *Politics and Passion*, 74; Christiano, *Rule of the Many*, 268, 287. See the discussion in *Civil Society and Government*, ed. Nancy L. Rosenblum and Robert C. Post (Princeton: Princeton University Press, 2001).

73. Theda Skocpol, "Advocates without Members: The Recent Transformation of American Civic Life," in Skocpol and Fiorina, *Civic Engagement in American Democracy*, 499; Wilson Carey McWilliams, "The Meaning of the Election," in *The Election of 1996: Reports and Interpretations*, ed. Gerald Pomper (Chatham, NJ: Chatham House, 1997), 255; he attributes the oligarchic content of party politics to

the effect of the "progressive" politics of strong government on the local and communal roots of party politics.

74. Pettit, "Democracy, Electoral and Contestatory," 134.

75. Schattschneider, *Party Government*, 192ff., 196.

76. Walzer, *Politics and Passion*, 23, 104.

77. Schattschneider, *Semisovereign People*, 57, 58. This is a practical argument. Hans Kelsen argues that democracy necessarily means a party state, and that antiparty thinkers are antidemocratic. The only alternative to party democracy is corporatist groups. Interests cannot be avoided and must be compromised, but organization into political parties "means, in reality, creating the organizational conditions for such compromises." "On the Essence and Value of Democracy," in *Weimar: A Jurisprudence of Crisis*, ed. Arthur Jacobson and Bernhard Schlink (Berkeley: University of California Press, 2000), 106–7.

78. Without a designable majority, it is difficult to assign "aristocrats" or "monocrats," "the money power," or any other sinister and undue influence genuine political meaning.

79. Theda Skocpol, ed., *The New Majority: Toward a Popular Progressive Politics* (New Haven: Yale University Press, 1997), 503, 505.

80. Judith N. Shklar, *American Citizenship: The Quest for Inclusion* (Cambridge, MA: Harvard University Press, 1998), 25.

81. Cohen, "Deliberation and Democratic Legitimacy," 86. See too Cohen and Rogers, *On Democracy* (New York: Penguin, 1983), 154ff. Cohen commends political parties (supported by public funds) as crucial to making deliberative democracy possible. His principal concern is relatively egalitarian access to parties if the costs of party activities are assumed by government.

82. Dennis F. Thompson, *Just Elections: Creating a Fair Electoral Process in the United States* (Chicago: University of Chicago Press, 2002), 1.

83. Carl Friedrich: "We speak advisedly of influence rather than participation or control, since the large number of citizens is not very likely to participate in or effectively to control government action." *Constitutional Government and Democracy* (Waltham, MA: Blaisdell, 1968), 278. Contemporary political science and democratic theory have plumbed the difficulty behind accountability or control: citizens cannot discern whether governments are acting in their interest or in the public interest, and cannot sanction them appropriately; for a summary, see Adam Przeworski, "Minimalist Conception of Democracy: A Defense," in *Democracy's Value*, ed. Ian Shapiro and Casiano Hacker-Cordon (Cambridge: Cambridge University Press, 1999), 23–55.

84. Dennis and Owen, "Popular Satisfaction," 4–5, 10.

85. Arend Lijphart, "Unequal Participation: Democracy's Unresolved Dilemma," *American Political Science Review* 91, no. 1 (March 1997): 1–14, for a discussion and view that like the extension of the franchise, compulsory voting could be legislated in the United States.

86. Walzer, *Politics and Passion*, 8.

87. The exceptions are Hungary, Portugal, Slovakia, Greece, and Spain. Peter Mair and Ingrid van Biezen, "Party Membership in Twenty European Democracies, 1980–2000," *Party Politics* 7, no. 1 (January 2001): 5–21.

88. United States Elections Project at George Mason University: http://elections .gmu.edu.

89. Lijphart, "Unequal Participation," 5.

90. For a discussion of the controversy over measuring turnout, see Michael McDonald and Samuel Popkin, "The Myth of the Vanishing Voter," *American Political Science Review* 95, no. 4 (December 2001): 963–74. The thesis is that turnout since 1972 has not declined as a total of eligible voting population; decline is a function of the rise of noneligible voters as a percentage of the voting age population, due mainly to immigration and the exclusion of felons. "There are virtually no identifiable turnout trends from 1972 onward" (968). On the baseline issue, the authors say the 1950s were unusual in being the high point of participation outside the Jim Crow South.

91. He described nonparticipation as "by a wide margin the most important feature of the whole system . . . . Anyone who finds out how to involve the [then] forty million in American politics will run the country for a generation." Schattschneider, *Semisovereign People*, 103, 99.

92. Chronic nonparticipation is known to have a bias: there is a nexus between social class and turnout. For a summary, see Lijphart, "Unequal Participation."

93. Mark M. Gray and A. Wuffle, "Vindicating Anthony Downs," *PS: Political Science and Politics* 38, no. 4 (October 2005): 737–40.

94. G.W.F. Hegel, "Proceedings of the Estates Assembly in Wurtemberg," 264, and "The English Reform Bill," 318, in *Hegel's Political Writings*.

95. David M. Estlund, *Democratic Authority: A Philosophical Framework* (Princeton: Princeton University Press, 2008), 272.

96. Gerry Mackie makes this argument. His discussion shows that "voters say they intend to influence the outcome, and act as if they so intend." "The Nonparadox of Nonvoting," unpublished manuscript, 3, 29. He argues that voters may care by what margin their candidate wins or loses—they want a larger majority or larger minority; this alters motivation but does not change the problem of "perceptible effect."

97. Mark Franklin disavows this as well as political disaffection as cause and discredits too the "mobilization model." *Voter Turnout and the Dynamics of Electoral Competition in Established Democracies since 1945* (Cambridge: Cambridge University Press, 2004), 6. His complex explanation centers on whether the habit of voting is established early in life (12) and on the competitiveness of elections, which draws out voters who correctly perceive themselves as members of a potentially winning coalition if supporters vote (202).

98. Schattschneider, *Semisovereign People*, 105; he does not concur with this characterization.

99. Lijphart, "Unequal Participation," 7–8.

100. Franklin, *Voter Turnout and the Dynamics of Electoral Competition*, 215, 213.

101. Pelczynski, introduction to *Hegel's Political Writings*, 80.

102. James Bryce, *The American Commonwealth* (London: Macmillan, 1889), 51.

103. Schattschneider, *Party Government*, 49.

104. Schattschneider, *Semisovereign People*, 101. (The one-party South was the worst area of racial restriction, made possible by party monopoly.)

105. Ibid., 129.

106. Dionne, *Why Americans Hate Politics*, 15 (emphasis added).

107. For a study of public opinion of parties and correlation with nonparticipation, see Russell Dalton and Steven A. Weldon, "Public Images of Political Parties: A Necessary Evil?," *West European Politics* 28, no. 5 (November 2005): 931–51; the quote is from 936, 937.

108. A similar argument is made about independence as the result of party polarization; this is refuted by Luke Keele and James A. Stimson, "Polarization and the Mass Response: The Growth of Independence in American Politics," paper presented at the APSA meeting, Washington, DC, 2005. The authors reached this conclusion unhappily; they had hoped to show that the explanation for the trend toward independence lay in party polarization.

109. *McConnell v. Federal Election Commission*, 540 U.S. 92 (2003), Justices Stevens and O'Connor for the Court at 144.

110. *Victoria Adams v. Federal Election Commission*, jurisdictional statement, 2003, p. 5. Available at http://supreme.lp.findlaw.com/supreme_court/docket/2003/september.html, accessed August 6, 2007.

111. Disch, *Tyranny*, 111.

112. Frances Fox Piven and Richard Cloward, *Why Americans Still Don't Vote* (Boston: Beacon Press, 2000), 31. See too Disch, *Tyranny*, 113–15.

113. The best known case is the accusation leveled against Christine Todd Whitman in the 1993 New Jersey gubernatorial election, discussed in Pamela Karlan, "Not by Money but by Virtue Won? Vote Trafficking and the Voting Rights System," *Virginia Law Review* 80, no. 7 (October 1994): 1455–74.

114. "Wasteful" is from Schattschneider, *Party Government*, 95. Uncontested congressional races and races in which the incumbent is heavily favored result in parties concentrating their resources in a limited number of contests. In 2000, for example, only nine of four hundred House seats held by incumbents were listed as "toss-up" or "leaning" toward the challenger. Neither party financed a national media campaign. Gary Jacobson, *The 2000 Elections and Beyond* (Washington, DC: CQ Press, 2001), 28.

115. Schier, *By Invitation Only*, 7, 1. "The core logic of activation involves nudging those with the greatest marginal propensity to become active into motion" (32).

116. Ibid., 178, 31.

117. Aldrich, *Why Parties?*, 101ff., 103.

118. John Gertner, "The Very, Very Personal Is the Political," *New York Times Magazine*, February 15, 2004, pp. 42–47.

119. Dick Morris, *The New Prince* (Los Angeles: Renaissance Books, 1999), 220.

120. Schattschneider's phrase, *Semisovereign People*, 109.

121. Schlozman, Verba, and Brady, "Civic Participation," 430.

122. Harold Meyerson, "Politics with People, Reinvented," *American Prospect* 13, no. 7, September 23, 2002.

123. Beck and Sarouf, *Party Politics in America*.

124. Among the treatments, see Ginsberg and Shefter, *Politics by Other Means*, 21ff.; Piven and Cloward, *Why Americans Still Don't Vote*, 38ff.; Michael J. Avey, *The Demobilization of American Voters* (New York: Greenwood, 1989); Tom DeLuca, *The Two Faces of Political Apathy* (Philadelphia: Temple University Press, 1995).

125. Beck and Sorauf, *Party Politics*, 141.

126. Morris P. Fiorina, "Extreme Voices: A Dark Side of Civic Engagement," in Skocpol and Fiorina, *Civic Engagement*, 395–426, 405.

127. Schattschneider, *Semisovereign People*, 104.

128. Michael Kang, "The Hydraulics and Politics of Party Regulation," *Iowa Law Review* 91, no. 1 (October 2005): 131–88, 140.

129. "Because it is commonly believed that dissatisfaction with alternatives on offer causes widespread abstention from voting . . . it should be said that there is little or no respectable evidence sustaining this notion." *On Parties: Essays Honoring Austin Ranney*, ed. Nelson Polsby and Raymond Wolfinger (Berkeley: Institute of Governmental Studies Press, 1999), 42.

130. For a study of cross-over voting in connection with the blanket primary, see Mark Baldassare, "Context and Setting: The Mood of the California Electorate," in *Voting at the Political Fault Line: California's Experiment with the Blanket Primary*, ed. Bruce E. Cain and Elisabeth R. Gerber (Berkeley: University of California Press, 2002). Cross-over voting is also explained by the desire to vote for an incumbent. Thad Kousser, "Crossing Over When it Counts," in Cain and Gerber, ibid., 143–70, 155.

131. This is the research of Cohen, Karl, Noel, and Zaller, "Beating Reform."

132. *California Democratic Party v. Jones*, 984 F. Supp. 1288 (1997), at n. 34.

133. Bruce E. Cain and Elisabeth R. Gerber, "California's Blanket Primary Experiment," in Cain and Gerber, *Voting at the Political Fault Line*, 43.

134. Bruce E. Cain, "Party Autonomy and Two-Party Electoral Competition," *University of Pennsylvania Law Review* 149, no. 3 (January 2001): 793–814. In fact, studies suggest that the modification of the rules was favored by voters not because they subscribed to the ideal of maximum participation but because they considered themselves disadvantaged by them. Shaun Bowler and Todd Donovan, "Political Reform via the Initiative Process: What Voters Think about When They Change the Rules," in Cain and Gerber, *Voting at the Political Fault Line*, 36–58, 53.

135. *California Democratic Party v. Jones*, n. 34. (1302).

136. Samuel Issacharoff, "Private Parties with Public Purpose: Political Parties, Associational Freedoms, and Partisan Competition," *Columbia Law Review* 101, no. 2 (March 2001): 274–313, 279.

137. *California Democratic Party v. Jones*, 530 U.S. 567 (2000), Justice Scalia for the Court at 580.

138. Nor do standards like "orderly" or "clean elections" or the "integrity of elections." "The state's interest in . . . not restricting voting in the presidential preference primary to those who publicly declare and record their party preference is to preserve the overall integrity of the electoral process." But "preservation of the integrity of the electoral process" also justifies state-mandated *closed primaries*. In this case, it is said to guarantee that primary election results reflect the will of party members "undistorted by the votes of those unconcerned with, if not actually hostile to, the principles, philosophies, and goals of the party." *Nader v. Schaffer*, 417 F. Supp. 837 (1976), at 846.

139. Beitz, *Political Equality*, 191.

140. For a fuller discussion of these matters, see Thompson, *Just Elections*.

141. Pettit, "Democracy, Electoral and Contestatory," 134.

142. Beitz, *Political Equality*, 191.

143. Richard L. Hasen, "Do the Parties or the People Own the Electoral Process?," *University of Pennsylvania Law Review* 149, no. 3 (January 2001): 815–41.

144. *California Democratic Party v. Jones*, 530 U.S. 567 (2000).

145. John Dunn on voters: *The Cunning of Unreason: Making Sense of Politics* (New York: Basic Books, 2000), 292–93, 213. If the point is the opportunity to reject candidates, preoccupation with nomination procedures is mitigated. See Beitz, *Political Equality*, 165.

146. Cited in *California Democratic Party v. Jones*, 530 US 567 (2000), in case syllabus at 568.

147. Malcolm E. Jewell, "Parties and Candidate Recruitment in American Parties," in Polsby and Wolfinger, *On Parties*, 125.

148. California Secretary of State, 1996, cited in Bowler and Donovan, "Political Reform," 45.

149. Cain and Gerber, "California's Blanket Primary Experiment," 9. Minor parties exposed to the blanket primary have a similar fear that their hard-won ideological distinctiveness will be diluted.

150. *Nader v. Schaffer*, at 25. John R. Petrocik argues in "Candidate Strategy, Voter Response, and Party Cohesion" that candidates selected in closed primaries are more cohesive than those selected in open and blanket primaries and that candidates can use these primaries to overwhelm the preferences of partisans. In Cain and Gerber, *Voting at the Political Fault Line*, 270–302, 270–71.

151. *California Democratic Party v. Jones*, 530 U.S. 567 (2000), Justice Scalia for the Court at 579. Pildes's argument is that the division did not turn so much on social science facts and predictions as cultural judgments about political stability.

Richard H. Pildes, "Democracy and Disorder," *University of Chicago Law Review* 68, no. 3 (Summer 2001): 695–718, 704; 704. Issacharoff, "Private Parties," 279.

152. "California: Indies Allowed to Vote in White House Primary," *Roll Call*, October 23, 2003.

153. *Clingman v. Beaver*, 544 U.S. 581 (2005), in which Oklahoma's Libertarian Party challenged the state's semi-closed primary law, which made it unconstitutional for the party to invite voters registered with other parties to vote in their primary. The Court upheld the law on grounds that it was not a severe burden on the party's right of association.

154. Issacharoff, "Private Parties," 279.

155. Oral argument cited in Nathaniel Persily, "The Blanket Primary in the Courts: The Precedent and Implications of *California Democratic Party v. Jones*," in Cain and Gerber, eds., *Voting at the Political Fault Line*, 303–23, 313.

156. Kang reports that partisans of both parties supported the proposition. "Hydraulics and Politics," 27.

157. The content of rights of vote and association are not independent of the institutions in which they operate. They cannot be imported from areas of free speech or racial discrimination. They must derive from the purposes of these specific democratic institutions. Richard Pildes, "Foreword: The Constitutionalization of Democratic Politics," *Harvard Law Review* 118, no. 1 (November 2004): 28–154, 52.

158. The phrase, and the original impetus, is from John Hart Ely, *Democracy and Distrust* (Cambridge, MA: Harvard University Press, 1980).

159. Hibbing and Theiss-Morse cited in Cain and Gerber, "California's Blanket Primary Experiment," 38ff.

160. Ibid., 42.

161. Pildes, "Foreword," 130.

162. Hasen, "Do the Parties or the People Own the Electoral Process?," 816.

163. Daniel Hays Lowenstein, "Associational Rights of Major Political Parties: A Skeptical Inquiry," *Texas Law Review* 71, no. 7 (June 1993): 1741–92, 1783.

164. Ibid., 1779. In fact, Lowenstein points out, in *Jones* neither major party state central committee was plaintiff to the suit.

165. "The hydraulics of party regulation reveal reform for what it is—less a means of injecting popular control than an institutional modification of the political landscape to the advantage of certain leaders and to the disadvantage of others." Kang, "Hydraulics and Politics," 18.

166. The phrase is from Dalton and Weldon, "Public Images," 941; this article contains cross-country data on support for far right and far left parties.

167. Beck and Sarouf, *Party Politics*, 54 (quoting Steven J. Rosenstone, Roy L. Behr, and Edward Lazarus, *Third Parties in America* (Princeton: Princeton University Press, 1984), 162).

168. Whether activists are ahead of the major party (the George Wallace candidacy anticipated Republicans' shift toward conservative social policy and away from

exclusive identification with economic conservatism) or dragging behind (Ralph Nader's claim that the Democrats had abandoned their economic liberalism and had become a big business party indistinguishable from Republicans). See Gary Miller and Norman Schofield, "Activists and Partisan Realignment in the United States," *American Political Science Review* 97, no. 2 (May 2002): 245–60, 253–54.

169. Jacobson, *The 2000 Elections*, 3.

170. *Twin Cities Area New Party v. McKenna*, 74 F. 3rd 196 (1996), cited in Pildes, "Democracy and Disorder," 707.

171. *Timmons v. Twin Cities Area New Party*, 520 US 351 (1997), at 378.

172. Cited in Disch, *Tyranny*, 25–26.

173. This purpose was recognized by the lower court in *Twin Cities v. McKenna*, 199.

174. Illinois Board of Elections cited in *Eu v. San Francisco County Democratic Central Committee*, 489 US 214 (1989), Lawyer's Heading 4. Among the systemic arguments for the political uses of minor parties: "as an outlet for frustration, often as a creative force and a sort of conscience, as an ideological governor to keep major parties from speeding off into an abyss of mindlessness, and even just as a technique for strengthening a group's bargaining power in the future, the minor party would have to be invented if it did not come into existence regularly enough." Cited in *Timmons v. Twin Cities Area New Party*, nn. 10 and 11.

175. *Timmons v. Twin Cities Area New Party*, Chief Justice Rehnquist for the Court at 365.

176. *Burdick v. Takushi*, 504 U.S. 428 (1992), 439, 445.

177. *Ibid.*, 445.

178. *Timmons v. Twin Cities Area New Party*, Justice Stevens dissenting at 375.

179. Ibid.

180. *Ibid.*, 364. The Court "expressly concluded for the first time in its history, that the stated interest in political stability justified electoral regulations that 'favor the traditional two-party system.'" Pildes, "Democracy and Disorder," 708. Pildes traced the division of opinion on the Court to the justices' varying tolerance for political competition and set this observation in sweeping historical context: "Two great foundational crises confronted American democracy in the twentieth century. The first was the challenge to the economic order posed by the worldwide Depression of the 1920s and 1930s. . . . The second was the challenge to democratic order posed by the rise of fascism and totalitarianism in formerly democratic Europe. . . . In both contexts, the initial diagnosis and remedy were strikingly similar." The Great Depression was caused by "ruinous competition"; post-World War II democratic thought analogously located the causes of totalitarianism in an "overly competitive, overly chaotic and fragmented political system." Pildes, "Democracy and Disorder," 696, 716–17.

181. Dissent in *Timmons v. Twin Cities Area New Party*, 381.

182. Pildes, "Foreword," 125.

183. "We propose that a self-conscious judiciary should destabilize political lock-ups in order to protect the competitive vitality of the electoral process and facilitate more responsive representation." Pildes, "Democracy and Disorder," 704. The discussion in Kang, "Hydraulics and Politics," 6, cites Issacharoff and Pildes, "Politics as Markets," 649.

184. Pildes, "Democracy and Disorder," 704.

185. *Clingman v. Beaver*, 544 U.S. 581 (2005), Justice Stevens in dissent at 609.

186. Schattschneider, *Semisovereign People*, 135.

187. Beitz, *Political Equality*, 176.

188. Bernard Manin, "On Legitimacy and Political Deliberation," *Political Theory* 15, no. 3 (1987): 338–68.

189. The phrase is Helene Landemore's in a Ph.D. dissertation for Harvard University, "Democratic Intelligence."

190. Beitz, *Political Equality*, 185.

191. James S. Fishkin, "A Nation in a Room," *Boston Review*, March/April 2006: 10–12, 10.

192. Ackerman and Fishkin, *Deliberation Day*, 9.

193. Ackerman and Fishkin, *Deliberation Day*, 76–78.

194. Beitz, *Political Equality*, 179.

195. Bernard Manin, "On Legitimacy and Political Deliberation," trans. Elly Stein and Jane Mansbridge, *Political Theory* 15, no. 3 (August 1987): 338–68, 351.

196. Beitz, *Political Equality*, 179.

197. Thompson, *Just Elections*, 91.

198. Beitz, *Political Equality*, 115.

199. Dennis Thompson, "Public Reason and Precluded Reasons," *Fordham Law Review* 72, no. 5 (2004): 2073–88, 2082.

200. For surveys and assessments of these positions, see Jane Mansbridge, "Deliberative Neo-Pluralism," unpublished manuscript; Jane Mansbridge, "Deliberation and Self-Interest," in *Deliberative Democracy and Its Discontents*, ed. Samantha Besson and Jose Luis Marti (London: Ashgate, 2006); Simone Chambers, "Deliberative Democratic Theory," *Annual Review of Political Science* 6 (2003): 307–26.

201. Mansbridge, "Deliberative Neo-Pluralism," 17.

202. Ibid., 12ff.

203. Thompson, *Just Elections*, 89.

204. Beitz, *Political Equality*, 176–77. Beitz is one of the few theorists who thinks that under the right institutional conditions parties might "face incentives to compete on the basis of substantive programmatic commitments" and thus "contribute more to a fruitful process of public political deliberation than the parties that hold themselves aloof from such commitments" (184). Robert Goodin argues that the justification for parties is precisely that they provide a program backed by what he calls a "ratio" for political decisions, that is, the condition for saying legislation was "giving laws to ourselves." "The Philosophical Foundation of Party Government," unpublished manuscript.

205. Beitz, *Political Equality*, 186.

206. Bernard Manin, *The Principles of Representative Government* (Cambridge: Cambridge University Press, 1997), 332; Manin, "Deliberation across the Aisle," Judith Shklar Memorial Lecture, Harvard University, December 2, 2004, unpublished manuscript. When he speaks of "deliberation across the aisle," Manin alludes to parties as agents of deliberation, but he does not see parties as essential to democratic deliberation.

207. Phillip Pettit, "Deliberative Democracy and the Discursive Dilemma," *Philosophical Issues* 11: 268–299 at 269.

208. Joshua Cohen, "Procedure and Substance in Deliberative Democracy," in *Democracy and Difference: Contesting the Boundaries of the Political*, ed. Seyla Benhabib (Princeton: Princeton University Press, 1996), 95–119, 95.

209. Geoffrey Brennan and Philip Pettit, "Unveiling the Vote," *British Journal of Political Science* 20, no. 3 (July 1990): 311–33, 332. In Pettit's discussion, parties have no significant part and are notable mainly for perverting republicanism. Philip Pettit, *Republicanism: A Theory of Freedom and Government* (Oxford: Oxford University Press, 1997), 237.

210. For a summary of experiments and assessment, see Robert E. Goodin and John S. Dryzek, "Deliberative Impacts: The Macro-political Uptake of Mini-publics," *Politics and Society* 34, no. 2 (June 2006): 219–44.

211. For the most recent, see Shanto Iyengar, Robert Luskin, and James Fishkin, "Deliberative Preferences in the Presidential Nomination Campaign: Evidence from an On-Line Deliberative Poll," presented at APSA meeting, Washington, D.C., 2005, pp. 3, 9.

212. See the discussion in Manin, "Deliberation across the Aisle," and his proposal for a citizens' group in which participants listen to a debate that exposes them to conflicting positions by "policy experts, group leaders, moral authorities." He would allow politicians to participate, too, but "on the condition that their participation is decoupled from electoral campaigns" (15).

213. James Fishkin's deliberative poll in Greece was the first binding deliberation in electoral politics: nominating a candidate for the Pasok party in the mayoralty election of a Greek town, Marousi. Support from Papandreou led to the hope that as president of the Socialist International, the experiment might be tried on a EU plebiscite. See "Out of the Ruins," *Financial Times Weekend Magazine*, July 8, 2006, p. 18. A summary of the candidate selection poll (on file with the author) states that the participants "significantly changed their views on the candidates and the issues": against the baseline of pre-participation polling, this was a dramatic gain for the candidate selected and a shift in issue priorities. Another exception is the Citizens Assembly on Electoral Reform in British Columbia, Canada, established by the provincial government, which charged the assembly with deciding on a system of electoral rules and was committed to putting the proposal that resulted from deliberation to a popular referendum. It is worth noting that like the blanket

primary proposition put to California voters, this effort to change election law was initiated by party activists who felt they were disadvantaged under the current arrangement.

214. Goodin and Dryzek, "Deliberative Impacts," 226–27.

215. Presumably, the structure of the situation, particularly in settings with mediators and carefully chosen information materials, avoids the negative outcomes of discussion in small groups. Cf. Cass Sunstein's discussion of movement to the extreme and cascade effects. Cass Sunstein, "Deliberative Trouble? Why Groups Go to Extremes," *Yale Law Review* 110, no. 1 (October 2000): 71–119.

216. Goodin and Dryzek, "Deliberative Impacts," 221.

217. Ibid.

218. John Ferejohn, "The Citizens' Assembly Model," unpublished manuscript, 5. Forthcoming in *Designing Deliberative Democracy*, ed. Mark Warren and Hilary Pearse (Cambridge: Cambridge University Press, 2008).

219. For a critique of *Deliberation Day* in terms of incentives for participation, the problem of homogeneous deliberating groups, and above all the difference between Deliberation Day and the "deliberative polls" used as evidence for increasing participation and reducing ignorance on behalf of this proposal, see Joseph Mazor, "Implementing the Right Kind of Mass Citizen Deliberation: The Problem of Incentives," unpublished manuscript.

220. In everything from assessments of economic conditions to presidential performance to candidates' personal traits. It is "rational for observers to interpret what they see in light of what they already believe—for Democrats to find evidence of a Democratic scandal less credible than do Republicans." Larry Bartels, "Beyond the Running Tally: Partisan Bias in Political Perceptions," *Political Behavior* 24, no. 2 (June 2002): 117–50, 125, 130.

221. *New York Times* report cited in Larry Bartels, "Democracy with Attitudes," unpublished manuscript, 23.

222. Cited in ibid., 24.

223. Jane Mansbridge, "Rethinking Representation," *American Political Science Review* 97, no. 4 (November 2003): 515–28, 520.

224. For a historical view of these positions, see Samuel L. Popkin, "Changing Media, Changing Politics," *Perspectives on Politics* 4, no. 2 (June 2006): 327–41. The quote is from Jim Lehrer, 339.

225. John Stuart Mill, *On Liberty*, in John M. Robson, ed., *The Collected Works of John Stuart Mill*, vol. 18 (Toronto: University of Toronto Press, 1963–91), 225, 254. Keeping in mind the ambivalence in Mill's view of progressive deliberation, in chap. 3 I described his swing between "hostile banners" and independents.

226. Urbinati, *Representative Democracy*, 227.

227. Parties are "the best agencies yet devised . . . to formulate and to set before the whole electorate opinions that are held in common by a portion of it, to impress the merit of these opinions by concerted effort upon the whole body of voters, to

afford a means whereby responsibility for a policy shall be borne in common by all who advocate it." Munro, *Government of American Cities*, 155–56.

228. Schattschneider, *Semisovereign People*, 74.

229. The authors themselves simplify and say that parties transform this diversity into "one big residual difference of opinion." Bernard Berelson, Paul Lazarsfeld, and William McPhee, *Voting: A Study of Opinion Formation in a Presidential Campaign*, cited in Samuel L. Popkin, *The Reasoning Voter: Communication and Persuasion in Presidential Campaigns* (Chicago: University of Chicago Press, 1991), 216.

230. Nelson W. Polsby, "The American Party System," in *The New Federalist Papers: Essays in Defense of the Constitution*, ed. Alan Brinkley, Nelson W. Polsby, and Kathleen Sullivan (New York: W. W. Norton, 1997), 41. One theory of party realignment focuses not on the usual change of party fortunes at the polls but on parties creating new cleavages. Edward G. Carmines and Michael W. Wagner, "Political Issues and Party Alignments: Assessing the Issue Evolution Perspective," *Annual Review of Political Science* 9 (2006): 67–81.

231. Cited in Manin, *Principles of Representative Government*, 225, 222 n. 40.

232. Jurgen Habermas, "Popular Sovereignty as Procedure," in *Deliberative Democracy: Essays on Reason and Politics*, ed. James Bohman and William Rehg (Cambridge, MA: MIT Press, 1997), 35–66, 60.

233. Manin, "Legitimacy and Political Deliberation," 357.

234. Pettit, "Democracy, Electoral and Contestatory," 117, 125.

235. Manin, "Legitimacy and Political Deliberation," 357.

236. Bruce Ackerman has proposed a tri-partite framework—social movement/ "movement parties"/plebiscitarian presidency—as the "engine" of progressive reform. "The Broken Engine of Progressive Politics," *American Prospect* 38 (May–June 1998): 34–43; his concern is the waning of "movement parties."

237. The phrase is Bruce Ackerman's, *We the People*, vol. 1, 285.

238. John Hibbing and Elizabeth Theiss-Morse, *Stealth Democracy: Americans' Beliefs about How Government Should Work* (Cambridge: Cambridge University Press, 2002), 134ff.

239. Mutz details the two mechanisms—cross-cutting pressures and the social psychology that inclines to harmony, homogeneity, and conflict avoidance. The latter in particular makes it difficult for people "to negotiate their political and apolitical identities . . . . A highly politicized mindset of 'us' versus 'them' is easy so long as we do not work with 'them' and our kids do not play with their kids. But how do we maintain this same fervor and political drive against 'them' when we carpool together?" (126). See too Larry Bartels, "Campaign Quality: Standards for Evaluation, Benchmarks for Reform," in *Campaign Reform: Insights and Evidence*, ed. Larry M. Bartels and Lynn Vavreck (Ann Arbor: University of Michigan Press, 2000), 1–61.

240. Walzer, *Politics and Passion*, 105.

241. Ibid., 109.

242. Walter Dean Burnham, *Critical Elections and the Mainsprings of American Politics* (New York: Norton, 1970), 133.

243. Iyengar, Luskin, and Fishkin, "Deliberative Preferences," 13.

244. Popkin, *Reasoning Voter*, 222.

245. Didion, *Political Fictions*, 318.

246. "A radical chastening" of political authority spills over into "a fundamental lesson about the nature of all authority." George Kateb, "The Moral Distinctiveness of Representative Democracy," *Ethics* 91, no. 3 (April 1981): 357–74, 358.

247. Henry Adams, *Democracy: An American Novel* (New York: Henry Holt, 1880), 49.

248. Take President Clinton. The "morality" issue was proven not to grip the public imagination. The public was so unmoved by the Clinton impeachment hearings, so insufficiently outraged, that partisans and moralists declared the people feckless and complicit in Clinton's immorality and lies. As Joan Didion reported, this moralism was carted out again during the Bush/Gore election by Gore himself, again to no apparent effect. See Didion, *Political Fictions,* 232ff.

249. For the view that Wilson and the progressives inaugurated the idea of presidential plebiscitary nomination in which the candidate builds his own constituency and captures his party label—that the party is a coalition that forms around and serves a particular leader—see James Ceasar, "Political Parties and Presidential Ambition," *Journal of Politics* 40, no. 3 (August 1978): 708–39.

250. Robert Penn Warren, *All the King's Men* (New York: Harcourt Brace, 1926), 11, 97.

Chapter 7. Partisanship and Independence

1. Citizenship is the most important political identity, but it is not exclusive to democracy. I believe it is possible to work out the way in which the defining characteristics I attribute to partisanship derive from democratic citizenship, but that is beyond the scope of this chapter.

2. Michael E. McGerr, *The Decline of Popular Politics: The American North, 1865–1928* (New York: Oxford University Press, 1986), 17.

3. Cited in ibid., 56.

4. By illusion I do not mean that swing voters—Independents and weak partisans—do not decide certain elections, only that unlike partisanship the outcome is not the result of collective action, a point to which I return. It is certainly the case that neither party can win national elections by mobilizing only their base. On one estimate, Democratic candidates must capture "upwards of 60% of the moderate vote." William Galston and Elaine Kamarck, "The Politics of Polarization," a Third Way Report (The Middle Class Project), October 2005, available at http://www.third-way.com.

5. *California Democratic Party v. Jones*, 984 F. Supp. 1288 (1997), District Court at 1302.

6. James Albert Woodburn, *Political Parties and Party Problems in the United States* (New York: Putnam, 1924), 527.

7. Wattenberg attributes neutrality to voters' perception that parties are irrelevant for solving problems and are inconsequential for government outcomes. *The Rise of Candidate-Centered Politics* (Cambridge, MA: Harvard University Press, 1991), 88–89. Of course, indifference to a major institution implies a negative evaluation, however elusive.

8. Jesse Macy, *Political Parties in the United States, 1846–1961* (New York: Arno Press, 1974), 282.

9. Anthony Downs, *An Economic Theory of Democracy* (New York: Harper, 1957), 34.

10. Joshua Cohen, "Procedure and Substance in Deliberative Democracy," in *Deliberative Democracy: Essays on Reason and Politics*, ed. James Bohman and William Rehg (Cambridge, MA: MIT Press, 1997): 407–38, 412.

11. Lisa Jane Disch argues that political science is implicated in the maintenance of a two party system: "Whereas the two-party system was the effect of the regulation of parties by the state, that regulation in turn provided some of the requisite conditions for the formation of political science understood as a field in its own right. At its outset, then, political science was a party discipline; the two-party system, though no inheritance of the American founding, was intimately bound up with the founding of a new scholarly regime." *Tyranny*, 81.

12. Bruce E. Keith, David Magleby, Candice Nelson, Elizabeth Orr, Mark Westlye, and Raymond Wolfinger, *The Myth of the Independent Voter* (Berkeley: University of California Press, 1992), 10.

13. Leon Epstein, *Political Parties in the American Mold* (Madison: University of Wisconsin Press, 1986), 240. For a discussion of the relevance of party ID outside the United States, see Donald Green, Bradley Palmquist, and Eric Schickler, *Partisan Hearts and Minds: Political Parties and the Social Identities of Voters* (New Haven: Yale University Press, 2002), 20ff.

14. Green, Palmquist, and Schickler, *Partisan Hearts*, 166.

15. Joshua Freedman, "This Is Your Brain on Politics," *New York Times*, January 18, 2005, p. A25; Benedict Carey, "A Shocker: Partisan Thought Is Unconscious," *New York Times*, January 24, 2006, p. D1.

16. There are comparable trends in other advanced democracies. See Harold D. Clarke and Marianne C. Stewart, "The Decline of Parties in the Minds of Citizens," *Annual Review of Political Science* 1 (1998): 357–78, 363. Peter Mair and Ingrid van Biezen, "Party Membership in Twenty European Democracies, 1980–2000," *Party Politics* 7, no. 1 (2001): 5–21. "A recent study of parties in all advanced industrial democracies reveals that, with the one exception of Spain, the trend in membership numbers is downwards." Patrick Seyd and Paul Whitely, "British Party Members: An Overview," *Party Politics* 10, no. 4 (2004): 355–66, 356.

17. The decline of party ID is not just ascriptive, the result of observations of "behavioral independence" on the part of voters. In survey research it is a null point of nonpartisanship on a bipolar scale of partisan self-image. Researchers disagree about how to classify a reply of "no preference" for one party over another. As "apolitical"? Or as a separate classification of "no-preference nonpartisans"? Wattenberg, *Rise of Candidate-Centered Politics,* 43. Outside the hothouse world of surveys, however, these social science subtleties do not enter ordinary thinking about independence. Weakening party ID is a central thesis in explorations of major shifts in voting patterns (the phenomenon called "realignment," which some suggest is better described today as "de-alignment" or, less vividly, "the no majority realignment.") Paul Allen Beck, "Changing American Party Coalitions," in Green and Shea, *State of the Parties,* 28–49, 39. Warren E. Miller discusses the types of realignment: geographic, group-based, or numerical in "Party Identification and the Electorate of the 1990s," in *The Parties Respond: Changes in American Parties and Campaigns,* ed. L. Sandy Maisel (Boulder, CO: Westview, 1994): 103–21. For a recent summary of the evidence of resurgence in strong party identification and the waning of pure Independents, see Geoffrey C. Layman, Thomas M. Carsey, and Juliana Menasce Horowitz, "Party Polarization in American Politics: Characteristics, Causes, and Consequences," *Annual Review of Political Science* 9 (2006): 83–110, 102.

18. Center for Political Studies, 1996, cited by Steven E. Schier, *By Invitation Only: The Rise of Exclusive Politics in the United States* (Pittsburgh: University of Pittsburgh Press, 2000), 25. One exception to all this is race; black voters shifted dramatically to the Democratic Party beginning in the 1960s, and partisanship remains strong.

19. National Election Survey. The National Annenberg Election Survey of 2004 has released party ID by state, available at http://www.annenbergpublicpolicycenter .org/Downloads/Political_Communication/naes/2005_03_party-identification-by-state_02–15_pr.pdf, accessed August 13, 2007. For trends in advanced democracies, see Harold D. Clarke and Marianne C. Stewart, "The Decline of Parties in the Minds of Citizens," *Annual Review of Political Science* 1 (1998): 357–78, 363.

20. D. Sunshine Hillygus and Todd Shields, *The Persuadable Voter: Strategic Candidates and Wedge Issues in Political Campaigns* (forthcoming).

21. Clarke and Stewart, "Decline of Parties," 361.

22. On the seven-point scale and the question of unidimensionality, that is, the assumption that partisanship and independence are mutually exclusive (the alternative that party ID is multidimensional and involves partisan direction and nonpartisanship components), see Wattenberg, *Rise of Candidate-Centered Politics,* 29. See Jack Dennis, "Political Independence in America, Part I: On Being an Independent Partisan Supporter," *British Journal of Political Science* 18, no. 1 (January 1988): 77–109, and Jack Dennis, "Political Independence in America III: In Search of Closet Partisans," *Political Behavior* 14, no. 3 (1992): 261–96. Disputing the waning

partisanship thesis outright is Larry Bartels, "Partisanship and Voting Behavior, 1952–1996," *American Journal of Political Science* 44, no. 1 (January 2000): 35–50. Among his points is that declining partisanship is mainly among nonvoters and has reversed among voters (37).

23. Keith et al., *Myth of the Independent Voter*, 2, 4. And "what is to be explained is not a pattern of belief, behavior, or commitment. What is to be explained is a questionnaire response" (200). See too Steven Greene, "The Psychological Sources of Partisan-Leaning Independence," *American Politics Quarterly* 28, no. 4 (October 2000): 511–37, 511. Other scholars point out that the distribution of partisanship in 1996 looks much as it did in 1972 and that the proportion of the voting public identified with the two major parties was roughly the same as well. Green, Palmquist, and Schickler, *Partisan Hearts*, 14.

24. Most Independents are party "leaners." One study suggests that 15% of adults regard themselves that way and that another nearly 30% of adults, if allowed to choose nonattachment of either kind, will. Diana Owen, Jack Dennis, and Casey Klofstad, "Public Support for the Party System in the United States in the Late 1990s," in *The State of Democracy in America*, ed. William Crotty (Washington, DC: Georgetown University Press, forthcoming), 12.

25. Luke Keele and James A. Stimson, "Polarization and Mass Response: The Growth of Independence in American Politics," paper presented at the American Political Science Association Meeting 2005, p. 12. "For the reader who is keeping score, the picture is confused" (22).

26. Chuck Todd, "In Search of the Swing Vote," *New York Times*, December 29, 2003, p. A21.

27. Bartels, cited in Green, Palmquist and Schickler, *Partisan Hearts*, 16–17. "Strong partisan was the modal category in both 2000 and 2004—marking the only times this has happened since the NES began measuring party identification in 1952." Donald Baumer and Howard Gold, "Party Images and Partisan Resurgence," paper presented at the American Political Science Association meeting 2005, p. 3. Among many studies, see Keele and Stimson, *Polarization*; Jacobson, *2000 Elections and Beyond*; Morris P. Fiorina, "Parties and Partisanship: A 40-Year Retrospective," *Political Behavior* 24, no. 2 (June 2002): 93–115.

28. Keith et al., *Myth of the Independent Voter*, cited in Greene, "Psychological Sources," 513.

29. A. James Reichley, "The Future of the American Two-Party System after 1994," in Green and Shea, *State of the Parties*, 11–24, 11.

30. Green, Palmquist, and Schickler, *Partisan Hearts*, 85.

31. On persuadable voters, see Hillygus and Shields, *Persuadable Voter*; Samuel Popkin, *The Reasoning Voter: Communication and Persuasion in Presidential Campaigns* (Chicago: University of Chicago Press, 1991); Byron E. Shafer and William J. M. Claggett, *The Two Majorities: The Issue Context of Modern American Politics* (Baltimore: Johns Hopkins University Press, 1995).

32. Henry Adams, "The 'Independents' in the Canvas," *North American Review* 123, no. 253 (October 1876): 426–67, 426, 428.

33. Albert O. Hirschman, *Exit, Voice, and Loyalty* (Cambridge, MA: Harvard University Press, 1970), 17.

34. Disch, *Tyranny*, 127.

35. Keele and Stimson, "Polarization," 11.

36. See, e.g., Keith et al., *Myth of the Independent Voters*, 177. Dennis reports that "Independent Partisan Supporters" are relatively positive toward the party system (Dennis, "Political Independence, Part I," 109 and n. 38).

37. I am grateful to Dennis Thompson for suggesting this point.

38. Wattenberg, *Rise of Candidate-Centered Politics*, 88–89, ix. Another study reports: "as each new cohort of Americans has reached political maturity, we have observed . . . an increasingly complex set of attitudes towards parties in general . . . (containing) elements of greater indifference and hostility toward the party system." Owen, Dennis, and Klofstad, "Public Support," 2.

39. Wattenberg, *Rise of Candidate-Centered Politics*, 158. For the view that parties are consequential, see Steven J. Rosenstone and John Mark Hansen, *Mobilization, Participation, and Democracy in America* (New York: Macmillan, 1993), 151ff.

40. Wattenberg, *Rise of Candidate-Centered Politics*, 48; John Kenneth White and Phillip John Davies, *Political Parties and the Collapse of the Old Orders* (Albany: SUNY Press, 1998), 8. Opinion polls suggest that confidence levels in political parties lie at the bottom of the scale, lower than any other secondary association: 42.6% of respondents express "very little" and only 3.8% "a great deal" of confidence in them. Virginia A. Hodgkinson, Murray S. Weitzman, and the Gallop Organization, *Giving and Volunteering in the United States* (Washington, DC: Independent Sector, 1996). A Eurobarometer rating from 2004 shows political parties ranking at the bottom of trust in national institutions. Standard Eurobarometer 62/Autumn 2004—TNS Opinion and Social, published May 2005, available at http://europa.eu.int/comm/public_opinion/index-en.htm.

41. Cited in Disch, *Tyranny*, 25–26. *Timmons v. Twin Cities Area New Party*, 520 U.S. 351 (1997)

42. Henry Adams on Independents in the 1872 campaign. "'Independents' in the Canvas," 429.

43. Dave Denison applies a more differentiated typology that distinguishes independents from disengaged ("bystanders") and subcategories within the Democratic and Republican camp. "Reading the American Mind," *American Prospect* 11, no. 4 (January 3, 2000): 58–61, 58; 86–87. Studies repeatedly show that independent voters are not a homogeneous group.

44. "Survey Indicates More Americans without Faith," American Atheists, Inc., www.atheists.org/flash.line/atheist4.htm, posted November 22, 2001, accessed August 13, 2007.

45. Diana Owen and Jack Dennis, "Anti-partyism in the USA and Support for Ross Perot," *European Journal of Political Research* 29, no. 3 (April 1996): 383–400, 389.

46. Cited in John Kenneth White, "Reviving the Political Parties: What Must Be Done?," in *The Politics of Ideas: Intellectual Challenges to the Party After 1992*, ed. John K. White and John C. Green (New York: Rowman & Littlefield, 2001), 4–27, 5.

47. Steffens, *Letters*, vol. 1, 106.

48. Clarke and Stewart, " Decline of Parties," 368.

49. Cited in Michael Sandel, *Democracy's Discontent: America in Search of a Public Philosophy* (Cambridge, MA: Harvard University Press, 1996), 273.

50. William Galston, *Liberal Purposes: Goods, Virtue, and Diversity in the Liberal State* (Cambridge: Cambridge University Press, 1991), 222.

51. Judith N. Shklar, *American Citizenship: The Quest for Inclusion* (Cambridge, MA: Harvard University Press, 1991), 47.

52. Ibid., 68, 66.

53. Hamilton, Federalist No. 35, in *The Federalist* (New York: Modern Library, 1941), 214.

54. Steffens, *Autobiography*, 492–93.

55. Samuel L. Popkin, "Changing Media, Changing Politics," *Perspectives on Politics* 4, no. 2 (June 2006): 327–39, 329.

56. Edmund S. Morgan, *Inventing the People*, 162.

57. In vol. 3, chap. 37, of the online *Diary and Letters of Rutherford B. Hayes*, from the Rutherford B. Hayes Presidential Center. Available at http://www.ohiohistory .org/onlinedoc/hayes/chapterxxxvii.html, accessed August 13, 2007.

58. Cited in Carol Weisbrod, *The Boundaries of Utopia* (New York: Pantheon, 1980), 24.

59. *Rutan v. Republican Party of Illinois*, 497 U.S. 62 (1990) at 105, 103. These rulings restricted patronage to upper level policy-making positions where party affiliation is conceded to be a reasonable requirement for effective performance.

60. Adams, " 'Independents' in the Canvas," 427.

61. Cited in McGerr, *Decline of Popular Politics*, 19.

62. Ostrogorski, *Democracy and the Party System in the United States*, 216–17.

63. Steffens, *Shame*, 63.

64. Woodburn, *Politics Parties*, 527.

65. Steffens, *Autobiography*, 136.

66. James Bryce, *The American Commonwealth* (London: Macmillan, 1889), 321.

67. This and other speculative characteristics are in Dennis, "Political Independence, Part I."

68. Russell Dalton, Ian McAllister, and Martin Wattenberg, "The Consequences of Partisan Dealignment," in *Parties without Partisans: Political Change in Advanced Industrial Democracies*, ed. Russell Dalton and Martin Wattenberg (Oxford: Oxford University Press, 2000), 37–63, 60.

69. An early formulation is this praise for eighteenth-century Virginia farmer Edward Pendleton: "None of his opinions were drawn from personal views or party prejudices. He never had a connexion with any political party . . . so that his opinions

were the result of his own judgment, and that judgment was rendered upon the best unbiased estimate he could make of the publick good." Cited in White and Davies, *Political Parties*, 7.

70. Taft, *Liberty under Law,* 32.

71. One example is Richard G. Niemi and M. Kent Jennings's careful work across the first stages of the life cycle of political participation. "Issues and Inheritance in the Formation of Party Identification," *American Journal of Political Science* 35, no. 4 (November 1991): 970–88. They demonstrate that partisan identification is the most stable element of political orientation and that early learning in the family is a major determinate of both initial and enduring political direction. "Parents' affiliations are still a greater influence on the offspring than any single issue" and the influence of parental partisanship "was always present to a significant degree" into adulthood. From early on influences other than the family affect party identification, most notably school peers. They also find erosion (or "defection") in the connection between parental and offspring partisanship: very high at the onset of adulthood, parental influence seems to decrease and the effects of issues increase. But the study shows too that partisanship becomes less responsive to current political forces as individuals age. In short, there is a small window for "life-cycle" or "political event" influences on party identification, but partisan identity is not persistently malleable.

72. Albert Stickney, *The Political Problem* (New York: Harper and Brothers, 1890), 33.

73. Angus Campbell, Philip E. Converse, Warren E. Miller, and Donald Stokes, *The American Voter* (New York: Wiley and Sons, 1960), 135.

74. Cited in Green, Palmquist, and Schickler, *Partisan Hearts*, 26.

75. Warren E. Miller and J. Merrill Shanks, *The New American Voter* (Cambridge: Harvard University Press, 1996), 495.

76. Wattenberg, "The Rise of Candidate-Centered Politics," cited in Larry M. Bartels, "Beyond the Running Tally: Partisan Bias in Political Perceptions," *Political Behavior* 24, no. 2 (June 2002): 117–50, 118.

77. Morris P. Fiorina, "Parties and Partisanship: A 40-Year Retrospective," 97.

78. For a critical account of the literature on public opinion in ideological terms, see Christopher Achen and Larry Bartels, "Ignorance and Bliss: Party Competition with Uninformed Voters," unpublished manuscript, p. 3. "In our model, voters do not know the candidates' positions, do not know other voters' positions, and do not know their own positions—indeed they do not even know there is an ideological dimension on which they might have positions" (5) On the different question whether issue preferences can be reduced to a single ideological dimension, see Edward G. Carmines and Michael W. Wagner, "Political Issues and Party Alignments: Assessing the Issue Evolution Perspective," *Annual Review of Political Science* 9 (2006): 67–81, 72ff.

79. Cited in Green, Palmquist, and Schickler, *Partisan Hearts*, 214.

80. Morris P. Fiorina, *Retrospective Voting in American National Elections* (New Haven: Yale University Press, 1981). Against this: Partisanship "is not merely a

running tally of political assessments, but a pervasive dynamic force shaping citizens' perceptions of, and reactions to, the political world in." Bartels, "Beyond the Running Tally," 138.

81. Christopher Achen, "Social Psychology, Demographic Variables, and Linear Regression: Breaking the Iron Triangle in Voting Research," *Political Behavior* 14, no. 3 (September 1992): 194–211. Jane Mansbridge calls this "anticipatory representation," where representatives try to please future voters' underlying interests as well as present preferences. "Rethinking Representation," *American Political Science Review* 97, no. 4 (November 2003): 515–28, 515. Revisionists ascribe importance to voters' *perceptions* of what parties deliver as distinct from expert analysis; subjective understanding of the state of the economy as measured by the Consumer Sentiment Index and not "hard economic indicators," for example. Green, Palmquist, and Schickler, *Partisan Hearts*, 94.

82. Popkin, *The Reasoning Voter*, 7, 43.

83. An interesting question is the assessment voters make of their own level of knowledge. Ackerman argues that the normal voter "is under no illusions about the quality of reflection that lies behind her ballot" and that "voting decisions do not measure up to their own standards of deliberateness." *We the People*, vol. 1, 241ff.

84. Larry Bartels, "Homer Gets a Tax Cut: Inequality and Public Policy in the American Mind," *Perspectives on Politics* 3, no. 1 (March 2005): 15–31. Party ID can be saved from instability but at the partial expense of the position that appears to have just been won—the salience of programs and policies and perceptions of their consequences. The "biased learning" hypothesis allows that voters are politically attentive and update information but argues that they are not rational learners. In assessing their proximity to party positions or performance, they reason poorly because partisanship skews their perceptions. When Democrats and Republicans record divergent reactions to new information, it is the result not of conscious ideological disagreement but of perceptual bias or screens. Green, Palmquist, and Schickler, *Partisan Hearts*, 126ff.

85. Popkin, *Reasoning Voter*, 97.

86. Separation of powers is one factor. Another is divided government, which exacerbates the problem of legislative and executive branches contesting to take credit or lay blame. Parties without cohesion make collective responsibility difficult too. Against collective responsibility is the argument that there is "a causal relation between 'nonresponsible' parties and government stability," that is, cross-sectional and nonideological parties. See Gerald M. Pomper, "Toward a More Responsible Two-Party System? What, Again?," *Journal of Politics* 33, no. 4 (November 1971): 916–40, 918. This is a fairly common claim: broad-based parties "supply an essential coherence and flexibility to the American political scene." Justice Powell, in *Democratic Party v. Wisconsin,* 450 U.S. 107 (1981), at 133.

87. Christopher H. Achen and Larry M. Bartels, "Blind Retrospection," paper presented at the 2002 American Political Science Association meeting, Boston, 5.

88. Ibid., 6.

89. James Fearon, "Electoral Accountability and the Control of Politicians: Selecting Good Types versus Sanctioning Poor Performance," in *Democracy, Accountability, and Representation*, ed. Adam Przeworski, Bernard Manin, and Susan C. Stokes (Cambridge: Cambridge University Press, 1999), 55–97.

90. Keith et al., *Myth of the Independent Voter*, 24.

91. Campbell et al., *American Voter*, 143ff.

92. Keith et al., *Myth of the Independent Voter*, 166–67, 41–55.

93. See the useful summary in Christiano, *Rule of the Many*, 110ff.

94. "Huge Democracy Geek Even Votes in Primaries," *Onion* 38, no. 36, October 2, 2002. Available at http://www.theonion.com/content/node/38535, accessed August 13, 2007.

95. Jim Lehrer quoted in Popkin, "Changing Media, Changing Politics," 339, a position Popkin describes as "cultural protectionism."

96. Dalton, McAllister, and Wattenberg, "Consequences of Partisan Alignment," 60.

97. See Shafer and Claggett, *Two Majorities*, 185ff. Or more likely to be moved by attraction or aversion to candidates on the basis of personality and direct communication.

98. Miller and Shanks, *New American Voter*, 117.

99. Green, Palmquist, and Schickler, *Partisan Hearts*, 52, 204. On p. 9, they suggest asking "what type of person comes to mind" when you think of Democrat or Republican to elicit the social stereotypes ascribed to parties. One conclusion is that "the partisan stereotypes of the New Deal are alive and well." Other empirical work points more specifically to the image of party activists: Gary Miller and Norman Schofield, "Activists and Partisan Realignment in the United States," *American Political Science Review* 97, no. 2 (May 2003): 245–60.

100. The distinction between attitudes toward parties and identification as a partisan is not always sharp in practice. Preferences or attitudes or ideology and social identification may be fused, "so that what looks like ideologically motivated reasoning is in fact achieved by reacting favorably or unfavorably to reference groups." The drift of western Democrats to the Republican Party in the 1930s may have occurred because they did not identify with Roosevelt Democrats as liberals, or it may be that they did not agree with liberals because they associated them with immigrants. Some combination of ideology and social aversion was at work. Green, Palmquist, and Schickler, *Partisan Hearts*, 107.

101. Ibid., 138.

102. Ibid., 6. In the 1980s the mobilization of Christian conservatives on behalf of a conservative social agenda altered the Republican Party, and how Republicans were perceived, though there was a pre-history of mobilization efforts (and forecasts) from the Second World War (11–12).

103. Hillygus and Shields, *Persuadable Voter*.

104. Russell J. Dalton and Steve Weldon, "Partisanship and Party System Institutionalization," *Party Politics* 13, no. 2 (2007): 179–96, 182.

105. Green, Palmquist, and Schickler, *Partisan Hearts*, 2.

106. Walzer, *Passion and Politics*, 12.

107. Green, Palmquist, and Schickler point out that party switching from Democrat to Republican and vice versa is rare; the rate increases if one adds in switches to and from independence, "creating the misleading impression that party attachments in the United States are subject to frequent change" (*Partisan Hearts*, 167). See Jeffrey Graynaviski and Melissa Harris Lacewell, "Shifting Alliances: Are Black Voters Ready to Rethink Allegiance to the Democratic Party?," paper presented at American Political Science Association meetings, Washington, DC, 2005.

108. Clarke and Stewart, "Decline of Parties," 371.

109. For the argument against convergence across partisans in response to shared political experience, emphasizing significant partisan biases even in response to exceedingly straightforward factual matters, see Bartels, "Beyond the Running Tally." "Partisan loyalties have pervasive effects on perceptions of the political world" (138).

110. Green, Palmquist, and Schickler, *Partisan Hearts*, 8, 133–34, 137.

111. Rosenblum, *Membership and Morals*.

112. Amy Gutmann, *Identity in Democracy* (Princeton: Princeton University Press, 2003), 13, 14, emphasis added.

113. Russell Hardin, *One for All: The Logic of Group Conflict* (Princeton: Princeton University Press, 1995), 217.

114. See Brian Barry, *Culture and Equality: An Egalitarian Critique of Multiculturalism* (Cambridge, MA: Harvard University Press, 2001).

115. Mansbridge, "Rethinking Representation," 523.

116. Gianluigi Galeotti and Albert Breton, "An Economic Theory of Political Parties," *Kyklos* 39, no. 1 (February 1986): 47–65, 56, 54.

117. For an assessment of competing "underlying social cleavage" and "institutional" accounts, see Susan C. Stokes, "Political Parties and Democracy," *Annual Review of Political Science* 2 (1999): 243–67.

118. Kalyvas draws attention to the "microfoundations" of religious parties, offering a contextual examination of the discrete decisions made by political actors, both lay and clerical, in their own interests. Among them are the decision to create a party or ally with an existing party, or none; and to direct voting among a number of parties or for "Christian" candidates. I have drawn liberally on his work. Stathis N. Kalyvas, *The Rise of Christian Democracy in Europe* (Ithaca: Cornell University Press, 1996). Also see Margaret L. Anderson, "Piety and Politics: Recent Work on German Catholicism," *Journal of Modern History* 63, no. 4 (December 1991): 681–716, 690. See too Mario Caciagli, Lieven de Winter, Albrecht Mintzel, Joan Culla, and Alain de Brouwer, *Christian Democracy in Europe* (Barcelona: ICPS, 1992), and Mario Einaudi and Francois Goguel, *Christian Democracy in Italy and France* (Notre

Dame, IN: University of Notre Dame Press, 1952). Carolyn M. Warner, *Confessions of an Interest Group: The Catholic Church and Political Parties in Europe* (Princeton: Princeton University Press, 2000), 18.

119. Failure to develop religious political identity and organization is costly: "to insist that one's creedal or denominational theology . . . defines and occupies the entire content and space of the religious spirit is to pay high costs in a religiously pluralistic and democratic society. Self-distancing removes the religious community, its institutions and ideas, from participation in the larger spiritual and intellectual life of the nation and, through that, of one's own time." Eldon Eisenach, *The Next Religious Establishment: National Identity and Political Theology in Post-Protestant America* (New York: Rowman & Littlefield, 2000), 41.

120. We see this in the United States today. The Christian Right was the creation of conservative political strategists who were not religious fundamentalists but who saw the potential of a new conservative movement based on social and moral issues. Steve Bruce, "The Moral Majority: The Politics of Fundamentalism in Secular Society," in *Studies in Religious Fundamentalism*, ed. Lionel Caplan (New York: Macmillan Press, 1987), 177–94, 182. Also Sara Diamond, *Not by Politics Alone: The Enduring Influence of the Christian Right* (New York: Guilford Press, 1998). Evangelical preachers are an integral part of this movement. But they are also often in tension with political organizers who have divergent purposes: to expand the political agenda, to urge political accommodation, and to temper overzealous allies vulnerable to being labeled "extremist." John C. Green, "The Christian Right and the 1994 Elections," *P.S.: Political Science & Politics* 28, no. 1 (March 1995): 5–6, 6.

121. Nancy L. Rosenblum, "Religious Parties, Religious Political Identity, and the Cold Shoulder of Liberal Democratic Thought," *Ethical Theory and Moral Practice: An International Forum* 6, no. 1 (March 2003): 23–53.

122. McCormick, *Party Period and Public Policy*, 182–83. Parties have been defined as coalitions of interest groups by Cohen, Karol, Noel, and Zaller, "Political Parties and Presidential Nominations," unpublished manuscript, 24.

123. Margaret Weir and Marshall Ganz, "Reconnecting People and Politics," in Greenberg and Skocpol, *The New Majority*, 149–71, 153.

124. For a summary of literature on the change from parties as membership organizations rooted in social networks to parties geared to a general electorate, using evidence from Europe, see Ingrid van Biezen, "On the Theory and Practice of Party Formation and Adaptation in New Democracies," *European Journal of Political Research* 44, no. 1 (January 2005): 147–74, 149.

125. Green, Palmquist, and Schickler, *Partisan Hearts*, 52, 204.

126. Partisanship may be more stable if we look at the incessant splitting of churches, especially in the United States, where religious "musical chairs" is a well-documented phenomenon described as a "belief bazaar" with people picking and choosing among competing denominations.

127. Popkin, *Reasoning Voter*, 64.

128. Though it may have an effect on the issues about which those who are group-conscious choose to be active. Sidney Verba, Kay L. Schlozman, and Henry E. Brady, "Reply to Reviews," *American Political Science Review* 91, no. 2 (June 1997): 427–30, 429.

129. Green, Palmquist, and Schickler, *Partisan Hearts*, 2, 166.

130. Alan Wolfe, "The Tyranny of the Undecided Voter," *New York Times*, October 22, 2000.

131. Cited in Walzer, *Passion and Politics*, 128.

132. Henry David Thoreau, "Resistance to Civil Government," in *Thoreau's Political Writings*, ed. Nancy L. Rosenblum (Cambridge: Cambridge University Press, 1996).

133. Shklar, *American Citizenship*, 189.

134. Henry Adams on Independents in the 1872 campaign, "The 'Independents' in the Canvass," 429.

135. Woodburn, *Political Parties*, 521.

136. Bernard Manin, "Deliberation across the Aisle," Judith Shklar Memorial Lecture, Harvard University, December 2, 2004, unpublished manuscript, 8.

137. Taft, *Liberty under Law*, 35.

138. John Stuart Mill, "Considerations on Representative Government," in *Collected Works of John Stuart Mill*, vol. 19, ed. John M. Robson (Toronto: University of Toronto Press, 1977), 489.

139. Ostrogorski, *Democracy and the Party System*, 409, 411.

140. Shklar, *American Citizenship*, 60.

141. Hans Kelsen, "On the Essence and Value of Democracy," in *Weimar: A Jurisprudence of Crisis*, ed. Arthur Jacobson and Bernhard Schlink (Berkeley: University of California Press, 2000), 350 n. 24.

142. Munro, *Government of American Cities*, 155–56.

143. Macy, *Political Parties in the United States*, 170.

144. Theodore Roosevelt, *American Ideals and Other Essays, Social and Political* (New York: G. P. Putnam's Sons, 1907), 39, 59–60.

145. Stickney, *Political Problem*, 32–33.

146. Steffens, *Letters*, 108.

147. Theodore Lowi, "Toward a Responsible Three-Party System: Prospects and Obstacles," 42–60.

148. Woodburn, *Political Parties*, 521.

149. Munro, *Government of American Cities*, 155–56.

150. Edmund Burke, *An Appeal from the New to the Old Whigs* (New York: Library of Liberal Arts, 1962), 52. "Thoughts on the Cause of Present Discontents," in J.A.W. Gunn, *Factions No More: Attitudes to Party in Government and Opposition in Eighteenth-Century England* (London: Frank Cass, 1971), 201–2.

151. Harvey C. Mansfield Jr., *Statesmanship and Party Government* (Chicago: University of Chicago Press, 1965), 187.

152. Macy, *Political Parties*, 282.

153. John Stuart Mill, "On Liberty," in *The Collected Works*, 225, 254. Keeping in mind the ambivalence in Mill's view of progressive deliberation, and his swing between "hostile banners" and independents.

154. Morris Fiorina is one of many who defends parties as blunt but irreplaceable instruments of democratic accountability. "The Decline of Collective Responsibility in American Politics," *Daedalus* 109, no. 3 (Summer 1980): 25–45, 27.

155. Larry D. Kramer, "Putting the Politics Back into the Political Safeguards of Federalism," *Columbia Law Review* 100, no. 1 (January 2000): 215–93, 278–79. On the "successive waves of reform [that] maimed and nearly killed this system," see 280ff.

156. Aldrich, *Why Parties?*, 9. For parliamentary, presidential, and semi-presidential systems and the way in which parties permit or inhibit their functioning, see Cindy Skach, *Borrowing Constitutional Designs: Constitutional Law in Weimar Germany and the French Fifth Republic* (Princeton: Princeton University Press, 2005).

157. Munro, *Government of American Cities*, 155–56.

158. The 1996 U.S. presidential election had the second lowest turnout in the history of mass democratic politics in this country; the 2000 election was only a slight improvement. Figures are far lower—less than a third of eligible voters—for primary elections, and rock-bottom for young voters. For a discussion of the controversy over measuring turnout, see Michael McDonald and Samuel Popkin, "The Myth of the Vanishing Voter," *American Political Science Review* 95, no. 4 (December 2001): 963–74. "There are virtually no identifiable turnout trends from 1972 onward" (968).

159. Shklar, *American Citizenship*, 25.

160. For a summary of this literature, see Andre Blais, "What Affects Voter Turnout?," *Annual Review of Political Science* 9 (June 2006): 111–25. Mark Franklin argues that party ID does not generate high turnout but does prevent turnout from falling as much as it might in a low-turnout election. *Voter Turnout and the Dynamics of Electoral Competition*, 164–65.

161. On interestedness generally, see Joanne M. Miller and Wendy Rahn, "Identity-Based Feelings, Beliefs and Actions: How Being Influences Doing," unpublished manuscript.

162. Jack C. Doppelt and Ellen Shearer, *Non Voters* (Thousand Oaks, CA: Sage Publications, 1999), 22.

163. Arend Lijphart, "Unequal Participation: Democracy's Unresolved Dilemma," *American Political Science Review* 91, no. 1 (March 1997): 1–14, 10. A similar cautionary argument has been made for voters loosed from partisanship, who vote subject to the pressures of ethnic or religious leaders.

164. Bernard Manin, *Principles of Representative Government* (Cambridge: Cambridge University Press, 1997), 218.

165. L. Laurence Moore, *Selling God: American Religion in the Marketplace of Culture* (New York: Oxford University Press, 1994), 120ff.

166. Green, Palmquist, and Schickler, *Partisan Hearts*, 219.

167. Franklin, *Voter Turnout*, 215, 49, 41–42, 56.

168. Seyd and Whitely illustrate the point with the British Liberal party ("British Party Members," 360–61).

169. Nadia Urbinati, "What Makes Representation Democratic?," presented at the American Political Science Association meeting, Washington, D.C., 2005, p. 4.

170. On catch-all party, Otto Kirchheimer, "The Transformation of Western European Party Systems," in *Political Parties and Political Development*, ed. Joseph La Palombara and Myron Weiner (Princeton: Princeton University Press, 1966), 177–200.

171. In the United States, "any group of people who have virtually the same views on political questions, the same political loyalties and identifications, is certain to be a *minority*." So "to win national elections, even to win influence over national policies, every group must participate somehow in the politics of coalition building." Any aggregate large enough to constitute a majority of voters is necessarily heterogeneous, with views coinciding on some questions but diverging on others. Robert Dahl, *Pluralist Democracy in the United States: Conflict and Consensus* (New Haven: Yale University Press, 1967), 455.

172. Ibid., 226. Analysts agree that the parties are less class-based than they were historically. The standard view of Ranney and Kendall is that "the great accomplishment of the American party system has been that it created agreement in the face of great diversity. By their cross-sectional and non-ideological character, the parties were able to encompass all groups, or at least some of every group" (cited in Pomper, "Toward a More Responsible System," 918).

173. See Russell Muirhead, Nancy L. Rosenblum, Daniel Schlozman, and Francis Shen, "Religion in the 2004 Presidential Election," in *Divided States of America: The Slash and Burn Politics of the 2004 Election*, ed. Larry J. Sabato (New York: Longman, 2005).

174. A process of polarization among activists has been noted: "In the 1960s Republican activists were about 20% more conservative than independent voter. By 2002 . . . they were almost 40% more conservative." In Jacob S. Hacker and Paul Pierson, *Off Center: The Republican Revolution and the Erosion of American Democracy* (New Haven: Yale University Press, 2005), 27. Increasingly, liberals and conservatives line up with Democrats and Republicans. Galston and Kamarck, "Politics of Polarization," 3, 46.

175. Miller and Schofield, "Activists and Partisan Realignment," 249.

176. Potential voters are members of *potentially winning electoral coalitions*, who believe their coalition will win if every member voted. The argument depends on members of an electorate seeing themselves this way. Franklin, *Voter Turnout*, 202–3.

177. Tocqueville, *Democracy in America*, 230.

178. Morris, *New Prince*, 230.

179. Schattschneider, *Party Government,* 98. I mean to use narrative as a term not of art but of coherent positions on important problems and national direction. That is, a story that has more continuity than we would expect from individuals on their own or as members of particularist groups with shifting involvements.

180. Moore, *Selling God,* 82.

181. John Rawls, *A Theory of Justice* (Cambridge, MA: Harvard University Press, 1999), 195; Rawls, "The Idea of Public Reason Revisited," in *Collected Papers,* ed. Samuel Freeman (Cambridge, MA: Harvard University Press, 1999), 573–615, 585.

182. Rawls, *Theory of Justice,* 195; Rawls, "Public Reason," 585, 576, 578, 581. For a full discussion of Rawls on parties, see Russell Muirhead and Nancy L. Rosenblum, "Political Liberalism vs. 'The Great Game of Politics': The Politics of Political Liberalism," *Perspectives on Politics* 4, no. 1 (March 2006): 99–108.

183. Beitz, *Political Equality,* 176–77. Under the right institutional conditions parties might "face incentives to compete on the basis of substantive programmatic commitments" and thus "contribute more to a fruitful process of public political deliberation than the parties that hold themselves aloof from such commitments" (184).

184. This is less stringent than Robert Goodin's justification for parties: providing a "ratio" for laws, where this comprehensive ratio is the defining characteristic of law in contrast to coercion. "The Philosophical Foundation of Party Government," unpublished manuscript, 17.

185. I believe this point is consistent with John Petrocik's interesting argument about campaigns, which explains voting in terms of "issue ownership"—"framing a vote choice as a decision to be made in terms of problems facing the country that he is better able to 'handle' than his opponent." My argument is about partisanship generally, not restricted to campaigns. But it is consistent with Petrocik's insofar as he says that reputation for "handling" issues is tied to a "history of attention, initiative, and innovation toward these problems"; perceptions of a party's issue competence change very slowly if they change at all; and partisans consistently cast their party as "more competent" across a range of problems not specific issues. "Issue Ownership in Presidential Elections, with a 1980 Case Study," *American Journal of Political Science* 40, no. 3 (August 1996): 825–50, 826.

186. For a detailed case study, see Edward G. Carmines and James A. Stimson: "The ultimate evidence of an issue evolution, however, is not to be found in the halls of Congress, the behavior of party activists, or even the ideological orientations of the electorate. It is to be found in the link between issues and citizens' partisan identifications," *Issue Evolution: Race and the Transformation of American Politics* (Princeton: Princeton University Press, 1989), 138.

187. The phrase is Urbinati's in *Representative Democracy,* 31.

188. Bernard Berelson, Paul Lazarsfeld, and William McPhee, *Voting: A Study of Opinion Formation in a Presidential Campaign,* cited in Popkin, *Reasoning Voter,* 216.

189. Richard Hofstadter, *The Idea of a Party System: The Rise of Legitimate Opposition in the United States, 1780–1840* (Berkeley: University of California Press, 1969), 72.

190. For a discussion of the parameters of justifiable compromise, see Dennis Thompson, "Mill in Parliament: When Should a Philosopher Compromise?," in *J. S. Mill's Political Thought: A Bicentennial Re-assessment* (Cambridge: Cambridge University Press, 2007), 166–99.

191. Walzer, *Politics and Passion*, 92, 93.

192. Christiano, *Rule of the Many*, 169ff. However, Christiano, an advocate of proportional representation, also insists on party choice understood as a ranking of ends, a more onerous demand: "the choice of aims model requires that citizens choose a schedule of trade-offs between all the ends that they have" (198). Christiano assigns this to parties whose packages of aims and trade-offs should be clear (199).

193. Don't Independents have to compromise, perhaps even more? My point is that forced to choose a party candidate, Independents may have to compromise with *themselves*; partisans compromise with others. Their compromise is not guided by identification, aimed at sustaining an association, or moved by considerations of the group's effectiveness.

194. William Galston, *Liberal Purposes: Goods, Virtues, and Diversity in the Liberal State* (Cambridge: Cambridge University Press, 1991), 227.

195. Ostrogorski, *Democracy and the Party System*, 408.

196. I am indebted to the important work of George Kateb, "The Moral Distinctiveness of Representative Democracy," *Ethics* 91, no. 3 (April 1981): 357–74.

197. Veit Bader, "Religious Pluralism: Secularism or Priority for Democracy?," *Political Theory* 27, no. 5 (October 1999): 597–634, 617.

198. Schattschneider, *Party Government*, 91.

199. George Kateb, *The Inner Ocean: Individualism and Democratic Culture* (Ithaca, NY: Cornell University Press, 1992), 37.

200. Harvey C. Mansfield, "Whether Party Government Is Inevitable," *Political Science Quarterly* 80, no. 4 (December 1965): 517–42.

201. Tocqueville, *Democracy*, 185.

202. Russell Muirhead, "Left *and* Right: A Defense of Partisanship," paper presented at Dartmouth Politics Colloquium.

203. Manin, *Representative Government*, 226.

204. Rawls, *Theory of Justice*, 196.

205. Sidney Milkes, *Political Parties and Constitutional Government: Remaking American Democracy* (Baltimore: Johns Hopkins University Press, 1999), 3.

Chapter 8. Centrism and Extremism and an Ethic of Partisanship

* An early version of this chapter was published as Nancy L. Rosenblum, "Liberalism and Illiberalism: 'Extremism' and Anti-Extremism in American Party Politics," *Journal of Contemporary Legal Issues* 12, no. 2 (2002): 843–85.

1. Pat Buchanan to Nixon in 1971. Cited in John Kenneth White, "Reviving the Political Parties: What Must Be Done?," in *The Politics of Ideas*, ed. John K. White and John C. Green (New York: Rowman & Littlefield, 1994), 17.

2. Robin Toner, "In This Race, It's the Center against the Middle," *New York Times*, March 17, 1996, sec. 4, p. 3.

3. James Q. Wilson, "Polarization in America: Politics and Polarization," the Tanner Lectures at Harvard University, 2005, p. 1.

4. Jacob S. Hacker and Paul Pierson, *Off Center: The Republican Revolution and the Erosion of American Democracy* (New Haven: Yale University Press, 2005), 2.

5. Or, popular insight into distinctions between the parties coupled with complaints that the parties are "virtual carbon copies of one another"? John R. Hibbing and Elizabeth Theiss-Morse, *Stealth Democracy: Americans' Beliefs about How Government Should Work* (Cambridge: Cambridge University Press, 2002), 25.

6. Hacker and Pierson, *Off Center*.

7. Jim Hightower cited in James MacGregor Burns and Georgia J. Sorenson, *Dead Center: Clinton-Gore Leadership and the Perils of Moderation* (New York: Scribner, 1999), 161.

8. Cited in Wilson Carey McWilliams, "The Meaning of the Election," in *The Election of 1996: Reports and Interpretations*, ed. Gerald Pomper (Chatham, NJ: Chatham House, 1997), 241–72, 252.

9. Burns and Sorenson, *Dead Center*, 167, 154.

10. Bruce Ackerman, "The Broken Engine of Progressive Politics," *American Prospect*, no. 38 (May/June 1998): 34–43, 42.

11. Hacker and Pierson, *Off Center*, 48.

12. Robert Dahl's ingredients of severe conflict in *Pluralist Democracy in the United States: Conflict and Consensus* (New Haven: Yale University Press, 1967), 282.

13. Bob Herbert describing House majority whip Tom Delay in "The True Believer," *New York Times*, November 30, 2000, p. A31.

14. Hofstadter, *Idea of a Party System*, 6.

15. Burns and Sorenson, *Dead Center*, 270.

16. Frank Rich, "Happy Anniversary, Mr. Presidents," *New York Times*, December 2, 2000, p. A31.

17. David Brooks, "Party No. 3," *New York Times*, August 10, 2006, http://www.nytimes.com.

18. Fiorina, cited in Hacker and Pierson, *Off Center*, 43. Other academics judge only one party to be extremist, and characterize GOP "power brokers" as "monsters in B-grade horror flicks" always ready to spring back to life (210).

19. Hofstadter, *Idea of a Party System*, 244.

20. Ibid., 138.

21. *New York Times*, November 19, 2000, sec. 1, p. 25.

22. Michiko Kakutani, "Polarization of National Dialogue Mirrors Extremists of Left and Right," *New York Times*, November 26, 2000, sec. 1, p. 29.

23. Rosenblum, *Membership and Morals*, 283.

24. Michael Kelly, "The Road to Paranoia," cited in ibid., 280.

25. Ibid., 283.

26. The phrase is Alison Mitchell's, "The Election: Trying to Escape the Purgatory of Parity," *New York Times*, November 26, 2000, sec. 4, p. 3.

27. Roderick P. Hart, *Campaign Talk: Why Elections Are Good for Us* (Princeton: Princeton University Press, 2000), 114. He observes that the convention acceptance speech is long, cautious, and busy with the practical, concrete, and numerical: Clinton's speech "reads like a political road map, with each sentence identifying the pressure group likely to be offended by the idea it embraces."

28. Manin, *Representative Government*, 138.

29. Hart, *Campaign Talk*, 114.

30. Jon Margolis, "Chamber of Horrors," *American Prospect* 11, no. 16 (July 17, 2000): 18–22, 21.

31. David C. King, "Congress, Polarization, and Fidelity to the Median Voter," unpublished manuscript, 11.

32. Charles O. Jones, "The Separated System," *Society* 33, no. 6 (September 1996): 18–23, 22.

33. James Bennet, "Liberal Use of 'Extremist' Is the Winning Strategy," *New York Times*, November 7, 1996, p. B1.

34. For a historical discussion of the origin and development of the "left"/"right" topography, see Marcel Gauchet, "Right and Left," in *Realms of Memory: Rethinking the French Past*, vol. 1: *Conflicts and Divisions*, ed. Lawrence D. Kritzman (New York: Columbia University Press, 1996), 241–98. Gauchet traces the topography from its revolutionary and parliamentary origins to its emergence as an indispensible simplifying symbolism and signal of political identity with mass democracy in the twentieth century. For an example of the spatial model, Lyman Sargent opens his Introduction to *Extremism in America: A Reader*: "The varied social movements and political thought produced in any country may be imaged as existing along a line with midpoint and ends" (New York: New York University Press, 1995), 1.

35. Ronald Inglehart, *Culture Shift in Advanced Industrial Society* (Princeton: Princeton University Press: 1990). Which is why Inglehart predicts that new, "postmaterialist" cleavages will be assimilated to the standard spectrum, albeit with difficulty and unacknowledged modification (296, 298). Inglehart observes that the emergence of post-materialism has been much more stressful for party identification and alignments: activists "seek goals that the existing political parties are not well adapted to pursue" (333, 373).

36. Ibid., 293.

37. Gauchet, "Right and left," 248, 260. Gauchet indicates that the Larousse dictionary records the first use of the term "extremism" in 1922, when the extremes were ideologically dominant (275).

38. The spatial model may be absorptive, and the connotations of spectrum labels may vary in the short term with current events (Inglehart, *Culture Shift*, 293ff). But it is not static. The whole spectrum may shift over time. Even a relatively short-term perspective on issues from antidiscrimination policy to abortion rights reveals the moving center in American politics and with it, insofar as off-center positions are designated "extremes," shifting extremes.

39. Maurice Duverger, *Political Parties: Their Organization and Activity in the Modern State* (New York: John Wiley & Sons, 1963), 45.

40. Susan Scarrow, "Politicians against Parties: Anti-Party Arguments as a Weapon for Change in Germany," *European Journal of Political Research* 29, no. 3 (April 1996): 297–317, 297.

41. Seymour Martin Lipset, "What Are Parties For?" *Journal of Democracy* 7, no. 1 (January 1996): 169–175, 174.

42. Cited in *Anderson v. Celebreezze*, 460 U.S. 780 (1983) at n. 17.

43. Aldrich, *Why Parties?*, 54.

44. See, e.g., John C. Green, James L. Guth, and Clyde Wilcox, "Less Than Conquerors: The Christian Right in State Republican Parties," in *Social Movements and American Political Institutions*, ed. Anne N. Costain and Andrews S. McFarland (New York: Rowman & Littlefield: 1998), 117–36.

45. Ranney and Kendall, cited in Gerald M. Pomper, "Toward a More Responsible Two-Party System? What, Again?," *Journal of Politics* 33, no. 4 (November 1971): 916–40, 918. Generally, the two parties do not divide up the spatial territory that would otherwise be occupied by many parties—creating counterparts in distinct portions of the spectrum. Instead, a number of divisions and antitheses are likely replicated within both parties.

46. Hofstadter, *Idea of a Party System,* 72–73.

47. Letter to potential contributors, paid for by Nader 2000 General Committee, Inc. "Here Comes the Donkephant," *New York Times*, October 8, 2000, Week in Review sec., p. 5.

Note that this perception of ideologically indistinct parties coincided with a period from the 1960s to the present in which political scientists show that roll-call votes in Congress were split on "the basic liberal-conservative dimension" and the dispersion of positions increased. Nolan McCarty, Keith T. Poole, and Howard Rosenthal, *Polarized America: The Dance of Ideology and Unequal Riches* (Cambridge, MA: MIT Press, 2006), 23.

48. Otto Kirchheimer, "The Transformation of the Western European Party Systems," in *Political Parties and Political Development*, ed. Joseph LaPalombara and Myron Weiner (Princeton: Princeton University Press: 1966), 177–200, 192–93, 195.

49. A Pew Research Center poll taken before the November 2000 elections found that a bare 51% of voters were aware that the two major candidates have different positions. After a year of campaign coverage, the number of voters who think the presidential candidates' stands are "similar" had grown by more than a third. Mark

Danner, "The Shame of Political TV," *New York Review of Books*, September 21, 2000, p. 101. Convergence does not necessarily mean that the general public's *perception* of the major parties is that they are similar, however; stereotypes of differences may have a strong hold. There is evidence that increasing numbers of voters do not see these differences as politically significant. Aldrich, *Why Parties?*, 169.

50. Lowi agrees but takes the view that a multiparty system, not a two-party system, is required to force parties to be more clearly programmatic. Lowi, "Toward a Responsible Three-Party System," 42–60. The "responsible party government" argument did not confront divided government in which neither party is in control of governing—cohesive parties in divided government or polarized parties may result not in policy making but in gridlock.

51. Ackerman, "Broken Engine of Progressive Politics," 42.

52. David R. Mayhew, *Electoral Realignments: A Critique of an American Genre* (New Haven: Yale University Press, 2002), 148, 151.

53. This is said to be one mark of critical elections and realignments, hence specific and periodic, not the norm for party relations. For a summary, see ibid., chap. 1 and 21–24. For a discussion of polarization and the restructuring of party coalitions, see Geoffrey C. Layman, Thomas M. Carsey, and Juliana Menasce Horowitz, "Party Polarization in American Politics: Characteristics, Causes, and Consequences," *Annual Review of Political Science* 9 (2006): 83–110. The authors argue that what has changed today is that it is not just one major policy issue that is polarizing (slavery, cultural and moral concerns) but "conflict extension" to a number of issues.

54. This point is made by Mayhew, *Electoral Realignments*, 94–96.

55. The fact that the United States has never had strong European-type labor or fascist parties suggests that even if parties can be differentiated in ideological terms, this does not mean that they are positioned away from the center. Specific country comparisons reveal the relative absence of ideological parties, left and right, in America. But this should not be overstated. Lipset points out that the GOP is the only major libertarian party in the democratic world ("What Are Parties For," 170). Moreover, by itself, without a discussion of the political spectrum, the existence of social democratic parties does not signify an absence of convergence. In advanced industrial democracies centrism appears to be widespread. Among the explanations is the absence of alternatives to mixed capitalist systems. Roger Cohen, "Is Germany on the Road to Diversity? The Parties Clash," *New York Times*, December 4, 2000, p. A14.

56. *Democratic Party v. Wisconsin*, 450 U.S. 107 (1981) at 132. Note 9 adds: "Of course, the National Party could decide that it no longer wishes to be a relatively nonideological party, but it has not done so." Powell continues, "insofar as the major parties do have ideological identities, an open primary merely allows relatively independent voters to cast their lot with the party that speaks to their present concerns."

57. *Democratic Party v. Wisconsin*, 450 U.S. 107 (1981) at 133, Justice Powell in dissent.

58. Hibbing and Theiss-Morse, *Stealth Democracy*, 38. The authors find similarity between the distributions of people's policy self-placement and perceived placement of policies—with 71% preferring moderate policies in the middle and 70% placing actual policies there (27). But they suggest that this result is less careful analysis than that moderation is the simplest answer to survey questions (241).

59. William Galston and Elaine Kamarck, "The Politics of Polarization," A Third Way Report (The Middle Class Project), October 2005, available at http://www.third-way.com, 45ff. This is confirmed in the analysis of the literature by Layman et al., "Party Polarization." What is new is party division along multiple policy dimensions, but these do not comprise a coherent ideological stance or ideological realignment on a single left-right dimension (92). "There is no obvious reason why individuals who support tax cuts and reductions in social welfare spending also should oppose abortion rights except that those are all positions taken by most Republican leaders, candidates, and elected officials" (95). McCarty, Poole, and Rosenthal agree but cast the time frame backward and see this as a development over 30 years (*Polarized America*, 1, 71–72).

60. Hibbing and Theiss-Morse, *Stealth Democracy*, 33.

61. Lipset cites data for 54 political parties in 12 industrialized nations from the 1870s to 1960s suggesting that nonleftist parties moved steadily leftward; there is evidence of declining average difference in party positions for later dates as well. America is a "puzzling exception." Lipset uses this data to support an "end of ideology" thesis in *Consensus and Conflict: Essays in Political Sociology* (New Brunswick, NJ: Transaction Books, 1985), 101ff.

62. Cited in Lipset, *The Politics of Unreason: Right-Wing Extremism in America, 1790–1966* (Chicago: University of Chicago Press, 1978), 503.

63. Sargent, *Extremism in America*, 2, describing the beliefs of those in the middle.

64. Anthony Downs, *An Economic Theory of Democracy* (New York: Harper, 1957).

65. Downs cited in Paul Frymer, *Uneasy Alliances: Race and Party Competition in America* (Princeton: Princeton University Press, 1994), 30.

66. For a discussion of the expansion of the nation's issue agenda and that "issue preferences cannot be reduced to "a single ideological dimension," see Edward G. Carmines and Michael W. Wagner, "Political Issues and Party Alignments: Assessing the Issue Evolution Perspective," *Annual Review of Political Science* 9 (2006): 67–81. On single issues the thesis still holds. Consider Frymer's discussion of the median voter in the context of support for specific measures to reduce racial inequality and the consequent electoral strategies on the part of both parties that eclipse black issues and even black leaders.

67. Kenneth Shepsle cited in Frymer, *Uneasy Alliances*, 200.

68. Byron E. Shafer and William J. M. Claggett, *The Two Majorities: The Issue Context of Modern American Politics* (Baltimore: Johns Hopkins University Press, 1995), 185 ff.

69. Fiorina, "Extreme Voices," 411.

70. William Galston and Elaine Kamarck document this ("Politics of Polariza-tion," 3). They insist on the remarkable stability of ideological self-identification in the electorate between 1976 and 2004, which has varied within a very narrow range averaging 20% liberal, 47% moderate, and 33% conservative (42).

71. McCarty, Poole, and Rosenthal, *Polarized America*, 203, confirming the claim in Morris Fiorina, Samuel J. Abrams, and Jeremy C. Pope, *Culture War? The Myth of a Polarized America* (New York: Pearson Longman, 2005).

72. Alan Wolfe, *One Nation, After All: What Americans Really Think about God, Country, Family, Racism, Welfare, Immigration, Homosexuality, Work, the Right, the Left and Each Other* (New York: Penguin, 1999), 277.

73. Gordon Wood, *The Radicalism of the American Revolution* (New York: Knopf, 1991), 347. Religion is another case. Alan Wolfe identifies a coherent "*mentalite*—a cluster of attitudes, beliefs, practices, and lifestyles," including commitment to "quiet faith" and revulsion at politicizing religion, and consistent with this consensus he characterizes groups that use religion to push political agendas "extremist." Wolfe, *One Nation, After All,* 3. Wolfe does not focus on the significance of core values for electoral politics or party positioning. In fact, he asserts, "middle class morality . . . has no politics. It is an outlook on the world that grows up from personal experi-ence, not down from ideological commitment" (315). Wolfe consistently finds a pattern of opinion in which "the middle category dominates and the two extremes are smaller and roughly equal in size . . . a large group of people whose opinion was qualified between the two extremes" (141).

74. Everett C. Ladd, "1996 Vote: The 'No Majority' Realignment Continues," *Po-litical Science Quarterly* 112, no. 1 (Spring 1997): 1–28, 6.

75. See Stephen Skowronek, "The Risks of Third-Way Politics," *Society* 33, no. 6 (September/October 1996): 32–36, 32, 33.

76. Morris, *New Prince*, 48, 328.

77. McWilliams, "Meaning of the election," 252.

78. Fareed Zakaria, "Whimper on the Right," *New Yorker*, June 5, 2000, pp. 85–90, 90.

79. David King cited in Schier, *Invitation Only*, 92. See too Aldrich, *Why Parties?*, 186ff.; Morris Fiorina, "Whatever Happened to the Median Voter?," unpublished manuscript 15; the baseline problem discussed, 18.

80. Cited in Seymour Martin Lipset, review of Aldrich, *Why Parties?*, in *Journal of Democracy* 7, no. 1 (January 1996): 169–175, 174.

81. Further intensifying extremism, on this account, is the fact that major indi-vidual donors to parties, candidates, and above all legal entities created in the inter-stices of campaign finance law engaging in independent expenditures "are extrem-ists." McCarty et al., *Polarized America*, 156ff. They note that extremist candidates are not better funded than moderates, however (160).

82. Fiorina, "Extreme Voices," 396, 416.

83. Ibid., 410.

84. For discussion of recent change and "conflict extension," see Layman, Carsey, and Horowitz, "Party Polarization."

85. James Q. Wilson says otherwise: "These activists are not a tiny part of the population; they make up about one quarter of all the people in the country." Wilson's most interesting argument is that higher education, postgraduate education in particular, produces ideological liberalism, so that there is an educational divide between liberals and conservatives that outweighs division based on wealth. Tanner Lecture I, pp. 23ff.

86. Schier, *Invitation Only*, 16–17. Hyperactivists comprise "only 5% of the adult population" and are biased toward upper income and education; see Shafer and Claggett, *Two Majorities*, 117.

87. Schier, *Invitation Only*, 92.

88. Ronald Inglehart describes active political involvement on the part of "cognitively mobilized" people, geared to issue-specific participation and to "elite-directing" rather than "elite-directed" modes of participation (*Culture Shift*, chap. 10, esp. 363, 367).

89. Aldrich, *Why Parties?*, 182.

90. Fiorina, "Extreme Voices," 410.

91. "It is that capacity to alter the party platform and wrest control from the centrist tendencies that fuels partisan activism." Samuel Issacharoff, "The Role of Political Parties in Partisan Competition," unpublished manuscript, 18.

92. For an extended discussion of the position of activists, "the war inside the parties," see Shafer and Claggett, *Two Majorities*, chapter 6.

93. Cass Sunstein reviews the literature, cognitive and social psychological, explaining polarization in groups in "Deliberative Trouble? Why Groups Go to Extremes," *Yale Law Journal* 110, no. 1 (October 2000): 71–119, 97.

94. Aldrich, *Why Parties?*, 184.

95. Pettit, "Democracy, Electoral and Contestatory," 134.

96. Schattschneider, *Party Government*, 192ff., 196.

97. "As a class, extreme positions tend to be more confidently held. This point is an important complement to the persuasive argument theory: The persuasiveness of arguments depends not simply on the grounds given, but also on the confidence with which they are articulated." Sunstein, "Deliberative Trouble," 92.

98. John Petrocik, "Candidate Strategy, Voter Response, and Party Cohesion," in Cain and Gerber, *Voting at the Political Fault Line*, 270–302, 275.

99. Hacker and Pierson argue that the Republican *party leadership* generally is extremist, recruits extremist candidates, and pushes the party off-center—with successful results; Galston and Kamarck argue differently: that a powerful *wing* of the Democratic party leadership and activists have pushed the party off-center, with devastating results. Layman Carsey, and Horowitz argue that party activists are the polarizers ("Party Polarization," 96ff.). Taken together, the argument is not that parties are stronger, more disciplined, and thus more able to take off-center positions but that activists and agendas have changed.

100. Galston and Kamarck, "Politics of Polarization."

101. The mean differences in American Conservative Union (ACU) scores in Congress are increasingly divergent, especially during the last decade. Fiorina, "Whatever Happened to the Median Voter?," 5.

102. Hacker and Pierson, *Off Center*, 74.

103. Dionne, *Why Americans Hate Politics*, 332.

104. A somewhat different explanation diminishes the importance of recruitment and two-stage elections. McCarty, Poole, and Rosenthal trace polarization over 30 years; it is not a new development. They agree that polarization is the work of elites but emphasize posing policy choices, and party identity, in terms of income. This account, with its attention to economic positioning, is closer to the standard notion of polarization in spatial models. *Polarized America*, 72ff.

105. This analysis was offered by Alan Wolfe in oral presentation at a panel: Alexis de Tocqueville Lecture on American Politics, "Democracy and Christianity in America," Harvard University, March 2–3, 2006. The original stimulus for the organization of extremes within the Republican Party was in response to Democratic policy and coalitions in the 1970s and '80s.

106. About every five years, the Pew Research Center conducts a public opinion survey to sort out the country's major ideological groupings. In 1999, Pew found that liberals and New Democrats each accounted for nearly one-quarter of the Democratic base. By the next survey in 2005, New Democrats had completely disappeared as a group and the liberals had doubled their share of the party. Noam Schieber, "The Centrists Didn't Hold," *New York Times*, op-ed, July 28, 2007, available at http://www.nytimes.com/2007/07/28/opinion/28scheiber.html.

107. McCarty, Poole, and Rosenthal, *Polarized America*, 1. They emphasize movement to the right of Republicans north and south, and the liberalization of northern Democrats.

108. Fiorina, Abrams, and Pope, *Culture War*, 100.

109. Theda Skocpol, "Advocates without Members: The Recent Transformation of American Civic Life," in Skocpol and Fiorina, *Civic Engagement*, 461–510, 503, 505.

110. Ibid., 503, 505; Fiorina, Abrams, and Pope, *Culture War*, 5, 103. For a discussion of the controversy regarding the extension of polarization to the electorate generally, see Layman, Carsey, and Horowitz, "Party Polarization."

111. Beitz, *Political Equality*, 152. This literature compares systems on the basis of the number of parties, the threshold for seats, the consequences of coalition governments for governing and stability.

112. Leibholz, *Politics and Law*, 55.

113. Most advocates today favor not party list systems but transferable vote arrangements that favor candidates over parties; the antipartyism of many proportional representation theorists is latent but there, beginning with Mill.

114. Mill, "Considerations on Representative Government," 432.

115. Frymer, *Uneasy Alliance*, 198.

116. Sebastian Mazzuca and James A. Robinson discuss the Colombian system of "incomplete vote," which guarantees the minority in a majoritarian system a percentage of seats regardless of the percentage of the vote, in "Political Conflict and Power-Sharing in the Origins of Modern Colombia," National Bureau of Economic Research, Working Paper Series, Working Paper 12099, March 2006. Available at http://papers.nber.org/papers/w12099.pdf, accessed August 22, 2006.

117. One concern of proportional representation theorists is political equality, variously understood. See also Christiano, *Rule of the Many*, and Beitz, *Political Equality*, who argues against the necessity of PR for political equality or fairness based on a distinction between opportunity to elect vs. opportunity to effect outcomes.

118. Galston and Kamarck, "Politics of Polarization," 3.

119. McCarty, Poole, and Rosenthal, *Polarized America*, 101.

120. Hibbing and Theiss-Morse, *Stealth Democracy*, 10.

121. McCarty, Poole, and Rosenthal, *Polarized America*, 32, 33.

122. Hibbing and Theiss-Morse, *Stealth Democracy*, 20, 19.

123. In the context of increased inequality of income, tax policy engineered large transfers of wealth in the form of reductions in federal income taxes from the lower and middle classes to the rich. See Larry Bartels, "Homer Gets a Tax Cut: Inequality and Public Policy in the American Mind," *Perspectives on Politics* 3, no. 1 (March 2005): 15–31.

124. Ibid., 21. The argument does not change appreciably if instead of preference or interest we substitute judgment about the general good.

125. Beitz, *Political Equality*, 179.

126. Adam Przeworski, *Capitalism and Social Democracy* (Cambridge: Cambridge University Press, 1985), 101, cited in Frymer, *Uneasy Alliance*, 21 n. 56.

127. Morris, *New Prince*, 48, 328.

128. James Bennet, "Liberal Use of 'Extremist' Is the Winning Strategy," *New York Times*, November 7, 1996, p. B1.

129. McCarty, Poole, and Rosenthal, *Polarized America*, 24.

130. Fiorina, Abrams, and Pope, *Culture War*, 28, 103–4.

131. Duverger, *Political Parties*, 230.

132. Cited in Sidney Milkis and Jerome M. Mileur, *Progressivism and the New Democracy* (Amherst: University of Massachusetts Press, 1999), 13.

133. Hacker and Pierson, *Off Center*, 133.

134. Burns and Sorenson, *Dead Center*, 157.

135. Fiorina, "Extreme Voices," 405.

136. Layman, Carsey, and Horowitz, "Party Polarization," 103.

137. Hibbing and Theiss-Morse, *Stealth Democracy*, 23.

138. If not, "the mounting ambiguities of national policy might . . . set in motion more extreme tendencies in the people." Pomper, "Toward a More Responsible Two-Party System," 928.

139. Hibbing and Theiss-Morse, *Stealth Democracy*, 25.

140. King, "Congress, Polarization," 14.

141. Frymer, in *Uneasy Alliances*, makes the "capture" argument, along with deliberate exclusion of African American participation and avoidance of appeals to them when it threatens coalitions or the ability to attract "swing voters."

142. Didion, *Political Fictions*, 148.

143. Schier, *Invitation Only*, 7, 1.

144. Didion, *Political Fictions*, 153, 17.

145. Lani Guinier, *The Tyranny of the Majority: Fundamental Fairness in Representative Democracy* (New York: Free Press, 1994), 132.

146. Lani Guinier and Gerald Torres, *The Miner's Canary: Rethinking Race, Resisting Power, Transforming Democracy* (Cambridge, MA: Harvard University Press, 2002), 174, citing Justice O'Connor from *Shaw v. Reno*, 509 U.S. 630 (1993). The court discussion is in the context of racial gerrymandering. The authors are critical of the "representational theology" and are proponents of proportional representation.

147. Jack Dennis and Diana Owen, "Popular Satisfaction with the Party System and Representative Democracy in the United States," paper presented at the IPSA meeting, Quebec City, August 1–5, 2000, pp. 4–5 and 10.

148. Hofstadter cited in Rosenblum, *Membership and Morals*, 276.

149. Brandice Canes-Wrone and Kenneth W. Shotts, "When Do Elections Encourage Ideological Rigidity?," *American Political Science Review* 101, no. 2 (May 2007): 273–88, 284.

150. For a summary of recent literature on party polarization in Congress, see Layman, Carsey, and Horowitz, "Party Polarization," 87ff.

151. Norman Podhoretz, cited in Sam Tanenhaus, "When the Left Turns Right, It leaves the Middle Muddled," *New York Times*, September 16, 2000.

152. Norman Ornstein quoted in Hacker and Pierson, *Off Center*, 7. On polarization and gridlock, see McCarty, Poole, and Rosenthal, *Polarized America*, 181.

153. Cited in Burns and Sorenson, *Dead Center*, 273.

154. Morris, *New Prince*, 100.

155. Dahl, at 288, *Pluralist Democracy*, 279–81.

156. Amos Oz, *How to Cure a Fanatic* (Princeton: Princeton University Press, 2002), 8.

157. Hofstadter, *Idea of a Party System*, 76; citation at 119.

158. Wolfe, *One Nation*, 272, 294, 300.

159. Wood, *Radicalism*, 359, 357.

160. Inglehart, *Culture Shift*, 92.

161. Cited in Sidney Milkis, "Remaking Government Institutions in the 1970s: Participatory Democracy and the Triumph of Administrative Politics," in *Loss of Confidence: Politics and Policy in the 1970s*, ed. David Brian Robertson (University Park: Penn State Press, 1998), 51–74, 54. See too Fiorina, "Extreme Voices," 413.

162. This is the thesis of Shafer and Claggett, *Two Majorities*.

163. McWilliams, "Meaning of the Election," 243.

164. Shafer and Claggett, *Two Majorities*, 178.

165. Harvey C. Mansfield, Jr., *Statesmanship and Party Government* (Chicago: University of Chicago Press, 1965), 13.

166. For a recent discussion, see Adrian Vermeule, "Submajority Rules: Forcing Accountability upon Majorities," *Journal of Political Philosophy* 13, no. 1 (March 2005): 74–98. The author emphasizes minority role in agenda setting and in ensuring transparency and accountability—not substantive decision making.

167. Dahl, *Pluralist Democracy*, 295.

168. Burns and Sorenson, *Dead Center*, 167–68.

169. Dennis F. Thompson, "Mill in Parliament: When Should a Philosopher Compromise?," in *J. S. Mill's Political Thought: A Bicentennial Reassessment*, ed. Nadia Urbinati and Alex Zakaras (Cambridge: Cambridge University Press, 2007), 166–99, 168.

170. Ibid., 171.

171. Ibid., citing Bruce L. Kinzer, Ann P. Robson, and John M. Robson, *A Moralist In and Out of Parliament: John Stuart Mill at Westminster, 1865–1868* (Toronto: University of Toronto Press, 1992), 295.

172. McWilliams, "Meaning of the Election," 251.

173. Wolfe, *One Nation*, 294.

174. King, "Congress, Polarization," 15.

175. This is the thrust of Henry Adams's charge against Republican and Democratic parties in the 1870s. "The 'Independents' in the Canvass," *North American Review* 123, no. 253 (October 1876): 426–67, 426, 443.

176. Albert O. Hirschman, *Exit, Voice, and Loyalty* (Cambridge, MA: Harvard University Press, 1970), 78.

177. Cited in Hofstadter, *Idea of a Party System*, 78.

178. McWilliams, "Meaning of the Election," 254.

179. Cited in Adam Clymer, "Politics and the Dead Arts of Compromise," *New York Times*, October 22, 1995, sec. 5, p. 1.

180. Hibbing and Theiss-Morse, *Stealth Democracy*, 66, 142, 54.

181. Adams, "The 'Independents' in the Canvass," 440.

182. Cited in Hofstadter, *Idea of a Party System*, 21.

183. See Judith N. Shklar, *Ordinary Vices* (Cambridge, MA: Harvard University Press, 1984), 50.

184. Dennis F. Thompson, "Hypocrisy and Democracy," in Thompson, *Restoring Responsibility*, 209–26, 214ff.

185. Hacker and Pierson, *Off Center*, 3.

186. Oz, *How to Cure*, 44.

Chapter 9. Militant Democracy: Banning Parties

1. *New York Times*, October 17, 2000, p. C30.

2. *Communist Party of Indiana v. Whitcomb*, 414 U.S. 441 (1974).

3. *New York Times*, October 17, 2000, p. C30. The *Times* cites *Izvestia* reporting in 1992 that Hall had been the recipient of $40 million in assistance between 1971 and 1990.

4. Cited in Guenter Lewy, *The Cause That Failed: Communism in American Political Life* (New York: Oxford University Press, 1990), 133.

5. *Abrams v. U.S.*, 250 U.S. 616 (1919), Justice Holmes dissenting at 630; *United States v. Dennis*, 183 F.2d 201 (1950), at 212; Justice Douglas dissenting in *Dennis v. United States*, 341 U.S. 495 (1951), at 582–83. A survey of current third parties indicates that avowedly antidemocratic parties are a rarity. Directory of U.S. Political Parties, http://www.politics1.com/parties.htm.

6. The U.S. Supreme Court first attended to the First Amendment during World War I, handing down six decisions; during the Cold War it handed down sixty. Geoffrey R. Stone, *Perilous Times: Free Speech in Wartime from the Sedition Act of 1798 to the War on Terrorism* (New York: W. W. Norton), 396.

7. Ibid., 340.

8. *Scales v. U.S.*, 367 U.S. 203 (1961), at 236.

9. *Dennis v. United States*, 341 U.S. 494 (1951), Justice Jackson concurring at 567.

10. Walter Murphy puts it this way: "Government by consent is not the same as government chosen by and responsible to the people, for the people may consent to any kind of government they wish." "Excluding Political Parties: Problems for Democratic and Constitutional Theory," in *Germany and Its Basic Law*, ed. Paul Kirchoff and Donald P. Kommers (Baden-Baden: Nomos Verlagsgesellschaft, 1993), 175.

11. Aharon Barak, "A Judge on Judging: The Role of a Supreme Court in a Democracy," *Harvard Law Review* 116, no 1 (November 2002): 16–166, 44.

12. Hans Kelsen, "On the Essence and Value of Democracy," in *Weimar: A Jurisprudence of Crisis*, ed. Arthur Jacobson and Bernhard Schlink (Berkeley: University of California Press, 2000), 84–109, 94.

13. I have spoken of banning parties, but it deserves noting that innumerable electoral regulations and registration requirements inhibit party organization in practice or make it impossible for minor parties to have ballot access. Parties can be effectively stopped by withholding public funding or access to state-controlled television and other media, as the Belgian court did with the Flemish far-right Vlaams Blok party, the most popular party in Flanders. Besides prohibition, there is always intimidation and threats against party candidates from authorities or from hostile social groups, in the face of which the persistence of candidacies is heroic. Most common of all, parties can be legal yet effectively marginalized and rendered impotent—excluded from governing coalitions or ministerial posts or seats on courts. Even legal bans on parties can take various forms. Parties can be banned from participation in elections but not dissolved, or dissolved entirely and prohibited from reorganizing under another name; membership in the party can be criminalized; successful candidates can be refused their seats (as Jean-Marie Le Pen was from the European Parliament after

assaulting a French socialist during the 1988 electoral campaign); or election results can be annulled.

14. Political philosophers offer defining elements of constitutional democracy. Rawls, for example, focuses on reciprocity, the priority of basic rights and opportunities, and the means to make effective use of freedoms. John Rawls, "The Idea of Public Reason Revisited," in *Collected Papers*, ed. Samuel Freeman (Cambridge, MA: Harvard University Press, 1999), 140–41.

15. See Nancy L. Rosenblum, "Banning Parties: Religious and Ethnic Parties in Multicultural Democracies," *Law and Ethics of Human Rights* 1 (2007): 18–75.

16. Maurice Duverger's *Political Parties: Their Organization and Activity in the Modern State* (New York: John Wiley & Sons, 1963), 61–62.

17. Islam in Europe has been taken up as "an ideology of the downtrodden." Craig S. Smith, "Europe's Muslims May Be Headed Where the Marxists Went Before," *New York Times*, December 26, 2004, Week in Review sec., p. 7. "In Germany, the first Islamic fundamentalist association, the Cologne-based Califate State, has already been outlawed by the Federal Secretary of the Interior. . . . The anti-fundamentalist mechanisms contained in the Basic Law . . . are equally valid if the fight against the free democratic basic order is fought by reference to cultural imperatives." Peter Niesen, "Anti-Extremism, Negative Republicanism, Civic Society: Three Paradigms for Banning Political Parties, Part II," *German Law Journal* 3, no. 7 (July 2002): 7. Available at http://www.germanlawjournal.com/article.php?id=169, accessed August 17, 2007.

18. *Communist Party of Indiana et al. v. Whitcomb*, 414 U.S. 441 (1974), Justice Brennan for the Court at 448, 450.

19. Judith Wise, "Comment: Dissent and the Militant Democracy: The German Constitution and the Banning of the Free German Workers Party," *University of Chicago Law School Roundtable* 5 (1998): 301–44, 307. The phrase was introduced by a German exile in the United States, Karl Loewenstein, in 1937 to defend a democratic constitution from political extremism. See Meindert Fennema, "Legal Repression of Extreme-Right Parties and Racial Discrimination," in *Challenging Immigration and Ethnic Relations Politics*, ed. Ruud Koopmans and Paul Statham (New York: Oxford University Press, 2000), 119–44, 127.

20. Barak, "A Judge on Judging," 44.

21. Vali Nasr, "The Rise of 'Muslim Democracy,'" *Journal of Democracy* 16, no. 2 (April 2005): 13–27, 23.

22. For current examples of this application, see Richard Bernstein, "What Is Free Speech, and What Is Terrorism," *New York Times*, August 14, 2005, Week in Review sec., p. 14.

23. Walzer, *Passion and Politics*, 42.

24. A recent multination study shows that religion remains "more strongly and more consistently related to voting choice today than any of the various indicators of socioeconomic status" (and is associated with ideologies of the "Right"). Pippa Norris and Ronald Inglehart, *Sacred and Secular: Religious Politics Worldwide*

(Cambridge: Cambridge University Press, 2004), 201–2. However, it should be noted that in the United States, in contrast to other democracies, the foundation of party building is degree of religious observance regardless of faith, and religious identity as "Christian" or "Judeo-Christian," or simply "religious values" replaces denominational and sectarian religious orientations defined in contrast to others.

25. Kanchan Chandra, "Ethnic Parties and Democratic Stability," *Perspectives on Politics* 3, no. 2 (June 2005): 235–52, 236.

26. Gary Jacobsohn, "'By the Light of Reason': Corruption, Religious Speech, and Constitutional Essentials," in *Obligations of Citizenship and Demands of Faith: Religious Accomodation in Pluralist Democracies*, ed. Nancy L. Rosenblum (Princeton: Princeton University Press, 2000), 294–320, 296–97.

27. Yusuf Sevki Hakyemez and Birol Akgun, "Limitations on the Freedom of Political Parties in Turkey and the Jurisdiction of the European Court of Human Rights," *Mediterranean Politics* 7, no. 2 (Summer 2002): 54–78, 57–58, 60.

28. Oz, *How to Cure a Fanatic*, 91.

29. Parliamentary Assembly: Resolution 1308 (2002), "Restrictions on Political Parties in the Council of Europe Member States," Council of Europe Portal, http://assembly.coe.int. UDHSR and ECHR provide the right to vote and to be elected without specifying parties, but participatory rights are interpreted to entail party competition. For discussion, see Christian Tomuschat, "Democratic Pluralism: The Right to Political Opposition," in *The Strength of Diversity*, ed. Allan Rosas and Jan Helgesen (Dordrecht: Martinus Nijhoff Publishers, 1992), 27–48; and Gregory H. Fox and Georg Nolte, "Intolerant Democracies," *Harvard International Law Journal* 36, no. 1 (Winter 1995): 1–70.

30. Kelsen discusses this phenomenon, describing parties as "one of the most important elements of real democracy" ("On the Essence and Value," 92).

31. The question of the existence of parties per se was taken up in the 1973 Party Finance Law, which, despite its title, speaks not of parties but of "parliamentary factions." Dan Avnon, "Parties Laws in Democratic Systems of Government," *Journal of Legislative Studies* 1, no. 2 (Summer 1995): 283–300, 289.

32. Report by the General Counsel for the State, State Legal Services Offices, regarding the illegality of Batasuna political party. Http://www.spainemb.org/novedades/legal/legalreport.htm, accessed April 4, 2004.

33. The legal and theoretical literature on this interpretive point is extensive. For a discussion, see Rosenblum, *Membership and Morals*.

34. This is the International Covenant on Civil and Political Rights; see Fox and Nolte, "Intolerant Democracies," 46.

35. Mustafa Kocak and Esin Orucu, "Dissolution of Political Parties in the Name of Democracy: Cases from Turkey and the European Court of Human Rights," *European Public Law* 9, no. 3 (September 2003): 399–423, 403–4. Dicle Kogacioglu, "Progress, Unity, and Democracy: Dissolving Political Parties in Turkey," *Law and Society Review* 38, no. 3 (September 2004): 433–61.

36. Fox and Nolte, "Intolerant Democracies," 29, 41.

37. Ibid., 51.

38. Niesen, "Anti-Extremism, Part II."

39. Peter Niesen, "Anti-Extremism, Negative Republicanism, Civic Society: Three Paradigms for Banning Political Parties, Part I," *German Law Journal* 3, no. 7 (July 2002). Available at http://www.germanlawjournal.com/article.php?id=164, accessed August 17, 2007.

40. The ECHR recognized this explicitly in *Leyla Sahin v. Turkey*, 44774/98 [2004] ECHR 299 (29 June 2004): "The role of the Convention machinery is essentially subsidiary . . . [T]he national authorities are in principle better placed than an international court to evaluate local needs and conditions." Decision available at http://cmiskp.echr.coe.int////tkp197/viewhbkm.asp?action=open&table=F69A27 FD8FB86142BF01C1166DEA398649&key=11423&sessionId=1795523&skin=hudo c-en&attachment=true.

41. During wartime this encompassed Italian, German, and Japanese nationals (and of course internment of Japanese American citizens).

42. Cited in *Dennis v. United States*, 341 U.S. 494 (1951), Justice Frankfurter concurring at 555. This is the theme of Stone's *Perilous Times: Free Speech in Wartime*.

43. Nancy L. Rosenblum, "Constitutional Reason of State: The Fear Factor," in *Dissent in Dangerous Times*, ed. Austin Sarat (Ann Arbor: University of Michigan Press, 2005), 146–76.

44. Remark by an EU representative, cited in David Makovsky and Elizabeth Young "Toward a Quartet Position on Hamas: European Rules on Banning Political Parties," *PeaceWatch*, no. 515 (Washington Institute for Near East Policy, September 12, 2005). Available at http://www.washingtoninstitute.org/templateC05 .php?CID=2369, accessed August 17, 2007. My subject is parties operating within democracies, and I leave aside the case of parties that turn to arms during the transition to democracy or when a country's military or leadership voids elections. For examples, see Leonard Weinberg and Ami Pedahzur, *Political Parties and Terrorist Groups* (London: Routledge, 2003).

45. Cited in Makovsky and Young, "Toward a Quartet Position." The Hamas charter declares, "We must spread the spirit of jihad among the *umma*, clash with the enemies, and join the ranks of the jihad charter." Note that Great Britain did not ban Sinn Fein.

46. Walzer, *Passion and Politics*, 64.

47. Article 21 of the German Constitution, for example, mandates that political parties' "internal organization shall conform to democratic principles." Spain: "Their internal structure and working must be democratic." Portugal: "Political parties shall be governed by the principles of transparency, democratic organization and management, and participation by all their members." Turkey: "The activities, internal regulations and operation of political parties shall be in line with democratic principles."

48. For a detailed discussion of the ambiguous nexus between government and parties, especially on matters of party finance, see Donald P. Kommers, *The Constitutional Jurisprudence of the Federal Republic of Germany* (Durham, NC: Duke University Press, 1997). It is through parties that the popular will is produced and popular sovereignty exercised by the formation of a government. This view is attributed to Leibholz: the people are incapable of acting except in parties; the people are not differentiated from the parties; the will of the majority party is equated with the general will. Leibholz, *Politics and Law.*

49. Weinberg and Pedahzur, *Political Parties*, 63. "Of the almost 400 terrorist groups in our data collection a total of 124 (31 percent) were described in our source texts as having links of one kind or another with political parties" (28). Links are more common on the left (30) and, most surprising, most common in Western Europe (32). Since the mid-1980s religion has become the most common basis for terrorist attacks, but not linked to parties (43–44).

50. Ibid., 77.

51. *New York Times,* cited in Kenneth Craig Dobson, "The Spanish Government's Ban of a Political Party: A Violation of Human Rights?," *New England Journal of International and Comparative Law* 9, no. 2 (2003): 637–50, 649. The General Counsel report interprets European norms as denying protection to parties that do not respect "the fundamental values of democracy and *social harmony*"—a more severe test than association with terrorism and a standard that should not be defended. Parties are inherently divisive.

ETA violence increased after Spain's transition to democracy and the legalization of parties; "the principle of majority rule may promote a transition to peaceful party politics for groups that can make a logical claim to represent the majority. But the situation may be quite different for violent organizations rooted in ethnic minority populations." Weinberg and Pedahzur, *Political Parties*, 62.

52. Report by the General Counsel for the State, State Legal Services Offices, regarding the illegality of Batasuna political party.

53. This element appears in *Refah Partisi (The Welfare Party) vs. Turkey,* 41340/98 [2003] ECHR (13 February). Available at http://cmiskp.echr.coe.int////tkp197/viewhbkm.asp?action=open&table=F69A27FD8FB86142BF01C1166DEA398649&key=3516&sessionId=1816510&skin=hudoc-en&attachment=true, accessed August 17, 2007.

54. My references to Israeli cases are indebted to the citations and translation in the senior honors thesis of Eric Robert Trager, "Subversive Parties in Israeli Politics," Honors Thesis, Government, Harvard College, 2005.

55. Larry Derfiner, "A Show of Confidence—In Himself," *Jerusalem Post*, February 26, 1999, p. 16, cited in Trager, "Subversive Parties," 79.

56. Cited in Trager, "Subversive Parties," 80.

57. *Central Election Committee for the Sixteenth Knesset v. Tibi and Bishara* (57 PD [*Piske Din*] IV 1 [2003]), cited in ibid., 89. See Dan Izenberg, "High Court

Overturns Disqualifications of Tibi, Bishara," *Jerusalem Post*, January 28, 2003, available at http://info.jpost.com/C002/Supplements/Elections2003/ld_03_1201.html, accessed August 17, 2007.

58. *Central Election Committee for the Sixteenth Knesset v. Tibi and Bishara* (57 PD [*Piske Din*] IV 1 [2003]), p. 35, cited in Trager, "Subversive Parties." Bishara denied meeting with Hezbollah leaders in Syria (asserting that they were simply under one roof for the ceremony).

59. Ibid., 103.

60. The best discussion is Stone, *Perilous Times*, 408ff.

61. Ibid., 523. In the same vein, Yael Tamir has written about restrictions on religious hate speech, even when it consists of readings by religious leaders of passages from sacred texts in religious spaces. Religious hate speech is more likely to produce harm than nonreligious speech insofar as the words of religious teachers have the status of commands, making "clear and present danger" at least plausible. "Remember Amalek: Religious Hate Speech," in Rosenblum, *Obligations of Citizenship*, 321–34, 332.

62. Vinson's majority opinion in *Dennis v. United States*, 341 U.S. 494 (1951), at 508–9.

63. Rawls invokes it in *A Theory of Justice*, 215ff. Israel's High Court has employed something very close to this rule. In *Neiman v. Chairman of the Central Elections Committee* the Court unanimously ruled that there was insufficient proof that PLP sought "the liquidation of the state." One Justice was explicit that the party did not present "a clear or immediate" threat. Justice Shamgar, *Ben-Shalom*, cited in Trager, "Subversive Parties," 72.

64. *Dennis v. United States*, 341 U.S. 494 (1951), Justice Douglas dissenting at 583. And along with other "totalitarian groups" the Communist Party "here and abroad perfected the technique of creating private paramilitary organizations to coerce both the public government and its citizens." *Dennis v. United States*, 578. Justice Black points out that the same language was used in 1798 against the "Jacobins," meaning the Jeffersonians, as allegedly subservient to France: they were "trained, officered, regimented, and formed to subordination, in a manner that our militia have never yet equaled," and they will "take arms against the laws as soon as they dare." *Communist Party v. Control Board*, 367 U.S. 1 (1961), at 162.

65. *Refah Partisi (The Welfare Party) vs. Turkey*.

66. Tomuschat, "Democratic Pluralism," 27. Similar reasoning guided the decision in the Yeridor case before the Israeli Supreme Court, which I discuss below.

67. Ibid., 33–34.

68. Irving Howe and Lewis Coser propose that the internal "stalinization" of the party and the end of all free discussion began earlier than is generally thought, by the mid-1920s. *The American Communist Party: A Critical History* (New York: Praeger, 1962), 152. It is also clear that the Cominterm from the start urged both a legal party and an underground apparatus; Lewy, *Cause That Failed*, 6.

69. In the context of labor unrest, unwelcome immigration with its foreign language presses and federations, a war-time draft and a rash of bombings, a wide range of dissenting groups were charged with subversion and subject to the Wilson administration's Espionage Act of 1917.

70. Stone, *Perilous Times*, 322.

71. Howe and Coser, *American Communist Party*, 425. In 1945 at the direction of Moscow, Browder was expelled and his heretical course reversed.

72. The government successfully warded off the charge that the Subversive Activities Control Act was an unconstitutional "bill of attainder" aimed solely at the Communist Party. Federal legislation enforced against the party included immigration laws excluding and deporting aliens who advocate overthrow of the government: the Hatch Act (1939) prohibiting government employment of members of groups advocating overthrow; the Voorhis Act (1940) requiring registration of political organizations subject to foreign control; the section of the Taft-Hartley Act excluding communists from positions of leadership in labor organizations (1947); and the Smith Act (1940) criminalizing membership in an organization that advocates the overthrow of government by force—under which there were over a hundred convictions of Communist leaders by 1956 including Gus Hall, who served eight years in jail.

73. Stone, *Perilous Times*, 313.

74. It was amended in 1954 to add "communist infiltrated" organizations. This law passed over Truman's veto, and prohibited those acting on behalf of the organization to use the mails or commerce for publications without designating it a communist organization publication, broadcasting without a statement that the message is sponsored by a communist organization, holding nonelective office or office or employment with any labor organization, and using or attempting to obtain a passport or visa. See Herbert Aptheker, *Dare We Be Free? The Meaning of the Attempt to Outlaw the Communist Party* (New York: New Century Publishers, 1961), 32, 71.

75. Ibid., 55. *Communist Party v. Control Board*, 367 U.S. 1 (1961), at 142.

76. Howe and Coser, *American Communist Party*, 478.

77. *Communist Party v. Control Board*, 367 U.S. 1 (1961), Justice Black in dissent at 138.

78. Duverger, *Political Parties*, 366–37.

79. *Dennis v. United States*, 341 U.S. 494 (1951), Chief Justice Vinson for the Court at 498. "The Party is rigidly controlled. . . . Communists, unlike other political parties, tolerate no dissension from the policy laid down by the guiding forces, but that the approved program is slavishly followed by the members of the Party" (510, 563).

80. See Rosenblum, *Membership and Morals*, 246ff., on secret associations.

81. Joseph R. Starobin, *American Communism in Crisis, 1943–1957* (Cambridge, MA: Harvard University Press, 1972), ix, 8, 221.

82. Appendix to Congress's 1961 *Guide to Subversive Organizations and Publications*, prepared and released by the Committee on Un-American Activities, U.S. House of Representatives, Washington, DC.

83. Ibid., 5, 6.

84. Aptheker, *Dare We Be Free?*, 38.

85. *Dennis v. United States*, 341 U.S. 494 (1951), Justice Jackson concurring at 563.

86. *United States v. Dennis*, 183 F.2d 201 (1950), at 212–13.

87. Stone, *Perilous Times*, 409.

88. Howe and Coser, *American Communist Party*, 188. For example, "If we were to read the nine dailies and twenty-one weeklies of the Worker Party carefully," wrote John Pepper, "one would get the complete picture of all European countries, but a very incomplete picture of the political life of America"(104 n.).

89. For statistics, see ibid., 528.

90. Lewy, *Cause That Failed*, 295.

91. For one argument, see Yigal Mersel, "The Dissolution of Political Parties: The Problem of Internal Democracy," *I-Con* 4, no. 1 (2006): 84–113. His principal reason for mandatory internal democracy seems to be that parties represent society by "reflecting and channeling the social currents within it," which requires that party ideology and politics is produced "by large and representative groups within society" (96). This standard provides little guidance as to organizational requirements. He also insists on "the real ability of the individual to participate and influence the party" (104). Again, this provides little guidance; cf. earlier discussions of closed/ open/blanket primary elections.

92. Whose members engaged in street violence and in more sophisticated attacks on Arabs. Weinberg and Pedahzur, *Political Parties*, 101.

93. Cited in Trager, "Subversive Parties," 26.

94. Cited in Fox and Nolte, "Intolerant Democracies," 310.

95. Fennema, "Legal Repression," 129.

96. Wise, "Comment," 322.

97. Belgium, "Anti-Racism Law," at http://www.diversiteit.be/CNTR/EN/legislation, accessed August 20, 2007.

98. Tamir, "Remember Amalek," 323.

99. One academic commentator distinguishes the ban on Kach from the Court's rejection of the proposed ban on the Moledet Party on democratic grounds: Kach proposed the deportation of all Arabs, including citizens, while Moledet advocated the transfer of noncitizens only. Yoav Peled, "Ethnic Democracy and the Legal Construction of Citizenship: Arab Citizens of the Jewish State," *American Political Science Review* 86, no. 2 (January 1992): 432–43, 438.

100. Jacobsohn, "Light of Reason," 296–97.

101. Walzer, *Passion and Politics*, 42.

102. Hofstadter, *Idea of a Party System*, 12.

103. David Hume, "Of Parties in General," in *Hume: Political Essays*, ed. Knud Haakonssen (Cambridge: Cambridge University Press, 1994), 33–40, 39.

104. Oz, *How to Cure a Fanatic*, 27.

105. R. Quinn Mecham, "From the Ashes of Virtue, a Promise of Light: The Transformation of Political Islam in Turkey," unpublished manuscript, 21.

106. See Kent Greenawalt, "Five Questions about Religion Judges Are Afraid to Ask," in Rosenblum, *Obligations of Citizenship*, 196–244. See the discussion of these questions in Nancy L. Rosenblum, "Amos," in ibid., 165–95.

107. Clear and present danger is invoked in some cases, among them the predominant assessment of Algeria's 1991 electoral crisis, in which the government/army annulled elections likely to bring "radical Islam" in the form of the FIS (Islamic Salvation Front) to power as a parliamentary majority capable of ratifying constitutional amendments. On divisions within the U.N. Human Rights Committee about whether an FIS victory would justify derogation, see Fox and Nolte, "Intolerant Democracies," 57.

108. Sabrina Tavernise, "Ruling Party in Turkey Wins Broad Victory," *New York Times*, July 22, 2007, www.nytimes.com/2007/07/22/world/europe/22cnd-turkey.

109. The government's position invokes equality, though no non-Muslims were subject to disciplinary proceedings in university cases. Jews were not prohibited from wearing skullcaps or Christians the crucifix in a key case involving students at the national university. A sign of severity is the very unusual statement that secularism is "a precious asset for atheists, agnostics, skeptics, and the unconcerned." Cited in *Leyla Sahin v. Turkey*.

110. M. Hakan Yavuz, "Political Islam and the Welfare (REfah) Party in Turkey," *Comparative Politics* 30, no. 1 (October 1997): 63–82, 70.

111. Hakyemez and Akgun, "Limitations," 60.

112. Government supported "soft Islam" by expanding religious high schools, Qur'anic seminaries and Islamic colleges, foundations, and an interest-free Islamic banking system. Yavuz, "Political Islam," 64.

113. The ECHR cited Refa Partisi and Dogru Yol Partisi in *Leyla Sahin v. Turkey*.

114. *Refah Partisi (The Welfare Party) vs. Turkey*.

115. Kocak and Orucu, "Dissolution of Political Parties," 423; Hakyemez and Akgun, "Limitations," 74.

116. *Refah Partisi (The Welfare Party) vs. Turkey*.

117. Soli Ozel, "Turkey at the Polls: After the Tsunami," *Journal of Democracy* 14, no. 2 (April 2003): 81–94, 93. AKP disavows integralist purposes, and political science accounts confirm that the party's version of politicized religion had support not only among fundamentalists but also among those without strong religious identity.

118. *Leyla Sahin v. Turkey*.

119. Kogacioglu, "Progress, Unity," 445–46.

120. Asher Cohen and Bernard Susser, "From Accommodation to Decision: Transformations in Israel's Religio-Political Life," *Journal of Church and State* 38, no. 4 (Autumn 1996): 817–39.

121. See translations in Trager, "Subversive Parties," 49.

122. President Agranat in *Yeridor v. Central Elections Committee*, 19 PD [*Piske Din*] III 365 [1965] at 386, translation in ibid., 48.

123. Kach, interview with Eric Trager, in ibid., 59. See also Peled, "Ethnic Democracy," 437.

124. For a discussion of the justices' positions, see Dan Brown, "Limits on Extremist Political Parties: A Comparison of Israeli Jurisprudence with That of the United States and West Germany," *Hastings International and Comparative Law Review* 10 (1987): 347–400.

125. *Scales v. United States*, 367 U.S. 203 (1961).

126. Fox and Nolte, "Intolerant Democracies," 59.

127. Michael Herzog, "Can Hamas Be Tamed?," *Foreign Affairs* 85, no. 2 (March/ April 2006): 83–94, 86.

128. Robert Goodin has argued that the "affected interests" argument is incoherent as a standard for distributing political rights. Who is affected depends on what decisions are taken and how it turns out, and that depends on the identity of "the demos" that decides what gets decided in the first place. Goodin, "Enfranchising All Affected Interests, and Its Alternatives," *Philosophy and Public Affairs* 35, no. 1 (Winter 2007): 40–68.

129. For an overview, see Thomas Ertman, "Democracy and Dictatorship in Interwar Western Europe Revisited," *World Politics* 50, no. 3 (April 1998): 475–505.

130. Noel Cary, *The Path to Christian Democracy: German Catholics and the Party System from Windthorst to Adenauer* (Cambridge, MA: Harvard University Press, 1996), viii; Stathis Kalyvas, *The Rise of Christian Democracy in Europe* (Ithaca, N.Y.: Cornell University Press, 1996); Carolyn M. Warner, *Confessions of an Interest Group: The Catholic Church and Political Parties in Europe* (Princeton: Princeton University Press, 2000).

131. Herzog, "Can Hamas Be Tamed?," 84.

132. Nasr, "Muslim Democracy," 15 on the comparison; 20, 23.

133. Ibid., 15. Even in Iraq, which does not meet the conditions of party democracy, in the 2005 elections Shi'ite ayatollah Ali Sistani—an advocate of a unified Shi'ite candidates' list—reminded women of their religious duty to vote even if their husbands forbade them. The imperative of electoral victory, not religious reform, compelled it. Ibid., 26.

134. Kalyvas, *Christian Democracy*, 255.

135. There are specific compilations, including Louis Massicotte, Andre Blais, and Antoine Yoshinka, *Establishing the Rules of the Game* (Toronto: Toronto University Press, 2004), on the formal rules of candidacy. Some case studies provide a general overview: Dan Avnon, "Parties Laws in Democratic Systems of Government," *Journal of Legislative Studies* 1, no. 2 (Summer 1995): 283–300; Wise; Fox and Nolte, "Intolerant Democracies," though their focus is international law on the subject. Most writing has to do with party bans reviewed by the European Court: Kocak and Orucu, "Dissolution"; Hakyemez and Akgun, "Limitations."

136. Nancy L. Rosenblum, "Religious Parties, Religious Political Identity, and the Cold Shoulder of Liberal Democratic Thought," *Ethical Theory and Moral Practice: An International Forum* 6, no. 1 (March 2003): 23–53.

137. For some, justice is "political not metaphysical," and public debate should involve only secular issues, should be conducted solely in terms of public reasons (recognizing that not all nonreligious reasons are public reason), and should appeal only to secular, civic grounds for policy, as John Rawls argues in *Political Liberalism* (New York: Columbia University Press, 2005), 215, 776. Bhikhu Parekh advises: "Reasons are public not because their grounds are or can be shared by all, as the secularist argues, but because they are open to inspection and can be intelligently discussed by anyone with the requisite knowledge or willingness to acquire it." *Rethinking Multiculturalism* (Cambridge, MA: Harvard University Press, 2000), 327. On Rawls and parties, see Russell Muirhead and Nancy L. Rosenblum, "Political Liberalism vs. 'The Great Game of Politics': The Politics of Political Liberalism," *Perspectives on Politics* 4, no. 1 (March 2006): 99–108.

138. Rawls, *A Theory of Justice*, 195.

139. John Rawls, *Justice as Fairness: A Restatement* (Cambridge, MA: Harvard University Press, 2001), 118.

140. Hume, "Of Parties in General," 33–39.

141. Raphael Cohen-Almagor, "Disqualification of Political Parties in Israel: 1988–1996," *Emory International Law Review* 11, no. 1 (Spring 1997): 67–109. "Most of the atrocities, genocides, and ethnic cleansings in our century have been legitimized by secularist ideologies." Veit Bader, "Religious Pluralism: Secularism or Priority for Democracy?," *Political Theory* 27, no. 5 (October 1999): 597–634, 597.

142. Arend Lijphart, *The Politics of Accommodation: Pluralism and Democracy in the Netherlands* (Berkeley: University of California Press, 1975), 179.

143. Cohen and Susser, "From Accommodation to Decision."

144. Parekh, *Rethinking Multiculturalism*, 306, 340.

145. Judicialization is common "in fragmented politics facing deep ethnic, linguistic, and religious cleavages that may result in political crises of ungovernability or threats of political breakdown." Ran Hirschl, *Towards Juristocracy: The Origins and Consequences of the New Constitutionalism* (Cambridge, MA: Harvard University Press, 2004), 172.

Conclusion: "We Partisans"

1. Rawls, *A Theory of Justice*, 196.

2. Mill, "On Liberty," 252, 245.

INDEX

Abbas, Mahmoud, 423

Abrams v. U.S., 412

Ackerman, Bruce, 56, 204, 302, 475n134, 538n236

Adams, Henry, 10, 191, 217, 313, 325, 327, 408, 550n134

Adams, John, 4, 74, 90–91, 116–17, 145–46, 211

Addams, Jane, 177

advocacy groups, 255, 360; campaign finance and, 250–51; issue advertising and, 250, 258; moral majorities as, 12, 54; progressivism and, 190; religious, 259; theoretical interest in, 2, 15

African Americans, 182, 342–43, 344, 391, 428; Democratic Party and, 201, 346, 356

AKP (Justice and Development Party, Turkey), 442

Aldrich, John, 218, 279, 492n71, 494n99

Algeria, 574n107

Alien and Sedition Acts (U.S.), 115

Alien Registration Act (U.S.), 422

American Political Science Association, 133, 398

American Voter, The, 335, 340

Anderson, John, 215

Anthony, Susan B., 171, 331

Antifederalists (U.S.), 12, 91, 123

"anxiety of influence," 14–15, 254; campaign finance and, 241–48; competitiveness and, 248–51; cycling through, 238–41;

defined, 211; extremism and, 388; forces of nature and, 212–14; party cartel and, 228–33, 388; party collusion and, 227–28; party convergence and, 211, 214, 216–27; phases of, 214–16, 233–38; sinister interests and, 252–53

Arendt, Hannah, 38–40, 91, 110, 475n143

aristocracies: in America, 53, 79, 90–91, 211, 311, 502n25; in England, 81; in France, 95

Aristotle, 4, 27, 68, 76, 81–86, 141, 474n117

al-Asad, Hafez, 426

Assembly of Estates (Germany), 99, 127

association. *See* freedom of association; voluntarism

associational democracy, 102

autonomy, party, 233, 246, 284

Bagehot, Walter, 101, 132, 154

bans of political parties, 17, 412–55; baseline antipartyism and, 412–22; existential challenges to political/national identity and, 17, 415, 417–18, 437, 439–46; hate, incitement to, and, 17, 415, 417, 433–39; outside/foreign control and, 17, 415, 446–50; parties of virtue and, 37; political philosophy theory and, 453–55; violence and, 17, 415, 423–28. *See also specific parties and types of parties*

Barak, Aharon, 416

Batasuna (Spain), 424–25

Ba'thist Party (Syria), 44